MW00804724

THE
BANK CREDIT ANALYSIS
HANDBOOK

A Guide for Analysts, Bankers and Investors

THE
BANK CREDIT ANALYSIS
HANDBOOK

A Guide for Analysts, Bankers and Investors

Jonathan Golin

John Wiley & Sons (Asia) Pte Ltd

Singapore • New York • Chichester • Brisbane • Toronto • Weinheim

Published in 2001 by John Wiley & Sons (Asia) Pte Ltd
2 Clementi Loop, #02-01, Singapore 129809

Other Wiley Editorial Offices

John Wiley & Sons, Inc., 605 Third Avenue, New York, NY 10158-0012, USA
John Wiley & Sons Ltd, Baffins Lane, Chichester, West Sussex PO19 1UD, England
John Wiley & Sons (Canada) Ltd, 22 Worcester Road, Rexdale, Ontario M9W 1L1, Canada
John Wiley & Sons Australia Ltd, 33 Park Road (PO Box 1226), Milton, Queensland 4064, Australia
Wiley-VCH, Pappelallee 3, 69469 Weinheim, Germany

Library of Congress Cataloging-in-Publication Data
Golin, Jonathan L.
    The bank credit analysis handbook: a guide for analysts, bankers and investors/ Jonathan Golin.
        p.cm. – (Wiley finance)
    Includes bibliographical references and index.
    ISBN 0-471-84217-6 (cloth: alk. paper)
        1. Credit –Handbooks, manuals, etc. 2. Banks and banking – Handbooks,
        manuals, etc.
    I.   Title. II. Wiley finance series.
    HG3726.G63 2001
    332.1'753'0685—dc21

        2001026005

Typeset in 11 points Times by Cepha Imaging Pvt Ltd, India
Printed in Singapore by Craft Print International Ltd
10 9 8 7 6 5 4 3 2 1

To my parents and my grandmother, Mazie

TABLE OF CONTENTS

ACKNOWLEDGEMENTS

Many times I have casually suggested to someone in the course of conversation that they write a book about a topic which seemed intensely interesting at the time I was hearing about it. Until I became involved in this project, I never realized just how much easier that was said than done. No one actually made the suggestion to me to write this book. This is understandable. Bank credit analysis is not a conspicuously entertaining subject. *The Economist* led a recent article on the new proposal from the Basel Committee on Banking Supervision by stating that "bank capital requirements may sound arcane and achingly dull." Indeed, and the same can probably be said of bank credit analysis in general. Yet as the newspaper points out, the former is a highly important subject, and I would venture that the latter is as well. Perhaps Nick Wallwork of John Wiley and Sons was not entirely sure about the merits of a book on the topic as I regaled him about my idea after a visit to the Foreign Correspondents Club in Hong Kong in, as I recall, late 1998. My special thanks then to Nick for ultimately agreeing on the need for this book, and accepting my proposal for a work originally to be entitled *Bank Credit Analysis Demystified*.

It is a truism that the production of every book is a collaborative effort and that certainly rings true in this case in which several chapters were prepared by others. Yet the process of actually researching and writing a book can be a lonely and sometimes disheartening one. I would like to especially thank Darren Stubing for his work in preparing the original drafts of the chapters on liquidity and the distressed bank, for his help in reviewing various portions of the text, and for his support throughout the project. Anand Adiga, now with Brown Brothers Harriman in New York, also deserves special thanks for his very helpful comments on various draft chapters and for explaining a number of points relating to sovereign risk and macroeconomic analysis. Anand is a superbly astute sovereign risk analyst whose opinions I hold in the highest regard. His enthusiasm for this project and willingness to help throughout despite having no formal role helped me at critical times. Thanks also to Andrew Seiz of Goldman Sachs for his excellent contribution of Chapter 26 on fixed income analysis.

I would also like to express my gratitude to those who played a part at key points in my making the transition from the legal profession to finance, including Bina Jang at the E.I.U., Brian Lippey and Drake Pike at Tokai Asia, and Amy Lai of First Chicago Bank. I am especially grateful to Philippe Delhaise for offering me a position at Thomson BankWatch, for having confidence in me, and for generally being the best boss I have ever had. Others from whom I learned much at BankWatch, whom I would like to acknowledge, include Tom Gove, Joe Scott, Fred Puorro, Greg Root and Betty Starkey in New York, Paul Grela and Mark Jones in Sydney, Brett Williams in Hong Kong and Phil Jones in Japan.

A special note of thanks must be given to Greg Root, President of BankWatch until its acquisition by Fitch, for his support of this project and cooperating in allowing the use of BankWatch and BankStat materials in its creation.

I would also like to thank Josh Wang of Goldman Sachs for his thoughts on the chapters concerning the rating industry and Charles Ledesma of Thomson Ratings Philippines and the University of the Philippines for making some extremely valuable comments on an early draft of the manuscript. Not to be forgotten are Gael Lee at Wiley who put up with a lot of grief from me, especially as the turmoil at BankWatch prior to its acquisition compelled the deferral of publication several times, and Katherine Krummert at Wiley for her invaluable help in copyediting the manuscript. Many others have played a part in facilitating the production of the pages that follow. To you who remain unnamed, I also offer my thanks. Finally, I would like to thank my girlfriend, Suzanna Wong, for her patience as I devoted many weekends this winter on the book that would have been great for hiking in the environs of Hong Kong, and also for her help with indexing, preparing the list of sources and (in advance) for getting Bankinsights.com. up and running.

Of course, it is another truism that notwithstanding the help one has received as an author, responsibility for the quality of the end result rests with the author alone. That is certainly the case here.

PREFACE

In the autumn of 1994, while aboard a flight back to Japan from Vietnam, where I had been researching an article for the *American Bar Association Journal*, I pondered the next step in my career. Four years of working and traveling in Asia had led me in new directions, and I needed to decide what was next. In 1990, after a decade devoted to the study and practice of law, I had become more or less convinced that private legal practice was not to my taste. Fortunately, sometimes life has a way of giving you a kick in a new direction. In late 1989, with a recession taking hold, the New York firm with which I was associated lost one of its biggest clients, and a skiing accident that required surgery and subsequent recuperation gave me some quiet time to seriously think about whether it might be time to seek out an alternative to "the law." From an earlier stint in Japan in the mid-1980s as a "foreign legal associate," I knew it would be possible to find a teaching position in Japan, which would afford me the freedom and time to pursue other interests, something which was tantalizingly beyond reach in a career track position at a private law firm.

It proved to be the case. After an intensive summer course in Japanese during the summer of 1990, I was by September situated in a provincial city in the west of the country. Jobs teaching at nearby universities quickly followed. In retrospect, it had been a wonderful interlude. But now, after several years, the time had come to make a decision about the future. I had begun travel writing on the side, and had followed up my interest in Vietnam's rapid change, which resulted in an assignment to write about the country not from the traveler's point of view, but from a business and legal perspective. While researching the article, I met a number of analysts examining investment opportunities. Their work appealed to me, and also reminded me of being intrigued some years previous when a lawyer-turned-equity analyst I had met while living in Tokyo described his job. So by the time I got back to Japan, I had decided that investment research — in some capacity — was what I wanted to do.

By May 1995, I was on my way to Hong Kong. But my route into investment analysis was neither easy nor conventional and in hindsight, I perhaps bypassed opportunities that may have led more quickly to the work I desired. In the end, I leveraged my experience traveling and writing about Vietnam to an association with the Economist Intelligence Unit writing, and later editing, direct investment reports. My thoughts then turned to gaining some solid experience researching companies, and in April 1997 I landed a position as a bank credit analyst with Thomson BankWatch. It was not very long before I was appointed Vice President, and ultimately as events transpired became the *de facto* head of the Hong Kong office.

This was perhaps the best job I have ever had. Not only was it interesting work, it was an interesting time to be doing it. As I started, the rumblings of the Asian crisis were just beginning, with cracks beginning to appear in the Thai financial sector. The head of the office and of Thomson BankWatch Asia, Philippe Delhaise, was a former banker and had been an early investor in a local rating agency, Capital Information Services, which he sold to Thomson in 1994, staying on as its president. He proved to be an excellent, if sometimes elusive, mentor and afforded me a great deal of autonomy and responsibility. There was, however, little in the way of formal training at BankWatch in Hong Kong.

It was difficult at first. I had no background in banking, and little academic coursework to rely on, though a mere 2-credit accounting course and some basic economics classes stood me in a good stead. Still, it was a steep learning curve, and required a lot of outside reading, which was not easy because the workload was heavy from the outset. Philippe soon had me assisting on the bank credit workshops that he gave each year, and through these, the research I did on my own, and my daily work analyzing Asian banks, I steadily learned the craft of bank credit analysis. Nevertheless, it would have been nice at the outset to have had a book that explained the essentials. This is my attempt at writing that guide.

I must confess, however, that if I had realized at the start of this project how much time and effort would be involved, I doubt that I would have taken up the task. In addition, not long after I signed the contract with the publisher, BankWatch was thrust into turmoil as the parent company decided to put it up for sale. This soon meant more responsibility and the need to do the same job with fewer resources, while a long period of uncertainty followed. Finally, at the end of November 2000, BankWatch was acquired by a competitor, which fortuitously afforded me the time necessary to complete this project.

As a footnote I would add that prior to employment with BankWatch, I had never had a great deal of affinity for banks (although I probably have more sympathy for them now). Indeed, once ensconced in my work, I considered it a supreme irony that I ended up in a position evaluating financial institutions. Yet in retrospect, a critical attitude towards these institutions probably helps rather than hinders one's work as a bank credit analyst. In addition to a healthy dose of cynicism, my legal training was probably a major aid. One thing you learn at law school is to separate the wheat from the chaff and focus on the issues which are relevant. That, too, is crucial in bank analysis where basic principles are easily obscured by a mountain of detail. As a practicing lawyer, you learn to ferret out those pertinent facts from the mass of detritus with which you are presented. Wading through financial statements and meeting with the managers of the bank being evaluated, all in an effort to find out the home truths about the subject institution, appealed to the detective in me, I suppose. Over time, I realized that banks were a species of enterprise more fascinating than I had imagined. I came to understand why so much is obscured by jargon, and why banks are treated differently than other companies. I hope this book goes beyond demystifying banks to functioning as both a practical guide for novice bank credit analysts, and as a useful reference for their seniors.

INTRODUCTION

Having explained the origins of this book, let me discuss its organization and how readers can make the most of it. Chapter One answers the questions: What is a bank analyst, what does the bank analyst do, who does he or she work for, and what are the different types of bank analysts?

Chapters Two through Fifteen form the heart of the book, the how-to portion of bank credit analysis in which the process of analyzing a financial institution is outlined. This section starts with the financial statements, and moves onwards through the five basic elements of the CAMEL model, the mainstream model for assessing a bank's performance and financial condition, before setting the stage in a chapter on risk management for discussing banks in the larger context of regulation and policy. Chapter Two delineates the source materials for bank analysis and provides an overview of how it is done. Chapters Three and Four respectively deconstruct the two key bank financial statements: the income statement and the balance sheet. That is, in these chapters we explain the function of the financial statements — which is essentially the same for all businesses — and then look at the income statement and balance sheet line by line. One difference between bank credit analysis and corporate credit analysis is that the cash flow statement, so important to corporate credit analysis, is not of much concern when analyzing banks.

Chapter Five provides an introduction to the CAMEL model and the processes of peer and trend analysis. Chapters Six and Seven discuss profitability analysis, the "E" for earnings of the CAMEL model. Chapters Eight, Nine and Ten are concerned with what is probably the keystone of understanding bank creditworthiness: the issue of asset quality. Chapter Eight explains what non-performing loans are and why they are so detrimental to bank health. Also, it discusses the business cycle and its corollary, the credit cycle. Chapter Nine delves into the qualitative aspects of asset quality, including a bank's credit culture, its credit review procedures, its own credit analysis policies, and the composition of its loan portfolio. Chapter Ten approaches the subject from a quantitative perspective explaining and giving guidance on applying ratio analysis using indicators such as NPLs to total loans and loan loss reserves to NPLs.

Chapters Eleven and Twelve delve into an over-rated but highly important facet of bank creditworthiness: capital. Chapter Eleven explains just what capital is generally, and what bank capital is specifically. More importantly, it distinguishes between equity capital and regulatory capital, two different concepts which are often confused. It also discusses traditional measures of capital. Chapter Twelve explores the concept of risk-weighted capital, the 1988 Basel Capital Accord and the 1999 proposals for change. (The January 2001 proposals are discussed in Appendix C.)

Chapters Thirteen and Fourteen, prepared by Darren Stubing, Chief Bank Analyst at Capital Intelligence, a major specialist bank rating agency based in Cyprus, explain liquidity, why it is a pivotal factor in bank health and how it is measured. Chapter Thirteen explains the techniques of interest rate sensitivity analysis and maturity gap analysis. Chapter Fourteen examines funding issues and also applies a variety of indicators to the analysis of liquidity. Finally, Chapter Fifteen completes the explication of the CAMEL paradigm with an examination of the role bank management play in affecting bank creditworthiness and how they can be appraised. While not amenable to quantitative analysis, an evaluation of management should not be given short shrift.

Chapters Sixteen through Twenty Seven go beyond the basics to deal with a variety of important related and supplementary topics. Chapter Sixteen, The Risk Management Context, explores the types of risks financial institutions face and the practical applications of bank credit assessment. Chapter Seventeen addresses the close relationship between sovereign risk and banking risk, and how an understanding of key sovereign risk issues is a prerequisite for a comprehensive analysis of a bank or banking system. The nexus between the two is one reason why governments regulate banks closely and often prop them up when they falter. Chapter Eighteen then turns to the specifics of government regulation of banking: prudential regulation. The most common types of prudential regulation are enumerated, as well as the variations which are frequently found from country to country.

Chapters Nineteen through Twenty Three deal with the problem of the distressed bank, a subject of significant concern to any bank analyst covering emerging markets, and especially so during the last few years in light of the Asian crisis. Based on an original chapter draft from Mr. Stubing, I have expanded this section to its present length, which I believe is merited due to the timeliness of the topic and its frequent presence in the news media, at least in this part of the world. Chapters Twenty Two and Twenty Three discuss restructuring, what it is and why it is needed, and provide an overview of the usual approaches, while Chapter Twenty Four discusses recapitalization methods and Chapters Twenty Five and Twenty Six the experiences of several of the most severely affected Asian countries.

Finally, Chapter Twenty Four and Twenty Five look at the rating industry, particularly in respect of how it treats banks. Chapter Twenty Four surveys the development of the industry, the role it plays in the financial sector, the charges that have been leveled against it, and a reasoned response based on the author's experience in the industry and research in the field. Chapter Twenty Five is a user's guide to rating symbology, a companion to understanding what the rating symbols mean, especially insofar as they are applied to banks, and how they compare. A discussion of the ratings methodology of Thomson BankWatch, which was the world's largest specialist bank rating agency prior to its acquisition by another rating agency during the course of the writing of this book have been left in this chapter for heuristic purposes, although the scope of the discussion has been condensed.

Chapter Twenty Six is a brief introduction to fixed income analysis of bank securities. Andrew Seiz, a BankWatch alumnus, and now a fixed income analyst with Goldman Sachs kindly prepared this chapter. Lastly, a book on bank credit analysis should not be written in this day and age without some reference to the Internet. So, I have included a brief Chapter Twenty Seven on how the Internet has affected the banking industry and the creditworthiness of banks, and how it is likely to do so in the future.

This ends the main text of the book, but this being a handbook, an extensive reference section — a virtual bank analyst's toolkit — has been included in the appendices for the readers' benefit. The largest portion of this is given over to a glossary, with over 700 definitions, that includes many of the terms that I have come across that figure significantly in bank credit analysis. Selected terms from sovereign risk, corporate and equity analysis have also been included, as the bank analyst must be familiar with sovereign risk terminology. It addition, a Ratio Compendium provides over 90 definitions of indicators used in bank credit analysis and comments on their use. Also, a brief discussion of the final proposal on a new Basel Capital accord which was issued on January 16, 2001 is provided.

Let me acknowledge two potential criticisms of the book at the start, and offer my response. First, although the book is intended as a general introduction to bank credit analysis, many of the examples provided are from Asia, and naturally reflect my own experience covering Asian banks. My response to this criticism would be that first, Asia itself encompasses a wide diversity of political, economic and banking regimes. Second, the Asian crisis of 1997-98 is the most recent example of a major turn in the business and credit cycle affecting financial institutions. By seeing banks under stress, the credit analyst is well prepared to catch an early glimmer of future potential problems in other regions and assess the risk and severity of default. Finally, my collaborator, Darren Stubing, has provided a number of examples from Africa and the Middle East in the chapters he prepared, that I hope rounds out the coverage to some extent. Another more valid criticism might be the comparatively few case studies. Indeed, it was my hope and intention to include a greater number of case studies to illustrate particular points. What I found, however, was just to cover the basics resulted in a much larger book than originally contemplated. Space and time simply did not permit the inclusion of more than what is provided.

While I have done my best given the particular circumstances and limitations under which I have labored, I regard this book as a work in progress and hope that future editions may remedy any flaws in this one. To that end, I have established a website, Bankinsights.com, to support this book and to function as a resource center on the credit analysis of financial institutions. It is my plan to use this website as a vehicle to provide updates to the book and supplementary information on bank credit analysis. I sincerely welcome any suggestions for improvements, corrections or other relevant comments. Readers can contact me at jonathan@bankinsights.com.

Jonathan Golin

Mid-levels
Hong Kong
March 28, 2001

PART ONE

CHAPTER ONE

THE ROLE OF THE BANK CREDIT ANALYST: ASSESSING THE CREDITWORTHINESS OF BANKS

A bank lives on credit. Till it is trusted it is nothing; and when it ceases to be trusted, it returns to nothing.

— Walter Bagehot

Credit is at the heart of not just banking but business itself. Every kind of transaction except, maybe, cash on delivery — from billion-dollar issues of securities to getting paid next week for work done today — involves a credit judgment ... Credit ... is like love or power; it cannot ultimately be measured because it is a matter of risk, trust, and an assessment of how flawed human beings and their institutions will perform.

— R. Taggart Murphy[1]

Bankers dress conservatively: they are risk-takers dressed as civil servants. Their main banking halls are marbled copies of the Parthenon or St. Peters in Rome: on entering the hallowed portals, the awe-struck client is supposed to be conclusively persuaded that the institution, like the edifice, is as solid as the Rock of Gibraltar.

— IBCA,[2] Special Report, Bank Capital: A Vale of Tiers

---

[1] Murphy, R. Taggart. *The Real Price of Japanese Money*. Weidenfeld & Nicholson, 1996.
[2] IBCA is now part of Fitch Ratings. "Bank Capital: A Vale of Tiers," Fitch IBCA, October 1997.

THE MEANING OF CREDIT AND CREDIT ANALYSIS

The word "credit" derives from the Latin "credere," meaning to trust or believe. Through the intervening millennia, the meaning of the term remains close to the original. Lenders, or creditors, extend funds (credit) based on the belief that the borrower can be trusted to repay the debt, according to the terms agreed. This conviction results from: (1) the belief that the borrower is willing to repay based on the lender's knowledge of the borrower and the borrower's reputation; (2) an appraisal of the value of collateral deposited with or pledged to the lender; and (3) an analysis of the borrower's financial condition, based on the assumption that the financial condition of the borrower has been honestly and openly represented to the creditor. The last involves a thorough examination of the borrower's financial statements, as well as its prospects for the future, that would support a conclusion that it will have adequate cash flow to pay back the loan. The lender or bank credit officer trusts that a customer will fully perform a loan agreement based on the conclusion that the borrower has the ability and willingness to do so. Ascertaining whether both capacity and willingness exist is the subject of credit analysis. By conflating the two inquiries into one, credit analysis seeks to answer the following question: What is the likelihood that a borrower will perform its financial obligations in accordance with their terms? Or conversely: What is the likelihood that it will default on these obligations?

With the evolution of financial systems, credit analysis has become increasingly important. The traditional banker knew with whom he was dealing (or thought he did) either locally with his customers or at a distance with correspondent banks whom he trusted. As Walter Bagehot, the 19th century English economic commentator wrote:

> "A banker who lives in the district, who has always lived there, whose whole mind is a history of the district and its changes, is easily able to lend money there. But a manager deputed by a central establishment does so with difficulty. The worst people will come to him and ask for loans. His ignorance is a mark for all the shrewd and crafty people thereabouts."[3]

For the old-fashioned local banker, knowledgeable about local business conditions and prospective borrowers, there was less need for formal

---

[3] Quoted in Martin Mayer, *The Bankers: The Next Generation*, Penguin, 1996, p. 10.

credit analysis. Reputation and personal knowledge of the borrower were sufficient grounds to accept or reject a loan application, and this banking practice was a cozy business. While some local bankers can still operate in this way, the growth of banks into regional, national, and global institutions has made inevitable the need for more rigorous and systematic mechanisms for gathering intelligence about a borrower's willingness and capacity to repay. Hence, credit analysis has developed as a professional function.

Willingness to Repay: Character, Moral Obligation, and Legal Obligation

Willingness to pay can be ascertained to a degree from the borrower's reputation and apparent character. The strength of the relevant legal system and the ability of a creditor to enforce a judgment against a debtor undoubtedly have an influence on the debtor's predisposition to fulfill its obligations. Assessing willingness requires making subjective, even intuitive, judgments about the borrower. The evaluation is essentially qualitative, taking into account information gleaned from a variety of sources, including, where possible, face-to-face meetings with the borrower. Although the ability to make such judgments comes more easily to some than to others, it can be honed with experience.

While willingness and ability to pay are both prerequisites to the lender for obtaining the expected benefits from the loan transaction, ability is usually of greater significance, at least in more developed markets. As long as there is ability, along with the existence of an effective legal system, a lack of eagerness to repay can often ultimately be overcome by judicial means.[4] A borrower who can pay but will not, can maintain such a position only in a legal regime that is ineffective or strongly favors debtors over creditors.[5] Cultural influences too may come into play in encouraging repayment or in supporting resistance to repayment.

Regrettably for lenders in emerging markets, effective protection of creditors' rights is not the norm. As was seen in the aftermath of the Asian financial crisis during 1997–98, the legal systems in a number of

---

[4] Full recovery may nonetheless be impossible, depending upon the borrower's access to funds and the worth of the collateral securing the loan.

[5] The effectiveness of a legal system encompasses many facets, including the cost and time required to obtain legal redress, the consistency and fairness of legal decisions, and the ability to enforce judicial decisions rendered.

countries were demonstrably deficient in this regard. Reforms that have been implemented, such as the new bankruptcy law enacted in Thailand in 1999, have gone some distance towards remedying the deficiencies in that country's insolvency laws. The efficacy of new legislation is, however, dependent upon a host of factors, including the attitudes of all participants in the judicial process. In Thailand, as well as other comparable jurisdictions where legal reforms are being implemented, it will probably be a number of years before changes are thoroughly manifested at the day-to-day level.

Weak legal and regulatory infrastructure and concomitant uncertainties concerning enforcement of creditors' rights mean that credit analysis in emerging markets often tends to be more subjective than in developed markets. Due consideration must be given not only to willingness to pay, but also to the variables that may affect the lender's ability to coerce payment through the legal system. To be sure, even in developed markets, this aspect of credit analysis inevitably involves an element of subjective evaluation.

Despite the not inconspicuous inadequacies in the legal frameworks of the countries in which they extend credit, during periods of economic expansion and prosperity bankers have in the past frequently paid scant attention to prospective problems they might confront. Reliance on often implicit government support for the borrowing institution (or should the government itself experience difficulties, upon the expectation that the International Monetary Fund would stand ready to provide liquidity to the governments concerned and thereby indirectly to the borrowers) has led to a certain degree of obliviousness to the difficulties involved in enforcing their rights as creditors through legal action. The expectation of such support gives rise to the issue of moral hazard, a topic we will explore in later chapters.

Capacity to Repay: Financial Strength, Collateral and External Support

The Corporate Context

Compared to willingness to pay, the assessment of capacity lends itself more readily to quantitative measurement, and financial analysis goes far to reveal whether the borrower will have the capacity to repay outstanding obligations when they come due. A corporate credit analyst or bank credit officer examining bread-and-butter loans to industrial and service enterprises will be particularly concerned with the following items, all of which are amenable to quantitative analysis:

❑ the borrower's cash flow coupled with the borrower's earnings capacity in the near-term business and industry environment

❑ the borrower's liquidity

❑ the borrower's capital

❑ the collateral, for example real property, pledged by the borrower to secure the loan, as well as any external support such as a guarantee.

The first three items represent aspects of a firm's financial strength. Cash flow is critical to debt repayment capacity, and is a better indicator of such strength than profits, which due to accounting conventions may not accurately reflect a firm's ability to repay its debts.[6] Liquidity refers to a company's immediate access to cash or cash equivalents (such as US Treasury bills or money-market securities) to fulfill current obligations. Capital or equity refers to the owners' residual claims on a corporation's assets. Where matching assets are inadequate to satisfy creditors' claims, owners' equity provides additional comfort to the most senior creditors who have first claim on the corporation's assets and equity.

Collateral refers to assets, such as real property, that are pledged to the lender in case the borrower is unable to repay its obligation out of cash or other current assets.[7] The intrinsic creditworthiness of a borrower may be low owing to a lack of financial strength, but risks can be mitigated through the pledge of collateral or the provision of external support from a more creditworthy entity, such as a parent company. If the borrower defaults, the lender can seize the property through foreclosure and sell it to satisfy outstanding obligations, or force the borrower into bankruptcy.[8] Another way to provide additional capacity is by having a requirement that a borrower's obligation be guaranteed by a third party. A guarantee is a form of external support since the creditor can demand that the guarantor repay the borrower's loan if the borrower defaults.

---

[6] For reasons to be discussed, while cash flow analysis is extremely important when analyzing non-financial firms, it has much less relevance when analyzing banks and other financial institutions.

[7] There are four basic types of collateral: real or personal property (including inventory, trade goods, intangible property), negotiable instruments (including securities) and other claims to receive funds, and business proceeds. A floating charge is collateral on all business assets.

[8] Unsecured creditors may also be able to initiate bankruptcy proceedings, but are less sure of compensation than the secured creditor.

The credit analyst assessing the creditworthiness of a non-financial company needs to consider each of the preceding four elements when estimating a company's default risk. Traditionally, banks place primary emphasis on collateral and guarantees when extending loans, and at least until the Asian crisis, this so-called "pawnshop mentality" was pervasive.[9] For contemporary credit analysts, however, cash flow analysis and an evaluation of the financial condition of the borrower are the usual starting place. These reflect the borrower's current and future ability to repay its obligation.

As the financial statements from which the analyst is compelled to draw conclusions are nearly always out of date to some extent, the quantitative aspect of credit analysis, like the qualitative assessment of willingness to repay, is in many ways as much an art as it is a science.[10] Based on data which lags behind the financial reality, the analyst must consider the possible scenarios that could unfold and take a critical look at bank management's often rosy view concerning the bank's prospects. Indeed, an important element of credit analysis common both to the credit appraisal of corporations and of banks is an evaluation of management, namely its competence, motivation and incentives, and the plausibility and coherence of its strategy. Assessing management's ability is necessarily a largely subjective undertaking.

Bank Credit Analysis: Basic Differences from Corporate Credit Analysis

The specifics of financial analysis in respect to banks will be discussed in due course. The elements of credit analysis applicable to banks display some similarities to those applied in the non-financial corporate context, although the business of banks, as we will see, differs in fundamental respects from non-financial businesses. Suffice it to say for the moment that the analyst examining the creditworthiness of a bank looks at several aspects of its financial strength, including:

❑ earnings capacity, i.e. the bank's ability to generate revenue and

---

[9] This term refers to an approach to credit review that focuses solely on the purported value of collateral as justification for making a loan instead of the borrower's ability to generate adequate positive cash flow to satisfy its financial obligations.

[10] In many Asian countries, for instance, banks publish their comprehensive financial status only once a year. Moreover, these annual reports may not be published until a year (or more) after the end of the fiscal year.

overcome difficulties

❑ liquidity, i.e. the bank's access to cash or cash equivalents to meet current obligations

❑ capital adequacy, i.e. the cushion that the bank's capital and liquidity reserves afford it against its liabilities to depositors and the bank's creditors

❑ asset quality, i.e. the likelihood that the loans that the bank has extended to its customers will be repaid, taking into account the value and enforceability of collateral provided by them.

CATEGORIES OF CREDIT ANALYSTS

The work of the credit analyst encompasses the collection and consideration of a broad array of information that may be relevant to the evaluation of both the willingness and capacity to repay a financial obligation according to its terms. Moreover, the role of the credit analyst necessarily embraces a wide range of situations and activities. For example, the credit officer at a small provincial bank may have to decide whether a loan should be extended to a retail shopkeeper whose establishment the officer visits regularly. At the other end of the spectrum, the head of credit at a multinational bank may be responsible for setting country risk limits and for determining the credit lines that may be extended to specific banks and corporations in that country. In addition, much of the evaluation undertaken by rating agencies such as Moody's Investors Service and Standard and Poor's of the creditworthiness of governments, corporations, financial institutions, and other entities, as well as of financial instruments, is devoted to what is essentially credit analysis.[11] Finally, "sell-side" and "buy-side" credit analysts, who work for investment banks, hedge funds and proprietary trading units, spend much of their time engaging in credit analysis as they assess the "relative value" of debt instruments.[12]

While all credit analysts seek to answer the same core question, specific functions may vary. Most credit analysts, however, can be

---

[11] We may sometimes refer to Moody's Investor Service as "Moody's" and to Standard & Poor's as "S&P".

[12] As will be discussed later, equity analysts often need to pay attention to credit considerations.

classified into one of the four following categories which can be further divided into two primary categories: risk management and fixed income analysis.

❑ In-house risk managers are credit analysts at banks or corporations, who seek to evaluate whether the bank should lend to or the company should do business with a financial or non-financial firm or in a particular country. They also may have responsibility for setting exposure limits.

❑ Ratings analysts are credit analysts who work for rating agencies to evaluate the creditworthiness of banks, corporations, and governments. They perform risk assessments that are distilled into ratings represented by rating symbols. Rating analysts who evaluate governments and government obligations are called sovereign analysts.

❑ Government bank and insurance examiners are essentially credit analysts who assess the riskiness of a bank or insurance company to determine the institution's eligibility to continue to do business, and whether, in that context, it should be compelled to undertake certain prudential measures required under the relevant regulatory regime.

❑ Fixed income analysts are credit analysts who evaluate both the creditworthiness and "relative value" of a fixed income security, resulting in a recommendation to buy, sell, or hold the security.

Credit analysis can be categorized not only by the role of the credit analyst, and by type of employer, but also by sector and region. Frequently, credit analysts specialize in particular industries or countries, especially those employed by multinational corporations, investment banks, and rating agencies. A credit analyst, for example, may focus on Hong Kong companies, emerging markets, Japanese banks, or on particular industrial or service sectors, such as utilities and retail sales chains.

PARAMETERS OF BANK CREDIT ANALYSIS

Credit Analysis vs Equity Analysis: In General and In the Banking Context

Before describing the work of bank credit analysts in more detail, it is important to understand the difference between credit analysts and equity analysts. The work of credit analysts generally differs from that of equity analysts in its main purpose.

Equity Analysis

Equity analysis concentrates on determining whether to invest in the shares of a particular firm. In other words, the core question that equity analysis seeks to answer is: Should an investor buy the securities of the subject company? Bank equity analysts, therefore, almost exclusively confine their analysis to publicly listed financial institutions (i.e. banks listed on a stock exchange), although they might also analyze a bank that is about to list or a government-owned bank that is about to be privatized. Generally speaking, the corollary question that the equity analyst attempts to answer is: What is the appropriate value of the company's securities, based on an accurate assessment of its present and future earnings?

Consequently, a primary indicator with which equity analysts are concerned in determining an appropriate valuation is return on shareholders' equity (ROE).[13] ROE reflects the equity investor's return on investment. Since ROE is closely correlated with leverage, higher profitability does not necessarily imply higher credit quality; instead, as common sense would dictate, risk often correlates inversely with return. Therefore, the credit analyst, in contrast to the equity analyst tends to give greater weight to a variety of financial ratios, including those that indicate a bank's asset quality, capital strength, and liquidity. Together, such indicators reflect the institution's overall soundness and ability to ride out harsh business conditions rather than merely its ability to generate short-term profits.

Equity analysis can be divided into two broad approaches: technical analysis and fundamental analysis. Technical analysis looks at patterns in share price movements to try to predict future movements. To the technical analyst, these patterns express common archetypes of market psychology, and technical analysis emphasizes the timing of the decision to buy or sell.

Fundamental analysis examines the factors affecting a company's earnings, including the company's strategy, comparative advantages, financial structure, and market and competitive conditions. It attempts to ascertain whether the firm's shares are undervalued or overvalued with respect to the firm's present and projected future earnings. This determination will

---

[13] Return on equity is but one of many measures of equity analysts utilize to measure return on investment and the fair value of shares. The analyst can choose from a number of other indicators such as the price earnings ratio (PER) and earnings per share (EPS), which takes account of valuation, or several ROCE (return on capital employed), EVA™ (economic value added) or CFROI (cash flow returns on investment) which attempt to compare returns to the true cost of capital.

result in a recommendation to buy, sell, or hold.[14] Relatively unconcerned with timing the market, fundamental analysis presupposes market ineffi- ciencies and a corresponding belief that the market will ultimately recog- nize the true value of the security. Most equity analysts, whether covering banks or other companies, employ fundamental rather than technical analysis as their primary tool, although technical factors will often be given some consideration. In emerging markets particularly, secular influences, funds flows from developed markets, and economic and political developments may play a significant role in the investment decision-making process.[15]

Credit Analysis

Unlike equity analysts, credit analysts traditionally are little concerned with the valuation of a company or its shares. Except for fixed income analysts, credit analysts do not particularly care whether a firm's securi- ties are a good investment; they are only concerned whether the firm will fulfill its financial obligations. Since most equity investments entail few obligations, if any, that management ensure a return to shareholders (preferred or preference shares being the main exception), equity analysts customarily tend to pay relatively less attention to credit matters. The distinction is not black and white, however. Some equity analysts do concern themselves to a great degree with creditworthiness.[16] The Asian crisis of 1997–98 highlighted the need for analysts in the region to take into account a company's financial strength and external support, as well as its profitability. Indeed, following the crisis, Lehman Brothers' analyst, Robert Zielinski, noted this trend:

> "In the past, most of the focus of an analyst's research was on the earnings line of the income statement. The analyst projected sales based on industry growth, profit margins, and net income. The objec- tive was to come up with a reasonable figure for EPS growth, which was the main determinant of stock valuation ... Today, the analyst

---

[14] It is common practice in contemporary markets to employ additional terms that are designed to prevent a company from taking offense and to reflect the gradations in the degree of enthusiasm the analyst has for a particular stock.

[15] "Secular" in this sense refers to long-term trends or developments, e.g. industrialization, the rise of the Internet.

[16] e.g. bank equity analysts.

places most of his emphasis on the balance sheet. Indeed the most sought-after equity analysts in the job market are those who have experience working for credit rating agencies such as Moody's."[17]

Similarly, some credit analysts keep a weather eye on a firm's share price as a proxy for impending difficulties that may manifest in credit problems. While credit analysts traditionally have been largely backward-looking, relying on historical financials instead of modeling and projecting earnings as equity analysts characteristically do, there is a trend among them toward placing more emphasis on earnings and other financial projections, at least through the current (and sometimes into the upcoming) fiscal year. In addition, a company's share price, of course, has an impact on the ability of a company to raise capital cheaply, which in turn has an influence on its prospective capital strength.[18]

Credit Analysts as Fixed Income Analysts

Credit analysts may be employed by an investment bank, a fund management company, or a proprietary trading unit (often within an investment bank) either as risk managers or fixed income analysts. Akin to their equity analyst counterparts, a relatively small proportion of credit analysts are employed by investment banks, securities brokerages, and asset management firms to analyze fixed income instruments of financial institutions. Fixed income analysts may specialize in banks or banks may just comprise a portion of their portfolio. Like equity analysts, fixed income analysts must make recommendations on whether to buy, sell, or hold a fixed income security such as a bond. That is, they must ascertain the relative value of the security. Is it undervalued and, therefore, a good buy, or overvalued and consequently best to sell?

In addition, like equity analysis, fixed income analysis can be divided into fundamental analysis and technical analysis. Fundamental analysis explores the same issues as does credit analysis for risk management purposes, i.e. the likelihood of default. Technical analysis looks at market timing issues, which are affected by the risk appetite of institutional

---

[17] Robert Zielinski, Lehman Brothers, "New Research Techniques for the New Asia," December 14, 1998.
[18] The share price also has the virtue of reflecting a wide variety of information available to market participants. KMV Corporation, among others, uses share price information as a significant indicator of default risk.

investors and market perception. The latter is often strongly influenced by headline events, such as political crises, foreign exchange rates, and rating actions. Ratings issued by credit rating agencies also play a critical role in fixed income analysis by providing independent credit assessments of issues and sovereign risk, establishing a benchmark yield curve, and helping to determine — in light of fundamental analysis — the relative value of particular fixed income securities. Accordingly, another difference between equity and fixed income analysis is that to a much greater extent than in equity analysis, fixed income analysis integrates fundamental and technical analysis.

Both equity and fixed income analysis vary in respect of the audience to which the analysis is targeted. In the case of investment banks and brokerages, analysis may be intended for clients, often institutional investors or asset managers, who will use the research to make their own trading decisions. Alternatively, to a greater degree than is customary in regard to equity analysis, fixed income analysis may be intended solely for a firm's own traders, i.e. its proprietary trading, who will use the research internally. Whether designed for a bank's customers or the bank itself, fixed income analysis requires a good understanding of: (1) the elements that affect creditworthiness, (2) how the issue (or issuer) is perceived by the market, (3) a sense of market movements and dynamics, (4) and how rating agencies operate. Often fixed income analysts have had prior experience working as in-house analysts or as rating agency analysts. Fixed income analysis of banks is discussed in more detail in a subsequent chapter.

Financial Institution Credit Analysis and Risk Management

Within the realm of financial analysis, the need for the analysis of the creditworthiness of banks is an especially important one. Although relatively few in number, bank credit analysts have a comparatively high profile. Three of the four key roles of bank credit analysts are mainly, if not exclusively, focused on risk management. This has to do with the special role that banks play within the financial system of all markets. In addition to their monetary function, which we will discuss later, banks act to facilitate payment among disparate market participants both domestically and internationally. To facilitate the creation of an interbank market for liquid and loanable funds, banks frequently lend to and borrow from other banks, or otherwise incur credit exposure by, for example, opening or accepting a letter of credit. Most banks of significance within a country have correspondent banking relationships with hundreds of financial institutions worldwide.

Exposure to individual banks is likely to be large for both multi-national corporations and financial institutions themselves. Unlike a bank's corporate customers, who in most cases are likely to be based in the same region as the bank's head offices, a correspondent bank may be located halfway around the world from a bank's home territory. The bank credit officers may not be as familiar with such institutions as they are with the bank's prime customers. Yet the high-leverage characteristic of entities that act as financial intermediaries makes them particularly vulnerable to distress, if not failure. While the total collapse of internationally active banks is quite rare, the level of leverage on both sides of a transaction makes each counterparty extremely sensitive to risk. Consequently, the analysis of the financial institutions with which a bank deals is of critical importance. Moreover, the failure of a bank is no simple matter. On the one hand, the collapse of a single, comparatively small bank can have repercussions far out of proportion to its size—the adverse effects can extend to the business climate and economy of a whole nation or region. On the other hand, the failure of a major bank can be catastrophic. As a consequence, governments tend to exert wide regulatory power over banks, although the quality of regulation and enforcement differs considerably from one jurisdiction to another.[19] For these reasons, banks tend to pay close attention to the credit analysis of their financial institution counterparties.

Thus, while credit analysts working within banks involve themselves with nearly all entities to which they have credit exposure, exposure to other financial institutions is a key concern, especially when such counterparties are located on the opposite side of the globe.[20] Given their role, it should not be surprising that banks are both the largest generators of credit analysis and among the largest customers for bank credit analysis provided by third parties such as rating agencies.

Whether the bank credit analyst works for a commercial bank, an investment bank, a fund manager, a rating agency, or a regulatory

---

[19] The unique role that banks play in a country's economic health is further discussed later.

[20] The vast majority of such analysis, however, covers industrial companies and other firms outside the financial sector. Credit analysis of non-financial institutions is outside the scope of this book, although we will discuss it briefly in certain contexts, such as in connection with the asset quality of bank loan portfolios.

authority, the analyst's main objective is to assess the creditworthiness of a universe of banks. If working for a bank or a corporation in a risk management capacity, the analyst will usually make a recommendation as to whether and to what extent the analyst's employer should have business dealings with the subject institution (establishing country limits or credit lines). The analyst employed by an independent rating agency will assign a rating to the bank, supported by an analytical profile, which through its letter or number designation will classify the rated institution as a strong, weak, or average credit, and various gradations in between.[21]

Credit Analysis of Banks (vs Credit Analysis Performed by Banks)

When we refer to "bank credit analysis," we mean the analysis of the creditworthiness of banks themselves (and frequently other types of financial institutions), and not the duties performed by credit analysts employed by banks to evaluate the risk of the non-financial firms to which the bank lends its funds. In fact, the majority of credit analysts employed by banks are largely, although not necessarily exclusively, engaged in the credit analysis of non-financial corporations. They are actually corporate credit analysts employed by financial institutions. The work of these credit analysts, whether employed by banks or other institutions, to the extent that it concerns evaluation of the creditworthiness of non-financial (e.g. industrial) companies, is beyond the scope of this book. Naturally, however, when examining the creditworthiness of a bank, the ability of that bank to evaluate the companies to which it lends must be taken into consideration. We look at that function, however, as part of understanding a bank's business and as part of the total credit assessment of the bank, rather than as a topic in itself.[22]

Primary vs Secondary Credit Research

Though the basic parameters of each role are similar, the amount of time and resources the analyst can spend on the analytical process depends on

---

[21] The in-house bank analyst will also often utilize a rating system, albeit an internal one.

[22] Owing to the nature of their business, banks employ the vast majority of credit analysts who concern themselves with the credit assessment of corporations and individuals. The credit analysis of non-financial companies is well addressed by other works, some of which are mentioned in the Sources and Further Reading section at the end of this book.

the nature of the position. An in-house analyst may very well be responsible for an entire continent or region, e.g. Asia, and his or her brief may extend to a hundred or more banks. Unsurprisingly, such an analyst will not be able to visit every bank within his purview, nor expend several days evaluating a single bank. In-house analysts, whether employed by a commercial bank or an investment bank, therefore rely heavily on secondary research such as those produced by rating agencies or investment banks. Although the in-house analyst ideally will conduct an independent review of the bank's financial statements, and may in some cases periodically call or visit the subject bank, much of the in-house analyst's work will be involved in researching the ratings produced by third parties, taking into account recent developments, and in utilizing all available sources of information to arrive at a synthesis of the institution's "credit story." Supporting text will often follow an abbreviated format as the analysis is purely for internal purposes and will not be published.

The credit analyst employed by a rating agency operates at the other end of the spectrum. As in-house analysts often rely upon the assessments made by rating agencies, rating agency analysts must engage in intensive primary research. Therefore, in addition to examining the bank's financials, they almost invariably visit the bank in question to form an independent conclusion as to the bank's creditworthiness. As bank visits are relatively time-consuming—due diligence visits can last a day or more, and additional time is needed to prepare the report and have it approved by the agency's rating committee—rating agency analysts typically cover a fairly small number of institutions, ordinarily, to ensure that enough resources are allotted to ensure a high-quality credit evaluation.[23]

Sovereign and Country Risk Analysis

A specialized form of credit analysis is sovereign and country risk analysis. Governments throughout the world engage in the issuance of fixed income securities in local and international markets. Sovereign risk analysts assess the risk of default on such obligations. Country risk analysts engage in a similar form of analysis, but country analysis connotes a

---

[23] The scope of the "due diligence" normally undertaken by rating agency analysts is discussed in a subsequent chapter.

greater emphasis concerning the effect of the country's political, legal, and economic regime on issuers of obligations within the country, as well as concerning the risks of foreign direct investment in the country. Although it is a separate field from bank credit analysis, because the strength of a financial system affects sovereign risk and because the level of sovereign risk affects bank credit, a bank credit analyst should have at least a passing familiarity with sovereign risk analysis (and vice versa). While many bank analysts engage in country risk analysis to a degree, forming their own views on the risk of default attributable to government actions or omissions, bank analysts, nonetheless, rely to a large extent upon sovereign risk ratings issued by agencies such as Moody's Investors Services, Standard & Poor's, and Fitch Ratings, whose sovereign risk ratings are used as a benchmark for their own ratings.[24] Additional analysis may be provided by the analyst's economist colleagues, economists at banks or at independent agencies (e.g. the Economist Intelligence Unit, Independent Strategy), or by the analyst directly.

Sovereign risk analysts, many of whom are employed by rating agencies, make use of tools that are analogous to those utilized by credit analysts in respect of private companies, but which take into account the peculiar characteristics of governments. (Technically, governments do not go bankrupt, although they may default on their obligations.) Instead of focusing on company financials, sovereign risk analysts examine macroeconomic indicators to determine whether a government will have the wherewithal to repay its financial obligations to local and international creditors. Most sovereign risk analysts have a strong background in economics. Sovereign risk also takes account of political risk, so the sovereign risk analyst should have an understanding of the political dynamics of the country he or she is analyzing. Sovereign risk analysis is discussed in greater detail in Chapter 17.

CHAPTER SUMMARY

Credit is the foundation of all business dealings, and credit analysis examines the question: What is the likelihood that a financial obligation will not be repaid? Credit analysts look at both capacity to pay and willingness to pay. Willingness to pay may correlate with the efficacy of the legal system in which the obligor resides. Credit analysts differ from

---

[24] See David T. Beers and Marie Cavanaugh, Standard & Poor's Rating Service, "Sovereign Credit Ratings: A Primer," December 1998, p. 1.

equity analysts in that they look at overall financial soundness and give only moderate attention to profitability and the valuation of the company, the latter being the core concern of equity analysts.

Credit analysts evaluate both financial institutions and non-financial corporations, and may concentrate on risk management or on fixed income analysis. Financial institution credit analysis is a particularly high-profile area of the field because of the importance of financial institutions in facilitating international and domestic trade. The high leverage that financial institutions typically employ makes them vulnerable to distress. Moreover, the nature of the banking business means that banks must often consider risks with counterparties located on the other side of the world about which their knowledge is limited.

The primary categories of analysts are rating agency analysts, in-house analysts, fixed income analysts and government regulators. Rating agency analysts engage in primary research, while in-house analysts at banks and at regulatory agencies (excepting bank examiners) tend to use a synthesis of secondary research to form their opinions. Agency analysts, analysts employed by regulators, and probably the majority of in-house analysts have a risk control perspective. In contrast, fixed income analysts, who typically work for investment banks, are opportunity-oriented, making recommendations to customers (or internally) as to whether to buy, sell, or hold a particular security.

CHAPTER TWO

An Overview and Introduction to Bank Credit Analysis: Source Materials and Disclosure

The incidence of bad and doubtful loans is a particularly sensitive aspect of a bank's operations. If the losses are material, they can reduce the capital resources of the bank and affect its ability to grow and develop its business. If large losses are disclosed in the financial statements, it may lead to a loss of confidence in the bank's management and a reduction in its credit ratings. This will lead to an increase in the bank's cost of borrowing and make it more expensive to raise capital.

— "Bank Reserve Accounting," Special Supplement to Development
Bank of Singapore's Annual Report for 1999, p. 2

Credit problems are like cockroaches: when you see a few, you know there are a lot more around.

— Paul Schulte, Asiawise, 2 Nov 2000

SCOPE AND DEPTH OF ANALYSIS

Approach: Quantitative vs Qualitative Analysis

Analyzing the creditworthiness of a bank has several facets. It is both a *qualitative* and a *quantitative* endeavor, involving a review of the bank's historical performance, its present condition, and future prospects. The quantitative aspect involves the comparison of financial indicators and ratios — for example, percentage rates of net profit growth or the bank's risk-weighted capital adequacy ratios — that allow the analyst to compare a bank's performance and financial conditions to a *peer group* of banks. Not all aspects of bank performance and financial condition can be reduced to numerical terms. Qualitative review, for example, of a bank's management or the plausibility of a bank's strategy, must also be considered. Indeed, one of the most important variables in bank creditworthiness is the competence of senior management. It is this team that must determine the bank's performance targets and how to reach them while effectively managing the bank's risks.

The line between quantitative and qualitative analysis cuts across key elements of bank creditworthiness. Asset quality can be measured quantitatively by non-performing loan ratios, but an assessment of the character of a bank's credit culture and the efficacy of its credit review procedures is very much a qualitative exercise. It is sometimes said that because accounting and regulatory standards and the scope and detail of disclosure vary so much around the world, analysis of banks in emerging markets requires a greater component of qualitative assessment. It has also been observed that in some markets, seemingly precise disclosure is not to be trusted. This too argues for more emphasis on qualitative aspects of credit analysis in such markets. Yet as transparency increases in emerging markets, the trend is likely to be in the direction of putting more emphasis on quantitative methods. The wide acceptance, for example, of the Basel Accord on Capital Adequacy, and the increasing convergence of prudential and accounting standards suggests that greater weight may be placed upon quantitative analysis of banks in emerging markets in the future.[1]

Putting the Bank in Context

The process of bank analysis cannot be done in isolation. Instead, the analyst must be aware of the risk profile of the country in which the bank is operating, as well as the business conditions in the banking sector as a whole, and judge the bank he is appraising with reference to its peers. Sovereign and systemic concerns must also be taken into account, a subject we will address later, as must the legal and regulatory

---

[1] Robert Morris Associates, *A Guide to Analyzing Foreign Banks*, p. 8.

environment and the quality of bank supervision.[2] Some aspects of the sovereign risk and banking environment are subject to quantitative analysis, for example, GDP growth rates or levels of non-performing loans. Others, such as the degree of ability of the central bank to supervise banks under its authority, are more qualitative in nature.

This said, when looking at a market for the first time, the question arises: Analyze the individual banks first or the banking system as a whole? The analyst confronts something akin to the chicken-and-egg problem. Since individual banks must be viewed in context, the banking system requires early attention. But the system or sector as a whole cannot be fully understood without knowledge about the problems and prospects of specific banks. In practice, gaining that understanding is an iterative process. The analyst might begin with research into the structure of the system as a whole for background purposes. This might be followed by a review of the major commercial banks. Then the analyst may return to a more "macro" perspective, preparing an analysis of the entire sector, and highlighting the impact of key players.

Following this approach, when analyzing a particular bank, it is a good idea to first gain an understanding of the level and nature of sovereign and country risk, subjects which are discussed in subsequent chapters. This should be followed by some basic research into the structure of the banking system and the quality of regulation, to roughly gauge where the bank fits in within the country's banking system and to gain an understanding of the scope and nature of bank regulation. Next, the analyst should undertake quantitative and qualitative reviews of the subject bank, comparing it when possible against its peers and with the bank's historical performance. The CAMEL model of analysis, introduced later in this chapter, provides a generally accepted framework for analyzing the creditworthiness of banks. Finally, a more rigorous comparison of the bank in relation to its peers might be carried out, in order to establish the bank's place

---

[2] While systemic concerns relating to the structure and strength of the banking system as a whole are clearly within the purview of the bank credit analyst, some would argue that bank analysis and sovereign risk analysis are inextricably intertwined and that a bank analyst must also be a sovereign risk analyst. The author agrees that bank analysis must be done with reference to sovereign risk analysis and vice-versa, and must have a general understanding as to how sovereign risk analysis is performed. But the two fields of analysis do require different skills sets and in practice are distinct. Sovereign risk analysis is essentially macroeconomic analysis and most sovereign risk analysts are trained economists. While it may be an advantage to have experience in sovereign risk analysis, so long as the bank analyst has access to competent sovereign risk analysis it is not necessary that he replicate the work. The scope of this book is consequently limited to bank credit analysis and only touches on sovereign risk analysis in a cursory way.

within a hierarchy of creditworthiness among comparable institutions in the banking system. For heuristic purposes, we will first focus on the process of evaluating the financial condition of a specific bank. When we have done this, we will step back and examine the forces that shape a financial institution's operating environment.

Scope and Depth of Analysis

While all bank credit analysis has the same basic goal — to come to a determination as to the creditworthiness of a bank or banks — the approach may differ according to the objectives of the analyst and role. For a rating agency analyst visiting a bank for the first time, the purpose will be to undertake an overall assessment of the creditworthiness of the bank and any securities it is issuing to determine a credit rating. The credit rating will be used by risk managers and investors to determine whether the exposure or investment is attractive or at what price it would be worth accepting. For the fixed income analyst, the purpose is to determine the value of any debt securities issued by the bank relative to perceptions about its present and future creditworthiness. This analysis will be used by investors to help decide whether to buy, sell, or hold the security. For the in-house credit analyst at a bank functioning in a risk management capacity, the purpose is to implement the institution's overall risk management policy generally, and to establish correspondent bank and counter-party risk credit limits specifically.

While time available and the depth of any accompanying written analysis may vary, the analyst's principal tools remain the same. Fundamental to any bank credit analysis are the bank's annual financial statements, preferably audited and preferably available for the past several years, accompanied by relevant annual reports, and any more recent interim statements. The analyst will also want to have access to some secondary sources. These may range from news clippings in paper or electronic form to reports from rating agencies and investment banks, prospectuses published in connection with securities issues, and material provided by regulatory authorities. Finally, the analyst may make a visit to the bank to meet with senior management to gain a better understanding of the bank's operating methods, strategy and the competence of its management and staff.

The amount of resources applied to each type of bank credit analysis will differ according to the analyst's situation and aims. At one end of the spectrum is the in-house analyst who is assisting in

Basic Source Materials for Bank Credit Analysis

Material	Contents	Remarks
Annual reports	Income statement, balance sheet, and supplementary statements.	Financial data for a minimum of three years is recommended.
Interim financial statements	Frequently these are limited to a balance sheet and income statement, and are often unaudited.	In some jurisdictions, these statements will be only a condensed or rudimentary version of the annual statements.
Notes from the bank visit and third parties	For rating agency analysts, this may include a questionnaire completed by the bank.	In addition to information formally obtained in the course of a bank visit, the analyst may also seek to obtain informal views about the bank from various sources.
Prospectuses	Prospectuses may include more detailed company and market data than provided in the annual report.	In many jurisdictions, prospectuses are not easily accessible or may not add much new data.
News	News articles concerning acquisitions, capital raising, changes in management and regulatory developments are important to consider in the analysis.	Newspaper and magazine clippings can be helpful but are time-consuming to collect; proprietary data services such as Reuters Business Briefing function as electronic clipping services. If not available, the Internet can provide much of the same information. Stock and bond prices may also be used for analytical purposes.
Other research reports	Reports from regulatory authorities, rating agencies, and investment banks.	In-house analysts will necessarily rely to a great extent on rating agency reports when preparing their own reports.

the process of establishing credit limits to particular institutions. The in-house analyst may rely largely on secondary source material, such as reports from rating agencies, or may undertake an independent review of the subject bank's credit from its financial statements. Because of time and resource limitations, the in-house analyst will ordinarily place heavy reliance on third-party reports. In effect, the in-house analyst is outsourcing part of the credit function to these outside agencies. Regulatory considerations may also come into play. Reference to the opinion of independent agencies may be required to satisfy rules governing the extension of credit or the making of investments at the organization at which the in-house analyst is employed.

The fixed income analyst will typically undertake some primary research, including making a bank visit, but will also refer to ratings established by credit rating agencies. Since the fixed income analyst is engaging in independent proprietary research for the eyes of his employer's customers or staff traders, use of third party research will be relatively minimal. The fixed income analyst, however, will likely make some use of reports prepared within his organization, such as those prepared by staff economists or equity analysts. Finally, the bank rating analyst, upon whom both the in-house analyst and fixed income analyst may rely, will focus on independent primary research. In addition to examining the bank's annual reports and financial statements, he or she will typically visit the bank, submit a questionnaire to management, and perform a due diligence investigation.[3] Where a due diligence visit is made, the analyst may submit written questions or a questionnaire to the bank, and visit management. The visit can be an informal discussion or a formal due diligence meeting in connection with establishing a rating for the bank. Of course, both the fixed-income analyst and in-house analyst may make bank visits and undertake intensive primary research. For the bank rating analyst, however, such visits will normally be made whenever possible.[4]

---

[3] As we discuss subsequently, the rating agency's role is similar to but distinct from that of a bank's auditor or that of a bank examiner.

[4] Note that unless the analyst is working in the capacity of bank examiner, there is normally no right of access to bank management. When performing a solicited (i.e. paid) rating, rating agencies will ordinarily enter into an agreement that ensures analyst access to management. Otherwise, such visits are made on a courtesy basis only and in exceptional cases the analyst may be unable to meet in person with management. In-house analysts, in particular, may have difficulty or may be shunted off to the investor relations or correspondent bank relations staff who often will be able to add little to the data provided in the bank's annual report.

Use of Source Materials

Use of Research Sources	Rating Agency Analyst	In-house Analyst	Fixed Income Analyst
Annual reports	Yes	Yes	Yes
Interim financial statements	Yes	Yes	Yes
Bank visit	Yes, if feasible	To a limited extent	Frequently
Bank website	Yes	Yes	Yes
Informal sources	Yes	Yes	Yes
Prospectuses	To a limited extent	To a limited extent	Yes
News	Yes	To a limited extent	Yes
Stock and bond prices	To a limited extent	To a limited extent	Yes
Regulatory agency reports	Yes	To a limited extent	Yes
Rating agency reports	Limited to reports from the agency at which the analyst is employed	Yes	Yes
Investment bank reports	Rarely	To a limited extent	Limited to reports from the bank at which the analyst is employed

RESEARCH SOURCES: COLLECTING DATA FOR THE BANK CREDIT ANALYSIS

The Annual Report

Although the annual report may be full of glossy photos and what appears to be corporate propaganda, its text should not be ignored. Much can be gleaned about the culture of the bank, how the bank views business and economic conditions, and its strategy. As it is prepared in most cases for the bank's shareholders, the emphasis of the annual report will be on putting the bank's operating performance in the best possible light. An understanding of the bank's side of the story can be a useful counterpoint to a more critical examination of bank performance. Moreover, the annual report will not infrequently contain highly useful data about the country concerned or other information relevant to bank analysis.

In addition to such intangibles, the bank's annual report will sometimes supply information on particular aspects of the bank's operations not available in the financial statements. Similarly, factual information relevant to the analyst, may be buried in the body of the report. Likewise, significant information relating to the economic and regulatory environment, as well as more mundane factual information, such as the number of bank branches and employees, can frequently be found in the annual report.

The Principal Financial Statements

Like companies in other industries, the bank will ordinarily issue a *balance sheet*, also known as *statement of condition*, and an income or profit and loss statement (also known as a *report of income*). These are the most important components of the financial statements provided. Typically, a bank will also issue a funds-flow or *cash flow statement* and a *statement of stockholders' equity*, both of which may be combined into one statement. These financial statements, in audited form, will appear in the bank's annual report. Unfortunately, as discussed in a preceding chapter, banks, especially in certain markets, do not always issue their annual reports on a timely basis. Publication of annual reports can follow anywhere from two months to in extreme cases two years following the end of the subject fiscal year. Under circumstances where the report is delayed, the analyst might attempt to obtain directly from management, copies of the audited financial statements (the annual report itself may be delayed for printing or production reasons) or unaudited financial statements. Management may or may not agree to provide such preliminary data.

The Income Statement

The income statement records and categorizes for a particular time period (e.g. one year) gross revenue, from which is deducted gross expenses. The remainder — the bottom line — is net income. The income statement reflects profits, and numerous ratios and indicators can be derived from the income statement to compare the revenues, expenses and profit of one bank with another.

The Balance Sheet

The balance sheet records assets on one side and liabilities and equity on the other. The two sides must balance, hence the term balance sheet. From the balance sheet, ratios and indicators can be derived to measure liquidity, capital strength and asset quality. By constructing ratios utilizing both the income statement and balance sheet, a number of profitability indicators can be calculated.

The Statement of Cash Flows

The statement of cash flows records inflows and outflows on a real (i.e. non-accrual) basis. Highly important in analyzing non-financial companies, the statement of cash flows is of little use in analyzing banks and financial companies since cash is the bank's stock in trade.

The Statement of Changes in Capital Funds

This statement registers changes in shareholders' equity. Because banks are highly leveraged, determining their capital position is critical to bank credit analysis.

Interim Financial Statements

Depending upon the country, interim (i.e. more frequently than annual) disclosure of financial statements may or may not be available. If available, it may be in abridged format. Nevertheless, a little information is better than none, and if a bank report is being undertaken during mid-year, interim reports should be sought and reviewed.

The Bank Website

The advent of the Internet has made the bank credit analyst's job easier. No longer is it always necessary to request a bank annual report and wait weeks for its arrival. Annual reports, financial statements, and a great deal of background information on the bank and its franchise can be obtained from the Web. Moreover, the depth, interactivity and overall quality and style of the site will say something about the bank as well as its Internet strategy.

The Bank Visit and the Rating Agency Questionnaire

Rating agency analysts and fixed income analysts will almost invariably make bank visits, while in-house analysts tend to make them less frequently. Because the evaluation by an agency or fixed income analyst can have a large impact on the ability of the bank to raise financing, it is generally easier for these analysts to gain access to senior managers than for the in-house analyst.[5] The in-house analyst will have a more difficult time gaining access to senior officers, and will tend to be relegated to less senior staff, whose role it is to manage correspondent and counterparty banking relationships. In view of the larger universe of banks in-house analysts generally cover, they will in any case often have less time available to make bank visits. Handling the bank visit is discussed in greater detail in a subsequent chapter.

News, the Internet, and Securities Pricing Data

Annual reports are just about out-of-date the day they are published. In numerous markets, there will be a delay of two to three months after the end of the financial year before the reports are published. Much can happen within this period, and prior to preparing a report, the analyst should run a check to see if any material developments have transpired. A check of the bank's website can be very helpful here, but alternatively, web-based news searches or proprietary electronic data services such as Reuters Business Briefing or Lexis-Nexis can be extremely valuable in turning up changes in the bank's status, news of mergers or acquisitions, changes in capital structure, new regulations, or recent developments in the bank's operations.

---

[5] This is not always true, however. Where the rating is unsolicited and the bank desires to maintain a low profile, access may be quite difficult, with mutually convenient times elusive.

Bond pricing data will be of key concern to the fixed income analyst, but in-house and rating agency analysts can make constructive use of both bond and equity price data when the bank is publicly listed or an issuer in the debt markets. Anomalous changes in the prices of the bank's securities can herald potential risks. The market will be the first to pick up news affecting the price of the bank's securities, and in this sense it can function as a kind of early warning device to in-house and agency analysts. Real-time securities data in emerging markets, as provided by Bloomberg for example, can be costly, but the Internet again is making such information more widely available. Sources for bond and equity pricing data of securities in emerging markets can be found in the back of this book.

Prospectuses

Prospectuses can be, but are not always, rich sources of information about a bank. This depends a great deal on the market and upon the type of securities issue for which the prospectus was prepared. Prospectuses for equity and international debt issues may add substantial data beyond that was included in the latest annual report. In contrast, prospectuses for bank loan syndications and local bond issues may add relatively little information. Also, prospectuses, particularly those prepared for the latter category, are not always easily accessible.

Secondary Analysis: Reports by Rating Agencies, Regulators, and Investment Banks

The use of secondary research will depend on the type of bank credit report being prepared. Rating agency analysts will often review official reports from central banks and government regulators, but, like fixed income analysts, will not depend upon their competitors for research. In-house analysts, however, will rely much more heavily on such secondary research sources and less on primary sources. The reports prepared by equity analysts, although they take a different perspective than bank credit reports, can nevertheless be useful in helping to form a view concerning a bank. Since investment bank reports are ordinarily prepared for their investor-customers, very recent ones may not be easy to obtain. Such reports, may be purchased, sometimes on an embargoed basis, from services such as Multex and Investext.

REQUISITE DATA: THE FINANCIAL STATEMENTS

An essential prerequisite to performing a credit analysis of a bank is access to its financial statements. Without these, unless the analyst has access to a secondary source of financial information about the institution such as the BankStat or BankScope service, quantitative analysis will of course be practically impossible.[6]

The Auditors' Report or Statement

The analyst should turn to the auditor's report at the start of analysis to determine whether or not the auditor of the bank's accounts provided it with a *clean* or *unqualified opinion*.[7] The auditor's report will normally appear just prior to the financial statements. In essence, a clean opinion communicates that the auditor does not disagree with the financial statements presented by management. It does not mean that the auditor might not have presented the financial information differently, choosing a different accounting approach or disclosing additional data. A clean opinion means that the financial statements as presented meet at least the minimum acceptable standards of presentation.[8]

The clean opinion will vary in length depending upon the jurisdiction in which the audit was performed and the standards applied. Normally a clean auditor's report will state:

❑ That the auditors have audited specified financial statements of a certain date.

❑ That the financial statements are the responsibility of the management of the company.

❑ The accounting standards applied (e.g. generally accepted accounting standards) n.b. reference may be made here to local company law as well.

❑ That the standards require that financial statements are free from material misstatement.

---

[6] See the resource section at the end of the book.

[7] "Unqualified" means that the auditor has attached no additional conditions to its opinion; i.e. the opinion is without further qualification.

[8] John A. Tracy, *How to Read a Financial Report: For Managers, Entrepreneurs, Lenders, Lawyers and Investors*, John Wiley & Sons, 5th Ed., 1999.

❑ That the audit involved examining evidence supporting the statements on a test basis.

❑ That the audits provide a reasonable basis for the auditors opinion.

❑ That in the opinion of the auditors, the financial statements present that financial position fairly in all material respects as of the date of the audit.

While the wording and the number of paragraphs may vary — in the United States, three paragraphs is standard — these are points that will ordinarily be covered by an unqualified auditor's report.

A clean auditors' report does not ensure against fraud or misrepresentation by the company audited, and the fairly standardized language of the auditors' report, although varying from country to country, has evolved to emphasize the limitations in what should be drawn from it. The reason for the existence of these qualifications is to provide a defense against litigation that would seek to hold the auditor liable for any fraud or misrepresentation subsequently discovered in the financial statements. Although audits could arguably be more thorough, the expense involved in checking every item in the bank's financial statements, i.e. other than on a test basis, would be prohibitive.

A *qualified opinion*, i.e. one in which the auditors' limit or qualify in some way their opinion that the financial statements provide a fair representation of the bank's financial condition, can be discerned in cases where additional items other than those mentioned above are added. Typical situations in which an opinion will be qualified by the auditors include the following:

❑ the existence of unusual conditions or event that may have a material impact on the bank's business.

❑ the occurrence of related party transactions.

❑ a change in accounting methods.

❑ where substantial doubt exists about the bank's ability to continue as a going concern.

Of course, the last type of qualification is the most serious and will justifiably give rise to concern on the part of the analyst. Not all qualifications are so serious and should be considered in the context of the financial statements, what else is known about the bank's prospects, and the prevailing business environment. An extremely rare phenomenon is the adverse opinion, in which the auditors set forth their opinion that the financial statements do not provide a fair picture of the bank's financial condition.

Finally, mention should be made of the organizations that perform audits. The accounting profession has consolidated globally into a few major firms, who often have local affiliates with different names. Although there may be no significant difference in quality vis-à-vis a less well-known firm, an audit by one of the major international accounting firms may be perceived as affording a certain imprimatur on a bank's financial statements. In some countries, however, independent local firms may have most or all domestic banks as their clients. While privately-owned banks are usually audited by independent accounting firms, government banks sometimes are not. Special government audit units may perform the audit, or they may not be audited at all.

Finally, it is sometimes perceived that where a company changes auditors it may be because of disagreement about the presentation of financial statements or because the particular accounting firm is unwilling to provide a clean opinion. This is certainly not always the case, and the reasons for a change in auditor may be entirely different. Nonetheless, changes in auditors should be noted by the analyst for possible further inquiry.

The Balance Sheet vs The Income Statement

The Balance Sheet as a Snapshot

The balance sheet is a snapshot as of the end of the financial period which indicates the composition of a bank's assets on the one side of the balance sheet and its liabilities and shareholders' equity on the other. The two must be in balance, hence the term. If a bank's liabilities (excluding shareholders equity) exceed the value of its assets after a write-down of loan loss provisions and capital, such as might occur if many of the bank's assets which are in the form of loans that turn bad, then the bank will be insolvent.[9]

---

[9] A bank that is in trouble will try to put the best face on its situation, however, and may not disclose that in fact 37% of its loans are worthless. Rather, the balance sheet is likely to show that the bank is solvent, even if in reality it is not. The footnotes to its financial statements can be helpful in coming to a better determination as to the value of the bank's outstanding loans.

The Income Statement as a Movie

The income statement, which will be dated the same as the balance sheet, is also in a sense a snapshot, but one whose will vary considerably over time. It may be better thought of as a movie, or perhaps as a sequence of time-lapse photography. Imagine a washbasin. It is completely empty. There are two faucets above the basin, and a drain with a valve at its bottom, which allows movie of water flowing from a tap into a basin. The basin has a drain at the bottom, but which at the moment is only partially open. This is the sort of washbasin that can be found in any bathroom. Next to the washbasin at eye level is a clock. It reads 11:59 pm. A video camera is recording this exciting scene.

Now this is a symbolic movie. The inflowing water represents income. Representing interest income is the right hand tap, representing non-interest income is the one on the left. The water flowing out through the drain represents expenses. Promptly at midnight water begins flowing into the basin first through one tap and then through the other. At times the water flows in more rapidly. At other times it slows to a trickle. Similarly, the drain, seemingly of its own accord, sometimes opens wide allowing water to escape rapidly, but then suddenly it returns to a position where water flows out of the basin at a measured pace. However, the water is flowing in more quickly than it escapes the basin. Gradually the level in the basin rises. At 3 am it is 3 centimeters deep. At 6 am the depth is 5 centimeters. At 9 am it is 8 centimeters, but the drain seems to have opened a bit more widely by 10 am and by midday, the level of the water has receded to 7 centimeters.

Imagine that at each three-hour interval we have measured the volume of water that has entered the basin from each tap and we have measured the volume of water that has flowed out of the basin. The water in the basin symbolizes profit, while each hour has symbolized one month. The measurements taken at each quarterly interval can form a symbolic income statement, showing the volume of interest income and non-interest income that has entered the basin, the volume which has escaped, and the remainder left in the basin as profit. We can see that the statement varies significantly with time, generally showing rising income and expenses as time goes by, but a variable (though generally increasing) profit. Of course, we can also imagine a somewhat different case in which the volume of water rose less quickly or more quickly or perhaps did not fill the basin at all. The last would symbolize a loss.

Thus, rather than representing the balance between assets, liabilities and equity as of a given date, the income statement represents the net inflows and outflows during the financial period, ordinarily the previous year but sometimes the most recent six-month or three-month period. Unlike the balance sheet, at the beginning of the income statement period all item tabulations are effectively reset to zero and unless there is dramatic change in the rate of change affecting a particular item (or a reversal in the direction of change), the amount of each item will normally correlate to a greater or lesser degree with the amount of time elapsed. In other words, assuming that income and expenses are generated and incurred at a constant rate, profits or loss over a six month period will be double that registered over a three month period. The balance sheet, absent highly unusual circumstance, is, however, to show a relatively marginal change over the same period.

Items such as expenses and income can be said to "pass through" the income statement during the period reported and are subsequently reflected on the balance sheet. For example, in the case of a bank, the sum of net interest and non-interest income will customarily be accrued and reflected on the income statement at the end of the year, hopefully, after non-interest expenses and taxes have been deducted, leaving some measure of profit. Profits are then allocated; some are paid out as dividends, others retained building up the bank's capital, a balance sheet item. Meanwhile, assets will have increased — an increase of 10–15% would amount to a fairly significant rate of growth in most markets — and to fund that lending growth, additional deposits will also have been required resulting in a corresponding increase in liabilities.

The income statement, in contrast, does not look at assets, liabilities or equity but simply registers income, expenses, and profit (or loss). The increase or decrease in assets or liabilities will normally have some impact on profit or loss, with an increase in assets often being associated with an increase in profits. But it is not necessarily so. Assets and liabilities can remain unchanged, and profit or loss can change as a result of increased or reduced spreads, as a result of an increase or decrease in non-interest income, or as a result of increased or reduced costs or any combination of the three. The only direct link between the two is that profit or loss must be allocated against the balance sheet, increasing or decreasing shareholders' equity, unless in the case of profits entirely paid out in dividends or in the case of loss written off against existing provisions. To be sure, changes in the balance sheet can also have an impact on the income statement, where, for instance, the diminution in the value of assets requires loan loss provisions to be subtracted from income.

Two additional points should be borne in mind. First, our metaphor of the wash basin is an abstraction. The actual income statement maps the movement of what are conceptual items. Profit is an accounting concept. It is not cash on hand. The income statement is almost always constructed on the accrual principle, meaning that it does not map the actual flow of cash — that is the function of the cash flow statement (see below) — but when the item of expense or income is booked, i.e. entered in the bank's accounting ledger based on when the liability is incurred or the asset become receivable. The reality is that the receivable asset, e.g. an interest payment, may not ever be received even though it is recorded on the income statement as if it had been. Under most accounting regimes and international best practices, there will be an adjustment made subsequently if it is determined that the loan generating the putative interest is non-performing. The interest payment will then be "clawed back," an adjustment made in retained earnings, and ultimately the balance sheet will be restated. But not all jurisdictions impose clawbacks of interest income previously booked and the adjustment on the balance sheet may not be visible for a number of months. The analyst should therefore pay attention to the applicable rules and make his own adjustments when appropriate when comparing banks on a cross-border basis or to an international benchmark.

Lastly, it occasionally happens that banks change the duration of their financial year. This most often occurs following a merger between two banks having different fiscal year ends, although it may sometimes occur in other situation. In this case the analyst should make appropriate adjustments when comparing the increase or decrease in income statement items over two or more years.

OTHER FINANCIAL STATEMENTS

While the income statement and the balance sheet are the primary tools that the bank analyst uses in evaluating a bank, other financial statements may also be utilized.

Statement of Cash Flows

The statement of cash flow, though much less important in bank analysis than in the analysis of non-financial companies, may be helpful in observing changes among accounts and also in locating line items, such as depreciation, that might not be specified in other financial statements.

Illustration: Statement of Cash Flows, Bank of the Philippine Islands

CONSOLIDATED STATEMENTS OF CASH FLOWS FOR THE YEARS ENDED DECEMBER 31, 1998, 1997 AND 1996 (In Thousands of Pesos)			
	1998	1997	1996
CASH FLOWS FROM OPERATING ACTIVITIES			
Net income fo the year	P 4,602,731	P 4, 559,742	P 4,012,899
Adjustments to reconcile net income to net cash			
provided by (used in) operating activities			
Provision for probable losses	2,018,491	1,682,458	397,802
Provision for deferred income tax	(532,417)	(881,061)	(6,160)
Depreciation and amortization	609,973	589,640	511,992
Minority interest in subsidiaries	41	(42)	(49)
Equity in net income of unconsolidated subsidiaries	(52,162)	(45,777)	(70,038)
Changes in operating assets and liabilities			
(increase) decrease in:			
Due from Bangko Sentral ng Pilipinas	3,605,455	1,361,098	(2,182,380)
Trading account securities	(2,388,451)	152,449	2,271,759
Other resources	(2,567,527)	1,409,439	(6,124,903)
Increase (decrease) in:			
Due to Bangko Sentral ng Pilipinas	(258,264)	144,363	(436,613)
Manager's checks and demand drafts outstanding	501,052	(37,726)	(395,744)
Accrued taxes, interest and othe expenses	138,664	310,638	344,759
Deferred credits and other liabilities	(592,803)	2,113,814	(541,339)
Net cash provided by (used in operating) activities	5,084,673	11,054,137	(2,218,015)
CASH FLOWS FROM INVESTING ACTIVITIES			
(increase) decrease in			
Investment securities	(38,222,836)	(3,675,885)	(7,343,231)
Loans and advances	8,648,821	(9,518,273)	(18,376,568)
Bank premises, furniture, fixtures and equipment	923,934	(1,018,820)	(784,966)
Net cash used in investing activities	28,650,081	14,212,978	(26,504,765)
CASH FLOWS FROM FINANCING ACTIVITIES			
Cash dividends	(1,793,284)	(989,550)	(505,304)
Collection on stock subscriptions	60,604	28,980	1,706,527
Increase (decrease) in:			
Deposit liabilities	19,410,814	25,444,989	15,693,319
Bills payable	(9,248,416)	(4,520,036)	6,596,268
Due to other banks	39,680	(128,850)	162,580
Net cash provided by financing activities	8,469,378	19,835,533	23,653,390
TRANSLATION ADJUSTMENT, net	(9,937)	198,763	939
INCREASE (DECREASE) IN CASH AND CASH EQUIVALENTS	(15,105,967)	16,875,455	(5,068,451)
CASH AND CASH EQUIVALENTS (Note 3)			
January 1	30,236,301	13,360,846	18,429,297
December 31	P15,130,334	P30,236,301	P13,360,846
SUPPLEMENTAL DISCLOSURE OF CASH FLOW INFORMATION			
Cash paid during the year			
Interest	P13,962,608	P10,885,523	P10,556,582
Income taxes	2,271,323	935,039	1,015,239
SUPPLEMENTAL SCHEDULE OF NON-CASH INVESTING ACTIVITY			
Purchase of real property on installment from an affiliate (Note 6)	P —	P 1,890,439	P —
(See accompanying notes to financial statements.)			

Depreciation can be found on the statement of cash flows

The reason that the cash flow statement is little used in bank credit analysis (notwithstanding that it is one of the most important tools in evaluating the creditworthiness of non-financial companies) is due to the typical bank's extremely high leverage (the Basel CAR establishes a maximum benchmark gearing ratio of 12.5 to one). A bank that is expanding its lending rapidly will tend to look as if it is hemorrhaging cash flow. As banking analyst Anthony Lok explains:

> "This abnormality occurs because rapid loan growth consumes a large volume of working capital, which results in negative operating cashflow. Conversely, when recession (or crisis) hits, loan demand plummets while deposits rise (due to falling investment and consumption), meaning cash flow turns hugely positive."[10]

This perverse quality of bank cash flow as a performance measure is exacerbated by the fact that the adverse impact of loan loss provisioning due to increasing non-performing loans is not reflected in the cash flow statement, because provisions are a non-cash item.

For illustration purposes, BPI's statement of cash flows is shown on previous page.

Statement of Changes in Capital Funds

A review of the Statement of Changes in Capital Funds assists in determining how the bank's profit was allocated. What portion of a bank's profits, for example, was paid-out in dividends and in what form, cash or stock? What portion was allocated to equity reserves, and what portion was retained earnings? BPI's Statement of Changes in Capital Funds is shown on next page. Note that what we term "surplus" is referred to as "paid in surplus" by BPI, and "surplus" is the term given to retained earnings (undivided profits).

CHAPTER SUMMARY

Bank analysis is both a quantitative and a qualitative exercise. Some critical elements, such as capital ratios or profitability, are relatively easily reducible to numerical data allowing one bank to be easily

---

[10] Anthony Lok, Regional Banking: Banking Guidebook, Nomura International Equity Research, Nov. 1, 1999, p. 4.

Illustration: Statement of Changes in Capital Funds, Bank of the Philippine Islands

STATEMENTS OF CHANGES IN CAPITAL FUNDS
FOR THE YEARS ENDED DECEMBER 31, 1998, 1997 AND 1996
(In Thousands of Pesos)

	1998	1997	1996
CAPITAL STOCK (Notes 1, 9 and 10)			
Issued			
Preferred stock — nil in 1998 and 1997, 53,873,999			
Class A shares in 1996 at P10 par value	P —	P —	P 538,740
Common stock — 802,898,967 shares in 1998,			
615,834,213 shares in 1997 and 561,960,184 shares			
in 1996 at P10 par value	8,028,990	6,158,342	5,619,602
	8,028,990	6,158,342	6,158,342
Subscribed			
Common stock — 7,714,970 shares in 1998, 4,541,970			
shares in 1997 and nil in 1996 at P10 par value	77,150	45,420	—
Subscriptions receivable			
Common stock	(69,850)	(43,102)	—
	8,036,290	6,160,660	6,158,342
PAID-IN SURPLUS (Note 1)	4,281,313	4,225,690	4,199,028
TRANSLATION ADJUSTMENT (Note 3)	213,090	223,027	24,264
SURPLUS			
Balance, January 1 (Note 1)	12,357,920	9,361,906	6,105,913
Net income for the year	4,602,731	4,559,742	4,012,899
Transfer to surplus reserve	(505,000)	(574,178)	(251,602)
Cash dividends (Note 9)			
Common stock	(1,793,284)	(903,345)	(419,410)
Preferred stock	—	(86,205)	(85,894)
Stock dividends (Note 9)	(1,870,649)	—	—
Balance, December 31	12,791,718	12,357,920	9,361,906
SURPLUS RESERVE			
Balance, January 1 (Note 1)	1,753,005	1,178,827	927,225
Transfer from surplus	505,000	574,178	251,602
Balance, December 31	2,258,005	1,753,005	1,178,827
	P27,580,416	P24,720,302	P20,922,367

(See accompanying notes to financial statements.)

compared with another. Other key elements, however, such as the quality of management or the quality of a bank's loan portfolio are not so amenable to quantitative analysis and must be viewed qualitatively, i.e. subjectively. In addition, a bank cannot be viewed in isolation. The business and cultural environment in which it operates, including the regulatory regime and legal infrastructure, must be considered. In emerging markets, particularly, these considerations loom large. An otherwise strong bank operating in a country where borrowers are prone to resist repayment, where the legal system is ineffective in enforcing creditors' rights, and where the government sees banks as tools to advance its development policies by directing lending to particular sectors will be see its creditworthiness diminished relative to an institution with identical characteristics in a country more conducive to commercial bank operations. In short, while analyzing the bank as an individual company, the bank analyst must bear in mind relevant systemic and sovereign risks as well.

How the bank analysis will be performed and the sources of the data utilized depends in large part upon the role of the analyst. Ratings agency analysts and fixed income analysts will engage in more primary research, while in-house analysts functioning as risk managers will rely more upon the research produced by the former in making their assessments. In analyzing a bank, the most critical inputs are the bank's financial statements. Other data include securities prospectuses and securities pricing data (for listed banks or issuers in the debt markets), news services and the Internet, and bank visits. The key financial statements are the balance sheet and income statement, while the statement of cash flows and statement of changes in capital funds are of secondary importance. Despite their primacy, financial statements are nearly always out of date to some degree, and the extent and accuracy of disclosure vary considerably from bank to bank and from country to country. The auditor's statement deserves attention not because it provides any guarantee, but because qualifications to it or changes in auditors may flag deficiencies in financial reporting and more severe underlying problems. Because of the multiple variables that need to be taken into account, a number of which are qualitative in nature, bank credit analysis is as much art as science, especially in emerging markets.

CHAPTER THREE

DECONSTRUCTING A BANK'S FINANCIAL STATEMENTS, PART ONE: UNDERSTANDING THE INCOME STATEMENT

Banking is a business like any other — a raw material (in this case money) goes into the process we call banking, and hopefully, a profit ... comes out ... the other end.
— Howard Palmer, *Bank Risk Analysis in Emerging Markets*[1]

Income for most individuals is the cash they receive. Income for companies is anything but the cash they receive.
— Ian Griffiths, *Creative Accounting: How to Make Your Profits What You Want Them To Be*[2]

To allege that making a provision against bad and doubtful losses was outside the ordinary activities of a bank and therefore not expected to recur ... seemed to fly in the face of reality. Bad debts are of course a normal part of banking, and had been an even more regular feature of Midland's performance.
— Terry Smith, *Accounting for Growth*, on Midland Bank's attempt in 1987 to classify its provisions for lending to less developed countries as an extraordinary rather than as an exceptional item.

---

[1] Howard Palmer, *Bank Risk Analysis in Emerging Markets*, Euromoney Publications, p. 1.
[2] Ian Griffiths, *Creative Accounting: How to Make Your Profits What You Want Them To Be*, Unwin, London 1987.

The income statement (also known as the profit and loss account, or P&L), measures a bank's income, or revenue, and to determine net income or loss. As we explained in the preceding chapter, it registers this revenue or lack thereof, by summing up financial flows, as distinguished from cash flows, over a period of time. Financial inflows consist of interest income, as well as non-interest income. A bank's non-interest income is composed of foreign exchange and securities trading gains, fees and commissions, and other miscellaneous revenue. Financial outflows consist of interest expense, including interest paid on deposits and borrowings used to fund loans and securities purchases, compensation costs, occupancy costs, taxes and licenses and miscellaneous income. Profit results when financial inflows exceed financial outflows; loss results when financial outflows exceed financial inflows. It bears repeating that financial inflows and outflows, as recorded, will in most cases be only approximations of actual financial inflows and outflows, a phenomenon epitomized in the treatment of interest income.

Income can be exaggerated and losses can be masked where financial inflows are recorded that are not subsequently matched by corresponding inflows. This can occur where non-performing loans are not recognized as such, and interest income is accrued and thereby passed through the income statement, but is never ultimately received by the bank. Suppose that economic conditions begin to rapidly deteriorate towards the end of the financial year so that the number of borrowers who fail to pay back their loans in accordance with the loan terms exceeds estimates. In such case, the bank will record a certain amount of interest income, which may in fact exceed the actual amount of income received. For this reason, best practices in bank accounting require that interest income on non-performing loans be put into a suspense account and that interest already accrued be "clawed back" i.e. deducted, where such interest is not ultimately forthcoming from the borrower. Best international practice, however, is not the rule in all jurisdictions and income statements may be distorted as a result.

In the previous chapter we made the common observation that a balance sheet is like a snapshot and added that the income statement is resembles a movie, or a sequence of time-lapse photography. The income statement, however, has a much narrower focus than the balance sheet. The latter is a snapshot of the bank's overall financial position at a given moment in time. The income statement, in contrast, is only concerned with changes in one aspect of the bank's financial condition: the change in its earnings between two moments in time. To be sure, this is an aspect of the bank's financial condition that is of great interest to shareholders and prospective investors, but it is merely part of the picture from the point of view of the credit analyst.

While the income statement is intuitively easier to understand than the balance sheet, especially in the case of banks to which loans are assets and deposits liabilities, it can be better thought of as an appendage to the balance sheet. Indeed, it can be viewed as a special footnote to it explaining in detail the elements that contributed to and detracted from the bank's profits. Some analysts term these elements value creators and value destroyers because they have a direct impact on the profit stream of the bank, which in turn affects the value of the bank as a whole and the price that individual shares command in the market. The income statement is linked to the balance sheet in that it seeks to explain changes in a bank's earnings, specifically in its retained earnings after distribution of profits to shareholders between two periods of time: the date of the most recent balance sheet and the date of the balance sheet previous to that.

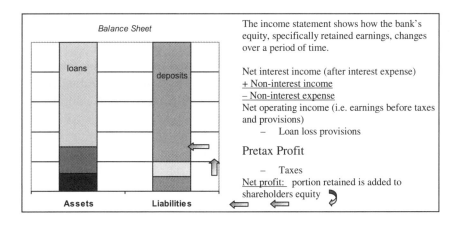

INCOME STATEMENT ITEMS

The income statement lists income and expense items in columnar form, typically beginning with interest income, followed by interest expense, non-interest income, non-interest expense, and income taxes. The example below is the consolidated profit and loss account (i.e. income statement) for fiscal year 1998 (FY98) of Dah Sing Financial Holdings Limited,

ANNOUNCEMENT OF 1998 FINAL RESULTS

The Directors of Dah Sing Financial Holdings Limited (the "Company") announce that the audited results of the Company and its subsidiaries (the "Group") for the year ended 31st December 1998 are as follows:

Consolidated Profit and Loss Account

for the year ended 31st December

	1998	1997	Variance
	HK$'000	HK$'000	%
Interest income	**3,649,049**	2,269,736	
Interest expense	**(2,687,378)**	(2,123,494)	
➤ Net interest income	**961,671**	1,146,242	−16.1
➤ Other operating income	**458,930**	375,361	22.3
Operating income	**1,420,601**	1,521,603	−6.6
Operating expenses	**(717,133)**	(698,134)	2.7
➤ Operating profit before provisions	**703,468**	823,469	−14.6
Charge for bad and doubtful debts (Note 1)	**(255,172)**	(66,819)	281.9
Operating profit after provisions	**448,296**	756,650	−40.8
Profit on disposal of fixed assets and long-term investments	**68,815**	8,551	
Operating profit before exceptional items	**517,111**	765,201	−32.4
Exceptional items (Note 2)	**(192,510)**	—	
Profit on ordinary activities	**324,601**	765,201	−57.6
Share of net losses of associated companies	**(2,223)**	(1,551)	
Profit before taxation	**322,378**	763,650	−57.8
Taxation (Note 3)	**(50,356)**	(88,404)	
Profit after taxation	**272,022**	675,246	−59.7
Minority interests	**(16,007)**	(12,025)	
Profit attributable to shareholders	**256,015**	663,221	−61.4
Dividends	**(145,565)**	(273,968)	
Profit for the year retained	**110,450**	389,253	

Interest income and interest expense will vary substantially depending upon prevailing interest rates and economic conditions. The number to focus on is net interest income, which ignores these changes to provide an indication of how much profit the bank's lending and investment operations are generating. Non-interest income includes income from all other sources.

Operating income = net interest income + non-interest (other) income.

Deducting non-interest (other) expenses from operating income leave net profit before provisions and taxes.

a diversified financial services company based in Hong Kong that has a large commercial banking operation there. Notes have been omitted.

Notice that the income statement for Dah Sing Bank, like all income statements, shows line items for income and expenses, and proceeds with inexorable logic to subtract the one for the other to arrive at the net profit attributable to shareholders. This is the so-called bottom line. Proceeding further, we see that out of net profits, dividends are distributed to shareholders, and the sum remaining constitutes the bank's retained profits. Retained profits are internally generated capital, and, as mentioned, form the nexus between the income statement and the balance sheet.

Let us look at the component parts of an income statement. We will use the income statement for HSBC, a UK based financial services company with global aspirations that is the majority shareholder of Hongkong Bank, the largest in that special administrative region of China. In the following chapter, we will also use HSBC's balance sheet for illustrative purposes. Because the bank's operations constitute the major source of the group's revenue, Hong Kong accounting standards have been followed and the statement is quite similar to that of Dah Sing Bank.

INTEREST INCOME

The first line item is *interest income*, sometimes referred to as *gross interest income*. Interest income includes income from loans and securities, and comprises the bulk of income for most banks. In the case of HSBC, net interest income comprises about 70% of operating income (net interest income + non-interest income). This is typical. Net interest income usually constitutes between 50% and 80% of operating income at most banks. Gross interest income, it should be noted, is of limited relevance to the analyst as it fluctuates in line with interest rates, as does interest expense. A more relevant figure is net interest income, which substantially absorbs fluctuating interest rates. The mere increase in general interest rates will cause a bank's interest income to rise, even though net interest income remains the same. It is worth noting that a rise in either interest income or net interest income does not necessarily imply a rise in profitability.

Some banks will break down interest income into subcategories by source in the income statement, such as interest income from commercial loans, interest income from consumer loans, interest income from short-term securities and so on. It is more common practice to categorize the sources of interest income separately, which is HSBC's policy. Footnotes 4(a) and 4(b) in the group's annual report show these figures. The bulk of interest income is actually categorized as "other interest income," notwithstanding that it is the primary category. This actually refers to interest income from loans and other advances to customers, in contrast to interest income from investments in fixed-income securities such as treasury bills and bonds.

INTEREST EXPENSE (EXPENSE ITEM)

The second line item is interest expense. This refers to the interest the bank must pay to its depositors and creditors from whom it has borrowed funds to on-lend to bank customers. In other words, interest expense constitutes the bank's cost of funding. As with interest income, interest expense can be categorized by its source; e.g. consumer deposits,

THE HONKONG AND SHANGHAI BANKING CORPORATION LIMITED

Consolidated Profit and Loss Account for the Year Ended 31 December 1999

	Note	1999 HK$m	1999 £m	1999 US$m	1998 HK$m
Interest income	4a	**90,656**	*7,220*	*11,684*	103,884
Interest expense	4b	**(55,703)**	*(4,436)*	*(7,179)*	(70,696)
Net interest income		**34,953**	*2,784*	*4,505*	33,188
Other operation income	4c	**15,282**	*1,217*	*1,969*	15,714
Operating income		**50,235**	*4,001*	*6,474*	48,902
Operating expenses	4d	**(19,236)**	*(1,532)*	*(2,479)*	(18,619)
Operating profit before provisions		**30,999**	*2,469*	*3,995*	30,283
Provisions for bad and doubtful debts	4e	**(7,847)**	*(625)*	*(1,011)*	(12,531)
Provisions for contingent liabilities and commitments	28b	**(143)**	*(11)*	*(18)*	(222)
Operating profit		**23,009**	*1,833*	*2,966*	17,530
Profit/(loss) on tangible fixed assets and long-term investments	5	**1,822**	*145*	*235*	(289)
Deficits arising on property revaluation	21d	**(263)**	*(21)*	*(34)*	(971)
Share of profits less losses of associated companies		**127**	*10*	*16*	182
Profit on ordinary activities before tax		**24,695**	*1,967*	*3,183*	16,452
Tax on profit on ordinary activities	6a	**(3,625)**	*(289)*	*(467)*	(3,102)
Profit on ordinary activities after tax		**21,070**	*1,678*	*2,716*	13,350
Minority interests		**(3,165)**	*(252)*	*(408)*	(2,565)
Profit attributable to shareholders		**17,905**	*1,426*	*2,308*	10,785
Retained profits at 1 January	31	**45,314**	*3,609*	*5,840*	44,542
Exchange and other adjustments		**(155)**	*(12)*	*(20)*	(690)
Transfer of depreciation of premises revaluation reserve		**274**	*22*	*35*	379
Realisation on disposal of premises and investment properties		**15**	*1*	*2*	49
Dividends (including amounts attributable to non-equity shareholders)	8	**(22,088)**	*(1,759)*	*(2,847)*	(9,751)
Retained profits at 31 December	31	**41,265**	*3,287*	*5,318*	45,314

	Note	1999 HK$m	
Interest income	4a	**90,656**	To the analyst, (gross) interest income says little about the bank's interest earning business since it will fluctuate with prevailing interest rates. The key figure is net interest income.
Interest expense	4b	**(55,703)**	
Net interest income		**34,953**	

a	Interest income	1999	1999
		HK$m	HK$m
	Interest income on listed investments	1,707	1,622
	Interest income on unlisted investments	7,128	6,056
	Other interest income	81,821	96,206
		90,656	103,884

b	Interest expense	1999	1999
		HK$m	HK$m
	Interest expense on loan capital, other debt securities in issue, customer deposits and deposits by banks maturing after five years	1,100	1,178
	Other interest expense	54,603	69,518
		55,703	70,696

interbank borrowing, medium- and long-term borrowing. Most commercial banks obtain the bulk of their funding from deposits. Some institutions, wholesale banks for example, tend to rely to a great extent on commercial borrowing for funding.

In the case of HSBC, again other interest expense, referring to interest on customer deposits is the primary category.

NET INTEREST INCOME

Subtracting interest expense from interest income leaves net interest income as the remainder. Net interest income is a crucial figure to any bank, as it ordinarily represents the majority of a bank's revenue. Significant increases or decreases in net interest income are of particular interest to the analyst. In general, moderate and continuous increases in net interest income, in line with or somewhat above average relative to the bank's peers, is the ideal.

NON-INTEREST INCOME

Income that is not derived from interest-earning assets (earning assets) is categorized as non-interest income and is sometimes referred to as other income. The main sources of non-interest income are fees and commissions (e.g. for providing guarantees, letters of credit, trust services, arranging financing, rental of safe deposit boxes; check clearing fees and automatic teller machine fees) and gains on securities and foreign exchange trading. Other categories of non-interest income run the gamut from stock broker-age fees to ATM charges depending upon the permitted activities in which banks may engage in a particular jurisdiction.

c Other operating income	1999 HK$m	1999 HK$m
Dividend income		
Listed investments	175	271
Unlisted investments	131	85
	306	356
Fees and commissions (net)		
Fees and commissions receivable	11,141	10,124
Fees and commissions payable	(1,762)	(1,712)
	9,379	8,412
Dealing profits		
Foreign exchange	2,640	3,657
Interest rate derivatives	413	707
Debt securities	70	290
Equities and other trading	43	(6)
	3,166	4,648
Rental income from invetment properties	260	291
Other	2,171	2,007
	15,282	15,714

Although non-interest income is referred to as "other operating income," HSBC is otherwise fairly typical in the composition of its non-interest income stream. Dividend income and rental income are minor components, while fees and commissions, which like trading gains (dealing profits) are netted out by deducting fees and commissions pay-able (trading losses in the case of trading gains), are the chief constituents. "Other income" constitutes a significant portion of non-interest income, and might be worth further inquiry in a meeting with management.[3]

OPERATING INCOME

Operating income is the sum of net interest income and non-interest income. It represents the entire pool of revenue from which the bank must pay for its operations and generate a profit.

---

[3] This refers to miscellaneous income.

	Note	1999 HK$m	Net interest income plus non-interest income (other operating income) gives us (gross) operating income. This is the pool of revenue out of which profit is derived after deducting non interest expense. Note that interest expense and expenses directly attributable to fees and commissions (i.e. fees and commissions payable) and trading losses will already have been netted out from non-interest income at this point.
Interest income	4a	90,656	
Interest expense	4b	(55,703)	
Net interest income		34,953	
Other operating income	4c	15,282	
Operating income		50,235	

NON-INTEREST EXPENSES[4]

Non-interest expenses are the costs to the bank of running its business, including staff salaries and benefits (compensation expenses), occupancy expenses (i.e. rent on the bank's premises and utility costs) and other expenses, such as office supplies. Banks will often provide additional disclosure concerning the source of expenses, including categories for compensation and occupancy expense. Significant changes in non-interest expenses is of key interest to the analyst, as higher expenses normally mean lower profits and vice versa.[5]

			From (gross) operating income, operating expenses (i.e. non-interest income expenses) are deducted to obtain operating profit before provisions (i.e. earnings before provisions and taxes — EBPT), a key indicator that reflects core profit generating capacity.
Operating income		50,235	
Operating expenses	4d	(19,236)	
Operating profit before provisions		30,999	

In HSBC's income statement, like that of many banks, operating expenses are a single line item. A more detailed breakdown can be found in the footnotes to the financial statements, in this case, footnote 4d.

For most banks, compensation costs are the main expense, and HSBC is no exception. More than half of the bank's non-interest expenses derive from staff costs. As is usually the case, the runner up is occupancy expense, in this case denominated as "premises and equipment." Depreciation, an

---

[4] These are sometimes referred to as "operating expenses."
[5] Non-interest expense ordinarily includes depreciation. To provide a better picture of actual, as opposed to financial outflows, depreciation may be broken out of expenses when spreading the bank for analytical purposes.

d Operating expenses	1999 HK$m	1998 HK$m
Staff costs	10,124	9,570
Salaries and other costs	1,146	1,248
	11,270	10,818
Premises and equipment		
Depreciation (Note 21a)	1,883	1,883
Rental expense	1,380	1,281
Other premises and equipment expenses	1,305	1,276
	4,568	4,440
Other	3,398	3,361
	19,236	18,619

accounting construct, comprises a significant portion and for credit analytical purposes might permissibly be set aside when making analytical calculations. Other expenses likewise are significant, and again some inquiry might be made of bank management as to the composition of this category.

OPERATING PROFIT BEFORE PROVISIONS, TAXES AND EXTRAORDINARY ITEMS

Subtracting operating expenses from operating income, we arrive at operating profit before loan loss provisions, taxes and extraordinary items. Because loan loss provisions are both volatile and often highly discretionary, a bank's net profit can vary considerably from one year to another. It is not unusual for a bank to show a decline in profits or even a loss after provisions are deducted, at the same time that operating profit before provisions has increased. Underlying profitability is frequently better reflected in a bank's operating profit before provisions.

Similarly, bank management may use provisioning charges to smooth out profits. To be sure, it is prudent to provision when times are good and draw down those provisions when times are hard. While the analyst prefers to see steady rather than erratic line entries for profit and expenses, an eyebrow should be raised when it appears that loan loss provisioning is mainly used to manipulate the bottom line. If in such a case the analyst has the opportunity to meet with management, the topic of loan loss provisioning policy may be further explored.

LOAN LOSS PROVISIONS
(CHARGE FOR BAD AND DOUBTFUL DEBTS)

Loan loss provisions are a financial outflow, although they are a non-cash expense.[6] Hence, they are listed separately from non-interest (operating) expenses. Loan loss provisions include general provisions applied on a statistical basis to all loans and specific provisions designed to account for the probability of losses among classified or problem loans. Such general or statistical loan loss reserves are meant to function as reserves against probable loan losses, and are essentially a deduction designed to account for the costs arising from credit or default risk among customers (credit risk). Specific provisions, in contrast, are assigned to specific loans deemed problematic, typically weighted according to the loan classification, which in turn is linked to the likelihood of non-payment.

Operating profit before provisions		**30,999**	Loan loss provisions may eat away a significant chunk of operating income. The analyst should beware of banks that under-provision, or over-provision in an attempt to manipulate the bottom line.
Provisions for bad and doubtful depts	*4c*	**(7,847)**	
Provisions for contingent liabilities and commitments	*28b*	**(143)**	
Operating profit		**23,009**	

Loan loss provisions can be viewed as a means to adjust for a bank's inevitable "mistakes" in extending credit. In fact, a certain proportion of defaults is expected and should be provided for as a cost of doing business. For this reason, they are sometimes termed *credit costs*. Banks know from experience what their expected default rate is and ideally will set aside adequate provisions in advance to cover the costs of loss from default, making adjustments as necessary. While the principal of setting aside loan loss reserves to account for credit costs is almost universally accepted by banks and bank regulators throughout the world, determining the appropriate amount of loan loss provisioning can be difficult. In actuality, banks often, as we will see, underestimate these costs and under-provision. Because provisions cut into the bottom line, management often has an incentive to keep provisioning costs to a minimum in order to prevent profits from being reduced and drawing the ire of shareholders and equity analysts. In other circumstances, banks may

---

[6] Loan loss provisioning in accounting terminology is referred to as a "contra account."

over-provision in order to reduce tax liability, or as mentioned, to smooth out profits. Needless to say, provisioning is not always undertaken for the purpose for which it is intended.

e	*Provisions for bad and doubtful depts*		
	Net charge/(release) for bad and doubtful debts	**1999**	
		HK$m	
	Advances to customers (Note 16a)		
	... Specific provisions		
	New provisions	**10,282**	
	Releases	**(1,754)**	
	Recoveries	**(307)**	
		8,221	
	... General provisions	**(364)**	
		7,857	
	Placings with banks maturing after one month		
	... Net specific (release)/charge (Note 10c)	**(10)**	
	Net charge to profit and loss account	**7,847**	

Loan loss provisioning for the year will be deducted from operating income. Its placement in the income statement varies with some banks deducting it from directly from net interest income.

The loan loss provisioning charge is calculated as follows:

new specific provisions
−provisions released that are no longer required (e.g. loan that was considered substandard subsequently returned to performing status and has since matured)
−recoveries (e.g. on loss loans)
+ general provisions*

*HSBC also separately identifies specific provisions against placements with (i.e. loans to) other banks.

The foregoing excerpt from the notes to HSBC's financial statements shows the breakdown of provisioning charges into *general provisioning* and *specific provisioning*. Note that requisite specific provisioning was reduced by "releases" of provisions previously set aside (the reason could be the change in classification of a group of loans from a more severe category to a less severe category, or due to the loans maturing). Additionally, the net specific provisioning charge has been further reduced "recoveries," which refer, for instance, to recoveries on loans previously deemed to be loss loans and fully provided against. HSBC, in this case, has also reduced its general provisioning requirement and has returned those funds into general use by subtracting them from the loan loss provisioning charge that would otherwise be made, resulting in a lower net charge. The reason was likely the contraction in the bank's loan book between in FY98 and FY99, possibly coupled with the prospect of more salutary business conditions. Note that HSBC has also provided for contingent i.e. off balance sheet liabilities.

Remember that provisioning, an income statement line item, differs from provisions or loan loss reserves. Loan loss reserves are a cumulative item that usually appear on a footnote to the balance sheet. Cumulative loan loss provisions, of course, change according to the amount of net new provisions added or subtracted. This provides another link between the income statement and the balance sheet in addition to that of retained earnings and capital. This should not be surprising because loan loss provisions share a similar cushioning function to capital and, as we shall see, are indeed considered in certain cases to be capital for regulatory purposes.

OPERATING PROFIT BEFORE EXTRAORDINARY ITEMS

From one year to the next, a bank's profits may be subject to major fluctuations, if, for example, the institution sells a subsidiary and books an one-time gain or a one-time loss. Such "extraordinary" or "exceptional" gains or losses may make a bank's bottom line appear much better or worse than is justified by its ongoing business. When the result is positive for the bank and where reporting standards are lax, there is little incentive to bring attention to the fact that it such income is unlikely to be recurring. It is important therefore for the analyst to make special note of any significant extraordinary items, positive or negative. Note that some degree of discretion exists on management's part to determine whether an item is extraordinary or not. Some unusual items, although perhaps not contravening local accounting rules in being characterized as such, may be arguably viewed by the analyst as non-recurrent, yet deemed by the bank to be non-extraordinary. In similar fashion, to boost poor earnings, a bank may engage in a series of "extraordinary" transactions, whether characterized as such or not, and its managers may argue that because the bank is engaging in them so frequently that they are akin to a recurring business.

Note that "extraordinary" and "exceptional" items have basically the same impact in that they represent non-recurrent income or expenses. The difference is that an extraordinary gain, for example, arises outside of the bank's ordinary business (e.g. through the one-off sale of a subsidiary), while an exceptional gain, for instance, would be an unusual windfall arising in the course of the bank's ordinary business (e.g. a loan syndication fee as an arranger for a bank which rarely plays that role and has no intention of pursuing the loan syndication business). Determining whether an item is an extraordinary or exceptional item involves reference to applicable accounting guidelines and in the end may be a judgment call.

Operating profit		**23,009** —	
Profit/(loss) on tangible fixed assets and long-term investments	5	**1,822**	
Deficits arising on property revaluation	21d	**(263)**	
Share of profits less losses of associated companies		**127** —	
Profit on ordinary activities before tax		**24,695** —	

Although not specifically noted as such on the bank's income statement, HSBC has separately identified three items that are of a sufficiently exceptional nature such that discrete line items have been made, notwithstanding that they occurred in the ordinary course of the bank's operations. They are 1) the net gain realized from the sale of property and investments; 2) a revaluation of property that resulted from a decline in appraised value; and 3) net profits from associates (i.e. affiliates).

Turning back to Dah Sing's income statement, we can see that the bank's share of net losses of associated companies was treated somewhat differently. Instead of being identified as an above-the-line "exceptional" income item, these losses are treated as a below the line "extraordinary" item.

PROFIT ON ORDINARY ACTIVITIES (NET INCOME BEFORE TAXES)

After deducting non-interest expense, provisioning, and extraordinary items from operating income, what is left is income (earnings) before taxes. As with extraordinary items, since taxes can fluctuate for reasons independent of bank operating performance, variance between pre-tax profit and after-tax profit should be noted by the analyst.

TAXATION

This item refers to corporate profits (income) tax. In jurisdictions where other local taxes apply, they may be included as a subcategory of non-interest expense. The bank's tax burden can have a major impact on the bottom line and some banks may attempt to use taxes, like provisioning, to smooth out net profits by taking a more or less aggressive approach to calculating tax liability. In Hong Kong, out of which HSBC derives most of its profit, the tax regime is quite simple and would probably not be amenable to such manipulation.

			Tax in this line item generally refers to corporate income or profit tax. Other miscellaneous taxes and license fees usually are categorized as part of non-interest expense.
Profit on ordinary activities before tax		24,695 −	
Tax on profit on ordinary activities	6a	(3,625) _	
Profit on ordinary activities after tax		21,070	

PROFIT AFTER TAXATION (NET PROFIT)

Deducting taxes from this gives the bottom line: net profit. Net profit is the item ordinarily used to calculate return on equity and return on assets. Here it is referred to as "profit on ordinary activities after tax." Note that for the years in question HSBC showed no extraordinary gains or losses, but presumably if it had, any entries would be made below this line. In some markets, extraordinary gains (or losses) might be entered before calculating net profit. The analyst should flag such a practice and take it into account when evaluating profitability and especially when making cross-border comparisons among jurisdictions where accounting rules differ.

MINORITY INTEREST

Minority interest refers to the allocation of profits to those who hold minority interests in bank's subsidiaries. Minority interest deductions from the income statement only arise in the case of consolidated financial statements in which the bank owns subsidiaries that are other than wholly owned. That is, subsidiaries that are majority owned by the bank will normally be incorporated within the bank's consolidated financial statements. It is therefore necessary to take account of the ownership interest of the minority shareholders of the subsidiary by making an adjustment for those profits (or losses) that are attributable to shareholders other than the bank (and indirectly the bank's shareholders). For example, if Bank X and Y Co own a subsidiary Z Ltd., on a 60:40 basis, Y Co, which is not a shareholder of Bank X, is entitled to 40% of the profits of Z Ltd. This item is deducted from Bank X's consolidated income as a minority interest.

		Minority interests represent the share of income from subsidiaries not attributable to the bank's shareholders. The category therefore represents a deduction from net income.
Profit on ordinary activities after tax	21,070	
Minority interests	(3,165)	
Profit attributable to shareholders	17,905	

On the HSBC income statement, minority interests appear as a deduction from "profit on ordinary activities after tax" (net profit). The counterpart of minority interest is the net income the bank receives from affiliates (associates) in which it holds a minority interest. As a minority shareholder, these affiliates are not encompassed within the consolidated financial statement, but the income they generate will contribute to the bank's bottom line, as would any other investment in the ordinary course of business.

			Share of profits of associated companies represents the net contribution from the bank's ownership in affiliates not consolidated within the bank's financial statements, while *minority interests* represent the profit from subsidiaries consolidated in the financial statement that are attributable to shareholders of the subsidiary other than the bank. They are two sides of the same coin: one corresponding to income from minority-held affiliates, the other representing the share of income paid out to minority shareholders of the bank's majority-held (or 50% held) subsidiaries.
Share of profits less losses of associated companies		127	
Profit on ordinary activities before tax		24,695	
Tax on profit on ordinary activities	6a	(3,625)	
Profit on ordinary activities after tax		21,070	
Minority interest		(3,165)	
Profit attributable to shareholders		17,905	

The illustration on next page may make the concept of *minority interests* clearer.

PROFITS ATTRIBUTABLE TO SHAREHOLDERS

Net profits less minority interest equals profits attributable to shareholders. Some of this profit may be paid out in the form of dividends to shareholders.

DIVIDENDS

Dividends are discretionary payments to common shareholders, and in the case of preferred (preference) dividends, obligatory payments to

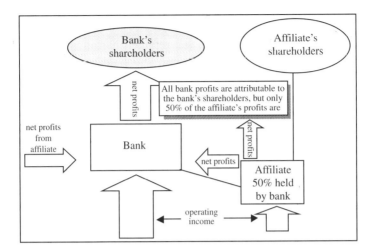

preferred (preference) shareholders. Preferred shareholders are normally entitled, depending upon the terms of the security instrument, to a fixed dividend ahead of common shareholders, but behind creditors.

HSBC's income statement shows retained profits attributable to the bank's shareholders at the end of the fiscal year as HK$17.9 billion (US$2.3 billion). Below this line adjustments are made for some extraordinary and miscellaneous items including foreign currency translation, an adjustment to revaluation reserves, and a disposal of premises outside the ordinary course of business. The main deduction, however, is for dividends which represent a direct payout to the bank's shareholders. A breakdown of dividends is provided in a footnote (note 8, not shown here).

Retained profits at 1 January	*31*	**45,314**
Exchange and other adjustments		(155)
Transfer of depreciation to premises revaluation reserve		274
Realisation on disposal of premises and investment properties		15
Dividends (including amounts attributable to non-equity shareholders)	*8*	(22,088)
Retained profits at 31 December	*31*	**41,265**

PROFIT FOR THE YEAR RETAINED (RETAINED EARNINGS)

Taking away dividend payouts leaves retained earnings. Retained earnings represent profits plowed back into the bank's business. In other words, they represent a component of the bank's capital that has been internally generated. In HSBC's financial statements, an accounting of retained earnings (sometimes referred to by banks as undivided profits) appears in a footnote to the balance sheet line item entitled reserves.

ILLUSTRATION: THE INCOME STATEMENT, ALTERNATIVE PRESENTATION

While the same basic information is normally contained in the income statement, details and presentation can differ. Some financial statements will be presented with most of the detail in accompanying notes, while others will include more items in the statements themselves. The example below is that of the Bank of the Philippine Islands, one of the largest banks in the Philippines.

We can see that BPI presents its income statement somewhat differently from Dah Sing. First, in contrast to Dah Sing, interest income is broken down into several components as is interest expense. Second, there is a line item for a "gross receipts tax," presumably a tax that does not exist in Hong Kong. There is an accompanying Note 13, which we would expect provides additional data about the tax. Third, rather than tally up "operating income" which helps show underlying profitability the reader is left to do this on his own. The emphasis in the BPI income statement is arriving at the bottom-line figure. A final difference is that BPI's income statement does not show the allocation of profit and dividend payouts. This information is provided elsewhere.[7]

CHAPTER SUMMARY

The income statement delineates the items that caused the bank to make a profit or a loss. In a sense, it is footnote to the balance sheet, that by virtue of its special importance to shareholders, describes in some detail the elements that contributed and detracted to a bank's profits.

---

[7] The reader may also observe that the BPI statement indicates earnings per share. This data was in fact provided in Dah Sing's statement, but is omitted from the presentation here.

CONSOLIDATED STATEMENTS OF INCOME FOR THE YEARS ENDED DECEMBER 31, 1998, 1997 AND 1996 (In Thousands of Pesos, Except Per Share Amounts)			
	1998	1997	1996
INTEREST INCOME (Note 3)			
...On loans and advances	P18,519,302	P16,950,055	P14,048,041
...On investments and trading account securities	6,831,911	3,650,002	3,724,241
...On deposits with banks	851,939	549,272	577,182
	28,203,152	21,149,329	18,349,464
GROSS RECEIPTS TAX (Note 13)	835,310	663,988	577,982
INTEREST EXPENSE			
...On deposits	13,713,451	10,466,666	8,322,223
...On bills payable and other borrowings	361,068	646,276	1,057,600
	14,074,519	11,112,942	9,379,823
NET INTEREST INCOME	11,293,323	9,372,399	8,391,659
PROVISION FOR PROBABLE LOSSES (Note 3)	2,018,491	1,682,458	397,802
NET INTEREST INCOME AFTER PROVISION ...FOR PROBABLE LOSSES	9,274,832	7,689,941	7,993,857
OTHER INCOME (Note 3)			
...Service charges and commissions	1,477,780	1,602,665	1,683,170
...Income from foreign exchange trading, securities			
......trading and investments (Note 12)	1,155,831	1,333,005	564,163
...Other income (Notes 7 and 11)	1,464,793	732,648	996,589
	4,098,404	3,668,318	3,243,922
OTHER EXPENSES (Note 3)			
...Compensation and fringe benefits (Note 16)	3,351,090	3,229,175	2,991,908
...Occupancy and equipment-related expenses			
......(Notes 6 and 14)	1,796,120	1,702,844	1,538,896
...Other operating expenses (Note 13)	2,094,044	1,795,302	1,578,368
	7,241,254	6,727,321	6,109,172
INCOME BEFORE INCOME TAX AND MINORITY ...INTEREST	6,131,982	4,630,938	5,128,607
PROVISION FOR INCOME TAX (Notes 3 and 15)			
...Current	2,061,627	952,299	1,121,917
...Deferred (Note 7)	(532,417)	(881,061)	(6,160)
	1,529,210	71,238	1,115,757
INCOME BEFORE MINORITY INTEREST	4,602,772	4,559,700	4,012,850
(INCOME) LOSS APPLICABLE TO MINORITY ...INTEREST	(41)	42	49
NET INCOME FOR THE YEAR	P 4,602,731	P 4,559,742	P 4,012,899
EARNINGS PER SHARE (Note 3)	P.........5,69	P.........5,68	P.........5,01
(See accompanying notes to financial statements.)			

Note that the sequence of presentation in this income statement for the Bank of the Philippine Islands differs from that of Dah Sing Financial Holdings and HSBC. While main categories are broken down into additional subcategories, the essential elements are the same.

By examining the various cost and expense items on the income statement, the analyst can determine to what causes an increase or decrease in profits — or in rare cases a loss — is attributable. To simplify analysis, the items of the income statement are customarily classified into a relatively small number of key categories. These categories are: 1) net interest income (gross interest income less interest expense); 2) non-interest income (income other than net interest income); 3) non-interest expense;

4) loan loss provisioning (a category sometimes combined with non-interest expense but which is typically broken out as a separate category); and 5) taxes, extraordinary gains or losses and minority interest. The bottom line, net profit attributable to shareholders, is calculated by adding 1) and 2) and then subtracting 3) and 4). Sometimes 5) will also be subtracted, although it is better analytical practice not to include extraordinary items when calculating financial performance indicators.

Using these simplified categories, changes in net profits or losses can be ascribed to one of a finite number of combinations. For example, an increase in profits can be attributed to a) an increase in either or both of net interest income and other income; b) a decrease in loan loss provisioning; c) a decrease in other non-interest expenses; or d) a decrease in taxes or the reduced adverse effect of extraordinary items or minority interest on net profit. Each of the income statement items can, of course, be broken down into further detail and positive or negative changes in a particular item can be further ascribed to such component items. For instance, non-interest expense can be divided into occupancy expense, compensation expense, and general and administrative expense. A decline in non-interest expenses may be composed of a modest increase in compensation expense, flat general and administrative expenses, and a substantial decline in occupancy expense. In addition to the items mentioned above, various aggregated items are commonly reviewed by analysts. Such aggregate items include: i) operating income (net interest income + non-interest income); ii) net operating income — also known as earnings before provisions and taxes or EBPT (operating income — non-interest expenses); and iii) pre-tax income (net income before taxes). Probably the most important is earnings before provisions and taxes, which takes into account non-interest expenses but excludes the often distorting impact of loan loss provisioning on core profitability.

The income statement is linked to the balance sheet through the shareholders' equity account. If the bank earns net profits, the portion of those earnings remaining after distribution to shareholders will be added to retained earnings, which itself constitutes a part of shareholders' equity. Shareholders' equity will thus rise, bolstered by the internally generated capital. Conversely, in the event of a loss, the shortfall between income and expenses will correspondingly cause a decline in retained earnings and in shareholders equity.

CHAPTER FOUR

DECONSTRUCTING A BANK'S FINANCIAL STATEMENTS, PART TWO: THE BALANCE SHEET

[A] typical bank's balance sheet presents, on the face of it, an alarmingly precarious situation.: its liabilities are mostly short term, but most of its assets are realizable only in the long term, and it is highly geared or 'leveraged.' Depositors and other creditors must be persuaded that the whole pack of cards will not come crashing down at a moment's notice.
— Fitch IBCA, Bank Capital: A Vale of Tiers, October 1997.

UNDERSTANDING THE BALANCE SHEET (STATEMENT OF CONDITION)

The balance sheet, or statement of condition, is a snapshot on a given day — very often December 31 — which indicates the composition of all assets and liabilities of the bank, including shareholders' equity. Assets usually appear on the left hand side of the balance sheet, while liabilities

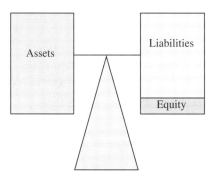

appear on the right. By definition, both sides must balance. That is, assets must always equal liabilities plus shareholders' equity.

This is just another way of saying that all the company's assets are claimed by somebody. What is left over after all the claims of depositors, bondholders, and other creditors have been satisfied, is claimed by the shareholders. (Shareholders' equity can be viewed as a special type of liability in that it represents the claims of the owners on the assets of the company they own.)

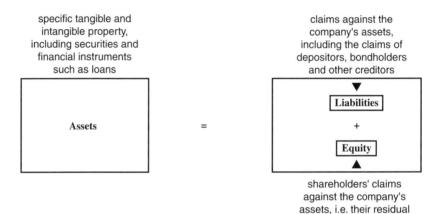

The assets, in turn, represent the company's ownership of specific property (e.g. premises and equipment) or claims against others, including ownership of securities or other financial instruments, which may generate revenue such as investment in stocks and bonds and loans. What is an asset to one entity may be a liability to another. This can be clearly

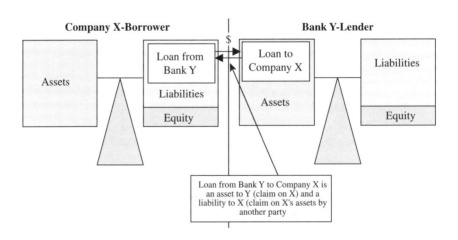

seen in financial assets, such as loans, which represent claims on another entity for the payment of interest or principal. For example, to a bank a loan is an asset, but to the borrower it is a liability. Likewise, to a bank, its investment in bonds is an asset but to the company which issued the bonds, they are liability. Similarly, to a bank its equity investment in Company X is an asset. On the company's books, however, that investment is recorded as a liability, since it is a claim of the bank against the assets of Company X. Finally, on the other side of the equation, my deposits with Citibank are an asset to me. They are, however, a liability to Citibank.

Assets

In the banking context, assets (sometimes referred to as resources) are items of value owned by the bank, or claims the bank may have against others. Normally, most of a bank's assets are in the form of (interest) earning assets such as loans and securities and non-earning assets. Non-earning assets include cash in the vault, which does not earn interest, as well as items deemed fixed assets such as the bank's premises, furnishings and equipment like desks and computers. Also included in the category of non-earning assets will be foreclosed assets, such as other real estate owned and other collateral or repossessed property.

Categories of Assets

Quasi-Liquid Assets*	Liquid Assets	Most Liquid Assets	❑ Cash ❑ Due from the Central Bank ❑ Due from Other Commercial Banks ❑ Government Securities[1]	Relatively risk-free
		Moderately Liquid Assets	❑ Marketable Securities (listed or unlisted securities for which a secondary, i.e. trading market exists) ❑ Other government obligations (e.g. government guaranteed obligations) ❑ Deposits with other banks[2]	Relatively low risk
		Less Liquid Assets	❑ Loans and advances ❑ Other securities and financial obligations, including direct investment, which generally are not easily liquefiable	Usually Moderate to high risk
		Other and Fixed Assets	❑ Premises and equipment ❑ Goodwill, intangibles, and miscellaneous other assets	Non-interest earning

* The definition of liquid and quasi-liquid assets varies.

---

[1] This is a general rule. Not all government securities are marketable. In some countries, commercial banks are obligated to hold certain portion of such securities and in some instances, government securities used to recapitalize a bank may be non-marketable and non-transferable.
[2] Term deposits are obviously less liquid than demand deposits.

UNDERSTANDING BALANCE SHEET ITEMS: AN OVERVIEW

Assets are customarily listed on the bank's balance sheet in order of decreasing liquidity, or the rapidity with which they can be liquefied or transformed into cash. Cash is obviously the most liquid asset, while loans and fixed assets are generally considered to be the least liquid. In between are readily negotiable assets such as government securities (assuming a liquid secondary market exists) and other debt securities. In some jurisdictions, banks may hold equity securities and these are often readily liquefiable. Together the first two categories are sometimes referred to as quasi-liquid assets, although the definition is not precise. The distinction between quasi-liquid and liquid assets, however, is sometimes blurred by disclosure and definitional issues.[3] For example, funds on deposit with another bank are normally deemed "quasi-liquid," but where such deposits are term deposits, they may in fact lack a degree of liquidity.

Balance Sheets Illustrated

Note the following examples of a bank balance sheet. The first is that for the Hongkong and Shanghai Banking Corporation, now known as HSBC, as published in the bank's fiscal year 1999 annual report shown on next page.

The second is the Bank of the Philippine Islands, one of the largest banks in the Philippines and one of the oldest in Asia, for fiscal year 1998. (Balance Sheet shown on page 68.)

Categories of Assets and Liabilities

As suggested, we can see that in both balance sheets, assets, referred to here as resources, begin with the most liquid type, cash, and proceed downwards in order of decreasing liquidity. How the bank's assets are categorized as to their liquidity is an important factor in determining the liquidity position of the bank as a whole. In the first table below are liquid and quasi-liquid assets.

---

[3] Thomson Financial BankWatch, prior to acquisition by Fitch, defined quasi-liquid assets as: cash + near cash + interbank assets + government securities + marketable securities. The company's BankStat product defined liquid assets similarly as "assets immediately available to cash, e.g. Cash, Trading Securities, Government Securities, Due from Banks and Short-term Marketable Securities."

Balance Sheet, The Hongkong and Shanghai Banking Corporation Limited (FY99)

Consolidated Balance Sheet at 31 December 1999

	Note	1999 HK$m	1999 £m	1999 US$m	1998 HK$m
ASSETS					
Cash and short-term funds	9	**416,922**	*33,184*	*53,637*	379,451
Placing with banks maturing after one month	10	**169,126**	*13,461*	*21,758*	120,401
Certificates of deposit	11	**32,308**	*2,571*	*4,157*	21,120
Hong Kong SAR Government certificates of indebtedness	12	**76,994**	*6,128*	*9,905*	57,384
Securities held for dealing purposes	13a	**24,258**	*1,931*	*3,121*	19,518
Long-term investments	14a	**130,226**	*10,365*	*16,754*	92,888
Advances to customers	15	**636,251**	*50,641*	*81,854*	682,638
Amounts due from fellow subsidiary companies	18	**23,056**	*1,835*	*2,966*	8,117
Investments in associated companies	20a	**1,480**	*118*	*190*	1,543
Tangible fixed assets	21a	**42,666**	*3,396*	*5,489*	40,886
Other assets	22	**84,605**	*6,734*	*10,885*	57,218
		1,637,892	*130,364*	*210,716*	1,481,164
LIABILITIES					
Hong Kong SAR currency notes in circulation	12	**76,994**	*6,128*	*9,905*	57,384
Current, savings and other deposit accounts	23	**1,263,359**	*100,554*	*162,532*	1,167,534
Deposits by banks	24	**47,198**	*3,757*	*6,072*	50,298
Dividends payable	8	**8,217**	*654*	*1,057*	2,551
Amounts due to fellow subsidiary companies	26	**6,813**	*542*	*877*	6,246
Amounts due to ultimate holding compnay		**452**	*36*	*58*	462
Other liabilities	27	**121,834**	*9,697*	*15,674*	82,118
		1,524,867	*121,368*	*196,175*	1,366,593
CAPITAL RESOURCES					
Loan capital from ultimate holding company	29a	**2,915**	*232*	*375*	2,905
Other loan capital	29b	**14,567**	*1,159*	*1,874*	13,982
Minority interests		**16,057**	*1,278*	*2,066*	18,185
Share capital	30	**16,258**	*1,294*	*2,092*	16,258
Reserves	31	**63,228**	*5,033*	*8,134*	63,241
Shareholders' funds		**79,486**	*6,327*	*10,226*	79,499
		113,025	*8,996*	*14,541*	114,571
		1,637,892	*130,364*	*210,716*	1,481,164

Directors	*Secretary*
David G Eldon	M W Scales
Kenneth H Fang	28 February 2000
Rosanna Y M Wong	

Balance Sheet, Bank of the Philippine Islands, 1998 and 1997

CONSOLIDATED STATEMENTS OF CONDITION
DECEMBER 31, 1996 AND 1997
(In Thousands of Pesos)

	1998	1997		1998	1997
RESOURCES			**LIABILITIES AND STOCKHOLDERS' EQUITY**		
CASH AND OTHER CASH ITEMS	P4,505,602	P4,896,462	DEPOSIT LIABILITIES		
			Demand	P17,963,356	P6,577,018
DUE FROM BANKO SENTRAL NG PILIPINAS (Note 4)	8,891,320	12,496,775	Savings	123,194,986	115,889,575
			Time	34,939,010	34,219,945
DUE FROM OTHER BANKS	6,369,167	20,487,260		176,097,352	156,686,538
			BILLS PAYABLE (Note 8)	1,899,675	11,148,091
			DUE TO BANGKO SENTRAL NG PILIPINAS	295,808	554,072
INTERBANK LOANS RECEIVABLE	4,255,565	4,850,579			
			DUE TO OTHER BANKS	124,844	85,184
TRADING ACCOUNT SECURITIES (Note 3)	5,799,290	3,410,839			
			MANAGER'S CHECKS AND DEMAND DRAFTS OUTSTANDING	1,607,814	1,105,752
INVESTMENT SECURITIES (Notes 3 and 17)	67,087,571	28,864,735	ACCRUED TAXES, INTEREST AND OTHER EXPENSES	2,039,899	1,901,345
LOANS AND ADVANCES (Notes 3 and 5)	100,950,871	111,618,183			
			DEFERRED CREDITS AND OTHER LIABILITIES (Note 6)	9,202,718	8,016,284
BANK PREMISES, FURNITURE, FIXTURES AND EQUIPMENT (Notes 3 and 6)	5,989,738	5,690,723	Total liabilities	191,258,110	179,498,276
			MINORITY INTEREST IN SUBSIDIARIES	5,483	5,442
OTHER RESOURCES (Notes 3 and 7)	15,004,885	11,906,464	CAPITAL FUNDS (Notes 1, 3, 9 and 10)	27,580,416	24,720,302
	P218,854,009	P204,224,020		P218,854,009	P204,224,020

(See accompanying notes to financial statements.)

Liquid and Quasi-liquid Assets: Comparison of Two Balance Sheets

HSBC	BPI	Remarks
Cash and short-term fund	Cash and Other Cash Items	This category encompasses cash in the bank's vault, cash items being collected, and in some markets may include overnight funds lent through the interbank market and deposits with the central bank.
Placings with banks maturing after one month	Due from Bangko Sentral ng Pilipinas (refers to deposits with the Philippine central bank)	This category broadly includes interbank deposits or borrowings and funds due from the central bank. Note that the order varies between banks.
Certificates of Deposit	Due from Other Banks (refers to deposits with other commercial banks)	
Hong Kong SAR Gov't Certificates of Indebtedness	Interbank Loans Receivable (refers to funds lent to other banks)	
Securities held for dealing purposes	Trading Account Securities	Refers mainly to short-term debt such as treasury bills.
Long term investments	Investment Securities	Refers to securities, including equity securities, held for investment purposes.

Non Liquid and Fixed Assets: Comparison of Two Balance Sheets

HSBC	BPI	Remarks
Advances to Customers	Loans and Advances	Refers mainly to loans made or leases extended to customer
Amounts due from subsidiary companies		Refers to equity investments
Amounts due from fellow subsidiary companies		
Investments in subsidiary companies		
Investments in associated companies		
Tangible fixed assets	Bank Premises, Furniture, Fixtures and Equipment	The banks' fixed assets
Other assets	Other Resources	

Quasi-liquid assets

Quasi-liquid assets refer to assets that are less liquid than cash, cash equivalent or deposits with other banks. The category consists mainly of government and marketable securities, although as mentioned in reality not all government securities are necessarily marketable. The term "marketable securities" embraces listed securities and over the counter securities for which a market-maker is willing to quote a bid and offer. Unquoted securities, or those for which no ready market exists, are excluded from the category of quasi-liquid assets. It should be mentioned that categories "trading account securities" and "investment securities" are sometimes applied to a bank's securities holdings. Trading account securities are necessarily marketable securities. Investment securities may be marketable or unquoted. The latter are as a matter of conservatism in the analytical approach deemed to be non-marketable.

Liabilities and Capital: Comparison of Two Balance Sheets

Presentation of liabilities differs more between HSBC and BPI than does the presentation of assets. HSBC has an unusual item resulting from its role as a provider of local currency in Hong Kong on behalf of the government. It also gives more attention to liabilities to subsidiaries, affiliates and the ultimate holding company (as shown in table next page).

THE BALANCE SHEET IN MORE DETAIL: ASSETS

Let us explore the balance sheet in more depth.

Liquid Assets and Quasi-Liquid Assets

Cash and Cash Equivalent

This refers to currency in the bank's vault, in ATM machines, and ordinarily includes checks in the process of collection, bullion, and other items of a similar character.

Note that HSBC's balance sheet is unusual in that it provides entries in three different currencies. Only Hong Kong dollar entries, however, are provided for 1999 and the preceding year.

	Note	1999 HK$m	1999 £m	1999 US$m	1998 HK$m
ASSETS					
Cash and short-term funds	9	416,922	33,184	53,637	379,451

Details of the composition of this category of assets is provided in Note 9, reproduced on page 73.

HSBC	BPI	Remarks
Hong Kong SAR currency notes in circulation[4]	—	An unusual item resulting from HSBC's role in providing currency on behalf of the Hong Kong government
Current, savings and other deposits	Deposit Liabilities	Refers to obligations to repay depositors their deposited funds
Deposits by banks	Bills Payable (e.g. bankers' acceptances[5]) Due to [the Central Bank]	
	Due to Other Banks Manager's Checks and Demand Drafts Outstanding Accrued Taxes, Interest and Other Expenses	It is helpful when deposits by banks are separated from core customer deposits
Dividends Payable	Deferred Credits and Other Liabilities	—
Amounts due to subsidiaries, affiliates and ultimate holding company	Minority Interest in Subsidiaries	—
Other liabilities		
Capital resources loan capital from holding company other loan capital share capital reserves shareholders' funds	Capital Funds	HSBC provides more detail in the balance sheet while limited additional detail is provided by BPI in the notes to the financial statements

---

[4] This is an unusual item resulting from HSBC's role as a provider of currency in Hong Kong.
[5] A banker's acceptance is "a negotiable time draft financing international trade." Thomas Fitch, Barron's *Dictionary of Banking Terms*, 3rd ed.

Due From Banks (Interbank Assets)

This category encompasses deposits with other banks, both domestic and foreign. Amounts due from the central bank may come under the same rubric, or be categorized separately. Similarly, short-term instruments purchased from another bank through the interbank market fall under this umbrella.[6] In the case of HSBC, we can see from this excerpt from the balance sheet on page 67 that interbank assets of less than one month maturity are deemed current and those having a longer term are classified separately.

Placing with banks maturing after one month	10	**169,126**	*13,461*	*21,758*	120,401

Interbank placements (i.e. interbank assets) are broken down by HSBC in Note 10 to the balance sheet reproduced on page 74. Subsection *a* classifies these assets by maturity. Note that not only loan assets can go bad and be required to be provisioned against, placements with other banks (i.e. effectively interbank loans) can also become problematic. As can be seen from Note 10, a very small portion of the bank's interbank placements required provisions. The problematic portion is delineated in subsections *b* and *c*.

Other quasi-liquid assets include certificates of deposits, which are negotiable instruments and marketable securities.

HSBC includes line items for certificates of deposits, Hong Kong SAR certificates of indebtedness, securities held for dealing purposes (i.e. trading securities) and long-term investments. Negotiable CDs are generally marketable and therefore quasi-liquid in nature. Hong Kong SAR certificates of indebtedness are a special asset not common to most

Certificates of deposit	11	**32,308**	*2,571*	*4,157*	21,120
Hong Kong SAR Government certificates of indebtedness	12	**76,994**	*6,128*	*9,905*	57,384
Securities held for dealing purposes	*13a*	**24,258**	*1,931*	*3,121*	19,518
Long-term investments	*14a*	**130,226**	*10,365*	*16,754*	92,988

---

[6] In the case of BPI, the following items are encompassed by the broader category, due from banks:
- ❑ Due from Bangko Central ng Pilipinas (refers to deposits with the Philippine central bank)
- ❑ Due from Other Banks (refers to. deposits with other commercial banks)
- ❑ Interbank Loans Receivable (refers to funds that BPI has lent to other banks)

9 Cash and short-term funds

	Group		Bank	
	1999	1998	**1999**	1998
	HK$m	HK$m	**HK$m**	KK$m
Cash in hand and current balances with banks	**24,063**	14,809	**18,620**	10,981
Placings with banks with remaining maturity				
of one month or less	**293,780**	286,990	**171,030**	180,553
Treasury bills	**99,079**	77,652	**91,266**	60,149
	416,922	379,451	**280,916**	251,683

Deposits required by overseas government regulations are included in the above figures as follows:

	Group		Bank	
These items are listed for regulatory	**1999**	1998	**1999**	1998
purpose	**HK$m**	HK$m	**HK$m**	KK$m
Cash in hand and current balances with banks	**1,990**	1,876	**1,799**	1,545
Treasury bills	**3,560**	1,432	**3,560**	1,432
	5,550	3,308	**5,359**	2,977
Treasury bills are analysed as follows:				
Held for dealing purposes				
— at fair value	**18,491**	15,985	**16,773**	14,033
Held to maturity				
— at amortised cost	**80,588**	61,667	**74,493**	46,116
— fair value	**80,640**	61,728	**74,540**	46,151

Treasury bills intended to be held to maturity with an amortised cost of HK$2,389 million *(1998: HK$2,084 million)* were disposed for prior to maturity or transferred to the held for dealing purposes catergory. The related profit recognised amounted to HK$3 million *(1998: HK$ nil)*. Such disposals and transfers amounted to 1% of total held to maturity treasury bills *(1998: 1%)*, were approved by Asset and Liability Management Committees, and were generally made to improve liquidity, lengthen the maturity profile of portfolios or reduce the risk portfolios.

Treasury bills are classified both by whether held to maturity and by term

	Group		Bank	
	1999	1998	**1999**	1998
	HK$m	HK$m	**HK$m**	KK$m
Treasury bills				
Remaining maturity:				
— three months or less	**87,831**	53,764	**83,450**	43,568
— one year or less but over three months	**11,061**	23,888	**7,629**	16,581
— over one year	**187**	—	**187**	—
	99,079	77,652	**91,266**	60,149

10 Placing with banks maturing after one month

commercial banks that arises through the bank's unusual role as an issuer of currency in Hong Kong. HSBC issues currency notes, together with the Bank of China and Standard Chartered Bank, on behalf of the Hong Kong government that serve as Hong Kong's legal tender and the certificates of indebtedness represents the government's backing for the notes issued. Trading securities include mainly government and corporate debt securities, although a small portion are equity securities or unlisted securities. The same applies to the bank's long term investments. In respect to both categories, unlisted or unquoted securities would properly be deducted from the pool of assets deemed liquid or

10 Placing with banks maturing after one month				
	Group		Bank	
	1999 **HK$m**	1998 HK$m	**1999** **HK$m**	1998 HK$m
a Remaining maturity:				
— three months or less but over one month	**130,189**	74,720	**87,194**	35,462
— one year or less but over three months	**35,959**	39,738	**8,369**	12,379
five years or less but over one year	**2,468**	5,464	**2,391**	5,311
— over five years	**510**	490	**510**	490
Gross placings with banks maturing after one month	**169,126**	120,412	**98,464**	53,642
Provisions for bad and doubtful debts	—	(11)	—	(11)
	169,126	120,401	**98,464**	53,631

	Group		Bank	
	1999 **HK$m**	1998 HK$m	**1999** **HK$m**	1998 HK$m
b Included in the above are gross placings with banks, net of interest in suspense: Non-performing placings	—	11	—	11
Placings overdue with respect to either principal or interest for periods of over three months	—	14	—	14
Rescheduled placings	**73**	229	**73**	229

c Specific provisions for bad and doubtful debts				
	Group		Bank	
	1999 **HK$m**	1998 HK$m	**1999** **HK$m**	1998 HK$m
At 1 January	**11**	—	**11**	—
Net (release)/charge to profit and loss account (Note 4e)	**(10)**	45	**(10)**	45
Amounts written off	**(1)**	(34)	**(1)**	(34)
At 31 December	—	11	—	11

quasi-liquid in nature. As the notes supplying additional details about these assets are rather lengthy, they are omitted.

Government Securities

Treasury bills and notes, and other securities issued by the national, provincial or local government, constitute government securities. Note that in many countries, there is a secondary market for national government securities. However, sub-national government entities will not necessarily issue debt and there may be no secondary market in such paper.

Marketable Securities

This refers to debt or equity securities for which there exists a liquid secondary market. It may or may not include government securities, if those are not classified separately.

Unquoted Securities

Unquoted securities are unlisted securities or securities for which no effective market exists.

Illiquid Assets

The term "illiquid" (a comparative term) embraces a bank's loan portfolio as well as its fixed assets. Loans (and unquoted or unlisted securities) although they may in certain cases be marketable, are the major component of a bank's non-liquid assets. Fixed assets comprise the remainder.

Loans and Advances

The bulk of a bank's assets will be composed of its loans. Advances include overdraft facilities and leases. Ideally, these assets will generate funds for the bank in the form of interest payments. Some percentage of loans will inevitably become non-performing, and the bank will need to set aside provisions for them. The total amount of loans made minus loan loss reserves equals net loans.

| Advances to customers | 15 | **636,251** | 50,641 | 81,854 | 682,638 |

While advances to customers of HSBC were the largest category of assets at the end of 1999, as a percentage of total assets the bank was relatively liquid. This was partly the result of the Asian crisis. The bank, which has a high proportion of its business activity in Asia, reduced loan growth along with most commercial banks in the region.

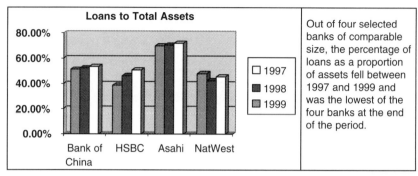

Data: BankStat

In Note 15 on next page, HSBC breaks down assets by maturity. The remainder of the note provides additional detail concerning asset composition. Observe that provisions, which are deducted from operating profit on the income statement are correspondingly deducted from loans to obtain net loans.

Investments In And Assets In Respect Of Subsidiaries And Affiliated Companies

Where a bank has substantial investments in affiliates and subsidiaries and holds assets in respect of such companies, such as an internal loan, these assets may be itemized separately. This is the case for HSBC which has large investments in bank and non-bank subsidiaries and affiliates as can be seen in this balance sheet excerpt.

Amounts due from fellow subsidiary companies	18	**23,056**	*1,835*	*2,966*	8,117
Investments in associated companies	20a	**1,480**	*118*	*190*	1,543

Fixed Assets

In the case of a bank, fixed assets are normally comprised of the banks premises and investment properties. This normally includes land and buildings, if owned freehold or by means of long-term leases, and associated equipment and furnishings.

Tangible fixed assets	21a	**42,666**	*3,396*	*5,489*	40,886
Other assets	22	**84,605**	*6,734*	*10,885*	57,218

15 Advances to customers

a *Advances to customers*

	Group		Bank	
	1999	1998	**1999**	1998
Remaining maturity:	**HK$m**	HK$m	**HK$m**	HK$m
— repayable on demand or at short notice	**52,369**	53,678	**38,250**	39,316
— three months or less but not repayable on demand or at short notice	**103,012**	121,651	**78,231**	97,347
— one year or less but over three months	**79,046**	79,757	**55,698**	58,242
— five years or less but over one year	**191,048**	192,778	**110,615**	115,930
— over five years	**194,935**	220,498	**94,760**	112,809
— non-performing advances and overdue for more than one month	**44,974**	38,833	**33,634**	28,874
Gross advances to customers*	**665,384**	707,195	**411,188**	452,518
Provisions for bad and doubtful debts (Note 16a)	**(29,133)**	(24,557)	**(22,510)**	(18,685)
	636,251	682,638	**388,678**	433,833

Included in advances to customers are:	Group		Bank	
	1999	1998	**1999**	1998
	HK$m	HK$m	**HK$m**	HK$m
Trade bills	**24,013**	27,416	**19,326**	22,069
Specific provisions for bad and doubtful debts	**(921)**	(855)	**(862)**	(818)
	23,092	26,561	**18,464**	21,251

Other Assets

Other assets is a catch all category for classes of assets which are not listed separately.[7] Examples are prepayments and goodwill. Categories of other assets for HSBC are itemized in Note 22 on next page.

THE BALANCE SHEET IN MORE DETAIL: LIABILITIES

On the right hand side of the balance sheet are liabilities and capital. Liabilities are claims upon the assets of the bank. Liabilities represent the bank's obligations to other entities, most of which have provided the funds to the bank enabling it acquire the larger part of its assets. This majority embraces depositors and creditors, including other banks, which have lent the bank funds. These liabilities, including also obligations to the central bank, may be deemed "funding liabilities." Funding liabilities are often, although not always, interest-bearing.

---

[7] In some jurisdictions, these may be listed separately.

22 Other assets

	Group		Bank	
	1999 **HK$m**	1998 HK$m	**1999** **HK$m**	1998 HK$m
Assets, including gains, resulting from off-balance sheet interest rate, exchange rate and other derivative contracts which are marked to market				
— third parties	**13,100**	25,970	**11,582**	24,583
— fellow subsidiary companies	**6,194**	3,378	**3,231**	2,870
— subsidiary companies	—	—	**2,462**	1,041
Current taxation recoverable	**276**	420	**250**	402
Deferred taxation (Note 28a)	**146**	85	**141**	68
Items in the course of collection from other banks	**17,343**	11,325	**13,324**	8,803
Prepayments and accrued income	**11,676**	10,816	**11,469**	9,804
Long-term assurance assets attributable to policyholders (Note 27)	**30,583**	—	—	—
Goodwill	**86**	59	—	—
Other accounts	**5,201**	5,165	**2,446**	3,259
	84,605	57,218	**44,905**	50,830
Remaining maturity:				
— three months or less	**39,853**	37,638	**32,728**	32,370
— one year or less but over three months	**7,461**	9,748	**6,233**	8,875
— five years or less but over one year	**5,349**	7,594	**5,005**	7,426
— over five years	**31,942**	2,238	**939**	2,159
	84,605	57,218	**44,905**	50,830

The remaining liabilities are those in respect of check clearing, obligations to vendors of goods and services, internally to subsidiaries and affiliates, and to the government in the form of taxes. These last would also include miscellaneous claims such as those of the landlord who leased property to the bank for its premises, the computer company which leased computer equipment and the other vendors who provide contracted services to the bank. Liabilities can also be said to include the claims of the shareholders, who are the owners of the bank. Their claims rank last after creditors. Creditors rank in order of priority from depositors and senior secured debt holders at the top to unsecured creditors at the bottom of the totem pole.

Funding liabilities can be broadly divided into customer deposits and purchased funds. Customer deposits represent retail deposits, while purchased funds are made up of commercial deposits (often in the form of large denomination certificates of deposit), and interbank and other borrowings.

Shareholders claims consist of their contributed equity (share capital), retained earnings not needed to satisfy the claims of creditors and various other items that represent the residual difference between assets and liabilities. The sum of share capital and these residual funds comprise capital, a term which, it should be emphasized, has a variety of definitions depending upon the context. Of course, if liabilities (excluding shareholders' claims) exceed assets, then the bank may be deemed insolvent with the result that, in theory if not always in practice, the shareholders will be left with nothing.

Liabilities are ordinarily presented in order of decreasing seniority with depositors at the top and shareholders at the bottom. In the case of HSBC, customer deposits are lumped together on the balance sheet, although an accompanying note groups deposits by maturity. Deposits made by other banks, which are sometimes referred to as interbank borrowings, are listed separately. Again, an unusual aspect of HSBC's balance sheet is the line item for Hong Kong SAR currency notes in circulation, which exactly corresponds to the asset item mentioned above that reflects the Hong Kong government's obligation to the bank.

LIABILITIES					
Hong Kong SAR currency notes in circulation	12	**76,994**	*6,128*	*9,905*	57,384
Current, savings and other deposit accounts	23	**1,263,359**	*100,554*	*162,532*	1,167,534
Deposits by banks	24	**47,198**	*3,757*	*6,072*	50,298

Customer and Interbank Deposits

Deposits (Deposit Liabilities)

This category in the main refers to retail (core) deposits. The following subcategories are common, although others may sometimes be seen. In the USA, so-called NOW and Super NOW accounts (interest-bearing checking accounts) and money market accounts are commonplace.

Demand Deposits

Demand deposits are current or checking account deposits. Traditionally, they bear no interest.

Savings Deposits

Saving deposits are equivalent to passbook deposits. They pay interest, but there is no fixed term.

Time Deposits

Time deposits are deposits for a certain term. They usually pay a higher interest rate than savings deposits.

Interbank Deposits (Due to Other Banks); Large Denomination/ Negotiable Certificates of Deposit; Short-Term Borrowings

This category together with short-term borrowings, and large-denomination certificates of deposits, constitutes "purchased funds" or so-called "hot money."

Long-Term Liabilities

This category refers to borrowings for a term exceeding one year. Under most bank accounting and regulatory systems, so-called loan capital (subordinated debt) may be classified in the equity or capital portion of the balance sheet if it has a tenor of five years or more and meets certain other criteria. This is the case with HSBC which as can be seen below groups borrowings from its ultimate holding company and long-term borrowings in the capital markets with capital. Capital is discussed in greater depth in Chapters 14 and 15.

Other Liabilities

Another catch-all category, other liabilities embraces those items that may or may not be grouped separately, depending upon customer and regulation. Examples include:

- Checks and demand drafts outstanding
- Accrued taxes, interest, and other expenses
- Dividends payable
- Liabilities in respect of subsidiaries and affiliates
- Miscellaneous liabilities

With regard to HSBC, several of the foregoing items are broken out separately as can be seen in the following excerpt.

Dividends payable	8	**8,217**	*654*	*1,057*	2,551
Amounts due to fellow subsidiary companies	26	**6,813**	*542*	*877*	6,246
Amounts due to ultimate holding company		**452**	*36*	*58*	462
Other liabilities	27	**121,834**	*9,697*	*15,674*	82,118
		1,524,867	*121,368*	*196,175*	1,366,593

THE BALANCE SHEET IN MORE DETAIL: EQUITY CAPITAL

Equity capital refers to the residual claims upon the assets of the bank, which if not needed to satisfy outstanding claims of creditors — senior, subordinated and unsecured — become those of the bank's shareholders. In other words, capital represents both the ownership interest in the bank and a cushion against losses. In reference to the balance sheet equity capital can be viewed as essentially synonymous with shareholders' equity (excepting minority interest in subsidiaries in the case of consolidated banking groups), including equity reserves. Shareholders equity is comprised of share capital (of common and preferred shares), retained earnings (undivided profits), and equity reserves. As such, equity capital embraces the following items in an unconsolidated balance sheet.

Observe that, if certain criteria are met, long term borrowings may be deemed capital both as matter of regulation (regulatory capital) and will so appear on the balance sheet. HSBC provides a good illustration.

CAPITAL RESOURCES					
Loan capital from ultimate holding company	29a	**2,915**	*232*	*375*	2,905
Other loan capital	29b	**14,567**	*1,159*	*1,874*	13,982
Minority interests		**16,057**	*1,278*	*2,066*	18,185
Share capital	30	**16,258**	*1,294*	*2,092*	16,258
Reserves	31	**63,228**	*5,033*	*8,134*	63,241
Shareholder's funds		**79,486**	*6,327*	*10,226*	79,499
		113,025	*8,996*	*14,541*	114,571

Putting aside regulatory capital for the moment, let us look at the components of share-holders' equity.

Share Capital

Share capital or paid-in capital refers to the value of the assets contributed by the shareholders. It is comprised of the par value of the bank's shares,[8] preferred or common,[9] and the surplus, which represents the difference between par value of those shares and the funds paid in.

Common Shares

Common shares represent the equity ownership of the bank. Common shareholders have no guaranteed right to dividends.

Preferred Shares

Preferred shareholders usually have limited voting and ownership rights, but are guaranteed a specified dividend. Preferred shares in that sense are akin to debt and are actually a hybrid between debt and equity.

Retained Earnings

Also known as undivided profits, retained earnings represent the earnings of the bank that have been plowed back into its business. They may be unutilized in the form of cash, or utilized to fund loans, securities or business expansion. Retained earnings are the source of internally-generated capital.

Equity Reserves

Equity reserves, not to be confused with loan loss reserves, are reserves designated for special purposes.

Minority Interest in Subsidiaries

In consolidated reporting for a bank that has subsidiaries, the investment of outside shareholders as minority owners in the bank's subsidiaries will be counted as part of the consolidated group's capital. To illustrate, suppose Oak Bank has a subsidiary Acorn Insurance, of which it holds

---

[8] That have no necessary relation to the actual value of the contribution.

[9] Preference shares or ordinary shares.

80% of the shares. The remainder are held by Stone Corporation. Since Stone is a minority shareholder, its equity in Acorn Insurance is counted as part of Oak Bank group's capital. However, a portion of Oak Bank group's earnings must be designated to Stone Corporation rather than to the shareholders of Oak Bank Group.

Equity Capital, Diagrammatic

This diagram shows the components of equity capital. Note that terminology may vary from one jurisdiction to another.

Unconsolidated Bank

Funds Paid in Exchange for Shares			Funds Generated from the Bank's Business	
Share Capital				
Common Shares (par value)	Preferred Shares (par value)	Surplus (Paid in Surplus)	Retained Earnings	Equity Reserves

Consolidated Bank

Funds Paid in Exchange for Shares			Funds Generated from the Bank's Business		Funds Paid in by Non-Bank Shareholders
Share Capital					
Common Shares (par value)	Preferred Shares (par value)	Surplus (Paid in Surplus)	Retained Earnings	Equity Reserves	Minority Interest in Subsidiaries (if any)

The diagram above refers only to equity capital, it excludes the inclusion of long-term debt as capital. It bears repeating that the components of balance sheet capital funds diverge from capital as defined for regulatory purposes. From an analytical perspective, as we discuss later, it is preferable to take a more conservative view of capital.

Off-Balance-Sheet Items

Off-balance sheet items, as one would infer, do not appear on the balance sheet, but may appear in notes to the financial statements. They do not appear on the balance sheet because they do not represent certain obligations but are instead merely contingent upon certain conditions occurring. Examples of off-balance sheet items are loan commitments (the promise that a bank will make a loan if the bank customer so opts), letters of credit, guarantees (the bank's promise, in exchange for a fee, to pay if a customer defaults), and various types of financial derivatives such as interest rate swaps and foreign exchange forwards. Because off-balance sheet commitments create contingent risk for a bank, they are under international best practice and many regulatory regimes factored into the calculation of regulatory capital.

RELATIONSHIP BETWEEN THE BALANCE SHEET AND THE INCOME STATEMENT

We began the discussion of a bank's financial statements with the income statement because it is the easiest to understand. While the income statement is highly important, the balance sheet presents a much more comprehensive picture of a bank's financial condition. How do the two relate

How the balance sheet and income statement link together

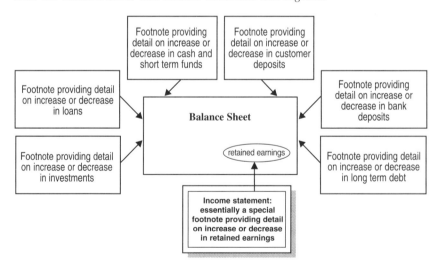

to each other? In simplest terms, what the income statement does is explain in some detail how the bank's operations caused its equity (via retained earnings) to increase or decrease before and after dividend distribution. In a sense it can be seen as a footnote to the balance sheet just like footnotes that explains how net loans, deposits, loan loss reserves or any other line item on the balance sheet increased or decreased.

CHAPTER SUMMARY

The balance sheet is the primary financial statement as it provides the most comprehensive description of a bank's financial condition. It is a snapshot which depicts the composition of a bank's assets and the claims on those assets. As with all companies, a bank, a banking corporation, is merely a vehicle for doing business. All of its assets are actually owned by creditors or shareholders. The income statement and the balance sheet do not exist in isolation. The income statement can be viewed as an explanation as to how a bank's net earnings before dividend distributions were achieved, and why capital increased or decreased, just as other footnotes to the financial statements explain other line items such as net loans or deposits.

Presentation of the balance sheet — sometimes called a statement of condition or statement of resources — may vary to some extent, but generally banks group items in a similar fashion. Assets, may be classified by liquidity or by whether they are interest earning or non-interest earning. For nearly all commercial banks, advances to customers, i.e. loans, comprise the lion's share of a bank's total assets.

Liabilities are claims upon the bank, and broadly speaking include the subcategory known as capital or equity. Liabilities are normally listed in the order of their seniority or priority of claim on the bank's assets. Most bank's fund their assets primarily through deposits, which usually form the bulk of a bank's liabilities. Deposits may be divided into core deposits, or customer deposits, and bank or institutional deposits. The latter are sometimes called "purchased funds" and represent a less stable source of funding.

A bank may also obtain funding from borrowings either directly or through the capital market. From the perspective of corporate law and conventional equity analysis, such debt funding is a liability comparable to that which a bank has towards its depositors, although depositors will invariably rank above other debtholders. Equity capital or shareholders' equity, represents the residual claims upon a bank's assets. The shareholders, in other words, are entitled to what is left over when depositors and creditors have been repaid. The concept of "regulatory capital," however, sometimes causes financial reporting of banks to diverge from that of non-financial companies. Under certain conditions, long term subordinated debt may be classified as "capital" equivalent to "equity" even though it is clearly not from a traditional perspective. Somewhat similarly, off-balance sheet commitments, as one would infer, do not appear on the balance sheet but may nonetheless be factored into a calculation of a regulatory capital.

CHAPTER FIVE

INTRODUCTION TO BANK CREDIT ANALYSIS: THE CAMEL MODEL

Though the principles of the banking trade appear somewhat abstruse, the practice is capable of being reduced to strict rules. To depart upon any occasion from those rules, in consequence of some flattering speculation of extraordinary gain, is almost always extremely dangerous, and frequently fatal, to the banking company which attempts it.

— Adam Smith, Wealth of Nations[1]

The underlying concept of financial ratio analysis is valid regardless of the system to which it is applied. The problem comes in developing appropriate standards with which these ratios can be compared. In other words, there is no debate over whether ROA measures the efficient employment of assets; rather the debate concerns what number should be viewed as an acceptable ratio.

— Robert Morris Associates, *Analyzing Foreign Banks*[2a]

Bank credit analysis ... is a discipline in which quantitative tools and qualitative judgment are used to predict the risk of default on both specific debt obligations and on classes of obligations.

— Moody's Special Comment, "Moody's Approach to the Credit Analysis of Banks and Bank Holding Companies," April 1993

With bank financials presented in a consistent format, analysis can begin. By comparing a bank with its peers and with its historical performance, the relative strengths and weaknesses of the bank and emerging or reversing trends can be discerned. The heart of the analytical inquiry, as always, is to evaluate the bank's creditworthiness in general, and

---

[1]Book Five, Chapter One.
[2a] p. 8.

specifically, to determine its strength, diversification, and prospects of its business franchise, the quality and diversification of its loan portfolio, its vulnerability to economic shocks or business reverses, and its ability to absorb such shocks and return to sustainable growth.

CAMEL IN A NUTSHELL

Bank credit analysts almost universally employ the so-called CAMEL approach to credit analysis. Most rating agencies and credit analysts within the financial industry utilize the CAMEL model or a variant when evaluating bank creditworthiness. Even many equity analysts use the CAMEL model to assist them in making recommendations concerning the valuation of bank stocks. It is the system we explain in this book.

CAMEL is an acronym which stands for the five most important attributes of bank financial analysis. It derives from a system developed by bank examiners in the US and has become the international approach by which bank creditworthiness is evaluated. It should be emphasized, however, that the financial services industry is rapidly evolving as banks engage in new activities. Refinements and alternative models to bank credit analysis, therefore, cannot be ignored. Some of the variants to the CAMEL model and alternative credit assessment methodologies that may be applicable to banks are discussed in greater detail in a subsequent chapter.

The CAMEL model attempts to categorize the key elements of a bank's financial condition that affect its creditworthiness. The five elements are:

C for Capital
A for Asset Quality
M for Management
E for Earnings
L for Liquidity

The meaning of these facets of financial ratio analysis and the ratios used to measure them will be discussed in detail in the chapters that follow. All but the assessment of the quality of "management" are amenable to ratio analysis.

Capital refers to capital adequacy, which goes beyond the traditional definition of bank capital as equity capital. Capital as defined by applicable prudential regulations may include more than shareholders' equity, retained earnings and equity reserves. Such *regulatory capital*, as we observed when we examined the bank balance sheet in the previous chapter, may also include items such as subordinated debt, general loan loss provisions and hidden reserves in the balance sheet. Capital adequacy refers to the sufficiency of the cushion of equity and other accounts that function to absorb any shocks the bank may experience as a result of losses or diminution of its assets. If the capital cushion is exceeded, a bank is by definition insolvent, although technically insolvent banks can continue to operate if they have access to external sources of liquidity, as government-owned banks frequently do. Capital indicators include ratios such as shareholders' equity to assets and the risk-weighted Capital Adequacy Ratio (CAR), as developed and promulgated by the Basel Committee.[2]

Asset quality refers primarily to the credit quality of the bank's earning assets, the bulk of which comprises its loan portfolio, but will also include its investment portfolio (usually fixed income securities and rarely equity securities), as well as off-balance sheet items. Quality, in this context, means the degree to which the loans that the bank has extended are performing (i.e. being paid back in accordance with their terms) and the likelihood that they will continue to perform. As asset quality decreases, increased credit costs, i.e. loan loss reserves that the bank must set aside, cut into profits and loan write-offs may eat into a bank's regulatory capital. A bank with excellent asset quality will normally be able to maintain sufficient profits and capital adequacy.

Management refers to the competency of the bank's managers, a necessarily subjective judgment as to their expertise, strategic vision and experience, as well as other relevant qualities. An evaluation of management may also include other qualitative concerns such as the bank's ownership structure and organizational structure, including items such as staff training and experience, as well as compensation and incentives. The operating environment in which the bank operates is sometimes considered as a separate factor in gauging creditworthiness, but when not may be subsumed within the category of management.

Earnings refer to both profits and profitability, but with an emphasis on the latter. A bank with strong earnings capacity and high profitability will be able earn its way out of trouble by building up capital and continuing to invest in and grow its business.

---

[2] The Basel Committee on Banking Supervision.

Liquidity refers to the ability of a bank to access liquid funds (i.e. cash) in order to meet the current — or more specifically an acute — need for such funds. An acute need can arise if depositors panic, justifiably or not, and seek to withdraw their funds. A lack of sufficient liquidity is the proximate cause of most bank failures.

WEIGHTING OF THE CAMEL ELEMENTS

Different analysts and rating agencies weight the CAMEL components differently. From a credit standpoint, the components are not weighted equally. A hypothetical weighting is illustrated on next page.

PEER AND TREND ANALYSIS

Peer Comparisons

Once the bank's financial statements have been studied and placed into a standardized form, the process of peer and trend analysis can begin. Because all banks perform largely similar functions of financial intermediation, it is advantageous to compare banks to banks of similar size and character to see how they measure up to each other. This process is called "peer analysis." A large commercial bank is matched with several of its peers and various financial ratios, as well as qualitative facets of bank performance, are examined. In this way, a bank's relative strengths and weaknesses, and more importantly the trade-offs the bank has made, can be discerned. Since most financial indicators, as we will see, are interlinked, through analysis of key financial ratios (ratio analysis) it becomes possible to ascertain what choices a bank has made or failed to make, and whether management has made optimal use of its resources.

Discerning Trends

In addition to peer analysis (i.e. comparing a bank with banks of a similar class), bank credit analysts utilize trend analysis. Very simply, this means, determining whether a specific area of financial performance is improving over a two to three-year time horizon, or getting worse. Of course, whether a change in a single ratio has a positive or negative credit impact often depends upon the interplay of a variety of factors. Positive growth in assets is generally favorable, but if growth is too rapid, if it outpaces growth in capital or profits or occurs during an economic downturn when non-performing loan rates are rising, it may be viewed negatively.

Hypothetical Weighting of CAMEL Elements

CAMEL Components	Typical Weighting	Impact	
Largely Quantitative Factors	75	*Strong*	*Weak*
Capital	20	Deep cushion against loan losses; reduced perception of risk; reduced funding costs	Bank is highly leveraged and prone to insolvency if non-performing loans reach a relatively low threshold
Asset Quality	25	Reduced credit costs and improved earnings; can access liquidity and capital more easily	Requisite provisions and reduced income eat into profits, while write-offs eat into loan loss reserves and capital; bank vulnerable to insolvency
Earnings	10	Feed internal capital growth and liquidity; ability to rebound from problems	Feeble internal capital growth; difficulty attracting new capital; lack of resilience in bouncing back from problems
Liquidity	20	Ample cash to meet current liabilities; key to bank survival external liquidity compensates for weak capital in overall creditworthiness	Subject to cash shortages which could trigger bank failure through a "run" absent external sources of liquidity
Largely *Qualitative* Factors	25		
Management and related items	25	Able to drive earnings, attract capital, and employ robust risk management policies to maintain asset quality and sufficient liquidity	Inability to drive sustainable earnings; lack of or inadequate risk management policies make the bank vulnerable to asset quality problems, followed by capital or liquidity deficiencies
	100		

PEER ANALYSIS: DEFINING THE PEER GROUP

Peer comparison is an expression of the principle of comparing like with like. While banking at first glance is a relatively homogenous industry, banks differ from one another in size, nature of their franchise, commercial objectives and the regulations under which they operate. In attempting to discern deviation from a norm, choosing the subject bank's peers should be undertaken with some care. The concept of a peer group, however, is a flexible one. Members of a peer group will ordinarily have at least one characteristic in common, and ideally will have more than one. For example, a peer group could include any of the following:

- ❑ all banks within a country
- ❑ all commercial banks within a country
- ❑ all private commercial banks within a country
- ❑ all mid-sized private commercial banks within a country
- ❑ all mid-sized private commercial banks which have a fiscal year ending December 31 and which have reported results for the most recent fiscal year.

To a degree, a course, the selection of the peer group is constrained by the number of banks within a country of interest to the analyst. In some markets, Australia or Canada for example, the number of possible peer group members is quite limited. In others, such as the United States, the number is much greater. In other markets, the number of banks sharing similar characteristics, e.g. state ownership, may be relatively few. Below we list the main variables in defining a peer group.

Type of Bank

The character of a bank's business can be categorized in several different ways. Each country has its own regulations defining the roles of specific types of financial institutions and the activities they may engage in, as well as its own terminology. The categories can be quite numerous, ranging from large commercial banks to small rural institutions, and definitions and meanings will vary from market to market. Usually, smaller institutions will be of little interest to the majority of bank analysts. Broadly speaking, banks can be divided into three types: state-owned banks, which often have policy or development objectives; commercial banks: and thrift or savings banks. Most analysts will confine their coverage to major development and commercial institutions, unless special circumstances warrant.

Key Categories of Banks

BankStat the quantitative database product used by Bankwatch classified banks into 13 categories. This classification may be helpful in classifying financial institutions into appropriate peer groups. They are:

❑ Bank Holding Companies
❑ Building Societies (Savings & Loans)
❑ Commercial Banks
❑ Cooperatives
❑ Credit Unions
❑ Deposit Taking Companies
❑ Development Banks
❑ Finance Companies
❑ Industrial Banks
❑ Investment Banks
❑ Mortgage Banks
❑ Offshore Banks
❑ Specialized Banks

In addition to the BankStat categories, universal banks, merchant banks, and trust banks are terms that are frequently seen. A simplified list combining types that are similar to one another is provided below. As noted, regulatory definitions and roles may vary from place to place, but the following definitions may be helpful. They are listed in order of the probable degree of interest to the analyst.

Commercial Banks

Commercial banks are deposit-taking institutions that traditionally emphasize short-term commercial lending to businesses for working capital purpose. Funding conventionally comes from demand deposits, as well as savings and time deposits and commercial borrowings. A variant of the commercial bank, the universal bank, is common in European countries. Universal banks provide a wide variety of financial services in addition to traditional commercial banking activity, such as insurance, stock brokerage and consumer finance. Commercial banks are sometimes referred to in the United States as full-service banks, although the range of services will not necessarily be as broad as that of universal banks.

Savings Banks, Building Societies and Savings & Loans

The category "savings banks" is both a broad and narrow definition. Generally, it refers to institutions that focus on obtaining savings deposits from individuals for the purposes of financing home ownership through residential mortgage loans. The term, in this sense, encompasses thrift banks and in the United States what are termed savings and loan associations, as well as savings banks. In the 1980s, deregulation of savings and loans allowed them to engage in high-risk lending and investment activities that ultimately resulted in the US$150 billion savings and loan crisis. The industry was restructured, and while S&Ls now are more similar to commercial banks, they still retain an emphasis on home mortgage lending. Variants of savings banks, in the broad sense of the term, can be found globally. Building societies in the UK, for instance, are similar to savings and loan associations in the United States. In the United States, the term savings bank has a more specific definition, referring to savings banks or mutual savings banks that engage in home mortgage lending and investment in high-grade securities.

Bank Holding Companies

Bank holding companies, common in the United States, are companies that own one or more banks. Holding companies can own commercial banks, savings and loan associations and savings banks. Similar structures can be found elsewhere in the world.

Development and Industrial Banks

Development banks are banks with a specific policy role that emphasizes some form of economic development, such as agricultural, rural, or industrial development. They often have a component of state ownership, although in some countries, nominally private banks are not infrequently compelled by the government to engage in some development lending. Lending for development purposes that would not justify lending on commercial for-profit terms is termed policy lending or directed lending. Banks wholly-owned by the state frequently have a development function, often in conjunction with a commercial banking function.

State ownership, incidentally, commonly translates into some degree of state support.

Similar to development banks are industrial banks, which provide long-term finance to industrial companies. Typically they were funded by issuing bonds or borrowing from the government. Note that in the United States, the term industrial bank has a different meaning, referring to a form of consumer finance company.

Finance Companies

Finance companies typically provide short- to medium-term financing to individuals or companies. They are generally non-deposit taking institutions, but obtain their financing through commercial borrowing or through the capital markets. Finance companies may be associated with banks, bank holding companies or manufacturers. When associated with manufacturers, their prime focus is to finance the purchase of that company's products. For example, the General Motors Acceptance Corporation (GMAC) finances the purchase of GM cars by consumers. Likewise, GE Capital originally focused on financing the purchase of that firm's industrial goods, but subsequently diversified into various forms of consumer and commercial finance. In Thailand, finance companies lent heavily into the property sector and were implicated in helping to cause that country's financial crisis in 1997. Many were subsequently closed by the authorities.

Investment and Merchant Banks

The traditional role of an investment bank is to finance the sale of securities by underwriting the offering and assuming, to varying degrees, the risk of placing and distributing those securities with investors. Investment banks, depending upon the jurisdiction, may engage in a variety of other activities including securities brokerage, merger and acquisition advisory services, proprietary trading, and merchant banking, among other products and services. Merchant banking, which traditionally was a distinct category, involves the use of the bank's capital to finance acquisitions, originate loans, engage in structured finance transactions, and make equity investments, all with a view to earning a fee or selling the asset or investment for a significant gain. Today, however, the two terms investment bank and merchant bank are generally synonymous. Note that neither investment banks nor merchant banks ordinarily take retail deposits, but rely largely on the capital of their principals or shareholders.

Specialized Banks

There are number of types of financial institutions that can be found throughout the world. As suggested, as a rule these will be outside the scope of most bank analysts' work. It is nonetheless useful to be aware of these institutions and and the usual scope of their activities.

Mortgage Bank

Mortgage banks are banks that concentrate on mortgage lending, both commercial and residential. Unlike savings banks, they obtain their funding not from retail depositors, but through the sale of bonds in the capital markets. The bonds may be secured by the mortgages that the bank originates.

Trust Banks

Trust banks or trust companies manage trust accounts as a fiduciary to the trust beneficiaries. In other words, they manage assets (often inheritances) held in trust. In addition to their primary function as asset managers, trust bankers may also provide investment advisory services. Many commercial banks offer trust services, while trust banks may also offer some commercial banking services.

Offshore Banks or Offshore Banking Unit

Offshore banks are banks (usually owned by non-resident banks) established in certain "offshore" financial centers. The function of offshore banks is to accept deposits from foreign banks and make loans in the essentially unregulated Eurocurrency market. They are generally prohibited from accepting local deposits. Although subject to obtaining a license and paying a licensing fee, offshore banks ordinarily are exempt from local reserve and prudential requirements, exchange regulations, and income taxes.

Cooperatives and Credit Unions

Member-owned, the purpose of these institutions is to take deposits and provide financing within the member group.

Rural Banks

In some countries, small institutions designed to serve remote or provincial areas may be permitted by regulation.

Size

The banks should be within the same approximate size range. Within a country, banks often appear to fall into three tiers. The table below shows the size in assets of commercial banks in the Philippines.

Graph, Size Rankings of Commercial Banks in the Philippines

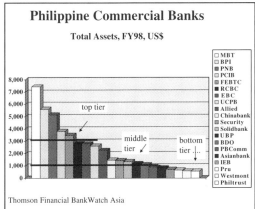

Thomson Financial BankWatch Asia

As of 1998, in the Philippine commercial banking system, three tiers of banks by asset size could be easily discerned: a top tier comprised of banks having more than US$3 billion in assets; medium-sized banks with assets of between US$1–3 billion in assets; and small commercial banks of less than US$1 billion in assets. Each tier could be used by the analyst as a discrete peer group or a pool from which to select a peer group, although banks which were fully or partly state-owned could themselves be grouped separately. Note that in response to a more competitive environment and policy incentives mandated by the central bank, the banking system was subsequently engulfed by a wave a consolidation during which numerous banks were merged or acquired.

Creating the Peer Group

Having identified the relevant categories of banks within a country and the size of each bank, a peer group can be identified. This might be all banks of a certain type, or often more practically, a group of between three and ten banks that share a similar character and size range.

For purposes of illustration, let us look at the banking market in Australia. Suppose that our purpose is to prepare a credit analysis of Westpac Bank. In order to create an appropriate peer group, we need to select a number of banks that are comparable to Westpac Bank. BankStat covered 65 institutions in Australia in 1999. Many of these are comparatively small foreign branches or specialized financial institutions and would be of little use in a peer comparison. Australia's banking system is fairly well consolidated with a small number of large commercial banks that dominate the sector. The table below includes all Australian commercial banks having more than A$10 billion in assets. It can be seen that the four largest form a clear peer group, each having assets of between A$130 billion and A$260 billion, in which our subject bank, Westpac, ranks third with total assets of A$150 billion.

Illustration, List of Australian Financial Institutions covered by BankStat with Total Assets over A$10 billion

		TOTAL ASSETS	FISCAL YR	
NATIONAL AUSTRALIA BANK, LTD. (C)	Melbourne, Australia	254081	9/30/99	Peer Group 1
AUSTRALIA & NEW ZEALAND BANKING GROUP LTD (C)	Melbourne, Australia	149007	2/28/99	
WESTPAC BANKING CORP. (C)	Sydney, Australia	140220	9/30/99	
COMMONWEALTH BANK OF AUSTRALIA (C)	Sydney, Australia	138096	6/30/99	
ST. GEORGE BANK LTD. (C)	Kogarah, Australia	45017	9/30/99	Peer Group 2
MACQUARIE BANK LTD. (C)	Sydney, Australia	23389	3/31/00	
STATE BANK OF NEW SOUTH WALES LTD (C)	Sydney, Australia	23140		
SUNCORP-METWAY LTD (C)	Brisbane, Australia	21496	6/30/99	
BANK OF WESTERN AUSTRALIA LTD (C)	Perth, Australia	17446	2/29/00	

Data: BankStat

As can be seen, a second peer group is discernable among the five smaller banks, each having between A$10 billion and A$50 billion in assets. These banks are more regional rather than national players within the Australian banking system. Note that the fiscal year-ends for Australian banks varies considerably, which makes comparison more difficult than it otherwise would be.

Having chosen the peer group, the next step is to do a peer comparison, to see what trends are evident in the group's performance. If data is available and if practicable, these trends should be compared with the industry as a whole. In succeeding chapters, we will examine trends of particular significance for which we will be on the look out. The illustrations on the following pages provide examples of the type of trends in which we are interested.

Peer Group Comparison, Australian Banks: Selected Indicators

The table on next page illustrates the data required to perform a peer group and trend analysis. It examines one or more key ratios in each of the key CAMEL categories, other than management, which as we have indicated is not amenable to quantitative analysis.

From this table, considerable information can be gleaned. For the moment, we shall illustrate in a broad-brush manner the type of issues that can be detected by looking at some graphs showing how particular indicators have fluctuated over time. In the charts that follow, ANZ Bank is represented in (▦), Commonwealth Bank in (▨), Westpac Bank in (■) and National Australia Bank in (▨). A line graph is used to smooth out the differences from one year to the next to display the trends more conspicuously.

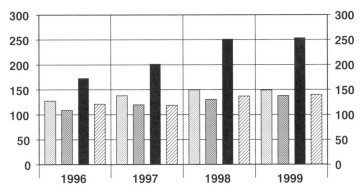

Source: BankStat

Total Assets

From the graph above, it can be seen that the three banks have maintained the same relative ranking in asset size over the past five years. Asset growth was rapid between 1995 and 1998, especially at National Australia Bank, which grew from A$150 billion to over A$250 billion during that period. Our subject bank, Westpac, actually declined in asset size between 1996 and 1997 before growing again 1998. All the banks leveled off in growth in 1999.

From this picture, we can begin to form some questions that our analysis should ultimately answer. First, why did the growth of all three banks slow in 1999 (although it appears that Westpac did grow slightly)? Second, what caused the decline in Westpac's total assets in 1997? Obviously, in the course of a full-fledged analysis, we would look at other trends affecting the four banks collectively and respectively, and come up with additional questions to which we would seek answers. The graphics on the succeeding pages will provide a taste of the types of trends we might examine.

LATEST FISCAL YEAR + THREE YEARS OF HISTORY												
ORDERED BY: BANKNAME		1	2	3	4	5	6	7	8	9	10	11	12
DISPLAYED IN: MILLION AUD			Key Items			Earnings			Liquidity	Asset Quality		Capital	
	FY	Total Assets	Total Deps.	Sh. Equity	Net Profit	ROA	NIM	Op Exp to Net Op Inc	Liquid Asset Ratio	NPLs to Gross Loans	LLRs to NPLs & Prob. Loans	IGRC	BIS Ratio
ANZ	1999	149,007	105,560	9,429	1,480	0.99%	3.16%	63.76%	9.15%	1.54%	119.65%	6.67%	10.70%
Melbourne, Australia	1998	149,720	93,292	8,391	1,106	0.77%	3.15%	69.52%	15.01%	1.72%	113.90%	4.67%	10.70%
	1997	138,241	87,675	6,993	1,024	0.77%	3.22%	70.34%	20.58%	1.02%	166.93%	4.94%	9.80%
	1996	127,604	80,940	6,336	1,116	0.93%	3.47%	70.16%	22.26%	1.59%	82.86%	8.81%	10.50%
Commonwealth	1999	138,096	96,058	6,962	1,422	1.06%	3.15%	60.90%	9.26%	0.62%	160.09%	5.18%	9.38%
Sydney, Australia	1998	130,544	83,438	6,889	1,090	0.87%	3.30%	63.80%	10.92%	1.02%	111.43%	1.94%	10.49%
	1997	120,103	77,863	7,024	1,078	0.94%	3.59%	63.06%	13.55%	1.10%	76.94%	1.90%	10.89%
	1996	109,285	70,360	7,367	1,119	1.02%	3.80%	62.84%	16.68%	1.57%	61.33%	3.90%	12.71%
Natl Australia Bank	1999	254,081	162,823	18,520	2,821	1.12%	2.95%	61.04%	12.18%	0.89%	144.59%	7.21%	10.40%
Melbourne, Australia	1998	251,714	158,642	15,761	2,014	0.89%	3.22%	62.05%	12.06%	0.87%	151.22%	4.35%	9.20%
	1997	201,969	131,114	12,381	2,223	1.18%	3.49%	61.41%	13.93%	0.97%	90.51%	7.62%	8.70%
	1996	173,710	112,866	12,267	2,102	1.31%	3.99%	61.64%	15.09%	1.28%	77.28%	7.53%	9.30%
Westpac	1999	140,220	83249	8,884	1,456	1.05%	3.26%	66.57%	10.06%	0.62%	179.86%	6.80%	9.30%
Sydney, Australia	1998	137,319	81,822	8,467	1,272	0.99%	3.57%	66.76%	10.12%	0.84%	132.89%	5.09%	9.40%
	1997	118,963	71,388	8,004	1,291	1.07%	3.58%	66.53%	11.73%	0.99%	127.04%	7.16%	10.50%
	1996	121,513	74,188	7,631	1,132	1.00%	3.67%	68.34%	12.83%	1.52%	102.50%	6.46%	10.80%

Data: BankStat

Return on Average Assets

The first illustration shows ROA, i.e. return on average assets, which is the key measure of profitability and how it varied among the four banks over a four-year period. Westpac ranked third at both the beginning of the period and the end of the period depicted. In its favor, however, its ROA has been remarkably stable while its peers have shown more fluctuation in profitability by this measure.

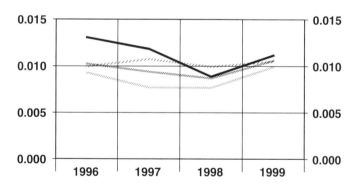

Source: BankStat

Comparing Westpac Bank against its peer group, we can see from the immediately preceding illustration that although it ranked third

Westpac Bank vs. Peer Group [Westpac in (▨), peers collectively in (▨)]

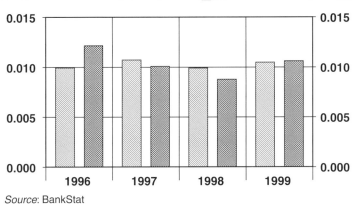

Source: BankStat

both at the outset and end of the four-year period, on a weighted basis relative to its peers as a whole, it improved its comparative profitability over that time.

Net Interest Margin

Another measure of profitability is the bank's net interest margin, which corresponds to the core profitability of its lending and investing activities. In respect to this indicator, Westpac improved its rank from third of four to first over the four-year period. The succeeding table also shows how the bank improved its position relative to its peers.

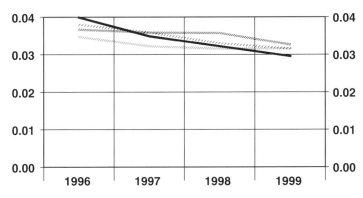

Source: BankStat

NIM — Westpac Bank to Peer Group [Westpac in (▨), peers collectively in (▩)]

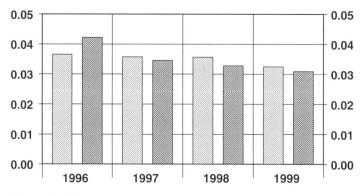

Source: BankStat

Liquid Assets Ratio

Turning to liquidity, Westpac Bank ranked clearly at the bottom of its peer group at the start of the period in terms of a key ratio: liquid assets to total assets. By the end, it ranked second and again had improved its position more significantly compared with its peers as a whole.

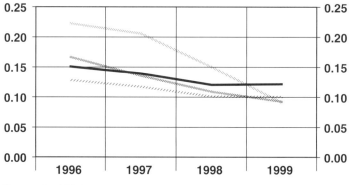

Source: BankStat

NPL Ratio & Asset Quality

Looking at another component of the CAMEL model — asset quality a key indicator is the NPL ratio, or the ratio of non-performing (problematic) loans as a proportion of gross or total loans. Here, lower is better and we can see that at the start of the period, Westpac's NPL ratio

Liquid Assets Ratio — Westpac Bank to Peer Group

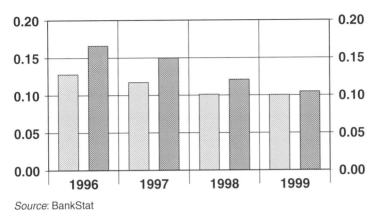

Source: BankStat

was about as high as its peers. Over the four years, however, it displayed significant relative improvement, ending the period tied for first place with the lowest NPL ratio.

NPL Ratio — Illustration

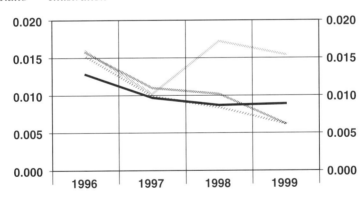

Source: BankStat

Capital Adequacy Ratio

Although indicators suggest that Westpac has generally improved compared with its peers in respect of profitability, asset quality, and liquidity, it is rare that a bank can improve in every respect without showing some trade-offs. Capital adequacy, as measured by the so-called Bank for International Settlements (or BIS) capital adequacy ratio — to be discussed in

NPL Ratio — Westpac Bank vs. Peer Group

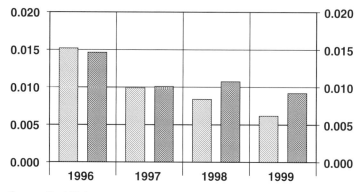

Source: BankStat

detail in a succeeding chapter — received somewhat short shrift by the bank's management as the graphs below indicate. Westpac Bank began with relatively strong capital adequacy, but this ratio declined during the four-year period. Compared to its peer group, the bank went from being better-than-average to weaker-than-average in terms of capital adequacy.

Capital Adequacy Ratio — Graph

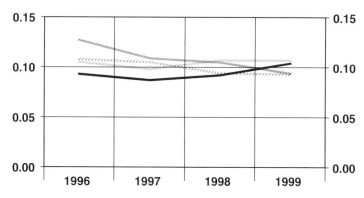

Source: BankStat

The foregoing illustrations are not meant to form a comprehensive bank analysis, but instead, are to give the reader a flavor of how bank credit analysts look at banks and the criteria that they consider. In practice, a greater number of indicators would be examined and questions raised

Capital Adequacy — Westpac Bank vs. Peer Group

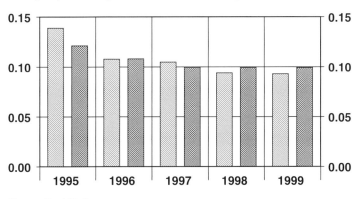

Source: BankStat

would be explored with management or be factored into the analysis possibly raising potential credit issues. In the following chapters, we shall explore the elements of the CAMEL model in greater detail.

CHAPTER SUMMARY

The CAMEL model is used almost universally as the framework for mainstream bank credit analysis. The acronym CAMEL stands for capital, asset quality, management, earnings (and profitability), and liquidity. Except for management, each component can be analyzed in large part using quantitative indicators. Weightings of each element vary but usually give greater emphasis to asset quality, capital and liquidity and relatively less emphasis to earnings and to management. Although the CAMEL model is by far the most widespread approach to bank credit analysis, variants and alternative and supplementary methods have been developed.

Because of the large and unavoidable qualitative aspect to bank credit analysis, the methodology used by analysts tends to be fairly uncomplicated. Relevant financial indicators are examined for trends and compared with banks in a defined peer group. Peer groups can be defined in any number of ways, but usually share commonality as to one or more criteria, including most often country (i.e. country or jurisdiction in which the bank does the majority of its banking business, asset size, and type of institution).

CHAPTER SIX

EARNINGS & PROFITABILITY: EVALUATING OVERALL PERFORMANCE

Earnings are essential to absorb loan losses, they finance internal growth of capital and they attract investors to supply new capital from the outside.
— Davis International Banking Consultants Manual[1]

The keys to banking are as follows: Charge high enough lending rates to cover default risk and yield a hefty profit. Leverage your capital and customer relationships by providing services ... in areas where you have a comparative advantage. Maintain a strong enough balance sheet so that counterparty credit concerns don't impinge on sour ability to do business. Avoid businesses where you have no competitive advantage ...
— Walter Altherr, *Japanese Banks: False Dawn*,
Jardine Fleming Securities (Asia) Ltd., November 1998

INTRODUCTION

The Importance of Profits

Profits are the lifeblood of any commercial firm. Although not all banks are purely commercial institutions, the vast majority fall into this category. By making adequate earnings, a bank, like any other firm, will be able — barring exceptional circumstances — to maintain solvency, survive, and, in a suitable environment, grow and prosper. Robust profits enable a bank to build up its capital internally through retained income and thereby absorb economic shocks, attract outside capital and to earn

---

[1] Cited in Robert Morris & Associates, *Analyzing Foreign Banks*, p. 25.

107

its way out of problems. Ample earnings provide the bank with the where-withal to make investments that may be necessary for it to flourish within a competitive environment. A commercial bank's ability to generate profits and thereby become self-sustaining is critical to its longer-term credit-worthiness. At the same time, by managing risk effectively and lending to those borrowers that can most effectively use the capital obtained, a bank performs a larger role by allocating credit efficiently within an economic system.

A fair number of banks, however, are not solely profit-oriented. In some economic systems, government policies direct bank credit to chosen sectors, such as agriculture or particular industries. But even in the case of those banks that play a policy role and rely upon government support or subsidies, avoiding excessive losses and producing a modicum of profits is viewed as desirable both by participants and analysts. Though external support, by the government for example, may underpin a bank's creditworthiness, a reasonable level of profitability is always a positive factor in assessing its credit standing.

Credit Analysts vs Equity Analysts

All investment activity, indeed all business activity, involves some element of risk and return. These components tend to be correlated. Low risk is associated with low returns and high risk with high returns. Returns on high-risk investments are high to compensate for the comparatively large chance that the investment may return nothing at all, or worse, that the investor may lose the capital invested altogether. Debt investment, in US government treasury bills for instance, may be effectively risk-free. Near risk-free and low-risk investments generate modest rates of interest and modest returns. Conversely, high-risk investments such as high yield or junk bonds have correspondingly higher rates of default. These invest-ments may pay an interest rate of 5% per annum or more in excess of US Treasury bills. High-risk investments also include many equity invest-ments ranging from widely held stocks to dicey venture capital projects.

While we have discussed some of the differences between equity and credit analysts in Chapter 1, the contrast is most conspicuous in terms of their respective approaches to profitability analysis and bears further examination here. Equity and credit analysts are both concerned with an enterprise's position on the risk-return frontier. But because credit analysts generally are employed to make evaluations in connection with investments or obligations having (comparatively) fixed rates of return, and consequently a limited upside, the aspect of risk looms much larger to the credit analyst — whether employed in a risk management or a fixed income analytical capacity — than it does to the equity analyst. Returns on equity investments are highly variable, and thus the equity analyst pays a great deal of attention to the return that such investments will produce over time.

Both equity analysts and credit analysts are consequently concerned with profits and profitability, but for different reasons and with differing degrees of emphasis. In short, equity analysts are focused on an investment's upside potential, credit analysts on downside potential, or risk of loss. For an equity analyst, profitability is the pre-eminent concern, because higher profits will tend to increase an investment's value and the amount that can be realized from its sale. The equity analyst, therefore, spends a great deal of time constructing earnings models and producing detailed projections of profit in order to establish the present value of a bank's shares. These form the basis of rendering a decision to buy, hold or sell such shares, and are the major element of his or her work.

Compared to an equity analyst, the credit analyst's focus is on how a company's earnings-generating activities affect its ability to meet its obligations. In the banking realm, the credit analyst is relatively little interested in constructing detailed earnings forecasts to establish a valuation of a bank's stock. While robust earnings and profitability are certainly desirable, because return is intrinsically correlated to risk, high returns cannot be considered in isolation. Indeed, unduly high returns may cause the bank credit analyst to raise an eyebrow and suspect that the bank might be *too* profitable as a result of taking excessive risks. In the short term, a bank may take any number of actions, such as lending to dodgy customers at high rates of interest, or engaging in speculative investments, that will temporarily inflate profits. When such customers stop paying back their loans or the asset bubble bursts, a different picture will emerge. Consequently, the primary concern from a credit perspective is the sustainability or "quality" of a bank's earnings. Extraordinarily high profits can in such circumstances warn against future problems.

The equity analyst is primarily concerned with how a bank's earnings' prospects will affect its valuation and correspondingly its stock price, while the credit analyst attempts to assess to what extent its earning capacity, in conjunction with other aspects of its financial condition, will affect the bank's ability to fulfill its obligations to creditors.

The Treatment of Provisioning on Bank Profits

The contrast between the two approaches is often highlighted in terms of treatment of loan loss provisioning expenses.[2] When a bank suffers a decline in asset quality in a particular year, either through a rise in non-performing loans or due to an increase in write-offs, it will ordinarily increase its loan loss provisioning, i.e. set aside more loan loss reserves that year. The increase in provisioning will show up in a reduced bottom line. For that reason, equity analysts frequently view an increase in loan loss provisioning as a negative, since profit and hence return to shareholders is correspondingly diminished.

To the bank credit analyst, in contrast, the institution's setting aside a greater amount of provisions means that it is doing the right and prudent thing, notwithstanding that profits are temporarily dampened. In the same manner, while large profits are usually good news to the equity analyst, the credit analyst will wonder whether or not some unnecessary chances are being taken to achieve those profits. The credit analyst may wonder whether adequate provisions have been set aside, whether loan growth has been too rapid or whether the higher profits are at the expense of some other component of creditworthiness, such as capital or liquidity.

Illustration, Loan Loss Provisioning Cuts Into the Bottom Line

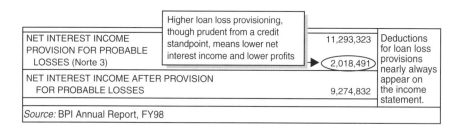

The illustration above, drawn from a bank income statement, shows how higher provisions reduce operating income, and hence net profit.

---

[2] Loan loss provisioning is discussed in more detail in chapters on asset quality that follow.

This is not to minimize the significance of earnings and profitability in credit analysis, nor is it to say that equity analysts pay no attention to credit concerns. Profitability is important to credit analysts because robust profits enable a bank to absorb inevitable losses from loans, to build up reserves against such losses and to enhance capital through retained earnings. In addition, a profitable bank can more easily attract capital in the equity and bond markets, facilitating expansion directly or through mergers and acquisitions.

What both credit and equity analyst would certainly agree on is that a bank should set aside sufficient reserves to meet anticipated credit costs. The challenge is determining in advance what those credit costs will be and therefore distinguishing between real profit and profits that, on a mark-to-market basis will ultimately transmute into losses on loan assets. Particularly in emerging markets, provisioning is subject to abuse by bank managers. There is a tendency to either use provisioning as a means to smooth out profits from year to year, as well as to under-provision. Tax regulations in some jurisdictions that are unsympathetic to the need for provisioning can also play a part in encouraging banks to underprovide for their asset quality problems.

Tip: In emerging markets, reported profits can be very deceptive. Watch out for banks that under-provide for credit costs. Underprovisioning means that asset quality problems are not being addressed, and that profits registered now will magically disappear when the value of the bank's loan assets fall and must be provided for out of profits, or written off against capital in the future.

Nonetheless, because the credit analyst and equity analyst have different missions, it can be expected that the weight equity and credit analysts place upon profits and other aspects of performance will differ. To equity analysts, there is no getting around the notion that profits and profitability are by far their most important concern. Although some attention may be paid to asset quality, liquidity and capitalization as risk factors, these elements are secondary to the bank's ability to produce revenues. For a credit analyst, however, profitability is of lesser importance, and must always be weighed against other aspects of the bank's financial condition. Bank credit analysts might give profitability a weighting of between 10–20%, relative to other financial characteristics.

The difference in emphasis is exemplified in the case of government-owned banks, which will often be evaluated as creditworthy solely on the basis of government support, irrespective of any profits they may create.[3] As a result of recent developments, however, such as the Asian financial crisis of 1997–98, equity analysts have tended to give a greater emphasis to the tools of credit analysis when assessing bank stocks. They, too, are placing more emphasis on the quality of earnings. A review of reports from major investment banks, such as Goldman Sachs, shows considerable attention being paid to credit concerns.[4] The table below compares the approach of credit and equity analysts, therefore, in a rather broad-brush manner, for illustration purposes.

Table: Bank Credit Analysts vs. Bank Equity Analysts

Bank Credit Analysts vs. Bank Equity Analysts		
	Credit Analysts	*Equity Analysts*
Importance of Profits	Secondary consideration. Profits are important because they support the bank's creditworthiness by enabling it to write off losses, build up loan loss reserves, and generate or attract capital.	The dominant consideration. Profits are important because they determine the value of the bank and hence of the bank's shares; hence profit trends will support a decision to buy, sell or hold the bank's shares.
Focus of Analysis	Sustainability or quality of earnings; review of historical (last 2–5 years) profit performance, qualitative assessment of future performance.	Earnings projection over next; 1–5 years quantitative valuation of shares
Key Profitability Ratios	Return on average assets; net interest margin; net interest spread	Return on equity; earnings per share; price earnings ratio

---

[3] Note that banks that have relatively poor profitability may be in no immediate danger of collapse if asset quality, capital, and liquidity relatively strong. Government-owned banks, of course, will be of no interest to equity analysts, unless there is some private ownership component or a privatization is contemplated.

[4] Indeed, a number of equity analysts incorporate the CAMEL model into their valuation of bank shares.

To summarize, the fundamental question the bank credit analyst[5] seeks to answer is not what is the value of the bank's stock and whether an investor should purchase or sell shares, but simply whether the bank will have sufficient funds over the foreseeable future to meet its financial obligations. This in fact is the essence of credit analysis. Projections, to the extent that they are employed, consequently tend to be of a more qualitative nature, with the relevant issue being whether there is any likelihood that the bank's earning ability could be impaired in the near- to medium-term. As a result, while the credit analyst must keep an eye on future prospects, he or she tends to focus more attention on historical results over the last two to three years, particularly as reflected in the bank's most recent financial statements, as past performance provides some indication of an institution's ability to generate sustainable earnings.

In general, for the credit analyst, a company's track record is far more important than its earnings projections; for the equity analyst, it is the opposite. This said, it should also be noted that credit analysts have been criticized for being preoccupied with historical performance at the expense of a more forward-looking view. As credit analysis evolves, it can be anticipated that some of the forecasting tools and techniques used by equity analysts will be adapted for credit evaluation, just as equity analysts have adopted some credit analytical techniques.

ANALYSIS OF OVERALL PROFITABILITY

To begin the process of analysis, a number of key financial ratios are examined. Some of these ratios are different than those employed by credit analysts to evaluate non-financial companies, since financial institutions differ in critical ways from their non-financial counterparts. Evaluating a bank's profitability requires an understanding of how banks make money, and an awareness of how banks differ from non-financial institutions.

As financial intermediaries, banks generally derive earnings not from commerce in manufactured goods but largely from their financial assets: their loans, securities holdings and the use of their capital to render financial services.

When considering earnings and profitability, it must be remembered that an increase in absolute profits does not necessarily mean an increase

---

[5] This is especially true of the credit analyst engaged in a risk management capacity. Of course, a fixed income analyst will make a recommendation whether to buy, sell or hold a fixed income security, but this done largely with reference to the issuer's creditworthiness relative to comparable issuers and the relevant credit rating assigned to it. We discuss fixed income analysis in greater detail in Chapter 26.

in profitability. Output must always be related to inputs, whether those inputs be measured in the form of shareholder funds (equity) or the assets the bank holds. For both the equity and credit analyst, profitability and not mere profits are the important element. For the credit analyst, an examination of profitability concentrates on understanding differences between the subject bank and its peers, as well as comprehending changes in earnings trends.[6]

> Tip: An increase in profits does not necessarily mean an increase in profitability. Outputs must always be related to inputs. A bank can increase its net interest income simply by adding assets, i.e. loans. But this can be at the cost of profitability, if not financial strength.

Composition of Operating Revenue: Interest Income vs. Non-Interest Income

Fundamentally, and as we have seen from the review of a bank's income statement in Chapter 3, all of a bank's income can be divided into two categories: interest income and non-interest income. Simply put, interest income is generated by lending funds, a function that produces the bulk of most bank revenue, while fees and commissions charged on activities ranging from check-clearing to merger advisory work, as well as gains from the trading or sale of assets, comprise non-interest income. As with income, all expenses can be similarly divided: interest expense and non-interest expense. Interest expense is the cost of funds borrowed to on-lend to customers, while non-interest expense encompasses the costs of running a bank as a business: i.e. compensation to staff, occupancy costs, services, and other administrative and operating expenses, as well as taxes.

> Tip: All bank income can be divided into two categories: (net) interest income from earning assets, and non-interest income. The most creditworthy banks tend to have a diversified revenue flow, although interest income will normally be larger than non-interest income. A good rule of thumb is that net interest income will generally be 60–80% of operating income.

For an ordinary commercial bank, the bulk of its interest income will come from loans, including lending to other banks (interbank deposits).

---

[6] The equity analyst will, unsurprisingly, focus on return on investment. Ratios such as return on equity and earnings per share thus weigh more heavily in the equity analyst's calculus than they do in that of the credit analyst.

Exploiting its own creditworthiness, the bank attracts deposits and borrows from the market at a lower rate than that at which it lends to customers. The difference between the two is the bank's spread, and traditionally the source of the lion's share of its profits. Commercial banks, however, also typically generate a substantial amount of interest income from fixed-income securities, including notes, bonds and preferred shares. The financial obligations (loans, securities and advances) invested in or purchased by the bank are the bank's *earning assets* that generate interest income for the bank.

In addition, a bank may earn income from fees generated through services, for example, from providing a letter of credit to an exporter, or for processing a loan. This category of non-interest income is referred to as *fees and commissions*. Another key source of non-interest income is trading. Trading in foreign exchange or marketable securities is the most common form of such activity. Additionally, a bank may earn income from its subsidiaries and affiliates, both financial and non-financial. In certain countries, so-called universal banks may carry out these activities directly. Finally, income may be generated from the sale of fixed assets, including assets acquired through foreclosure. As a rule, net interest income and non-interest income are clearly distinguished on the income statement. A breakdown of the sources of interest and non-interest income may be provided, frequently in the notes to the statement rather than on the statement itself.

Within the two basic categories of income and expense, there are a relatively small number of sub-categories. For the moment, we can observe that just about all bank income can be put into one of the following categories and sub-categories.

Income: Key Categories

A. Interest Income
1. Income from Loans
2. Income from Securities
3. Income from Interbank Deposits (Interbank Lending)
B. Non-Interest Income
4. Fee & Commission Income
5. Foreign Exchange Trading Gains
6. Securities Trading Gains

The same can be said for expenses:

Expenses: Key Categories

> A. Interest Expense
> B. Non-Interest Expense
>   1. Occupancy Expenses
>   2. Wages & Compensation
>   3. Overhead
>   4. Taxes

Much of bank earnings' analysis involves understanding the relationship between these items of income and expense, and how changes in their composition affects and is affected by bank financial performance and condition.

Illustration: Sources of a Bank's Revenue: Broad Categories

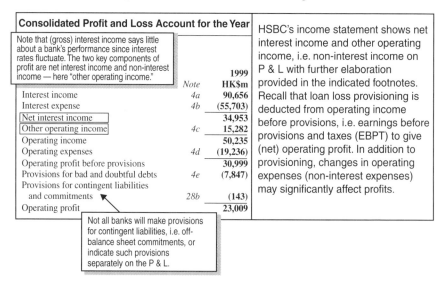

The sources of a bank's revenue are usually broken down on the income statement into broad categories while further categorization will ordinarily be found in the footnotes to the financial statements. Returning to HSBC's income statement, we can see that the bank follows this pattern.

Illustration: Further Detail on the Sources of Bank Revenue and Expenses (HSBC, FY 1999)

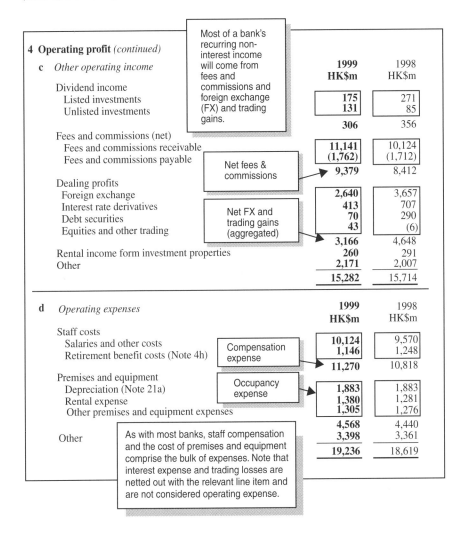

		1999 HK$m	1998 HK$m
4 Operating profit *(continued)*			
c *Other operating income*	Most of a bank's recurring non-interest income will come from fees and commissions and foreign exchange (FX) and trading gains.		
Dividend income			
Listed investments		**175**	271
Unlisted investments		**131**	85
		306	356
Fees and commissions (net)			
Fees and commissions receivable		**11,141**	10,124
Fees and commissions payable	Net fees & commissions	**(1,762)**	(1,712)
		9,379	8,412
Dealing profits			
Foreign exchange		**2,640**	3,657
Interest rate derivatives	Net FX and trading gains (aggregated)	**413**	707
Debt securities		**70**	290
Equities and other trading		**43**	(6)
		3,166	4,648
Rental income form investment properties		**260**	291
Other		**2,171**	2,007
		15,282	15,714

		1999 HK$m	1998 HK$m
d *Operating expenses*			
Staff costs			
Salaries and other costs	Compensation expense	**10,124**	9,570
Retirement benefit costs (Note 4h)		**1,146**	1,248
		11,270	10,818
Premises and equipment			
Depreciation (Note 21a)	Occupancy expense	**1,883**	1,883
Rental expense		**1,380**	1,281
Other premises and equipment expenses		**1,305**	1,276
		4,568	4,440
Other	As with most banks, staff compensation and the cost of premises and equipment comprise the bulk of expenses. Note that interest expense and trading losses are netted out with the relevant line item and are not considered operating expense.	**3,398**	3,361
		19,236	18,619

Proportion of Net Interest Income to Non Interest Income

Usually the bulk of a bank's earnings will come from interest-generating business, although the percentage varies. A degree of diversification between interest income and non-interest income is desirable, since the latter can supplement the former during periods when demand for loans is constrained. The analyst should be wary of a bank that derives income almost exclusively from interest-earning activities. Likewise, a bank which derives too high a proportion of its revenue from non-interest income sources deserves a close look.

Sources of non-interest income vary. Some are fairly stable such as income from fees and commissions. Others are more volatile. Proprietary trading by a bank in foreign exchange and securities frequently results in erratic flows of income. It is not at all unusual for a bank to experience a substantial decline in trading gains (or even a loss) in one year, which may be followed the next year by a substantial gain.

Percentage of Net Interest Income to Operating Income, Selected Countries

As the chart below suggests, net interest income as a percentage of operating income (net interest income + non-interest income) has been on a generally downward trend as deregulation and intensified competition for deposits and financing has put pressure on margins. While banks in developed markets are generally farther along this curve, banks in some emerging markets, particularly in Asia, have been adversely affected by high levels of non-performing loans which have both depressed profits (and in some instances resulted in losses) while temporarily distorting the importance of non-interest income in the banks' revenue streams.

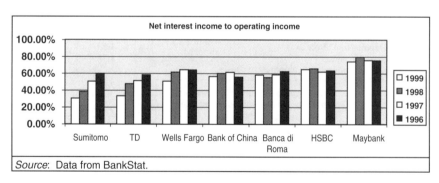

Source: Data from BankStat.

Measures of Overall Profitability: ROA and ROE

As is the case for non-financial firms, profits are defined as revenues less expenses.

$$\text{Profits} = \text{Revenue} - \text{Expenses}$$

Whether profits are high or low in absolute terms is relevant, but the absolute level of profits is not the key issue to the credit (or equity) analyst. It is, as suggested, comparatively easy over the short term for a bank to increase its profits. For instance, a bank merely has to increase its volume of loans to cause profits to grow. Nevertheless, attention should be paid to the year-on-year change or quarter-to-quarter change in absolute profits. To take account of the inputs used to obtain the increase, in this case the quantity of financial assets, some measure of profitability is employed. Such indicators enable the credit analyst to determine the degree to which a firm is generating revenue from some specified input or resource.

Illustration: Output of profit must be assessed in relation to "inputs" of assets and capital

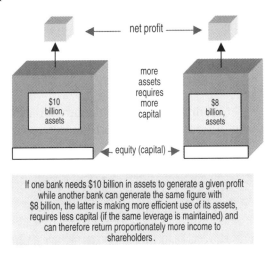

net profit

more assets requires more capital

$10 billion, assets

$8 billion, assets

equity (capital)

If one bank needs $10 billion in assets to generate a given profit while another bank can generate the same figure with $8 billion, the latter is making more efficient use of its assets, requires less capital (if the same leverage is maintained) and can therefore return proportionately more income to shareholders.

Key Indicators of Overall Profitability: ROA and ROE

There are two basic measures of overall profitability, neither of which is limited to financial firms.[7] One is *return on equity*, the other *return on assets*. Return on equity measures net profits against equity inputs (i.e. the amount of capital contributed by shareholders). It is consequently of particular interest to equity investors as it measures the return on their investment. Return on assets measures net profits against total assets, which for a bank consist largely of financial assets such as loans. Return on assets indicates how effectively the bank's assets are being managed to generate revenues. The two are mathematically related, differing only by the degree of *leverage* or *gearing* employed by the bank. In general, the ideal profitability profile is reflected in a bank that consistently generates above average profitability for its peer group, without incurring undue levels of risk.

Let us first examine return on equity as an indicator of profitability. Return on equity measures the return on the shareholders' investment.

Return on Equity

$$\frac{\text{Return on Equity}}{\text{Shareholder's equity}} = \text{Net Profit}$$

For example, ABC Bank has shareholders' equity of $10 m, assets of $50 m and net profits of $1 m. Its return on equity is $1 m/$10 m or 10%.

Return on Assets

The other key profitability indicator is return on assets. Return on assets measures the efficiency with which an enterprise is employing its assets.

$$\text{Return on Assets} = \frac{\text{Net Profit}}{\text{Total Assets}}$$

Since ABC Bank's assets amount to $50 m, and its net profits are $1 m, its return on assets is equal to $1 m/ $50 m or 2%.

Return on equity and return on assets are mathematically correlated. Since net profits is the numerator in both ratios, we can see that the variable that accounts for differences between them is that *ratio between equity and assets, or leverage*. This variable is the equity multiplier and is basically equivalent to the leverage ratio.

$$\text{Return on Assets} \times \text{Equity Multiplier} = \text{Return on Equity}$$

Illustration: Leverage and ROE

To illustrate, suppose that ABC Bank increases its leverage by expanding its loan book *without* increasing its capital. Hypothetically, suppose that the bank has no fixed assets, that all of its assets are in the form of loans, and that by doubling its loans it can double its income. If ABC Bank doubles its loans, its assets will increase to $100 m from $50 m and profit to $2 m from $1 m. Equity remains unchanged at $5 m. In such case, since the increase in profit is proportional to the increase in assets, ABC Bank's return on assets should remain the same as previously. Dividing the new level of profit of $2 m by the new level of assets ($100 m), we get 2/100 or 2%. The return on assets ratio has indeed not changed.

ABC Bank, $ m	Scenario 1	Scenario 2	
Assets (Assume all are loans)	50	100	Assets double ...
Equity	5	5	Equity stays the same ...
Assets/Equity (Leverage or gearing)	10	20	But gearing doubles ...
Net Profit	1	2	As does net profit.
Return on Assets	2%	2%	Return on assets is the same ...
Return on Equity	20%	40%	Return on equity, however, doubles

What about return on equity? Equity is still $10m, but profit has increased to $2 m. Return on equity is now $2 m/$10 m or 20%. Return on equity has doubled. Why? The increase is a direct result of the increase in leverage. Since equity remains at $10 m while assets have increased, the bank's leverage has likewise increased proportionally. In the first example, equity to assets was $5 m/$50 m or 10%. To put it the other way around, we can say that the *leverage* of the bank was 10 times (assets are 10 times equity.)[7] In the second example, the equity to assets ratio has fallen to $5 m/$100 m or 5%. Again, we can say that leverage has increased to 20 times. (Assets are 20 times equity.) The relationship between the two ratios can be clearly seen below. Total assets divided by

---

[7] Leverage may also be defined as the ratio between equity and assets, i.e. shareholders' equity divided by total assets.

equity, of course, represents the leverage or gearing of the bank. It may also be referred to as the equity multiplier.

Relationship between Return on Equity and Return on Assets

$$ROE = ROA \times \frac{Total\ Assets}{Equity}$$

$$ROE = ROA \times Equity\ Multiplier$$

Because of the ease with which ROE can be manipulated, bank credit analysts normally focus on return on assets (ROA). By separating leverage, or capital structure, from profitability, the credit analyst is able to gain a better understanding of changes in both. In actuality, bank analysts normally use a similar ratio called *return on average assets* (ROAA), but often abbreviated as (ROA). This ratio is exactly the same, except that the denominator is composed of the average of the current year's assets and the previous year's assets.[8] The reason average assets are used is to attempt to reduce the distortion that results when assets are increasing (or decreasing) over the course of a year, but are compared against income for the entire year. In addition, use of average assets as the denominator helps to discern core profitability by smoothing out fluctuations in asset growth that may occur from one year to another. Longer-term trends are then more readily apparent.

Return on Average Assets

$$\frac{Return\ on\ Average}{Assets\ (ROAA)\ (\%)} = \frac{Net\ Profit^*}{(Assets,\ current\ year + Assets,\ previous\ year) \div 2} \times 100$$

* extraordinary items should be subtracted

Note that ROAA can be averaged monthly rather than yearly or by other time periods. Banks will often have such data available internally.

---

[8] Returns can be averaged over any period of time, but generally the outside analyst will only have access to sufficient data to perform this rough and ready calculation of average assets.

Because such data is not normally disclosed, for the sake of consistency, the formula above is the most practical to use. (N.B. Henceforth, when we use the term ROA or return on assets, we are actually referring to return on *average* assets.)

While a crucial ratio for bank analysis, two points should be kept in mind concerning returns on asset. First, while it ideally should measure

---

Illustration: Prudential Capital Regulation, ROA and ROE

Because of the three-way correlation between return on assets, return on equity and leverage, prudential regulations governing capital adequacy (such as that imposed by the 1988 Basel Accord) have both a direct and indirect impact on ROE. Assuming a minimum capital requirement of 8% to risk assets, the imputed ceiling on leverage is 12.5. Since secular factors within particular banking markets will tend to limit ROA to an average range, ROE will also be constrained. This may have two types of adverse impact.

Direct impact. Return on equity can be easily manipulated by changing the degree of leverage employed by the bank. When ROA is difficult to raise, ROE can be pumped up by increasing leverage to the hilt and by utilizing forms of regulatory capital, such as long-term subordinated debt, which minimizes the need to employ shareholders' equity.

Indirect impact. Assets with lowrisk weightings will be favored and within a risk weighting category the highest yielding (and most risky) assets will also be favored. For example suppose in Country A as a conse-quence of the economic and regulatory structure banks on average will be able to earn an ROA of 0.7–0.8%. Country B has a more relaxed regulatory regime and a rapidly growing economy. Banks in Country B earn an ROA averaging 1.4–1.6%. Both countries adhere to the Basel norms and allow 12.5% leverage. Bank X in country A is a typical bank in that country with average management. It earns an ROA of 0.75% and hence an ROE of 9.37%. Bank Y in Country B earns an ROA of 1.5% and hence an ROE of 28.13%.

Fund Manager Z lives in Country C. All other things being equal, whose securities is he more likely to buy? The consequence of this rigid relationship between leverage, ROA and ROE is that the managers of Bank X may try to increase both ROA and ROE by allocating capital towards lower-weighted risk assets, such as real estate mortgages or bank debt, riskier assets within the same risk weighting category or increasing non-interest income (e.g. trading gains). Within limits this is acceptable, but if pushed too far, prudential regulations like the CAR can have untoward effects, distorting bank behavior and elevating rather than reducing risk.

recurrent profitability, it is easy to neglect to exclude extraordinary, (or exceptional items if a more conservative approach is taken) items, such as gains from the disposal of subsidiary, in calculation, thus distorting comparisons. Similarly, when the bank has a high proportion of revenues that are not asset-based, such as brokerage commission, the comparative ability of the ratio will be weakened.

EVALUATING CHANGES IN PROFITS AND PROFITABILITY: INITIAL ASSESSMENT

What is the Bank's Overall Profitability Picture?

Financial analysis in general seeks to break down the financial results of firms into their component parts. In the context of bank profitability, analysts examine those factors that drive and constrain earnings to ascertain what is causing changes in financial performance. Because banking is a comparatively homogeneous business — most banks make money in fundamentally the same way — it is not particularly difficult to isolate those variables that tend to increase earnings and those which tend to reduce earnings.

Before analyzing the elements that make up bank earnings, it is useful to get an overall picture of how the subject institution's net revenues have changed since the last fiscal period. To start, begin with the bottom line, the bank's most recently reported net profit figure.

❏ How does it compare with the previously reported period and on a year-on-year basis?

❏ Have profits increased?

❏ If so, by what percentage?

❏ How does the percentage change compare with historical performance over the last two or three years?

❏ How does it compare with the bank's peers?

❏ If there has been a decrease, is this the continuation of a trend, or the result of an economic downturn? Have other banks been affected similarly?

Losses are comparatively rare, but obviously raise red flags when they occur.

Substantial changes in the bottom line will ordinarily be reflected in the key measure of general bank profitability: return on average assets. How does this ratio compare with peers and with the industry average? Note that prevailing levels of profitability vary considerably from market to market, in large part the result of the extant bank regulatory regime. Again, trends and deviance from industry peers should be observed.

The following indicators will be useful in discerning changes in earnings: growth in net profit and growth in net interest income.

Net profit growth (%)	= (Net profits in Year 2/Net profits in Year 1) −1
Growth in net interest income (%)	= (Net interest income in Year 2/Net interest income in Year 1) −1
Growth in non-interest income (%)	= (Non-interest income in Year 2/Non Interest income in Year 1) −1

Steady and moderate increases over an extended period form the ideal growth profile from a credit perspective. Excessively high rates of growth and erratic income darken the credit picture, but beware of any indications that a bank is manipulating its financial statements to present an inviting picture of steady improvement. When looking at net profit growth or similar ratios, watch out for distortions that arise from changes off a low base. This can cause the growth rate to appear better than it actually is.

Example: Distorting Effects of Relatively Small Absolute Changes that Translate into Large Percentage Gains

For example, in Years 1 and 2, Adams Bank records net profits of $90 m and $100 m respectively. In Year 3, amid a recession, Adams Bank records a profit of just $10 m. In Year 4, it records a profit of $60 m. In Year 5, its profit is $110 m. The change in profit is shown below.

$m	Yr 1	2	3	4	5
Net profit	90	100	10	60	110
% change	n/a	11%	− (90%)	500%	83%

Year 4 was a good year, but the 500% growth makes it look better than it was. Profits were actually the third lowest in five years, and the increase looks large because it is jumping off a low base. Had the recession year 3 resulted in just $1 m in profit, the increase would have been 5000% for the same Year 4 earnings. Changes in provisioning policy, exceptional items recorded as recurrent income, and the years following recessions can cause similar effects. Watch out for amplified percentage changes that result from increases off a low base, and which, notwithstanding the high percentage changes, may indicate relatively lackluster results.

Checklist for Overall Profitability

Item	Remarks	Red Flags
Profit growth, year on year	Look for change in trend, differences from peers, secular factors.	Significant decreases in profits, losses.
ROA, trend and peer comparison	Same as above; ROA: less than 0.5%: weak 0.5%–1.0%: fair 1.0%–2.0%: good >2.0%: high	Declining or consistently low ROA; ROA over 2.5% suggests either: 1) cartel; 2) high risk portfolio; or 3) exceptional items (e.g. gain on sale of subsidiary).
ROE, trend and peer comparison	Basel Committee international minimum capital requirements limit maximum, leverage, depending upon how capital adequacy ratio is defined and achieved.	ROE over 20–25% range suggests excessive leverage is being employed.

WHAT ARE THE TRENDS DRIVING THE BANK'S PROFITABILITY?

Once the bank's profitability position in its market has been established, and relative trends ascertained, the analyst's next step is to explain why the bank is more or less profitable than its peers, and what is causing the bank's earnings and profitability to increase, decrease or remain constant. To do this, the analyst must look at those earnings drivers and constraints alluded to earlier. An understanding of the bank's business is helpful in this respect, but much can be gleaned solely from its financial statements and concomitant ratios.

Divergence in Profitability Among Peer Banks

As the graphs on the next page indicate and as one would expect, banks vary in their degree of profitability. These deviations are not random, however, and can usually be traced back to bank operations and strategy. The analyst's task is to explain, insofar as possible, the causes of these variations and to differentiate banks within the peer group.

Illustration, Divergence in Profitability, FY 99, Hong Kong Banks

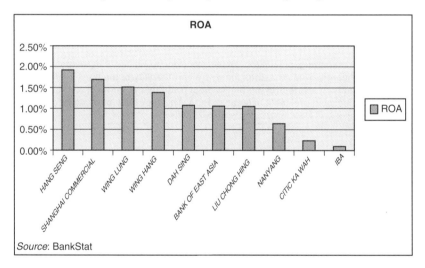

Source: BankStat

Causes of Variations in Profitability

To understand what is causes a bank to be more or less profitable than its peers, or to experience increases or decreases in profitability relative to them, the analyst can take comfort in the fact that there are while there are any number of potential causes, these can be divided generally into two broad scenarios and into a limited number of common categories of causes: The two broad scenarios are: 1) an alteration in condition is due

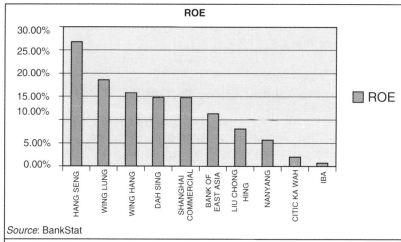

Source: BankStat

Hong Kong banks vary considerably in respect of their profitability as measured by return on average assets, or ROA.

Return on average equity or ROE tends to correspond to return on average assets. Differences can be ascribed to varying degrees of leverage among the banks.

The net interest maring, or NIM (not shown), of Hong Kong banks correspondingly varies significantly. NIM measures the overall profitability of the bank's interest-generating activity. Note that the banks most profitable in terms of NIM are not necessarily the most profitable in terms of ROA. This may be in part because ROA takes account of loan loss provisioning while NIM does not.

to a secular change in the industry; and 2) changes in conditions or operations affecting a particular bank. If the former, there is a strong possibility that the change is due to changes in the business or economic cycle or in the regulatory/policy environment.

Secular Changes in Profitability

Scenario one: All banks in the peer group are experiencing an increase or decrease in profitability. What are the potential causes? Here are a few:

Economic and Business Conditions

Increase in profitability: One possibility — is that the economy is booming, demand for credit is high, banks are able to obtain high spreads (especially where savers have few alternatives to bank savings) and fee business is strong.

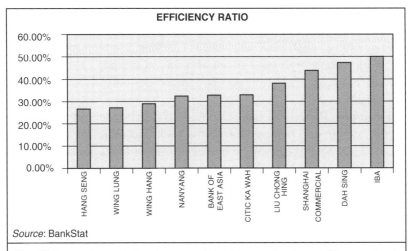

EFFICIENCY RATIO

Source: BankStat

The efficiency ratio, non-interest expense divided to operating income (the sum of net interest income and non-interest income) varies inversely with profitability. A higher ratio indicates a higher expense burden, and unsurprisingly lower profits, all other factors remaining equal. Perhaps it should be termed the "inefficiency ratio."

Decrease in profitability: The economy is strong, but changing business conditions are making it hard for banks to maintain thick spreads due to new market entrants, or additional financing options for companies in need of capital (disintermediation). Or, the credit cycle is turning and an asset bubble has burst.[9] There is a surplus of supply, a dearth of demand, companies are not expanding, demand for credit is slack and banks are preoccupied with rebuilding their own capital.

Change in Regulatory or Policy Environment

Another possibility is that new government regulations or directives make it harder or easier for banks to make profits. As simple a measure as changing prevailing interest rates through central bank actions may affect profits significantly. If loans are more interest sensitive than deposits, an upward move in interest rates means that loans will re-price faster than deposits, increasing spreads and bank profits. If deposits are more interest

---

[9] The business cycle is described in a succeeding chapter.

sensitive than loans, the reverse will be true. Observe, however, that if interest rates move too high, both demand for loans will decline and the credit quality of applicants will tend to decline. Creditworthy customers will avoid paying high rates of interest unless the need is urgent and if the need is urgent the likelihood is that the customer is not among the most creditworthy.

Example: The central bank imposes a tighter monetary policy raising interest rates in an environment where loans are more interest-sensitive than deposits. The result will be higher profits. If loans are more interest-sensitive than deposits, a downward move in interest rates conversely will narrow spreads reducing bank profits. If deposits are more interest-sensitive than loans, spreads will widen, with the corresponding positive impact on bank profits.

Example: The central bank imposes a loose monetary policy, lowering interest rates in an environment where deposits reprice more quickly than loans. The result will also be higher net income.

Finally, regulatory changes increasing or restricting competition, requiring higher or lower levels of capital or loan loss provisions, or limiting or expanding the types of business banks can engage in are all apt to have some impact on profits.

Example: Deregulation permits new market entrants, such as foreign banks, who compete fiercely for business. This results in pressure on spreads among all participants, generally decreasing net income.

Affecting the Subject Bank More than Other Banks

Scenario two: The alteration in condition is affecting the subject bank more significantly than the peer group. What are the potential causes? There are five key potential causes. These five types of causes are briefly mentioned here and the first three items relating to a bank's expense level are discussed in some detail. To keep this chapter to a reasonable length, the discussion is resumed in the following chapter, where income items are examined in more depth.

❑ Operating costs are higher/lower than its peers. (Sample indicator: efficiency ratio)

❑ Provisioning is higher/lower than its peers. (Sample indicator: NPL ratio)

❑ Funding costs are higher/lower than its peers. (Sample indicator: average cost of funds)

❑ Yields are higher/lower than its peers. (Sample indicator: average yield)

❑ Non-interest income business is more robust/less robust than its peers.

Note: For the first three categories, + means higher costs, − means lower costs. This, naturally, corresponds to lower and higher profits respectively. For the second two categories, deferred until the succeeding chapter, + means higher income, − means lower income. This, of course, corresponds to higher and lower profits respectively.

Operating Costs are Higher/Lower than Peers
Possible causes

(−) Management is keeping a tight rein on expenses.

(+) Management is too spendthrift.

(+) Management is too top-heavy.

(−) Management is hiring second-class staff or not hiring enough staff with deleterious effects possible down the line.

(+) Management is investing in information technology or other capital intensive initiatives.

(−) Management is not spending enough on staff training.

(+) Exogenous conditions have caused costs to rise (e.g. preparation for Y2K).

(+) The bank's franchise has special characteristics that cause it to have higher or lower costs than average (e.g. far flung branch network; wholesale banking).

Provisioning Costs are Higher/Lower than Peers
Possible causes

(+) The bank has poorer asset quality than its peers due to inadequate credit control and therefore has high provisioning costs.

(−) The bank is not provisioning as much as it should, given the state of its loan book.

(+) Because of a strongly conservative management, the bank is provisioning more than it needs to, notwithstanding that asset quality is at reasonable levels.

(−/+) There has been a regulatory directive narrowing the bank's discretion in provisioning (other banks are already in compliance).

Funding Costs are Higher/Lower than Average

We will return to funding again in a succeeding chapter. Possible causes of higher or lower funding costs include:

(+) The bank's branch network is not as wide as its peers and therefore it cannot tap sub-markets that are less interest sensitive (e.g. rural markets) as effectively as its peers.

(+) The bank relies heavily on the interbank market for funding and market conditions caused rates to rise.

(+) The bank relies heavily on the interbank market for funding and its declining creditworthiness has caused its funding costs to rise.

(−/+) The bank has/does not have the benefit of government support and therefore can/must pay lower/higher rates for deposits and funding.

(+/−) There has been a change in the bank's status vis-à-vis the prospect of external support.

Extraordinary Gains & Losses and Exceptional Items

In addition, there is the possibility of some extraordinary gain or loss affecting the bank that year. A typical extraordinary gain might be the sale of a subsidiary. A typical loss might be a write-off of an equity investment. Finally, there is the possibility that both secular changes and internal factors are combining to have a positive or negative effect. The subject bank may be less or more vulnerable to business cycle, regulatory or policy changes.

Note: In the next chapter, we will discuss two additional categories of causes: 1) where yields are higher/lower than the bank's peers; and 2) where non-interest income is higher/lower than the bank's peers.

MEASURING OVERALL COSTS: THE EFFICIENCY RATIOS

As mentioned in the preceding section, differences in the expense burden a bank bears can make a significant difference in its profitability vis-á-vis its peers and explain why one bank has performance superior or inferior to them.

Assessing Efficiency

Before examining ratios, the analyst should ascertain how non-interest expenses have changed over the previous fiscal period. Have expenses increased or declined? Is the rate of change in line with changes in operating revenue? How does it compare with the bank's peers?

The Concept of Efficiency

A bank's non-interest expense level reflects its efficiency. A bank with high efficiency — i.e. one that makes efficient use of the inputs that its non-interest expenses such as staff compensation represent — will have an efficiency indicator that is a low number. A bank with poor efficiency will exhibit a higher number. There are two basic indicators of efficiency. The first is the cost to income ratio. This measures non-interest expenses as a proportion of operating income. The other is the cost to assets ratio, which measures non-interest expenses as a proportion of total assets. Efficiency, in other words, gauges administrative or non-interest expenses in terms of revenue or assets. A bank with high efficiency is able to spend less on inputs (other than interest) than one with low efficiency.

Efficiency Indicators

The two primary efficiency indicators are defined below.

Cost to Income Ratio

$$\text{Cost to Income Ratio} = \frac{\text{Non-Interest Expenses (excluding loan loss provisions)}^{10}}{\text{Net Interest Income + Non-Interest Income}}$$

A variation of this ratio is to use net assets as the denominator.

Cost to Assets Ratio

$$\text{Cost to Assets Ratio} = \frac{\text{Non-Interest Expenses (excluding loan loss provisions)}}{\text{Total (Average) Assets}}$$

---

[10] As a general rule, when we refer to non-interest expense, we are not including loan loss provisioning costs.

Both ratios are useful, but the cost to assets ratios (sometimes called the cost-margin) is less easily manipulated, and better reflects a bank's core efficiency. Significant changes in these ratios from previous periods, or substantial deviations from the industry and the bank's peer group should

Efficiency: Selected Banks	FISCAL	Cost Margin	Efficiency Ratio
Selected Australian Banks			
AUSTRALIA & NEW ZEALAND BANKING GROUP LTD	1999	2.31%	55.21%
Melbourne, Australia			
COMMONWEALTH BANK OF AUSTRALIA	1999	2.40%	56.43%
Sydney, Australia			
WESTPAC BANKING CORP.	1999	2.91%	63.75%
Sydney, Australia			
Selected Hong Kong Banks			
BANK OF EAST ASIA	1999	1.33%	32.85%
Hong Kong, Hong Kong			
DAH SING BANK	1999	1.99%	47.28%
Hong Kong, Hong Kong			
HANG SENG BANK LTD	1999	0.93%	26.65%
Hong Kong, Hong Kong			
Selected Japanese Banks			
BANK OF TOKYO-MITSUBISHI, LTD. (THE)	2000	1.35%	65.08%
Tokyo, Japan			
SANWA BANK, LTD.	1999	2.97%	124.32%
Osaka, Japan			
SUMITOMO TRUST & BANKING CO., LTD.	1999	2.87%	70.27%
Osaka, Japan			
Selected Philippine Banks			
BANK OF THE PHILIPPINE ISLANDS	1999	2.96%	51.76%
Manila, Philippines			
LAND BANK OF THE PHILIPPINES	1999	3.05%	41.38%
Manila, Philippines			
METROPOLITAN BANK AND TRUST CO.	1999	2.87%	63.78%
Manila, Philippines			
Selected US Banks			
BANK ONE, NA	1999	8.03%	84.09%
Columbus, Ohio, USA			
CITIBANK, N.A.	1999	4.25%	67.24%
New York City, New York, USA			
WELLS FARGO BANK, N.A.	1999	5.88%	71.19%
San Francisco, California, USA			

be noted. The table below illustrates how efficiency ratios vary from bank to bank but is also suggestive of how efficiency ratios vary from market to market. Efficiency ratios in Hong Kong, for instance, tend to be good, reflecting the high volume of transactions, small market area, strong emphasis on bank profitability and high level of technology. Ratios in Japan are generally not as good as a result of traditional labor practices and less investment in technology.

The efficiency of US banks is hampered by high labor costs and a fragmented banking market, while Philippines' banks' efficiency is impaired by low transaction volumes and inadequate infrastructure. Australian banks benefit from economies of scale in a consolidated banking market. The varying environments in which banks operate is one reason that cross-border comparisons are often inapt.

CHAPTER SUMMARY

Evaluating bank profitability, while not the *sine qua non* of bank equity analysis, is an important component of bank credit analysis. Earnings enable the bank to attract outside capital, generate capital internally, and produce a reasonable return on the investment of shareholders. From a credit perspective, bank profitability is generally measured historically, although attention must be paid to future earnings prospects. Detailed earnings forecasts and concomitant valuations of the bank as an enterprise, however, are usually left to bank equity analysts.

All bank profits derive either from interest generating activities or non-interest generating activities. The latter include revenue generated from fees and commissions or trading gains. Profits must be distinguished from profitability, which relates profits to inputs, be they equity or assets. The most important indicators of overall profitability for the bank credit analyst are:

❑ return on average assets (ROA), and

❑ efficiency, which is commonly measured by the so-called efficiency ratio and by the non-interest expense to operating income ratio

It is also important to look at earnings' growth when evaluating a bank's profitability.

ROA measures the overall profitability of the bank and is mathematically correlated to return on average equity (ROE). All other things being equal, the latter indicator will vary according to the bank's leverage. Two banks with same ROA but different degrees of leverage will exhibit ROE that will be a multiple of the difference in their leverage. NIM measures the profitability of the interest-earning side of the bank's business. Efficiency measures the burden of non-interest expenses. Profitability in general and component indicators will vary from bank to bank and from market to market, a fact which makes cross-border comparisons of banks somewhat problematic. It is the analyst's job to discern the variations and understand their causes.

Although there are any number of reasons why such variations exist, they generally fall into two basic scenarios: differences that affect all banks in a given market, and those that affect one (or a few) banks. Each group can be further subdivided into a relatively small number of categories that tend to explain why one bank's profitability is superior or inferior to another. For example, Bank A may have below average asset quality requiring it to set aside more loan loss provisions, thus eroding profits. Bank B, on the other hand, might benefit from superior cost control, reducing the burden of administrative expenses on the bottom line.

CHAPTER SEVEN

EARNINGS & PROFITABILITY: EVALUATING THE INTEREST INCOME AND NON-INTEREST INCOME COMPONENTS OF REVENUE

How interest income is recognized depends upon two accounting principles in particular: whether the income is quantifiable and how probable it is it will actually be received. Whether to stop accrual and reverse accrued interest depends for most ... banks largely on the length of the past-due period and banks' qualitative judgment of debtors' ability to pay.
— Chaiyapat Paitoon & Bradford K. Ti, *Bank Accounts Made Easy, Report Summary — Vol I: Recognition of Interest Income.* Salomon Smith Barney, Feb 9, 2001, p. 2.

Evolutionarily, banks are accidental accretions of history. They have become an unwieldy combination of investment and commercial banking services, trading activities, and portfolio management. Both nurtured and neutered by regulation, banks comprise heterogeneous constituencies with conflicting objectives.
— James McQuown and Stephen Kealhofer, KMV Corporation, "A Comment on the Formation of Bank Stock Prices"

After examining overall changes in earnings, the analyst can begin to break down the income stream and the relevant deductions into constituent categories. For most banks, net interest income makes up the larger part of operating income (net interest income + non-interest income), so let us begin there.

In examining the interest income component of a bank's revenue stream, looking at the level of gross interest income by itself is not very useful. Gross interest income varies considerably as interest rates change, and changes in gross interest income say as much about prevailing business conditions and interest rates as they do about an individual bank's performance. The same can be said about gross interest expense. The most significant item to consider when looking at a bank's interest income generating activities is not its interest income (i.e. gross interest income), but its net interest income.

Illustration: Interest Income and Interest Expense Fluctuations

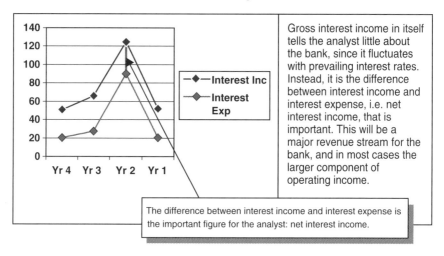

Gross interest income in itself tells the analyst little about the bank, since it fluctuates with prevailing interest rates. Instead, it is the difference between interest income and interest expense, i.e. net interest income, that is important. This will be a major revenue stream for the bank, and in most cases the larger component of operating income.

The difference between interest income and interest expense is the important figure for the analyst: net interest income.

NET INTEREST INCOME

Net interest income is equal to the difference between interest income and interest expense.

> Net Interest Income = Total Interest Income − Total Interest Expense

Since interest income and interest expense tend to rise and fall together, focusing on net interest income allows the analyst to separate the quality of bank performance from changing economic conditions. Although a bank's net interest income levels will vary as prevailing rates of interest change and economic conditions change, the effect is much less pronounced than with gross interest income levels.

> **Example:** To illustrate, suppose DEF Bank in Year 1earns $10 m in interest on earning assets of $100 m, providing an average yield of 10%. Imagine further that the bank funds these assets from deposits on which it pays 3% interest, and interest expenses are $3 m for the year. This leaves net interest income of $7 m. Let us ignore market risk and assume that earning interest assets and interest bearing liabilities reprice immediately. Now in Year 2, suppose interest rates increase by 2%. Average lending rates are now 12%, while deposit rates are 5%. The bank now earns $12 m on the same assets, but pays $5 m. Net interest income is still $7 m. The fact that gross interest income rose by $2 m is essentially irrelevant.

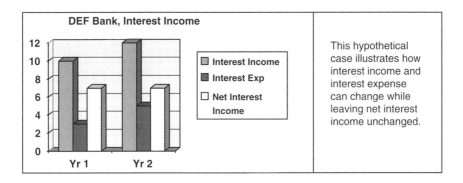

This hypothetical case illustrates how interest income and interest expense can change while leaving net interest income unchanged.

Monitoring Funding Costs and Funding Expense

It is interesting, however, to observe the relative changes between gross interest income and gross interest expense. If gross interest income increases by a greater percentage than gross interest expense, then net interest income will rise. Conversely, if gross interest expenses increase by a greater percentage than gross interest income, net interest income will fall. Whether total interest income growth outpaces growth in gross interest expense, or vice versa, will depend upon changes in the bank's average cost of funding vis-à-vis its average gross yield. Funding costs and yield then are two additional elements affecting bank profitability. These elements are reflected in corresponding indicators: 1) the average cost of funding; and 2) the average gross yield. More particularly, these indicators measure the average cost of interest-bearing liabilities and the yield on average-earning assets. A third indicator, the net interest spread, measures the difference between them.

Average Cost of Funding

$$\text{Average Cost of Funding} = \frac{\text{Gross Interest Expense}}{\text{Average Interest Bearing Liabilities}}$$

Average Gross Yield

$$\text{Average Gross Yield} = \frac{\text{Gross Interest Income}}{\text{Average (Interest) Earning Assets}}$$

Net Interest Spread

$$\text{Average Cost of Funding} - \text{Average Gross Yield} = \text{Net Interest Spread}$$

Table: Comparative Funding Costs, Yields and Net Interest Spreads for Selected Banks

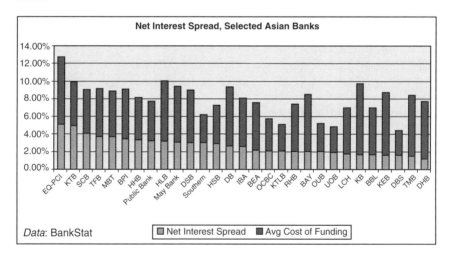

These ratios are also useful in discerning whether a bank enjoys a lower cost of funding than its peers, or than it has historically, or whether its cost of funding is comparatively high. Similarly, it is helpful to ascertain whether a bank is able to achieve higher yields than its peers or than it has in the past. Increases in funding cost or decreases in yield likewise inform the analyst about trends in profitability. The difference between the average funding cost and the average yield is the net interest spread, a key indicator of the profitability of the bank's interest-generating business.

Why Funding Costs Vary

To continue the discussion that we began in the previous chapter, there are a variety of reasons why one bank might have the advantage of lower funding costs, and hence higher spreads, assuming yields are the same as other banks. A bank with a wide branch network will normally have a lower cost of funds than one with a small branch network, as the wide branch network will typically include regions where there is less competition among banks for deposits, and interest paid on deposits will be correspondingly lower, absent regulation. Through a wide branch network, the bank will be able to tap more deposits from customers who value convenience over a fraction of a percentage-point-better interest rate. In addition, a bank with a large number of branches is likely to be able to extend its network into areas where there is little or no competition for deposits. Consequently, when interest rates change, the bank with a broader customer base will tend to see less outflow of deposits than a smaller one, all other things being equal. In addition, a large bank may very well be perceived as being stronger, and may be able to exploit its associated brand image. As a result, the bank will probably have less need to access the interbank or capital markets for funds. Accessing these markets will inevitably be more costly than acquiring funds from depositors.

Another reason for low funding costs may be that the bank benefits from external support and is thereby able to obtain cheaper funding than a bank that must rely exclusively on its own balance sheet for its creditworthiness. Finally, it may be that the bank entered the capital markets at a propitious time and was able to fund its loans when interest rates were comparatively low. As interest rates rise, its funding costs will be comparatively lower than banks that were not so lucky in their timing. Naturally, the reverse can also occur.

The graph on next page shows the net interest spread for three major Asian banks — Development Bank of Singapore (DBS), Bangkok Bank (BBL), and Metrobank (MBT) — over a five-year period. DBS has experienced stable spreads, which rose significantly in FY99. BBL registered declining spreads although it exhibited some improvement in FY99. MBT's spreads, in contrast, rose between FY96 and FY98, but fell rather than increased in FY99. What causes yields net interest spreads to vary?

Table Showing Changes in Net Interest Spread over Time: Development Bank of Singapore, Bangkok Bank, and Metrobank

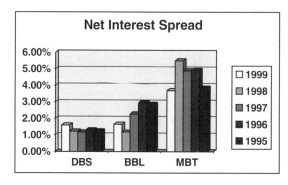

In the previous chapter, we deferred discussion of two key factors affecting a bank's profitability — variation in yields and variation in non-interest income. It is these items that have a direct impact on a bank's net interest spread, and we address them below.

Why Yields Vary

As is the case with funding costs, there are a variety of possible explanations for comparatively high yields. The sector as a whole may be affected by economic developments, or individual banks may register changes as a consequence of the success or failure of their own business strategies. Of particular importance is the degree of success the bank achieves in balancing risk and return in the composition of its loan portfolio. A bank with a conservative portfolio, in other words one in which most of its interest earning assets are in the form of loans to blue-chip corporations or in government securities (or other liquid assets), will tend to earn less interest on its assets, and therefore have a lower yield on interest-earning assets, than a bank whose lending is concentrated on smaller companies and individuals. Another factor that may influence gross interest income is the level of non-performing loans. If the ratio is high, then interest from those loans deemed non-performing will either be not forthcoming, or if there is a subsequent collection, it will be recorded as a non-interest income item.[1]

---

[1] Note that this depends on properly recording interest income on non-performing loans as interest in suspense. In some less developed markets, interest income may be accrued through the income statement for a considerable period of time despite being uncollectable.

Of course, banks that have high-return portfolios also tend to suffer higher risks, so there is a correlation between both variables. It may take one to two years before the high-risk loans display higher levels of non-performance, so a bank that has recently changed its portfolio to reflect a higher risk/return level, should be monitored closely for volatile funding costs. Nevertheless, a bank that properly provisions against loss may still net higher yields from a higher risk loan portfolio, despite greater loan losses. A final reason for higher average yields may be superior management. A bank which is better able to spot problem credits and target customers not well served by its competitors may have a comparative advantage over its rivals that enables it to earn more on its interest-generating assets. In addition, a bank that invests in government or blue-chip fixed income securities when interest rates are high will show better yields without commensurate risk than competitors who forego such opportunities.

The Importance of Provisioning

Provisioning may be conceptually seen as, 1) a type of non-interest expense, 2) a credit cost to be deducted from the bank's stream of revenue generated from interest, or as 3) a discrete item to be examined separately. However it is viewed, the level of provisioning that a bank takes in a given year will also have a significant impact on its bottom line for that period. As we touched upon in the previous chapter, the amount of additional loan loss reserves that a bank will set aside depends upon several factors. The most important influence on the amount of loan loss provisioning an individual bank must take relative to its peers is the bank's asset quality. A bank that sought high yields from consumer and middle market loans will have to pay the piper when a portion of those loans turn bad, perhaps exacerbated by an economic downturn.

With regard to banks within a particular market, the regulatory environment, including the amount of discretion allowed to bank management, as well as any changes affecting loan loss reserve requirements, will be a strong influence. Other regulations, such as those governing the taxability of provisions or write-offs, will also have an effect. Beyond these considerations, the level of non-performing loans the bank is experiencing, management's belief as to future prospects for asset quality, and management's conservativeness will also play a part in determining the amount channeled into credit costs.

Because ample provisioning is an important aspect of bank credit-worthiness, when reviewing bank profitability the credit analyst should perform a profitability analysis using pre-provision net profit figures (earnings before provisions and taxes) as well as ordinary net profit figures. This will better reveal the bank's underlying profitability, and what proportion of profit has been siphoned off either to prepare for anticipated loan losses or to repair damage that has already occurred.

EVALUATING THE PROFITABILITY OF A BANK'S INTEREST EARNING OPERATIONS

Net Interest Margin

Perhaps the most important single ratio for the purpose of evaluating the profitability of a bank's interest-generating business is the net interest margin (NIM). The name is something of a misnomer since what it really measures is the bank's return on average (interest) earning assets.

$$\text{Net Interest Margin} = \frac{\text{Net Interest Income}}{\text{Average Earning Assets}}$$

Table Average Net Interest Margin and Return on Average Spread: Selected Countries

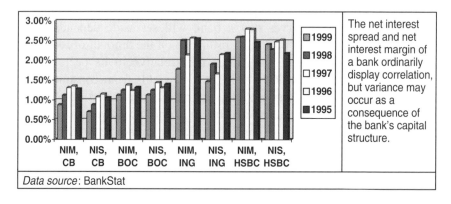

Data source: BankStat

The net interest margin is similar to the net interest spread. Prevailing net interest margins vary from market to market as well as from bank to bank. At the sectoral level, the banks' average net interest margin depends upon a number of variables including the level of competition and regulations governing bank activities. Again, depending upon government policy, interest rates are subject to fluctuation as a consequence of economic forces operating at both a country and global level. All other things being equal, a high demand for credit relative to supply will increase interest rates; a low demand will depress rates. The supply of credit as influenced by government policy, the state of banks' balance sheets and business confidence will have a corresponding impact in affecting the supply of credit. Whether an increase in interest rates has a positive impact on a bank's net interest margin depends upon whether deposits reprice faster than assets, or vice versa.

Other influences on interest rates, and thereby on the net interest margin, include: the level of prevailing business activity, the propensity of consumers to save or spend, the amount of competition in the financial sector, and government policy. Government policy can influence interest rates directly or indirectly through a variety of mechanisms, including reserve requirements (the percentage of funds required to be deposited in the central bank). Similarly, competitive conditions will have a bearing on the interest rates that can be obtained and charged. Some banking markets are highly competitive, which tends to narrow spreads. Others are cartels, quasi-cartels or are otherwise externally regulated in order to enable banks to maintain relatively fixed spreads. The upshot is that there are many influences on the interest rates that banks can charge on loans and which they pay on deposits or other funding. Hence a bank's "spreads" are affected both by external factors such as government policy and general business conditions, as well as by the institution's strategy.

Since governmental policy and market factors will ordinarily affect all banks in largely the same way, a credit analyst, as previously noted, will look for anomalies between a bank and its peers. It is a bank's individual strategy and management competence that will enable it to perform more or less successfully than its competitors. Having observed, for example, that a bank's ROA and NIM is lower than its peers and declining more rapidly, the credit analyst will seek explanations.

With respect to the individual bank, both its net interest spread and net interest margin will vary according to the approach it takes to the market. An aggressive bank seeking to gain market share may cut lending rates or raise borrowing rates above that of its peers in order to expand its loan book or mobilize additional deposits. Similarly, a bank might open new branches, allowing it to capture low cost deposits. Perception

Summary of Factors Affecting the Profitability of a Bank's Interest-Generating Business

In addition to the reasons mentioned above for changes in the profitability of a bank's interest-earning business, other factors affecting interest revenue are summarized below.

Asset Mix

A bank's asset mix may explain above or below average yields. Other things being equal, a greater proportion of funds being placed into higher risk assets, e.g. loans, will cause a bank's NIM and ROA to rise. A greater proportion of funds being placed into low-yielding liquid assets will cause the NIM and ROA to fall. Similarly, making higher-yielding but riskier loans will push the NIM and ROA upward, while a more conservative policy concentrating on lending to blue-chip companies at prime rates of interest will keep the NIM and ROA at lower levels. Bank supervisors may encourage banks to maintain higher levels of liquidity by raising mandatory liquidity thresholds. Likewise, during harsh economic conditions, bank management may seek to hold a higher proportion of its assets in easily liquefiable assets and in relatively safe but lower-yielding loans.

Deposit Mix

A bank's asset mix may explain above or below average funding costs. An increased proportion of demand (checking) deposits means lower funding costs; in contrast, an increase in time deposits and more particularly in "purchased" interbank funds will tend to push up funding costs.[2] A bank with a large branch network is also likely to have lower funding costs than a bank that maintains only a few branches. The wider the bank's branch network, the more probable it is that its network will encompass areas where there is comparatively little competition for deposits. Normally, non-urban residents are less interest-rate sensitive than depositors who live in large cities.

Asset Quality and Provisioning Levels

A bank's asset quality may help to explain comparatively higher or lower net yields. A higher level of non-performing loans (i.e. low asset quality) means less net interest income received. Moreover, the accounting treatment of NPLs is such that once a loan is deemed non-performing, typically any income ultimately received will no longer be categorized as interest income. Conversely, a lower level of non-performing loans (NPLs — i.e. a loan book with high asset quality) — translates into a higher level of net interest income for a given portfolio of loan assets, all other criteria being equal. Note that asset quality as well as a number of other factors may cause a bank to take a higher or lower level of provisions. This will have a direct impact on net profit and profitability.

---

[2] But note that a bank with negligible interbank deposits, while it may have an advantage in lower funding costs, may not have established the necessary relationships with counterparties to borrow additional funds in times of need.

of the bank's creditworthiness may play a role. Other banks might become less willing to lend to a bank believed to have problems, forcing up the cost of funds obtained through interbank borrowing.

Asset-Liability Mismatch

The proportion of interest-sensitive versus floating rate assets and liabilities will affect a bank's net interest income. For example, banks typically borrow short (from depositors) and lend long, causing a mismatch in time. If interest rates rise rapidly and the bank is saddled with a high percentage of fixed rate long-term loans, spreads will decline and could turn negative. Conversely, in such a circumstance, a bank that is blessed with a large core of cheap deposits that can find opportunities to lend in the interbank market can profit handsomely on fat spreads. In a world of greater interest rate volatility, asset-liability management has become increasingly important to bank managements. Frequently, however, analysts are not provided with sufficient data to enable a thorough examination of the impact of asset-liability management upon bank profitability. This is especially the case in emerging markets. Unless required to do so by regulation or demanded by equity investors, banks seem to regard this data as proprietary in nature, and perhaps are reluctant to disclose information that might be of use to competitors. Asset liability management is discussed in more detail in Chapters 13 and 14 which review liquidity.

EVALUATING THE NON-INTEREST INCOME COMPONENT

Having looked at overall profitability and then focused on the profitability of a bank's interest-earning business, we will now turn to the other component of a bank's revenue stream, its non-interest income.

Overview of Non-Interest Income

In addition to the interest generated from loans and advances, as well as interest obtained from fixed income securities held, nearly all banks generate some of their income from other sources. Such non-interest income helps banks to diversify their earnings streams, which are becoming increasingly important sources of revenue in their own right.

In theory, non-interest income can help supplement a bank's bottom line during periods when net interest income is low. But in practice it is often much more erratic than interest income, and is also not necessarily counter-cyclic. One undeniable advantage for a bank in expanding its non-interest income business, however, is that non-interest income is generally less capital intensive, both in actuality and in respect of meeting banks' regulatory requirements. This enables banks to supplement their returns on equity, making them more attractive to shareholders.

Commercial banks can generate non-interest income from a variety of sources. These can be divided into several basic categories, and are often so classified on the bank's income statement. These categories are:

❑ Fees & commissions

❑ Trading gains (and losses)

❑ Income from subsidiaries or affiliates

❑ Gains from equity or real estate investments or holdings.

Fees & Commissions

Among the most common types of fees or commissions collected by banks are:

❑ Fees for letters of credit issued or confirmed; fees for standby letters of credit.

❑ Investment and pension fund management (trust banking) fees.

❑ Fees for providing guarantees.

❑ Safe deposit box fees.

❑ Custodial and trusteeship fees for holding equity and fixed income securities.

❑ Fees for loan syndications.

❑ Underwriting fees.

❑ Corporate and merger advisory services.

❑ Brokerage commissions for the retail sales of mutual funds or other securities.

❑ Estate administration fees.

Trading Gains (and Losses)

Nearly all major commercial banks engage in some degree of trading activity. These ordinarily include foreign exchange trading, trading in money market instruments and fixed income securities, and in some countries and markets, trading in equity securities or other instruments. Foreign exchange trading is the most common sort of such trading activity, since by virtue of providing foreign exchange services, banks take positions on foreign exchange risk. Banks often trade in money market securities, either on a proprietary basis or as an adjunct to their funding operations. In some markets, banks trade in fixed-income and equity securities. A critical point to ascertain is to what extent do banks engage in trading as adjunct to customer business, and to what extent the bank trades on its own account.[3]

Income from Subsidiaries and Affiliates

A bank may own or partly own, through stockholdings, financial, as well as non-financial subsidiaries. Some jurisdictions, however, impose strict limitations on the extent of ownership a bank may have in affiliates engaged in a business other than banking. The rationale for such strict limitations is that it imposes undue risk on depositors, who have placed their funds with the bank for safekeeping. In other jurisdictions, restrictions are less strict, and banks' equity investments have been viewed as a way to better align the interests of creditors and shareholders, and to create a greater degree of stability in the financial system, thus allowing for more effective long-term planning. For example, in Germany and Japan, it has been common practice for banks to have large shareholdings in the non-financial businesses of their customers and their affiliates. Still, in other countries, non-financial investments are a customary form of diversification, and are seen as legitimate way of banks boosting their profits. For instance, in some countries such as Taiwan and Bangladesh, banks have attempted to raise their profits through investments in the stock market, and, in the Philippines for example, through investments in real estate. Mention should also be made of the phenomenon in Asia, particularly among family-controlled business groups, in which ownership of a bank by the group as a whole provides both prestige and a means by which the group can leverage its capital and finance members

---

[3] This also raises risk management concerns which are discussed in Chapter 16.

of the group with minimum public disclosure. Needless to say, some of these practices may be subject to abuse and should be viewed critically by the analyst.

Evaluating the Performance of a Bank's Non-Interest Income Business

Evaluating non-interest income is similar to evaluating any service business; attention must be paid both to revenues and expenses. We have already discussed non-interest expenses. While it is possible to assess the profitability of a bank's non-interest income separately using ratio analysis, it is equally if not more important to understand a bank's strength and weaknesses in this area. Does it, for example, have a healthy trust business that enables it to shore up profits when commercial lending activity is slow? In addition, to evaluate a bank's non-interest income business from a credit perspective, especial attention should be paid to any income components that are not likely to be recurrent. Extraordinary gains from the sale of property or businesses are the most obvious items in this category. A bank, however, may have had an extraordinarily good year in foreign exchange trading that masks declines in other categories. Since it is difficult to ensure repeat performance in such cases, declines in areas such as fees and commissions should be more closely scrutinized than trading gains or losses, unless the gains or losses are of great magnitude. Fees and commissions tend to be the bread-and-butter of a bank's non-interest income business more so than trading activity, which embodies substantial volatility and will likely fluctuate materially from year to year.

ANALYZING OVERALL PERFORMANCE

The foregoing tools enable the analyst to reveal a broad brush picture of a bank's performance relative to its peers. While this is often sufficient because it highlights the bank's strong and weak points, it is sometimes necessary to develop a more complete rendering. This can be done by measuring key income statement items against a common denominator. Since return on average assets functions as an indicator of banking performance, measuring revenues and expenses against average assets serves to highlight a bank's strengths and weaknesses relative to its historical performance and that of its peers.

Dupont Analysis

To better understand the relationship between component revenue streams and concomitant expenses, they can be systematically deconstructed. An analysis of this kind is called a Dupont analysis. Most often used by bank equity analysts, the Dupont analysis can also help bank credit analysts to better grasp the links between profitability and risk. Strictly speaking, a Dupont analysis does not address risk factors, although the degree of leverage it highlights implies a greater or lesser degree of risk. The two diagrams that follow show how the analysis of risk and return fit together and also provide an example of a Dupont analysis of a Latin American bank in the mid-1990s.

Beginning with ROE, which reflects "the ability of [a] bank to compete with other banks and non-financial companies for private sources of capital,"[4] a Dupont analysis shows the correlation between ROE, ROA

Illustration, Dupont Analysis: Conceptual Model

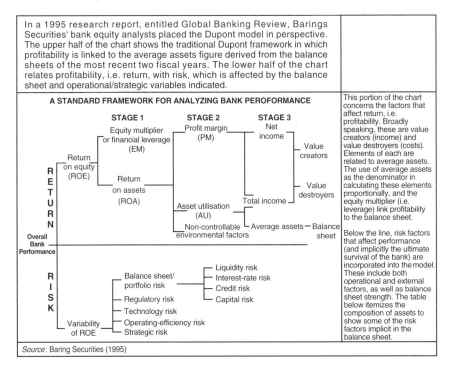

In a 1995 research report, entitled Global Banking Review, Barings Securities' bank equity analysts placed the Dupont model in perspective. The upper half of the chart shows the traditional Dupont framework in which profitability is linked to the average assets figure derived from the balance sheets of the most recent two fiscal years. The lower half of the chart relates profitability, i.e. return, with risk, which is affected by the balance sheet and operational/strategic variables indicated.

Source: Baring Securities (1995)

---

[4] Baring Securities, Global Banking Review, September 1995, p. 8.

Dupont Analysis: Banco de Bogotá

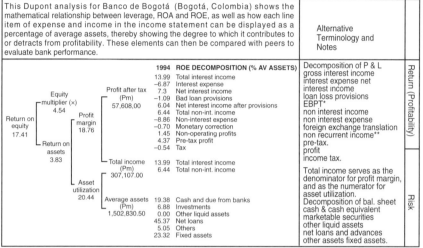

				1994	ROE DECOMPOSITION (% AV ASSETS)	Alternative Terminology and Notes
				13.99	Total interest income	Decomposition of P & L
				−6.87	Interest expense	gross interest income
			Profit after tax	7.3	Net interest income	interest expense net
	Equity		(Pm)	−1.09	Bad loan provisions	interest income
	multiplier (×)		57,608,00	6.04	Net interest income after provisions	loan loss provisions
	4.54	Profit		6.44	Total non-int. income	EBPT*
Return on		margin		−8.86	Non-interest expense	non interest income
equity		18.76		−0.70	Monetary correction	non interest expense
17.41				1.45	Non-operating profits	foreign exchange translation
	Return on			4.37	Pre-tax profit	non recurrent income**
	assets			−0.54	Tax	pre-tax.
	3.83		Total income	13.99	Total interest income	profit
			(Pm)	6.44	Total non-int. income	income tax.
			307,107.00			Total income serves as the
		Asset				denominator for profit margin,
		utilization				and as the numerator for
		20.44	Average assets	19.38	Cash and due from banks	asset utilization.
			(Pm)	6.88	Investments	Decomposition of bal. sheet
			1,502,830.50	0.00	Other liquid assets	cash & cash equivalent
				45.37	Net loans	marketable securities
				5.05	Others	other liquid assets
				23.32	Fixed assets	net loans and advances
						other assets fixed assets.

This Dupont analysis for Banco de Bogotá (Bogotá, Colombia) shows the mathematical relationship between leverage, ROA and ROE, as well as how each line item of expense and income in the income statement can be displayed as a percentage of average assets, thereby showing the degree to which it contributes to or detracts from profitability. These elements can then be compared with peers to evaluate bank performance.

Return (Profitability)

Risk

and leverage, and then proceeds to decompose ROA by measuring each element of costs and revenue against a common denominator. The common denominator is average assets.

The decomposition of ROA separates profitability into two additional components: the bank's profit margin, defined as net profit divided by total income, and asset utilization, defined as operating income divided by average assets. The first varies according to the degree to which the bank is able to maximize spreads through optimizing yields on interest earning assets, non-interest income and through controlling costs, including both interest expense and non-interest expense. Asset utilization refers to the proportion of total assets generating income measured against total income.

EVALUATING BANK PROFITABILITY: A CHECKLIST

In general, the credit analyst wants to account for differences in profitability between the subject bank and its peers, and its divergence from historic performance. What trends can be elucidated?

Changes in Net Profits

How have net profits changed? By what percentage upward or downward? Does this represent a continuation of prior trends or a break with them? How does the subject bank compare with its peers?

Return on Average Assets

How has the bank's ROA changed? Note that ROA will be adversely affected by high levels of loan loss provisions. Compare trends in pre-tax, pre-provision ROA with after-tax, after-provision ROA to determine changes in core profitability.

Extraordinary (or Exceptional) Items & Loan Loss Provisioning

Are there any extraordinary items, either extraordinary (or exceptional) income or expenses, that account for a significant change in the bottom line? Examples include high levels of loan loss reserves set aside (will cut into profits), sales of real property or subsidiaries (will inflate profits). Has the bank under-provisioned? If so, what would profits and profitability be if the appropriate level of loan loss reserves had been set aside?

Net Interest Income

Separate the net interest income component of the revenue stream from the non-interest income component. How does the rate of increase (decrease) in net interest income compare with past trends and peers? Tie it to changes in the volume of loan assets, funding expense (average funding cost) and gross interest income (average yield). The Net Interest Margin reflects the bank's profitability of its earning assets. Account for changes and discrepancies as a result of changes in the bank's Net Interest Spread, asset utilization, asset-liability mismatch and changes in the asset mix. Note that high levels of non-performing loans will adversely affect net interest income.

Non-Interest Income

What changes can be observed in the bank's non-interest income level? Bear in mind that non-interest income categories such as securities and foreign exchange trading tend to be more erratic than net interest income.

Operating Efficiency

How does the bank's operating efficiency compare with past performance and peers? How does cost control compare with past experience and peers? Observe any substantial changes in occupancy, compensation or other expenses. Key ratios include non-interest expenses to average assets, non-interest expenses to operating income, and operating revenue per staff member.

CHAPTER SUMMARY

In this chapter, we have broken down net operating income into its component parts, interest income and non-interest income. Further, we have looked at the items, including both revenue and expense, which make up each stream of income, and seen how key elements that contribute or detract from profitability are reflected in particular financial indicators. These are summarized in the table next page.

Using the Dupont model, we have also examined how return on investment is linked to profitability and observed how costs and revenues can be compared among banks by calculating them in proportion to a common denominator: average assets. The Dupont framework also provides a graphical way to link the income statement to the balance sheet, as we can see that profitability whether expressed as return on assets or return on equity requires the use of both financial statements in relation to each other.

Summary of Factors Affecting Bank Profitability, Relevant Queries,
and Selected Remarks

Operating Costs Are Higher/Lower Than Its Peers. Query:	Remarks
Is management keeping a tight rein on expenses/too spendthrift?	Compare efficiency with peers.
Is management hiring second-class staff/ not hiring enough staff with deleterious effects possible down the line?	Check staff costs as % of assets.
Is management too top-heavy/staffed too leanly?	
Is management investing in information technology or other capital-intensive initiatives?	Is investment likely to bring gains in future?
Is management spending too much/too little on staff training?	Check staff costs as % of assets. Inquire about training when meeting with bank.
Have exogenous conditions caused costs to rise (e.g. regulatory requirements, Y2K prep)?	Are non-interest costs rising materially at all banks? Check for mention about cost rise in annual report. Will the expenses improve other aspects of the bank's financial condition?
Does the bank's franchise have special characteristics that cause it to have higher or lower costs than average (e.g. far flung branch network, wholesale banking)?	Compare number of branches and branch growth to peers.
Provisioning Costs Are Higher/Lower Than Peers? Query:	Remarks
Is provisioning higher/lower than its peers? Is it because the bank has higher/lower NPLs? Is it because the bank is acting prudently anticipating a downturn in the credit cycle? Is it because the bank has lower/higher than average NPL coverage and wants to bring levels more in line with peers? Is it because the bank has a more/less aggressive policy than peers in suspending interest on loans?	Look at NPL ratio, provisioning to loans ratio, and NPL coverage. Compare interest in suspense against provisioning and loan loss reserve levels.
Does the bank have poorer asset quality than its peers due to inadequate credit control and therefore has higher provisioning costs?	Compare NPL trend & levels, coverage levels.

Table continued

Provisioning Costs Are Higher/Lower Than Peers? Query:	Remarks
Is the bank not provisioning as much as it should, given the state of its loan book?	Compare coverage levels.
Is the bank provisioning more than it ought, notwithstanding that asset quality is at reasonable levels?	
Has there been a regulatory directive narrowing the bank's discretion in provisioning?	Check for news on changes in central bank policy; inquire of subject bank.

Are funding Costs Higher/Lower Than Its Peers? Queries:	Remarks
Is the bank's branch network smaller than its peers therefore preventing it From effectively tapping sub-markets that are less interest sensitive (e.g. rural markets)?	Compare size and scope of branch network with peers
Does the bank rely heavily on the inter-bank market for funding and therefore pays more for deposits than peer banks with more extensive branch networks? Is the bank paying more for funding due to deterioration in its credit rating?	Check balance sheet, composition of liabilities (deposits vs. borrowed funds).
Is the bank paying more for funding due to the deterioration of the credit ratings or market perception of the creditworthiness of banks in the country generally (e.g. the Japan premium) or due to a decline in the sovereign rating? Is the bank paying less for funding due to propitious issues in the capital? Are the markets allowing it to obtain longer term funding at exceptionally low rates?	Compare ratings and rating actions. If available, compare spreads for the securities of the bank or securities of banks in the country against a stable benchmark. Note history of money and capital markets issues.
Does the bank have/not have the benefit of government support and therefore can pay/must pay lower/higher rates for deposits and funding?	What is bank's ownership?
Has there been a change in the bank's status vis-á-vis the prospect of external support?	What perecentage of the bank is owned by the national government or a major bank? Beware of minority share-holding, especially when less than 25% of shares.

Table continued

Are Yields Higher/Lower Than Its Peers? Query	Remarks
Is the bank utilizing funds more efficiently, placing a higher proportion in risk assets?	Compare proportion of assets in risk assets such as loans and securities.
Does the bank have—or has it shifted more assets into—a high yield business such as consumer finance?	Examine composition of loan portfolio and any material changes to it.
Has the bank shifted a higher proportion of funds into more liquid assets? Is the higher yield attributable to good credit management, avoiding problem loans and keeping extant loans performing?	Check asset composition, liquid assets ratio. How does credit management compare with the bank's peers?
Is non-interest income business more/less robust than its peers?	Substantial non-interest income will boost overall profitability (ROA), but not NIM.
Does the bank have adequate non-interest income to help diversify its revenue stream?	Over-reliance on interest-generation (less than 20% of operating income from non-interest earning activities) increases risk.
Has the bank benefited from any extraordinary/exceptional gains or suffered from any extraordinary/exceptional losses recorded as non-interest income during the year?	Check the income statement for exceptional and extraordinary gains and footnoted items for any increases or decreases that are unusually large.
Did the bank have an exceptional gain the previous year, resulting in a false decline in non-interest income during the most recent fiscal year?	A large increase or decrease in the year prior to the fiscal year being examined can make the most recent fiscal year look unusually negative or positive. This applies to most financial statement items.

CHAPTER EIGHT

AN INTRODUCTION TO ASSET QUALITY: NON-PERFORMING LOANS AND THE CREDIT CYCLE

Thus, bank credit expansion sets in motion the business cycle in all its phases — the inflationary boom, marked by expansion of the money supply and by malinvestment; the crisis, which arrives when credit expansion ceases and malinvestments become evident; and the depression recovery, the necessary adjustment process by which the economy returns to the most efficient ways of satisfying consumer desires.
— Murray N. Rothbard, *America's Great Depression*[1]

What about all the bad investments made during the boom? Well, that was so much wasted capital. But there is no obvious reason why bad investments made in the past require an actual slump of output in the present. Remember ... economic slumps are not punishments for our sins, pains we are fated to suffer.
— Paul Krugman, *Return of Depression Economics*[2]

Asset quality, or the credit quality of a bank's interest-earning portfolio, is one of the most important criteria in establishing the creditworthiness of a bank. It is also one of the most difficult for an analyst to measure, especially during periods of economic prosperity when even the dodgiest

---

[1] Murray N. Rothbard, *America's Great Depression*, Richardson and Snyder, 1963, p. 20 cited in Dr. Jim Walker, "Asianomics: The Unbearable Knowledge of Impotence: From Austria to Asia," Credit Lyonnais Securities Asia, May 11, 1998, p. 3.
[2] Paul Krugman, *Return of Depression Economics*, Penguin Books, 1999, p. 71.

of borrowers can make their loan payments without difficulty. Disclosure is also an issue that frequently arises in connection with asset quality. Although bank managers generally recognize an obligation to reveal profits, unless required to do so by regulation, they may be reluctant to disclose in detail the volume and sources of the bank's dud loans.

While non-interest income business is becoming increasingly important, banks, we have observed in the preceding chapters discussing the income statement and profitability, still make most of their income from lending money to individuals and businesses, and loans comprise the lion's share of most banks' assets. In the United States, where disintermediation is further along than in most countries, on average, more than half of a bank's total assets will be in the form of loans, and interest from loans will constitute over 60% of a bank's gross revenues. Other forms of (interest) *earning assets* include government and other fixed income securities, equipment leases and other obligations that generate fixed returns. Asset quality, more specifically, refers to the likelihood that the bank's earning assets will continue to perform.

Loans, however, are the primary category of earning assets, and while investment securities, leases and other earning and non-earning assets are also subject to default risks, bank loans are the focus of most asset quality concerns. (Remember that loans to a bank are *assets* rather than the *liabilities* they are to an industrial company, for it is the interest generated from these loans which is paid by borrowers to the bank that constitutes the primary revenue stream for most banks.[3]) As with any asset, bank assets must be paid for, or funded, by corresponding liabilities (i.e. deposits, interbank and other borrowings, as well as from bank capital), which represent claims of creditors or the owners on those assets.[4]

---

[3] Of course, when a bank borrows money from another bank — an interbank borrowing — such a loan is indeed a liability. Typically, most of a bank's liabilities, as we will discuss later, are the obligations it has towards its depositors, some of whom will also be other banks.

[4] There is no free lunch. The funds that were extended will have either come from deposits or borrowings, both of which will continue to bear interest. Even if the funding was from deposits that do not bear interest, e.g. checking deposits or from equity, the funds would still have costs associated with them. The bank also suffers the opportunity cost from having extended a loan that, as a result of default, does not generate interest.

ASSET QUALITY AND NON-PERFORMING LOANS: AN INTRODUCTION

What Are NPLs?

Not all of the bank's customers will pay back the loans extended in full. In bank jargon, not all loans will *perform*. Some will perform for a time and then become non-performing. When a particular borrower is unable or unwilling to pay the loan extended by the bank, then the loan is referred to as *overdue*. After a certain period of time, an overdue loan may become *non-accruing* or *non-performing*, subject to the definitions utilized by the bank and the regulatory authority that supervises it.[5] These definitions vary considerably in emerging markets and are in a process of flux as regulatory authorities seek to improve applicable standards. Moreover, in many jurisdictions, banks have considerable discretion in determining whether a loan is non-performing or not. Note that the terms overdue loans, classified loans, non-performing loans, non-performing assets and bad loans are often used loosely, and the imprecise use of terms can easily give rise to confusion.

Under common international practice, a loan in which interest (or principal) is more than 90 days overdue is classified as a *non-performing loan*, or as an *NPL* for short.[6] NPLs are themselves a subset of problem loans, which are often classified into three or more categories by regulatory authorities. A loan need not be non-performing or even overdue to be "classified." On the basis of economic changes or changes in the financial condition of a customer, a bank may *classify* a loan, even if payments or principal are still current. *Classified loans* include loans considered to be *substandard*, *doubtful*, and losses (i.e. *loss* loans). A non-performing loan is one form of *non-performing asset*. Such *problem assets* become a burden to a bank, and a bank with an increasing proportion of problem assets can be said to be experiencing *deterioration of its asset quality*.

Loan classification definitions can be fairly complex and vary from country to country although customary global standards do exist, based largely upon definitions used in the United States and other developed countries with similarly stringent regulations. Definitions may be based

---

[5] What is referred to as a *non-accruing loan* in the United States, will typically be referred to as a *non-performing loan* elsewhere.

[6] In reality, the risks to an industrial firm tend to be somewhat different, but for banks the risk that some loans will go sour is nearly inevitable.

upon a qualitative or a quantitative standard, or a combination of the two. We will come back to loan classifications in the next chapter, but the following table will give the reader a basic definition of the most commonly seen categories.

Loan Classifications Vary

Loan Classifications as of 2000				
Classification	**Customary inter-national standard**	**Examples of aging basis criteria**		**Deemed an NPL?**
		India	**Philippines**	
Non-perfor-ming loan	Past due more than 90 days	6 mo	3 mo	
Specially mentioned	Not past due more than 90 days, but borrower has experienced deteriorating financial conditions	n/a	Qualitative definition	Generally not
Substandard	Past due more than 90 days and the loan has a well-defined weakness, of borrower e.g. vulnerability to incapacity to pay in full or inadequacy of collateral to fully secure loan	6 mo past due	3 mo past due	Generally
Doubtful	Past due more than 90 days and given apparent weakness collection in full is improbable	24 mo past due	12 mo past due	Generally
Loss (Bad loans)	Past due more than 90 days and deemed uncollectable, notwithstanding that some partial recovery may be obtained in the future	24 mo past due + expecta-tion of loss	12 mo past due + expecta-tion of loss	Always

The Harm NPLs Cause

Although it might seem obvious, it is important to keep in mind just why *non-performing loans* or more generally *non-performing assets* (*NPAs*) are undesirable for banks.[7] Simply put, loans are the assets out of which a bank generates its profits. Because margins on bank loans are low — money is, after all, merely a commodity — and because banks are so highly leveraged, the complete loss of a single bad loan can wipe out the profits generated from dozens of performing loans. It is as if a manufacturing firm loses a factory through fire or other calamity. Imagine, for instance, that an industrial company finances and constructs a manufacturing facility incapable of producing saleable products — for example, through defective construction or design. Or imagine that the design defect is such that when certain outside conditions occur, a fire is triggered causing the facility to quickly burn to the ground. The asset, effectively destroyed, would be unable to generate revenue for the company. Instead, it would become a cost. The company would still bear the liabilities it undertook to construct the plant. It would have to repay the funds it borrowed to build the facility, and the costs of maintaining it would be an ongoing burden that the company would be compelled to carry. In other words, not only would the asset no longer be generating income, but maintaining the property on which it was established would be an added expense to the company. It would likely be worth a fraction of its putative value at best, perhaps to be sold as scrap, or perhaps nothing at all.

Loans, too, are assets that can be impaired or destroyed. A non-performing loan is not unlike such a non-performing manufacturing facility, whether non-performing as a result of an internal flaw, external forces or both.[6] A bank's assets, including its loans, must be funded, just like the assets of an industrial company. The money extended as a loan, whether money owed to depositors, outside borrowers or belonging to shareholders, must be repaid. Although not all bank deposits earn interest, deposits in general are not free money. The bank, as we have seen, effectively borrows from its depositors. The funds that the bank borrowed from its depositors to extend a loan that subsequently becomes *delinquent* must still be repaid, in interest and principal, irrespective of whether the loan is generating revenues for the bank or whether the

---

[6] See p. 161

[7] Indeed, a bank that has negligible non-performing loans may be overly-conservative. While credit analysts may find little to complain about in such an institution, equity analysts might opine that such a bank is not maximizing the value of its franchise.

principal has been repaid. The bank's other funds — those borrowed from other banks or investors, or those invested by shareholders — likewise bear a cost. The ongoing interest and operating expenses associated with the bank's funding remain a burden on the bank, and, even if the deposit is not interest-bearing, principal must be repaid. Compensating for the hole in a bank's balance sheet created when a loan goes bad — like a factory destroyed by fire and without insurance — can place a heavy burden on a bank's bottom line and ultimately wipe out its capital.

Poor Loan Quality Is the Salient Underlying Cause of Bank Failure

Asset Quality Problems Can Trigger Other Problems

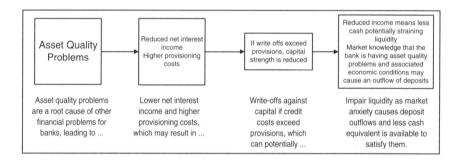

That some portion of a bank's loans will become non-performing is practically certain. It is an inherent risk and a cost of banking.[7] But it is also this *credit risk*, that when poorly managed, most often triggers liquidity problems as revenues decline, costs rise and capital is impaired, and is therefore ultimately responsible for the majority of bank failures.[8] Again, because banks operate on comparatively thin margins and are highly leveraged, the impact of a substantial volume of NPLs can have dire consequences. It only takes a comparatively small proportion of NPLs before a bank's capital is entirely consumed and the bank is rendered technically insolvent. According to a study by the US Office of the Comptroller of the Currency (OCC), the consistent element in bank

---

[7] See p. 163.
[8] "Poor loan quality [has been] the main factor in … US bank failures [in the mid-1980s to mid-1990s]." *Bank Management*, DATE, p. 370.

failures in the United States has been poor control of credit risk, including the following elements.[9]

❏ Lack of compliance with loan policies

❏ Lack of clear standards and excessively lax loan terms

❏ Over-concentration of lending

❏ Inadequate controls over loan officers

❏ Loan growth in excess of the bank's ability to manage

❏ Inadequate systems for identifying loan problems

❏ Insufficient knowledge about customers' finances

❏ Lending outside the market with which the bank was familiar

Each of the foregoing elements is a potential precursor of poor asset quality. Indeed, it is precisely these items that the analyst must be on the lookout for, especially those that can be readily identified from disclosed data about the bank's loan book, namely over-concentration and foreign lending. Standards, controls and the overall credit culture can, if the opportunity exists, be explored in discussions with management or gleaned from conversations with those familiar with the institution.

To be sure, in reality there are degrees of performance and the fact that a loan is non-performing does not mean that a bank will recover nothing from it. The borrower may be able to make partial payments, or the bank may be able to foreclose the loan and obtain security which it can sell to mitigate its losses.[10] But even if it is able to regain some fraction of the value of the loan, the bank is unlikely to come out ahead when loans fail to perform. While the bank may be able to foreclose the loan and obtain title to the security, which typically will be in the form of real property, it is not unlikely that the circumstances that led the bank's customer to default occurred in less than sanguine economic conditions. Property values may very well be depressed or falling, and collateral when sold may be insufficient to cover the outstanding principal and interest. It may end up recovering only a portion of the funds that it extended. The bank may be reluctant to attempt to sell the

---

[9] Paraphrase of items in a study by Joseph F. Apadoford, "Credit Quality: CEOs Set the Tone," *Magazine of Bank Administration*, June 1988 cited in *Bank Management*, p. 371.

[10] To continue the analogy with the defective manufacturing plant, the industrial company might have legal recourse against an outside engineering firm or supplier and also recover a portion of its expenditure.

loan security during depressed market conditions, hoping for a rise in property values. In some markets, the bank may have considerable discretion in holding on to loan collateral. But until sold, the property must be maintained, rented out or, if not ready for occupancy, protected against decay and vandalism. Maintaining the property may very well be a drag on the bank's earnings — in taking title to it, through foreclosure for example, the bank will become responsible for taxes, utilities and security. Moreover, banks normally lack expertise in property investment and management and may not do a good job in maximizing returns from sale or lease of the collateral.[11] The challenge for bank management is to minimize the risk of loan defaults and to price loans so that returns are more than sufficient to cover loan losses. It is fair to say that managing credit risk is a commercial bank's most critical function, and asset quality is probably the element of bank financial performance that is of most importance to a bank credit analyst.

Illustration, The Harm NPLs Cause

To illustrate the problems NPLs pose for a bank, imagine the following scenario. The community of Bay City has experienced several years of prosperity, and the Bay City Bank (BCB), a bank with $10 m in equity, and $100 m in deposits that pay on average 3% per annum (0.25% monthly) has built up its loan book to $100 m that on average pay 9% per annum or 0.75% monthly. This is an extremely robust spread on loans. Another $10 m of the bank's assets are in liquid assets, comprising $5 m one-year Treasury bills that pay on average 5% per annum; $3 m in reserves deposited with the central bank that pay no interest; and $2 m in cash or cash equivalent. The default rate is almost zero. Now suppose a recession strikes the region in which Bay City is located. The largest employer in Bay City, Bay City Gear Corporation, suddenly goes bankrupt early in the year, while another major firm BC Spark Plug Corporation, closes down its Bay City plant and moves production to Mexico.

Although BCB had no loans outstanding to Bay City Gear, customers of the bank, including suppliers to the company and its employees, start to experience problems and cannot make their interest payments.

---

[11] The calculation of NPLs and the use of recovery rates in their measurement is discussed in the next chapter.

Other local companies, like Bay City Metals, to which BCB did have a working capital loan of $2 m, shut down, and clothing shops, restaurants and other retail outlets also close their doors. Property values fall by one third and real estate developers to whom BCB has lent funds experience cash flow problems. With each passing month, BCB's loan default rate increases by 2%. Assume further, that BCB has no non-interest income. The result is that the actual profit (if booked on a cash basis) steadily dwindles as overdue loans rise.

In actuality, a prudent bank would maintain some level of general loan loss reserves. But under the dire circumstances assumed, this would not much help the bank defer disaster. As above, assume that after 90 days the overdue loan is deemed non-performing and must be written off from the balance sheet. Let us imagine that BCB maintained 1% general reserves, i.e. $1 m that had been built up from retained earnings. As the overdue loans are classified non-performing, the assets are written off and the write-offs must be charged from the bank's provisions and equity to keep the balance sheet in balance. Such reserves would only delay the wiping out of equity by two weeks, and once equity and reserves are gone, the bank is insolvent. By August, that is the case with BCB.

However, dwindling net interest income just represents a small part of BCB's problem. Although not calculated in the above example, in reality, customers with accounts at BCB would be drawing down their funds to deal with the crisis. So long as they have their funds deposited with the bank, the interest paid to them is simply a book-entry item, but if funds are withdrawn, liquidity is required. In other words, there is no change in cash flow in respect of deposits, unless a depositor withdraws funds from the bank either by taking out cash or making payment to another party or account. In contrast, third party borrowers must be paid at the time interest payments become due. However, as depositors' funds are withdrawn, cash is reduced and the bank will be forced to sell loans or securities to raise additional liquid funds, unless the central bank offers the bank a liquidity facility. If depositors panic, the bank's $2 m in cash and $5 m in T-bills will be quickly depleted. A mere contraction of deposits by 7% would exhaust the bank's liquid funds (10% if statutory reserves are included). Even if the bank is supplied with additional liquidity or deposit insurance prevents a run, gradually the bank's cash flow will dwindle to zero and the bank will not be able to pay its depositors. During this period, of course the bank will be loath to make new loans.

Illustration: Hypothetical: Bay City Bank

Bay City Bank

× $m	Jan	Feb	Mar	Apr	May	June	July	Assumptions:
Assets								Assets remain constant
Marketable Securities	5	5	5	5	5	5	5	
Total Loans	100	100	100	100	100	100	100	2% of the loan portfolio becomes overdue each month
Other Assets	5	5	5	5	5	5	5	e.g. Fixed assets
Overdue	0	2	4	6	8	10	12	Loans overdue but not yet non-performing
NPLs	0	0	0	2	4	6	8	There is a 3 month lag before overdue loans register as NPLs. NPLs exceed equity from August onwards
Loans classified as "performing"	100	100	100	98	96	94	92	Total loans less loans deemed NPLs
Other	5	5	5	5	5	5	5	Assumptions:
Total Assets	110	110	110	110	110	110	110	remains constant
Deposits	100	100	100	100	100	100	100	remains constant
Equity	10	10	10	10	10	10	10	Liabilities and equity remain constant
Total Liabilities + Equity	110	110	110	110	110	110	110	

× $m	Aug	Sep	Oct	Nov	Dec	Year	Assumptions:
Assets							Assets remain constant
Marketable Securities	5	5	5	5	5	5	
Total Loans	100	100	100	100	100	100	2% of the loan portfolio becomes overdue each month
Other Assets	5	5	5	5	5	5	e.g. Fixed assets
Overdue	14	16	18	20	22	22	Loans overdue but not yet non-performing
NPLs	10	12	14	16	18	18	There is a 3 month lag before overdue loans register as NPLs. NPLs exceed equity from August onwards
Loans classified as "performing"	90	88	86	84	82	82	Total loans less loans deemed NPLs
Other	5	5	5	5	5	5	Assumptions:
Total Assets	110	110	110	110	110	110	remains constant
Deposits	100	100	100	100	100	100	remains constant
Equity	10	10	10	10	10	10	Liabilities and equity remain constant
Total Liabilities + Equity	110	110	110	110	110	110	

Table continued

Bay City Bank								
x $m	Jan	Feb	Mar	Apr	May	June	July	
Net Int Income (A)	0.78	0.78	0.78	0.76	0.75	0.73	0.72	Int income still recorded until loans overdue 3 mo
Non-Int Exp	0.26	0.26	0.26	0.26	0.26	0.26	0.26	remains constant
Profit	0.52	0.52	0.52	0.50	0.49	0.47	0.46	Profit less than if no NPLs
Actual Int Income	0.775	0.76	0.745	0.73	0.715	0.7	0.685	Actual int income even less
Actual Int Exp	0.25	0.25	0.25	0.25	0.25	0.25	0.25	remains constant
Actual Net Int Inc	0.53	0.51	0.50	0.48	0.47	0.45	0.44	Actual net int income declines as NPLs increase
Non Int Exp	0.26	0.26	0.26	0.26	0.26	0.26	0.26	remains constant
Cash Flow	0.27	0.25	0.24	0.22	0.21	0.19	0.18	Cash flow is less than profit and approaching zero even without taking into account the likely circumstance that deposits would be withdrawn
Equity less NPLs	10	10	10	8	6	4	2	By August, the bank is technically insolvent

x $m	Aug	Sep	Oct	Nov	Dec	Year	
Net Int Income (A)	0.70	0.69	0.67	0.66	0.64	8.63	Int income still recorded until loans overdue 3 mo
Non-Int Exp	0.26	0.26	0.26	0.26	0.26	3.12	remains constant
Profit	0.44	0.43	0.41	0.40	0.38	5.51	Profit less than if no NPLs
Actual Int Income	0.67	0.655	0.64	0.625	0.61	8.31	Actual int income even less
Actual Int Exp	0.25	0.25	0.25	0.25	0.25	3	remains constant
Actual Net Int Inc	0.42	0.41	0.39	0.38	0.36	5.31	Actual net int income declines as NPLs increase
Non Int Exp	0.26	0.26	0.26	0.26	0.26	3.12	remains constant
Cash Flow	0.16	0.15	0.13	0.12	0.10	2.19	Cash flow is less than profit and approaching zero even without taking into account the likely circumstance that deposits would be withdrawn
Equity less NPLs	0	-2	-4	-6	-8		By August, the bank is technically insolvent

In any event, it will be difficult for the bank to fund new loans. As still-healthy customers repay principal, the bank will have an incentive to maintain those assets in liquid form. If many banks experience the same problem, the amount of credit circulating within the economy will remain at a comparatively low level, and business activity will stay subdued.

ASSET QUALITY AND THE BUSINESS CYCLE

NPLs Vary with Business and Economic Conditions

During periods of strong economic growth, non-performing loans will tend to fall or rise slowly for two primary reasons. First, during periods of rising prosperity, borrowers will probably be doing good business and earning sufficient cash flow to service their debts. Second, as banks rapidly expand lending during such periods, the volume of non-performing loans will appear to contract on a proportional basis. There will be some lag time before new loans go bad, as borrowers will probably be able to service the debt initially out of the cash infused as result of the loan. In contrast, during periods of economic recession, non-performing loans will rapidly rise for reasons corresponding to those that reduced NPLs during periods of robust economic growth. In times of falling demand, borrowers will confront reduced cash flow and will have more difficulty servicing their debt. NPLs will shoot up, as latent problem loans emerge and, the NPL ratio will be given a further boost amid a static or contracting bank loan book.

Masking Effect of Loan Growth and Revealing Effect of Loan Contraction

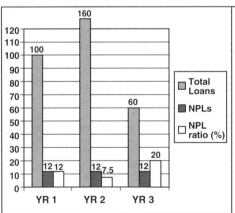

Loan growth and loan contraction serve to respectively mask and reveal non-performing loans. In this hypothetical illustration, NPL remain constant at 12, but the NPL ratio varies with the size of the loan book. When it stands at 100, the NPL ratio is a mediocre 12%. When it rises to 160, the NPL ratio declines to a more acceptable 7.5%. When lending contracts to 60, the NPL ratio balloons to 20%. In the real world, NPLs would likely not stay the same in absolute terms. More likely they would initially fall with a flood of new lending (it takes time for loans to become non-performing) and be rising in the wake of a recession when the bank would be most likely to be cutting back on lending. Thus, what is at heart a purely arithmetic phenomenon acts to dampen the rise in the NPL ratio in an expansionary environment and amplify its rise in a recession.

In the following chart, we can see an illustration of what is more likely to happen in real life. During an expansionary phase, NPLs will climb slowly and the modest increase will appear even more modest. In a recessionary phase, NPLs will balloon, and an accompanying loan book contraction will simply make the swelling appear that much more rapid. We can see that of three banks in Hong Kong, loan growth was rapid in FY96 and FY97 but NPL growth was minimal; in FY98 and FY99, the situation reversed. NPLs grew quickly and the banks' NPL ratio expanded even more sharply.

> Tip: It is easy after a period of sanguine economic conditions to underestimate a bank's potential to register a substantial erosion in asset quality as reflected in NPLs and the bank's NPL ratio. Once a bank's loan book is bruised, rot is apt to set in quickly.

Three Hong Kong Banks: Loan Growth and NPL Ratio Expansion

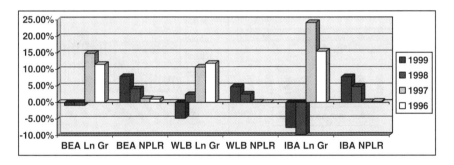

Actual Growth of Loans And NPLs at Three Hong Kong Banks

	BEA Total Loans	BEA NPLs	WLB Total Loans	WLB NPLs	IBA Total Loans	IBA NPLs
1999	81,931	6,701	13,525	1,089	31,926	1,508
1998	83,384	3,473	15,942	779	31,562	1,396
1997	84,895	979	19,811	34	32,885	220
1996	65,423	640	13,356	36	24,956	228
Data sourced from BankStat						

The cycle of growth and recession, known as the business cycle, varies from time and place in duration and magnitude.[12] The charts below show a long cycle in the Philippines that began in the late 1980s as the country's economic and political situation began to stabilize following the overthrow of dictator Ferdinand Marcos, and the banking and economic crisis that was still occurring. NPLs fell from a peak of over 20% and declined rapidly as the country partook of the Asian boom when economic reforms were implemented under the Fidel Ramos administration (1992–96). Bottoming out at below 3%, NPLs shot up again with the onset of the Asian crisis in mid-1997. Prudential regulations promulgated by the new central bank put a lid on banking excesses and NPLs appear to have peaked in 2000 at under 15%.

Illustration: NPLs in the Philippines

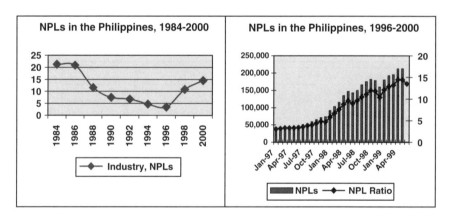

The Banking Credit Cycle and the Business Cycle

The banking business is traditionally cyclical, tracking the business cycle through recovery and expansion, boom and peak, contraction and recession. Business cycle theory is a somewhat arcane corner of macroeconomics that need not be addressed in any detail here, but its application can be seen in the commonsense experience of economic change. Although business cycles are associated with periods of boom and bust,

---

[12] See Charles P. Kindleberger, *Manias, Panics and Crashes: A History of Financial Crises,* John Wiley & Sons, 3rd Ed., 2001, p. 1.

bull and bear markets, ups and downs in the business cycle as it affects a particular economy do not necessarily lead to financial crises. But financial crises occur frequently enough, and when they do occur they highlight in their aftermath the causes that engendered them.[13] The cycle illustrated below uses one of these more extreme paradigms to illustrate the flow and ebb of the cycle more clearly.

Recovery and Expansion

During the recovery and expansion phase, improving business conditions lead firms to expand, hiring new workers to respond to increased orders and capital improvements. Banks, sensing the more salutary business climate and flush with deposits, begin lending to fund the expansion. Additional employment leads to more consumer spending, which leads to more orders for retail and wholesale goods, which leads to further expansion in a virtuous cycle. Increasing trade leads to greater demand for trade finance. Amid emerging prosperity and a growing economy, companies require new capital to fund further expansion. The greater income and investment opportunities attracts additional capital seeking to benefit from the associated rise in prices for assets, that are now able to generate higher profits. The generation of new capital internally or through infusions by shareholders enables further growth and allows banks to lend to such enterprises more safely.

Boom

Perceiving the possibility of gains through price appreciation, more investors put their capital at risk investing in assets such as real estate and stocks. As these rise in value, investors sitting on unrealized gains feel richer and are more willing to spend on all manner of goods and services. Meanwhile, banks, still earning good returns with few loans defaulting under the beneficent economic conditions continue to lend in attractive sectors. But, increasing competition among banks leads banks to shave interest rates to the bone in order to win more business. Credit standards are relaxed. By means of the money multiplier effect, the expansion in bank credit results in a ballooning money supply, which eventually triggers price inflation. Interest rates, already low in real terms, may become

---

[13] For an accessible discussion of the anatomy of a financial crisis from an historical economic perspective, see Charles P. Kindleberger, *Manias, Panics and Crashes: A History of Financial Crises*, John Wiley & Sons, 3rd Ed., especially Chapter 2.

even more attractive to borrowers seeking to profit from price appreciation in real and financial assets, which are rapidly increasing in price. The upward trend attracts investors and speculators who are able to leverage moderate down payments into substantial gains from price appreciation.

Ultimately, too much capital chasing too few investment opportunities causes prices to spiral aloft further feeding a boom, which by now has clearly become speculative. New players are drawn into the market, including among them those who had previously avoided such endeavors. As the exuberance becomes widespread and valuations reach unprecedented highs, even skeptics begin to be persuaded by an increasing number of market pundits opining that this time things are different, and that some new concatenation of circumstances justifies the elevation in market values. For others, the "greater fool theory" starts to take hold as they, no longer believing that valuations are defensible, purchase only with the intention of unloading the asset to a "greater fool" once an incremental gain is achieved. In any case, notwithstanding a jeremiad or two (dismissed as being hopelessly out of touch), a euphoria descends upon the mass of investors leading to a final frenzy of irrational exuberance.[14] Inevitably, the resultant asset bubble bursts, pricked by news of a firm that has not achieved its expected earnings, the failure of a noteworthy bank or corporation, or external economic shock, such as a rise in the price of oil.

Crash or Contraction

The prices of real and financial assets typically crash at this point, bringing about a sudden change in the mood of investors. Looking to preserve gains already made or to mitigate losses, many speculators and investors exit the market, selling their property or stock. Some resist panic, believing that the rapid drop in market prices is merely a temporary dip and therefore a buying opportunity. Disproportionate sales to purchases, however, further depress prices, causing even more investors to decide to cut their losses. Sensing that market conditions have really changed, they also exit the market leading to further downward pressure on prices. Eventually, most in a position to exit do so, and market prices stabilize.

---

[14] The title of the book by Yale University's economics professor Robert J. Shiller on March 15, 2000, just as the US'NASDAQ market reached a peak.

Recession

But the destruction in wealth caused by the crash in real estate and securities prices dampens consumer spending considerably as consumers no longer feel so affluent. Businesses are by now contracting on reduced consumer spending and laying off workers or even shutting down. As they do so, demand for loans for productive purposes falls off, while bad loans begin to rise as investments conceived during a period of exuberance fail to make projected returns. Unable to service their debt, or entering bankruptcy, borrowers default on their bank loans. Some banks at this point will halt lending to new customers and will begin to focus on preserving their balance sheet. Meanwhile, unemployed borrowers, like their corporate counterparts, may not have the funds to pay off loans assumed in more prosperous times. Those who have borrowed to purchase dwellings secured by mortgages may find that as prices have plunged, they have "negative equity" in their property. That is, the face value of their mortgage exceeds the market value of their homes. In such cases, homeowners are more likely to default on their mortgages, allowing banks to seize their property and sell it in lieu of the underlying debt. Or, if unemployed for an extended period, with savings depleted, they may simply have no choice. As more workers are made redundant, demand for goods and services falls further creating a vicious cycle.

Declining business conditions lead to even higher levels of non-performing loans, which, due to provisioning needs reduces banks' net profits. Meanwhile, with loans spinning off less interest income (as a higher proportion become non-performing), little new loan growth and a higher percentage of operating income needed to be set aside for loan loss provisions, net profits fall. If the bank has not lent its funds prudently, NPLs may rise to a level where they eat into bank capital. If they have not done so already, most banks will by now have essentially stopped lending altogether, called in many existing loans to increase liquidity, and placed a higher proportion of their deposit and other funding into liquid assets such as government securities. With high demand for safe government securities, interest rates decline. Prevailing interest rates, though they may be nominally low, are likely to be high in real terms as inflation falls. Price deflation may even take hold, as depressed demand and less money circulating through the economy will keep downward pressure on prices. To stimulate demand, the government may seek to inject more funds into the economy through public works spending and by lowering interest rates.

Although some prospective borrowers with potentially profitable projects may exist, they will be hard-pressed to obtain funding for them. Where deposit insurance is non-existent or weak, depositors may become anxious and the bank may become vulnerable to a bank run. Even if this is not a concern, the bank will become preoccupied with shoring up capital and liquidity, by building up loan loss reserves, and stanching the loss of interest income. As a first step, banks will step up collection efforts and seek to enforce their collateral through foreclosure. Following a property crash, however, the collateral may no longer cover the outstanding principal and interest on the loan. Some banks may now find their capital depleted. Unless the bank is privately held, equity capital may not be available at this point, since the bank's need for capital will coincide with a sliding stock market. In any case, if their capital is consumed, shareholders may be unwilling to throw good money after bad, and may hope for a government bailout. More prudently run banks will benefit from a flight to quality, as depositors seek a safe haven for their funds. Bank deposits in quality banks will rise, with consumers having cut spending to the minimum and businesses seeking to bolster their liquidity. Banks having few opportunities to lend funds reduce interest rates in order to discourage deposits. Business and investor confidence declines.

Renewal

The duration of such depressed economic conditions may be short or long, depending upon the severity of the decline, government policy and many other factors. What turns the business cycle around? Government intervention through stimulus programs such as through public investment may ultimately be successful in "priming the pump" and stimulating demand. Low interest rates may encourage banks to begin lending. Other government actions, including recapitalization of weak banks, may also help them to start lending again enabling their customers to expand. Or some external shock may create new business opportunities.

Classically, the economic malaise following a financial crash is dislodged by an exogenous shock to the system. The "outbreak or end of war," creating new demands or releasing pent-up ones, "a bumper harvest or crop failure," or " the widespread adoption of an invention with pervasive effects," or any number of other sufficiently large "displacements"

Illustration: Diagram of the "Business Cycle"

expansion / contraction recovery / recession	Recovery: business confidence improves, businesses expand, hire workers, liquid banks resume lending to fund working capital and capital expenditure, real interest rates are low. Expansion: bank credit further expands, expanding money supply triggers inflation depressing real interest rates, appreciation in the price of real and financial assets encourages further consumer spending and capital investment, ultimately resulting in a speculative frenzy.
	Contraction: external shock or disappointment in results of investments triggers a crash in the price of real and financial assets, demand drops and companies experience cash flow shortfalls.
	Recession: NPLs rise as companies lack liquidity, banks cut back on lending, companies halt new investment, shrinking money supply and falling demand stanches inflation and may trigger deflation; bank profits decline as provisioning needs and write-offs increase, consumers save rather than spend pushing interest rates down and increasing bank liquidity.

may change market sentiment and create new opportunities for profit. Investors seek to exploit those opportunities and capital begins to flow into new sectors.[15]

Losses from Non-Performing Loans Ultimately Must be Subtracted from Provisions or Capital

The level of average asset quality as reflected in key indicators — such as the volume of non-performing loans and in the proportion of NPLs to total loans — improve and deteriorate with changing economic conditions. During periods of economic turmoil, asset quality issues come to the fore as average NPLs, a key indicator, inevitably rise. What happens to NPLs? Basically, there are three possible outcomes. A non-performing loan can return to performing status, perhaps as a result of *restructuring*, or it can be *written off*. To write off loans means to remove them from the balance sheet. When a loan is written off from the asset side of the balance sheet, an equivalent adjustment must be made from the liability side. Since funding obligations are not affected by the

---

[15] Kindleberger, p. 12, citing Hyman Minsky (Hyman Minsky, John Maynard Keynes. Columbia University Press, 1975.

fact that a loan has become non-performing, the adjustment must come from capital. The loan loss is deducted first from loan loss reserves, which constitute a form of capital, and if that is insufficient to cover the losses, then from core or equity capital.

Restructuring means to adjust the terms of the loan so that it can return to performing status. A bank may determine, for example, that a long-time customer's business is fundamentally sound, but that extreme economic conditions have led the borrower to experience temporary payment problems. In such case, the bank may extend the term of the loan or provide the borrower with some relief in respect of the interest rate. Restructuring may enable the borrower to resume repayment and, depending upon regulatory and accounting guidelines, the loan will be reclassified performing after some period of time.[16] Some loans will nonetheless relapse to their previous state, again becoming non-performing. Loan restructuring can be subject to abuse by banks seeking to make their asset quality appear better than it is. Restructuring may be used as a way to avoid high nominal NPL rates and write-offs against capital. Such *cosmetic restructuring* is at heart just extending loan terms without regard to the viability of the borrower's business.[17]

CHAPTER SUMMARY

Not only is asset quality important in its own right, but the quality of a bank's loan portfolio will have an impact on all the other quantitative measures of bank creditworthiness, including profitability, capital and liquidity. Poor asset quality will affect profitability, since a high percentage of NPLs means less net interest income to the bank relative to equity and assets than would otherwise be the case. Elevated NPL levels also tend to engender a high level of provisioning, which cuts directly into profits as a bank sets aside more reserves to cover dud loans.[18] Weak asset quality also threatens core capital, which is the last line of defense against loans that are written off. Loans must be written off against something,

---

[16] Note that in some markets, a loan that is restructured will be immediately reclassified as performing. These markets, banks will be encouraged to restructure to reduce their nominal NPL rate.

[17] Even greater abuses have been known to occur as when two banks arrange to extend loans to each other's customers. The new infusion of cash allows the loans of both to return to performing status, at least for a while.

[18] Provisions properly account for problem loans, by setting aside reserves against probable and estimable loans and deducting them from the book value of the loans to estimate their actual value.

and if loan loss reserves prove insufficient and are exhausted, bank capital, including shareholders' equity is next in line to cover further write-offs. Unfortunately, a bank with mediocre asset quality will have a hard time attracting additional capital. Existing shareholders will be loath to throw bad money after good, while outside investors will be discouraged from doing so, since returns on a bank with high NPLs will be depressed relative to other investment opportunities. Liquidity will also be affected. Loans are relatively illiquid, but performing loans are considerably more liquid than loans which are not being paid back.[19] Moreover, a bank with a high level of NPLs will have to maintain a superior degree of liquidity compared to a bank with excellent asset quality, all things being equal. Sophisticated depositors and investors will be more wary of a bank with mediocre asset quality, and to compensate for the perceived risks, the bank may feel obliged to maintain a higher proportion of its assets in liquid form. This will, of course, impede the generation of above-average returns. Thus, a bank's performance is inextricably intertwined with its asset quality, and managing the bank's loan portfolio to minimize defaults is consequently of primary importance.

---

[19] Non-performing loans are in effect frozen assets that may shrink to a fraction of their former volume before they are eventually reliquefied, or even disappear entirely.

CHAPTER NINE

QUALITATIVE REVIEW OF ASSET QUALITY

[T]he concept of a high-quality loan cannot exist in the absence of objective credit standards.

— R. Taggart Murphy[1]

Asset quality is perhaps the most important factor in determining the credit risk of financial institutions. Given the fact that banks rarely achieve return on assets greater than 1%, the charge-off of even a relatively small amount of assets can quickly eliminate bank earnings and eat up capital or reserves.

— Robert Morris Associates, *Analyzing Foreign Banks*[2]

"[T]he institutional inefficiency of a bank is extremely high. A bank's balance sheet is not marked to market. There is scope for inefficient — and sometimes even destructive — behavior by banks. ...[T]he bank can be motivated to cover this up and take on greater risk; doubling the bet has only upside and no downside for such a bank. This tends to exaggerate the business cycle. The accumulation of bad assets in the banking system decreases the real cost of capital to the economy and encourages overinvestment. The payback is a period of underinvestment. The bank is the institution of the boom-bust investment cycle. This is why almost every economic crisis is also a banking crisis."

— Andy Xie, Bankless Economies: Banks and the IT revolution, Morgan Stanley Dean Witter, Asia Pacific

The bank credit analyst must measure the asset quality of a bank, as always against its peers and past performance. The analyst also has to evaluate the extent to which any impairment of the bank's loan book is

---

[1] *Japanese Money*, p. 55.
[2] p. 26.

moderated by the bank's ability to generate profits, and more importantly the degree to which loan losses are cushioned by loan loss reserves and equity. At the same time, the analyst must keep in mind general economic and business conditions. Has the economy in the subject country been in an expansion phase for several years? Have banks on average been expanding their lending rapidly? Has total bank credit to GDP been rapidly rising? An affirmative answer to these questions may make the analyst wary about bank asset quality. Correspondingly, if banks appear to be relatively healthy in terms of capital, liquidity and with generally low NPL ratios, the analyst's concerns about expansion in bank credit will be lessened, especially if the economy is entering a recovery phase.

QUALITATIVE REVIEW

Analysis of a bank's asset quality can be divided into two parts. The first is a qualitative review of the bank's credit policies and the value of the bank's credit management, as well as an assessment of the composition of its loan portfolio. The second is a ratio analysis of key indicators.

Portfolio Review

Qualitative review of the bank's portfolio begins with an examination of the composition of the bank's loan portfolio, which it should be noted encompasses the use of some quantitative criteria. This includes:

- a review of the countries, geographic areas, industries and companies to which the bank is lending

- a review of the type of customers to which a bank is lending and the tenor of the loans

- determining whether the bank is exposed to any foreign currency risk as a result of its lending

- ascertaining whether the bank is exposed to high sovereign or country risk as a result of cross-border lending activities

The fundamental concerns here are the degree of diversification and the level of foreign or foreign currency lending; or, in other words, the avoidance of excessive concentrations of lending in any one sector or category. In conducting this review, the analyst is looking for signs of over-concentration within the loan portfolio (or preferably an adequate level of diversification). Over-concentration can be in respect of a particular industry (e.g. real estate), borrower (e.g. large amount lent to a single borrower) or geographic (e.g. high proportion of loans extended to a particular foreign country). Qualitative review takes into account the relative financial health of the industry, borrower or geographic area in question.

Credit Policies and Credit Culture

The second major component of the qualitative review of asset quality concerns a bank's credit policies and credit culture. Credit policies refer whether the bank has in place adequate credit controls and credit risk management policies to avoid undue default risk, insider dealing, as well as a potential lack of diversification in its loan book. Credit culture refers to less tangible elements that underlie those policies, including attitudes of management towards risk, incentives affecting the treatment of risk, the experience and training of credit personnel, and the character and competence of key management. Implicating both is the bank's approach to the lending process, and particularly how it deals with problem loans.

Quantitative review includes an appraisal of the bank's level of non-performing loans relative to its loan loss reserves, its equity and its ability to internally generate profits. It also involves a review of the bank's reserve policy and cover of problem loans. In respect to both qualitative and quantitative review, the analyst, to render an accurate assessment of asset quality, needs adequate and accurate data. A serious difficulty that an analyst may face, however, is a lack of disclosure both in regard to qualitative and quantitative information concerning a bank's credit controls and the composition of its loan book. This lack of transparency can be significant problem in emerging markets.

Assessing Asset Quality: The Problem of Transparency

"The incidence of bad and doubtful loans is a particularly sensitive aspect of a bank's operations. If the losses are material, they can reduce the capital resources of the bank and affect its ability to grow and develop its business. If large losses are disclosed in the financial statements, it may lead to a loss of confidence in the bank's management and a reduction in its credit ratings. This will lead to an increase in the bank's cost of borrowing and make it more expensive to raise capital."

— "Bank Reserve Accounting," Special Supplement to Development Bank of Singapore's Annual Report for 1999, p. 2

As the quote above makes clear, banks have rational reasons to limit disclosure of their true financial conditions especially with respect to their level of non-performing loans when asset quality is in decline. Full disclosure can impair shareholder, investor and depositor confidence, impel a downgrade in credit ratings and have a consequent adverse impact on the bank's business, especially with regard to the cost of funding. In short, it can aggravate a situation that is already difficult. It is understandable then why banks are inclined towards opacity rather than transparency when asset quality issues are concerned. As a consequence, where the bank regulatory environment is frail, and where the local culture encourages less disclosure rather than more, the quantity and quality of information provided about asset quality can be quite sparse.[3] In certain countries, for example, some or all banks may not disclose their level of NPLs and other problem assets. Some banks will reveal the composition of their loan portfolio in their annual report. Others will not. Although banks almost universally will reveal their volume of assets, capital and net income, the crucial issue of asset quality is given short shrift in some markets.

In many cases, learning about and evaluating a bank's credit policies is difficult without making a bank visit and meeting with management. In some cases little will be revealed, although this in itself says something about the nature of the bank. Certainly, if feasible, the analyst should attempt to meet with bank management to gain a better understanding of the bank's credit approval process and the analytical skill of the bank's credit officers. On most visits, some worthwhile information will be gained. When qualitative analysis resulting from such a visit is coupled with ratio analysis, the analyst should be able to get a clearer picture of the bank's potential asset quality problems.

Sometimes, for reasons of practicality, the analyst will be unable to meet with management and will have to rely upon publicly available information and the bank's financial statements. Assuming a modicum of disclosure, the analyst ought to be able to make a rough assessment of the bank's asset quality using only ratio analysis. Depending upon the level and reliability of disclosure, as well as the regulatory environment, such assessments should be viewed as provisional, and it may be wise for the analyst to err on the side of conservatism when data is lacking.

---

[3] In less developed markets, lack of compliance is a major concern. In many such markets, rules and laws may exist on the books, but as a result of lack of supervisory resources, lax operations, or corruption, the rules and laws may not be consistently enforced.

QUALITATIVE REVIEW STEP-BY-STEP

In this section we will review the three steps of qualitative review:

Step one: Review of Loan Portfolio Composition
Step two: Appraisal of the Bank's Credit Culture
Step three: Review of Credit Policies and Procedures

Step One: Review of Loan Portfolio Composition

An examination of the composition of a bank's loan book can allow the analyst to draw some conclusions about the bank's asset quality going forward. When a bank's loan portfolio is profiled by loan duration, industry category, and borrower type, much can be inferred about potential for asset quality problems. While ratio analysis is backward looking, loan portfolio composition may suggest problems that have yet to be captured in asset quality indicators.

Duration

There are many different types of loans that banks ordinarily make. First, loans may be classified by duration or *tenor*, another word for term. By tenor, loans are typically grouped as short-term, medium-term or long-term.

- short-term loans: term of one year or less
- medium-term loans: term of one to five years
- long-term loans: term in excess of five years

A large portion of bank loans will ordinarily be short-term. This is partly a function of the fact that the majority of bank funding is short-term. Banks rightly seek to avoid an excessive *mismatch* between their earning assets and funding liabilities, although some mismatch is inevitable. (Asset-liability mismatch is discussed again in the context of funding and liquidity.) In addition, while it is not always the case, short-term exposure is frequently regarded as being less risky than medium- or long-term exposure. From an analytical perspective, a proportion of medium- and long-term loans that is significantly greater than the bank's peers calls for further inquiry.

Review of the Loan Portfolio by Borrower Type
Wholesale or Retail Lending

Lending can be *wholesale* or *retail* in nature. *Wholesale lending* means that the bank is lending in large denominations mainly to businesses, including financial institutions such as finance companies and other banks.[4] *Retail lending* refers to lending made mainly to individuals, families and small or family-run businesses. Note that retail lending is not synonymous with consumer lending. Retail lending encompasses consumer lending, but not the converse.

Borrower Type

Another useful distinction is by *borrower type*. There are a variety of ways in which loans can be categorized. A distinction can be made between corporate and consumer lending, which corresponds broadly to the distinction between wholesale and retail lending just noted. In some countries, lending to the *corporate market*, referring to larger (blue-chip) companies, may be differentiated from lending to the *middle-market*, referring to small- and medium-sized enterprises (SMEs), with the two being seen as distinct business franchises. On average, larger companies are apt to be more creditworthy than SMEs (yields will be lower on corporate lending than on middle-market lending) so a bank that concentrates on lending to mid-sized and small-companies may be prone to a higher level of NPLs.

Lending to SOEs

Lending to state-owned enterprises (SOEs) raises somewhat difficult issues of analysis since it is regularly linked to the problem of policy lending (lending for non-commercial purposes in furtherance of government policy ends). SOEs, which may comprise a substantial portion of the economy in countries with a socialist legacy, are frequently poor credit risks. Often loss-making, almost invariably inefficient and reliant on state subsidies — of which policy lending is the primary one — SOEs have a tendency to "not service their debt obligations in a timely manner."

---

[4] Note that the meaning of the term wholesale lending may differ somewhat from that of *wholesale banking*. Wholesale banking may connote a banking business which eschews deposit-taking business from small depositors, and in which funding is obtained from large depositors and through the capital markets. Wholesale banking may also connote a banking business in which the bank provides for a fee significant value-added services, for example in related advisory work. See glossary.

As Robert Morris Associates' *A Guide to Analyzing Foreign Banks*, well puts it:

> In many countries, the banking regulators allow banks to treat assets to these companies as fully performing despite massive delays in payments. More important, poor performance in the non-governmental sector of a bank's portfolio may be masked by the continuous accrual of interest on non-performing government loans until it is too late, catching foreign creditors by surprise.[5]

Policy lending, the lending for non-commercial purposes, commonly is associated with an implicit or explicit promise that support will be provided by the government for the bank engaging in this otherwise risky activity. The promises, however, may not be as sweeping as creditors sometimes assume. When a local or provincial government is the primary backer of the enterprise, decisions at the national government level will take precedence over local authorities, and support may be withdrawn. In evaluating the presence of high SOE lending in a bank's portfolio, special attention must be paid to the relationship between the bank and the government, and particularly to the scope and depth of government support. Generally speaking, banks wholly-owned by a national government and dedicated to a specific policy purpose are the safest bets for government backing. They are frequently regarded by bank credit analysts as being quasi-sovereign risks.

Customer Category

Another way of categorizing loans by borrower type is by dividing loans into functional groupings. Default rates vary considerably within each category and from market to market.

Commercial and Industrial Loans

These are loans made either on a short-term basis to provide working capital to meet seasonal or specific needs, or less frequently, medium- and long-term loans used to fund project or infrastructure construction. Trade finance, which includes off-balance sheet finance such as the contigent liability-represented by letters of credit or financing based on a letter of credit, while often seen as a separate category of lending, can be

---

[5] Robert Morris Associates, *A Guide to Analyzing Foreign Banks*, p. 27.

viewed as a subset of commercial and industrial loans. Project finance, which often includes other types of financing besides bank finance, is usually medium- to long-term in nature, although bridge loans for project finance purposes may be short-term.

Consumer Loans

This category, comprising loans to individuals and families, spans a wide variety of types, including credit card loans, personal loans, and auto loans.

Real Estate Loans

Loans to finance all types of real estate, including development of and investment in residential and commercial property, as well as for the purchase of houses, apartments and other real property. Home mortgage loans are sometimes put into this category, but may also be classified as consumer loans.

Agricultural Loans

Includes loans to farmers and ranchers to fund seasonal planting and livestock raising operations, among other things. Such loans may be secured by the crops harvested.

Interbank and Financial Institution Loans

This category includes loans made to other banks, as well as to finance companies, securities houses and other financial organizations.

Borrower Type—By Industry

Bank loans may be further classified by a more detailed sectoral break-down, and each country has its own customary classifications. These are often designated by the local bank regulator.

Making Sense of Loan Composition: Over-Concentration and Other Warning Signals

The types of loans a bank makes will depend upon the market (and sub-markets within which it operates), the bank's size and strategy. In Hong Kong, for example, because the property industry is so important

Pie charts, showing classification of loans, for HSBC, FY 1998–1999 (Source: Annual report)

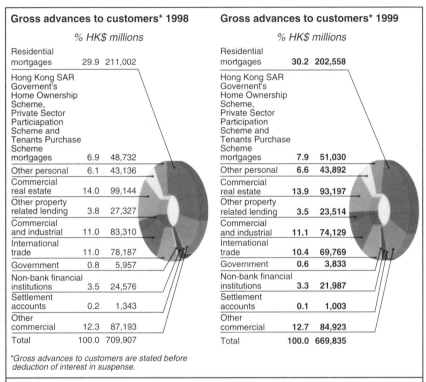

Gross advances to customers* 1998		
	%	HK$ millions
Residential mortgages	29.9	211,002
Hong Kong SAR Governent's Home Ownership Scheme, Private Sector Particiapation Scheme and Tenants Purchase Scheme mortgages	6.9	48,732
Other personal	6.1	43,136
Commercial real estate	14.0	99,144
Other property related lending	3.8	27,327
Commercial and industrial	11.0	83,310
International trade	11.0	78,187
Government	0.8	5,957
Non-bank financial institutions	3.5	24,576
Settlement accounts	0.2	1,343
Other commercial	12.3	87,193
Total	100.0	709,907

Gross advances to customers* 1999		
	%	HK$ millions
Residential mortgages	30.2	202,558
Hong Kong SAR Governent's Home Ownership Scheme, Private Sector Participation Scheme and Tenants Purchase Scheme mortgages	7.9	51,030
Other personal	6.6	43,892
Commercial real estate	13.9	93,197
Other property related lending	3.5	23,514
Commercial and industrial	11.1	74,129
International trade	10.4	69,769
Government	0.6	3,833
Non-bank financial institutions	3.3	21,987
Settlement accounts	0.1	1,003
Other commercial	12.7	84,923
Total	100.0	669,835

Gross advances to customers are stated before deduction of interest in suspense.

These charts show the composition of HSBC's loan portfolio, applying the Hong Kong Monetary Authority's loan classification system. Note the high proportion of property-related land. While ordinarily a danger sign, the high concentration is mitigated by the fact that much of the property-related lending is actually comprising of mortgage loans for owner-occupied housing which historically has had an extremely low default rate. It is also an unavoidable consequence of the nature of the Hong Kong market which lacks diversified lending opportunities. HSBC has a large part of its operations there as well as about three-quarters of its loan exposure.

in the local economy, a very high proportion of bank loans are made to fund home purchases and for other property-related purposes. In other markets, savings and thrift banks specialize in home mortgages, and commercial banks do comparatively little business in the field. Similarly, based on their history and strategy, some banks have developed specialties in trade finance, while others have garnered a large market share in consumer finance.

It is hard to generalize about the credit implications of particular categories of lending without reference to the historical experience in the country and the expertise that a specific bank has developed. Within particular markets, however, an analyst will soon gain some understanding of what sort of lending tends to be problematic. We make some generalizations below, but there is no substitute for familiarity with the local environment. Much depends upon local market conditions and the bank's level of experience and expertise in the particular type of lending. Probably the most salient consideration in evaluating the character of a bank's loan portfolio is whether there is adequate diversification. One generalization which can be safely made is that over-concentration brings with it potential dangers. As with all investment, diversification is a key to minimizing risk. The opposite of diversification is over-concentration, and, as suggested at the beginning of this chapter, the analyst should be on the lookout for over-concentration in any of its various manifestations.

Over-Concentration by Industry

When too high a percentage of loans is made to a particular industry, the bank becomes vulnerable to a downturn in that industry.

Over-Concentration by Geography

A high percentage of loans made in a particular region within its franchise area makes a bank vulnerable to an economic downturn or a cataclysm affecting that locale. Depending upon the size of the bank, the over-concentration may be in one urban or rural district, city, province, or even a country.

Over-Concentration by Individual Borrower

Too a high a percentage of loans made to a single individual or company holds a bank hostage to the fortunes of that borrower.[6] The analyst should also beware of a hidden over-concentration achieved through cross-holdings and the use of nominee companies; however, such veiled linkages may be difficult for the analyst to ferret out.

---

[6] Ratings analysts may ask for the identity of the 10 or 20 largest borrowers to identify such an over-concentration. It is important to take note of any cross-shareholdings among companies, although such information may be difficult to come by. Some countries are dominated by a few families, which through cross-shareholdings, holding and nominee companies, may in fact control a panoply of apparently separate firms.

Over-Concentration by Size

A small number of large loans is intrinsically more risky than a large number of small loans. In addition to over-concentration, substantial lending to cyclical or vulnerable industries or to related-parties should be viewed as red flags. Some common warning signals include:

Excessive Real Estate Lending

The property market tends to be highly cyclical in nature. Long boom periods are usually followed by steep and rapid busts. Unfortunately, over the decades, banks have demonstrated a fatal attraction to lending to the property market. There are several types of properly-related exposure and both definitions and associated levels of risk vary. Care needs to be taken when comparing banks that define "real estate exposure" differently. An example of a difference is noted by HSBC in the text accompanying the preceding charts. It notes that "there are a number of significant differences between the categories of advances used by HSBC and by the [regulatory authority]." One is that the bank includes loans to non-property companies for the purchase of properties for use in their own business to be "property lending," while the regulatory authority classifies such advances differently.

However defined, the analyst should be wary of a bank that relies heavily upon financing real estate, particularly of those that focus on lending to real estate developers. Developers may be subject to severe cash flow problems when the market turns negative. Lending to purchase existing real estate for investment purposes is less risky than real estate development. Finally, home mortgage lending to finance owner-occupied housing, which is often categorized as consumer lending, is likely to be comparatively low risk, shelter being a basic human need and homeowners with positive equity in their dwellings being highly inclined to make their mortgage payments.[7]

Excessive Lending to Other Cyclical Industries

The real estate industry is just one sector, one common to nearly all markets, that is prone to wild swings between boom and bust. Others examples include the oil and gas, computer chip and construction industries.

---

[7] The situation may be different when the homeowner has negative equity, i.e. where the market value of the dwelling is less than the face value of the mortgage.

Kinds of Bank Real Estate Exposure

Type of Real Estate Exposure	Description	Risk Level	Remarks
Real estate development	Development of raw land or redevelopment of existing developed areas for sale or lease	High	Real estate development is subject to numerous risks including the developer's ability to service debt and complete project, construction risks, location and marketing risks, and economic risks.
Real estate investment & management	Leasing and management of commercial or residential real estate	Medium	No completion risk. Loan may be secured by real estate or by contract cash flow.
Commercial or residential mortgage lending (for investment purposes)	Lending for the purchase of commercial or residential structures for investment purposes	Low-medium	Main risk is inability to rent at level to cover debt service or decline in market values.
Owner-occupied residential mortgage lending	Lending for owner-occupied single-family occupancy of a residential unit	Low	Need for housing and the limited cost savings of alternatives reduce defaults. Watch out, however, for situations where "negative equity" may arise and where high unemployment levels may make it impossible for home-owners to service their mortgage. This type of lending is sometimes classified as consumer.
Collateral against non-real estate loans	Use of real estate as security	Depends upon the risk level of the underlying loan	In itself not real estate lending and not generally classified as such, as the real estate provides security only. Decline in value of property may impair value of security (collateral).
Hidden real estate loan	Loan ostensibly for other purposes diverted into real estate development or speculation	High	Issues of loan security and risk management.

Lending to Industries in Decline or Subject to Imminent Deregulation

Another area to be on the lookout for is excessive lending to a mature industry that is in decline, or is about to be negatively affected by new regulations, or just as often, deregulation (loss of tariff protection can be deadly to a coddled industry). The analyst should watch out for deregulation affecting a substantial portion of the bank's customers. Similarly, when banks themselves are the target of deregulation, the results can be catastrophic. Government banks that have been privatized are especially vulnerable to this danger. Prior to privatization they are likely to have developed a franchise lending to large but inefficient state-owned enterprises or regulated private corporations. They nonetheless survived by virtue of an implicit government guarantee of deposits and occasional cash injections. Their credit culture is not apt to change immediately with privatization, and mistakes will be made. If support continues, it may be difficult for a new culture to take root. If it does not, lack of experience in making commercially viable loans and the lingering effects of a state bank credit culture may result in the bank making lethal mistakes.

Related party or insider lending. Related-party lending means lending to individuals or entities that are related to the bank's shareholders. Related-party lending would occur for instance if a bank lent to a company, not otherwise affiliated with the bank, but owned by one of the bank's shareholders. There may be good economic reasons for providing credit to a related party, but in general such loans are suspect. During the recent Asian crisis, a number of bank failures were associated with excessive related-party lending. In many jurisdictions, bank regulators require related-party lending to be disclosed or limit such lending to a specified percentage of a bank's total portfolio. Unfortunately, related-party lending is often accomplished by subterfuge, and regulations proscribing it are thereby circumvented.

A Special Category—Foreign Currency Lending

Finally, a distinction can be made between local currency and foreign currency lending. In developed markets, this is rarely an issue. However, as the recent Asian crisis has made clear, excessive borrowing in foreign currency to fund foreign currency lending can pose a severe threat to the health of individual banks and a country's banking system as a whole.

Step Two: Appraisal of the Bank's Credit Culture

Evaluating a bank's approach to credit risk management encompasses both an examination of its formal procedures, as well as the informal credit culture which underlies them. Formal procedures may very well appear prudent, but it will be hard for an analyst to discern how they are being applied in practice. What is the attitude of the bank's managers towards credit review? What incentives, institutional or pecuniary, may affect credit decisions?

Ideally, a bank should have developed a sophisticated credit culture that imbues its lending function, and which is expressed in both written credit policies and established operational credit approval and loan monitoring procedures. Evaluating a bank's credit culture may be difficult without meeting bank management in person, although much can be gleaned from a bank's annual report, and from third parties.

Credit Culture

What is a credit culture? It has been defined as:

> A bank's credit culture is, in the broadest sense, the unique combination of policies, practices, experience and management attitudes that defines the lending environment and determines lending behavior acceptable to the bank.[8]

Credit culture, like the term corporate governance, is an implicitly normative term. It ordinarily refers to a set of shared beliefs as to the desirability of lending being done on the basis of prudent, commercial, and profit-oriented criteria.[9] A strong credit culture is likely to be apparent in some or all of the following:

❑ a comprehensive approach to asset quality management

❑ centralized lending policies

❑ efforts to diversify risk and avoid overconcentration in particular segments, sectors or firms

---

[8] G. Root, P. Grela, M. Jones and A. Adiga, "Financial Sector Restructuring in East Asia" [Restructuring in East Asia], p. 217.

[9] Non-commercial lending often involves a conflict of interest between the person responsible for making the loan and the interests of the bank's creditors and shareholders. When a loan that appears to be made for non-commercial reasons is also supported by a sturdy commercial rationale, such lending is less reprehensible than when it is done for non-commercial reasons alone.

❑ an explicit approval system for granting loans, with clear delegation of authority and accountability

❑ separation of the loan marketing function from the credit function, and the independence of the latter from the former

❑ the incorporation of credit quality concerns into the staff performance review process[10]

It is probably easier to understand what is meant by credit culture by observing its absence. A bank that lacks a credit culture, or has a weak credit culture, is likely to be characterized by a significant proportion of its lending being done for non-commercial reasons. At an extreme, state-owned banks are often said to lack a credit culture or to have a weak credit culture. Policy banks, almost invariably state-owned, can be said lack a credit culture because their raison d'être is non-commercial, i.e. to achieve the government policy objective. In this case, there may be an explicit directive or implicit guidance that the banks are to engage in business according to non-commercial criteria. For example, the bank may have been in fact set up to lend to state-owned companies, whether they are profitable or not. Similarly, loans may be made on the basis of government policy favoring, for example, particular industries or even specific enterprises. The usual *quid pro quo* for such directed or policy lending is that a bank will receive support from the government in the event of difficulty.[11] Thus, poorer asset quality may well be mitigated by the prospect of shareholder (i.e. government) support.

Yet policy banks at least have a clarity of purpose. More problematic is the commercial bank in which lending for non-commercial reasons is pervasive. Non-commercial reasons could include among other things: family relationship, acquaintanceship, the social or political stature of the borrower; or the prospect of an individual rather than the bank enjoying the main benefit of the loan either directly, or through kickbacks or recip-rocal favors owed. It may be difficult for bank officers, who may owe their jobs to political patronage or who may suffer negative career prospects if they do not cooperate, to refuse such requests. Political considerations, perhaps a legislator's request that a company in this representative district be favored with a loan, also can impinge on the

---

[10] Restructuring in East Asia, p. 217.
[11] This is discussed in more detail later. Support can, for example, take the form of additional liquidity or a capital infusion.

loan approval process.[12] The rejection of commercial criteria as the basis for lending may not be explicit. Nonetheless, non-commercial considerations may permeate the credit approval process with the expected deleterious effects. Whether the result of explicit government policies or more nebulous political criteria, such *directed lending* is often associated with a high proportion of NPLs and a correspondingly low level of asset quality.

Credit culture, however, goes beyond abstaining from *directed lending*. A bank with a strong credit culture will tend to be characterized by strong implicit and explicit guidelines and standards that govern the bank's lending. In contrast, the absence of such a credit culture suggests that loans may be made without rigorous concern for criteria that take account of willingness and ability to repay the loan. This lack of concern may be the result of an over-aggressiveness on the part of bank's management, who have become preoccupied with expansion and gaining market share at the expense of prudent credit control.

Sometimes, insidious considerations may gain sway, that are not outright directed lending or related-party lending, but which nonetheless may have adverse effects on credit quality. For example, a loan may be granted on the basis of the perceived standing of the borrower, or because of personal relationship, e.g. because the bank's chairman plays golf with the director of the firm seeking the loan. In milder manifestations, *name lending* or *relationship lending* is not necessarily a bad practice. Certainly, knowing the character of the borrower is relevant to the credit process.

It should be observed, in this context, that so-called *relationship banking* is distinct from *relationship lending*. Relationship banking accepts as a premise that the bank's lending business may not be profitable in itself, but seeks to offer customers loans essentially at cost (or even as a loss-leader) in order to acquire more profitable fee-based business. In an earlier manifestation of relationship banking, it encompassed a business model in which loans were made to large corporate customers at a profitable rate, but many "free" or subsidized services were offered to customers in order to cement the relationship and reduce the overall cost to the customer while preserving an adequate return for the bank. In its more modern manifestation, relationship banking is particularly common in the private client arena where high net-worth individuals

---

[12] In the Philippines, this practice is termed "behest lending."

are offered the full array of lending to trust/investment services as the bank pursues that all-encompassing relationship. In this expression, relationship lending does not necessarily imply any subsidies to the customer, and when pursued as a strategy ordinarily involves an explicit calculus of the overall costs and benefits to the bank. This type of relationship lending does not necessarily compromise good risk management.

In contrast, name or relationship *lending* as it is often practiced in emerging markets and not a few developed markets is typically undertaken without proper financial analysis of the loan applicant, lacks the checks and balances that a systematic credit review process imposes and is therefore subject to abuse. Collateral, when taken in such cases, may be insufficient, or in the prevailing legal infrastructure and political environment, difficult to foreclose upon. In more extreme cases, the basis for the loan may be more than a social relationship, involving the recip-rocal giving of favors; e.g. a loan on the one hand, and some business favoritism or political dispensation from a politically well-connected individual on the other. These practices in their more egregious forms come under the rubric of "crony capitalism," a phenomenon often associated with emerging markets which was highlighted and widely criticized in the aftermath of the Asian crisis.

As mentioned earlier, a particular peril occurs when state-owned banks are privatized. Bank staff brought up in an environment where loans were made to state-owned companies or other large enterprises with few questions asked are likely find it difficult to make the transition to one where credit risks must be rigorously examined and the concomitant returns sufficient to justify the risks. Similarly, deregulation can pose a threat to hidebound banks that practice name and "good old boy" lending. Deregulation allows the entrance of new players into the financial market, including foreign players, who are often able to opti-mize their risk/return ratios and outperform stodgier institutions. Deregu-lation has been correlated with bank failures; banking crises are more liable to occur within a few years after deregulation than before, as banks that were once protected by central bank support and artificially high profit margins are unable to cope in the more competitive environment that ensues.[13]

---

[13] Similarly, deregulation is often accompanied by the granting of new banking licenses. New entrants may rapidly exceed their ability to manage credit risk and suffer the consequences.

Credit Culture and Local Banking Practices

The credit culture of an individual bank will be hard to separate from the environment in which the bank operates. For instance, some bank managers may boast of the collateral that secures their loans. Certainly, in many markets, particularly developing ones, after relationship, collateral is the more or less the sole criterion in the decision whether or not to lend. This is the so-called "pawnshop mentality" of which some emerging market banks have been accused. "Pawnshop mentality" refers to an over-reliance on collateral (at the expense of credit analysis that examines cash flow and financial condition) to secure and justify a loan. It might seem that adequate collateral would mitigate any lack of a methodical cash flow and credit analysis. To be sure, the proportion of collateral to the amount lent — the loan to value ratio — is relevant to its asset quality, but purported collateralization should nonetheless be viewed skeptically by the analyst when reviewing the caliber of a bank's loan book. The collateral may be over-valued, and when an economic crisis occurs, collateral that once appeared to be sufficient may be worth a fraction of its prior value.

Sound banking and prudential practice imposes a maximum loan to value ratio in respect to the value of collateral. The loan to value ratio operates most conspicuously in home mortgage lending. In making mortgage loans, banks will typically require that the property being financed be appraised, and as a policy will limit their lending to some percentage of its appraised value. This is the loan to value ratio. Its function is to protect the bank against a downturn in property values. A frequently used benchmark loan to value ratio is 70%. For example, on a dwelling appraised as having a value of $1 m, the bank will lend a maximum of $700,000 secured by a first mortgage on the property. This protects the bank against a 30% drop in property prices at a minimum. Despite such ceiling loan to value ratios, often mandated by regulators, aggressive banks may attempt to circumvent such rules by offering additional financing through separate loans for, as an example, furnishings. In addition to mortgage lending, thornier issues of collateralization may emerge in the case of secured loans for working capital or project finance to business enterprises. Here, compared with real estate, the collateral (e.g. specialized sugar milling machinery) may find little or no secondary market and, if personal property rather than real property is involved as security, it may be harder to sell.

Even if the value of the collateral is adequate, in a number of jurisdictions the prevailing legal infrastructure may be so weak, or fraught with corruption, that enforcing the security is difficult or infeasible. Laws governing bankruptcy or insolvency may be antiquated or unduly biased towards debtors. Or the laws may exist on paper, but are all but impossible to enforce in a timely manner in practice. The process may be so time-consuming and expensive as to make a mockery of the time value of money. In such cases, justice delayed is justice denied. Lastly, in certain countries, some individuals or the companies they own may be so powerful as to, in realistic terms, be immune from legal process. In short, the environment in which a bank operates will generally have a strong impact on its asset quality.

Step Three: Review of Credit Policies and Procedures

Corollary to the assessment of a bank's credit culture is the qualitative review of the policies and procedures it has put into place to maintain the value of its loan book. A systematic lending strategy can enable a bank and its shareholders to meet their earnings' goals with acceptable levels of risk. Lending policies will vary over time and place. What is prudent in one market may not be in another. Similarly, as banks have diversified their activities, a wider range of lending activities may be viewed as reasonable. Credit policies may also change throughout the business cycle. Following a collapse in asset prices, a bank may stop lending altogether and enter into a period of consolidation as it attempts to rebuild its capital adequacy. It being easier to cut back on lending than to locate new sources of capital, the bank may call in existing loans and refuse to grant new ones in an attempt to bring the ratio of assets to equity in line with more prudent standards. In contrast, during a period of robust expansion, credit officers in the same institution may relax lending standards, believing a more liberal lending policy to be consistent with the reduced default rate that a period of prosperity brings.

Strategy

Bank management should be able to articulate its goals and objectives in clear terms to the analyst. For example, one Asian bank recently indicated to an analyst that it had changed its strategy to develop a portfolio that is 40% large corporate, 40% middle market and 20% consumer, in the process reducing its emphasis on corporate and middle market lending.

Similarly, management should be able to describe its current franchise and the type of lending it wishes to target and avoid. For instance, a bank may want to emphasize consumer credit card business and home mortgage loans, but avoid auto loans, which in many markets have elevated default rates. Likewise, in the SME sector, a bank may want to focus on working capital and trade finance, but avoid medium- and longer-term project finance.

It is, of course, possible that because the bank's business strategy may be of use to its competitors, banks can be understandingly reluctant to disclose their strategy in great detail. Yet insofar as possible the analyst should attempt to establish the bank's present and intended composition of its loan portfolio, if not delineated in the annual report or other public statements. Specific lines of inquiry include:

❑ In what geographic or *trade area* does the bank do or intend to do business?

❑ Does it have international exposure? To what countries?

❑ Is it highly concentrated in one city?

❑ In what sectors does the bank have a competitive advantage?

❑ In what sectors does the bank plan to increase or reduce its exposure?

In some markets, the US being the most noteworthy example, the banking system is highly fragmented and many banks are associated with particular towns, cities and counties. This structure tends to work against the diversification of a bank's loan book, especially geographic distribution. In other markets, such as Thailand, Canada, and Australia, a small number of banks dominate the entire country. Another factor to consider is the relative aggressiveness of the bank. New banks often want to grow their loan books very rapidly, while more mature players are content with more modest growth. The degree of aggressiveness, of course, will have some bearing on the amount of attention that is paid to credit quality. At least, the analyst should be able to obtain some projection from management of the coming year's loan growth.

Policies and Procedures

Beyond a bank's strategy for achieving a particular mix of loans in its portfolio, a bank should have policies in place to properly manage credit risk at all stages of the loan cycle. Adequate procedures would normally include:

- Establishing appropriate lending criteria and policies and procedures for loan approval.
- Avoiding problem credits by ensuring procedures are followed and that good judgment is exercised in making decisions about which loans to extend.
- When possible, securing the loan by obtaining collateral or security in the form of real or other property to which the bank can take title in the event of default.
- Monitoring the loan portfolio, and keeping abreast of problem loans, while setting aside reserves to take account of foreseeable losses.
- Taking appropriate steps when a problem appears with a particular credit, for example: calling in the loan, restructuring its terms, or, if the loan is in default, foreclosing on the collateral securing the loan; and
- Taking prompt measures to write off defaulted loans, to pursue collection efforts or sell the right to do so, and disposing of any property obtained through foreclosure to optimize overall recovery.

The foregoing represent the ideal. In reality, not all banks give due attention to the preceding steps. The less developed the banking system, the less sophisticated the bank, the less likely it will approach the management of credit risk in a methodical and commercially-oriented manner.

Written Loan Policy

There is no guarantee that a written loan policy will be followed. But at least the existence of one suggests that the bank's managers have given some thought to better managing their credit risks. The outline below, derived from a well-known banking textbook, will give the analyst a benchmark against which to review a bank's stated credit policy.

In addition to having articulated loan policies, the analyst should attempt to discern how the bank approaches the decision to grant a loan. Does the bank engage in *name lending*, extending credit on the basis of a borrower's perceived status in the business community, or because the chairman is an acquaintance of members of management? As we have

---

Outline for a Written Loan Policy

Outline for written loan policy[14]

I. General policy statements
    A. Objectives
    B. Strategies
        1. Loan mix
        2. Liquidity and maturity structure
        3. Size of portfolio
    C. Trade area
    D. Credit standards
        1. Types of loans
        2. Secured vs. unsecured guidelines
        3. Collateral
        4. Terms (tenor)
    E. Loan authorities and approval

II. Principles and procedures
    A. Insurance protection
    B. Documentation standards and security interest
    C. Problem loan collections and write-offs
    D. Legal constraints (on lending) and compliance (requirements)
    E. Loan pricing
    F. Financial information required from borrowers
    G. Ethics and conflicts of interest
    H. Loan Review

III. Parameters and procedures by type
    A. Parameters & procedures
        1. Loan description
        2. Purpose of loan proceeds
        3. Preferred maturities
        4. Pricing: rates, fees and balances
        5. Minimum and maximum amounts
        6. Insurance requirements
        7. Perfection of collateral
        8. Channels of approval
    B. Types
        1. Real estate mortgage loan
        2. Interim construction financing
        3. Accounts receivable loans
        4. Inventory loans
        5. Term loans
        6. Securities purchase loans
        7. Agricultural loans
        8. Small business loans
        9. Personal loans

---

[14] Bala Shanmugam, Craig Turton & George Hempel, *Bank Management* (Milton, Australia: Jacaranda Wiley, Ltd., 1992), p. 288.

observed, name lending is not necessarily bad, but it does raise questions. There are two sides to such a practice, especially in emerging markets where companies are not in the habit of disclosing a great deal about their business and may maintain three sets of books: one for the tax authorities, one for the public shareholders, and one for controlling shareholders. Name lending and relationship lending at best evince an understanding of the borrower's character and earnestness, as well as a sensitivity to the customer's sensitivity to disclosing its finances in detail. More often, however, they are a poor substitute for systematic credit analyst, and at worst, mask cronyism and poor credit practices.

Credit Control Procedures

While a detailed knowledge of the criteria a bank's applies in granting loans will not be sought by most bank credit analysts — a credit analyst is not a bank examiner — the analyst will want to see evidence of a sensible loan approval policy. Typically, this takes the form of various loan committees composed of increasing numbers and ranks of management for specified lending limits. Warning signs in this context include too much loan-approving authority at the branch level, and a mingling of the marketing and credit functions. The latter occurs, for example, where the bank officer originating the loan is also responsible for approving it. Where marketing staff have a significant role in credit decisions, there will be an incentive to give the benefit of the doubt to the loan applicant. This is not apt to result in strong asset quality.

In addition to having created effective credit approval procedures, a prudent bank will maintain pristine loan files, with full documentation. Again, a detailed examination of this aspect of credit control is more the work of the bank examiner than the bank analyst. Bank analysts will rarely have the time or inclination to examine a bank's individual loan files.

Credit Monitoring

Credit review goes beyond the mere scrutinizing of the loan applicant before credit is extended. The bank should also have in place policies and procedures for an ongoing and periodic review of its loans. The purpose of this monitoring is to recognize problem loans at an early stage, and to take appropriate actions. While late payments are conspicuous signs of loan problems, ideally the bank's ongoing credit monitoring will take account of developments that may adversely affect the customer's business. The degree of attention that can be given to particular loans will necessarily depend upon the size of the bank and the average size of its loans. In general, the riskier the loan, the more frequently it should be reviewed. The table below gives some indication of a desirable loan review policy. At the same time, the credit department responsible for the loan should keep abreast of the state of the borrower's business and external events that may have an adverse impact on that business. (Obviously, this applies mainly to business borrowers.)

Specific review of loans will properly be done at regular intervals. Such a review would ordinarily seek to confirm that the borrower's financial condition has not materially changed for the worse and it remains able to repay the loan. In particular, the loan

- Documentation is complete and the bank has perfected any relevant security interests in collateral.

- Is in compliance with laws and regulations affecting the bank.

- Conforms with the bank's loan policy and is likely to be profitable for the bank.

Depending upon the size of the bank and the average loan size, a bank may deem certain loans unworthy of regular review as the cost is not likely to be justified by the benefits. Similarly, some banks may undertake review of certain classes of loans only at random. Clearly, however, large loans should be subject to a regular review in any event.

CHAPTER SUMMARY

Asset quality, perhaps the most important aspect of bank credit analysis, requires both a qualitative and quantitative assessment. The qualitative review of asset quality is a critical part of bank credit analysis and should not be given short shrift. It encompasses an appraisal of the bank's loan portfolio, its credit culture and its credit policies and procedures. An awareness of these qualitative elements will alert the analyst to prospective asset quality problems that have not yet materialized in numerical ratios. Remember that non-performing loan ratios are lagging indicators that are prone to mushroom after asset quality has already been compromised.

As was introduced in the preceding chapter, at the country level, the analyst should be aware of the state of the economy, prudential regulations governing asset quality — for example, how non-performing loans are defined and how much discretion is allowed to individual bank management. In addition, the analyst should be aware of the legal infrastructure governing creditors' rights: how easy or difficult is it for a bank to enforce the terms of a loan agreement to foreclose on security and recover funds due. At the bank level, the analyst should attempt to discern the strength of the institution's credit culture, its credit strategy, the rigor of its credit controls, and the health of its loan portfolio. With regard to the last, the analyst is advised to pay special attention to signs of over-concentration, particularly in sectors that are prone to cyclical downturns.

Special problems are presented in countries in which non-commercial considerations play a significant part in lending decisions. These non-commercial considerations may be explicit and targeted to direct finance to particular enterprises or economic sectors. Or, they may be implicit, favoring well-known borrowers, trading for personal or political advantage, or the consequence of an extremely tight nexus between government and the business community. The analyst should attempt to fathom the extent to which these considerations influence those decisions at the subject bank. Often in countries where these practices are present, disclosure concerning asset quality is quite limited making the task even more difficult.

To sum up the qualitative portion of a review of a bank's asset quality, the analyst should in principle be able to answer the following questions prior to or in the process of preparing a bank credit report:

Credit Culture

❑ What is the bank's credit culture? In general, what are the primary considerations governing the granting and monitoring of the bank's loans?

❑ Are loans extended on commercial criteria? If not, to what extent do non-commercial criteria affect the loan approval process?

❑ Is the bank obliged by the government to engage in policy lending?

❑ Has the bank been recently privatized? Has it undergone any major shift of ownership over the past five years, and if so, how has that affected its credit culture?

❑ Is there any indication that the bank engages in significant related-party transactions or name lending? (loans to insiders — employees, directors or stockholders)?

❑ Is money being lent for speculative purposes?

Credit Policies and Procedures

❑ Does the bank appear to have coherent loan approval procedures? Are they in writing?

❑ Do credit officers appear to have sufficient experience or training in credit analysis?

❑ What credit training programs does the bank operate? How much is expended annually for this purpose?

❑ Do marketing staff have credit assessment and approval responsibilities?

❑ Is there adequate ongoing monitoring of outstanding loans? (How often are loans reviewed?)

❑ Is there an effort to minimize over-concentration in the bank's portfolio, by loan size, borrower and industry?

❑ What performance incentives or disincentives exist for a credit officer to engage in a stringent review of loan applications and loans under his or her purview?

❑ To what extent are the bank's credit policy and procedures integrated into broader risk management policy and procedures?

General Lending Strategy

❑ Does the bank appear to have a coherent lending policy?

❑ Is it articulated in writing?

❑ What are its lending targets in terms of percentage of lending to specific sectors and in terms of loan growth?

❑ Is the bank satisfied with the current composition of its loan portfolio?

❑ Is the bank entering (or has it entered) any new sector? If so, does the bank have adequate experienced staff?

❑ How does the bank handle problem loans? Are these managed by a separate division or agency within the bank? Generally speaking, what procedures are followed when managing problem assets?

Portfolio Composition

❑ Is there evidence of an over-concentration in the bank's loan portfolio, particularly in respect of a particular industry or borrower?

❑ Is a high percentage of loans made outside the bank's main franchise area, particularly in risky markets? What is the bank's proportion of international loans?

❑ Does the bank engage in substantial real estate lending, especially to real estate development or construction companies?

❑ Has the bank made a significant portion of its loans to declining or highly cyclical industries?

❑ Is the bank exposed to major problem credits?

❑ What sectors are responsible for the bulk of the bank's NPLs?

❑ Are there any sectors that the bank avoids for lending purposes?

❑ Does the bank engage in substantial foreign currency lending? If so, how is it funded?

CHAPTER TEN

QUANTITATIVE REVIEW OF ASSET QUALITY

Evaluating the quality of a bank's assets is both the most important — and normally the most difficult — facet of bank analysis.
— Moody's Investors Services, Global Credit Analysis[1]

Any loan must be priced high enough to permit the bank to maintain its capital cushion.
— R. Taggart Murphy[2]

[A]sset quality is the most important fundamental dimension of bank analysis. Asset quality ultimately drives everything, including margins, capital adequacy, underlying profitability, investment sentiment and valuations.[4]
— Roy Ramos, Head of Banking Analysis, Goldman Sachs, Hong Kong

INTRODUCTION TO RATIO ANALYSIS OF ASSET QUALITY

Qualitative analysis of a bank's credit culture must be coupled with a quantitative or ratio analysis of key indicators that are reflective of its asset quality. In many jurisdictions, the annual report and accompanying financial statements will provide the necessary figures. As we have mentioned, however, asset quality is an element of financial performance where disclosure is most often lacking, and in some markets little or no relevant information will be provided in the financial statements. Sometimes the requisite data will not be disclosed formally, but can

---

[1] David Stimpson, Editor, *Moody's Investor Service — Global Credit Analysis*, IFR Books, London 1995.
[2] *Japanese Money*, p. 43.

209

be obtained from the bank on request. Much of the necessary information may be available in the bank's audited financial statements, or in information provided by the central bank. The remainder can be sought by query or during a visit to the bank. It may not, however, always be forthcoming.

Key Asset Quality Data and Indicators

Since comprehensive information might not be available, especially in emerging markets, the analyst may be limited to very basic data to evaluate asset quality on a quantitative basis. Nonetheless, a few ratios can tell the analyst a lot about the bank being examined. The most critical figures to obtain for the periods being examined are:

❑ Total loans[3] (this will almost always be available in the annual report)

❑ Total *non-performing loans* (often referred to as *NPLs*)

❑ *Provisioning* (annual)

❑ Total *loan loss reserves* (cumulative), also known as *provisions*

❑ Total equity

The analyst can make do with absolute figures, but it is also advantageous as a backup check to get the bank's own calculation of relevant percentages, such as the percentage of NPLs to total loans, as discussed below.[4] A number of ratios will enable the analyst to get a handle on the bank's asset quality, assuming the relevant data is available.[5] With the foregoing data and the information normally supplied in the bank's audited financial statements, the ratios below can be easily calculated. They are:

❑ Year-on-year loan growth

❑ Non-performing loans to total loans

❑ Loan loss reserves to non-performing loans

❑ Loan loss reserves + equity to non-performing loans

---

[3] Note that the terms gross loans, total loans and net loans ordinarily have somewhat different definitions. Gross loans refers to the loan principal plus unearned (interest) income — for a new loan this would be principal plus total interest. Total loans refers to the face value of the loan, i.e. loan principal. Net loans refer to total loans minus loan loss provisions.

[4] Definitions may vary. For example, a bank may subtract provisions or collateral from NPLs to arrive at a net figure. While this may be customary in a local market, it does not accord with standard ways of comparing asset quality across markets. Make sure that the NPL figure refers to gross NPLs. Definitions of basic terms such as gross loans or total loans may also vary.

[5] In some emerging markets, banks are still not obliged to publicly disclose data concerning non-performing loans and other relevant asset quality indicators.

Checklist: Asset Quality

Definition and discretion. How are non-performing loans (NPLs) defined? What is the difference between NPLs and overdue loans? What degree of discretion does the bank have in defining NPLs?

Amount of NPLs. What is the volume of NPLs in absolute terms and the ratio of NPLs to total loans? How do these compare with the previous period? What are projected NPLs for the current year?

Amount of classified loans. What is the volume of classified loans (substandard, doubtful and loss) in absolute terms and their respective ratios to total loans?

Restructured loans. What is the volume of restructured loans in absolute terms and their ratio to total loans? What criteria, if any, must be satisfied before restructured loans are considered to be performing?

Foreclosed assets. What is the volume of foreclosed assets in absolute terms and in relation to total loans?

Security. What percentage of loans is secured? What percentage of problem loans?

Write-offs. What was the volume of loans written off in the last fiscal year? What were the net write-offs?

Loan loss provisioning. What amount of provisioning was set aside in the last fiscal year? How does it compare with the previous year? Are there any regulations or regulatory guidelines requiring provisions or disincentives limiting provisions?

Loan loss reserves and coverage. What is the bank's total stock of (cumulative) loan loss reserves? What is it in relation to total loans and problem loans (NPL coverage)?

Banks must establish an allowance for loan and lease losses because there is credit risk in their loan and lease portfolios. The allowance, which is a valuation reserve, exists to cover the loan losses that occur in the loan portfolio of every bank. As such, adequate management of the allowance is an integral part a bank's credit risk management process. .... A bank that fails to maintain an adequate allowance is operating in an unsafe and unsound manner.

— Comptroller's Handbook[6]

---

[6] Comptroller's Handbook, Allowance for Loan and Lease Losses, p. 2–3.
Agency is U.S. Comptroller of the Currency Administrator of National Banks.

PROVISIONING, LOAN LOSS RESERVES AND CLASSIFICATION

Before exploring the use of asset quality ratios, it is worthwhile to return to first principles and discuss in more detail the function of loan loss provisions and how they work. *Provisions* or *loan loss reserves* are amounts set aside from earnings to adjust for the probable decline in the value of the bank's loan assets. In accounting terms, as we have noted, they are *contra-assets*. When deducted from total loans they give us net loans.[6] Loan loss reserves do not necessarily appear on the balance sheet, but are ordinarily referred to in footnotes to it. The balance sheet will include line items for reserves, but these are for so-called equity reserves and are distinct from loan loss reserves.

General Reserves vs. Specific Reserves

The purpose of loan loss reserves is to identify and provide for probable, but as yet unconfirmed, loan losses. Clearly, the degree of probability that loans in general and certain loans in particular, will become loss loans varies with the type of loan, purpose, creditworthiness of the customer, and economic and market conditions.[7] Consequently, loan loss reserves are divided into two categories: *general provisions*, sometimes called *allowance for loan losses*, to provide against the possibility that any loan in the bank's portfolio will go bad; and *specific provisions*, to provide against problem or classified loans, i.e. loans that have been identified as problematic. (We discussed classified loans briefly in a preceding chapter, and will return to the topic in greater depth below.) Specific provisions vary with each class of loans. The higher the probability of non-performance, the higher the provision should be. The percentages required are established by regulation. Once a loan is identified as loss, it ideally will be written off, and the loan loss reserve account will be adjusted to reflect the write-off, which is expressed as a deduction from the account.

General provisions, sometimes called statistical provisions, are reserves set aside against all loans. General reserves are intended to account for probable but as yet unidentified loan losses. That is, general reserves are designed to take account of expected loan losses. They are not tied to a particular class of loans, but function as reserves for any loan

---

[6] Comptroller's Handbook, Allowance for Loan and Lease Losses, p. 2–3.
Agency is U.S. Comptroller of the Currency Administrator of National Banks.
[7] Comptroller's Handbook, Allowance for Loan and Lease Losses, p. 4.
Agency is U.S. Comptroller of the Currency Administrator of National Banks.

that may turn sour. In the words of the *Comptroller's Handbook*, a US regulatory guide intended for bank examiners and bank management:

> The allowance is a valuation reserve maintained to cover losses that are probable and estimable on the date of the evaluation. The allowance is not a cushion against possible future losses; that protection is provided by capital.[7]

Notwithstanding the approach of US regulators, in some markets, through custom or regulation, banks set aside a percentage, e.g. 1% of reserves, as non-specific provisions. While theoretically designed to cover expected losses, in many countries and among many institutions they are calculated by rule of thumb rather than forecast in any systematic way. When benchmark requirements for general provisions exist, they will typically range from between 1–2%.

Classification of Loans

Classifications of problem loans vary by country, but as we mentioned briefly in Chapter 9, a typical breakdown has at least four categories: normal (or pass), substandard, doubtful or loss, which reflect an increasing probability that the loan will not perform according to its terms. A fifth category, "specially mentioned" (or "special mention") is sometimes added. The amount of specific provisions required will vary according to the classification and provisioning scheme applicable to the subject market. By and large, loss loans require 100% provisions, while each class of loans from the more problematic to less problematic requires progressively less provisions to be set aside.

Classifications may be on a functional or aging basis (how long the loan as been non-performing) or a combination of the two. In practice, most banks will employ an aging framework on smaller loans, e.g. consumer loans, as it is not efficient to review each one separately on a functional basis.[8] Common international definitions for the most conventional loan classifications are as follows:

Special mention loans

Loans which are not yet past due over 90 days (i.e. non-performing), but where collection in full is questionable as a result of adverse circumstances

---

[8] Larger or more technically sophisticated banks may analyze their loans in pools bearing certain defined characteristics. Historical loss rates are determined using techniques such as "migration analysis."

affecting the borrower and its ability to make complete repayment on a timely basis. Special mention loans may or may not require specific provisioning under local regulation. If they do, the amount of provisioning required will be small, e.g. 5% of the face value of the loan.

Substandard loans

The first category of problem or non-performing loan, substandard loans are generally those 1) overdue between 3 months and 6 months or 2) where impaired collateral or a specific weakness in the borrower jeopardizes the ability of the bank to collect the debt in full on a timely basis.

Doubtful loans

Doubtful loans are loans which 1) are overdue between 6–12 months or 2) where collection in full is doubtful.

Loss loans

Loss loans are loans which 1) are overdue over 1 year, or 2) which are deemed substantially uncollectible and having so little value that they cannot properly be considered viable financial assets.

An Illustrative Functional Framework

The table on the next page shows the scheme used in by Development Bank of Singapore in 1999, which embodies four categories of non-current loans. It employs functional criteria to determine loan classification. Collateral and the valuation of such collateral play an important role in this framework. Note that DBS has no "special mention" category, but does have a category called "substandard/loss" which is common in some countries.

Terminology: Provisioning and Provisions

One last point on terminology should be reiterated. It is important to distinguish between *provisions*, used to refer to the cumulative pool of loan loss reserves, and *provisioning*, which refers to the amount set aside and added to the total pool in a particular time period. Provisioning will normally appear in the bank's income statement as a deduction.

Development Bank of Singapore
Loan Grading & Provisioning Framework

Grade Assigned to a Loan	Functional Criteria	Provision Level	Examples of Collateral Valuation
Substandard	Fully secured or expected loss is less than 50% of the unsecured amount	If fully secured: no provision against principal, but 100% provision against interest. If shortfall in security: principal provision of 10 to 50% of unsecured amount and 100% provision against interest. Plus general provision on outstanding principal.	Property: discount to approximate a forced sale valuation. Shares/ deposits: marked-to-market. Debentures: discount ranging from 1/3 to 2/3 book value
Substandard/ Loss	Primary source of repayment is collateral which is inadequate to fully cover the loan	100% provision against unsecured principal amount and against interest. Plus general provision on outstanding principal.	
Doubtful	Indeterminable security value but expected to be significant Expected loss is 50% to less than 100% of the loan	50–100% provision against principal amount and 100% provision against interest. Plus general provision on outstanding principal.	n/a
Loss	Loan recovery is assessed to be insignificant with no security available as alternative recourse	100% provision against principal amount and against interest. Plus general provision on outstanding principal.	n/a

Source: Development Bank of Singapore.

Loan Loss Provisions & Reserves: Terminology	
Current: Deducted from operating or net interest income on the income statement	Cumulative: Ordinarily appears as a contra-asset in a footnote to the balance sheet; although some portion of loan loss reserves may count towards regulatory capital, loan loss reserves do not appear in the equity portion of the balance sheet
Provisioning loan loss provisions or loan loss provisioning LLPs	Terms: provisions loan loss reserves LLRs

Aging Framework

In some jurisdictions or at their own discretion, banks will abide by an aging framework instead of a functional framework to classify loans. The definitions of loan classes delineated at the start of this chapter showed both functional and time-based definitions for the five basic loan classifications. Actually, many jurisdictions use both functional and aging definitions, setting forth the functional definitions in broader regulations while providing time-based guidelines to be used unless exceptional circumstances are present. Generally, time-based frameworks consider a loan substandard and non-performing after three to six months (depending on the jurisdiction), doubtful after six to twelve months, and loss after twelve to twenty four months.

Liu Chong Hing Bank, a medium-sized bank in Hong Kong, in its 1999 annual report, classified its problem loans according to a time overdue. Although the terms substandard, doubtful and loss are not used in the bank's annual report, they conform with HKMA standards on loan classification which are defined both in functional and aging-basis terms as can be seen in the table on page 218. The table following page shows some of the variation among a number of Asian countries circa mid-1998. Note that regulations were in flux at the time and the figures given may have been changed in the intervening period. In general, there has been a convergence toward a more conservative international standard. The table is therefore intended for illustrative rather than reference purposes.

Time Based Framework in Asia: Varying Rules

Time Period Past Due*:	Thailand	Malaysia	Indonesia	Philippines	Korea	Singapore	Hong Kong	Taiwan	India
Special Mention	n/a	n/a	1 day-3 mo past due	–	3–6 mo	3 mo	–	n/a	n/a
Substandard	3–6 mo**	3–6 mo (now: 6–12 mo)	3–6 mo past due	>3 mo*	6 mo	–	>3 mo	>3 mo	>6 mo
Doubtful	>6 mo*	6–12 mo (now 12–24 mo)	>6 mo past due	>12 mo*	>6 mo	–	>6 mo	>6 mo	substandard for >24 mo
Loss	>12 mo	>12 mo (now >24 mo)	>12 mo past due	>6 mo* or >12 mo*	–	–		>24 mo	doubtful for >36 mo
Remarks	Distinction between NPLs and "classified" loans; add'l category "doubtful loss" is used.	Regulations were loosened during the Asian financial crisis.	Parameters are basically quantitative.	Some loans overdue less than 90 days may be deemed non-performing	These criteria were applicable as of mid-1998.	After initial determination of NPL, judgment is largely quantative the loans.	Time periods subject to bank discretion and other specific aspects of the loans.	Regulations distinguish between NPLs (overdue > 6 mo) and "past due loans"	These criteria were applicable as of mid-1998.

n/a means that the category did not exist in that country as of 9/98; – means that there is no formal time based criterion specified; * this table is highly simplified; additional criteria may apply altering the time period; ** changed July 1998. Data sourced from Warburg Dillon Read; Salomon Smith Barney; Hong Kong Monetary Authority.

Liu Chong Hing Bank, Hong Kong, FY99: Loan Classification and Specific Provisioning

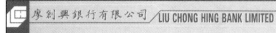
廖創興銀行有限公司 / LIU CHONG HING BANK LIMITED

UNAUDITED SUPPLEMENTARY FINANCIAL INFORMATION
for the year ended 31 December 1999

4 OVERDUE AND RESCHEDULED LOANS
Overdue and rescheduled advances

	1999			
	Gross amount of Advances HK$'000	Percentage to toal advances	Specific provison HK$'000	Net amount of advances HK$'000
Advances overdue for				
— 6 months or less but over 3 months	100,103	0.5	9,182	90,921
— 1 year or less but over 6 months	301,325	1.6	22,819	278,506
— over 1 year	872,918	4.5	300,233	572,685
	1,274,346	6.6	332,234	942,112
Rescheduled advances	149,905	0.8	—	149,905
Total ovedue and rescheduled advances	1,424,251	7.4	332,234	1,092,017

	1998			
	Gross amount of Advances HK$'000	Percentage to toal advances	Specific provison HK$'000	Net amount of advances HK$'000
Advances overdue for				
— 6 months or less but over 3 months	157,162	0.9	1,291	155,871
— 1 year or less but over 6 months	434,718	2.4	113,194	321,524
— over 1 year	245,705	1.4	90,957	154,748
	837,585	4.7	205,442	632,143
Rescheduled advances	289,199	1.6	—	289,199
Total overdue and rescheduled advances	1,126,784	6.3	205,442	921,342

Out of the gorss amout of total overdue advances (net amount of advances is HK$942,112,000) (1998: HK$632,143,000), HK$1,092,497,000 (1998: HK$633,367,000) is secured by collateral with estimated market value of approximately HK$988,797,000 (1998: HK$1,060,592,000).

The gross amount of total rescheduled advances of HK$149,905,000 (1998: HK$289,199,000) is secured by collateral with estimated market value of approximately HK$222,566,000 (1998: HK$420,030,000).

The amount of advances to customers include the following:

	1999 HK$'000	1998 HKS'000
Amount that are overdue for more than 3 months and on which interest is still being accrued	89,317	163,526
Amount that are overdue for 3 months or less and on which interest is being placed to suspense or on which interest accrual has ceased		

In an unaudited supplement to its FY99 financial statement, Liu Chong Hing Bank displays the breakdown of its problem loans. The first three categories to the left correspond to the classifications of

– substandard
– doubtful, and
– loss

Rescheduled loans are also included as a separate category within problem loans.

The bank also notes that it was still accruing interest at year end on a portion of its NPLs

Illustration, Provisions and Provisioning

The diagram below shows graphically how provisions work. Imagination helps to understand the concept. Recall the washbasin we conjured up to understand the income statement and how it differs from the balance sheet. Imagine a hose which siphons water (funds) from the sink into a tank. The tank is a tank of funds, a reservoir of loan loss reserves which enables a bank to avoid touching core equity capital when it is obliged to write off bad loans. Part of the tank consists of general provisions designed to deal with the statistical likelihood that a certain portion of a bank's loans will inevitably go sour.

Specific provisions are reserves set aside against identified problem loans. Some are only required to have a percentage of reserves set aside; other more serious problem loans will have to be fully reserved against. When it needs to build up its loan loss reserves, revenue that would otherwise be termed profit is diverted. In other words, provisioning is deducted from operating income. When bad loans must be written off, the loan loss reserve tank is emptied by the amount that must be written off.

Think of loan loss provisions as a pool or reservoir used to make up for the diminuition in the value of loans as a result of non-performance. The reservoir is composed of two strata: general loan loss provisions are meant to reserve against generally expected loan losses; specific provisions are those associated with particular problem loans. The bank is filled with funds diverted from net profits.

How Provisions Work

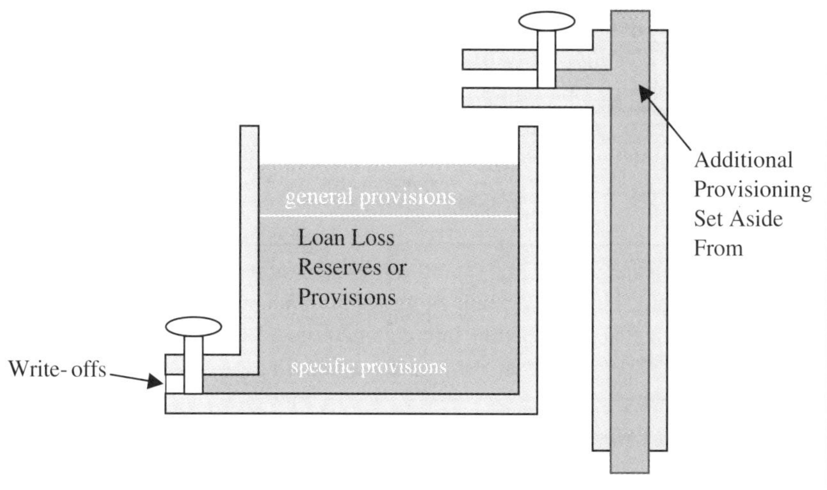

general provisions

Loan Loss
Reserves or
Provisions

specific provisions

Additional
Provisioning
Set Aside
From

Write-offs

Source: After Thomson Financial Bank Watch

ACCRUAL OF INTEREST INCOME, INTEREST IN SUSPENSE, AND CLAWBACKS

[T]wo main criteria are used to decide whether and when interest accrual should be stopped, or accrued interest receivable should be reversed: (1) how long the payment is past due; and (2) the bank's subjective judgement of the debtor's ability to repay.[9]

In addition to provisions, the analyst must be aware of the role of *interest in suspense* and other aspects of bank interest income accounting. Normally, a bank is entitled to obtain interest income generated on a loan until it is repaid or the obligation of the borrower to pay is otherwise extinguished. Because virtually all financial institutions operate on an accrual accounting basis and will therefore record interest income as it accrues, a bank will register interest income generated on a performing loan on its income statement as it falls due, whether the interest payment has been collected or not.

In the case of non-performing loans, accounting guidelines and regulatory requirements may require the bank to either provision against the non-payment of interest, or credit an *interest in suspense account* when the interest payment is overdue for some specified period of time. Note that the suspending of interest performs the same function as setting aside loan loss provisions, and may be written off in the same way as provisions if the loan is deemed a loss loan.

In the United States, for instance, if principal or interest is overdue 90 days or more, banks *must* suspend interest. Rules governing suspense of interest income vary from country to country. In some jurisdictions, banks may prefer to record interest on the income statement, but provision against it. Net income will be the same as if the interest was put into a suspense account, but banks that provision against interest will show higher provisions. Therefore, the analyst should take account both of general and specific provisioning together with interest in suspense when evaluating a bank's reserve against loan losses.

> Tip: Interest in suspense is equivalent to a like amount of loan loss provisions and in any event, net income will be the same. When interest is suspended, however, it does not appear as interest income on the income statement. Discretion to suspend interest varies among jurisdictions.

---

[9] Salomon Smith Barney, February 12, 2001, p. 5. C. Paitoon & B.T., Bank Accounts Made Easy, Vol. 1, Recognition of Interest Income.

Clawbacks

Clawbacks are reversals of interest already accrued. Usually they come into play after a loan has been overdue for a period of time, typically 90 days or three months, after which the loan is deemed non-performing. As with classifying loans, the bank may have some discretion in determining whether it must cease accruing interest and reverse interest already accrued. In Hong Kong, for example, if the loan is fully secured and overdue more than three months but not yet 12 months, the bank may choose to continue to accrue interest income. In contrast, in Singapore, after three months has elapsed, the bank may no longer continue to accrue interest income, unless the bank fully provides (loan loss provisions) against the amount accrued. It may only recognized any interest received on a cash basis. Another option permitted the bank is to accrue the interest as interest-in-suspense. If put into the interest-in-suspense account, the "accrued interest" does not appear on the bank's financial statement as interest income and as observed, the effect is essentially the same as if the bank had set aside loan loss provisions against accrued interest income. The actual details of the accounting treatment of clawbacks vary from country to country, and differences in such treatment may distort cross-border comparisons of banks. A detailed discussion of these nuances of bank financial accounting is outside the scope of this book. The point is to alert the bank analyst to these issues and it is recommended that the analyst become familiar with the relevant differences in accounting treatment of banks in the countries for which he or she is responsible.

Write-Offs

When there is no reasonable prospect of a loan being repaid, it should be written off. When a loan is written off, provisions are reduced and the bank will need to rebuild its reserve of provisions. If there are insufficient provisions, loans must be written off against capital. (Note that if certain criteria are met, some portion of loan loss reserves may be deemed a part of regulatory capital. We discuss this in Chapter 14 and 15.) In practice, as noted, banks do not always write off loans on a timely basis. If disclosure is accurate, a bank that does not write off loans rapidly will show a higher level of non-performing loans than a bank that writes off loans quickly. In general, banks in emerging markets will often write off

---

How Clawbacks Work

Example: Willow Bank, the largest bank in Port Willow, lent $10,000 to Jones on an unsecured basis at a rate of 12% simple interest per annum ($1200 interest per year) in March 1999. The loan agreement called for semi-annual payments payable on September 30, and March 31. On September 30, Jones made a payment of $600, which was duly recorded as interest income. (The bank debited cash $600 and credited interest income.) On December 31, the end of Willow Bank's fiscal year, 3 months' interest had accrued on Jones' loan even though payment was not due until March 31, 2000. The bank therefore recorded $300 on December 31, 1999 as accrued interest income, accruing the interest on a monthly basis. (It had debited its accrued interest income account by $300 and credited its interest income account $300 at year end.) On March 31, 2000 Jones paid the bank another $600. This reduced the accrued interest income attributable to Jones to zero. (The bank debited cash an additional $300 and credited accrued interest income by $300.) On September 30, 2000 he made payment again. Again on December 31, 2000 Willow Bank showed $300 in accrued interest income attributable to Jones on its books.

In January 2001, however, Jones suffered financial reverses and soon found himself in difficult financial straits. He was unable to make payment to Willow Bank on March 31, 2001. By June 30, three months had passed and as payment had still not been made, Willow Bank therefore deemed the loan to Jones to be non-performing. It had to cease accruing interest and reverse any interest already accrued under the regulations prevailing in Marshalia, the country in which Port Willow was situated. Thus, by June 30, six months of accrued interest receivable had accumulated on the bank's books. Obliged to cease interest accrual and reverse that had occurred, the bank credited its accrued interest receivable account by $600 and recognized a loss of that income by debiting its loss from accrued interest receivable account in the same amount.

---

loans more slowly than banks in the United States or other developed markets.

Recoveries

Recoveries refer to the sums received by a bank from loans that have already been written off. Typically, revenue from recoveries will be shown as a reduction in provisioning on the income statement. They are not normally shown as interest income.

WHY DON'T BANKS PROVISION ADEQUATELY?
WHY DON'T BANKS WRITE-OFF BAD LOANS?

What we have been describing is the way proper loan loss management should work. In practice, in many emerging markets banks do not:

- Fully identify and disclose problem loans;
- Set aside adequate amounts of both general and specific provisioning; and
- Do not write-off loss loans in a timely manner.

In certain cases, banks in some emerging markets have been able to defer writing off non-performing loans for considerable periods of time, years and even decades in some cases. Why is this the case? The motives for not recognizing such losses are varied. The companies to which the loans were made, frequently state-owned enterprises, may still be in operation and as arms of the state are theoretically capable of repaying the loans. Laws and regulations in the jurisdiction may make writing off loans a tedious and thorny process that requires court or regulatory approval. Underlying these reasons is the notion that recognizing historical non-performing loans may prove embarrassing, especially when NPLs exceed the bank's equity many times over. Writing off loans in such cases will put the bank's owners, whether government or private shareholders, in an untenable position. If equity is written down to zero, a bank must either be shut down or recapitalized. The government's laws will almost certainly require it. Even acknowledging that a bank is technically insolvent may have domestic or international repercussions. As obtaining new capital may be difficult, it is easier for all concerned to allow technically insolvent banks to continue to operate while maintaining the fiction that some non-performing loans are actually performing. A government guarantee of deposits and an occasional infusion of equity are all that is necessary to keep the bank open. Technically insolvent banks can continue to operate for many years in this fashion.

In addition, in some markets, the issue of saving face should not be minimized. Non-performing loans, loan losses and write-offs imply the failure of management, both of the bank and that of its customers. When non-performing loans reach a certain level, as we have said, a bank becomes technically insolvent and in theory shareholders' equity should be written down, management replaced, and shareholders' ownership rights dissolved. In reality, both management and shareholders have an economic incentive

---

Reasons Why Some Banks Do Not Write Off Loans

- First, identifying problem loans requires adequate credit analysis and management skills that may be beyond the bank's capability.

- Second, the regulatory regime may not meet international best practices, or if the regulations exist, regulators may not have sufficient resources or the will to enforce existing rules.

- Third, where the regulatory regime is weak, or where regulators collaborate with bank managers, problem loans may not be fully disclosed because the result could be a lack of confidence among depositors, both domestic and foreign, in the bank or the banking system as a whole.

- Fourth, setting aside adequate amounts of provisions will reduce the bank's stated profits, to the apparent detriment of shareholders.

- Fifth, in many markets, provisioning above a nominal amount is not tax-deductible.[10] If not, the bank will be paying tax on earnings without corresponding profits to show for it. Shareholders and managers therefore have an incentive to minimize provisioning.

- Lastly, write-offs reduce total loan loss reserves and, if reserves are insufficient, shareholders' equity. Shareholders will naturally not be keen to write off loans so long as there is any possibility of their being repaid.

---

to retain their grasp on the bank irrespective of theory. They may be abetted in this by cultural and political factors.

ASSET QUALITY IN THE FINANCIAL STATEMENTS: AN ILLUSTRATION

Provisioning Appears on the Income Statement

The level of loan loss provisioning set aside during the year will normally appear on the income statement. In the income statement below, that is of Development Bank of Singapore, S$1,063,000 were deducted from profits and set aside as new loan loss provisions.

---

[10] In the United States, "few banks provided reserves for bad debts until the Internal Revenue Service (IRS) allowed the additions to such reserves to be deducted on a bank's tax return". This was first permitted in 1921, but formal guidelines were not established until 1965. OCC Comptroller's Handbook, Allowance for Loan and Lease Losses, p. 1.

Development Bank of Singapore, FY99, Income Statement

		DBSH GROUP - CONSOLIDATED PROFIT AND LOSS ACCOUNT	

DBS GROUP HOLDINGS LTD
Consolidated Profit and Loss Account
of the year ended 31 December 1999

		DBSH Group	
	Note	**1999** **(S$'000)**	1998 (S$'000)
Interest income		**4,607,872**	4,931,259
Less: Interest expense		**2,573,197**	3,501,256
Net interest income	5	**2,034,675**	1,430,003
Fee and commission income	6	**423,053**	274,130
Dividends	7	**31,297**	37,032
Rental income	8	**30,747**	37,660
Other income	9	**509,152**	97,012
Income before operating expense	43	**3,028,924**	1,875,837
Less: Staff costs	10	**529,258**	333,588
Other operating expenses		**535,423**	420,779
Total operating expenses		**1,064,681**	754,367
Operating profit		**1,964,243**	1,121,470
Less: Provision for possible loan losses and diminution in value of other assets	12	**1,063,224**	996,428
Add: Share of profits less losses of associated companies		**901,019** **140,372**	125,042 (80,931)
Net profit before tax		**1,041,391**	44,111
Less: Taxation		**345,150**	64,390
Share of taxation of associated companies		**34,313**	73,143
Net profit after tax		**661,928**	(27,593)
Less: Minority interest		**(409,855)**	(139,557)
Net profit attributable to members	19.4,43	**1,071,783**	111,964
Earnings per ordinary share of S$1/- each	16		
- Basic		**Cents 97**	Cents 10
- Fully diluted		**Cents 87**	Cents 10
US/S$ exchange rate 31 December		**1.67**	1.65

(See notes on page 62 to 108, which form part of these financial statements.)

Annotation (boxed): Loan loss provisioning is deducted from operating profit. It amounted to S$1,063 m in 1999.

Total Loan Loss Provisions Are Footnoted to the Balance Sheet

Loan loss provisions ordinarily do not appear directly on the balance sheet. Instead, they are deducted from loans and advances and shown in a footnote. In the balance sheet below, the reader is referred to Notes 28,

29 and 42. Note that reserves shown on the balance sheet in the liability column are equity reserves, separate and distinct from loan loss reserves. In Note 28, we can see that total general provisions of $2,924 m and specific provisions of S$1,145 m have been deducted from gross loans and receivables of S$58,438 m to arrive at (net) total loans and receivables of S$53,370 m. Subtracting bills receivable, a net total loans figure of S$53,168 m is reached. The latter figure is the one that appears in the asset column of the balance sheet below.

Balance Sheet Excerpt, DBS

		DBSH GROUP - CONSOLIDATED BALANCE SHEET	
			DBSH Group
		1999	1998
	Note	**(S$'000)**	(S$'000)
ASSETS			
Cash, and balances and placements with central banks		**6,943,841**	8,720,463
Singapore Government securities and treasury bills	26,30,42	**8,813,799**	6,949,915
Trading securities	27,30,42	**3,334,664**	2,733,092
Balances, placements with, and loans and advances to banks	42	**26,493,664**	20,751,947
Bills receivable from non-bank customers	28-29,42	**1,201,881**	2,056,912
Loans and advances to non-bank customers	29-94,42	**53,167,650**	54,158,482
Investment securities	31	964,640	315,559
Other assets	32	**2,244,914**	1,644,613
Associated companies	34	**1,479,546**	1,087,531
Fixed assets	35	**1,820,465**	1,618,878

The calculation of total loans can be seen in Note 28. (The line below the circled line is the total of net loans and bills receivable.)

Calculation of Cumulative Loan Loss Reserves

The calculation of the total stock of loan loss reserves can be seen in Note 29 on the next page. The balance from December 31, 1998 is brought forward to January 1, 1999. Provisions obtained through the acquisition of other banks is added in, while provisions utilized through write-offs and other transfers are deducted. New provisions are added (charged to profit and loss account) less some general provisions (S$57 m) that were

DBS, FY99, Note 28 to the Financial Statements

28 LOANS TO, AND BILLS RECEIVABLE FROM NON-BANK CUSTOMERS

In S$'000	DBSH Group 1999	1998
Gross	58,437,720	59,194,664
Less: Specific provisions (Note 29)	2,923,661	1,907,509
General provisions (Note 29)	1,144,528	1,071,761
Net total	54,369,531	56,215,394
Including:		
Bills receivable	1,201,881	2,056,912
Loans	53,167,650	54,158,482
Net total	54,369,531	56,215,394

reduced resulting in a lower overall deduction from operating income. Interest in suspense, which is a quasi-reserve, is also included (although in this case — in contrast to the prior year — it is negative suggesting a recovery of interest income) resulting in a new total loan loss reserves of S$4,068 m. This is the amount that deducted from total loans and advances to arrive at total net loans and advances.

DBS, FY99, Note 29 to the Financial Statements

29 PROVISION FOR POSSIBLE LOAN LOSSES AND INTEREST-IN-SUSPENSE

In S$'000	Specific	General	DBSH Group Total	interest-in-suspense
1999				
Balance at 1 January	1,907,509	1,071,761	2,979,270	62,475
On acquisition of subsidiary companies	171,030	131,300	302,330	—
Utilisation/transfers during the year	(199,388)	(1,258)	(200,646)	(15,597)
Charge to profit and loss account (Note 12)	1,046,509	(57,275)	989,234	—
Interest suspended during the year	(1,999)	—	(1,999)	39,158
Balance at 31 December	2,923,661	1,144,528	4,068,189	86,036
1998				
Balance at 1 January	154,632	741,467	896,099	12,102
On acquisition of business undertakings and subsidiary companies	875,666	152,978	1,028,644	117
Utilisation/transfers during the year	(36,773)	1,168	(35,805)	(480)
Charge to profit and loss account (Note 12)	897,087	176,148	1,073,235	—
Interest suspended during the year	16,897	—	16,897	50,736
Balance at 31 December	1,907,509	1,071,761	2,979,270	62,475

Total reserves from the previous year become the starting point for the new year

Included in 1999 specific provision charged to the profit and loss account is 55495 million (1998: S$Nil) in respect of losses arising from the termination of loan arrangements in DTDB. Of this amount, 55353 million is

Note 12 shows a breakdown of provisioning (i.e. total provisions taken during the year), and the portion that comprised new specific provisions.

DBS, FY99, Note 12 to the Financial Statements

12 PROVISION FOR POSSIBLE LOAN LOSSES AND DIMINUTION IN VALUE OF OTHER ASSET		
	DBSH Group	
In S$'000	**1999**	1998
Specific provision for loans (Note 29)	**1,046,509**	897,087
Specific provision for diminution in value of investments and other assets (Note 30)	**4,788**	1,164
Release of specific provision for diminution in value of investments during the year arising from the change in methods of accounting (Note 2.7.2 & 30)	**—**	(83,884)
Release of general provison for loans (Note 29)	**(57,275)**	176,148
Provision/(write-back) of general provision for diminution in value of investments and other assets (Note 30)	**390**	(909)
Provision for contingencies and other banking risks (Note 30)	**68,812**	6,822
Total	**1,063,224**	996,428

Non-Performing Loans in the Financial Statements

Turning to non-performing loans, disclosure as we have emphasized varies from bank to bank and market to market. In the 1999 annual report for DBS, disclosure is relatively thorough, breaking down NPLs by loan grade, whether bank or non-bank, and by country. In addition to the FY99 figures shown on the next page in Note 41 to DBS' financial statements, FY98 figures (not shown) are also provided, to afford the basis for comparison. We can see that a high proportion of the NPLs came from one subsidiary, DBS Thai Danu Bank (DTDB), the bank's recent acquisition in Thailand. DTDB accounts for NPLs amounting to $3,206 m out of a total of S$8,149 m or 39%. This subsidiary had an extraordinarily high level of NPLs, 65%. NPLs in other regional countries were also elevated, but non-performing loan levels in Singapore were modest at 4.9%. For the group as a whole, NPLs of 9.3% were not at ideal levels but were also not surprising in the aftermath of the Asian crisis.

RATIO ANALYSIS: KEY ASSET QUALITY INDICATORS

We previously identified four ratios as being especially important to bank credit analysis. They are:

❑ year-on-year loan growth;

DBS, FY99, Note 41 to the Financial Statements

---

41 NON-PERFORMING LOANS AND PROVISIONS

41.1 At 31 December 1999, DBSH Groups total non-performing loans amounted to $S8,149.0 million (1998: S$7,086.0 million) Non-performing loans (NPLs) are loans, contingent facilities and debt instruments classified as Substandard, Doubtful or Loss in accordance with MAS Notice 612.

Out of the total NPLs of $S8,149.0 million:

— $S4,951.5 million (61%) [1998: $S3,799.1 million (54%)] were in the substandard category; and

— $S4,529.8 million (56%) [1998: $S4,021.8 million (57%)] were secured by collateral.

Total cumulative specific and general provisions at 31 December 1999 amounted to 118% (1998:103%) of unsecured NPLs.

Details of DBSH Group's NPLs and provisions as at 31 December 1999 were as follows:

In S$ million	DTDB[(a)]	Regional Countries Others	Singapore	Other Countries	Total	
Non-Performing Loans (NPLs)	3206.6	1364.6	2425.0	1152.7	8149.0	by
— Substandard	1170.7	910.1	2088.7	781.9	4951.5	country
— Doubtful	113.7	125.3	48.9	333.1	621.0	
— loss	1922.2	329.2	287.4	37.7	2576.4	
(NPLs) as a of:						
— Total loans in the respective countries	65.4%	22.9%	4.9%	4.2%	9.3%	breakdown
— Group total assets	3.0%	1.3%	2.3%	1.1%	7.7%	of problem loans
Non-bank NPLs as a % of non-bank loans in the respective countries	70.4%	47.4%	5.4%	11.3%	13.0%	
Total Cumulative Provisions	1923.9	947.2	938.6	476.2	4285.9	
— Specific provisions	1785.4	578.7	447.8	282.9	3094.8	
— General provisions	138.5	368.5	490.7	193.4	1191.0	
Total Cumulative Provisions						
— Total loans in the respective countries	39.2%	15.9%	1.9%	1.7%	4.9%	total loan
— Group total assets	1.8%	0.9%	0.9%	0.4%	4.0%	loss
— NPLs in the respective countries	60%	69%	39%	41%	53%	reserves
— Unsecured NPLs in the respective countries	133%	99%	118%	112%	118%	NPL coverage

❑ the ratio of non-performing loans (NPLs for short) to total loans (NPL ratio);

❑ loan loss reserves to non-performing loans (NPL coverage); and

❑ loan loss reserves plus equity to non-performing loans.

Year-on-Year Loan Growth

How rapidly a bank is growing can give the analyst an idea of the types of problems it is likely to face. There is inevitably a lag between the time a bank makes a loan and the time in which it becomes delinquent. Too rapid loan suggests that a bank is expanding its loan portfolio beyond its credit management capability and will ordinarily be a negative factor to the analyst making a credit assessment. In addition, it is always easy to find high risk customers — remember the principle of adverse selection. In addition, this is as good of a place as any to observe the herd mentality which is prevalent in the financial markets. All too often in the banking industry the herd follows the trail to perilous real estate lending, energy and infrastructure finance or developing markets. The story ends when the asset bubble is pricked, prices crash and banks (or in some case, taxpayers) are left to pick up the pieces.

Since most banks lend fairly short term, rapid growth in one year can lead to a high rate of NPLs the following year, especially if the economy begins to slow down. Excessive loan growth is consequently a good indicator of prospective asset quality problems. Certainly, low growth significantly higher than peer levels should be a warning to the analyst to look more closely.

$$\frac{\text{Loans in Year } 2 - \text{Loans in Year } 1}{\text{Loans in Year } 1} \times 100 = \text{YoY Loan Growth (\%)}$$

Example: Loans in Year 1 are \$325 m. Loans in Year 2 are \$388 m. YoY loan growth $= 388 - 325 = 63$; $63/325 = 0.194 \times 100 = 19.4\%$.

In emerging markets, rates of loan growth are often higher than in industrialized countries. This occurs for a number of reasons: the economy is developing from a low base and financial intermediation is expanding rapidly. In addition, because the capital markets in such countries are less evolved, companies must rely heavily upon bank finance. Finally, new banks will see huge loan growth at first, since they are escalating from a base of zero. Under such circumstances, many financial institutions in emerging markets have in recent times seen their loan books grow more quickly than prudent credit assessment would permit. During boom periods, 50–60% year-on-year loan growth for the banking industry in certain markets was not infrequent.

How much growth is too much? Circumstances vary, but in emerging markets, although growth in excess of 30% per annum was not uncommon in the recent past, it does suggest that expansion of the bank's loan book is exceeding its ability to internally generate capital or to effectively vet its borrowers or both. This is not always the case; ideally, the analyst should explore the reasons for the rapid growth and how well underpinned that growth is by solid management, a viable franchise and strong economic conditions. Is the bank maintaining sufficient liquidity and capital to support the asset growth?

Nevertheless, in an emerging economy, loan growth rates over 20% per annum should probably give the analyst pause, and 15% would be a more con-servative ceiling. Twenty percent is less worrisome if the industry average is 40%, but an average rate of 40% positive growth is a possible signal that an asset bubble is building and should be monitored. In a more mature economy, 10–15% should normally be the upper range of growth. In both emerging and mature markets, an exception of course occurs where high rates of loan growth occur as a result of a merger or acquisition and the financial statements of the entities have been consolidated. Other possible exceptions are the new bank or the bank that has just raised new capital and is growing from a relatively small base.

As a rough rule of thumb, assuming no consolidation, growth between 10–20% in an emerging economy would generally be viewed very favorably, assuming the economy is enjoying an upturn. Loan growth of 5–10% is respectable and characteristic of a mature economy experiencing stable economic conditions. Loan growth of 0–5% would tend to either indicate a very large bank, a mature economy experiencing less than robust economic conditions, or mediocre performance. Negative or extremely low rates of loan growth are characteristic of the period following the collapse of an asset bubble as banks work to consolidate and strengthen their balance sheets amid a rising tide of non-performing loans.

Tip: A loan growth rate significantly beyond the market norm suggests potential asset quality problems. Except in cases of merger or acquisition, a new bank, or a bank that has just received a capital injection, per annum loan growth over 20% should be scrutinized. Watch out for high rates of loan growth in the commercial real estate sector.

NPL Ratio

Perhaps the single most important indicator to ascertain a bank's asset quality is the ratio of NPLs to total loans. It signifies the degree to which a bank is lending money to borrowers who are not paying it back. This ratio, when available for individual banks, several peer banks, and preferably for the banking industry in the subject market as well, will provide an excellent picture of a bank's comparative asset quality.

It should, however, be emphasized that non-performing loans and the non-performing loan ratio are historical and lagging indicators. While short-term credits may manifest as NPLs sooner rather than later, it will necessarily take longer for medium and longer term loans to season. A five-year loan or may not go bad until three years into its term. The analyst should also be aware that loans that have been written off will no longer appear on the bank's financial statements as non-performing loans. For this reason, the NPL ratio should not be examined in isolation. Instead, it should preferably be viewed in conjunction with indicators of write-offs as well as broader definitions of non-performing assets which take in both NPLs together with foreclosed assets and restructured loans.

NPL Ratio, Definition

$$\text{NPL Ratio (\%)} = \frac{\text{Total Non-Performing Loans}}{\text{Total Loans}} \times 100$$

Example: Back Bay Bank in Year 1 has total outstanding loans of $798 m. Its non-performing loans amount to $49 m. Its NPL ratio = 49/798 = 0.0614 or 6.14%.

A ratio which is higher than the bank's peer group (and industry) trend is a salient indicator of inferior asset quality. Conversely, a bank that has an NPL ratio that is lower than its peers, increasing less rapidly or decreasing more rapidly than its peers, evinces superior asset quality.

In addition to observing the bank's comparative NPL ratio, and trends, it is essential to probe beneath the surface to determine what may account for differences among banks and trends. In many markets, banks have some degree — often a great deal — of discretion in deciding whether a loan is non-performing. Some banks take a more conservative approach to classifying loans, and as a result have seemingly higher NPLs. Some banks define NPLs more liberally and are reluctant to classify loans as non-performing. It is important not to take these figures at face value, but to take account of definitional differences that may be accounting for them. The true figure — or the figure that would be calculated if international standards were strictly applied — may not be clearly determinable, but it should not surprise the analyst if it is 50–100% or more above the disclosed figure.

> Tip: Higher than average or increasing NPLs suggests mediocre or deteriorating asset quality. But be aware of factors, such as the degree of discretion permitted the bank to define NPLs, that may account for figures that seem better or worse than peers.

In addition, the regulatory regime, which we will discuss in more depth in the following chapter, may give such a bank an alternative; by restructuring the loan, by initiating foreclosure proceeding or other means, the bank may be able to keep its NPL ratio lower than it otherwise would be. Clearly, then, a bank with a higher level of NPLs than a peer does not necessarily have inferior asset quality. The apparently better asset quality indicated by a higher NPL ratio may be a mirage, created by classifying problem assets in a more lax manner. In many emerging markets, disclosed NPL figures should be taken with a grain of salt.

> Tip: Sometimes differences in NPL data and ratios can be traced back to definitional differences. Is the bank applying the 90-day international standard when defining NPLs? Be consistent when comparing banks within a country and across borders.

Falling NPLs

Similarly, if a bank's NPL level is falling, the analyst should seek to ascertain the reason. Is it because:

❑ There has been a relaxation in the definition of non-performing loans?

❑ In the subject jurisdiction, restructured loans are not considered non-performing and the bank is thereby restructuring loans to make itself look better?

❑ NPLs are falling as a result of charge-offs to loan loss reserves or to capital?

❑ Some loans have been returned to performing status.

Relaxation in Definition of NPLs

Clearly, a change in definition, unless it is a relaxation from a standard stricter than international best practice, can be viewed as a form of *regulatory forbearance*, which is a form of window dressing to allow a bank's performance or financial condition appear better than it would under prior regulations. Regulatory authorities may nonetheless view regulatory forbearance as a strategy during a banking crisis. During the Asian crisis, for example, Malaysian banking authorities loosened the definitions of non-performing loans. By relaxing NPL definitions, provisioning and capital requirements are also lessened, and banks may thereby be encouraged to maintain open lines of credit to customers, preventing a credit crunch and concomitant economic contraction. All other things being equal, this will arguably allow banks to improve operating revenue and possibly earn their way back to profitability.

Cosmetic Restructuring

Where restructured loans are considered to be outside the definition of non-performing loans, banks may engage in hasty restructuring, in effect *rescheduling*, in an attempt to reduce nominal NPLs. In these cases, it is highly likely that many of these loans will ultimately return to a non-performing state, but in the meantime, under some regulatory frameworks, the bank's asset quality superficially appears better than it is.

More insidious types of cosmetic restructuring occasionally occur when two banks collude to make each other's balance sheets look better. It is not unknown for Bank X to extend a new loan to a customer of Bank Y so that the customer can resume or continue performance on its old loan from Bank Y. Bank Y may reciprocate the favor for Bank X. In this situation, four ostensibly performing loans are listed in place of two non-performing ones. These types of covert and arguably fraudulent restructuring are less seen these days than they once were, but the analyst should be alert to their potential occurrence particularly in markets with weak bank supervision.

Write-Offs (Charge-Offs)

NPLs, as noted, may fall as a result of write-offs of such loans against provisions or capital. Rapid write-offs the best practice approach to dealing with NPLs and should be viewed positively by the analyst. In this case, however, nominal NPLs may never rise to warning levels, and therefore the volume of write-offs functions as a proxy for real NPLs. A substantial rise in write-offs, although the appropriate way to handle loans that go sour, is still be a point of concern to be monitored. If prolonged, provisions will be depleted and capital can ultimately be impaired. The analyst should therefore pay attention both to NPLs and to net write offs.

Return of NPLs to Performing Status

Depending upon the jurisdiction, NPLs may return to performing status and be permitted to be classified as such, provided certain criteria are met. The situation is similar to that of restructuring, and indeed the restructured loans almost always returns to performing status, at least for a short while. If the definitional standards are sufficiently strict, the return to performing status is a positive development. Attention must be paid, however, to the relapse rate. The *relapse rate* is the rate at which loans that have returned to performing status, often following restructuring, return to non-performing status.

Rules of Thumb

What is an acceptable level of NPLs? It depends. The local market, economic conditions, and how strictly the bank classifies NPLs are all relevant. Nonetheless, with the foregoing caveat, as a rule of thumb, the following ranges applicable to emerging markets may prove helpful to the novice analyst. In developed markets, the percentages below should be halved.

Below 2%: excellent

2–5%:   good

5–10%:   fair

10–20%:   moderate to severe problems

over 20%: extremely severe problems

NPLs Are Masked During Times of Rapid Loan Growth

Analysts should also be aware of the distortion in NPL ratios that can occur during times of rapid loan growth or rapid loan contraction. During boom times, banks may build their loan books quickly, expanding their loan volume at the rate of 25% per annum or more. This fast rate of loan growth will swell the denominator of NPL ratio decreasing the overall ratio, while possibly masking a rise in NPLs in absolute terms.

Example and Illustration: Loan Growth Masks NPLs, NPLs Lag Behind Peak Loan Growth

Let us look at an imaginary bank in the Republic of Tropicola, an imaginary emerging market. Mango Planters Bank in Year 1 is growing at a rate of 43% per annum. Assume that at the end of Year 1, its NPL ratio is equal to 1.67%, and that the same year it begins a program of expanding its lending to small- and medium-sized enterprises and to finance automobile purchases by consumers and taxi purchases by small entrepreneurs. Competition for lending to blue chip companies is fierce and spreads are falling. But the SME and consumer loans are relatively high-risk credits, with higher default rates. Assume further that initially 2% of the low risk loans go to non-perform after the first year and 8% of high risk loans go to non-perform after the second year, but that poor economic conditions in Years 3 and 4 cause the rates to increase through Year 4.

During the first three years loan growth is rapid. Then, Tropicola is hit by a recession and the bank cuts back on lending. Years 4 and 5 see a contraction in the bank's loan book. An analyst looking at the bank in Year 1 might assume all is rosy. NPLs are a mere 1.67% and loan growth is brisk. But the rapid loan growth is itself a worry. The denominator (total loans) is growing faster than the numerator (NPLs), which are lagging 1–2 years behind. Even by Year 2, however, NPLs have jumped up over 4%. When the recession hits and the loan book contracts, the true picture is revealed as NPLs exceed 15%. In the aftermath of the recession, loans continue to sour at a rapid rate. In Year 5, this abates, but a contracting loan book pushes up the NPL ratio even more.

NPL Growth

Another indicator of asset quality is growth in NPLs in absolute terms. In addition to the NPL ratio discussed above, it is always helpful to look at total NPL growth. Beware of large increases in the rate of NPL growth due to a rise off a low base. For example, Bulletproof Bank had an NPL ratio in Year 1 of 0.1%. In Year 2, the bank's NPL ratio rose to 0.3%. The average among its peers is 1.9%. Despite the fact that Bulletproof Bank's NPLs tripled (rose by 200%), the bank remains relatively sound and it cannot reasonably be said to have an asset quality problem.

$$\frac{\text{NPLs in Year 2} - \text{NPLs in Year 1}}{\text{NPLs in Year 1}} \times 100 = \text{YoY NPL Growth (\%)}$$

Mango Planters Bank, Republic of Tropicola, a factious bank							
	Base Year	Year 1	2	3	4	5	
High Risk Loans*		200	400	600	630	567	High risk loans increase rapidly in FY3 and FY3
Low Risk Loans		944	1322	1388	1249	1062	Low risk loans increase rapidly in FY 1 and FY 2
Total Loans		1144	1722	1988	1879	1629	Total loans grow rapidly through Year 3 before declining somewhat through Year 5
New Loans			578	266	−109	−250	Rapid loan growth in Yr 3 & 4
Loan Growth, High Risk			100%	50%	5%	−10%	Loan growth from Yr 2 to 4
Loan Growth, Low Risk		18%	40%	5%	−10%	−15%	Rapid Loan growth Yr 1 & 2
Loan Growth, Overall		43%	50%	15%	−5%	−13%	Loan book contracts from Yr 4
New NPLs, High Risk		0	32	90	126	45	
New NPLs, Low Risk		19	66	97	100	22	New NPLs lag behind period of peak loan growth
Total NPLs for Year		19	98	187	226	67	
Cumulative NPLs assuming no write offs		19	117	304	530	597	Even NPL accumulation has write offs slowed, the NPL ratio rises sharply due to contraction in the loan book in Yr 4 and 5
NPL ratio		1.67%	6.79%	15.29%	28.21%	36.65%	
Assume Loan portfolio become non-performing at following rate		Yr 1	Yr 2	Yr 3	Yr 4	Yr 5	
Low Risk		2%	5%	7%	8%	2%	Rates decline in Yr 5 due to lack of new lending and expiration of extant loans
High Risk			8%	15%	20%	8%	

NPL Coverage

This ratio refers to the total (cumulative) level of loan loss reserves (not the annual provisioning) to NPLs. This ratio, sometimes referred to as NPL coverage, indicates the extent to which the bank's loan loss reserves will cover the default of all loans deemed non-performing. It may be high, and therefore afford a large cushion, because the bank has been especially prudent in setting aside loan loss reserves, even if the NPL ratio is average or above-average.

A heightened ratio of NPLs, while usually not desirable, does not necessarily mean that a bank has inferior asset quality overall. Bank management may have taken a decision to emphasize a sector such as the small- and medium-sized enterprise sector (SME) that will generate higher returns than, for instance, the blue-chip corporate sector, but at a higher expected rate of default. If the bank has provided adequate loan loss reserves to cover the higher *credit costs*, then its asset quality may, from a credit analysis perspective, be better than that of a bank with a lower rate of NPLs, but which has set aside a negligible level of loan loss reserves.

$$\text{NPL Coverage} = \frac{\text{Total Loan Loss Reserves}}{\text{Non-Performing Loans (NPLs)}}$$

Marigold Bank has NPLs amounting to $80 m. Its total loan loss reserves amount to $45 m. NPL coverage therefore is 45/80 or 56.25%.

Conversely, a bank may have lower than average NPLs, but if it has set aside a negligible level of loan loss reserves, NPL coverage could be unduly low. Such a bank, notwithstanding a low level of NPLs to total loans, may very well be viewed as having poorer asset quality overall. How much coverage is sufficient, as we have seen in our discussion of provisioning policy, above, the level of customary provisioning will vary from country to country. It depends upon the profitability of the bank and banking system as a whole, the stage of the economic cycle, as well as the character of the bank's business. Certainly, NPL cover that exceeds 100% can be regarded as fundamentally adequate. In emerging markets, many banks will not achieve that level, especially during depressed economic conditions. It might be said that an ordinary NPL coverage ratio of 50% can be regarded as minimally adequate during periods when a bank that is fundamentally profitable or particularly well-capitalized is aggressively provisioning against NPLs occasioned by a recession. In emerging markets, a ratio between 25 and 50% can be judged as having marginal asset quality, while one having less than 25% deserves careful inspection. The table below provides some rough benchmarks that should be applied with discretion.

Rule of Thumb: NPL Cover

NPL Cover	
>100%	Ample.
75–100%	Adequate
50–75%	Minimally satisfactory
25–50%	Weak
<25%	Poor

NPL cover

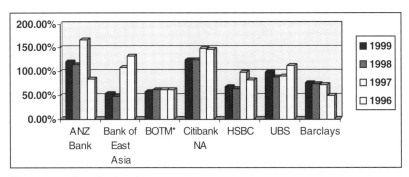

(Data source from Bankstat)

Example and Illustration, NPL Cover

The illustration below indicates the NPL and loan loss reserves for three hypothetical banks. Each has a loan book of $100 m. Carnation Bank maintains a very conservative loan book with just $3 m in NPLs or 3% of its total portfolio, a low ratio for the country of Floralia. (The average NPL ratio among banks in Floralia is 5% and the average NPL coverage ratio is 0.8 or 80%.) It has an equivalent amount of loan loss reserves, providing NPL coverage of 100%.

Orchid Bank's NPLs are just one percentage point higher than Carnation's at 4%. Its level of loan loss reserves is just $1 m or 25% of the outstanding NPLs. Magnolia Bank, in contrast, has significantly higher NPLs at 6% of book. Its coverage ratio is even higher than Carnations' at 133% of NPLs. Carnation's asset quality would seem to be significantly superior to that of Orchid, when NPL coverage is considered.

Although Carnation certainly appears to have good asset quality and strong provisioning, it cannot definitively be said that its asset quality is necessarily better than Magnolia's. To be sure, its NPL level is less than half that of Magnolia's, but Magnolia's NPL coverage seems to be more than adequate to cover any foreseeable loan losses. It may be that Carnation Bank has a franchise in blue chip corporate lending, where its spreads are thinning as a consequence of sharp competition, but that Magnolia has carved out a growing franchise in the consumer and middle markets, where it enjoys hefty profits.

Of course, more information would be needed to come to an opinion about which ranks better in asset quality. The point is that though that the bank with the lowest NPLs does not necessarily have the best asset quality.

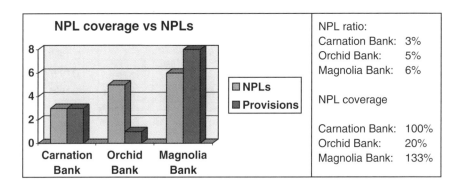

Tip: NPL coverage indicates the depth of the cushion of loan loss reserves relative to non-performing loans. A ratio of over 100% is good, and 50% to 100% generally satisfactory. Under 50% NPL coverage raises warning signals.

Another Coverage Ratio: Loan Loss Reserves Plus Equity to Non-Performing Loans '

Loan loss reserves are the first line of defense against a rash of NPLs. But if a bank has not provisioned adequately against dud loans, then it must dig into its capital. Shareholders' equity is the second and last line of defense against a rising tide of sour assets. Therefore, as a matter of principle, a bank should have a loan loss reserves + equity to NPL ratio that exceeds 100%. If it is less than 100%, this means that if all NPLs were total losses (0% recovery), then loan loss reserves and equity would be exhausted before outstanding obligations to depositors and other creditors would be satisfied. In other words, the bank would be technically insolvent. Hence, this ratio has been referred to as the "dead bank ratio."

$$\text{Dead Bank Ratio } (\%) = \frac{\text{Loan Loss Reserves} + \text{Equity}}{\text{Non-Performing Loans (NPLs)}} \times 100$$

Durian Planters Bank has NPLs of \$350 m. Its loan loss coverage amounts to \$200 m, and it has further shareholders' equity of \$100 m. Together, the bank's \$300 m of equity and reserves is less than its outstanding NPLs. With a dead bank ratio of 85.7%, it may be technically insolvent, depending upon the expected recovery rate on the non-performing assets.

Of course, realistically, not all NPLs will result in 0% recovery and so some degree of conservatism is built into the 100% benchmark. In addition, so long as the bank has access to liquidity, it can continue to operate as a going concern, notwithstanding a theoretical shortfall in its ability to cover problem loans. But as we have noted, it is hard to predict when NPLs will peak, so it is probably fair to insist that banks which are to be considered the most creditworthy meet or exceed this standard.

Key point: The Loan Loss Reserves + Equity to NPL ratio, including as it does both loan loss reserves and equity in the denominator, gives the analyst a reasonable idea of the bank's ability to survive a worst case scenario in which NPLs rise to unanticipated levels.

SUPPLEMENTARY ASSET QUALITY RATIOS

In addition to the preceding ratios, some additional formulae can aid the analyst in refining the asset quality profile of a bank.

Non-Performing Assets to Total Loans (or to Total Assets)

Because the NPL ratio, though commonly used, is subject to manipulation by the manner in which banks classify NPLs, substituting non-performing assets rather than NPLs in the foregoing three ratios will give the analyst an even better idea of the ability of the bank to withstand rapid erosion of the quality of its loan book. The reason we have not included it in the preceding section is that in many markets it can be difficult to obtain figures concerning "restructured loans." Data on foreclosed assets, too, is not always available. While NPL data is also not necessarily easily obtainable, it is one of the most popular indicators employed by regulators, analysts and the financial press in discussing bank asset quality, and is frequently available when figures on restructured loans are not.

Non-performing assets, as we define them here, are meant to be an approximation rather than a perfect calculation. Non-performing assets can be approximated by adding NPLs, foreclosed assets, and restructured loans. To be sure, some restructured loans may currently be performing, while foreclosed assets can be offset against loan losses. Yet, NPLs are a flawed measure of loan losses as well do not capture loan write-offs although this omission is offset to a degree by including foreclosed assets. In addition, the cost of maintaining foreclosed property will not necessarily be reflected in the financial statements of the bank as a credit cost. Instead, it may appear as "other non-interest expense. Although including all of these items as non-performing assets may seem unduly conservative, in many markets the prevailing tendency is to under-report non-performing assets so this measure may serve to compensate for that bias.[11]

Non Performing Assets and the NPA Ratio

$$\text{Non-Performing Assets (NPAs)} = \text{NPLs} + \text{Restructured Loans}^{12}$$
$$+ \text{Foreclosed Assets}$$

---

[11] In certain developed markets, notably the US, NPLs would normally encompass the items that NPAs as defined below attempts to take in, the "pure" NPL component being termed non-accruing loans. These differences in definition are responsible for much confusion and many seeming differences in figures, particularly in media reporting.

[12] Loan that have not returned to performing status optimally might be deducted.

$$\text{NPA Ratio} = \frac{\text{NPAs}}{\text{Total}} \quad \text{NPA Coverage} = \frac{\text{Loan Loss Reserves}}{\text{NPAs}}$$

Ratios corresponding to NPL coverage and Equity + Loan Loss Reserves/NPLs can be calculated as follows:

$$\text{Dead Bank Ratio (variant)} = \frac{\text{Equity + Loan Loss Reserves}}{\text{NPAs}}$$

The dead bank ratio although an asset quality ratio also reflects a bank's solvency and highlights the link between the two aspects of bank credit analysis. When non-performing assets exceed a bank's provisions and equity, it is technically insolvent and without a source of liquidity not far from collapse.

In order to obtain a clearer view of the breakdown of NPAs, the following sub-ratios can be tracked. Note that foreclosures and restructured loans typically lag behind NPLs, so that when foreclosures and restructured loans have peaked, a recovery is probably well underway.

Foreclosed Assets to Total Loans

Foreclosed assets are denominated in different ways and treated in different manners depending upon the market. In the United States, the term OREO is used to refer to Other Real Estate Owned, real estate being as in all countries, one of the most common forms of property used to secure a loan. Other terms are prevalent depending upon the jurisdiction. In the Philippines, for instance, the term ROPOA, real estate and other property owned or acquired, is a more all-encompassing term that is equivalent to foreclosed assets.

Restructured Loans to Total Loans

Although data on restructured loans can be more difficult to obtain than data on NPLs and foreclosed assets, if available, it is a helpful ratio to monitor, since cosmetic loan restructuring (i.e. mere loan rescheduling) is

---

How should the bank and the bank analyst account for foreclosed assets?

When a bank forecloses on a loan, it should recognize as a loss the difference between the value received through the sale of the foreclosed assets and the carrying value of the loan (i.e. the difference between the amount the bank should have received in interest and principal and the amount it had received). Best practice is for any foreclosed assets acquired to be disposed of quickly. Recoveries from such sales of collateral should be reported as *other income*.

In many emerging markets, however, foreclosure is deferred for long periods of time or their sale may also be delayed indefinitely. Consequently, loan losses may either not be recognized since the collateral is either not sold, or an estimated value is substituted for actual sale or appraised value in establishing the loss on the loan. In both cases, loan losses will probably be underestimated.

To remedy this, the NPA ratio defined above can be used in an attempt to bring asset quality measures more in line with those used in developed markets. In other words, by including all foreclosed assets held by the bank as part of the bank's non-performing assets, together with non-performing loans and restructured loans, whether performing or not, the analyst has at his disposal a conservative rule of thumb to measure the extent of erosion of the bank's asset quality.

---

one of the most common tactics banks in emerging markets employ to hide NPLs.

Net Write Offs to Loans

This ratio is of more assistance in gauging a bank's write off policy than in assessing asset quality. Banks vary in the aggressiveness of their write off policy, which is to a large degree dependent upon the regulatory and tax regime in which they operate. For instance, in the United States at present, write offs of bad loans are tax deductible while loan loss provisioning is not. In other markets, it is the reverse. Even where write offs are encouraged, the ratio does not indicate whether the write offs are the result of forward looking prudence or after the fact remedial action. Low write offs may mean that there is a disaster waiting to happen, while high write offs may mean that the loan book has been cleaned up. In addition, write offs will lag behind new loan growth so the significance of increasing write offs may be masked in the same way as rising NPLs.

Provisioning Ratios

Provisioning, as we have seen, should be distinguished from provisions, i.e. (cumulative) loan loss reserves. We have already discussed the ratio of loan loss reserves to NPLs or to problem assets, which are excellent indicators of the cushion the bank has built up against loan losses resulting from NPLs. When NPL data is not available, the analyst may only have access to provisioning figures. Unfortunately, provisioning ratios say little in themselves. Without knowing the bank's proportion of NPLs, it is impossible to discern whether a high level of provisioning evidences conservatism — that the bank is prudently building up its loan loss reserves against some potential adverse event — or whether it indicates that the adverse event has already occurred and the bank is scrambling to restore reserves that have been (or will soon be) lost due to write-offs. Nonetheless, an analyst may have to rely to some extent on the succeeding provisioning ratios to get a rough and ready measure of the bank's credit costs.

Loan Loss Reserves to Total Loans

This ratio measures the total level of cumulative loan loss reserves to total loans. In some markets, as mentioned, the regulators require banks to reach a certain level of gross provisions, while some regulators cap the level of gross reserves such that additional provisioning beyond that level is no longer tax deductible. This is a conspicuous disincentive to additional provisioning. By itself, the ratio does not tell the analyst very much, since the level of the NPLs is the key variable, but it can be useful for comparison purposes.

$$\text{Loan Loss Reserves to Total Loans (\%)} = \frac{\text{Loan Loss Reserves}}{\text{Total Loans}} \times 100$$

Loan Loss Reserves to Net Loan Write-Offs

This ratio is of limited use, because write-offs and the amount set aside for additional reserves can vary considerably from year to year for a variety of reasons. In addition, in countries that do not encourage the rapid write-off of impaired loans, it is even less useful. Longer-term averages can be beneficial, however, to show trends in the bank's credit costs and may reflect upon the adequacy of reserves.

Provisioning to Total Loans

This ratio shows how much a bank is provisioning in a given year relative to total loans. Again, this is not a particularly relevant indicator because it ignores both NPLs and cumulative reserves. But it does give some idea of how hard a bank is trying to raise its overall reserves.

$$\text{Provisioning to Total Loans } (\%) = \frac{\text{Provisioning}}{\text{Total Loans}} \times 100$$

Year-on-Year Increase in Provisioning[13]

Like provisioning to total loans, this ratio mainly indicates how aggressively a bank is attempting to reserve against bad loans. But, again, it says nothing about past performance or NPL coverage.

Recoveries to Write Offs

The ratio of recoveries to write offs is an indication both of how aggressive the bank's loan write off policy is and the legal environment in which it operates. If write off policy varies considerably globally, in particular markets, it may be useful in comparing write off policies among peer banks.

RELATION OF ASSET QUALITY TO PROFITABILITY

It bears repeating that bad asset quality can impinge upon bank profitability by reducing interest income revenue received and by burdening the bank with higher provisioning costs, thereby diminishing net profits. Correspondingly, bank profitability can be a factor in evaluating asset quality. In theory, a highly profitable bank should be able to absorb a high rate of loan losses and still come out ahead. This is another way of saying that a bank that focuses on high risk, high yield lending may have better asset quality than a bank with comparatively low risk, low yield earning assets, *if* it properly prices its credit costs and thereby its loans.

---

[13] Note that ratios not illustrated here for reasons of space can be found in the ratio compendium, part of the bank analyst's toolbox that can be found in the appendices to this book.

At heart, when we appraise asset quality, we are doing so to arrive at a judgment about total creditworthiness. In essence, we are looking at the extent of a bank's bad loan problem and the means it can bring to bear to overcome that problem. Loan loss reserves and shareholders equity are two bulwarks against bank failure. A third is profitability. A more profitable bank will be better able to withstand a crumbling loan portfolio by earning its way out of it, restoring capital and loan loss provisions in the process. Hence, all other things being equal, a highly profitable bank can be seen as having better asset quality than one that is less profitable.

A helpful ratio in this regard is pre-provision profits to net loans. Pre-provision profits, sometimes referred to as earnings before provisions and taxes and (EBPT) as we have seen, refers to net income prior to additional loan loss reserves (provisioning) being set aside. The term EBPT is synonymous with net operating income (so long as provisioning costs are not included as part of non-interest expenses). EBPT is a key indicator of a bank's underlying earnings capacity. The higher the EBPT to net loans ratio, the more bad loans a bank can afford to write-off in a given year. For example, a bank with a ratio of EBPT to net loans of 4% can to provide against or write-off 4% of its loan book every year. In other words, it can, in theory, afford an increase in its NPL ratio of 4% before it has to dig into existing reserves to cover loan write-offs.

$$\text{EBPT to Total Loans } (\%) = \frac{\text{Net Operating Income} + \text{Provisioning}}{\text{Total Loans}} \times 100$$

Observe, however, that a track record of high EBPT does not ensure that it will continue in the future. High loan yields may shore up EBPT, but as soon as loans begin to go sour, this figure may fall together with net interest income.

EBPT to Total Loans

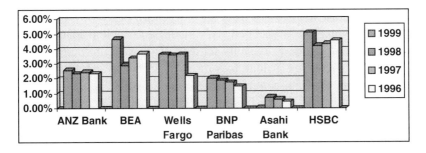

Earnings Coverage of Loan Losses

> (Operating Income i.e. EBPT + Loan Loss Provisioning)/Net Write Offs

This ratio also links asset quality to profitability. The problem with the indicator is that write off policies vary substantially for the reasons noted above, and may also vary from year to year. The principle of taking into account core profitability when assessing the significance of a given rate of problem loan creation remains valid, however.

CHAPTER SUMMARY AND CHECKLIST

In the previous chapter we examined asset quality, the key element of bank credit analysis, from a qualitative perspective. In this chapter, we look at it from a quantitative perspective. In the first part of the chapter, we explore the concepts of classified loans, provisioning, loan loss reserves, accrued interest and interest in suspense, interest income clawbacks and write-offs.

What is a problem loan? When a bank's loan to a customer becomes overdue for a certain period of time, it will be classified as problematic. The most common designations for classified loans are: substandard, doubtful and loss. In addition, in some countries, the classification "special mention" may apply to loans that are not overdue for the minimum time period but where there is an indication that the customer may face imminent financial problems affecting its ability to repay the loan to the bank.

Simplified Problematic Loan Terminology

Loan loss reserves are accumulated through loan loss provisioning that comes out of net profits. Most banks set aside both general provisions (reserves against loan losses affecting the entire portfolio) and specific provisions, which are associated with identified problem loans. When a loan is written off, the provisions set aside against it are deducted from total loan loss reserves. If loan loss reserves are insufficient, the must be deducted from the bank's equity.

Once a loan is deemed non-performing, interest income accrual normally ceases, and interest income already accrued must be reversed

Allowance Policies: Checklist for Bank Examiners

1. Has the board of directors, consistent with its duties and responsibilities:
    a. Established a comprehensive and well documented process for maintaining an adequate allowance?
    b. Established an effective loan review system that will identify, monitor, and address asset quality problems in an accurate and timely manner?
    c. Established procedures for the timely chargeoff of loans that are confirmed to be uncollectible?
    d. Defined collection efforts to be undertaken after a loan is charged off?

Loan Chargeoffs
2. Is the preparation and posting of any subsidiary records of loans charged off performed or reviewed by persons who do not also:
    a. Issue official checks and drafts singly?
    b. Handle cash?
3. Are all loans charged off reviewed and approved by the board of directors as evidenced by the minutes of board meetings?
4. Are notes for loans charged off maintained under dual custody?
5. Are collection efforts continued for loans charged off until the potential for recovery is exhausted?
6. Are periodic progress reports prepared and reviewed by appropriate management personnel for all loans charged oft for which collection efforts are continuing?

Allowance Evaluation Process
7. Does the bank have a written description of the process and methodology used by management to determine the adequacy of the allowance?
8. Does management review the adequacy of the allowance and make necessary adjustments at least quarterly and report the findings to the board of directors before preparing the report of condition and income?
9. Does management retain documentation of its review of the adequacy of the allowance?

Conclusion
10. Is the foregoing information considered an adequate basis for evaluating internal control in that there are no significant additional internal auditing procedures, accounting controls, administrative controls, or other circumstances that impair any controls or mitigate any weaknesses indicated above (explain negative answers briefly, and indicate conclusions as to their effect on specific examination or verification procedures)?
11. Based on a composite evaluation, as evidenced by answers to the foregoing questions, internal control is considered — (good, medium, or bad).

Source: Comptroller's Handbook

	Normal / Pass	Special Mention	Substandard	Doubtful	Loss
Functional Characteristics	OK	Borrower experiencing problems	Definite possibility of less than payment in full	Payment in full doubtful	Non-viable asset albeit some recovery may be made
Days overdue	< 90 Normal/ Pass	< 90 Special Mention	90–180 Substandard	180–360 Doubtful	>360 Loss

Classified Loans

Non Performing Loans/Problem Loans/Non Accrual Loans

Impaired Loans

Bad Loans

(clawed back). Accounting treatment varies from country to country. In some countries, after a loan is deemed non-performing interest accrued may be put into an interest in suspense account, which is equivalent to provisioning.

At its essence, quantitative analysis of asset quality is about assessing the bank's loan default rate and ascertaining whether it is covering its credit costs either through adequate provisioning or adequate pricing. Adequate pricing will only help the bank, however, if it results in net profits that are retained as internally generated capital.

Leaving aside analysis of loan portfolio composition discussed in the previous chapter, the most important quantitative indicators applicable to appraising asset quality are:

- Loan growth
- NPL growth
- The NPL ratio
- NPL coverage

As always, these indicators should be examined for the emergence of trends and compared among banks within a peer group through the lens of various ratios to discern trends and rank the bank against its peers. In addition, especially in emerging markets where detailed disclosure and

Interview and Questionnaire Checklist

❑ What was the bank's loan growth last year? What is projected in the current or forthcoming year?

❑ What is the bank's lending strategy?

❑ Does the bank have written lending policies and strategies?

❑ What sectors or business segments, in management's view, constitute the riskiest portions of the bank's loan portfolio?

❑ What is the composition of the bank's loan portfolio by borrower type, loan type and sector?

❑ Are there any types of borrowers, loans or sectors that the bank avoids?

❑ What is the bank's largest problem loan?

❑ What is the bank's largest commitment?

❑ How are loans approved? Is there a committee structure? How does it work?

❑ What are management's policies on loan underwriting, review, collection, write-off and recovery? Have there been any recent changes? Are any planned?

❑ How does management control sector exposure and avoid over-concentration?

❑ How does the bank classify loans? How does it define a non-performing loan?

❑ What is the total volume and percentage of loans are in each classification? What percentage is non-performing, restructured, or foreclosed?

❑ How much discretion does the bank have in loan classification vis-à-vis regulatory requirements?

❑ What is the bank's total percentage of NPLs?

❑ Has the percentage of NPLs increased? If so, why? How does the bank compare with its peers? Has it decreased? If so, why? What sectors or types of borrowers are responsible for a disproportionate volume of NPLs?

❑ What are the bank's provisioning policies? What is the bank's target NPL cover?

❑ Are there any disincentives (e.g. tax-related) to full provisioning?

❑ What amount was set aside for loan loss provisioning last year? How was this determined?

❑ What was the amount of loans written off last year? What is projected for the current year?

❑ What is the bank's policy on writing off loans? What time thresholds, if any, are employed?

❑ What are the bank's policies on restructuring and foreclosing loans?

❑ What percentage of the bank's total loans were restructured? What was the total number?

❑ What was the total amount of foreclosed assets on the bank's balance sheet?

❑ What is the bank's historical recovery rate on loss loans? How are recoveries accounted for?

❑ If a loan is restructured, what criteria, if any, must be met before that loan is deemed performing?

❑ What is the relapse rate on restructured loans?

Note: Many of the foregoing items, particularly quantitative ones, can be found in the bank's financial statements. If that is the case, the interview with management should focus more on policy-related matters.

best credit practices may be lacking, attention should be paid to non-performing assets including restructured loans and foreclosed assets that may not be included in NPL figures.

The analyst faces a number of potential difficulties in assessing a bank's asset quality. Disclosure may be limited. Regulatory standards and definitions of non-performing loans and relevant financial indicators may vary or change. Loan growth may mask the build up of NPLs. It may be difficult to ascertain whether an increase in provisioning evidences prudence or is making up for a lack of it. In emerging markets especially, evaluating a bank's asset quality is more art than science.

The checklist on the following page can be used by the analyst to assist in the process of evaluating a bank's asset quality, particularly during a meeting with bank management.

---

[i] Note that ratios not illustrated here for reasons of space can be found in the ratio compendium, part of the bank analyst's toolbox that can be found in the appendices to this book.

CHAPTER ELEVEN

CAPITAL: CUSHION AGAINST LOSS

Capital as an issue is more important in the financial centers than it is in emerging market countries, yet analysts reach for capital as a measure of bank performance before any other figure is considered.... [This is] due to a belief that a bank's capital is in some way linked to a bank's 'soundness', safety or performance ...[a corollary of] belief in 'the myth of capital' — that it is a panacea of a bank's ills and a supreme indicator of the market's confidence ....The nature of capital runs counter to these beliefs.
— Howard Palmer, *Bank Risk Analysis in Emerging Markets*[1]

One common misconception is that the higher the level of capital, the stronger the bank, regulatory solvency being considered as the defining factor for bank safety. This however is an analytical shortcut that most often leads nowhere and in fact has repeatedly been proven wrong. ... [There is] no automatic correlation between a bank's level of regulatory capital and its credit rating.[2]
— Moody's Rating Methodology

Because capital serves different purposes and because the relative importance of those purposes may differ among customers, managers, owners and regulators, complete agreement is lacking on exactly how capital should be defined.
— Mona Gardner & Dixie Mills, *Managing Financial Institutions: An Asset Liability Approach*[3]

THE IMPORTANCE OF CAPITAL

Much obeisance is given to the importance of banks maintaining robust levels of capital. Banks tout their capital levels as a sign of financial soundness, and indicators such as the Basel Committee's capital adequacy

---

[1] Howard Palmer, *Bank Risk Analysis in Emerging Markets* p. 101.
[2] Moody's Rating Methodology, p. 36.
[3] Mona Gardner & Dixie Mills, *Managing Financial Institutions: An Asset Liability Approach*, p. 481.

ratio, which was only established in 1988, have acquired talismanic significance.[4] But why is this so? What makes capital seem so important?

A number of reasons suggest themselves. First, as we have noted throughout this text, the exceptionally high leverage that banks employ — which, of course, is a function of a low capital to asset ratio — makes them extremely vulnerable to financial reverses. Because bank capital's primary function is its ability to absorb economic shocks — any losses a bank suffers ultimately can be written off against capital — an adequate supply would seem to obviate much of the need for more specific controls over risk.

Second, the nature of the fractional-reserve banking business — which is the type of banking business that virtually all commercial banks engage in — is such that in the event of distress, banks have few tangible assets with which to meet their obligations to creditors, while a large proportion of their financial assets will be comparatively illiquid and susceptible to erosion in value without constant monitoring. This elevates the importance of bank capital in times of difficulty.

Third, the allocation of capital figures strongly in the ability of banks to compete with each other. By reducing the amount of capital supporting its assets, a bank can increase its return on investment to shareholders and at the same time reduce the cost of new equity. Banks, consequently, have a natural inclination to minimize equity capital. Similarly, it follows that, absent any minimum global standards (which now exist) differences in capital requirements from one jurisdiction to another, through a lower cost of capital, can give banks in one country a competitive advantage over those in another.[5]

Finally, capital levels are perhaps the aspect of bank financial condition most easily subject to control by bank supervisors, and they have a long tradition of being used as measures of financial strength. The very perception that a bank is robustly capitalized is likely to increase the confidence of its depositors and creditors. Since confidence, wherever derived, is essential to the survival of fractional reserve banking, the

---

[4] The Basel Committee refers to the Basel Committee on Banking Supervision, a panel of regulators from the Group of Ten (G10) countries that usually convenes at the Bank of International Settlements (BIS) in Basel, Switzerland. The Committee established the first international standards on the capital adequacy of banks in 1988, in the form of a risk-weighted capital adequacy ratio (CAR). Although the standards and the CAR have nothing to do with the BIS per se, for convenience' sake the ratio is often referred to as the BIS ratio, the BIS capital adequacy ratio, or as the BIS CAR.
[5] This can occur in cross-border transactions or where banks having a lower cost of capital have entered into a foreign market.

mystique of capital survives. Whatever the reasons, there is no doubt that regulation of bank capital is a favored tool of regulators as a means to maintain the satisfactory financial condition of the banks under their charge.[6]

In view of its perceived significance and of the importance of the perception of confidence to a healthy banking system, it should be emphasized that relevant questions are raised when a bank has taken insufficient pains to build up capital to proportions comparable to its peers. Most bank analysts do therefore pay a great deal of attention to capital adequacy, even though from an analytical perspective it is but a single building block of bank creditworthiness.

Capital then, for the reasons given, certainly does have considerable importance. But it is not the be-all and end-all of bank financial creditworthiness, and it may be over rated as a measure of a bank's financial condition. To understand why, the analyst needs to comprehend the function capital fills for banks, how it is measured and whether high levels of capital will actually protect the bank in the event of difficulties. This is one area of bank analysis where it is especially important to keep in mind first principles, as well as to look behind the numbers and see how they were derived. The discussion that follows explores these issues.

INVESTMENT CAPITAL VS. BANK REGULATORY CAPITAL

Capital Defined

What is capital? The meaning depends on the context, and to some extent the country. Capital in the ordinary business sense of the word refers to funds invested in an enterprise. In this general sense, it encompasses both the debt and equity of a corporation. Hence, the term "loan capital" — used more often in British English than in American — is used to refer to financing acquired by a company from other than shareholders. (The term more common in American usage would be "debt.") In the milieu of accounting and investment, the term "capital" alone is usually synonymous with "net worth," "equity capital" or "share capital." As such, it refers to shareholders' legal claims upon a firm's assets. The claims of shareholders, of course, are subject to the claims of creditors and depositors, and form a residual right to all profits and (on liquidation) to all assets. But the shareholders must also absorb all losses and upon liquidation

---

[6] Commercial Bank Examination Manual, Section 3020.1

there may be nothing left for them after creditors claims have been satisfied. Remember, the company or bank as the case may be, is merely a legal creation, a vehicle which holds assets that are either subject to claims by creditors (including the government for taxes) or shareholders.

From an ordinary accounting perspective, therefore, "capital," meaning *capital stock*, is usually equated with equity and is the difference between a firm's assets and its liabilities. In both the investment and accounting contexts, capital or, to be more precise "equity capital" represents the shareholders' claims upon an enterprise's assets, and "capital accounts represent the owners' (stockholders') share of the business."[7] Used in this latter sense, capital is *initially* composed only of *paid-in capital* (also known as *share capital* or *contributed capital*), the amount that was paid into the company by its founding shareholders.

Paid-in capital equals *legal capital,* i.e. *stated capital*, or the number of issued shares multiplied by the par value of the shares plus *surplus.* Surplus refers to the amount contributed for shares in excess of stated capital or legal capital. Paid-in capital (stated capital + surplus) is not available for distribution to shareholders, except upon liquidation.

As the bank or other company grows and presumably prospers, it will earn profits. Some profits will be paid out as dividends. The remainder will be accumulated as *retained earnings*, or in bank terminology, *undivided profits.* (They are sometimes called *earned capital* or *earned surplus*, the last not to be confused with *surplus.*) Retained earnings form a part of capital, a part that is internally generated. Collectively, all these items constitute *shareholders' equity.*

Regulatory Capital: An Artificial Creation

The foregoing definitions of capital apply to corporations generally, and are often in everyday investment and accounting settings. These definitions of capital, applicable to corporations universally, however, must be distinguished from bank capital as defined by regulation for prudential purposes, i.e. *regulatory capital.*[8] Regulatory capital embraces shareholders' equity but goes well beyond the clear cut definition of capital as the shareholders' residual interest in the assets of the corporation.

---

[7] Peter S. Rose, Commercial Bank Management, p. 136.

[8] Bank regulatory capital is specifically defined for public policy and supervisory purposes, and is not to be confused with capital as the term is understood in normal investment and accounting contexts. Although there is substantial overlap between ordinary capital and bank regulatory capital, it may be better to think of the latter as a separate and artificial construct.

Illustration: Basic Bank Capital Structure

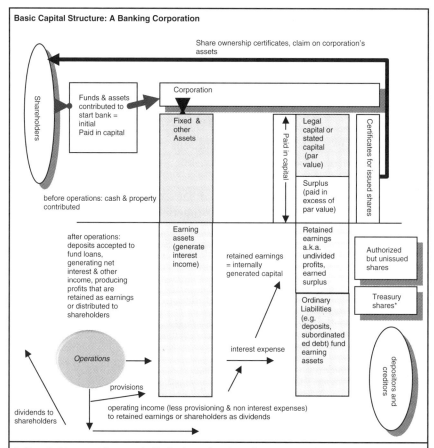

Basic Capital Structure: A Banking Corporation

1. Shareholders contribute capital in the form of cash and/or property to form bank in exchange for certificates of share ownership.
2. Paid in capital is comprised of legal capital, which equals the number of shares issued multiplied times the par value of each share (or alternatively, the stated value of the shares).
3. plus, Surplus, which is equal to the capital contributed less legal capital.
4. The funds and assets contributed as capital by the shareholders become the assets of the banking corporation, and represent claims on the bank's assets.
5. These assets are used to acquire premises and equipment, recruit staff and start operations
6. After operations commence, the bank acquires deposits to fund earning assets such as loans and securities, which generate interest income in addition to other revenue generated by commission and fee income operations.
7. Operations through off operating income, out of which interest expense to depositors and creditors and non-interest expense are paid. From net operating income, provisioning accounts for credit costs and the remaining net operating income is retained as internally generated capital or distributed to shareholders as dividends.

* Treasury shares are shares issued and then reacquired. Not all jurisdictions permit them.

For reasons we outline below, bank regulators in various countries and in international and regional bodies such as the Basel Committee on Banking supervision of the G-10 and the European Union have broadened the definition of capital to encompass considerably more than shareholders' equity. Bank regulatory capital, to be sure, includes the elements of shareholders equity which we have just discussed (paid-in capital, retained earnings, surplus and equity reserves), but it may also include a number of other line items that are not deemed to be capital other than from the frame of reference of bank accounting. Prior to the establishment of the 1988 Basel Accord, definitions of regulatory capital varied considerably from country to country, but in the years since there has been a considerable convergence.

The rationale for a broader view of bank capital has two bases. First, balance sheet items that have a similar function to shareholders' equity in affording a cushion against probable loan losses are deemed to be eligible to qualify as bank capital. One such item obvious item is *loan loss reserves*, also referred to as *loan loss provisions*.[9] Loan loss reserves, subject to limitations discussed in the succeeding chapter, may to some extent constitute part of bank capital under most various bank accounting regimes. As we mentioned in our discussion of the balance sheet, they are characterized in accounting terms as a *contra-account*, more particularly *contra-asset*, and represent a deduction from a particular category of assets, in particular a deduction from the asset category of loans.[10] Normally, as we observed, they will appear as a footnote to the asset side of the balance sheet. Note that although they are referred to as "reserves," loan loss reserves or provisions are wholly different from equity reserves, which fall within the category of capital.

Tip: Do not confuse shareholders' equity — capital as commonly understood in non-bank contexts — with bank regulatory capital. To understand the role of bank capital, it is critical to distinguish between capital defined as such for bank regulatory purposes, and capital that truly represents the owners' residual interest in the bank. Regulatory capital is an artificial construct, defined by bank regulators, and although it has a rationale for the elements it includes, it is a different creature than shareholders' equity.

---

[9] Note that loan loss reserves are distinct from equity reserves, which are defined as capital, even under the strictest definition of the term. They are funds set aside from earnings, and if unused, represent part of the shareholder's claims upon the bank's assets.

[10] A contra account, in this case a deduction against assets, allows the bank to report both the book value of its loan assets and their estimated net value (loan assets net of loan loss provisions).

Second, the inclination of banks to use of high levels of leverage unless constrained by regulation has induced regulators to include other balance sheet items as a defined form of capital that can be said to share some of the characteristics of equity capital as conventionally understood. On the one hand, this effort to broaden the definition of capital by banks can be characterized pejoratively as a form of window dressing, an attempt to make thinly capitalized entities appear to be better capitalized than they are in reality. On the other, it can be depicted as a legitimate attempt to both overcome the shortcomings of book value accounting — which limits the valuation of assets to their historical cost — by permitting the use of market-based accounting techniques. It can also be rationalized as looking at capital from a more functional than a formalistic vantage point, and as an attempt to answer the question: what is a capital standard attempting to accomplish?

In part, some of the items that have been allowed to be defined as capital by regulators do arguably embody capital-like qualities to a greater or lesser extent. Regulators have been persuaded that certain forms of long-term subordinated debt qualify as capital in this respect, subject to certain limitations. While long-term debt must be repaid just as depositors must be repaid, the long tenor means that there is little risk that immediate payment will be required. By providing additional funding, such debt affords some protection to depositors. Although it must be repaid eventually, arguably it does serve to stabilize funding to some extent and thereby provides some cushioning effect. Another more persuasive rationale for permitting some subordinated debt to be deemed to be regulatory capital is that subordinated debtholders are likely to keep a weather eye on the creditworthiness of the bank and provide an early warning signal should the banks credit situation deteriorate. These forms of subordinated debt consequently come under the rubric of what is known as Tier 2 capital under the 1988 Basel Accord and have been incorporated into the prudential regulations of numerous jurisdictions. The elements of regulatory capital will be delineated in detail when we examine the Bank of Basel Committee's Capital Adequacy Ratio and the corresponding definitions of Tier 1 and Tier 2 capital in the next chapter.

We have discussed how capital is defined in the ordinary corporate accounting and investment framework and how that definition differs from how capital is defined by bank regulators. There is still a third perspective to consider: what definition of capital makes sense from an analytical perspective? Just because certain balance sheet items are permitted to be defined as capital by regulators, and hence by bank accountants, does not mean that we as analysts should accept such a definition as holy writ. Not all accounting and regulatory definitions are meaningful from the credit analyst's point of view. For example, the concept of depreciation is well-accepted by accountants and regulators. Yet corporate credit and investment analysts often ignore depreciation and focus their attention on cash flow and the corresponding ability to service debt as a prime indicator of corporate creditworthiness. Similarly, as bank analysts, we need to have our own view as to how capital should be defined and how much is enough. Although we can make use of accepted accounting and regulatory definitions, we should not use them blindly. To arrive at a working definition of capital from an analytical perspective, let us re-examine in greater depth the purpose of capital and the function it performs.

THE PURPOSES OF CAPITAL

Why Banks Are Highly Leveraged

Banks are highly geared entities, and do not have much capital relative to their liabilities. When gearing is steep, the impact of small mistakes is greatly magnified. Consequently, banks must act with exceptional prudence to ensure their survival. But first why are banks so highly geared, second, what is the purpose of capital for a bank? The answer to the first question is easy. Banks are highly leveraged because banking is a commodity business, trafficking in the most fungible of all commodities: cash. The margins on supplying banking products to depositors and customers are extremely thin, much thinner than is characteristic of a manufacturing or service enterprise that arise as consequence of the bank's willingness to take risks on the basis of information it obtains as it intermediates between savers and borrowers. Consequently, in order for banks to make decent profits and compete for capital along with other industries, they need fairly high leverage to earn an adequate return on equity.

The Uses and Purposes of Bank Capital

To answer the second question, "what is the purpose of capital?" we can discern the following purposes.

- To purchase fixed assets and pay for start-up costs, and to fund expansion.

Illustration: Definitions of Capital

Capital	Capital as Equity	Bank Regulatory Capital
Everyday definition	Investment definition	Definition for bank regulation and supervision
❑ Funds invested or available for investment including equity or debt (e.g. loan capital)	❑ Shareholders or owners' claims on the assets of a business; their ownership interest	❑ Definitions vary with the regulatory regime, but typically include items that have a capital-like function, including core capital plus defined items:
	❑ Paid-in capital ❑ Undivided profits (retained earnings) ❑ Surplus ❑ Equity reserves	❑ Paid-in capital ❑ Undivided profits (retained earnings) ❑ Surplus ❑ <u>Equity reserves +</u> ❑ Loan loss reserves as defined by regulation ❑ Other defined items, including subordinated debt

- To function as a cushion against unforeseen future losses.

- To fulfill obligations to depositors (and other creditors) in the event of failure.

- To inspire confidence in depositors and creditors, regulators, and analysts.

To purchase fixed assets and pay for start-up costs, and to fund expansion

When a bank is formed, capital will be used to obtain a bank license purchase or lease the bank's premises, purchase equipment, pay staff obtain a bank license and for professional services, and begin operations. (In this respect, capital fulfills the same needs for a bank as it does for a non-financial corporation.) In a bank's early days, capital may even be used to deposit initial statutory reserves with the central bank, and to make loans and thereby start earning interest and revenues. From the day it opens its doors, however, the bank will start to borrow money by accepting deposits from depositors and other banks to fund its loans. As the bank grows, earning both interest and non-interest income, and becomes profitable, *internally-generated* capital will be added in the form of retained earnings. The shareholders may also inject additional capital in order to fund further expansion, or the bank may offer its shares to the public for the same purpose. Capital may be needed to finance the creation of new branches, acquisitions, or other fixed investment. Of equal importance, in order to maintain sufficient capital adequacy — whether demanded by regulators or the market — additional capital may be needed to fund loan growth. This can be accomplished directly by subscription in the case of an unlisted bank, or through a rights issue in the case of a listed one.

To function as a cushion against anticipated and unanticipated future losses

Capital is also necessary for a bank to be able to sustain operations, while absorbing losses such as those arising from non-payment of loans by customers. Loan losses reduce the value of the assets available to fulfill the claims of depositors and creditors. Such losses as discussed in the preceding chapters on asset quality can be aggravated during periods of economic shock or market volatility. Loan loss reserves act as a cushion, absorbing loan losses so that capital need not be tapped. Because they provide a similar loss-cushioning function to capital, loan loss provisions, subject to certain limitations, are included within the regulatory definition of capital. Indeed, it can be said that there are three lines of defense against loan losses: first, current profits (from which loan loss provisioning can be drawn); second, cumulative loan loss reserves; and finally, capital. (See illustration on following page.)

To fulfill obligations to depositors (and other creditors) in the event of failure

Closely related to the cushioning rationale is the need to provide some source of recovery for creditors should the bank be liquidated or reorganized. Bearing in mind that the proximate cause of most bank failures is a lack of liquidity, in the event of bank failure resulting from a liquidity shortfall, it is also highly likely (though not necessarily the case) that the bank will also be deemed insolvent.[10] In other words, its assets will be found insufficient to meet its liabilities (excluding shareholders' claims). In this case where a bank is liquidated, a bank's capital theoretically makes up for the deficiency and the bank will be able to meet its obligations to depositors. As in the previous case, current profits (if any) and loan loss reserves will be run down, followed by equity reserves, surplus, retained earnings and shareholders' capital until the claims of senior claimants are satisfied. If the shareholders are lucky, something may be left for them. In a worst case scenario, the depositors will come up short and nothing will be left for more junior creditors and shareholders.

Illustration: Lines of Defense Against Loan Losses

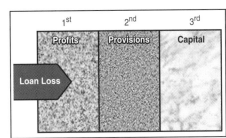

1st	2nd	3rd	Profits form the first line of defense against loan losses. New provisioning will be deducted from profit to compensate for identified likely loan losses or expected losses. Cumulative provisions (loan loss reserves) form the second line of defense. Write-offs of actual loan losses will come from here. Note that some portion of provisions is considered capital under current international guidelines. Finally, capital is the last line of defense before insolvency. Note also that loan capital may to some extent be classified as regulatory capital, but it will ultimately become additional claim against equity (rather than a defense) in the event of liquidation or reorganization.
Profits	Provisions	Capital	
Loan Loss			

To inspire confidence in depositors and creditors, regulators, and analysts

While the "myth of capital," as one commentator has referred to it, may inspire confidence on the part of depositors, regulators and analysts, there is a more plausible underlying explanation why superior capital may give greater comfort to each of these groups. The more capital bank shareholders have at risk, the more likely they will compel the bank's management to act prudently. Having their own capital at risk, shareholders' minds will be concentrated on the need to avoid risk. Another way of saying the same thing is that sufficient capital reduces moral hazard.[11] Likewise, the more capital the bank has at its disposal, the more likely it will gain the credibility of those who will be entrusting their own funds to it.

Once a bank has purchased its fixed assets, the purposes of capital can be conflated into a single phrase: *to provide a cushion against*

---

[10] See p. 258.
[11] See glossary.

(and reduce the risk of) collapse and thereby foster confidence in the bank.[12] Clearly, a measure of capital is necessary to accomplish this. The difficult part is gauging minimum and optimal capital strength relative to bank risks.

The Purposes of Capital

Bank Capital:

❏ serves as a **cushion** against losses — i.e. against the diminution in the value of the bank's assets through non-performance, when loan loss reserves fail to absorb estimable foreseeable losses — and ultimately against bank failure;

❏ initially provides start up funds to finance a bank's early **operations**

❏ reduces losses to state-sponsored deposit insurance programs by providing a means to **repay** the claims of depositors and creditors of a failed bank on termination; and[13]

❏ bolsters **confidence** in part by providing incentivizes for directors and managers to exercise the necessary prudence and impose reasonable controls.

Equity Capital

To reiterate, capital, in the conventional sense, what is often called shareholders' equity or equity capital, although other terms may also be used, represents the shareholders' claims upon the value of the business (assets — liabilities other than capital). This *core capital* is composed primarily of five primary elements.

Common stock (or ordinary shares) — common stockholders rank behind all other categories of stockholders and creditors in respect to their claims on the firm's assets and there is no entitlement to fixed dividend payment or to redemption of their investment; however, common stockholders have rights to all residual assets including ownership of the firm. For purpose of calculating capital on the balance sheet, common stock is valued at its nominal or par value.

---

[12] "The primary function of capital is to support the bank's operations, act as a cushion to absorb unanticipated losses and declines in asset values that could otherwise cause a bank to fail, and provide protection to uninsured depositors and debt holders in the event of liquidation." CBEM, Sec. 3020.1
[13] The figure of 8%, albeit in a different formula, was subsequently chosen by the BIS through the Basel Accord as a benchmark for bank capital adequacy among OECD member countries.

Preferred stock (or preference shares) — preferred stockholders are entitled to specified dividends that typically accrue if unpaid. Preferred stockholders have limited ownership rights; their shares, which are valued at par, may be perpetual or have a fixed duration. Some preferred shares closely resemble debt and to the extent they do, they may be viewed as a less pure or hybrid form of capital.

Surplus — gains from the sale of shares for more than their par value or stated values.

Retained earnings (undivided profits) — cumulative profits not paid out as dividends.

Reserves — cumulative reserves set aside from revenues. Equity reserves include contingency reserves, reserves set aside to pay dividends on preferred shares or to retire preferred shares or senior debt. They do not include loan loss reserves.

MEASURING CAPITAL STRENGTH: TRADITIONAL MEASURES

In the following traditional capital indicators, the terms "equity" and "capital" are used synonymously to refer to shareholders' equity.

Non-Risk Weighted Measures

The most basic ratios for measuring capital strength are *equity to assets,* and *equity to deposits.* The use of these ratios dates back at least to the early 1900s. In the United States, a ratio of one part capital to each ten of deposits became a rule of thumb of reasonable bank capitalization at the beginning of the century. The constraints of this rule became apparent as the American economy expanded after the Second World War, and the ratio came to be seen as outmoded.

Equity to Assets

Equity to total assets succeeded as the ratio of choice, and a ratio of 8% capital to total assets came to be favored as a benchmark within the US Federal Reserve system.[13] A variation of this ratio excludes preferred shares.

---

[13] See p. 264.

$$\text{Equity to Total Assets} = \frac{\text{Total Shareholders' Equity}}{\text{Total Assets}}$$

Leverage

The inverse of equity to assets is leverage. Leverage is defined as:

$$\frac{\text{Total Liabilities}}{\text{Total Shareholders' Equity}} = \text{Leverage}$$

The amount of leverage banks employ ranges widely among various banking systems and within sectors.

Illustration: Average Leverage Among Commercial Banks in Selected Markets, 1997

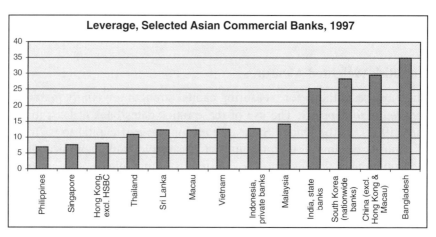

(Data Source: Thomson BankWatch, Survey of Asia's Commercial Banks, 1997.)

Analysts still use the equity to assets and leverage ratios especially in emerging markets, where if nothing else, a bank will invariably reveal its total assets and shareholders' equity in its annual report. They also remain of some use in making cross-comparisons within a bank peer group. The equity to assets ratios has a serious limitation, however. Keeping in mind that the purpose of capital is to provide confidence that the bank can absorb losses and maintain a cushion to meet its obligations (liabilities), the problem is that these ratios do not take account of the riskiness of the assets and the concomitant probability of loss. In other words, they are not risk-weighted capital adequacy measures. Under these traditional ratios, an asset is an asset no matter if it a US Treasury bill or a loan to Joe's Bar.

Traditional Capital Measures that Take Account of the Risk Level of Assets

Equity to assets and leverage to put it another way do not distinguish in any way among the type of the assets being compared with capital. Ratio analysis subsequently evolved to take account of the riskiness of a bank's assets to measure the relative strength of its capitalization. The first step in this evolution was the increasing use of two simple indicators: equity capital to total loans and equity capital to risk assets.

Equity to Loans

The rationale of using equity capital to total loans is that since loans are the riskiest assets banks generally hold, it is the proportion of capital to these assets that is relevant. Thus, the ratio of equity to loans above is a simple form of risk assets measure.

$$\text{Equity to Total Loans} = \frac{\text{Total Shareholders' Equity}}{\text{Total Loans}}$$

A slightly more refined approach, below, lumps loans and interest-earning assets other than government securities together.

$$\text{Capital to Risk Assets} = \frac{\text{Total Shareholders' Equity}}{\text{Total Assets} - (\text{Cash} + \text{Government Securities} + \text{Fixed Assets})}$$

IGRC: A Measure of the Link between Profitability and Capital

If a bank has an historic record of profitability and the ability to sustain similar earnings growth going forward, it will be able to earn itself out of most potential problems. Only a short-term liquidity crisis, most likely occasioned by a severe economic shock, could prove fatal. Otherwise, in most cases, over time, a bank will be able to rebuild its capital strength to satisfactory levels, again assuming reasonable profitability. Think about it this way. If, after dividend payout, a bank is able to generate a return on assets of 2.0%, it can effectively afford to write off at least 2.0% of its loan book each year, without impairing capital.[14]

Looking at it another way, assuming credit costs of 1.0% per annum, over a five-year period, the bank would be able to build up its capital roughly by 1.0% of assets per annum, increasing substantially over a period of time. Imagine that Freeport Bank, an imaginary institution, has to write off a substantial proportion of its loans against equity so that its equity to assets ratio is reduced from 9% to 6%. With ordinary credit costs of 1% and an ROA of 2%, 1% is left over to replenish capital. Year by year the bank would be able to rebuild its equity to asset ratio so that after three years it would be back to 9%.

Such a bank would probably have a high internal growth rate of capital (IGRC) enabling it to build or rebuild its capital base relatively quickly. Internal growth rate of capital, is closely linked to profitability, and refers to the rate at which a bank is able to retain its earnings and increase its capital. In other words, it is the retained earnings of the bank, i.e. net profit not paid out in dividends, as a percentage of shareholders' equity. As the hypothetical below illustrates, the IGRC can be viewed as equal to or of greater importance than indicators, such as equity to assets, which merely reflect the proportion of accumulated capital to risk assets at a particular time. It must be observed, however, that the IGRC is subject to large fluctuations and high historical rates of internal capital growth do not ensure future ability to replenish capital at the same rate as occurred in the past.

Definition of Internal Growth Rate of Capital

The internal growth rate of capital (IGRC), sometimes referred to as the equity generation rate, is equivalent to the retained earnings after dividend payout to shareholders as a proportion of shareholders' equity.

---

[14] Actually, return on loans would be the equivalent measure.

$$\frac{\text{After Tax Profit} - \text{Dividend Payout}}{\text{(Average) Total Shareholders' Equity}} = \frac{\text{Internal Growth}}{\text{Rate of Capital}}$$

The IGRC varies directly according to the dividend payout, which is sometimes itself used as an indicator of capital. It assumes greater relevance in the case of bank holding companies where the dividend payout from the bank to its parent holding company will be compared with that of other affiliates to the parent holding company and with the dividend payout of the parent holding company to its shareholders. An imbalance may be a sign of internal stress within the bank holding company.

$$\frac{\text{Dividend Payout}}{\text{After Tax Profit}} = \text{Dividend Payout Ratio}$$

Supplementary Traditional Capital Ratios

Other ratios which are sometime used to analyze equity capital include the following:

Equity Growth Rate and Asset Growth Rate

The overall rate of equity growth of the bank should be examined to understand whether shareholders' equity is rising or declining. The analyst might ask what are the sources of new equity? Has the bank been internally generating capital at a healthy rate, or has there been an infusion of new capital? Has the new capital come from a new public offering of shares, or have existing shareholders contributed more capital, for example, through a rights offering? Or, has capital increased through accounting legerdemain — through a revaluation of reserves for instance?[15] Similarly, the analyst should make note of any decline in capital, such as a weakening resulting from write-offs of loan losses.

---

[15] While an accounting revaluation may be justified as a result for example of the appreciation of real estate held by the bank for a long period of time, such revaluations should be scrutinized. In addition, other banks may have similar assets that could be revalued and if one bank revalues while the others do not, ratios may need to be adjusted before undertaking a peer comparison.

Example: The Importance of Internal Capital Generation

Imagine for example two financial institutions, Bank Lapin and Tortoise Bay Bank, both with assets of $1 billion. BL has an equity to assets ratio of 8%, while TBB has a ratio of 12% (equivalent to leverage of 12.5 × and 8.33 × respectively). Let us assume that 10% is the average equity to assets ratio for the banking sector, and that that level is considered to be a reasonable level of capital. In other words, BL has $80 m in equity and $1 billion in assets; TBB has $120 m in equity and $1 billion in assets. All other factors being equal, TBB would appear to have better capital adequacy. However, let us assume that TBB, the more conservative bank, has a return on assets of 0.8% while BL has an ROA of 2.0%. (Corresponding ROE would be 6.4%, i.e. 0.8% × 8.33 for TBB versus 25%, i.e. 2% × 12.5 for BL.)

Assume no dividend payout, no loan loss reserves, no taxes, and that capital is equal to shareholders' equity. With ROA of 1%, TBB's net profits are $8 m on $1 billion of assets while those of BL are $20 m on assets of $1 billion. The IGRC of TBB is 8/120 = 6.4%, while that of LB is 20/80 or 25%. In other words, if all earnings of TBB are invested back into capital, capital would grow from $120 m to $128 m, i.e. at a rate of 6.4%. Correspondingly, if all of LB's profits of $20 m are used to build capital, its shareholders' equity would grow from $80 m to $100, i.e. by 25%.

Suppose each suffers major deterioration in their loan books and has to write off 5% of its booked loans against capital: in other words, $50 m. TBB's capital is thus reduced to $70 m, while BL's is reduced to $30 m on total assets of $950 m. TBB thus has a new equity to assets ratio of just 7.4% (while LB's is reduced to 3.2%. If, however, each can maintain the same profitability as before, TBB will be able to earn $9.5 m per year while LB will earn $19 m per year on assets of $950 million. To achieve the target equity to assets level of 10%, TBB needs $30 m, while LB needs $70 m. Growing its capital at $8 m per year, it will take TBB more than four years to achieve the target, while LB will be able to do the same in just a little more than three years. In addition, with better returns available to investors, LB might be able to better attract new capital as well.

While equity to assets provides a good measure of a bank's static capital strength. IGRC is better able to show its resiliency. Although Tortoise Bay Bank appeared to be more robust. Lapin Bank's ability to bounce back from an economic shock meant that it could be viewed as comparably strong, despite having apparently weaker capital strength. Of course, in reality, numerous additional factors would come into play, such as the dividend payout ratio and LB's higher yield on assets probably comes at a cost. That cost might be a higher risk portoflio with higher credit costs. In addition, the IGRC tends to be higher the smaller the bank's capital base. All these considerations argue for applying the IGRC carefully. Nonetheless, this example illustrates the importance of taking account not just of present capital strength but also of the ability of the bank to earn its way out of trouble as reflected in its rate of internal capital generation.

Since capital provides support for assets, the rate of asset growth or decline should also be examined. Capital ratios can improve just as easily through a contraction in a bank's loan portfolio as they can from an infusion of new cash. Finally, a ratio that is sometimes used is that of long-term (i.e. subordinated debt to equity), which as we shall see in the next chapter is linked to the relationship between BIS Tier 1 and Tier 2 capital. This ratio mirrors the extent to which a bank can take on additional debt to meet anticipated funding needs.

CAPITAL VS. LIQUIDITY: INSOLVENCY RISK VS. LIQUIDITY RISK

Capital, in conclusion, forms a last line of defense against the risk of bank collapse or failure. When we look at capital, it is primarily for the purpose of measuring the strength and depth of that wall. Recall the types of risks a bank faces that could cause it to fail. Most notably, credit risk — the risk that a substantial proportion of a bank's customers will default on their loans — can cause the value of a bank's assets to become less than its liabilities thereby rendering the bank technically insolvent. Credit risk indeed is the most ubiquitous risk that banks confront and one that has the greatest potential to undermine their long-term survival.

But insolvency in and of itself will not bring a bank down, and will not necessarily result in a bank's failure, unless regulators force such an action. Unless a bank's retail or commercial depositors become convinced that there is a danger that their deposits will not be repaid and a bank run occurs, a bank's *technical insolvency* will remain latent. Absent regulatory action, banks can continue to function as long as they are supplied with sufficient liquidity. Accordingly, the manifestation of credit risk and accompanying solvency risk that may be engendered by a substantial portion of a bank's loans going bad will not be the proximate cause of bank failure.

A fairly sizeable number of Asian banks, as a matter of fact, are technically insolvent but continue functioning normally with state backing. As would be expected, unless strong supervision exists, banks that are technically insolvent, however, tend not to broadcast their true state of affairs, particularly in countries where appearances and saving face count for much. Instead, as capital has acquired a talismanic character, such banks are given an incentive to inflate capital indicators and to hide the volume of the non-performing loans (NPLs) in their loan book.

This accounts for much of the obfuscation and lack of disclosure in respect of NPLs, and for the skepticism with which capital ratios are justly viewed.

The Bank Run: Illiquidity Trumps Solvency

A bank run, however, can cause a bank to collapse. If depositors or creditors do panic, and a run on the bank is triggered, it is a shortfall of liquid funds that will cause a bank to close its doors. Let us assume hypothetically no deposit insurance exists in the relevant market, that a bank is technically insolvent and that this fact becomes known. Lines will form outside a bank's doors that may herald the beginning of a bank "run." Of course, once a panic begins, it feeds on itself, because the longer the line gets, the more probable that those who have not joined it will lose their deposits. Ultimately, the bank may very well fail and be forced to shut its doors. By the very nature of a fractional-reserve banking system, collapse though possibly triggered by a perceived technical insolvency will be the proximate result of a lack of liquidity.[16] Most of a bank's assets are in the form of illiquid loans, used to fund the purchase of fixed assets and provide working capital, and are not easily or rapidly liquefiable.

A bank, in theory, does not need to have any financial weakness whatsoever to experience a run. Even if, contrary to the hypothetical example, all loans are performing, as we have observed before, even the most prudent bank will not have sufficient cash in its vault or liquefiable on short notice to meet *all* depositors' claims. Suppose an entirely false rumor begins to circulate that Bank X was having financial problems. Bank X is actually in tip-top financial shape. Nonetheless, a line forms outside the bank's doors with depositors screaming for their deposits. If there is no lender of last resort to provide temporary assistance to Bank X, it will probably fail.

Nor does a bank run have to be the 1930s-style picture of panicked depositors queued up at the institution's entrance. Institutional lines of

---

[16] By fractional-reserve banking we mean ordinary commercial banking where banks lend out most of their deposits, and maintain only a fraction as a reserve against difficulties. Also note that though in our hypothetical example, the bank was technically insolvent, the critical point was that this fact became known, undermined confidence, and triggered the bank run. A rumor would have had the same effect, and bank runs can cause the collapse of a bank that is perfectly solvent.

credit can be called a bit more quietly, but the effects can be about as adverse to the bank concerned. A bank failure can, of course, result merely from the flight of commercial depositors, including other banks. The collapse of Continental Illinois and Franklin National Bank in the US during the 1970s and 1980s were triggered by the flight of such "hot money" or purchased funds rather than by runs by retail depositors, who were insured by public deposit insurance programs.[17] Whatever the cause, a run epitomizes the perils of liquidity risk, and it is this risk which is most often fatal to a bank's survival. Bank runs do not arise out of the blue, but are usually (though not always) based on legitimate concerns about a bank's financial condition. Obviously, liquidity risk and solvency risk are interlinked, and we shall address the subject of measuring liquidity in Chapters 13 and 14.

Because confidence counts for so much in banking, banks are highly zealous about maintaining their reputation. It is critical that a bank guard carefully against liquidity risk — the risk that it will not have sufficient current assets such as cash and quickly saleable securities to satisfy current obligations e.g. those of depositors — especially during times of economic stress. Effective risk management will permit the bank to avoid

---

The Importance of Confidence

Hong Kong is an example of a banking system where deposit insurance does not exist, and it comes as no surprise that Hong Kong banks maintain extremely high liquidity levels by international standards. The banks in the Special Administrative Region are also highly sensitive to the importance of maintaining depositor confidence. Some years ago, a local Hong Kong bank controlled by a foreign institution, was informed that its parent bank was planning a celebration to mark the anniversary of its founding, and had decided to provide a souvenir of the occasion to all of its depositors. Because of the close relationship between the two banks, the president of the parent bank suggested that the souvenir should be provided to the bank's Hong Kong depositors as well. The managing director of the local bank, however, objected. "If we offer our depositors a free souvenir, a line will form outside our doors. The public will think that there is a run on our bank!" The president's suggestion was quietly dropped.

---

[17] For an account of how Franklin National Bank failed, see Sanford Rose, "What Really Went Wrong at Franklin National", *Fortune Magazine*, October/November 1974, reprinted in Roger H. Hale, *Credit Analysis: A Complete Guide*, John Wiley & Sons, 1983.

liquidity shortfalls, except in the economic equivalent of a devastating cyclone, in which case government support may very well be forthcoming with the central bank functioning as a lender of last resort. This is crucial within banking systems that place strict limits on emergency funding or those in which deposit insurance has not been implemented.

CHAPTER SUMMARY

Capital has several definitions. In the context of bank credit analysis, it is important to make a distinction between equity capital (or equity) and regulatory capital. Regulatory capital is an artificial construct and can be defined in different ways. Under the Basel Committee's 1988 capital accord, in principle accepted by over 100 countries throughout the world, regulatory capital encompasses two key components. The first is core capital, or shareholders' equity, which includes paid-in capital, retained earnings and equity reserves. The second component includes other forms of defined capital including, to some extent, the bank's pool of loan loss reserves as well as, with limitations, subordinated debt. While regulators may define capital according to formulas of their own construction, bank credit analysts may legitimately take a more conservative view.

In addition to the functions capital performs in non-financial firms, i.e. to finance fixed investment, in a bank capital acts primarily as a cushion, absorbing losses, and providing a reserve out of which bank depositors and creditors may ultimately be repaid when losses can no longer be absorbed in case of bank failure. In many countries, retail depositors are provided insurance through any number of schemes, including government-financed programs. But in those markets where deposit insurance is non-existent or quite limited, bank capital, in principle at least, still fulfills this role. If deposit insurance does exist, the insurer will have a claim to the bank's assets and capital in place of the depositor, so the end result is the same. Because of capital's talismanic significance, it also bolsters confidence, a feature contributed to by the plausible assumption that the more shareholders have at risk in the bank, the more prudent they are likely to be in its management.

Current provisioning from profits and cumulative loan loss reserves provide initial lines of defense to absorb the bad loans that a bank will inevitably experience as mistakes are made and business conditions decline and improve. Bad loans can be written off against loan loss reserves without affecting shareholders' equity, and loan loss reserves thus function to smooth out the losses arising from the fluctuating value of its loan book. If a bank's asset quality problem becomes acute, however, the pool of loan loss reserves may be insufficient to permit all bad loans to be written off against them. The excess will have to be written off against shareholders' equity. This is where core capital becomes relevant to bank credit analysis. The greater the degree of the bank's capital strength, i.e. the higher the proportion of capital relative to the bank's assets, particularly to its risk assets such as loans, in general the better able the bank will be to survive and enable depositors and creditors to recover their funds in the event of its collapse. We can see that irrespective of regulatory formulations, the amount of capital a bank needs is to degree dependent upon its asset quality.

Capital can be measured in a number of ways and additional indicators are explored in the following chapter. Traditional capital measures assess shareholders' equity against assets or loans, or invert the formula to arrive at leverage or gearing. Such measures of capital strength must be applied carefully. A bank with seemingly higher capital ratios than another, but which has a lower internal growth rate of capital, may actually be the weaker of the two. The internal growth rate of capital is an important measure of the capital resilience, or the ability of the bank through its profits from operations to earn its way out of trouble. It is thus arguable that the more profitable the bank, the less capital it needs. The internal growth rate of capital directly correlates with the profit retained by the bank as returned earnings, and is therefore a function of the bank's profitability, its dividend payout ratio (the percentage of its profits it distributes to its shareholders as dividends) and the size of the bank's equity base. Paradoxically, the smaller the equity base, the larger the IGRC, so this ratio must be used with discretion and with reference to the bank's core profitability as measured by return on average assets.

CHAPTER TWELVE

CAPITAL ADEQUACY: THE BASEL ACCORD AND PROPOSED CHANGES

In the mid-1970s, American bankers began running into competition they could not understand. They encountered groups of banks that priced loans and extended credit in ways that made no sense. They were Japanese banks.
— R. Taggart Murphy[1]

"A well-managed bank needs no capital, whilst no amount of capital can save an ill managed bank."
— Walter Bagehot[2]

The capital of a bank should be a reality, not a fiction; and it should be owned by those who have money to lend and not by borrowers.
— Hugh Maculloch, US Comptroller of the Currency, 1863

Capital inadequacy in relation to the risks being run *is behind virtually every bank failure. ... That said, it is important to keep things in perspective. A bank's primary risks are not taken care of solely by throwing more capital at them. ... The most potent influence in boosting capital ratios has been the Basle framework itself ... Banks now have no choice but to maintain capital ratios possibly higher than economic need might otherwise suggest.*
— Eddie Cade[3]

---

[1] *Japanese Money*, p. 45.
[2] Quoted in Cades at p. 25.
[3] p. 25, 26, 29.

BACKGROUND TO THE 1988 CAPITAL ACCORD

Beginning in the mid-1970s, bankers in the United States and Europe began to face new and unprecedented competition. As R. Taggart Murphy, a former banker with Chase Manhattan recounts in his book, *The Real Price of Japanese Money*, Japanese banks were able to price loans at rates that Western bankers could not fathom. While Japanese manufacturing companies were becoming known worldwide as formidable competitors during the same period for their able to produce extremely high quality products for exports at affordable prices, the competitiveness of Japanese banks was something of a puzzle. The product of banks is a fungible commodity: money. How were Japanese banks able to price loans so low? It could not be efficiency. Anyone walking into a bank in Japan at the time could see that they were models of inefficiency — hugely over-staffed and lagging behind their Western counterparts in the adoption of technology. A simple retail banking transaction, like a foreign remittance, could take upwards of a half-hour. As bank analysis began to catch up with the increasing global reach and dominance of Japanese financial institutions the conclusion was reached that the reason Japanese banks could undercut their foreign competitors was that they were under-capitalized. With the firm promise of government support, these behemoth financial institutions were leveraged to the hilt.

Even before concerns, began to mount, efforts were already underway to strengthen international banking supervision. In 1974, following the fright inspired by the collapse of a small German bank active in the foreign exchange markets, the G10[4] central bank governors established the Basel Committee on Banking Supervision. In 1983, the Basel Concordat was formed by the G10 committee to provide a framework for international banking supervision through national banking authorities. By the mid-1980s, a consensus had formed among the G10 nations, given impetus by the perceived threat posed by Japanese banks, that a level playing field[5] concerning bank capital level was necessary. In December

---

[4] The G10 is actually a misnomer. Twelve countries comprise the group: 1) Belgium, 2) Canada, 3) France, 4) Germany, 5) Italy, 6) Japan, 7) Luxembourg, 8) the Netherlands, 9) Sweden, 10) Switzerland, 11) the UK and 12) the United States.

[5] French banks were also viewed as operating with unfairly low levels of capitalization. The Accord's "principal motivation was to ..persuade major Japanese and French banks to increase their equity capital, thereby achieving a more 'level playing field' ...." Fitch IBCA, untitled paper concerning frequently asked questions about the Basel Accord, 2000 ["FAQ"]

1987, initial proposals were published[6] and by June 1988, agreement was reached among the G10 to establish a minimum risk-weighted capital requirement for internationally active banks in the twelve countries. The Accord provided that by March 1993, the ratio of capital to risk weighted assets must be a minimum of 8%. To gain the assent of the Japanese authorities, a concession was made that allowed Japanese banks to count 45% of their "hidden reserves" as capital. At the time, the skyrocketing Tokyo stock market of which bank shares made up about 25% of the capitalization made this compromise attractive.[7]

Although the Accord was not enforceable by an international body — it has been remarkably successful. Even if not fully binding even on the original 12 members, it was implemented largely according to its terms. The European Union contributed to its acceptance by subsequently making the framework embodied in the Accord mandatory on all EU countries and required that member states enact national banking laws implementing it.[8] Ultimately over 100 countries worldwide have used the Accord (or a variant of it) as a bench-mark for their own national banking supervision, even though most of them did not participate in negotiating the accord and did not formally approve it.

THE CONCEPTS OF REGULATORY AND RISK-WEIGHTED CAPITAL AND THE 1988 ACCORD

The heart of the accord and the innovation that it made it so successful was its international standardization of a *risk-weighted* capital adequacy ratio. Until the accord was implemented, not only was there no international benchmark as to *how much* capital was a base minimum, there was not even agreement on what constituted capital for regulatory purposes. Countries varied widely in how they defined capital and reconciling the different approaches, even assuming that adequate disclosure was forthcoming which it often

---

[6] Basel Basel Committee on Banking Supervision, "International Convergence of Capital Measurement and Capital Standards" [The 1988 Basel Accord], June 1988. Two fundamental objectives lie at the heart of the Committee's work ... firstly ... to strengthen the soundness and stability of the international banking system; and secondly that the framework should be ... fair and have a high degree of consistency in its application to banks in different countries with a view to diminishing a source of competitive inequality among international banks." Section 3.

[7] The subsequent market crash in 1990 caused every Japanese bank to fall below the interim BIS guidelines by September of that year. *Japanese Money*, p. 190.

[8] FAQ, p. 2.

was not, was an analyst's nightmare. Whatever the deficiencies in the 1988 Accord's formula for defining capital and establishing a benchmark, by fostering a uniform definition and methodology for calculating regulatory capital adequacy, the Basel accord represented a great advance over what had existed before.

An Important Note on the Basel Accord

Methods of measuring capital adequacy are a work in progress. As this book was being written, The Basel Committee on Banking Supervision was in the process of revising its risk-weighted capital adequacy measures that have been in place since 1988. In June 1999 a preliminary proposal was published which engendered much controversy. In January 2001, the Committee issued a revised proposal for a New Basel Capital Accord that, once implemented, will replace the current 1988 Accord. If all goes as planned, the new Accord will go into effect in 2004. In Appendix C, we shall briefly discuss the new Accord and its ramifications. Meanwhile, however, the 1988 Accord (as amended by various revisions throughout the 1990s) remains in place, and therefore in this chapter we intend to explain how the capital adequacy rules as outlined in the 1988 Accord work, their impact on banks and the Basel committee's initial response to their deficiencies as expressed in its March 1999 proposal. It is not the intent to explicate the original accord in all its arcane detail, which in any case will be superseded by 2004. The Bank of International Settlements has made available numerous documents and hundreds of pages of text available concerning both the original accord, its amendments and proposed revisions. The reader is therefore referred to these materials for more detailed exploration. In this light, when we refer to regulatory capital in this book, unless otherwise specified, we are speaking of the approach to capital and the accompanying capital adequacy indicators set forth under the 1988 Accord and its amendments.

Components of Regulatory Capital

In the previous chapter, the importance of differentiating between core or equity capital, meaning shareholders' equity, and regulatory capital was noted. To put it in its most simple terms, what the Basel Accord did was to give an international importance to regulatory capital. It took what had been traditionally viewed as capital — shareholders' equity — and made that what is referred to in the Basel scheme as Tier 1 (core) capital. To equity capital, various other balance sheet items which arguably had capital-like characteristics were allowed to be defined as Tier 2 (supplementary) capital in the terms of the accord. The most salient of these were debt — namely debt junior to the claims of the bank's depositors and other senior creditors, i.e. subordinated debt — and so-called hidden reserves, which were of critical concern to Japanese bank regulators. By allowing these additional balance sheet items to be counted as capital, banks, of course, appeared to have more capital at their disposal than they had under the traditional measures.

At the same time, the concept of risk-weighting of assets reduced the bank's apparent assets, since certain types of securities and loans were deemed to have weightings of 0%, 20%, 50% or 100% of their actual balance sheet weight when calculating capital adequacy. This also tended to make the apparent capital to assets ratio of the bank look stronger.

For bank regulatory purposes, additional elements of capital qualify as Tier 2 capital, that may include:

❑ Loan loss reserves.

❑ Minority interests in consolidated subsidiaries.

❑ Subordinated debt — fixed income securities, the holders of which have claims against the bank's assets which are subordinated to, or follow, the satisfaction of all depositor claims; in some cases, such instruments may be convertible to common shares at the option of the holder.

❑ Equity commitment notes — a form of debt securities payable from the sale of equity securities; and, in some cases.

❑ Hidden reserves.

All capital, however, is not the same and the Basel arrangement implicitly recognized this by dividing regulatory capital into Tier 1 capital and Tier 2 capital. Tier 1 capital, or ownership capital, is more likely to function as an incentive to the owners to exercise prudent control of their managers, lest their own moneys be at risk. Indeed, it may seem somewhat odd to call debt "capital," since the debtholders certainly want their money back in the event of financial distress at a bank to which they have lent funds. This usage is actually not out of line with British usage of the term capital which often has the connotation of embodying "loan capital" (i.e. debt) and techniques such as EVA™ which looks to both debt and equity in valuing a firm and its return on capital. But Basel's inclusion of debt as a component of capital in the risk management context was something of an innovation for its time, notwithstanding some more rudimentary approaches to a broader definition of capital that had been adopted by various bank regulators.

From a credit analyst's perspective, Tier 1 capital or shareholders' equity still remains the key measure of the bank's ultimate capital cushion.

THE CAPITAL ADEQUACY RATIO

The Rosetta stone of the Basel Accord that enabled regulators, investors and creditors to divine whether an internationally active bank had sufficient capital strength, was the capital adequacy ratio. This ratio in a single number measured a bank's capital as defined against its assets to determine whether or not a bank met the threshold. The magic number above which a bank was deemed to have achieved satisfactory capital strength was set arbitrarily at 8%. Although under the accord the ratio was originally intended to apply to internationally active banks in countries within the G10, soon the 8% risk-weighted capital adequacy ratio became a near-universal measure of bank solidity. While, as we have said, the scheme represented a major advance over the confusion that had reigned before, form soon triumphed over substance, sometimes with paradoxical results. Following the crash of Japan's stock market in 1990, much of the hidden reserves with which the country's banks had expected to meet the 8% bar disappeared. In the early 1990s, an annual scramble began every spring as the country's banks sought to surmount the hurdle.

The Accord specified in precise detail how capital adequacy was to be calculated: what balance sheet items were to be included in which category of capital and how risk weightings applied. Some discretion, however, was left to national regulators in defining and implementing the scheme.[9] While sometimes complex in execution, the method of calculation was conceptually quite simple. The denominator, capital, was separated into *core (Tier 1) capital* and *supplementary (Tier 2) capital*. The numerator, assets, was divided into separate components based on defined risk weightings of 0%, 10%, 20%, 50%, and 100%. In addition, it was required that at least 50% of a bank's risk weighted capital should be core capital (Tier 1). The remainder was permitted to be Tier 2.[10]

$$\text{Capital Adequacy Ratio (\%)} = \frac{\text{Tier 1 Capital} + \text{Tier 2 Capital} \times 100}{\text{Risk Weighted Assets}}$$

Definition of Core (Tier 1) Capital and Supplementary (Tier 2) Capital

Core capital (Tier 1 capital) was defined as equity capital, i.e. issued and fully paid ordinary shares/common stock and non-cumulative perpetual preferred stock (but excluding cumulative preferred stocks), plus *disclosed (equity) reserves*, minus *goodwill* and investments in *unconsolidated* financial subsidiaries.[11]

The definition of supplementary (Tier 2) capital was rather more complex and problematic. It generally was deemed to include the following:

Undisclosed (hidden) reserves. Hidden reserves embody reserves that have been passed through the bank's P&L and which are accepted by local supervisory authorities.[12]

---

[9] One example: " in the UK, banks are allowed to issue forms of perpetual securities which can count as Tier 1 capital, whereas in Germany, banks are allowed to issue Tier 1 capital in dated format (silent partnership certificates) up to a certain limit of their Tier 1 ratio." Warburg Dillon Read, Europe, Credit Research: Credit — High Grade, February 2000, p. 5. Another example: "Whereas the norm in the EU is for holdings in insurance companies to be deducted from Tier 1 capital, banks in the UK, Switzerland and Denmark are allowed to deduct these holdings from total capital, which is a much more lenient treatment." Id. at p. 8.

[10] A transitional scheme provided flexibility on this and other items through end-1992. See Annex 4.

[11] Section 24.

[12] The rationale for including hidden reserves was that they were similar to retained earnings, but the Accord noted that "many countries do not recognize undisclosed reserves" and because of this fact and because of their non-transparent quality such reserves were excluded from core capital. Section 15.

Revaluation reserves. Revaluation reserves, permitted in some countries and which result when an adjustment to the historic cost of assets produces an unrealized gain, are permitted to be classified as supplementary capital, provided such assets are "considered by supervisory authority to be prudently valued, fully reflecting the possibility of price fluctuations and forced sale."[13]

General loan loss reserves, in contrast to specific loan loss reserves ascribed to particular assets (e.g. loans) are included within Tier 2 capital up to a limit of 1.25% of weighted risk assets.[14]

Hybrid debt instruments, e.g. long-term preferred shares in Canada, mandatory convertible debt instruments in the US, may be classified as Tier 2 capital, provided they meet specific criteria.[15]

Subordinated Term Debt, provided it has a minimum tenor of five years and appropriate amortization arrangements are included, may be categorized as Tier 2 capital.[16] In the last five years in which the issue is outstanding, the qualifying capital must be amortized (i.e. reduced) to reflect its increasingly current quality.[17]

Upper and Lower Tier 2 Capital[18]

Although ordinary subordinated debt, is permitted to be counted as regulatory capital (Tier 2) under the Basel Accord, applicable rules only permit such subordinated debt to amount to 50% of total Tier 1 capital. (This is notwithstanding that *total* Tier 2 capital can be as much as 100% of total Tier 1 capital.) Banks which are sorely in need of rebuilding capital therefore may wish to take advantage of the difference. To do so, they must issue qualifying debt which has sufficient equity-like characteristics so as to fall

---

[13] Where "very substantial amounts of equities" are held by banks at historic cost but which if sold could produce a gain, are permitted to be included in supplementary capital subject to a 55% discount. Section 17. This encompasses the exception sought by the Japanese banks, referred to above.

[14] The limitation was added by a November 1991 amendment to the Accord.

[15] The criteria generally involve their being able to support losses without triggering liquidation. Section 22 and Annex 1.

[16] Section 23. Further deductions by national authorities in respect of cross-holdings of bank capital by other banks. Sections 25–27.

[17] Consequently, as a matter of practice, many subordinated debt issues designed for issue by banks have call features allowing the bank the opportunity to repurchase the debt from investors during the last five years of the issue's term.

[18] The Special-Corporate Study, Asian Bank Subordinated Debt – A Primer, JP Morgan Securities Asia, January 24, 2000 (Analyst: Stephen Long), was helpful in the preparation of this section on Lower Tier 2 capital and Upper Tier 2 capital.

under the rubric of hybrid debt instruments and not fall a foul of the prohibition against exceeding the 50% of Tier 1 capital ceiling.

As a result, in practice, Tier 2 capital has come to be categorized into two categories: Lower Tier 2 and Upper Tier 2. Observe that these are terms used informally and which refer almost exclusively to types of subordinated debt rather than to other forms of Tier 2 capital mentioned above.

Lower Tier 2 Capital

Lower Tier 2 refers to ordinary subordinated debt that has no special features designed to allow the issuer to defer interest payments under certain circumstances and that may compel the debtholders to absorb some losses. In other words, Lower Tier 2 capital is pure conventional debt.

Upper Tier 2 Capital

In contrast to plain vanilla Lower Tier 2 capital, Upper Tier 2 capital is subordinated debt having special features that make it more akin to equity. Note that although it is termed *Upper* Tier 2, it is actually more like equity than *Lower* Tier 2, and that if one were to follow the vertical tiering analogy literally the terms are misnomers. (See the diagram on the following page.) These equity-like features include the following:

❏ the ability to defer interest payments at the option of the issuer under defined conditions so the obligation is not entirely fixed; and

❏ the ability of the issuer to impose losses on the upper Tier 2 debtholders in certain defined circumstances.

Typical circumstances triggering reduction in interest payments to investors include:

❏ the inability to pay dividends to shareholders

❏ the inability to meet regulatory capital requirements; and

❏ the recording of an accounting loss during the applicable year

To illustrate, in the case of one Asian debt issue, the bond agreement provided that if the issuer paid no dividends to its shareholders in the preceding year, it had the option to defer interest payments to bondholders.

The Rationale for Upper Tier 2 Capital

For banks:

❑ interest payments on debt are frequently tax deductible, thus potentially diminishing the institution's cost of capital on an after-tax basis

❑ enables banks to avoid diluting the interests of shareholders through equity issues at depressed prices

❑ upper tier 2 capital can function as bridge capital allowing a bank in a distressed situation to continue operating as a going concern until it can subsequently realize the value of its franchise and rebuild its capital through internal growth.

❑ where the upper tier 2 subordinated debt is issued in a stable foreign currency, the bank can reduce its foreign exchange risk

For Investors:

❑ higher nominal returns than lower tier 2 debt

❑ benefit of government's likely but not ensured support for its banking system and top-tier individual institutions

Source: JP Morgan

Bank Capital in Layers

Tokyo   J.P. Morgan Securities Asia Pte. Ltd.   page 2
January 24, 2000   Asia Credit Research - Financial Institutions
                    Stephen Long (81-3) 5573-1456
                    long_stephen@jpmorgan.com

Exhibit 1
Components of a bank's capita (hierarchical)

Risk Low			Return Low
	Senior debt	Fundingm not capital	
	Subordinated debt (Dated)	Tier III Trading Book only	
	Subordinated debt (Dated)	Lower Tier II (Up to 50% of Tier I)	
	Subordinated debt (Dated, with loss absorption features) Junior subordinated debt (Straight Perpetuals & Step-up Perps)	Upper Tier II (Up to 100% of Tier I)	
	Hybrid Tier 1 (Up to 15% of "core" capital) Preference shares Common shares Retained earnings	Tier I — 50% at least of minimum capital ratio of 8%	
High			High

("Core" capital "Suppleentary" capital labels on left vertical axis)

Note: Tier I can also include qualifiying reserves
Source: Basel Committee on Banking Supervision, J. P. Morgan Securities Asia pte. Asia

Source: JP Morgan

Tier 3 Capital

In addition to Tier 1 and Tier 2 capital, there is also a somewhat obscure category of capital known as Tier 3 capital. It came into being following the Basel Committee's 1996 revision to the Accord, "Amendment to the Capital Accord to Incorporate Market Risk."[19] A weak form of capital, Tier 3 capital is a form of short-term subordinated debt designed to support market risk exposure in trading and treasury activity by financial institutions. Tier 3 instruments must be unsecured, fully paid up, subordinated to senior creditors, have a minimum maturity of two years (being not repayable prior to maturity without the agreement of bank regulators), and be subject to a deferral of payment of interest or principal if a bank has not maintained its minimum capital requirements.[20] Tier 3 capital is generally permitted in Europe and in the US, but not elsewhere, but the market for this type of debt has been limited.

Definitions of Risk-Weighted Assets

Under the Accord, assets and off-balance sheet exposure is weighted according to imputed levels of risk. The risk weighting buckets were kept simple, which was an advantage, but are also quite broad in that asset classes that vary greatly in risk are put into the same class — for example, a loan to Joe's Bar and a loan to GE.[21]

In addition, off-balance sheet commitments, which until the 1980s had often escaped regulatory scrutiny, were captured under the Basel rules. Off-balance sheet commitments, i.e. contingent liabilities, were effectively treated as risk-assets under the Accord.

Risk weightings of assets and off-balance sheet items are shown in the tables next page.

Asset Weightings[22]

Note the low weighting on loans to bank within the OECD, and to short-term lending to banks generally. Note also that no distinction is made in

---

[19] Contemporaneously, it came into force in the EU in 1996 following the promulgation of the EU Capital Adequacy Directive. For a thorough discussion of Tier 3 capital, see Financial Institutions Special Report: "Tier 3 Capital — Well-named and unloved," Fitch, July 2000.

[20] Ibid. There are several quantitative restrictions on the amount of Tier 3 capital that may be employed, e.g. Tier 2 + Tier 3 capital may not be more than 100% of Tier 1 capital, but Tier 3 capital need not be amortized.

[21] See below for criticisms of the Accord.

[22] Annex 2.

0% Weightings

❑ cash

❑ local currency deposits with the central government/central bank

❑ deposits with OECD central governments and central banks[23]

❑ claims collateralized by cash, by OECD central government securities, or guaranteed by OECD central governments

❑ claims on domestic public sector entities other than the central government and loans guaranteed by such entities

20% Weightings

❑ claims on or guaranteed by multilateral development banks, or collateralized by the securities of such banks

❑ claims on banks incorporated in the OECD and loans guaranteed by OECD incorporated banks

❑ claims on banks incorporated outside the OECD or guaranteed by such banks having a residual maturity of one year or less

❑ claims on or guaranteed by non-domestic OECD public sector entities

❑ cash items in the process of collection[24]

50% Weighting

❑ Loans fully secured by mortgages on owner occupied residential property

100% Weighting

❑ Claims on the private sector

❑ Claims on non-OECD incorporated banks with a residual maturity of over one year

❑ Non local currency claims on central governments outside the OECD

❑ Claims on private sector commercial companies

❑ Fixed assets

❑ Real estate and other investments

❑ Capital instruments issued by other banks unless deducted from capital

---

[23] The Accord noted that some countries intended to apply a 10% weighting for short-term instruments in this category and a 20% weighting for long-term instruments. Annex 2.
[24] Added by an April 1998 amendment.

the case of ordinary private sector loans between companies whose, creditworthiness is high and those which are inferior credit risks. Finally, observe that fixed assets are included as risk assets.

Off Balance Sheet Items: Risk Weightings

RISK CATEGORIES OF OFF-BALANCE SHEET ITEMS

100% **Direct credit substitutes**
  Irrevocable off-balance sheet obligations which cany the same credit risk as a direct extension of credit.
    — guarantees, confirming of letters of credit, standby letters of credit serving as financial guarantees for loans, securities, acceptances (including endorsements with the character of acceptances) other than trade-related
    — Aval to bills, guarantees of loans, other guarantees
  Sale and repurchase agreements
  Arrangements whereby the authorized institution sells a loan, security or other asset to another person wit a conrmitment to repurchase the asset at an agreed price on an agreed future date.
  Assets sales or other transactions with recourse
  Assets sales where the holder of the asset is entitled to put the asset back to the authorized institution within an agreed period or should the value or credit quality of the asset deteriorate.
  Forward asset purchase
  Commitment to purchase a loan, security or other asset, including under a put option granted by the authorized institution to another party, at specified future date on pre-arranged terms.
  Partly paid-up shares and securities
  The unpaid portion of shares or securities which the issuer of such shares or securities may call for at a future date.
  Forward forward deposits placed
  Any agreement between the authorized institution and another party whereby the institution will place a deposit at an agreed rate of interest with that party at some predetermined future date.
  Outright forward purchases
  Asset sales, with and without recourse
  Committed facilities (to lend, to purchase securities, to provide guarantee or acceptance facilities)
  Overdrafts and other non-committed credit facilities

50% **Transaction-related contingencies**
  Contingent liabilities which involve an irrevocable obligation of the authorized institution to pay a beneficiary when a customer fails to perform some contractual, non-financial obligation.
    — performance bonds, bid bonds warranties and standby letters of credit related to a particular transaction
  Note issuance and revolving underwriting facilities
  Arrangements whereby a borrower may draw down funds up to a prescribed limit over a predefined period by making repeated note issues to the market, and where, should the issue prove unable to be placed in the market, the unplaced amount is to be taken up or funds made available by the underwriter of the facility.
  Other commitments with an original maturity of 1 year or over
  Customers' liabilities under acceptance
  Customers' liabilities under unmatured bills issued under L/C
  Claims against the bank not acknowledged as debts
20% **Trade-related contingencies**
  Contingent liabilities which relate to trade related obligations.
    — letters of credit, acceptances on trade bills, shipping guarantees and any other trade related contingencies

---

Figure continued

10%	Forward exchange purchase contracts
	Forward exchange sale contracts
	Interest rate transaction (reiated)

0.5%-5% Exchange rate contracts
  contracts with an original maturity of
    — under 1 year (2%)
    — 1 year and less than 2 years (5%)
    — 2 years or more, the factor for 1 year and less than 2 years plus for each additional year (3%)
  contracts with a residual maturity of
    — under 1 year (1%)
    — 1 year and over (5%)
  Interest rate contracts
  contracts with an original maturity of
    — under 1 year (0.5%)
    — 1 year and less than 2 years (1%)
    — 2 years or more, the factor for 1 year and less than 2 years plus for each additional year (1%)
  contacts with a residual maturity of
    — under 1 year(1%)
    — 1 year and over (5%)

0%	**Other commitments with an original maturity of under 1 year or which may be cancelled at any time unconditionally by the authorized institution.**
	Liabilities on accounts of outstanding forward exchange contract
	Forward contract
	Travellers' checks for sale

Source: Basel Accord; Thomson BankWatch

The Accord also took account of off-balance sheet risks, which had been causing increasing anxiety among bank regulations, when calculating mandatory capital. Although contingent, liabilities, off-balance sheet commitments sometimes required as much capital as ordinary loan assets.

How the CAR is Calculated

The calculation of the CAR is simple in concept but complex in execution. Typically analysts do not have adequate access to all relevant data to calculate the total CAR. Tier 1 capital is relatively easy to approximate, however, and in some cases, a good estimate of the total ratio can be made. Unless there is good reason not to, the analyst in most cases is likely to rely upon the CAR provided by the bank.

TOWARDS A NEW CAPITAL ACCORD

Problems with the 1988 Accord

The primary criticisms of the 1988 Accord, as it was implemented, was that it created distortions in the way banks allocated their funds, causing them to allocate credit exposure in ways that would not otherwise be economically justified. The risk weightings, although an improvement over earlier regulatory schemes, were highly arbitrary and did not accurately reflect the true risks involved in lending decisions. For example, a bank in an OECD country lending to a Thai bank for one year, for example, would only have to weight that exposure at 20%, while a bank's loan to a highly creditworthy company, such as America's General Electric (GE) would be weighted 100%. That is, the Accord deemed a hypothetical loan to GE to be five times more risky than a loan to a Thai bank. Just as perversely, a loan to Joe's Bar would, like GE, also have a risk-weighting of 100%. To put it in credit rating terms, under the Basel framework, a loan to a CCC rated company or an unrated company required no more capital as percentage of the assets lent than a loan to a AAA rated company.

The distorting effect of the original Accord has been recognized by commentators, as well as the Committee itself. In a speech given at a conference of banking supervisors in September 2000, William McDonough, president of the Federal Reserve Bank of New York and Chairman of the Basel Committee on Banking Supervision acknowledged that "in recent years... the (existing) Accord has exhibited serious shortcomings," adding that "One significant weakness is that the Accord's broad brush structure may provide banks with an unintended incentive to take on higher risk exposures without requiring them to hold a commensurate amount of capital."[25]

This situation encouraged banks to engage in interbank lending with other financial institutions. Of course, the banks that borrowed funds often lent to domestic corporations. In Thailand, such short-term foreign currency funding contributed to the onset of the Asian crisis. In other words, because the most creditworthy corporations were lumped in the same basket as the least creditworthy, banks are provided an added inducement to maximize their return on capital by making higher-yield loans to less creditworthy customers. Another result of the current risk weightings has been to induce banks, especially in the US, to securitize

---

[25] The Basel Committee in its own papers has recognized the shortcomings of the present framework noting that "a bank's capital ratio, calculated using the current Accord, may not always be a good indicator of its financial condition. The current risk weighting of assets results, at best, in a crude measure of economic risk, primarily because degrees of credit risk exposure are not sufficiently calibrated as to adequately differentiate between borrowers' differing default risks." A New Capital Adequacy Framework: Consultative paper issued by the Basel Committee on Banking Supervision, July 1999 [New CAF], Section 6.

their most conservative loans while keeping their higher-yielding but lower quality loans on their balance sheet.[26] In this context, it is worth observing that banks, particularly listed banks, are under great pressure to maintain levels of return on investment competitive with other financial and non-financial firms. Since the Accord in effect caps leverage — taking into account the risk weighting of assets and the inclusion of subordinated debt as capital, the 8% CAR is roughly equivalent to a leverage ratio of 12.5 — banks are enticed to achieve requisite levels of return on equity by looking for higher-yield. The paradoxical consequence is that the Accord actually undercuts in practice the objectives of soundness and security it is designed to achieve.

Benefits of the 1988 Accord

- Created a standardized approach to measuring capital adequacy

- Although risk-buckets were crude, precise definitions as to what qualified as core and secondary capital represented an improvement on the mishmash of definitions that previously existed

- Created a relatively level playing field, at least among OECD countries by establishing global standards

Key Problems with the 1988 Accord

- Meat-ax approach to risk weightings: too few gradations and distinctions not in line with reality

- No distinction made in creditworthiness of corporates: CCC requires no more capital than AAA borrower. Short-term lending to banks imputed to be 1/5 as risky as lending to non-financial corporations

- Unfair distinction between OECD and non-OECD countries

- Perverse incentives actually encourage riskier lending

THE JUNE 1999 PROPOSAL

In response to these criticisms in the recognition that the Accord was encouraging banks to behave in ways that undermined their financial strength, the Basel G10 committee proposed in June 1999 a revision of the accord. The proposal was designed to move international banking

---

[26] FAQ, p. 4.

regulation away from the mechanical formulation of the 1988 Accord towards a more holistic approach, one that incorporated three components. The first component represented a refinement of the crude risk weightings employed in the first accord. Like the original scheme, the 1999 proposal utilized a minimum capital ratio, but defined it in a manner to avoid the most negative effects of the 1988 formulation. Instead of the rough and ready risk weightings of the 1988 Accord, the proposal contemplated the use of internal ratings,[27] where certain conditions are met, or alternatively external ratings supplied by recognized credit rating agencies. The second and third components of the new system were intended to respectively strengthen supervisory review and employ the use of market discipline by compelling greater disclosure in order to encourage banks to maintain financial soundness. As stated in the document issued by the Basel Committee, the proposed revision of the Accord was designed to:

- continue to promote safety and soundness in the financial system by maintaining at least the current overall level of enhance competitive equality;
- provide a more comprehensive approach to addressing risks; and
- focus on internationally active banks.[28]

The Use of Ratings in the Regulation of Capital Adequacy

The heart of the proposed revision was the plan to allow banks to utilize internal or external ratings in establishing minimum capital requirements for specified types of exposures. As discussed below, this proposal gave rise to considerable controversy.

The Use of Internal Ratings

Under the plan, large sophisticated banks would be permitted to use internal ratings. It was contemplated that such banks would be have to assign an internal rating to each of its loans or exposures, correlated with the risks of the subject loan, and would also be required to assess the magnitude of likely loss should the borrower default on the loan. With regard to external ratings, the Committee proposed two variants schemes

---

[27] New CAF, Section 25.
[28] New CAF, Section 9.

as indicated in the table below. These, however, would only affect inter-bank borrowing. In the first, bank obligations would be automatically given the same rating as the sovereign in which they are domiciled. In the second, bank obligations would be rated separately.

External Ratings

Capital Requirements Based on Ratings-Derived Risk Weightings							
Claim		Assessment					
		AAA to AA−	A+ to A−	BBB+ to BBB−	BB+ to B−	Below B−	Unrated
Sovereigns		0%	20%	50%	100%	150%	100%
Banks	Option 1*	20%	50%	100%	100%	150%	100%
	Option 2**	20%	50% ***	50% ***	100% ***	150%	50% ***
Corporations		20%	100%	100%	100%	150%	100%

*Risk weighting based on risk weighting of sovereign in which the bank is incorporated.

**Risk weighting based on the assessment of the individual bank.

***Claims on banks of a short original maturity, for example less than six months, would receive a weighting that is one category more favorable than the usual risk weight on the bank's claims.

Source: Basel Committee, New Capital Adequacy Framework, June 1999.

Example of Risk Weighting of Capital

To illustrate the manner in which the capital requirements would work assuming Option 2, suppose a bank has a portfolio composed as follows:

10% of its portfolio is composed of sovereign obligations rated A+ to A−.

30% of its portfolio is composed of bank obligations, of which 1/3 are rated AAA to AA−, 1/3 are rated A+ to A−, and the remainder are unrated.

60% of its portfolio is composed of corporate obligations with 1/6 in each assessment category.

The sovereign obligations would have a risk weighting of 20%

The bank obligations would have a risk weightings of 20%, 50% and 50% respectively.

The corporate obligations would have risk weightings of 20%, 100% or 150% according to the table below.

Assuming a portfolio of US$10 billion dollars: the $1 billion of sovereign obligations would be calculated on a risk-weighted basis as $200 m; the bank obligations of $3 billion, as $1.2 billion ($0.2+$0.5+$0.5), and the corporate obligations capital of $5.7 billion ($0.2+$1+$1+$1+$1.5+$1). Total assets on a risk-weighted basis would therefore be $7.1 billion.

Bank's Portfolio	% of Portfolio	Risk Weighting	Risk Weighting % of All Assets	
Sovereign Debt, A + to A −	10.00%	20.00%	2.00%	0.2
Bank Debt, AAA to AA −	10.00%	20.00%	2.00%	0.2
Bank Debt, A + to A −	10.00%	50.00%	5.00%	0.5
Bank Debt, unrated	10.00%	50.00%	5.00%	0.5
Corporate AAA to AA −	10.00%	20.00%	2.00%	0.2
Corporate A + to A −	10.00%	100.00%	10.00%	1
Corporate BBB + to BBB −	10.00%	100.00%	10.00%	1
Corporate BB + to B −	10.00%	100.00%	10.00%	1
Corporate B − and below	10.00%	150.00%	15.00%	1.5
Corporate, unrated	10.00%	100.00%	10.00%	1
	100.00%		71.00%	7.1

Controversy Concerning the Proposed New Accord

While the present Accord had its faults, it did have the virtue of simplicity. The 1999 proposal, while it does attempt to remedy the meat-axe approach to risk-weightings of the present scheme, has drawn fire on several fronts. It is argued that the proposed revisions place too much emphasis on external ratings and consequently defer too much power to the rating agencies. Some of the rating agencies, in turn, have criticized the proposal on the grounds that its use of the ratings is contrary to the way they are designed to be used. Fitch, for instance, argued that the proposal would result in regulatory capital requirements that deviate from underlying risk assessments:

> When we assign a rating of, for example, 'A', we are doing this on the basis that the default characteristics ... whether [issued] by a sovereign, bank or corporate entity ... will be comparable. However, the Committee's proposal is, in effect, affirming that a sovereign rated between 'AA' and 'AAA' is a better credit risk than either a bank or sovereign with the same ratings.[29]

In addition, further criticisms were made in unless a borrower can achieve an external rating of AA, it is better off having no rating at all. Making this threshold so critical is arguably not only unjustified, but may

---

[29] "Special Report: Bank regulatory capital: a critical review of the new capital adequacy paper issued by the Basel Committee on Banking Supervision and its implication for the rating agency industry," Fitch IBCA, March 2000, p. 1.

put undue pressure on the integrity of rating agencies in cases where a borrower is borderline.

Status of the Accord

Given the deficiencies in the original accord and the controversy surrounding the 1999 proposal, voluminous comments concerning the proposed scheme were submitted to the Basel Committee by various interested parties, including financial institutions, rating agencies and regulators prior to the deadline of March 30, 2000. Taking account of these comments, the Committee issued a final proposal in January 2001. Following considerable review and discussion, taking account of the initial comments, the original proposal was modified in part. Following a final comment period, it is expected to be adopted by year-end and implemented substantially in its current form by 2004. We discuss the new scheme in Appendix C to this book.

CHAPTER SUMMARY

In the preceding chapter, we discussed the meaning of capital and its relative importance, as well as the application of traditional ratios to measuring capital adequacy. In this chapter, we discussed the background to the 1988 Basel Accord and the risk-weighted capital adequacy model it brought into widespread use globally. The 1988 Accord represented a major advance over previous non-risk asset based approaches to capital measurement and in effecting a global standard, it facilitated cross-border comparisons of bank capital strength.

The concept of the Basel approach was quite simple in concept, although sometimes complicated in execution. Fundamentally, the scheme was simply an adaptation of one of the oldest and simplest bank ratios: equity to assets. Instead of dividing shareholders' equity by total assets, however, the capital adequacy ratio under the Accord provided for adjustments in the numerator by class of capital and adjustments in the denominator by risk weightings. In the numerator were Tier 1 and Tier 2 capital (a third class, Tier 3, is rarely used) and all assets (as well as off-balance sheet commitments) were divided into one of several risk-weightings. If the end result were 8% or higher, an internationally active bank was deemed to have sufficient capital adequacy.

In its near universal acceptance by regulators and the impetus it provided towards improving capital adequacy globally, the Accord was a great success. The BIS capital adequacy ratio, as it is popularly called had substantial deficiencies however, which became increasingly apparent throughout the 1990s, especially after the Asian crisis. In particular, the Basel scheme created perverse incentives in which form triumphed over substance, and banks gravitated towards riskier rather than less risky behavior, in contrast to the intent of the Accord. Notably, the risk-weighting system set forth in the original accord was too unrefined and lumped together assets having widely disparate risk-profiles into the same risk buckets. The scheme also displayed a bias against non-OECD countries.

In 1999, the Basel Committee issued a new proposal in an attempt to improve on the 1988 Accord. Adopting a system of internal and external ratings to calibrate risk-weightings, the initial proposal was highly controversial and drew considerable comment from interested parties including financial institutions, their regulators and credit rating agencies. Taking into account these comments, a final revised proposal was issued in January 2001, and following further public comment, is expected to be implemented by 2004.

CHAPTER THIRTEEN

FUNDING AND LIQUIDITY, PART I: LIQUIDITY AND ASSET-LIABILITY MANAGEMENT[1]

Illiquidity, rather than poor asset quality, is the immediate cause of most bank failures.[2]
　　　　— Robert Morris Associates, *A Guide to Analyzing Foreign Banks*

[The banking] institution's ability to finance itself under stress ... is best measured by the degree to which core assets that are illiquid are funded by core liabilities that are stable.
　　　　— Moody's Investor Service, Global Credit Analysis

A banker is a fellow who lends you his umbrella when the sun is shining, but wants it back the minute it begins to rain.
　　　　— variously attributed to either Robert Frost or Mark Twain

Poor liquidity is the proximate cause of bank failure, and the analysis of a bank's liquidity position is a crucial part of the bank credit analyst's role in determining overall creditworthiness. Adequate liquidity can allow an otherwise weak bank to continue operating. However, even a good bank with, say, a clean balance sheet, sound management and making solid

---

[1] The author expresses his sincere thanks and appreciation to Mr. Darren Stubing, Chief Bank Analyst at Capital Intelligence, a major specialist bank rating agency based in Cyprus, for his contribution of Chapters 16 and 17 respectively entitled Funding and Liquidity, Part I: Liquidity and Asset-Liability Management and Funding and Liquidity, Part II: Funding the Bank and Ratio Analysis. These chapters comprise a critical component of the application of the CAMEL model to bank credit analysis and the author gratefully acknowledges Mr. Stubing's work and contribution.
[2] RMA. p. 28.

returns, can quickly face severe problems and ultimately collapse if liquidity weakens or dries up.

It is important to define what we actually mean by liquidity, by no means an easy task due to the wide interpretation of the word and of a financial institution's liquidity position. It is best if we first define satisfactory liquidity and this can be defined as "the ability to refinance maturing liabilities at or below market rates". Conversely, banks possessing poor liquidity will struggle to refinance liabilities and, if it is achieved, will be at a cost that is above market rates. Banks finding themselves in this position will only be able to operate in this situation for a certain period of time before either liquidity evaporates or earnings come under pressure.

> Satisfactory liquidity is the ability to refinance maturing liabilities at or below market rates.

A bank's liquidity management policy will aim to ensure that the bank has sufficient funds available to meet its operational needs, as well as to ensure compliance with regulatory guidelines. Liquidity risk includes the risk associated with an increase in funding costs and the risk of being unable to honor deposit withdrawals, make repayments at maturity of other liabilities and being unable to liquidate a position in a timely manner and at a reasonable cost. Accordingly, a bank will endeavor to maintain a significant amount of local and foreign currency demand deposits in order to respond quickly to its funding needs. Markets where the exchange rate is volatile, inflation is high or political uncertainty is prevalent, are most vulnerable to liquidity problems. In these types of markets, cash and deposit flight — a euphemism for panic — are common.

COMPONENTS OF BANK LIQUIDITY

Bank liquidity has three components:
- ❑ The stock of readily marketable, high quality *liquid assets*
- ❑ Expected *cash flow*
- ❑ The *capacity to borrow* in the markets

Liquid Assets

Readily marketable, high quality liquid assets usually mean government securities and central bank balances. However, even with government securities, one needs to examine the securities to determine whether they are really liquid. In some emerging markets, for example, domestic government securities are not liquid because there is no secondary market. Or, on the other hand, if they are marketable, they may only be saleable at deep discount. Illiquid government securities are found in many emerging markets (see later discussion on Kuwait). Moreover, it is for these reasons, and the often volatile interest rate movements of domestic government paper in some emerging markets, that analysts will risk-weight these securities at 10% or 20% despite local requirements of zero risk-weighting.

> Tip: Assets considered to be liquid in developed markets, such as government securities, may not be in some emerging markets because of a lack of a secondary market or limits on negotiability. When evaluating liquidity in emerging markets, especially in the Middle East and South Asia, check concerning the negotiability of government securities.

High quality liquid assets provides an important cushion for banks in times when there is an interruption to their expected cash flows. Qualifying liquid assets should have the following characteristics:

❏ nil or very low credit risk

❏ (if securitized) regularly traded in sizeable amounts in deep markets

❏ (if not securitized) very short maturity

An important aspect of liquid assets will be whether the monetary authorities are by convention prepared to provide funds against these instruments in their normal money market operations. Most advanced regulators require banks to maintain eligible liquid assets as a minimum proportion of liabilities maturing within eight days. Usual ratios are within the 5–25% range.

Expected Cash Flow

Expected cash flow is determined by the bank's asset quality and is influenced by the level of non-performing loans. A bank's net interest margin is a reflector of cash flow as net interest income comprises such a high proportion of commercial bank revenues.

Kuwait Bonds

Following the Gulf War in 1990, the Central Bank of Kuwait purchased Kuwaiti banks' non-performing assets and issued to them long-term government debt bonds (GDBs). By end-1992, the central bank had issued US$16.6 billion of GDBs, which represented 52% of the banking sectors' balance sheet. By end-1999, this percentage had fallen to 15%.The GDBs pay an interest rate equal to the cost of funds for the whole banking sector.

Although these are government securities of a quite highly rated sovereign, and thus it would seem appropriate to classify them as liquid assets, the GDBs are in fact illiquid as there is no secondary market where they can be traded. As such, the true liquid assets ratio would exclude these GDBs. Nevertheless, in a crisis situation, it is believed that the Central Bank of Kuwait would provide liquidity for the GDBs through discount and swap facilities.

Apart from the liquidity issue of the GDBs, the presence of the paper on the Kuwaiti banks' balance sheets exposes the institutions to an asset/liability maturity mismatch on account of the short-term nature of the customer deposit base and the long-term dates of the GDBs.

Interruption to Cash Flow

A good base of high quality liquid assets acts as an important cushion for banks in case there is some interruption in their expected cash flows. Cash flow pressure on a bank may be caused by delays in the maturity of assets or from an accelerated maturity of liabilities. This scenario may well be linked to a sudden change in sentiment affecting a bank's ability to borrow in the market. In such a case, the bank's public image will be damaged and its cost of funds will rise sharply. If the problem is perceived to be sector-wide, then all banks within the system are likely to face the same challenges.

The Bank of England describes the factors that determine minimum liquidity requirements for each bank as:

❑ The perceived strength of a bank's expected cash flow

❑ The stickiness of its retail deposits

❑ Holdings of assets against which a central bank may be prepared to provide refinancing facilities in exceptional circumstances

Capacity to Borrow in the Markets

The capacity to borrow in the market is largely a function of the bank's own credit standing and reputation together with its credit rating and that of the country. Other issues that need to be examined include the maturity and depth of the capital markets, as well as the depth, management and liquidity of the interbank market.

The ability of the bank to finance itself, especially under stress, is crucial. When markets are stable and sentiment is positive, the institution is unlikely to have any liquidity or funding difficulties. However, the real test comes when, either due to internal or external challenges, market sentiment changes and a bank's liquidity position can be squeezed. This scenario has happened many times in the past, especially for banks in markets where there is a heavy reliance on foreign funding such as international credit lines. If sentiment changes for the sovereign, and international banks become more risk-averse, international banks will quickly cut credit lines and this may place some banks under severe pressure. This may also happen if banks have significant syndication loans from foreign banks. If these syndicated facilities come due at unfortunate times, for example if markets are negative on the country and funding has been squeezed, then the bank needing to repay the facility may face pressure, particularly if the facility cannot be rolled over.

CORE ASSETS AND CORE LIABILITIES

The ability to finance under stress is best measured by the degree to which core assets that are illiquid are funded by core liabilities that are stable. The analyst needs to determine if there is a match or an imbalance. If there is an imbalance, is it at a reasonable level or is it too high? Core deposits ideally should at least match total loans. Also, the analyst needs to determine the proportion of stable customer deposits as against funds purchased in the open market.

> Tip: For good liquidity, core deposits ideally should at least match total loans.

Diversification of Funding Base

The key question the analyst needs to ask himself/herself about the bank being analyzed is, if because of concerns about this bank it was no longer able to refinance itself in the markets, how would it meet its obligations as they mature.

❑ Does the bank have a diversified funding base? Or is it reliant on one or two sources?

❑ Is there stability and strength in domestic funding?

❑ Is there flexibility in the balance sheet?

❑ Has the bank the resources, credit standing and distribution network to change its funding mix, say from domestic customer deposits to international sources?

❑ Does it have the franchise strength to shift its customer deposit base away from more expensive time deposits to cheaper demand deposits?

❑ On the other hand, is their potential liquidity within the bank's investment portfolio?

Sources of Funding

Funding sources need to be analyzed carefully. Where is the bank's funding coming from? The analyst needs to look at the relative sensitivity of funding sources. The most sensitive funding sources are from the *interbank market*, whether it be domestic or foreign. Funding from the interbank market can be both volatile and expensive. Many problems arise in emerging markets due to the tendency of banks in these countries to rely too heavily on interbank funding. For example, the 1994 crisis in Turkey exposed many Turkish banks' over-reliance on international credit lines and bank-syndicated borrowings from overseas. When the country's sovereign risk rating was downgraded in the early part of 1994, sentiment soon changed as the economic crisis took hold. International banks cut credit lines, squeezing many domestic banks liquidity positions, which then led to rumors regarding some banks' solvency. This eroded confidence in the banking sector and customer deposits were soon withdrawn in large quantities to the point where the government stepped in and placed a blanket guarantee on all deposits to restore the system's liquidity. Turkish banks realized from the crisis the advantage of possessing a good base of domestic deposit funding as it is the most stable source of funds for banks.

Alternative Sources of Liquidity

The more confidence-sensitive the bank, the more precisely defined its alternative liquidity should be. *Flight to quality* does indeed happen in times of market turmoil as depositors seek safe havens in well regarded and highly rated banks. The Asian crisis saw such much deposit flight from weaker banks to stronger perceived banks (in most cases to strong foreign-owned banks that were deluged with new depositors). Weaker or less-regarded banks need clear access to alternative funds as a deeper cushion is needed. Alternative sources of liquidity may come from the central bank, sister banks both within or outside the country, or even the bank's free capital position.

Not all banks are in a position to rely solely on interbank relationships; much depends on the receiver of fund's creditworthiness, importance domestically and/or internationally, dependence on confidence-sensitive funds (for example commercial paper) and overall country status or sovereign rating. The safest source of alternative liquidity is a committed line allocated for a specific issuance program such as commercial paper provided by a highly-rated bank for a longer time period and without clauses.

INTEREST RATE SENSITIVITY AND BALANCE SHEET MATCHING

In addition to examining straight forward liquidity issues, three other important factors figure in the bank's specific liquidity position and profile. These three factors are:

❑ Interest rate sensitivity

❑ Maturity matching

❑ Currency matching

Interest Rate Sensitivity Analysis

Interest rate sensitivity or interest rate risk can be defined as the exposure of the bank's net interest income to adverse movements in interest rates. Interest rate risk arises as a result of mismatches in the repricing term characteristics of a bank's assets and liabilities. The analysis of interest rate risk is performed by gap analysis and earnings-at-risk modeling. Gap analysis measures the volumes of assets and liabilities subject to repricing within a given period, ideally on a monthly or three-monthly basis (see illustration on Plus Ultra Bank, Table 1) basis. Accordingly, assets and liabilities are classified according to their contractual repricing characteristics. In addition, the cumulative position is ascertained whereby the gap between rate-sensitive assets to rate-sensitive liabilities at monthly intervals are accumulated, say up to five years and over, in order to pinpoint any possible large mismatches.

Banks use balance sheet stress testing and net interest income simulations for a variety of possible interest rate scenarios, with which the effect of interest rate movements can be measured. The analyst will ideally want to know the impact of a 1%, 2%, and 5% change in short-term interest rates on earnings. For example, a bank's exposure to an adverse 1% movement in interest rates may have a 2% overall impact on net interest.[3] Banks calculate the projected change in bank equity over a forecast period based on the most likely high and low interest rates scenarios for the period. The bank will then implement strategies for the mitigation of such risks. Lending operations within a bank that run interest rate risk will do so within formal risk exposure limits and in accordance with appropriate risk monitoring and reporting requirements.

Interest Rate Risk: From Trading vs. From Operations

Banks should make a clear distinction between interest rate risk arising from the balance sheet management of trading versus banking activities in its risk management process. The banking book is defined as all assets and liabilities that are intended to be held to maturity in order that they generate an income over time. These activities are subject to the bank's asset-liability committee. The balance sheet items that are acquired for trading purposes — the trading book — are managed by mark-to-market and risk quantification methodologies that form part of the market risk management process.

Interest Rate Sensitivity: Asset Sensitive vs. Liability Sensitive

A bank's interest rate sensitivity strategy may also take into account not only the rates of return and degree of underlying risk, but also liquidity needs, mandatory liquidity ratios, withdrawal and maturity of deposits and additional demand for funds. A bank's sensitivity to interest rate changes may be limited to the extent of the amount of short-term assets on its balance sheet. For example, a bank with a predominance of short-term

---

[3] For example, if the bank's assets profile contains a significant fixed interest rate element while within liabilities there is a greater mix of variable rate deposits or funding, then a 1% rise in interest rates may have an even greater adverse impact on the bank's net interest income performance as it is forced to raise rates paid to depositors but is unable to immediately raise rates for existing borrowers.

assets on its balance sheet is likely to be *less sensitive* to adverse interest rate changes than a bank in the same market with a low percentage of short-term assets on its balance sheet. In volatile operating environments with extreme interest rate fluctuations, a prudent bank is likely to reprice interest rates on new domestic currency-denominated assets daily. In such operating environments, which are usually characterized by high rates of inflation, domestic currency loans are mainly callable on one day's notice.

> Tip: A bank with predominantly short-term assets on its balance sheet is likely to be less sensitive to adverse interest rate changes than a bank in the same market with a low percentage of short-term assets on its balance sheet.

In highly volatile, high interest rate economies, banks tend to be *liability sensitive* (i.e. liabilities are maturing earlier or liabilities, e.g. deposits, are repricing earlier than assets). This is because success in volatile economies is largely dependent on the bank's ability to manage its liabilities and hence funding costs well. Also, in a declining interest rate environment, the bank will try and maintain a liability sensitive position (again liabilities are repricing sooner and the bank will adjust rates paid to depositors at a lower rate in line with falling interest rates). Conversely, in a rising interest rate environment, banks will be endeavoring to be *asset sensitive* whereby assets are repricing faster with the bank trying to capitalize on higher interest rates that can be passed onto borrowers quickly.

US Savings and Loans Institutions

A classic example of poor interest rate sensitivity management was the American savings and loans institutions (S&Ls) of the 1970s. The savings and loans were borrowing on a short-term basis at variable interest rates but lending long at fixed rates. Interest rates then rose significantly, exposing the S&Ls to severe interest rate risk. The spread between the institutions' yield on earning assets and their cost of funds turned negative as rates paid on short-term deposits quickly outstripped their long-term, fixed-rate mortgage portfolio yields. High interest rates also reduced loan demand at the time. These factors ultimately led to the collapse of numerous S&Ls. Ideally, loans over one year in tenor should be at floating rate.Similarly, if a bank has a fairly large mortgage book, all of this lending should be done at variable rates, or at the very least, only a small proportion done at longer term fixed rates.

The table below illustrates an example of a bank's interest rate sensitivity profile by looking at the repricing of assets and liabilities at various time frames:

Illustration: Interest Rate Sensitivity Analysis

Five-Step Process

To perform an interest rate sensitivity analysis, divide assets and liabilities into maturity categories (sometimes called buckets). Then:

1. Add up liabilities by maturity to arrive at Total Liabilities in each maturity category.

2. Do the same for assets to arrive at Total Assets for each maturity category.

3. Subtract Total Assets from Total Liabilities in each maturity category, adjusting for off-balance-sheet gaps. Gaps for off-balance sheet items are calculated in the same way as balance sheet items.

4. Add gaps for each maturity category to reach cumulative gap.

5. Divide the cumulative gap by total assets to obtain cumulative gap as a percentage of total assets.

Maturity Matching

Maturity matching is similar to interest rate sensitivity analysis. Again, the analyst looks at maturing assets and liabilities broken down over various time periods. The cumulative position is also calculated to determine whether the bank is carrying a positive (assets in excess of liabilities) or negative (liabilities in excess of assets) gap. The analyst needs to know if there is any large mismatch whereby the bank is funding long-term assets with short-term liabilities. The extent of the gap position is measured against the total assets of the balance sheet. A negative gap greater than 10% of the asset base starts to be on the high side and the position needs to be examined more closely to determine if there are likely to be any problems. However, it should be borne in mind that maturity mismatches are part and parcel of banking — often because of the short-term nature of deposits and long-term nature of loans. Nevertheless, the bank needs to avoid an excessive maturity mismatch. For example, a high negative

Plus Ultra Bank — Interest Rate Risk Analysis

1. Add up liabilities by maturity to arrive at Total Liabilities in each maturity category.
2. Do the same for assets to arrive at Total Assets for each maturity category.
3. Subtract Total Assets from Total Liabilities in each maturity category, adjusting for off-balance sheet gaps.
4. Add up gaps for each maturity category to reach cumulative gap.
5. Divide the cumulative gap by total assets to obtain cum. gap as % of total assets.

US$ m	Interest Sensitive					Non-Interest Sensitive	
	< 3 months	3 months– 6 months	6 months– 1 year	1 year– 5 years	> 5 years	Non Interest Sensitive	Total
Shareholders' funds	0	0	0	0	9,000	9,000	
— L/T Subordinated Debt				500		500	
Deposits by banks	5,000	0	0	0		0	5,000
Deposits by customers	48,000	1,500	2,500	13,000	1,000	0	
NCDs and Repos	5,000	1,500	500	500		0	7,500
Other liabilities						7,000	7,000
Deposit, current and other accounts	58,000	3,000	3,000	13,500	1,000	7,000	
Cash and S/T funds						7000	7,000
Other S/T securities	5,000	200	100				5,300
		48,000	1,500	2,500	13,000	1,000	
	5,000	1,500	500	500			
Total Liabilities	58,000	3,000	3,000	13,500	1,500	16,000	95,000
Cash and S/T funds							
Other S/T securities	5,000	200	100				
Government securities	1,000	800	200	1,000	1,000		
Advances	53,000	3,500	3,200	11,000		5,000	
Loans to banks	4,000						4,000
Loans to customers	49,000	3,500	3,200	11,000		4,000	
Other assets						1,000	1,000
Customers' indebtedness						500	500
Associates/investments						1,500	1,500
Fixed Property					1,000	1,000	
Total Assets	59,000	4,500	3,500	12,000	1,000	15,000	95,000
Off-balance sheet items	3,000	− 100	− 100	− 2800			
Interest rate sensitivity gap	4,000	1,400	400	− 4,300	− 500	− 1,000	
Cumulative gap	4,000	5,400	5,800	1,500	1,000	–	
Percentage of total assets	4.2	5.7	6.1	1.6	1.1		

position may present problems if the funding environment becomes more difficult. An additional factor when examining maturities is the need to look at the maturity structures of long-term debt, if any. Long-term debt should be spread out so earnings can retire the debt. Also, if large amounts are coming due within the year, the analyst should be comfortable with the bank's liquidity to meet obligations coming due.

In the table on the following page illustrating Delta Bank's asset liability maturity profile, it is evident that the bank is asset sensitive at all time frames, that is, the assets have shorter maturities than the liabilities.

Delta Bank-Balance Sheet Maturity Profile

	Up to 1 month US$ m	1–3 months US$ m	3–6 months US$ m	6–12 months US$	12+ months US$ m	Total US$ m
Cash and due from banks	268,453	5,829	13,983	2,646	21,641	312,552
Reserves deposits with central bank	144,804	–	–	–	–	144,804
Net loans	347,124	444,884	524,859	393,130	166,627	1,876,624
Marketable securities — repurchase	–	59,584	–	–	–	59,584
Securities portfolio	353,950	88,432	47,537	1,378	102,105	593,402
Equity participations	–	–	–	–	55,495	55,495
Property, plant and equipment	–	–	–	–	102,634	102,634
Accrued interest and other assets	76,237	119,607	53,112	22,925	14,504	286,385
Total Assets	1,190,568	718,336	639,491	420,079	463,006	3,431,480
Deposits	511,977	635,962	514,741	733,715	–	2,396,395
Funds borrowed from banks	25,402	9,724	20,359	43,355	125,085	223,925
Import transfer orders	7	2,585				2,592
Accrued interest expense+other liabs.	96,247	98,590	16,098	8,673	28,391	247999
Taxation on income	2,965	–	–	–	–	2,965
Employment termination benefits	–	–	–	–	5,515	5,415
Deferred tax liability	–	–	–	–	37,873	37,873
Total Liabilities	636,598	746,861	551,198	785,743	196,764	2,917,164
Net liquidity gap	553,970	−28,525	88,293	−365,664	266,242	514,316
Cumulative liquidity gap	553,970	525,445	613,738	248,074	514,316	–
Percentage of total assets	16.2	15.3	17.9	7.2	15.0	

Note how Delta Bank's assets are heavily biased towards short term assets with assets with maturities of less than one month far outweighing liabilities in this category. With a high proportion of the bank's assets having less than 6 mo. maturity, liquidity is strong.

514,316/
3,431,480 =
15.0%

This is quite unusual and is due largely to two factors. First, Delta Bank's loan portfolio consists largely of short-term lending, particularly of terms of up to six months. This suggests that the bank is operating in quite a volatile market, particularly in respect to interest rates. Second, the bank's deposit base consists of a significant percentage of more stable (and more expensive) time deposits. This fact aids Delta Bank's liquidity profile as it extends the tenor of funding. The difference between assets and liabilities in this example is the bank's capital, which of course could be considered as long-term funding. Overall, Delta Bank displays a sound liquidity profile.

CURRENCY MATCHING: ANALYZING THE BANK'S FOREIGN CURRENCY POSITION

An important part of the bank's funding position is the degree to which foreign currency liabilities match foreign currency assets. Put simply, does the bank possess a well-matched currency position? A bank can have one of two types of foreign currency positions. If a bank has an excess of foreign currency liabilities over assets, the bank is said to be running a *short position*. Likewise, a bank holding an excess of foreign currency assets over foreign currency liabilities is running a *long position*.

It is preferable for a bank to run a closely matched foreign currency position. There are two ways a bank can have other than a matched position.

1. Foreign currency liabilities exceed assets: short position.

2. Foreign currency assets exceed foreign currency liability: long position.

An unmatched position exposes the bank to foreign currency risk — loss and gain:

1. Long position benefits if foreign currency gains strength and value rises vis-a-vis local currency obligations. It loses if the foreign currency weakens.

2. Short position benefits if foreign currency loses strength and value falls vis-a-vis local currency assets. It loses if the foreign currency gains strength.

If the bank is running an unmatched position, it is exposing itself to currency risk which can, if the movement is adverse, add significantly to the bank's cost of funds through a large foreign currency translation loss. Many banks in emerging markets strategically run short foreign exchange positions as part of their overall asset-liability policy.[4] This is particularly the case where domestic interest rates are high and thus funding locally through either deposits or the interbank market is expensive compared with low interest rates in hard currency economies. The yield difference between borrowing in the high interest rate domestic market against the low interest rate hard currency market is highly tempting and will boost substantially the bank's interest differential; the bank will borrow at, say, 7% in US dollars and on lend in local currency, say at 25%. This will be very profitable providing the local currency does not devalue significantly against the US dollar.

Prior to the Asian crisis, some countries, such as Indonesia, had high foreign currency exposure through borrowing overseas, and when the Indonesian rupiah fell sharply against the dollar, many local banks suffered heavy losses. In high inflation economies, short foreign currency positions tend to be very common. This strategy tends to be very lucrative (usually in these economies a lot of bank funding goes to high yielding domestic government securities) providing that the rate of devaluation of the local currency is below the inflation rate.[5] Even taking into account the loss on the foreign currency position through the devaluation of the local currency, the yield differential will more than make up for it. To truly reflect the real funding cost, when banks strategically run short foreign currency positions, it is recommended that the analyst include any translation loss from the foreign currency position as part of normal interest expense. An example is given in the next page.

Accepting asset/liability mismatches and playing interest rate differentials are at the essence of banking and the pursuit of profitability. Borrowing short and lending long has long been the adage of banking; however, sudden changes in interest rates can negatively impact a bank if it is poorly positioned and without proper hedging. Funding costs may rise, causing a squeeze in margins, or liquidity may tighten, threatening the overall survival of the bank in a worst case scenario.

---

[4] Bank in developed countries may run currency positions from time but interest rate differentials are usually not wide enought to make this a part of overall funding strategy. Moreover, hedging strategies are far more sophisticated which will reduce the risk.

[5] High yielding domestic government securities are usually a function of large fiscal deficits and hence high borrowing requirements.

Illustration: Assessing Foreign Currency Exposure

Bank Beta is located in a volatile, high interest rate, high inflation rate country, has an interest on average earning assets ratio of 22.47% and a funding cost ratio of 10.11%, culminating in an interest differential ratio of 12.36%. However, the bank consistently runs a short foreign exchange position as part of its funding strategy in order to obtain cheap foreign funding, and directs the funds to government paper and/or loan customers where the domestic interest rates are substantially higher. The foreign exchange translation loss (the domestic currency is depreciating consistently against the US dollar due to high domestic inflation) amounts to US$127 million. Including this translation as part of interest expense sees the adjusted interest expense rising to US$430 million from US$303 million and net interest income falling to US$231 million from US$358 million unadjusted. As a result, the adjusted funding cost increases to 14.34% and the adjusted interest differential falls to 8.13%.

Bank Beta-Cost of Funds

	Unadjusted	Adjusted
Foreign Currency Translation Loss (US$ m)	127	NA
Interest Expense (US$ m)	303	430
Net Interest Income (US$ m)	358	231
Funding Cost (%)	10.11	14.34
Interest Differential (%)	12.36	8.13

ASSET-LIABILITY MANAGEMENT

Asset and liability management therefore is a crucial part of today's banking operations. Bank management must actively monitor and manage the bank's asset and liability position, in addition to the size and extent of its interest rate and currency exposure, in order to minimize the effect of these risks on profitability.

The Role of the Asset-Liability Management Committee

At a bank, the asset and liability committee (ALCO) is responsible for implementing asset and liability management . ALCO's main objective is to plan and control financial flows and to structure and develop the bank's balance sheet in order to achieve target levels for profitability while providing for adequate liquidity, capital and risk management. The ALCO will set interest rate levels and terms for both assets and liabilities and make decisions regarding maturity and pricing of assets and liabilities. In managing the bank's assets and liabilities, a bank's ALCO considers issues such as interest rates and yields, the size of the loan and investment portfolios, loan maturities, time deposits and investments, foreign currency positions, exchange rates, and inflation rates together with other macroeconomic factors. The ALCO ideally will strive to ensure that acceptable levels of financial risk, excluding credit and operational risk, are identified and effectively managed, while still aiming to achieve the financial objectives of the bank.[6] Aggregate risk exposure is usually set to a limited amount of capital. A conservative aggregate risk exposure limit of 5% of capital and reserves is considered prudent. The ALCO will meet on a daily, weekly or monthly basis.

Liquidity risk management forms an integral part of balance sheet management. Other important objectives include cash flow forecasting and strategic planning, maintaining a strong presence in selected target markets, maintaining an adequate pool of high quality marketable assets and liability diversification. The ALCO will examine the risk and correlation within the bank's investment and trading portfolios, as well as the loan book, allocating funds in the process.

MARKET RISK AND VALUE-AT-RISK

A bank's trading activities within the financial markets create the risk of loss due to adverse movements in rates and prices of currencies, interest rates in the domestic and international capital and money markets, equities, and commodities, as well as option volatility. The bank controls these market risks by setting *"stress loss" exposure limits* for each trading desk. Stress exposures are decided by measuring the potential losses that would be incurred on *open positions,* should rates, prices and volatilities change according to specified ranges, which are set to reflect potential market conditions.

Market risk is usually quantified by the *value-at-risk methodology,* that is, by ascertaining the value of market risk at certain confidence

---

[6] In some banks, credit and operational risk may be within the broad remit of the ALCO.

levels (usually either 99% or 95% confidence levels). Value-at-risk methodology measures the probability of trading loss on both capital and earnings at the given confidence level. A daily value-at-risk of US$10 million with a 99% *confidence level* means that in one day out of 100 can the bank be expected to lose more than US$10 million. Behind the value-at-risk tool is the theory that markets move in correlation; however, as was seen in international markets during the third quarter of 1998, markets do not necessarily move in correlation. Despite highly sophisticated value-at-risk modeling tools, Long Term Capital Management became caught up in the market turmoil that ensued in the wake of the devaluation of the ruble and the default on Russian debt in August 1998. Poor market liquidity will also distort normal market scenarios and correlations. Moreover, to some extent, the data assumptions that go into the model may be incorrect. Banks are continuing to refine the tools to measure value-at-risk through stress testing and different market scenarios.

CHAPTER SUMMARY

Liquidity analysis is an essential area of bank credit analysis. Without the liquidity and funding in place to meet obligations, the bank may quickly fail unless external support is given. Liquidity has many facets but is based largely on the bank's holding of liquid assets, its cash flow and ability to borrow in the market. Satisfactory liquidity is the ability to refinance maturing liabilities at or below market rates. Interest rate sensitivity, and both maturity and currency matching, are important elements of a bank's overall liquidity and funding position.

CHAPTER FOURTEEN

FUNDING & LIQUIDITY, PART II: FUNDING THE BANK AND RATIO ANALYSIS

This illiquidity problem arises even if the banks are solvent and profitable. If depositors come to doubt the soundness of banks, they will run on them. The banks must start unloading their assets to get the cash to satisfy depositors. If many banks do this, the simultaneous dumping of assets into the market depresses asset prices with the ironic result that banks can become insolvent as a result of the run — thereby justifying the public's decision to run in the first place.[1]

— G. Thomas Woodward

FinOne did not die from financial failure, it died from [a lack of] liquidity. It was a plain and simple run on deposits.

— Pin Chakkaphak, on the collapse of Finance One, Thailand's largest finance company which he headed at the time.[2]

A term loan is nothing but an illiquid junk bond.

— Joseph Grundfest, former SEC commissioner[3]

---

[1] G. Thomas Woodward, Money and the Federal Reserve System: Myth and Reality, Congressional Research Service Library of Congress CRS Report for Congress, No. 96-672 E (1996).
[2] Quoted in Tim Noonan, "Running on the Spot," *South China Morning Post Magazine*, October 1, 2000, p. 12.
[3] Quoted in *The Bankers*, p. 211.

FUNDING THE BANK: THE RELATIONSHIP BETWEEN FUNDING AND LIQUIDITY

Funding and liquidity are usually discussed and analyzed together because a bank's sources of funding have a major impact on its liquidity profile. Since most of a bank's funding ordinarily comes from deposits, an assessment of a bank's deposit base is a key step in the appraisal process. A higher percentage of customer deposits comprising the bank's total funding base normally indicates a more stable and reliable funding profile. More stable funding in turn enhances liquidity, since it means that it is far less likely that the bank will have to scramble for liquid funds to meet current liabilities.

Deposit Base

Commercial banks, therefore, benefit from the stable source of funding that deposits provide. Here, large retail banks have an advantage over their smaller counterparts as a result of their deep customer deposit bases gained through their large branch networks and other distribution channels. Wholesale or investment banks, in contrast, do not have a significant customer deposit base and their funding profile is generally regarded as higher risk and possessing greater volatility. Because of their less stable funding profile due to their lack of retail customer deposits, investment banks often carry lower credit ratings.[4]

Composition of Deposits

Demand Deposits vs. Savings and Term Deposits

In the case of deposit-taking institutions, it is important to look at the customer deposit profile and mix. Are deposits largely "at call," able to be withdrawn on demand? Most deposits are like this not withstanding that they tend to be rolled over. However, for purposes of stability, it is important to have a base of longer-term deposits.

Source of Deposits

Also, are deposits sourced from individuals or corporations? Corporate deposits and wholesale deposits tend to be a more volatile source of income. The large banks in South Africa, for instance, rely heavily on

---

[4] Investment banks concentrate on wholesale and bank funding and usually their banking licenses prohibit them from taking retail deposits.

wholesale deposits. Again, traditionally, these are rolled over, but in times of a crisis are subject to withdrawal.

Deposit Concentration

Deposit concentration needs to be examined to determine if there is a dominance of large depositors whose funds withdrawal may cause liquidity problems. A state-owned bank will often rely heavily on deposits from the government and its agencies. However, if the bank is privatized, these deposits may be withdrawn. Banks may also receive significant deposits from related parties. This may be both good and bad depending on the reasons behind the funds as well as the strength of the related party. On one hand it may represent a concentration of deposit funding and lack of ability to obtain additional deposits. On the other hand, it is likely to be a fairly stable funding source as the related party is unlikely to withdraw funds, especially if the bank is suffering liquidity problems.[5]

Medium- and Long-Term Debt

The access to, and the appearance of medium- and long-term funding on the balance sheet, is a tremendous advantage for banks. Medium- and long-term debt provides the bank with very stable funding, giving it greater flexibility and diversity. The bank is able to manage its projected balance sheet better and to match its medium- and long-term assets. The appearance of medium- and long-term funding on a bank's balance sheet usually elicits rating advantages for the bank in the eyes of the analyst. It is particularly an advantage in emerging markets as usually banks in these operating environments find it difficult to obtain medium-/long-terms funds as other institutions are not willing to take on longer term risk in markets of high volatility. Thus it tends only to be the very highly regarded banks or highly rated institutions that are able to gain access to these funds. However, as was mentioned earlier in respect to loan syndications, the analyst must be aware of the date when repayments are due to ascertain whether the bank can comfortably meet its obligations. Especially in times of market volatility and negative sentiment, the bank will not be able to roll over the medium-/long-term debt that may put pressure on its liquidity position.

> Tip: Some medium- and long-term funding is usually beneficial as it enhances funding stability and thereby improves liquidity.

---

[5] If the related party runs into problems, then obviously the funds will be quickly withdrawn.

Repurchase Commitments

Repurchase commitments (repos) connected to government fixed income securities have become an important off-balance sheet source of funding for banks in many countries.[6] Under a repo agreement, a bank agrees to sell fixed income securities, usually government treasury bills or bonds, with guarantee to repurchase them later at a predetermined rate and price. The effect is the same as if the bank borrowed the equivalent of the purchase price on a fully secured basis. Repos generally have maturities of less than one week. Repos create both liquidity and interest rate risk due to the mismatch in maturities between the repos and the longer maturities of bank's interest-earning assets, as well as pricing differences. For example, market interest rates may be 10% but the overnight repo rate may be 11%. For a bank holding a large repo portfolio, the loss could be significant. Liquidity risk occurs because government securities held as assets accrue interest for many months, while banks continue to make cash interest payments on their repo liabilities, thereby increasing the cash outflow in the short-term. In a situation where there is a significant fall in demand for repos, those banks relying on repos as a principal source of funds could face a funding shortage, particularly in the short-term.

A Note on Investment Banks

The liquidity and funding profile of investment banks is generally inferior to that of commercial or retail banks. Their funding tends to be less stable and less assured. If market sentiment turns against investment banks, they can quickly lose access to the unsecured debt market and thus need to rely on the market as a secured borrower. For the generally higher probability of funding loss, an investment bank must have in place a contingency plan for times of funding stress, and be fully aware of its realizable assets and how quickly they can be liquidated to meet maturing liabilities.

EVALUATING LIQUIDITY

Asset Profile and Liquidity

The overall asset profile of the bank is an important determinant of balance sheet liquidity and the aim is to gain a feel for the

---

[6] If repos are judged to be an integral part of a bank's funding, the bank's auditors may require that the repos be on-balance sheet.

complete liquidity picture. The analyst should ask a number of questions.

❑ Does the bank have an adequate level of liquid assets that can be easily sold in times of need?

❑ Are government securities easily marketable and is there a deep market for them?

❑ What is actually held in marketable securities and could these be sold in times of liquidity need?

Securities

The bank's holding of shares may be a source of liquidity, but they may have to be sold at below purchase or book value if there is market turbulence. Corporate securities and shares also may not be very liquid in developing markets, as the depth of the local market may be weak.

Tenor of Loans

The loan portfolio also should possess an appropriate level of short-term loans. A dominance of short-term lending will aid the overall liquidity position of the bank, especially in developing markets, as cash flow will be high as loan turnover is high. Also, with loans exiting the portfolio quickly, the potential for non-performing loans is lower.

Capital

A bank's funding and liquidity position will also be affected by its capital base. The bank may be funding a large part of its asset base by its own capital that will help to augment the liquidity position (i.e. free capital). Note also that subordinated debt, which ostensibly functions as Tier 2 capital, may play a similar role.

Size of the Institution

Size will have a bearing on the bank's liquidity and funding options. A larger bank may well have a more diversified funding base than a smaller bank. Moreover, the larger bank will usually have at its disposal more funding options than a smaller bank. Its treasury department will be able to utilize hedging instruments more efficiently. A larger bank is likely to have greater access to the international markets, attract medium-/long-term funding more easily and, if retail-oriented, is likely to have a large distribution network that can attract retail deposit funding. All things being equal, a large bank is likely to obtain a higher credit rating than a smaller bank and is likely to possess access to market funding, such as the interbank and fixed-income securities. Generally, smaller banks often rely more heavily on a narrow funding base and are therefore more vulnerable to liquidity risk.

Funding for troubled banks facing liquidity problems may be provided from a government or central bank wishing to avoid systemic problems and further liquidity problems for other banks if there is market panic in the banking system. This may be more likely at larger banks with a substantial number of deposit customers.[7]

Tip: Large retail banks tend to have more stable funding and liquidity than smaller retail banks and wholesale banks due to the deep customer deposit bases gained through their large branch networks. Larger banks may also have access to more alternative sources of funding.

Liquidity and Regulation

Domestic bank regulations dictate reserve requirements and other liquidity guidelines and these will influence the overall adequacy of liquidity in a market. Minimum reserve requirements differ from country to country. The analyst needs to be aware of this to see whether minimum requirements are above, below or at generally accepted levels. Some examples of various regulatory liquidity requirements are outlined on the next page.

Additional Funding and Liquidity Considerations

Securitization

Banks are increasingly securitizing assets, such as mortgages, in order to diversify funding, reduce capital needs and improve their return on equity. Securitization is the process whereby a financial

---

[7] The authorities are likely to deem the bank "too big to fail."

Sample Liquidity Requirements

Saudi Arabia	Banks must maintain liquid assets equal to at least 20% of their deposit liabilities. Banks must also maintain statutory deposits with the Saudi Arabian Monetary Authority amounting to 7% of their average demand and 2% of their average savings and time deposit liabilities.
Philippines	Banks are required to set aside a certain portion of their peso deposit liabilities as reserves in the form of liquid assets. At least 25% of the liquidity reserve must be kept in the form of deposits with the central bank of the Philippines. Banks can keep up to 75% in cash in vault and/or eligible government, or foreign securities. Banks also have to maintain a 10% reserve requirement on their peso-denominated common trust funds and other similar managed funds. The reserve requirements are as follows:
	Regular Reserves: 9% for deposits and deposit substitutes for commercial banks. Liquidity Reserves: 3% on government and quasi-government deposits.
Czech Republic	Banks are required to keep a minimum cash reserve balance with the central bank equal to or greater than 2% of primary deposits. Other minimum liquidity ratios are also utilized.
Source: Darren Stubing	

institution that owns a loan portfolio and is looking at funding them through securitization will pool the assets, recognizing the ownership of the assets though classes of tranches. Generally it is more expensive for a bank to securitize assets against obtaining funds from the wholesale market. The extra cost can be 40 basis points and above. Banks tend to securitize only if they can obtain capital relief (i.e. free the balance sheet of a corresponding value in capital required against the value, of, say, the mortgages funded through the securitization issue). If the bank needs to increase the yield of the issue to attract investors to the securitization issue to a greater level than the equity relief, then the securitization deal is not cost-effective funding.

Nevertheless, securitization does have funding, liquidity and asset/liability management advantages. It increases the liquidity of some assets by creating a secondary market for them. Asset liquidity management is enhanced through transferring the risk of some of the assets to the market.

Securitization provides an extra funding source for the bank apart from commercial paper and deposits to fund, say, its retail mortgage book. As mentioned in Chapter 13, one of the challenges facing a bank is managing its asset/liability maturity profile. Through securitizing part of its loan book, the uncertainty regarding loan repayment is transferred to the purchasers of the securitization issue. The secondary market is also strengthened in the securitization process and *inter alia*, other advantages are derived such as an actual market valuation of assets. The loan assets in effect become a marketable, and liquid, commodity which, in turn, aids the financing of loan assets thereby enhancing the overall liquidity profile of the financial institution, providing there remains market appetite for these securitized assets. At the same time, a bank may become over-dependent on the securitized market. If there is a lack of demand, then this will have negative consequences for the institution's liquidity profile. Securitization can improve a bank's balance sheet liquidity profile through the creation of a secondary market, and enhance its funding profile. Assets move off balance sheet, thereby freeing capital, while at the same time, payment risk is transferred.

In most emerging markets, however, the depth of the capital and financial markets, as well as the extent of, say, mortgage lending, restricts the use of classic asset securitization techniques. In addition, the risk profile of the assets makes them unattractive for investors. On the other hand, another advantage of securitization is that it can provide longer term funds for banks which have some difficulty gaining funds over one-year, particularly in emerging markets. For example, the securitization of future receivables has been used as financing tool in non-investment grade countries since the late 1980s.[8] The underlying assets are usually in the form of export receivables, credit card receivables, and remittance receivables.

Securitizing future receivables is very advantageous for banks in countries whose sovereign rating is below investment grade. A good bank with a low domestic credit risk seeking funds on the international market will be constrained by its country's sovereign rating and hence

---

[8] Source: Dresdner Kleiwort Benson Global Fixed Income Credit Research Note, April 2000.

its own rating will be capped at the sovereign ceiling, thereby affecting costs and availability. The capping of the bank's rating at the sovereign level reflects sovereign risk factors such as the host country's ability and willingness to meet obligations and *inter alia* the servicing of foreign debt. Through certain securitization techniques, the bank can achieve a higher rating than the sovereign rating by structuring the issue so as to partly overcome and reduce the related risks. For example, in a future financial flow transaction, the interest and principal repayments under a debt instrument are paid out of, and secured by, the cash flows from transactions such as credit card receivables. The important factor in these transactions is that they capture hard currency cash flows offshore and pay the debt service on the bonds before transferring excess funds back to the originator.[9]

Bank Facilities

It is important for the bank analyst to analyze bank facility agreements in place. The overall reliability and assuredness of bank facilities will differ depending on the type of arrangement. As a result, the bank's liquidity and funding profile will be subject to the actual type of back-up facilities. A bank may have in place a contractual lending commitment from another bank that is legally binding. In times of need, such as a liquidity squeeze, this type of committed facility will be very important. On the other hand, a bank may have a similar type contractual lending commitment, again legally binding, but with an escape clause which will come into play in certain circumstances. Clauses such as these are known as material adverse change clauses. A bank may well have commercial paper backup lines and revolving commitment vehicles but these may be of little value if the material adverse change clauses are attached to their legal agreement. Again, any support for the bank's liquidity position and funding profile may evaporate. If market sentiment to the bank changed for whatever reason, then the funding facility could be quickly withdrawn. This will exacerbate the potentially already tightening liquidity position of the bank in question. The facility document may also include financial covenants that the bank must adhere to. If the bank fails to meet any of these covenants, then again the funding facility may be withdrawn quickly and the bank's liquidity position may be dangerously weak.

---

[9] Source: Dresdner Kleiwort Benson Global Fixed Income Credit Research Note, April 2000.

Although the move in international banking today is towards transactional banking, whereby the correspondent bank is looking for reciprocal business that the other bank can generate, it is still important to examine the bank's relationship with correspondent banks and the borrowing facilities they provide, as well as to ascertain the credit profile of these correspondent banks. Not all banks require committed back-up facilities in order to provide comfort in times of stress. Highly rated, strong and large institutions with a significant franchise and distribution network will obviously not need these commitments. Banks with this type of profile should be able to continue sourcing funds from the interbank market.

Central Banks and Lenders of Last Resort

Central banks function as "lenders of last resort" or the final source of liquidity for a distressed bank. A bank may face difficulties because poor asset quality has depressed cash flows, or face a run on deposits because of negative news about the bank or the banking system. Even the financially soundest of banks can be hit by deposit runs. The original Basle Accord commented on the subject of lenders of last resort. It describes the intention of intervention by lenders of last resort as providing financial support to banks under temporary liquidity pressure, not to cover the losses of badly managed banks at the expense of the entire national community. A central banker's decision — as lender of last resort — whether or not to support a distressed bank often depends upon two questions:[10]

1. Would the failure of the bank cause unacceptably high disruption to the national financial system?

2. Is the bank solvent?

Governments and central banks cannot tolerate significant disruption to banking systems. Temporary facilities from a central bank are usually secured against sound loans. Alternatively, the central bank will discount credits of a solvent bank. The regulators may choose to allow a relatively small insolvent bank to fail, with shareholders and depositors suffering the losses. However, governments may choose to save even insignificant banks for political reasons. For larger banks, this is especially true.

---

[10] See Chapter 19: *The Distressed Bank, Part I: Introduction to Restructuring.*

Deposit Guarantees

Many countries have deposit insurance schemes in place. These guarantee the nominal value and liquidity of deposits up to a certain size. Deposit insurance schemes suffer, to a certain extent, from moral hazard. This is the risk that insured depositors are no longer concerned with the overall quality and financial soundness of any given bank as they are insured against any loss. Deposit schemes are designed to prevent deposit runs from starting, and lender-of-last-resort facilities are designed to prevent runs from spreading. Turkey implemented a full 100% deposit guarantee in the midst of its banking crisis in 1994 to halt the spread of deposit runs in the sector. The blanket scheme caused many problems over the years largely through moral hazard. Weaker and poorly run banks have been able to survive on the back of the guarantee scheme by offering above market rates to depositors. Often the deposit funds have been directed to Turkish government paper where high real yields have prevailed or, in some exceptional cases, to related party loans. The full deposit guarantee particularly adversely affected the well-run and financially sound banks through an overall higher market cost of fundings and had the indirect affect of having weak banks supported in the system.[11]

Key Liquidity Ratios

Before we examine the main liquidity ratios in detail, we should be clear what a ratio is, and what it is designed to tell us. Ratios express one thing in terms of another or, most often, as a percentage of another; they are a numerical expression of the relationship between two values. Their usefulness in analysis is as a tool that allows us to compare aspects of a bank's performance, either internally, over time, or with those of other banks, or with industry benchmarks.

Allowing for known characteristics of the particular market we are dealing with (for example competition, large changes in interest rates, behavior of the securities markets etc), we should be looking for any departures from steadily increasing balances. If there is no discernible trend, or if there are marked departures from trends, we would want to try to ascertain the reasons for such deviations. The cause could be something as simple as year-end distortions, or pure window-dressing, but it could be a factor that would seriously affect the view of the bank's credit status.

---

[11] The full deposit guaranteed was reduced in June 2000 to a maximum of 100 billion Turkish lira.

Net Loans to Total Deposits

$$\text{Net Loans to Total Deposits (\%)} = \frac{\text{Net Loans}}{\text{Total customer deposits} + \text{Interbank deposits}} \times 100$$

This ratio is the basic measure of overall liquidity. It indicates to what extent are depositors' funds tied up in lending (as opposed to liquid assets).

Net Loans to Customer Deposits

$$\text{Net Loans to Customer Deposits (\%)} = \frac{\text{Net Loans}}{\text{Total customer deposits}} \times 100$$

This is a more precise measure of liquidity as the ratio looks at net loans purely against *core customer deposits* and not *total deposits* as in the above ratio that may include *bank deposits*. The ratio may also use *total loans* (i.e. ignoring provisions) against total customer deposits. Customer loans refer to loans other than interbank lending (interbank deposits). Note: we are using total to mean face value of loan plus unearned interest income.

Net Loans to Stable Funds

This is a rather more sensitive and realistic liquidity measure. It looks at to what extent are the bank's own unencumbered capital and less volatile deposits tied up in lending.

$$\text{Net Loans to Stable Funds} = \frac{\text{Net Loans}}{\text{Stable Funds}} \times 100$$

Stable funds are defined as total *customer deposits* plus *official deposits* plus *medium/long-term liabilities* plus *free capital funds*. Free capital funds are defined as total equity capital minus financial and non-financial subsidiaries minus fixed assets. Official deposits are deposits or borrowings from central governments/banks. Medium/long-term liabilities include loans and notes with more than one year to maturity.

Under normal economic conditions, we would expect a well-run bank to grow steadily, with most measures increasing roughly in line with the overall expansion of the balance sheet. In some developing countries, especially where liberalization of the banking market has started and there is a growing middle class with rising expectations, we would expect the lending portfolio to expand more rapidly than total assets; the corollary of this would be a decline in liquid assets, and perhaps an increasing reliance on interbank funding.

Customer Deposits to Total Deposits

The customer deposits to total deposits ratio is a measure of the strength of the bank's customer deposit base or, conversely, of the extent to which it relies on generally more volatile interbank funds. Multi-branched retail banks will have high ratios whilst specialist institutions, such as development banks, may have very low ratios. However, the latter are likely to have access to other funding, particularly medium/long-term facilities such as bonds or debentures.

$$\text{Customer Deposits to Total Deposits (\%)} = \frac{\text{Total Customer Deposits}}{\text{Total Deposits}} \times 100$$

Customer deposits include short-, medium-, and long-term deposits, foreign currency deposits, cash margins (collaterals) and certificates of deposits placed by a bank's core clients.

Liquid Asset Ratio[12]

The liquid asset ratio is the basic measure of asset liquidity. The ratio indicates what percentage of total assets consists of instruments that can easily be sold in time of crisis. The criterion is liquidity, therefore high quality items having short-term maturities that can easily be converted into cash are included here (i.e. cash, deposits with the central bank, treasury bills, government securities and interbank funds sold).

---

[12] Some analysts may prefer to use a tighter definition and only look at "liquid assets."

$$\text{Liquid Asset Ratio (\%)} = \frac{\text{(Total liquid assets + deposits with banks)}}{\text{Total assets}} \times 100$$

Quasi-Liquid Asset Ratio

The quasi-liquid asset ratio is a somewhat looser measure of asset liquidity than the liquid assets ratio although there may not in fact be any difference between two. It looks at the proportion of total assets that are made up of readily available instruments, including securities such as corporate commercial paper or corporate debentures, which can ordinarily be easily be sold.

As mentioned, some securities which appear as liquid or quasi-liquid assets, particularly government securities, may not in fact be liquid, especially in difficult times, and may in actuality have long maturities. Where this is known, they are properly deducted from the numerator of the formula.

$$\text{Quasi-Liquid Asset Ratio (\%)} = \frac{\text{Quasi-liquid assets}}{\text{Total assets}} \times 100$$

Caution: The market for many securities may dry up at exactly the time it becomes necessary to liquidate them. Going into the 1997–99 Asian crisis, Korean banks' headline liquidity ratios appeared to be conservative. Many banks displayed prudent loans to deposits ratios of 65% and below. However, much of the banks' exposure to the *chaebols*[13] was classified under marketable securities. Taking this into account, the Korean banks' liquidity position was much tighter. Commercial paper is usually categorized as "marketable securities," but may in fact be equivalent to short-term unsecured lending.

Foreign Currency Assets to FX Currency Liabilities

$$\frac{\text{Foreign Currency Assets to}}{\text{FX Currency Liabilities (\%)}} = \frac{\text{Foreign Currency Assets}}{\text{Foreign Currency Liabilities}} \times 100$$

---

[13] *Chaebols* are large South Korean conglomerates that dominate the country's economy, and at least up until the Asian crisis of 1997–98 were the primary recipients of bank financing.

Foreign currency assets to foreign currency liabilities attempts to measure to what extent foreign currency assets and liabilities are matched. If there is a significant imbalance, and particularly if the bank runs a "short" position, this can be dangerous.

Foreign Currency Loans to Foreign Currency Deposits

$$\text{FX Currency Loans to FX Currency Deposits (\%)} = \frac{\text{Foreign Currency Loans}}{\text{Foreign Currency Borrowings} + \text{Foreign Currency Deposits}} \times 100$$

If loans in foreign currency are not well covered by similar deposits, the bank will be forced to fund itself in the international money market, with potentially disastrous consequences.

Interbank Assets to Interbank Liabilities

What is the bank's net position in relation to the interbank market? Is it a net lender (good) or a net borrower (not so good)? Net interbank Assets (total deposits with banks minus total interbank liabilities) gives an indication of the size of the bank's net interbank position. If interbank assets divided by interbank liabilities yield a number over 1, the bank is a net lender. If they yield a number less than 1, the bank is a net borrower.

Interbank assets include time deposits with banks, placements, deposits due from banks, certificate of deposits and asset backed securities. Interbank liabilities should include deposits from banks, call loans from other banks, vostro accounts, overdrafts, funds borrowed from banks, repurchase agreements, drafts and remittances outstanding.[14] Banks that rely heavily on interbank funding are sometimes said to be relying upon "purchased funds" or "hot funds," a more expensive and volatile source of funding than core deposits. These markets are subject to rapid changes in investor sentiment, and a bank that depends heavily on purchased funds can easily find itself facing a liquidity crunch should market conditions turn adverse.

---

[14] Account used by a bank to describe a demand deposit account maintained with it by a bank in a foreign country. It is the vostro account of the other bank, and used mainly to arrange foreign exchange transfers between the two banks.

$$\text{Interbank Assets to Interbank Liabilities (\%)} = \frac{\text{Total deposits with banks}}{\text{Total interbank liabilities}} \times 100$$

From a credit perspective, it is therefore preferable that a bank be a net lender in the interbank market than a net borrower. Analysts should be aware, however, that year-end figures must be treated with circumspection, as they may not reflect the typical position. If it is a large net taker of funds, it is likely to be more vulnerable in difficult times, as bank lenders are more likely to cut lines than customers are to withdraw their deposits.

> Tip: A bank which relies heavily on "purchased funds" will not only be paying more for funding than its peers with extensive branch networks, but it will also be more vulnerable to sudden withdrawals and to a liquidity crunch.

Another indicator that can be used to measure reliance on purchased funds is the ratio of *purchased funds to earning assets*.

Pledged Government Securities to Total Government Securities

What proportion of the government securities on the bank's books has been used as some form of collateral? In other words, how much of the stated amount of government securities is actually available in case of need?

$$\text{Pledged Government Securities to Total Government Securities (\%)} = \frac{\text{Pledged Government Securities}}{\text{Total Government Securities}} \times 100$$

In the illustration on the next page selection of countries, Greece's banking sector exhibits the highest average liquidity ratios. The banking sector in Greece has low net loans to customer deposits and to stable funds ratios while its liquid asset-based ratios are high. These liquidity ratios largely reflect the fairly weak lending environment in the past caused by poor economic fundamentals which saw high market interest rates. As a result, a high proportion of Greek banks' asset base comprised domestic government securities whilst their loan portfolios were relatively modest. Average liquidity ratios as depicted in

Illustration: Emerging Markets

Average sector	Greece	South Africa	Saudi Arabia	Bahrain	Malaysia	Indonesia	Thailand
Liquidity ratios at end 1999							
Net loans/ customer deposits	54.11	97.85	74.27	85.70	85.71	26.50	86.33
Net loans to stable funds	47.17	89.82	60.81	32.17	74.04	26.66	81.52
Liquid asset ratio	51.10	17.60	40.54	30.46	26.55	16.61	18.38
Quasi-liquid asset ratio	55.98	19.95	47.52	61.65	37.40	50.88	21.09

the above table for South Africa are comparatively tight. The representative bank sample for South Africa includes the big four banks — ABSA, Standard Bank of South Africa, FirstRand, and Nedcor — and all their loan portfolios comprise a high percentage of total assets. The relatively tight liquidity is a factor of the market whereby the banking sector is very well developed and sophisticated. Accordingly, the need for the Reserve Bank of South Africa to set high reserve requirements or liquidity ratios is unnecessary. Individual lending, such as home mortgages, is well developed. South African banks also rely heavily on wholesale deposits.[15] This reflects the sophisticated characteristic of the corporate sector with the large corporations placing their funds only with the main clearing banks. Generally, South African banks' liquidity ratios are more in line with those of developed markets.

Saudi Arabia banks possess solid liquidity ratios, aided by well capitalized balance sheets. Banks included in the Bahraini sector are the offshore-licensed investment banks. Loan-based liquidity ratios are moderate due to the fact that lending is not a focus of these investments banks. In addition, the offshore banks in Bahrain cannot tap the local deposit market and rely quite heavily on interbank funding,

---

[15] Defined in this market as deposits over 100,000 Rand.

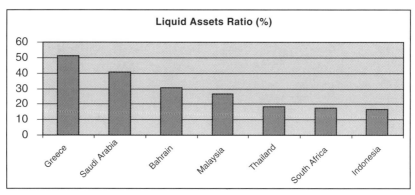

Source: Darren Stubing

particularly from Gulf-based institutions. Their assets profile includes significant portfolios of marketable securities and unquoted investments. The reason for the large jump between the liquid assets ratio (30.46%) and the quasi-liquid assets ratio (61.65%) is due to the large portfolios of *marketable securities*.

Malaysia's banking sector reflects overall sound liquidity ratios but the sector averages does overlook some noted variances. For example, a bank that was relatively unaffected by the crisis was Public Bank. This bank's management has traditionally been very conservative and Public Bank has always maintained very high liquidity with ratios being superior to the market. Through this practice, the bank recorded a much lower level of bad debt compared to the market.

Indonesia's low loan-based liquidity ratios is due to the restructuring that occurred when large volumes of non-performing loans were removed from the balance sheets and replaced with government paper (which is, in actual fact, illiquid). Thailand's liquidity ratios, although improved from a couple of years ago, are still relatively tight as much of the bad debt is still on banks' books and portfolios await further restructuring. In the years leading up to the Asian crisis of 1997, which begun in Thailand, Thai banks were registering very sharp loan growth rates. Many analysts thought this was not a problem as the high loan growth rates merely reflected the strong GDP growth rates in the economy. Exceptionally high loans to deposits ratios, in some cases as high as 125% at the end of December 1996, were recorded by banks such as Union Bank of Bangkok, Bangkok Metropolitan Bank, Siam City Bank and First Bangkok City Bank. Tellingly, all these banks suffered severe pressure when the crisis hit and international funding was withdrawn, placing significant liquidity

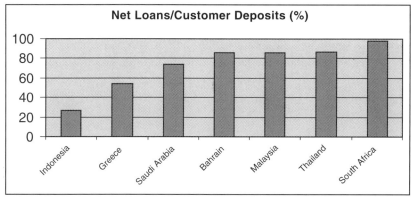

Net Loans/Customer Deposits (%)

Source: Darren Stubing

pressure on these institutions. All of these banks were subsequently taken over by the government's restructuring vehicle. Thai banks' pre-crisis liquidity positions were very poor. Even the basic customer deposits to loans ratios were extremely high, in some cases, over 120%.[16]

Illustration: Developed Markets

1998 (%)			
	Liquid assets/ Total assets	Gross loans/ customer deposits	Gross loans/ Total assets
Australia			
ANZ Group	14.14	77.24	151.04
Commonwealth Bank of Australia	12.47	79.97	137.65
National Australia Bank	12.84	78.58	150.19
Westpac Banking Corporation Canada	8.90	79.67	· 155.28
Canadian Imperial Bank of Commerce	8.90	77.24	156.20
Royal Bank of Canada	12.44	75.94	126.17
Toronto-Dominion Bank Germany	12.57	77.96	136.17
Bayerische Hypo-und Vereinsbank	27.36	67.91	210.56
Deutsche Bank	43.30	46.58	118.71
United Kingdom			
Abbey National	36.79	52.38	132.79
Barclays	42.37	44.20	91.97
Lloyds TSB Group	22.44	57.72	107.53

---

[16] This is considered high for an emerging market bank due to greater market volatility and less stable overall funding profile.

As can be seen in the table on the previous page, liquidity ratios in developed markets are much tighter than in emerging markets. This reflects the sophisticated nature of the market, the banks and the regulators. It also highlights the fact that their overall funding position is considerably stronger, and more diversified as they are able to tap many channels for funding, which, in turn, reflects their strong credit standing.

Other Ratios

Sometimes other liquidity ratios are seen in bank analysis. These include the ratios indicated below.

Illiquid Assets to Core Funding Sources

$$\text{Illiquid Assets to Core Funding Sources (\%)} = \frac{\text{Illiquid Assets}}{\text{Core Funding Sources}} \times 100$$

Liquid Assets to Purchased Funds

$$\text{Liquid Assets to Purchased Funds (\%)} = \frac{\text{Liquid Assets}}{\text{Purchased Funds}} \times 100$$

Window Dressing

It is important to remember that certain window dressing practices may change the apparent liquidity position of the bank at the year-end. These include:

❑ Overnight back-to-back transactions with banks to boost liquidity ratios;

❑ Transferring overdrafts or loans to or from associated companies over the end of the accounting period and since overdrafts or loans between associated companies and third parties are not consolidated in group financial statements, this may change the apparent liquidity of the group;

❑ Repaying a loan shortly before the end of an accounting period and re-borrowing it shortly afterwards, with a view to avoiding its disclosure;

❑ The temporary rearrangement of financing transactions, so that at the end of the accounting period they are dealt with as off-balance sheet items.

CHAPTER SUMMARY

The bank credit analyst must pay due attention to the assessment of a bank's liquidity position. Without the liquidity and funding in place to meet obligations, the bank may quickly fail unless external support is given. Liquidity has many facets but is based largely on the bank's holding of liquid assets, its cash flow and ability to borrow in the market. Interest rate sensitivity, and both maturity and currency matching, are important elements. Other factors such as the style of management (i.e. whether they aggressively position the balance sheet), the bank's operating environment, its own creditworthiness and reputation, will all, *inter alia*, have an impact on the strength, flexibility and diversity of the overall liquidity position.

The bank credit analyst must pay due attention to the assessment of a bank's funding position. The bank's size, market position, operating environment and regulatory system will all influence a bank's liquidity and funding profile. Other factors such as the style of management (i.e. whether they aggressively position the balance sheet), the bank's own creditworthiness and reputation will also, *interalia*, have an impact on the strength, flexibility and diversity of the overall liquidity position. Securitization offers the possibility of alternative, and important, funding sources. Asset liquidity management is enhanced through transferring the risk of some of the assets to the market. Securitizing future receivables is advantageous for banks in countries whose sovereign rating is below investment grade. Key liquidity ratios were examined. These can also be influenced by market characteristics and financial window dressing.

CHAPTER FIFTEEN

MANAGEMENT AND THE BANK VISIT

Evaluation of a foreign bank's management is perhaps the most difficult and subjective component of the credit evaluation process.
— Robert Morris Associates, *A Guide to Analyzing Foreign Banks*[1]

Although banks differ in many respects — some are larger than others, some are stronger in certain franchises, some specialize in particular products — many of the variables which determine the profitability of a bank's business are fixed, at least in the short-term. Prevailing interest rates, business conditions, and minimum capital requirements, as established by regulation are outside of a bank's control. Those variables over which the bank does have control are limited, but important. Among them: How much to lend and to whom? What credit controls and risk management policies will apply? What approach will be taken to addressing interest rate risk? Will the bank expand its branch network and how fast? What kind of staff will the bank recruit? What functions will it outsource? What kind of marketing strategy will the bank employ? These are many of the decisions that will literally determine a bank's future, and management will make them. Looking at two banks with roughly the same capital adequacy, asset quality, earnings and liquidity, disparity in management skills will determine which bank thrives and which bank merely survives. Management is the difference that makes the difference.

---

[1] RMA, p. 31.

THE IMPORTANCE OF MANAGEMENT

For these reasons, assessing management of a bank is one of the most critical elements of bank credit analysis, yet it is perhaps the most difficult to perform. It is also probably the aspect of bank credit analysis about which it is hardest to generalize. Yet the appraisal of management is important because, as noted, there is a direct link between a bank's condition, its prospects and the competence of management. Management is responsible for hiring, training and supervising staff, ensuring regulatory compliance, and ultimately generating a sustainable level of profits while minimizing risk.

Management must not only oversee day-to-day operations, but also plan for the future, developing a strategy to respond to the challenges presented by the economic, legal and competitive banking environment which the bank confronts. Management's objectives depend upon whether a bank is primarily a profit-making commercial institution, or whether it serves non-commercial policy objectives set by government or charter. While, in the commercial context, its overarching objective is to maximize returns for shareholders, the route to achieving this end is often not obvious.

DIFFICULTIES IN ASSESSMENT

Evaluating management is particularly hard because there are no clear-cut or easily quantifiable standards for appraisal, and the analyst, in any case, is likely to lack much of the intangible data necessary to form a complete picture of management's collective abilities. Equity analysts have a somewhat easier time of it here, because for them profitability and share performance is the best evidence of management skill. For the credit analyst, the task is harder as the credit analyst is looking for a balance between near-term performance and long-term financial strength that will ensure the bank's capacity to continue a function as a healthy going concern for a period of one to ten years — depending upon the time horizon of the credit analysis. Yet the analyst must make an appraisal of bank management based upon a relatively short interaction, or none it all, in a context that highlights certain skills in presentation and leadership but which downplays others.

BANK MANAGEMENT: A MORE CHALLENGING ROLE

While in a distant past and still in some markets, bank management was not so demanding, the increasing pace of change in the financial markets is presenting managers with greater challenges. Bank management is subject to demands from customers, depositors, shareholders and employees and must maintain an effective balance in responding to the demands from each. Each group seeks the maximum value relative to the competition. Customers and depositors want the cheapest rate on loans, the highest rate on deposits and the best ancillary services. Shareholders want to obtain the greatest return on their investment, but are generally highly sensitive to increased risk, and recognize the importance of maintaining an adequate degree of capitalization and liquidity. Staff wants to maximize compensation, but also takes into account a variety of other considerations such as working conditions, job satisfaction and security, and the opportunities for career development. Each group is also cognizant of the fact that all choices involve trade-offs and that changing from one bank, investment and employer to another necessarily involves transaction costs.

To some extent, the demands of one group can only be satisfied at the expense of another, but banking is not a zero sum game. The composition of the groups overlaps, while individuals within each group have different preferences. Customers are usually depositors, and despositors are often customers, that is, borrowers. Although money is a commodity, the ability of the banker to provide an attractive mix of products and services, as well as intangible benefits, in addition to its lending and deposit-taking functions can enable one bank to gain an advantage over another. Similarly, skillful marketing, risk management, and good customer service can also give an edge. By utilizing sophisticated risk management techniques, the bank may be able to price its loans more efficiently so as to optimize profits. Implementation of improved IT infrastructure can open new channels of product delivery, personalize marketing and reduce transaction costs.

At the same time, the entire scenario is a dynamic one, and banks must respond to a business landscape whose contours are in incessant movement. The products and services competing banks offer are not fixed. Investment opportunities are also in a state of flux and shareholders must continually evaluate the risk and return of present and prospective investments. Likewise, the employment market is not static, resulting in a lesser or greater degree of staff turnover. Compensation packages, too, vary a great deal in their make-up, with incentives that may to a greater or lesser extent be tied to organizational performance.

Management has choices and by making effective decisions can avoid mistakes and achieve higher returns relative to risk. Its goal should be to achieve the optimal combination of risk to return for its banking franchise, accounting for all relevant variables, and maintaining that mix through an effective business strategy. High-risk strategies in themselves do not necessarily impair creditworthiness, provided that effective risk management techniques are employed, and returns are commensurate to the risks taken. Similarly, a low risk strategy does not necessarily bolster creditworthiness, where returns are so disproportionately low so as to make the strategy unsustainable over the longer term.

QUANTITATIVE METHODS ARE OF LITTLE AID IN ASSESSING MANAGEMENT

Assessing management is not conducive to quantitative analysis. Certainly, there are quantitative indicators that can be proffered as proxies for the caliber of management. These include indicia such as:

❑ number of years of experience

❑ educational qualifications

❑ professional experience

❑ training expenditure per staff member

But these criteria hardly embrace the panoply of intangible qualities, including integrity, good judgment, and business acumen that will be found in first-rate management. Instead, the evaluation of management inevitably requires making subjective, even intuitive judgments, on the part of the bank analyst. It is difficult to make such an appraisal at a distance, which means that a bank visit is a near-necessity for even a partial assessment.

Yet the bank visit too has its dangers. The credit analyst must guard against being swayed by the charm, volubility or the ability of management to speak in the analyst's native language. Rating agency analysts in particular must be wary of the natural tendency of bank management to sell themselves and their bank. This is one reason why most rating agencies send a minimum of two analysts when performing a full rating of a bank. At the other extreme, particularly in developing markets, management may be reluctant to speak with the analyst, and will disclose comparatively little about operations or strategy. Unless management has solicited a rating from a ratings agency, it is under no obligation to meet with a particular analyst. The local business culture, moreover, may militate against frank disclosure of the bank's financial conditions as well as management's approach to the business. Similarly, the analyst may not have access to all key management, and the time available for a meeting may be limited. First impressions based on meetings with selected personnel may have to suffice.

MORE ART THAN SCIENCE

Presumably, before visiting the bank, the analyst will have obtained some knowledge of the bank's past performance, changes in top personnel during the previous several years, and the philosophy of present management. Management's track record says something about its ability to achieve future results, but is obviously not entirely predictive. In the bank visit, which may be as brief as a half-hour, the analyst cannot hope to evaluate management in a deep and comprehensive manner. Usually, the best the analyst will be able to do is to form some basic understanding of management's strategy, the plausibility of their plans, and likelihood that they can be carried out successfully, while in the process forming some impression of management's capability. To accomplish this, the analyst should seek to understand the corporate culture of the bank's management, while paying special attention to the ability of key managers to describe the bank's franchise and to voice a coherent strategy going forward. Beyond such generalities, there are some quantitative and qualitative guidelines that the analyst can utilize to make the task of assessing management easier. In the end, however, it must be emphasized that evaluating management almost always entails an element of intuition and subjectivity.

Assessing Management Indirectly

Ideally, before a bank visit (if one is contemplated) the bank analyst will be able to form a preliminary assessment of management through the review of written material received from the bank, including its annual report, as well as through background material obtained from news databases such as Reuters Business Briefing or other third party sources. In some cases, managers of controversial or well-known banks may be profiled in the local or international business press. However the analyst obtains preliminary data, initial hypotheses can then be confirmed or revised following the bank visit.

Evaluating management is probably best initiated during a bank visit by an attempt to gain a better understanding of the bank's business. Through background research and the bank visit, the analyst should attempt to understand the origins of the bank, its history, its corporate culture, the scope of its present franchise, and its future goals and plans. These can form the basis of lines of inquiry during the meeting with bank officers. Questions concerning these topics have the virtue of being non-threatening and serve two purposes. First, the analyst obtains critical information about the institution's relative position in the industry, and also learns something about the competency level of its managers in the process. For instance, the analyst will probably want to ask management about recent initiatives and the future direction of the bank's business. The answers to these questions, which will almost certainly bring up other questions, should demonstrate a coherent and sensible approach to developing the bank's business in a sustainable manner.

Whether during the bank visit or beforehand, the analyst will want to have answers to the following questions before preparing a written analysis:

❑ Is the bank a comparatively new one, or has it survived and prospered through many business and economic cycles? What is its main franchise and how has it evolved over the years?

❑ Is the bank owned in full or in part by the government? Was it founded as a government bank; if so, when was it privatized?

❑ What market does the bank primarily serve?

❑ Is it a global bank, or mainly local in focus, within its market, is it a first-tier, middle-tier or third-tier player?

❑ What does the management see as the bank's key competitive advantages?

❑ How well formulated is its strategic planning process? Does it address various possible scenarios?

❑ Has it grown internally or by acquisition?

❑ What is the current ownership structure: is it closely-held and dominated by a single shareholder or are a high proportion of shares owned by the public? Is it a family-owned and managed bank, or are professional management employed?

❑ Is the bank a finance arm of a larger non-financial conglomerate, or is its business primarily finance-related?

The image the bank tries to present can also offer clues as to management philosophy and corporate culture. A relevant issue in this regard is whether the bank's image is consistent with its position within the industry, and whether the bank is affirmatively attempting to change its image. An example of the latter is a newly privatized bank which is attempting to shed a stodgy bureaucratic image for a new more innovative one. The analyst should be alert for deviations between image and reality. The newly privatized bank, for example, may have the same workforce as it did when it was a stodgy bureaucratic institution. The same culture may still prevail notwithstanding a change in ownership.

Some additional questions the analyst may seek answers to include:

❑ Is the bank the historic, traditional player in the market known for doing things the way they've always been done, or does it pride itself on product and technological innovation? Is it a market leader or a market follower, responding to trends only when they are clearly apparent?

❑ Is innovation prompted by success in other areas or because its existing franchise is threatened or shrinking and profitability is falling?

❑ Does the bank have the resources to support its innovation, or does its reach exceed its grasp?

❑ Is the bank in a comfortable market niche, or is it striving to expand the scope of its operations?

Relevant information can be drawn from the annual report, the accompanying statements of the chairman and president, the appearance of the bank's headquarters and personnel and the ease with which information can be obtained.

Questions that seek answers to the preceding items may be perceived as somewhat intrusive, and for this reason are, as we have suggested, best posed indirectly. For example, rather than address the first point above directly — is the bank an innovator or a follower — the analyst might inquire as to what new products or initiatives the bank has introduced during the last year, or what are its plans to deal with the Internet banking phenomenon? Or perhaps the analyst can pursue a line of inquiry concerning the way in which the bank markets itself. Management's responses, when compared with those of its peers, will provide the analyst with an idea where the bank fits in the spectrum.

Direct Assessment

By discussing the bank's past, present operation, and future plans it is possible to indirectly evaluate management and the culture of the bank through the responses to the questions put by the analyst. Ideally, the analyst should go beyond a general discussion of the bank's business to gain an appreciation of the process by which decisions are made and the quality of the individuals comprising the bank's management team. Such topics are naturally more sensitive than those relating to a general discussion of the bank's franchise and it very well may not be appropriate for the analyst to pose these questions directly, but much can be gleaned through small-talk with the individuals concerned about their education, experience and current role. To be sure, questions relating to the caliber, credentials and compensation of bank staff, particularly at upper and middle management levels, are likely to be intrusive if made in blunt or interrogative fashion. Sensitivity is the watchword. Although such subjects may be hard to address, they should not be ignored.

While more quantitative indicators such as years of education and experience are, as noted earlier, by no means definitive, they may be helpful indicators of a manager's competence. Although excellent self-taught bankers no doubt exist, the nature of the business is such that rigorous education and training combined with well-rounded banking experience, preferably at first-rate institutions, may very well be the best external gauge of managerial excellence. Compensation levels are also often a sign of management quality. Although excessive compensation expenses are to be avoided, a bank that attempts to skimp on remuneration to its key managers is usually penny-wise and pound-foolish. As salary and bonus levels are primary markers of success in the financial industry, the unduly parsimonious bank will find that its best employees leave and that mediocre ones remain. In addition, learning what factors are considered to be most important in the performance review of bank staff and officers can suggest something about the qualities valued by the organization.

Rather than ask individual managers about their own situation, questions can be put in the institutional context. The nature of a bank's human resource management system, as well as of its bank's recruiting and training programs can also give some indication of the quality of its managers. As with any complex and risk-sensitive organization, management should have a clear organizational structure, clear job descriptions and reporting lines that permit adequate controls, well-planned recruiting strategies, suitable training, regular performance evaluations, and salary review. Finally, the process of decision making should be addressed. How is strategy formed? How are controls exercised? Is leadership dependent upon a particular visionary individual, or is it largely consensual in nature?

The following items will provide the analyst with some ideas for additional queries to elicit information useful to an assessment of management quality.

❑ Existence of an organizational chart; reporting lines and authority.

❑ Existence of a business/management plan; objectives over the next 3–5 years.

❑ Existence of a planning department and role within organization; use of outside consultants.

❑ Internal forecasting of economic and business conditions; use of outside economic forecasts; rating agencies.

❑ Formulation of strategies and policies: does senior management consult with directors?

❑ Frequency of meetings by top management; channels for communication between junior and senior management.

❑ Is the bank professionally managed?

❑ Marketing function (how is it handled)?

❑ Risk management function (how is it handled)?

❑ Recent changes in auditors, accounting methods.

❑ Performance evaluation of staff — how often, what are staff judged on?

❑ Training provided to staff, other than on-the-job.

❑ Opportunities for promotion; succession arrangements.

❑ Existence of a personnel department; is it actively involved in recruitment?

❑ Recruitment — internal and external.

❑ Incentive compensation; stock options.

❑ Salary levels relative to peers, including benefits.

❑ Internal controls and methods of regulatory compliance.

❑ Existence and revision of policy manuals.

❑ Reporting requirements of managers.

❑ If the bank is a subsidiary of a holding company, how much independence does it have vis-à-vis the parent?

The foregoing laundry list is designed to be suggestive rather than exhaustive and all questions will not necessarily receive answers. By formulating questions from it, however, the analyst should gain a better idea as to how the bank's managers conduct the bank's affairs and plan for the future. In addition, the analyst should certainly visit with other relevant participants in the bank's marketplace, e.g. foreign banks, accountancy firms, brokers and others, to understand these other key players' views of the bank's management and operations.

Without minimizing the substantive importance of the bank's strategy, it is also crucial that key decision makers have access to all the information necessary to make effective choices. The process whereby senior managers arrive at operational and strategic decisions should be given serious attention. Are decisions made in an authoritarian or consensual style? If authoritarian in nature, is there nonetheless an esprit de corps? Do managers give the appearance of having a high degree of motivation?

MANAGEMENT QUALITY AND CORPORATE GOVERNANCE

Corporate governance is a term which while objectively referring to the way in which a corporation is governed, i.e. how decisions are made and carried out, in practice often has a normative connotation. Good corporate governance, in the banking context, is associated with banks that: 1) operate for the benefit of shareholders (rather than for the benefit of management); 2) operate on the basis of commercial (i.e. for profit) criteria (instead of on the basis of gaining political favors) and 3) offer protection to minority shareholders and incorporate their interests into the decision making process.

Corporate governance is of particular interest to investors, especially to institutional investors in emerging markets. In these markets, law and regulation tend to favor the majority shareholder and minority shareholders are naturally concerned about corporate investments that appear to be made on the basis of non-commercial criteria or which benefit the majority shareholder at the expense of the minority. It should not be surprising that equity investors, and correspondingly equity analysts, are particularly sensitive to issues of corporate governance. Issues relating to the dilution of the minority shareholders' stake in the enterprise, or minority share-holders receiving less than fair value in exchange for their shares in a forced transfer are the typical sore points. There is evidence that investors will pay a premium for shares in companies perceived to have good corporate governance that pays due attention to the rights of minority shareholders.

While important, the issue of corporate governance is usually of less concern to fixed income investors and to counterparties, who are both potential creditors, of a bank. The bank's obligation to them is compara-tively fixed. It is nonetheless important insofar as the bank may make decisions on non-commercial criteria that affect the bank's risk profile. The bank, for example, that engages in extensive insider or related-party lending, or which extends credit to companies because their heads are the golf partners of the bank's president should raise a red flag to a bank credit analyst. Thus, while not as important to credit analysts as to equity analysts, the bank analyst should be cognizant of issues relating to corporate governance and on the lookout for issues that arise from them. The topic may also suggest lines of inquiry that may enable the credit analyst to glean further information to more fully appraise the management of the bank under review.

CHAPTER SUMMARY

The hump of the CAMEL model, quality of management and its assess-ment are both an extremely important aspect of bank credit analysis and one that is perhaps the most slippery. Management is important because it is both the key variable that determines a bank's success or lack thereof, and the most unpredictable. Although some quantitative indicators can be utilized as rather poor proxies for management quality, in the end analyzing management is a largely qualitative and subjective exercise. It is particularly difficult to assess management at a distance. Yet the bank visit is also subject to dangers, namely that the bank's managers will too effectively sell themselves or the bank to the analyst.

At best, we can suggest some lines of inquiry for the analyst that might be most appropriately pursued during a bank visit, but may also be helpful to the analyst working from his desk. Corporate governance issues, while of primary relevance to equity analysts, should not be ignored. A bank which has poor governance from the point of view of the equity analyst may also be engaging in practices that compromise its risk profile.

CHAPTER SIXTEEN

THE RISK MANAGEMENT CONTEXT: THE PRACTICAL APPLICATION OF CREDIT ASSESSMENTS

Let no loans be made that are not secured beyond a reasonable contingency. Do nothing to foster and encourage speculation. Give facilities only to legitimate and prudent transactions. Make your discounts on as short a time as the business of your customers will permit, and insist upon the payment of all paper at maturity, no matter whether you need the money or not. Never renew a note or bill merely because you may not know where to place the money with equal advantage if the paper is not paid. In no other way can you properly control your discount line, or make it at all times reliable. ... Pursue a straight-forward, upright, legitimate banking business. Never be tempted by the prospect of large returns to do anything but what may be properly done... "Splendid Financiers" in banking are generally either humbugs or rascals.

— Hugh Maculloch, US Comptroller of the Currency, 1863

More and more the bank is a "risk machine". It takes risks, it transforms them, it embeds them in banking products and services. ... Those banking which actively manage their risks have a decisive competitive advantage. They take risks more consciously, they anticipate adverse changes, they protect themselves from unexpected events, they gain the expertise to price risks. ...

— Joel Bessis, *Risk Management in Banking*[1]

---

[1] Managing Bank Risks, p. 2.

Risk management is not merely about reducing risks (although that is in many cases a necessity), but essentially about taking risks in an intelligent manner. Banking can be no more riskless than life itself.

— Eddie Cade, *Managing Banking Risks: Reducing Uncertainty to Improve Bank Performance*

In this chapter, we will look at some of the areas other than bank lending in which credit risk arises, examine some operational risk issues, and finally discuss very briefly some of the approaches to overall risk management. Risk management, it should be observed, is a very topical subject and one unto itself. Readers looking for an in-depth treatment will find some suggested references in Appendix A: Sources and Further Reading.

Although the bank credit analyst will not ordinarily delve very deeply into an examination of a bank's risks and risk management systems beyond those we have already discussed, it is important to be aware of a bank's risk environment for two reasons. First, it will enable the analyst — through a review of the bank's materials and a discussion with relevant officers — to make an appraisal of the quality and comprehensiveness of those systems. Second, if the analyst is asked to render an opinion concerning a particular transaction, he or she will be better placed to do so with an awareness of the comparative risks of those transactions.

OVERVIEW OF RISK

The tables provides an overview of the bank credit matrix. Note that within the five basic groupings, there is a great deal of overlap and the

Risk Category	Remarks/Examples
Credit Risk	Risk of loss through default on financial assets
Insolvency Risk	Risk that liabilities will exceed viable assets + equity capital
Liquidity (and funding) Risk	Risk that a bank will have insufficient liquid funds to meet its current obligations
Market Risk	Risk that a change in interest rates, foreign exchange rates or other market movements will adversely affect the bank
Operational Risk (Business Risk)	Business risks arising from day-to-day operations

Risk Subcategory	Remarks/Examples
Sovereign (country) risk	Risk of war, civil disorder, sovereign default (e.g. resulting in moratorium on foreign currency remittances); lack of diversification in economy resulting in over concentration in a sector. Note: sovereign and country risk can affect not only the bank's operations, but the bank's customers thereby affecting credit risk and other financial risks.
Systemic risk/ industry risk	Breakdown of banking system due to financial institution default and consequent "chain reaction"; risk of inadequate bank supervision; risk of industry decline or collapse due to secular factors affecting bank customers, e.g. textile industry, shipbuilding in the US; risk of calamity affecting bank customers e.g. epidemic affecting farmers' livestock.
Competition risk	Risk of change in strategic alliances, new product initiatives from the competition, new entrants into the industry including foreign banks; risk of key staff being poached by competitors.
Information risk	Risk of inaccurate information affecting bank decision e.g. cost projections.
Technology risk	Risk of change in technology requiring new investment to remain competitive; risk of technology failure.
Casualty risk	Risk of loss of premises, customer records, etc. through fire, flood, earthquake or other calamity; risk of loss of key employees.
Legal/regulatory risk	Risk of adverse change in law; risk of being a defendant in time-consuming or costly litigation; unexpected adverse legal decision; lack of effective enforcement (see sovereign risk); lack of effective bank supervision (see systemic risk); risk of errors in documentation.
Compliance risk	Risk that employees have not effectively complied with legal requirements subjecting the bank to liability or have made inadvertent clerical errors resulting in a loss to the bank.
Reputational risk (Public relations risk)	Risk of loss of reputation due to falling afoul of the law, bad decisions affecting customers etc.
Crime risk	Risk of fraud, embezzlement, computer crime, robbery.

sub-categories are meant to be suggestive rather than precisely defined discrete classifications. We shall return to these areas of risk later in the chapter.

OPERATIONAL RISKS

We have discussed the primary financial risks of banks, and have occasionally touched on salient operational risks. But like all enterprises, banks are subject to general operational risks. These have been summarized in the previous table, and we shall briefly address them here.

Competition Risk

Banking is a business with thin margins that requires substantial leverage in order to generate an acceptable return to compete for capital with other industries. Competition within the industry naturally may have a significant impact on bank profitability. Competition can manifest in various ways, from new entrants into the banking industry to existing players employing new technology to gain a competitive advantage. In its simplest form, an aggressive pricing policy on loans or offers of higher interest rates to attact deposits have a direct competitive impact.

Competition risk, however, refers both to the risks posed by competitors, new or existing, some of which can be anticipated, as well as to unexpected changes in the competitive landscape. Among the possible ways competition risk can pose a threat to a bank is through the appearance of new strategic alliances, highly competitive product initiatives from the competition, successful marketing and advertising campaigns or promotions, as well as risks occasioned by regulatory changes. For example, deregulation may allow new entrants into the industry including foreign banks. Another risk that could be classified as a competitive risk is that of rivals poaching key staff.

Compliance Risk

A subcategory of legal and regulatory risk is compliance risk. This is the risk of inadvertent errors in documentation resulting in loss or liability, or the risk that employees have not effectively complied with legal requirements internal rules or have made inadvertent clerical errors e.g. through negligence or wilfull intent, subjecting the bank to loss liability.

Reputational Risk (Public Relations Risk)

This is the risk of loss of reputation due to incurring civil or criminal liability, especially when aggravated by behavior that results in notoriety adversely affecting the bank's image and goodwill. Fiduciary activities such as trust business and asset management are especially vulnerable to reputational risk.

Information Risk

This is the risk that management will not have access to sufficient information to effectively plan and implement a coherent strategy, that such information as is available is inaccurate, or that confidential information may be obtained by competitors about the bank's own plans, operations or technologies. Because knowledge about the action of competitors can enable a bank to anticipate the potential consequences and quickly respond to them, information risk could be said to be a subcategory of competition risk. Information risk, however, has applications that may affect the gamut of a bank's operations, as well as its financial condition. We have made references to information as being a bank's stock in trade as a financial intermediary, and it is clear that insufficient or inaccurate information can easily have a harmful effect on a bank's asset quality through the taking of ill-advised credit decisions.

Technology Risk

This category of risk can be broadly described as the risk arising from new technologies, but older technologies as well. It can refer to the costs incurred when a change in technology requiring new investment to remain competitive (e.g. ATMs), the risk of technology failure or incompatibility, and the risk that purchased technologies may not accomplish the goals intended. Clearly, IT and computer technology gives rise to most of the technology risk that banks presently confront.

Casualty Risk

Casualty risks have long afflicted business, and include the risk of loss of premises, customer records, and other important assets through fire, flood, earthquake or other calamity. These risks may be addressed through insurance, but the consequential damages arising from a catastrophic event may be impossible to insure against. Casualty risk also includes the risk of loss of key employees through accident or natural causes.

Legal/Regulatory Risk

Another broad category, legal and regulatory risk encompass the negative impacts resulting from, among other things: the risk of adverse change in law; the risk of being a defendant in time-consuming or costly litigation; and, the risk of an unexpected adverse legal decision. Legal risk is closely related to sovereign and systemic risk, because the legal framework in the country in which a bank operates will affect its operations and financial condition. For example, an inability to enforce its rights as a creditor may handicap a bank in recovering losses from non-performing losses and have a direct impact on asset quality, capital and profitability.

Crime Risk

This encompasses the risk of fraud, embezzlement, computer crime, robbery or other illegal activities resulting in loss or impaired profits to the bank.

BANK COUNTERPARTY FACILITIES

Throughout this book, we have discussed the process of evaluating the creditworthiness of banks. Bank credit analysis, as we said at the outset, has a number of applications. We discussed its application to bank debt issues and to counterparty risk. Depending upon their background, bank analysts will have varying degrees of familiarity with specific bank facilities. When the analyst is asked for an opinion, however, it will often be in connection with the approval of a particular facility. Note that many of the facilities described below will be found not only in interbank transactions, but also in bank-customer transactions.

In *Analyzing Foreign Banks*, Robert Morris Associates (now the Risk Management Association), an association of loan and risk control officers, lists the following categories of international bank facilities with which the bank credit analyst should be familiar.[2]

Selected International Bank Credit Facilities	
High-Risk Facilities	**Description**
Eurodollar Deposits	US dollar funds normally placed with financial institutions (outside the US)
Foreign Exchange Lines	A foreign exchange trading facility or a facility used to manage foreign exchange needs. (also made to non-financial firms)
Pass-Through and Clean Advance Lines	An unsecured credit line (also made to non-financial firms)
Hard Currency Backup Lines	A backup credit line in a reserve currency to a local foreign financial institution
Floating Rate Notes	A subordinated debt obligation from the issuing bank to the bank approving the facility
Medium-Risk Facilities Credit Enhancements Repurchase Agreement Facilities & Interest Rate Swap Lines	Usually an off-balance sheet committment to increase the creditworthiness of a customer
Repo	Fully collateralized lending of funds on a short-term basis
Low-Risk Facilities Letters of Acceptance Credit Bankers' Acceptances	Negotiable draft arising from a letter of credit/ documentary trade transaction

Source: categorization from RMA; description from RMA and other sources.

High-Risk Facilities

Eurodollar Deposits

Eurodollars are US dollar deposits deposited in institutions outside the US. They are used by banks that have received Eurodollar deposits and are seeking additional liquidity by making the funds available to be borrowed on tenors ranging from overnight to three months or more. Eurodollars are sought by banks seeking additional funding for US dollar

---

[2] Also helpful in informing the discussion in this section were: J. Holliwell *The Financial Risk Manual: A Systematic Guide to Identifying and Managing Financial Risk*, FT Pitman Publishing, 1997 and Federal Reserve Bank of Richmond, Instruments of the Money Market, 6th Ed. ed. T. Cook & T. Rowe, FRB of Richmond, 1986.

loans, to benefit from changes in interest rates, or to meet liquidity requirements.

Foreign Exchange Lines

A foreign exchange line is foreign exchange trading facility or a line of credit in foreign currency used to manage the customers foreign exchange needs. To illustrate, the customer of a bank might have a foreign exchange line that permits the company to enter into forward foreign exchange contrast of up to $1 m maturing on any given day. In addition to market risk discussed earlier, foreign exchange lines involve risks arising out of the failure of the counterparty bank before settlement is concluded. This is the same as Herstatt risk, named after the failure of a German foreign exchange bank in 1973.

Pass-Through and Clean-Advance Lines

Pass-through and clean-advance lines may be offered to bank, non-bank financial institutions and non-financial customers. "Clean" in this context means unsecured; "pass-through" means net of charges and fees. Similar to Eurodeposit facilities, *pass-through* and *clean-advance lines* connote longer term funding in a reserve currency such as US dollars, ranging from six months to one or more years, and may be used to fund loan growth rather than to compensate for weaknesses in temporary liquidity.

Hard Currency Backup Lines

In some emerging markets, banks may be obliged to have hard currency backup lines in place to meet regulatory requirements. These lines involve both credit risk to the local financial institution as well as foreign exchange risk.

Floating Rate Notes

Floating rate notes (FRNs) are a form of subordinated debt commonly used by banks to bolster their Tier 2 capital. Other banks may purchase these FRNs for their securities portfolios. Tenor of FRNs varies, but for capital building purposes, it is five years or longer. The size of the issues also tends to be relatively large. Marketability of FRNs varies by currency and locale according to the state of development of a secondary market in the instrument.

Risks involved in acquiring FRNs is both pure credit risk, i.e. the risk of default by the borrowing bank, and transfer risk resulting from the imposition of government controls on currency transfer.

Medium-Risk Facilities

Credit Enhancements

Credit enhancements are methods used to improve the creditworthiness and hence the credit rating of a debt security, frequently of an asset-backed security or a municipal bond. The purpose of credit enhancements can be to penetrate the "sovereign ceiling" in an emerging market or to improve the creditworthiness of a municipality or other local government unit. Credit enhancements are often effected through the use of bank guarantees or standby letters of credit, and that is the context with which we are concerned here. In reviewing the creditworthiness of the security, which will often have a tenor of from 5–10 years, the analyst will have to make a judgment as to the creditworthiness of the bank to which the investing entity will be exposed in the event that primary obligor defaults. Since the bank is a secondary source of repayment, it falls into the category of medium rather than high risk.

Repurchase Agreement Facilities (Repos) and Interest Rate Swap Lines

Repurchase agreements, or "repos" are mentioned in Chapter 14, agreements to sell and buy back securities at a fixed time and at a certain price. In selling the security, the seller receives the purchase price and then buys it back at a the market rate plus a premium, the premium being the *repo rate*. Functionally, this is the same as the seller borrowing funds, on a fully secured basis, and repaying them with interest on the repurchase. Example: Bank X sells to Bank Y securities with a market value of $10 m agreeing to buy back the securities the next day at a repurchase price of $10 m plus the one day repo rate, e.g. $10 m + ($10 m × .05 × 1/365) or approximately $1,400. Bank X has in effect borrowed $10 m from Bank Y on a fully secured basis.

A reverse repo is the mirror image of the repo. In fact, it is just viewing the same transaction from the point of view of Y. In a reverse repo, Y purchases $10 m in securities from X and agrees to sell them back to X the following day at a repurchase price of $10 m plus the one day repo rate, e.g. $10 m + ($10 m × .05 × 1/365) or approximately $1,400. Bank Y has in effect lent $10 m to Bank X on a fully secured basis.

Since repos and reverse repos are fully secured and usually short-term in nature, their risk profile is comparatively modest. Bank Y is subject to market risk if the market value of the securities falls and Bank X is subject to market risk if the market value of the securities rises.

Interest rate swaps are the exchange of two payment streams, usually one at a fixed rate and another at a floating rate. A bank may enter into swaps on their own account to hedge risk or less often in a proprietary trading capacity, or it may act as an intermediary for two counterparties. Swaps are subject to default risk and may be subject to market risk. In contrast to repos and reverse repos, swap transactions tend to have longer durations as long as the term of the underlying debt instruments which may continue for five years or more. Because of legal risk associated with swaps — although this risk has diminished as swaps have become better accepted during the 1980s and 1990s — default risk, and their usual longer duration, swaps can be generally said to involve more risk than repos or reverse repos.

Low-Risk Facilities

Bankers' Acceptances (Letter of Acceptance Credit)

The bankers' acceptance, sometimes referred to simply as an acceptance, is a money market instrument for the confirmation and refinancing of a trade letter of credit. It is created after a facility for a *letter of credit*, as described below, has been created, and the documentary letter of credit has been "accepted" by the *issuing bank* (*accepting bank*). The issuing/accepting bank in effect guarantees payment of the amount specified (subject to explicit terms and conditions) and thereby effectively lends its creditworthiness to that of its customer (the issuer or drawer).[3]

In this type of facility, the exposure to the issuing bank by the *nominated*, *paying*, *advising* or *confirming bank* is secondary (i.e. effectively contingent upon non-payment by the bank's customer — i.e. the issuer/drawer — which is that actual buyer. This is because the primary obligation is between the party (usually an importer or buyer), which has opened the letter of credit or *L/C*, and the issuing bank, which has issued

---

[3] The majority of bankers' acceptances are indeed created in this manner. It is possible, however, for an open account transaction to give rise to a bankers' acceptance.

the L/C on behalf of that party (its customer). Ordinarily, the issuing bank is merely a conduit for the funds. This payment will be used by the issuing bank to pay the confirming bank on behalf of the exporter. The obligation becomes that of the issuing bank upon the receipt of the proper documentation according to the terms of letter of credit.

> **Letter of Credit.** Also known as a documentary letter of credit, the letter of credit is an instrument formed by the agreement of a bank (e.g. the buyer's bank) to make payment on behalf of its customer, to another party (e.g. the seller's bank for the benefit of the seller), when certain documents evidencing compliance with the terms and conditions of the agreement are presented to the (buyer's) bank. Ordinarily, actual payment will be rendered by buyer, but the letter of credit, commonly known as an "L/C" is, in effect, a guarantee and is similarly a contingent liability to the bank which issues it.

Risk, however, arises at two junctures: (1) when the issuing bank is not paid by the importer, and in turn does not pay the confirming bank, although it is obligated to do so, or (2) if the issuing bank fails and is for that reason unable to make payment. The risk is actually ordinarily minimal because letters of credit are short-term in nature, ordinarily ranging from 30–60 days and because governments of emerging markets, where problems are potentially most likely to arise, are loath to allow the difficulties of a single bank to jeopardize their country's ability to source necessary imports from overseas. In view of the importance with which trade obligations are perceived, and the essentially uniform acceptance of UCP 500 which clarifies the obligation of issuing banks to pay on behalf of importers (irrespective of the importer's willingness or capacity to pay), risks to confirming banks of default by issuing banks are comparatively low.

Bank risk of default arising from an L/C

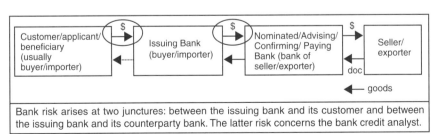

Bank risk arises at two junctures: between the issuing bank and its customer and between the issuing bank and its counterparty bank. The latter risk concerns the bank credit analyst.

Within the chain of payment, it is the issuing bank that bears the most risk in a letter of credit transaction. It is obliged to pay, even if its customer refuses to do so. The issuing bank, however, has a customer relationship and is in the best position to evaluate its creditworthiness. In most cases it will nonetheless have a claim against the customer, unless there is a material noncompliance with the terms of letter of credit. The advising and nominated banks normally bear little risk, but the confirming bank incurs an obligation to pay the beneficiary if the documentation is in order, even if the issuing bank fails to pay it. Conversely, if the confirming bank pays the beneficiary when the documentation is not in order, then it may not be able to recover from the issuing bank.

Types of Letters of Credit

A letter of credit may be revocable or irrevocable. The most common type is the irrevocable letter of credit which may not be modified by the issuer unless the beneficiary, issuing bank and confirming bank agree. A revocable letter of credit, in contrast, may be modified at the sole discretion of the issuer. This type of L/C, unsurprisingly, would not be very attractive to the beneficiary (often an exporter of goods) and therefore is little used in international trade.

A confirmed letter of credit is one in which a bank, most often the exporter/seller's bank, confirms that the beneficiary will receive payment according to the terms of the L/C. This is most often used where the exporter is unfamiliar with the issuing bank, and wants added comfort that it will be paid upon its satisfying the terms of the L/C. Whether an L/C is confirmed or not, however, does not affect the obligation of the issuing bank to remit funds to the *nominated, paying, advising* or *confirming bank,* as the case may be.

In addition, an L/C may be transferable, in which case it can be transfered from the original beneficiary to a second beneficiary. Notwithstanding whether an L/C is by its terms transferable or not, the beneficiary can effectively assign the benefit it would receive to another party by so instructing the nominating bank. Normally, an L/C is has payment terms which vary at sight, i.e. immediately to 180 days. If on a time basis, the L/C may nonetheless by sold immediately by discounting it.

The preceding types of letters of credit are normally used in international trade transactions. The standby letter of credit, mentioned above in

Illustration: The Life of a Typical Bankers Acceptance

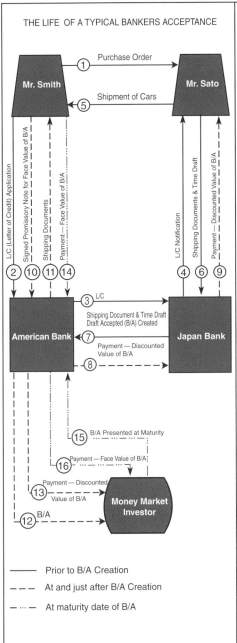

THE LIFE OF A TYPICAL BANKERS ACCEPTANCE

1. Mr. Smith, a customer of American Bank, desires to import some limited edition Japanese cars from Mr. Sato, the founder and CEO of Sato Special Vehicle K.K. Sato and Smith discuss the deal and Smith offers Sato $1 m payable 60 days after shipment.

2. Smith then requests American Bank to issue a letter of credit, which states the terms of trade and that American Bank in effect guarantees Smith's ability to pay Sato $1 m in 60 days.

3–4. American Bank pursuant to the L/C notifies Sat via Japan Bank o that his invoice for payment of $1 m 60 days hence (time draft) is eligible for "acceptance," if presented with the shipping and other documents listed in the L/C.

5. With the L/C in hand, Sato ships the cards to Smith endorsing the shipping documents transfering title to the holder.

6. Sato then sends the shipping documents (e.g. bill of lading) to Japan Bank and invoice, now a time draft, to Japan Bank.

7. Japan Bank then takes the shipping documents and time draft to American Bank's office, which duly stamps it "Accepted," creating a Bankers' Acceptance. This is a negotiable instrument indicating that American Bank has an unconditional obligation to pay the holder of the Bankers' Acceptance the face value of the instrument upon maturity.

8–11. Japan Bank can take payment immediately at a discount or, at its option, hold the bankers' acceptance to maturity. Assuming the former, Japan Bank then pays Sato the amount of the L/C less any relevant fees and before maturity Smith also pays American Bank the face value of the L/C plus any relevant fees and receives the relevant shipping documents and title to the vehicles.

12–15. Prior to maturity, in order not to tie up its own capital, American Bank may wish to sell the bankers' acceptance to a money market investor. In this way, the instrument functions similarly to a short-term debenture. The investor, for example, purchases it for $990,000 and receives $1 m back in 30 days, receiving $10,000 in interest.

Additional notes:
1. Tenor: The term of a bankers' acceptance (and underlying letter of credit) typically range from 30–270 days. 60–90 days is the most common.

2. Fees. The applicant will normally pay a fee of around 50 bp for the bank to issue the L/C. In connection with opening the L/C, the bank may provide advance funds (at interest) to the applicant, thereby providing finance to manufacture or produce the goods that have been contracted for.

Source: Federal Reserve Bank of Richmond [USA], Instruments of the Money Market, 1986.

How a trade letter of credit works:

Following discussion with personnel from Health Sciences Corporation ("Seller") in the country of Industria, Medical Supplies Co. ("Buyer") in the Democratic Republic of Agraria desires to purchase three new X-ray machines for use in hospitals in Capital City. Buyer and Seller agree to the price, specifications of the machines and other terms of trade. An important term of trade is the manner of payment. At Seller's request, Buyer agrees to obtain a letter of credit to be issued in favor of the Seller. Buyer (as an Applicant) then goes to the Industrial and Commercial Bank of Agraria, which is Buyer's main bank, to see if they will agree to issue a letter of credit in accord with the terms agreed to between Buyer and Seller. Industrial and Commercial Bank of Agraria will be exposing itself to a credit risk should Buyer fail to pay for the goods upon satisfaction of all documentary requirements. Buyer, however, is a good customer of the Bank's and the Bank, for a fee, agrees to take on the credit risk, which it regards as slight. The Industrial and Commercial Bank of Agraria thus becomes the Issuing Bank, and issues the letter of credit indicating seller as Beneficiary.

Buyer informs the Seller and contemporaneously, the Issuing Bank will then issue the letter of credit to the Seller's Bank and will also designate an Advising Bank or Confirming Bank (if a confirmation of the L/C is required), with which it has a correspondent relationship). These banks will normally be in the same country as the Seller's Bank. (Note that occasionally the Advising Bank and Confirming Bank would be different banks, if for example the Advising Bank already had substantial exposure to Agraria. It could then lay off exposure to another bank that had an appetite for Agrarian exposure.) Whichever bank which is designated to actually pay the beneficiary of the L/C (i.e. the Seller) is termed the Paying Bank or Accepting Bank. Note that the Advising Bank (or in the case of confirmation, the Confirming Bank), and the Paying Bank or Accepting Bank may all be the same bank. In this case, they are (although no confirmation is required). The Nominated Bank, Advising Bank, Paying Bank and Accepting Bank are the Seller's Bank, First National Bank of Electron City.

With the Beneficiary (i.e. Seller) having been advised of the issue of the letter of credit, the Seller proceeds to ship the goods from Industria to Agraria. Upon receipt of the proper documents, including for example the "bill of lading, evidencing that the goods have been shipped and describing them according to the terms of the letter of credit, the Paying Bank examines the documents, and if all is in order, pays the Beneficiary either on sight or at maturity, if so provided. If the Paying Bank is other than an Advising or Confirming Bank, the Nominated Bank may send the documents back to the Issuing Bank in order to receive payment, which it will then pay to the Seller. There are a number of variations on this basic pattern, which are beyond the scope of this book. This hypothetical example and the diagrams on the succeeding page, illustrate the most customary type of trade letter of credit transaction. For a detailed discussion of risks arising out of trade payments, see John Holliwell, *The Financial Risk Manual*, (FT Pitman Publishing, 1997), Chapter 2.

the context of credit enhancements, is a general purpose letter of credit that really functions as a sort of guarantee. It guarantees payment to the stated beneficiary by the issuing bank in the event of default or non-performance by the account party (the bank's customer). Unlike commercial documentary letter of credits which usually are not payable without the presentation of specified documents e.g a bill-of-lading, a standby letter of credit in contrast is typically unsecured. What triggers payment under a standby letter of credit is the simple non-performance or default by the account party, properly attested to or evidenced by the beneficiary. A standby letter of credit might be used for example to ensure the account party's performance under the award of a construction contract. A standby letter of credit will very often be more risky to the issuing bank than a commercial (documentary) letter of credit, especially no collateral has been required of the account party (the bank's customer).

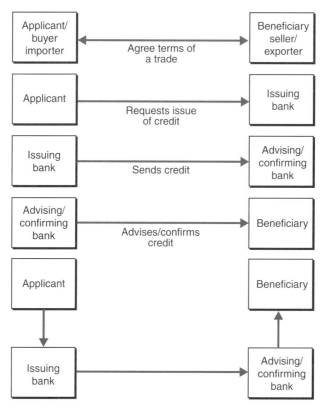

Source: Holliwell, Financial Risk Manual.

CHAPTER SUMMARY

In this chapter we have undertaken two somewhat disparate objectives. First, we stepped away from purely financial risks to provide an overview of the risks bank face and then later in the chapter to discuss the operational risks that banks, together with all enterprises, confront. (We will address country (sovereign) risk and systemic risk, which bridge both financial and operational risk, in a succeeding chapter.) The nature of the banking business, however, makes banks more vulnerable to some types of operational risks than others. Although a bank's apparent stock in trade is money, its real stock in trade could be said to be information. The risk of insufficient or inaccurate information is therefore one of especial importance to banks. This also explains the high profile of technology risk in banking. Money attracts crime, and banks are likewise particularly vulnerable to crime risk whether through robbery or through fraud. Because to operate effectively banks require a well-tuned legal system in which property rights and creditors rights are respected, legal and regulatory risk is another significant risk to banks.

Another portion of the chapter was given over to depicting a practical context for bank credit assessments. The majority of bank credit analysts are employed in a risk management capacity. How are the fruits of their labor used within a bank or other organization? We discuss some of the types of credit facilities in which bank credit analysis will be used to as a key input to determine whether approval is granted, and if so to what extent.

CHAPTER SEVENTEEN

THE BANKING ENVIRONMENT: SOVEREIGN RISK AND SYSTEMIC CONCERNS AND APPROACHES TO REGULATION

While the statement 'a bank can never be better than the country within which it is located' is not necessarily true in all cases (for example, if a bank has sizeable assets and liabilities beyond the home country's borders ...), in general, it is a pretty good rule to follow.
— Robert Morris & Associates, *A Guide to Analyzing Foreign Banks*[1]

[W]hen banks in emerging economies experience distress, they can be a huge contingent liability to the government, given their special status as deposit taking institutions. It is therefore critical to examine the health of the banking system in emerging markets when assessing a sovereign borrower's overall creditworthiness.
— JP Morgan Emerging Markets Bank Research Team, "Special Corporate Study — Financial Institutions: Bank Sector Risks to Emerging Economies," November 7, 1997, p. 1.

Periodically, business magazines publish a list of the top 100, 200, or 500 banks in the region they cover, or if they view the world as their beat, they come up with a global ranking. The list frequently purports to show which are the best banks. Like *Fortune Magazine*'s famous Fortune 500

---

[1] p. 11.

list, it is likely that lists of this kind are popular with readers. While these rankings can be of interest, they are rarely of much value. The problem with such rankings is that determining what makes the best bank is an elusive quest. Usually the editors rank the banks by assets, equity, profits or some composite ratio. But these provide little information out of context. If the criteria is return on equity or another profitability ratio, we have already seen that banks can easily enhance profitability at the expense of safety. If it is total assets, size tells us little about either profitability or creditworthiness. If it is equity, then the most well capitalized banks may be safe, but they are unlikely to be among the most profitable.

A greater problem with these rankings is that they rarely take into account the environment in which the bank operates. Banks cannot be analyzed in a vacuum. Some of the most profitable banks and best-capitalized banks in the world operate in developing countries with highly volatile economies. While their admirable financial ratios should not be overlooked, neither should the capricious environment in which they operate be ignored. The banks may very well be profitable because a banking cartel keeps deposit rates low and lending rates high. Capital may have been robust at the end of the previous financial year, but bank supervision may leave much to be desired and high levels of capital may be an effective requirement to survive in that market. Local accounting rules may allow the bank to show more impressive figures than an equally strong and profitable bank across the border. Just as an off-road vehicle needs high ground clearance and strong springs to absorb bumps and potholes, so banks in emerging markets frequently need a greater cushion of capital than they would in a more developed, less volatile economy and more power to drive themselves out of difficult situations. Rankings that rely solely on numerical ratios without adjusting for variations in the local operating environment and accounting treatment are, for this reason, mostly worthless.

Sovereign Risk Analysis, A Three Pronged Approach

An understanding of the banking system of the country in which a bank operates — together with the degree of systemic risk implicit in the banking system — and the level of sovereign risk in that country is critical to being able to fully evaluate the creditworthiness of a given bank. To assess the creditworthiness of banks in a particular country, the analyst must have an understanding of the:

❏ Political and economic environment; the
❏ Regulatory regime; and the
❏ Credit culture in which those banks operate.

The first element takes account of the political and economic environment that are the subject of sovereign risk analysis, which we touched upon in a previous chapter and will elaborate on here. The second and third elements affect both sovereign and systemic risk. A country's economic and political system have a major impact on a bank's ability to make good on its local currency and foreign currency obligations, a comprehensive discussion of sovereign risk is a book in itself, we must therefore limit ourselves to a brief consideration of the fundamental elements of sovereign risk analysis. This is followed by a discussion of some of the constituents of systemic risk, with a particular focus on approaches to regulation. In the next chapter, we will look at the specifics of bank regulation in more detail.

SOVEREIGN RISK AND COUNTRY ANALYSIS

Banks Are Affected by Sovereign Risk

No matter how robust an individual bank or banks, all financial institutions are subjects of the economic, legal and political environment in which they operate. Legal and regulatory constraints have a direct impact on bank operations, and are usually intended to improve the financial health of banking institutions. Laws and policies, however, do not always have a beneficent impact on banks. They may be directed towards other ends, such as converting banks into instruments of government policy, or attempting to create an egalitarian socialist society. Populist movements may result in the enactment of laws severely restricting creditors' rights. The absence of law or regulation entirely can have a highly negative impact. Civil disorder or revolution can render existing laws and regulations impotent to achieve their desired purpose.

Sovereign risk is the risk that the sovereign, i.e. the government, may default upon its financial obligations or cause other organizations or institutions, such as banks, to default upon theirs. A key difference between sovereign risk analysis and analysis of financial or corporate entities (although this difference is muted in countries that have weak or ineffectual legal systems) is that creditors' legal redress against a sovereign to coerce repayment is limited. Consequently, the sovereign's willingness to pay assumes a higher profile relative to its ability to pay. As Standard & Poor's analysts, David T. Beers and Marie Cavanaugh wrote in their article, "Sovereign Credit Criteria: A Primer," "a government can (and sometimes does) default selectively on its obligations, even when it possesses the financial capacity for timely debt service."[2] Sovereign risk is often used synonymously with country risk, although the latter may connote risk related to direct investment, while sovereign risk suggests risk related to government financial obligations or financial obligations of other entities, the nonpayment of which is attributable to government action or omission. Because government default and actions that force private organizations to default (e.g. the imposition of a general moratorium on repayment of foreign debt) are often the result of economic distress, analysis of macroeconomic conditions and prospects is a key constituent of sovereign risk analysis.

Sovereign risk analysis must also take account of political risk, such as the risk of war, civil disorder and expropriation. Sovereign risk ratings are used not only to evaluate the creditworthiness of debt instruments issued by a national government, but also to serve as a benchmark for the creditworthiness of firms, including banks, under the jurisdiction of the government. Since the government has the ultimate authority over private entities within its borders, in theory no private company can be rated higher than the sovereign. This concept is the "sovereign ceiling" which restricts the ratings of companies to that attained by the government. We will also refer to the sovereign ceiling again in a succeeding chapter on bank ratings.

Sovereign risk is also important to banks because risk managers ordinarily establish both country limits and country ratings in determining whether and to what degree their institution will deal with counterparties in such markets, as well as limits and ratings on individual banks. Country ratings may also determine the level of provisioning the bank will have to set aside against exposures in those countries. Those provisions, imposed by internal policies or external regulators, will have an impact on the profitability of particular transactions. Because banking is inextricably tied to government's implementation of monetary and economic policy, and because the creditworthiness of banks is highly

---

[2] David T. Beers and Marie Cavanaugh, Standard & Poor's Rating Service, "Sovereign Credit Ratings: A Primer," December 1998, p. 21.

dependent upon the regulatory environment in which they operate, bank credit analysis is closely linked to sovereign and country risk analysis.

The Health of a Banking System Influences Sovereign Risk

Indeed, the converse is also true: country and sovereign risk are to a great degree contingent upon banking system risk. Unhealthy banks that fail to exercise proper credit controls while funding themselves on short-term foreign currency debt, under the assumption that the government will come to their rescue, will ultimately be a drag upon the economy and government finances. The recent Asian crisis is a case in point and is now recognized as having been at heart a banking system crisis. While government macroeconomic fundamentals remained largely intact, profligate banks, often acting in alignment with government policy, brought the system down.

A BRIEF PRIMER ON SOVEREIGN RISK ANALYSIS

Sovereign ratings are frequently divided into foreign currency ratings and local currency ratings. The first measures the risk of default in respect of foreign currency borrowings, the second in respect to local currency borrowings. In general, the criteria for evaluating both are the same, although ratings may vary considerably because a government has a much greater scope of action in connection with local currency obligations. Since the sovereign controls the printing presses, in theory it can always satisfy its local currency obligations by printing new currency. Nonetheless, in practice, risks of non-payment or partial payment do exist and sovereign risk analysts take account of many of the same factors as they do with foreign currency obligations, placing particular emphasis however on the strength, stability and accountability of the country's political institutions. Since satisfying foreign currency obligations requires access to foreign currency, such risks are affected both by the sovereign's willingness to pay and capacity to pay. The country's foreign currency reserves, balance of payments, export capacity and external financial position assume greater importance in respect to foreign obligations.

Five Elements of Sovereign Risk

Criteria for assessing sovereign risk can be divided into several categories. The basic types of sovereign risk criteria are: 1) political, legal and regulatory risk factors; 2) the structure of the economy, the country's economic endowments and its overall performance; 3) the condition of its public finances; 4) the effectiveness of its internal monetary policy; and 5) its financial position vis-à-vis foreign countries, their investors and creditors. While these elements are interdependent on one another, such a grouping is convenient to better understand sovereign risk analysis. The political environment influences the structure of the economy and vice versa, while fiscal management is closely allied with monetary policy.

The first category is quite simple. The stability of a government's political institutions obviously have a major impact on the ability of a commercial bank to be able to meet its obligations. Is the country one in which populist or egalitarian sentiments cause banks to be handicapped in their attempts to generate returns for shareholders? A country racked by civil war, in which laws go unenforced or are enforced arbitrarily is hardly conducive to the business of banking. In terms of this group of criteria, stability is the watchword.

The second category refers to both the structure of the economy and its overall level of performance. Is it one which is dependent on one of income, tourism, for instance, or richly endowed with natural resources yet lacking in diversification? Is it one in which citizens are inclined to save or one in which they profligately spend? It is less easy to generalize about this category since much depends upon the facts of a particular situation and the linkages can be complex. To make a broad generalization, a country with a diversified economy, not too dependent upon any one sector, and one which has good prospects will have a better sovereign risk profile than one which has tied its fortunes to a single industry. In addition to structural aspects of the economy, if the past is prologue, its general level of performance is likely to provide some indication of its future prospects.

The third group of criteria concern a government's management of public finances or fiscal policy. The fundamental questions are: Does it collect enough in tax revenue to meet its current expenses, or must it issue debt to meet the shortfall? Can it manage its internal finances without creating an environment which is harmful to business?

The fourth category, price stability and monetary policy, refer to the ability of the government to effectively manage interest rates, inflation and the money supply. Monetary policy is linked to fiscal policy since large government deficits can force up interest rates and lead to inflationary pressures. The ideal, of course, is moderation in all respects: relatively low interest rates, low inflation and appropriate adjustments in the money supply.

Finally, the fifth category deals with trade accounts with other nations as well as the country's ability to meet its foreign currency obligations. This includes both a country's credit history and its debt burden relative to the resources at its disposal.

Although, there are numerous criteria that have an impact on sovereign risk, analysts tend to focus on a comparatively small number of indicators to get a rough idea of where a particular country ranks.

Sovereign Risk Criteria and Major Indicators		
1. Political Risk		Political risk, like the analysis of management within the CAMEL framework is largely qualitative, so no major indicators apply to it.
2. Economic:[3]	Gross domestic product (GDP) Investment and savings levels Unemployment rate	Corollary indicators include: GDP relative to other countries; Year-on-year (Yoy) percentage change in GDP (GDP growth per annum). Key indicators are: Savings to GDP (%) and Investment/GDP (%).
3. Fiscal Policy	Current Account (surplus or deficit)	Total debt to GDP (Debt ratio).
4. Monetary Policy	Inflation rate Interest rates Level of intermediation (Bank credit to GDP)	The primary indicators are the Consumer Price Index (CPI) and the Producer Price Index (PPI).
5. External Position[4]	External debt indicators: Trade account indicators:	Primary indicators are: debt service ratio (interest and principal payments to export earnings and short-term foreign currency obligations to GDP. Salient criteria are: foreign currency reserves and foreign currency reserves to imports.

[3] In addition to the economic indicators listed above which are the essential parameters of economic growth, this category includes structural considerations and thereby embraces some qualitative factors. The analyst will examine the relative contributions of agriculture, industry and services to an economy. This tells us how China is different from Japan. In contrast to Japan, which is already a mature industrial and service economy, China, like a number of its neighbors in Southeast Asia, has been industrializing and urbanizing rapidly. This is reflected in the relative increase in industry's contribution to economic growth. Similarly, the relatively small portion of services tells us that banking, transport, and other services still have a long way to go. A more qualitative factor is the level of economic diversification, a feature which has a direct impact on the banking business.

[4] An additional set of factors, which include qualitative aspects, include: exchange rate (volatility) and the exchange rate regime.

These include the following which can be classified along the lines of the five groupings mentioned above. Political risk, like the analysis of management within the CAMEL framework is largely qualitative, so no major indicators apply to it.

GENERAL ECONOMIC INDICATORS

Gross Domestic Product

Gross domestic product or GDP is probably the pre-eminent macroeconomic indicator because it is an all-encompassing measure of total economic activity within an economy. GDP per capita is a basic indicator of the state of a country's development. The rate of change in GDP expressed in percentage terms, however, is both the headline figure and that most relevant to analysts. It also tends to have an impact on financial markets. A moderately high rate of GDP growth is almost universally perceived as positive. When an economy is operating at full or near full capacity, however, and the GDP growth rate is very high (e.g. over 4–5% for a mature economy, more for an emerging economy), it can be said to be "overheating." The consequence will often be price inflation which is frequently negative for both the equity and fixed income since the monetary authorities will raise interest rates dampening stock prices and prices of existing bonds.

GDP rates vary globally. In a rapidly growing economy such as China in the early 1990s, annual GDP growth may be as high as 10% or more. In contrast, during a recession or economic crisis, an economy can contract as did that of Indonesia and Thailand following the Asian crisis. In a mature economy such as the United States, a GDP rate of 2–3% is considered by economists to be healthy and sustainable, while in emerging markets rates ranging from 3% to 7% would be viewed as desirable and sustainable over long periods of time. As a general rule, high GDP growth rates will tend to strengthen a country's currency relative to countries with less healthy growth rates. The table shows comparative rates of GDP growth during the mid-1990 in several countries, while the table that follows shows most recent GDP growth in rates for a wider sample of countries.

GDP is also useful because it gives us a benchmark against which to measure other economic indicators. For instance, the capacity to save is measured as savings to GDP; fiscal accounts are measured as public

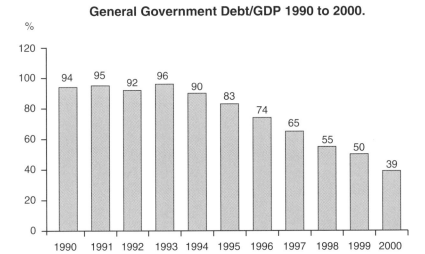

General Government Debt/GDP 1990 to 2000.

sector debt to GDP; and the bank sector's activity is measured as bank lending to GDP.

Unemployment Rate

The unemployment rate is the percentage of the eligible workforce that is unemployed. A countercyclical indicator, it goes up during an economic downturn and falls during periods of rising prosperity. The unemployment rate therefore tracks economic activity (albeit lagging to some degree) declining as demand for goods and services and demand for labor correspondingly rises and rising as demand for goods and services and labor declines. The unemployment rate is also a fairly smooth indicator (i.e. comparatively non-volatile) and is subject to only mild seasonal variations in most countries. From the vantage point of the market and monetary policy makers, like GDP growth, the unemployment rate should be neither too high nor too low. The number depends on the market: a rate between 4–5% is viewed as an optimal range. The reason is that policymakers therefore tend to prefer to see a relatively low unemployment rate, but not one that is so low that wages are pushed up substantially perhaps triggering inflation. A high unemployment rate is also negative since it signals a fragile economy and the continuation of weak demand as those who are without a job are not likely to be big consumers of new products and services.

Unemployment rate, 1989–2001 (seasonally adjusted)

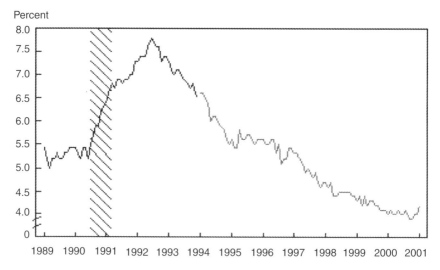

Source: Bureau of Labor Statistics
    Current Population Survey

Note: Shaded area represents recession. Break in series in January 1994 is due to
    the redesign of the survey.

Sourced from http://www.stern.nyu. edu/~nroubini/bci

Note that in emerging markets the unemployment rated is often understated since it may raise politically sensitive issues. In addition, this statistic does not capture underemployment, which occurs when people work at less than their full capacity or skill levels, and is also subject to variations in definition (e.g. who is classified as an eligible worker? does employment include part-time employment?).

Savings and Investment Rates

A country's investment rate is one of the most important determinants of economic growth. The other is productivity, but that is somewhat more difficult to measure. The investment rate closely correlates with a country's savings rate, and both are often measured as a percentage of GDP. The gap between the two is dependent upon how a country's savings are collectively allocated. They may be used to finance a government whose expenditures exceed its revenues, or capital flight may channel savings into offshore investments.

A high savings rate is normally viewed as beneficial and the East Asian miracle, which preceded the Asian crisis, was explained in large part by the high savings rates of the so-called "tiger" countries. Some of these countries achieved savings rates greater than 30% of GDP. It has also been argued that savings rates can be too high, and that investment disproportion to consumption created oversupply that contributed to the crisis. Nevertheless, a high savings rate is generally viewed favorably in sovereign risk analysis, particularly in respect of developing economies, unless circumstances warrant a contrary view. Savings rates are strongly influenced by government policy, and some would add, by cultural considerations. Among the forces that affect savings rates are: taxes, real interest rates on deposits or other investment vehicles, confidence in the formal financial system, the existence of social welfare programs, and government programs that affirmatively encourage or compel citizens to save.

High investment rates are also viewed favorably, although at the extreme they might raise questions about the sustainability of economic growth and potential overcapacity. A fairly low investment rate, for instance under 5–10% or less, would suggest that manufacturers are merely replacing machinery and other durable goods when they wear out. This does not bode well for economic growth.

FISCAL POLICY INDICATORS

Current Account (Surplus or Deficit)

A key indicator of fiscal health is the extent of a government's deficit, if any. The relative level of debt can be measured by the following ratio: public sector debt to GDP.

Public Sector Debt to GDP (Debt Ratio)

Public sector debt to GDP, also refered to as the (national) government debt to GDP or the debt ratio, measures the public sector debt burden of an economy. Note that this ratio differs from the total debt to GDP ratio, which includes private sector as well as public sector debt. Specifically, it measures a government's borrowing as a percentage of GDP. It may include the national government and all sub-national units or just the national government debt may be measured. Cumulative borrowing increases if a government spends beyond its means and is not able to compensate through increased tax revenue. The higher the ratio, the more of the government's revenue goes to interest payments and the less to goods and services, and the more vulnerable the economy is as the government may find it difficult to borrow further without crowding out private sectors borrowers which could better contribute to economic growth.

It should not be surprising that a lower rather than higher ratio is favorable from a sovereign risk perspective, although a rapidly growing economy may have a comparatively high ratio especially if it does not have a high savings rate. Particularly problematic is external debt, which includes funds either in local or foreign currency borrowed from non-residents. Where borrowings are in foreign currency, the government is vulnerable to foreign exchange risk as a result of a local currency devaluation and may need to scramble to obtain foreign currency for debt payments. The measures that may be needed to obtain such funds may have a deleterious effect on the local economy.

MONETARY POLICY INDICATORS

Interest Rates

The level of prevailing interest rates, as influenced by the central bank, will have an impact on bank performance and hence creditworthiness. It is critical to distinguish between nominal interest rates and real interest rates, i.e. the nominal interest rate less than the rate of inflation. Note that in a deflationary environment, nominally low interest rates can still mean high real interest rates. Interest rates that are volatile or a monetary policy which is erratic are both adverse from a sovereign risk perspective.

Bank Lending to GDP

Bank lending to GDP measures the degree to which an economy is leveraged. In other words, it reflects the extent to which formal financial intermediation has replaced informal finance networks. As emerging economies grow, intermediation expands rapidly and bank debt as a percentage of GDP rises. With the development of capital markets, however, other methods of finance become more important, including equity finance and finance through the issue of debt securities. At this point, bank lending as a percentage of GDP may begin to decline. A country that has a high level of bank lending to GDP — for instance over 100% — will tend to be heavily dependent on bank finance and vulnerable to distress in the banking system.

Other relevant indicators in this category include the country's savings rate, its investment rate and its Current account surplus or deficit to GDP.

INFLATION RATE

The rate of inflation is another pivotal economic indicator, which actually relates more closely to monetary policy than to general economic growth. Often referred to as the consumer price index (CPI), inflation is measured by comparing the price of a shopping list of items with the cost of the same goods at a certain time, which functions as the base period from which the rate of change is calculated. More than a very moderate degree of inflation (e.g. under 5%) is generally viewed as negative for both an economy and the financial markets. Periods of hyper inflation, during which annual inflation rates can exceed 100% or more, are associated with financial crises, while price deflation is also associated with crises as well as periods of prolonged economic malaise.

High rates of inflation tend to be followed by high interest rates, since inflation reduces the real return to lenders. Prolonged periods of high inflation will have an adverse impact on the stock market since investors will be drawn towards inflation-resistant real assets such as property. Deflation is also adverse to investors since consumers are not prone to buy when prices are likely to be lower a month hence. This discourages economic activity and does not bode well for stock prices. Fixed income investments may be comparatively attractive, however, since there is no such thing as a negative interest rate. Although interest rates will be low, real interest rates may be comparatively high. Bond investors, however, will be ware of conditions that are likely to raise interest rates thereby dampening prices of fixed income securities.

Another measure of inflation is the producer price index (PPI). It is similar to the CPI, but does not measure services and also encompasses a much different "shopping basket" than the CPI index, focusing on commodities and capital investment items. The impact is similar to the CPI, but there is less lag because changes in the price of commodities and of goods at the consumer level is more rapid than at the consumer level.

THE TRADE ACCOUNT

Another whole set of sovereign risk indicators measure a country's ability to service its financial obligations as well as its "external position" vis-à-vis other countries. These include the trade balance as well as a variety of ratios that relate debt and debt service levels to exports, which provide the foreign currency needed for imports. To begin with, a deteriorating trade imbalance in which a country imports more than it exports and thereby experiences a rising trade deficit is traditionally seen as an adverse indicator. In some cases, however, it may indicate that the country is borrowing to meet strong demand for productive investment, which is positive. A distinction then is sometimes made between trade deficits driven by excessive consumer spending and those which are driven by productive investment resulting in the import of commodities or capital goods.

A variety of other indicators reflect the ability of a country to meet its external obligations. We simply enumerate them here as space does not permit a detailed discussion.

Exchange rate (volatility), in view of exchange rate regime and dynamics

❑ Exports to GDP

❑ Growth in Exports

1. Current account surplus or deficit to Exports

2. Debt service ratio (interest and principal payments to export earnings)

❑ Reserves to Imports

❑ Short-term foreign currency obligations to GDP

Economic Diversification and Lending Opportunities

Closely linked to customary sovereign risk considerations are highly diversified economy will also allow local banks to diversify their lending. This will enable them to reduce the riskiness or volatility of their loan portfolios. In contrast, banks in a market where the economy is dominated by a few industries will find it much harder to diversify their lending. Banks in Hong Kong, for instance, are constrained by the fact that opportunities to engage in trade finance or to lend to manufacturers are very limited. The property industry represents a large portion of the economy of the "special administrative district." Consequently, Hong Kong banks are highly exposed to the property sector. Although such concentration is inherently risky — Hong Kong banks suffered during the Asian crisis when property values plunged — they really had few alternative sectors to which to lend.

SYSTEMIC CONCERNS

Systemic concerns are similar to sovereign risk considerations, and indeed there is no bright line between the two. However, while sovereign risk analysis is imbued with an examination of political and economic risk factors, systemic risk has more to do with the operation of a country's financial system, its strength and its resilience. Specific systemic issues include 1) the structure of the banking system, including its degree of consolidation, and openness to new entrants; 2) the financial regulatory environment (discussed in more detail in the following chapter), including the quality of bank supervision, as well as the overall legal framework and degree of protection afforded to creditors' rights; 3) substantive government policies bearing on banks such as those directing lending to specific sectors or enterprises; and 4) other related factors that affect the health of the banking system including tax policies, the capacity and willingness of the central bank to function as a lender of last resort and to assist in restructuring or recapitalizing sick banks, and the state of evolution of the capital markets and accompanying degree of disintermediation. All these have an impact on the level of ambient risk within a country's financial system and have a direct or indirect impact on bank financial condition and bank creditworthiness. We will address selected aspects of systemic risk below.

A Consolidated or a Fragmented Banking Industry

The structure of the banking system will also have a major impact on the probable strength of individual banks in the system. For example, a banking system that is highly fragmented and in which banks draw deposits and lend within small geographic areas is likely to be more prone to bank failure than a system in which there are a comparatively small number of large, well capitalized banks with nationwide distribution. To a large extent, the structure of a banking system is dependent upon the regulatory structure of the banking industry, which in turn is heavily influenced by political considerations. The structure of the banking industry in a particular country may be linked to the regulatory environment. For example, the federal system in the US as well as federal legislation encouraged a fragmented banking system. In some countries, geographic considerations may play a part in maintaining a more localized banking system. In other countries, the government has sought to compel the creation of a small number of major banking groups by fiat. Malaysia is a recent illustration of this phenomenon.

Depositor Confidence and Credit Culture

Another element that affects the health of a banking system and which may be properly termed systemic is the level of depositor confidence in banks and the development of a credit culture. In emerging markets, banks may be distrusted, due perhaps to previous failures, and savers may as a result keep their nest-egg under the proverbial mattress. Is there reliable deposit insurance? While deposit insurance tends to increase depositor confidence, it also increases moral hazard, allowing banks to engage in risky lending without having to worry about an outflow of retail deposits.

Similarly, the existence and state of evolution of a credit culture, though seemingly intangible, is a fundamental pillar upon which a robust banking system rests.

❑ Do borrowers take their financial obligations seriously?

❑ Do bankers take proper credit considerations into account when making loans or are relationships the prime criterion?

❑ Do borrowers recognize the consequences of default?

Historical patterns may shed light on potential problems in cultivating a credit culture. Countries making a transition from a command economy, where credit was actually a subsidy, to a commercial economy are likely to experience problems. Nations that were once part of the former Soviet Union have seen excesses and numerous bank failures arising from dramatic change in the role of banks. In the same way, countries that practice various forms of state-directed capitalism (e.g. Japan) or which remain nominally socialist (i.e. Marxist-Leninist) are prone to problems arising from the shifting function of credit within their economies.

THE RATIONALE FOR GOVERNMENT REGULATION OF BANKS

Banks play a significant role in facilitating economic growth and provide a mechanism for the transmission of government monetary policy. Because the banks, even where privately owned, take on a public policy function, their regulation and supervision by the government is justified. Moreover, the risks and vulnerabilities banks confront as a consequence of their very structure and function provides another reason for the authorities to monitor bank operations closely.

Conflict Between the Interests of the Bank's Shareholders and the Broader Public Interest

These risks are exacerbated by the fact that left to their own devices banks have commercial aims that may conflict with public policy goals. The extreme leverage that banks must employ to compete for investment capital brings with it a degree of moral hazard that calls for public oversight. From a bank shareholder's perspective, the more leverage, the better. The less capital at risk, the less to be lost if the bank collapses, while the upside returns can be spectacularly high. In purely economic terms, bank shareholders may have an incentive to minimize the amount of capital they put at risk and leverage it to the hilt. Indeed, given its typically high leverage, banking epitomizes the concept of making money with other peoples' money. Conceivably, a bank's shareholders could leverage their capital by 50 or 100 times. A return on assets of 2% would be transformed into return on equity of 100% or 200% — at least until a few customers defaulted on their loans.[5] As business and economic conditions are cyclical, loans eventually will turn sour and often do so in bunches. If too highly leveraged, a bank will ultimately fail, absent external support. So it has been over the past several centuries of economic history.

Nonetheless, with hypothetical ROE of 100%, even if the bank ultimately failed after several years, the shareholders might be better off in purely economic terms. Not so, of course, the bank's depositors and creditors. A similar phenomenon can come into play when a bank is already in difficulty. If a bank is on the verge of insolvency, its shareholders and managers may take riskier bets, figuring that a chance of success is better than the eventual loss of their investment. They may be encouraged to do so by the existence of deposit insurance, knowing that depositors will not

---

[5] See R. Hale, Credit Analysis, p. 168.

bear the risks of the perils they are tempting. Hence, through experience, governments have learned the virtue of placing strict constraints upon banks playing too free and loose with other people's hard-earned savings.

Ordinary Depositors are Unable to Effectively Monitor Bank Risk

Pure free-market theory would argue that it is incumbent upon the depositors to monitor the financial condition of banks into which they would consider placing their savings, and to only place their savings with those that show a requisite degree of financial strength and prudence. On paper, of course, depositors could monitor a bank's financial condition through disclosed statements, and a bank that failed to voluntarily disclose critical and complete financial data would be penalized, as circumspect depositors put their savings elsewhere. In other words, conceptually, the market could regulate banks without government intervention. In practice, the market fails to do so. The many risks of banking, many of which are difficult to quantify, make the task of assessing the creditworthiness of banks problematic even for sophisticated depositors.[6]

For the bank credit analyst, whose full time job is to assess banks' creditworthiness, the task of assessing bank creditworthiness is not an insuperable one. But the fruits of such analysis are ordinarily only available to institutional investors, commercial depositors and regulators. To expect small depositors to undertake a comparable evaluation — one which requires many of the skills the bank itself is offering as services — is highly unrealistic, not to say unjust. Because they do not have such skills or choose not to spend their time applying them is one reason that they contract out that task to banks. Banks are only too willing to oblige to earn their spread. Whether out of political expediency, or a genuine conviction that it is unfair to require small depositors to engage in credit analysis of the banks in which they place their deposits, most governments have put into place a formal or *de facto* deposit guarantee scheme, and concomitantly employ a number of measures to compel banks to act prudently, instead of relying on the discipline of the markets.

---

[6] It is not so much that the task of making such an assessment is unduly difficult. But it does require time and resources, as well as adequate financial disclosure on the part of banks. Moreover, the time requirements implicit in credit analysis of banks tend to conflict with the very services a bank offers. For one thing, key values that banks add as financial intermediaries is first, time-saving and convenience and second, their specialized ability to assess, monitor, and manage the risks they absorb. Banks are constantly evaluating the creditworthiness of diverse creditors and it is a bank management's expertise and trustworthiness in managing its loan portfolio that depositors rely upon to earn a modest but steady return on their savings.

MODELS OF GOVERNMENT REGULATION

For these reasons, governments have an important interest in maintaining the health, or at least the outward appearance of health, of their country's banks. This is even more so the case in emerging markets, where capital and money markets are probably poorly developed.[7] Those having authority over banks will consequently, in the interest of national economic development, attempt to support the strength of the banking system in any number of ways. Implementing prudential regulations restricting a bank's operations, setting threshold levels of financial strength and imposing minimum disclosure standards are a few, although in some markets the gap between law and practice may be quite large.

There are common elements of regulation in nearly all jurisdictions. As would be expected, the formation and structure of banking institutions, constraints on their business activities and procedural matters are addressed under virtually all schemes of banking governance. The devil is in the details, however, and the specifics of bank regulation, particularly insofar as they govern the incentives, disincentives or controls to which depository institutions are subject, can take a number of different forms. Fundamentally, though, two major approaches to bank regulation can be discerned. Both seek to enforce certain prudential standards upon banks. One is in the form of a dialog between the regulator and the bank, with the market essentially excluded; the other invokes the assistance of market mechanisms by compelling disclosure.

The Paternalistic Approach

The first model is paternalistic. The bank supervisory body exerts authority over the banks within its jurisdiction, compelling disclosure to the authority and requiring banks to meet its standards. In order to maintain public confidence, however, little external disclosure is required, however. Bank examiner reports are kept confidential. The bank supervisory authority sees itself as the guardian of the public's interest, but colludes with banks in revealing little about their operations to an ignorant public. Under such a regime, however, bank regulators may implicitly or explicitly promise to assist banks in trouble, thereby ensuring the safety of depositors' savings.

---

[7] Accessing finance through equity or debt issues is difficult in these circumstances for many firms, who must rely solely on bank finance. In such a business environment, banks become the sole or primary financial engines of economic growth.

Market-Assisted Models

A second model recognizes the need to impose prudential standards upon banks, but combines regulatory action with compelled public disclosure. By requiring banks to disclose key financial information, the market can assist (though not replace) regulators in rewarding "good" banks and punishing "bad" banks, thus encouraging appropriate risk management. Although bank shareholders still have an incentive to maintain minimal leverage, the countervailing pressure of credit and rating analysts who distribute their reports to market participants assists bank regulators in prompting banks to act more prudently than they might otherwise do.

Bank Bailouts

Neither model completely eschews assisting troubled banks. Instead, whether operating under a paternalistic or a market-assisted paradigm, authorities may go to great lengths to prevent any single bank from collapsing. The motive is, of course, not necessarily because of a desire to help a particular bank, but to maintain public confidence in the banking system as a whole. There are various means of rendering assistance when needed. One is to assist depositors rather than the bank itself. Another is to provide liquid funds in case of emergency. Finally, the government may need to become involved in recapitalizing a troubled bank or assisting in its disposal.

Lender of Last Resort

In addition, to prevent insolvency and the need to liquidate a failing institution, the government, through its central bank, may function as a lender of last resort. In other words, it will provide liquid funds in case of emergency. The bank's liquidity needs may be minor and occasional or acute. A bank that experiences a liquidity crunch necessitating a large injection of funds is not necessarily terminally ill, but those that are not are the exception. The fact that banking authorities will stand behind a bank tends to ameliorate both bank runs, and settlement risk.

Rehabilitation

Once a bank's critical liquidity needs have been relieved, the government may play a key role in rehabilitating the bank that has been assisted.

Taking the sick bank under its wing, rehabilitation can mean the government's taking over bad loans that the bank has accumulated, injecting capital, shopping the bank around to private investors, possibly providing state guarantees as a sweetener, or even nationalizing the bank with the hope that with a cleaner balance sheet (i.e. fewer bad loans and more capital) it can be privatized later. We will discuss bank recapitalization and rehabilitation in more detail subsequently. For the moment, it is important to observe that bank regulators typically employ an element of selectivity in deciding which banks to resuscitate.

Regulation of Banking: Policy and Structural Elements

The reasons for the heavy regulation of banking that prevail in most countries include the:

❑ Importance of banks within the financial system and the catastrophic consequences of systemic bank failures;

❑ Importance of banks to economic development through their credit-allocation function and the money-multiplier effect;

❑ Difficulty of relying on market mechanisms to monitor bank creditworthiness and the fact that assessing such creditworthiness requires time and an understanding of the business of banking; and

❑ Political interest of voters, most of whom are also bank depositors, in protecting their savings.

While the business of banking is similar all over the world, regulatory structures differ considerably. To be sure, the subjects of regulation are broadly comparable, but the specific rules governing banking practice and implementation vary in many significant respects. Regulatory bodies vary in their scope of responsibility and their power, as do the types of banking institutions permitted and the business in which they are authorized to engage. Likewise, methods of bank supervision, the nature of prudential regulation, accounting and tax treatment differ. In this section we will discuss banking regulation and regulatory institutions and how they diverge among various jurisdictions, with an emphasis on the impact specific regulations may have on bank creditworthiness.

Structure of the Banking System

Regulation of banking operates at several levels. Governments regulate the structure of the banking system. These include rules governing the formation and general operation of depository institutions, and may run the gamut from specifying the types of activities banks can engage in, the number and location of branches they may open to procedures concerning chartering new banks. For example, until the recent repeal of the Glass-Steagall Act, US banks were not permitted to engage in the securities business and securities firms were not able to engage in the banking business. In Japan, although reform is underway, the banking industry was divided into several categories of depository institutions each of which had a specified scope of activity in which banks of that class could engage. These groups included: ordinary commercial banks, which included so-called major "city" banks and regional banks; long-term credit banks; trust banks; rural and *shinkin* cooperatives; and, government financial institutions, including the Postal Savings Bureau and several government development banks.

From an analyst's perspective, one of the most important aspects of structural regulations is the extent to which they protect banks from competition. Although protection from competition detracts from economic efficiency, from a credit perspective, barriers to entry tend to allow the protected banks to maintain fatter margins and in turn bolster their creditworthiness. Barriers to entry can take many forms. Licensing and entry requirements are one manifestation. Restrictions on branching are another. Again in the US, until recently, banks in rural areas were protected from competition from branch banks. In Japan, city banks are generally not permitted to engage in trust banking activities; that is the prerogative of trust banks.[8]

Although protection may benefit banks in the short term, the lack of diversification in their loan portfolios that characterized such localized institutions made them more vulnerable to a downturn, and when barriers to entry are removed, banks previously protected from competition become exceedingly vulnerable. This can occur when state banks are privatized, and the cloak of government support is withdrawn, or where foreign banks are permitted to invade a country's banking market. The removal of obstacles to entry may be coupled with other deregulation initiatives. The analyst should be very careful when assessing the creditworthiness of banks that have recently been deregulated. Experience shows that deregulation is often destabilizing in the short-term, and deregulation initiatives are not infrequently followed by banking crises.

---

[8] A limited exception is made for Daiwa Bank.

In some countries, certain financial institutions are provided with special advantages that can sap the financial strength of competing institutions. Again, in Japan, the postal savings bank has a number of inherent advantages over commercial banks in attracting deposits. This has impeded the profitability of commercial banks, and contributed to the ultimately dire consequences that many of Japan's commercial banks confronted in the 1990s.

Policy or Directed Lending

Another issue that arises in the context of structural regulation is policy lending, which we will revisit in a succeeding discussion. Policy or directed lending refers to lending that is mandated by government policy. The extent to which bank lending is forcibly directed towards certain sectors or institutions varies considerably around the world. In "socialist market" economies such as China and Vietnam, banks, especially those owned by the government, are typically obliged to engage in lending to state-owned enterprises, notwithstanding the fact that many SOEs are loss making and will never be able to repay the loans. Such directed lending within a command economy really amounts to a subsidy, whereby the state, since it owns all relevant parties, is moving funds from one pocket to another. In India and Sri Lanka, another form of subsidy manifests in the form of bank loans to farmers that remain uncollected.

Sometimes the banks that engage in policy lending are state-owned, but often, privately owned commercial banks must perform some policy lending. In the United States, certain laws compel banks to engage in lending in poorer areas from which they take deposits. In other countries, like South Korea or Japan, even nominally private institutions were effectively commanded through so-called "administrative guidance" to lend to certain companies or sectors favored by the government. Throughout most of the post-WWII era, banks in both countries were encouraged to provide loans at low margins to the country's leading industrial enterprises.

In many countries, policy banks, whose charter provides that they were established to facilitate one policy mission or another, still play an important role. Typical examples are banks set up to fund agricultural development, community development or industrial development. A major part, if not the whole loan portfolio, of these institutions is devoted to policy lending. Although this type of lending is often subsidized finance in which the bank provides below-market interest rates, in some cases the object is to generate some level of profit. Policy banks, because of the subsidized infrastructure they have in place, may be able to enter markets that commercial banks have avoided. In the Philippines, for instance, Land Bank of the Philippines, an institution originally set up to finance land reform, has been developing a profitable and fairly risk-free business in lending to rural municipalities securing the loans with revenue sharing allotments received by these local governmental units by the national government.

Policy banks in developing countries also sometimes function as conduits for multilateral institutions such as the World Bank or Asian Development Bank, providing these larger institutions with greater distribution capability. In turn, the policy banks may receive long-term funding that has the benefit of improving their balance sheet.

What does it mean from a credit standpoint, when a bank engages in heavy policy lending? On the one hand, policy lending is generally seen as detrimental to the quality of the bank's loan portfolio (i.e. its asset quality) since the lending is not done for reasons of profit and consequently the credit risk is ordinarily mispriced. Default rates are likely to be high and in certain cases there may in fact be no expectation that the loans will be repaid. In these circumstances, the loans are loans in name only, and are actually pure, though disguised, subsidies rather than credit. On the other hand, a bank that is forced to make policy loans usually receives as a quid pro quo, either implicit or explicit, the promise of some government support, should the bank experience difficulties. Of course, this is only fair since the bank is foregoing opportunities to make a profit by providing loans at a rate that does not reflect their real risk, that its losses should made up when the loans it undertook on the government's behalf.

Policy lending is easy to recognize when a bank is wholly-owned by the government and its charter explicitly directs the institution to lend to a certain sector. Land Bank of the Philippines, mentioned above, is an example of such a 100% government-owned institution that has as its mission rural development, and lends a high proportion of its funds to that end, very often against non-commercial criteria. Policy lending is more difficult to discern when banks that have partial or no government ownership are compelled to lend to politically worthy borrowers. In such case, the level of support that can be expected by the government is usually more ambiguous. This makes placing much reliance upon government support in the event of need problematic. The situation becomes even thornier when the government in question is a local or provincial government that may not have the capacity or the political will or autonomy to provide the requisite degree of support. This was illustrated in recent years in China when the national government allowed a number of financial institutions supported only by local or provincial governments to collapse. The probability that support will be forthcoming and the quality of the support can only be determined by weighing the particular circumstances and announced policies of the government carefully.

> Tip: Policy Banks. Banks that engage in policy lending (lending in furtherance of a non-commercial purpose such as agricultural development) often benefit from an implicit or explicit promise of governmental support. The credit impact depends upon the strength of that support and the capacity of the government in question. In general, policy banks fully owned by the national government can be viewed as quasi-sovereign risk. Banks owned by local or provincial governments, only partly government owned, deserve much closer scrutiny.

Deposit Insurance

A deposit insurance scheme insures retail depositors, usually up to a certain limit, that their deposits will be repaid in the event of a bank failure. Limits vary globally. In the US, deposits at most banks are insured up to US$100,000, while Philippine bank depositors are only insured to PHP100,000 (US$2,500). Deposit insurance programs may be privately funded and operated, or run by the government. Premiums are ordinarily paid for by the insured banks, calculated as a percentage of total deposits. A number of countries have no deposit insurance program, while in others, especially in emerging markets, the government implicitly or explicitly guarantees bank deposits. For example, Thailand has no deposit insurance program but the government has nonetheless promised to make retail depositors whole in respect to banks that have failed.

Deposit insurance programs tend to boost depositor confidence. If depositors have faith in the program, bank runs will be discouraged and bank failures reduced. Where no program exists, as in Hong Kong, unjustified bank runs may occur. Even where a deposit insurance program exists, however, it may be prone to delays in repayment (e.g. Philippines), and the objective of maintaining depositor confidence may not be met.

Effective deposit insurance schemes create separate problems of moral hazard, as we have mentioned.

State Support for Troubled Banks

When good banks turn bad, governments, for the reasons we have discussed above, usually feel obliged to help. The help may extend to depositors if a bank shuts its doors, or the government may go further and provide assistance in the form of liquidity support to prevent the bank from shutting its doors. In addition, the government may become involved in rehabilitating a troubled bank, through a variety of means that are discussed in greater detail in the chapters on the distressed bank which follow.

When it comes to assessing the creditworthiness of a bank or banking system, the promise of government support is an extremely weighty factor. In effect, such a promise converts the risk of a bank or bank system failure as quasi-sovereign risk. When such support exists, the relative importance of the standalone performance of a bank or banking system is diminished.

While state support provides reassurance in assessing bank creditworthiness, state support is not without costs. The cost of fixing failed or failing banks is passed on to the country's taxpayers. At the same time, the knowledge that a bail-out may be available contributes, as we have observed, to moral hazard, with deleterious impact on industry efficiency and management competence.

State support is not necessarily a black or white proposition. Governments may come to the aid of some banks (e.g. those too big or too small to fail) and not to others. While government-owned banks are generally likely to be rescued, especially when owned by the national government, privately-owned banks may be allowed to fail and be liquidated. The level of support that may be forthcoming to partly government-owned banks and those owned by state enterprises, or by provincial or municipal governments, can be hard to ascertain. Cleverly, regulators may employ "constructive ambiguity" to keep bankers in the dark as to whether they will receive assistance, thereby decreasing moral hazard.

How can the probability and degree of state support for problem institutions be predicted? There is no easy answer, but the following questions and guidelines may be helpful.

Has the government expressly promised assistance to troubled banks or their depositors? Is there an implicit or informal promise relayed through regulators or bank officials? What is the history of government support for problem institutions? Is there an element of government ownership in the subject bank(s)? What would be the likely political and economic of the failure of the subject bank or banks?

CONDITION OF THE MAJOR BANKS WITHIN THE INDUSTRY

An estimation of the strength of a banking system is inextricably intertwined with the strength of individual banks. A strong banking system buttresses the strength of banks that operate within that system, while the vigor of the system depends in large part upon the financial condition, the stability of the franchise and the competence of management of the respective banks that comprise it.

SUMMARY: ASSESSMENT OF A BANKING SYSTEM—TWELVE QUESTIONS

A banking system cannot be evaluated without reference to the strength of specific players. In most countries, the number of key financial institutions are comparatively few, and their financial condition, management competence and the strength of their respective franchises will have a most important bearing on any appraisal of the banking system in which they operate. Consideration of key systemic and sovereign risks in a banking system, is also imperative. The legal and regulatory environment, together with the competence of bank supervision, is another important element to be contemplated. Additionally, the level of government and shareholder support available in case of need can be a critical.

Below is a checklist of questions to be weighed when evaluating the strength of a banking system:

❑ What is the strength of major players in the banking market in terms of health of their respective franchises, earnings, asset quality, liquidity and capital adequacy?

❑ What is the average financial condition of major and minor players with regard to profitability, efficiency, asset quality, capital strength and liquidity?

❑ What systemic and sovereign risks — including level of economic diversification, political stability and support for the financial system, and macroeconomic fundamentals — affect the banking system?

❑ Do historic patterns of deregulation or banking reform (e.g. former Soviet Union republics making transition from command to market economy) indicate any likely vulnerabilities in the banking system?

❑ What is the overall level of competence of bank regulation and supervision?

❑ To what extent do the country's bank regulations conform with international standards?

❑ To what degree is state support of particular banks available in case of need?

❑ What is the state of evolution of a credit culture within banks and among bank customers?

❑ How effective and fair is the legal system, particularly in respect to enforcement of creditors' rights?

❑ What is the degree of consolidation within the banking industry?

❑ What is the level of competition, including foreign competitions, and preparedness of existing banks to compete?

❑ How strong is the trend toward disintermediation and what other pressures on bank margins, if any, exist?

CHAPTER SUMMARY

In this chapter, we have tried to address several subjects. First, we have discussed the relationship between bank credit analysis and an analysis of sovereign risk and systemic risk issues. Sovereign risk influences bank health and bank health influences sovereign risk. The core of sovereign risk analysis involves exploring both political considerations, which are largely qualitative an unquantifiable, and macroeconomic considerations, which are amenable to quantitative review.

Key aspects of the macroeconomic aspect of sovereign risk analysis include examining a variety of ratios and indicators in an attempt to answer the following questions:

❑ How has the economy of the subject country performed and how is it likely to perform in the future?

❑ How well does the government manage public finances?

❑ How has the economy of the subject country performed and how is it likely to perform in the future?

❑ How well does the government manage public finances?

❑ How effectively does the government manage monetary policy?

❑ What is the level of the government's capacity and willingness to service its foreign debt obligations?

It can be seen that this line of inquiry in some respects parallels that of the CAMEL model. To make a very rough analogy, we can say that both political risk analysis and an assessment of management at the individual bank level are extremely important yet essentially qualitative in nature. The country's external position is similar to an individual bank's liquidity: will there be funds to satisfy creditors demands? Management of public finances is like earnings and profitability. Do incomings (tax revenue) exceed outgoings? At this point, it may be stretching the analogy a bit, but the structure of an economy could be said to be analogous to asset quality. What is the quality of the resources with which the country has been endowed? Finally, and admittedly, this may be stretching the analogy past its limit, but monetary policy may be said to resemble capital in that by effectively managing its monetary and financial system, the government creates the conditions that enables capital to flow and finance the economic system as a whole.

Finally, we turn to systemic risk — the structural factors that make one banking system more vulnerable than another — and finally to the rationale for and approaches to bank regulation. In the next chapter we shall look more closely at the prudential regulation of banks.

CHAPTER EIGHTEEN

THE REGULATORY REGIME: THE CONTOURS OF PRUDENTIAL REGULATION OF BANKS

The ... perverse incentives provided to creditors, coupled with shareholders' small investment and limited liability, create incentives for banks to assume excessive risks on behalf of owners, who receive the entire benefit from higher risk-taking, but have a relatively small investment to lose in case of failure.

— Virginia Manzer, Standard & Poor's,
"The Roots of Financial System Fragility"

A general collapse of credit, however short the time it lasts, is more fearful than the most terrible earthquake.

— Michel Chevalier[1]

The criticism of regulators has been that they arrive after the war is over and then shoot the wounded.[2]

— William Seidman, Chairman, FDIC (1989)

None of the risks to which banking is prone can be avoided entirely. They can only be minimized, mitigated or optimized; in other words: managed. No matter how diligent the bank's credit controls, eventually a customer will default. Similarly, the very nature of banking, which is based on

---

[1] Michel Chevalier, *Lettres sur l'Amerique du Nord*, 3rd ed. (Brussels, 1837), vol. 1, p. 37, cited in Kindelberger, Chapter 8, n. 21.
[2] Quoted in Gardner & Mills: *Managing Financial Institutions: An Asset/Liability Approach, 2nd Edition*, Dryden Press, 1991.

accepting short-term deposits in small, irregular amounts at erratic intervals and lending out the same funds in typically larger blocks for fixed terms, makes some gap in tenor between a bank's assets (loans) and its liabilities (deposits) inevitable, and the possibility of a shortfall in liquidity or a potential squeeze on profits inescapable.

The quality the regulatory regime governing banks has three elements. Two correspond to the two key approaches to modifying the natural tendency of banks towards opacity and excessive risk-taking. One is the use of market-mechanisms; a second the ability of government to command specific behaviors through its police power and the force of law. Thus, one element of the quality of a regulatory regime can be discerned in the extent regulators compel disclosure which enables the market to respond by effectively punishing a bank that appears to be sailing too close to the wind and in danger of capsizing. This the market can do by withholding funding or capital requiring that risky banks pay a premium to investors for their investment. A second element can be found in the degree to which regulators mandate substantive policies that require banks to maintain adequate loan loss provisions, for instance. A third element, which informs the first two, is the ability and will of the regulatory authorities to enforce their directives, whether disclosure-oriented or substantive in nature.

These three elements will also serve to organize this chapter. We will begin with a discussion of disclosure issues, then turn to prudential regulation, and finally conclude with a brief examination of enforcement issues.

Three Elements of a Regulatory Regime

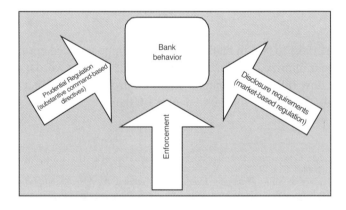

REGULATION OF BANKING: TRANSPARENCY AND REQUISITE DISCLOSURE

The level and quality of disclosure of financial data is critical to bank analysis, in the same way it is to banks when deciding whether or not to make a loan to a customer. If data is incomplete, late, or inaccurate, analysis may be negatively affected. In some countries, as we have mentioned, financial reports may be issued a year or more after the fiscal year reported upon ends. In others, crucial data such as the level of non-performing loans may not be disclosed. Figures reported may be inaccurate as a result of a high degree of discretion permitted to management, or in more extreme cases, as the result of incompetence or even fraud.

In a special report based on a speech delivered at the U.S. Securities and Exchange Commission in 1998, Donald Selzer of Moody's Investors Services identified a number of common disclosure failures.[3] These have particular applicability to the banking industry. The problems identified fell into four categories as indicated below:

1. Lack of Timeliness

❑ Delays in financial reporting of from 6 months to 2 years beyond the reports' due dates.

❑ Lack of interim financial updates or abbreviated interim reports.

❑ Failure to report information about material events at the time they occur.

2. Accounting Idiosyncrasies

❑ Non-standard loss and impairment definitions for financial assets.

❑ Non-homogeneous accounting standards.

❑ No consolidation of the financial results of related companies.

❑ Capitalization of ordinary and recurring expenses.

❑ The recognition of future cash flows as current income.

---

[3] Donald E. Selzer, Special Comment, "Disclosure and Transparency: Failures in Both Emerging and Established Markets," Moody's Investors Services, May 1998, based on material delivered in a speech to the U.S. Securities and Exchange Commission International Institute for Securities Market Development, April 29, 1998, Washington, D.C.

3. Undisclosed Relevant Financial Data

❑ Failure to disclose off-balance sheet derivatives activity.

4. Limits on Independence of Auditors and Freedom of Speech

❑ Lack of independence of auditors.

❑ Constraints on freedom of speech to openly discuss the financial problems of an issuer.

Let us look at each of these items in turn and provide some additional elaboration.

KEY DISCLOSURE PROBLEMS

Timeliness and Frequency

We have already mentioned how failure to disclose financial results on a timely basis tends to make credit analysis a difficult exercise. Related to timeliness is the issue of frequency of reporting. Interim results, if available, may be highly abridged, for example providing only limited balance sheet data and no information concerning income and expenses. Events having a material impact on the bank's financial condition, such as taking a charge for writing off losses, may not be announced at all, but instead left to be discovered following publication of annual results.

We have observed that banks have incentives not to disclose any more than the minimum financial and performance data. It therefore ordinarily falls upon bank regulators to set those minimum standards. From a bank analyst's perspective, quarterly or even monthly reporting would be near ideal. The majority of countries, however, merely require banks to report on an annual basis, although some lesser degree of interim disclosure may also be mandatory.[4] Unfortunately, in some countries (banks in South Asia are among the most egregious offenders), reports published a year to two years after the end of the financial year (or in extreme cases even more) are not unheard of. Plainly, such reports

---

[4] Banks listed on a stock exchange may under securities laws be obligated to separate reporting requirements affecting all listed companies.

have little predictive value.[5] Attitudes do appear to be changing, especially among the countries that were hard hit by the Asia crisis, as the value of disclosure is impressed upon banks and regulators. Taking into account the risk inherent in uncertainty, generally, the more frequent the reporting, the better and the more highly the analyst is likely to rate the sector and banking system as a whole.

Accounting Idiosyncrasies: Peculiar Accounting Standards

Consistency in accounting presentation aids comparison of the financial conditions of banks, and bank analysis as a whole. In markets that require International Accounting Standards (IAS) or Generally Accepted Accounting Principles (GAAP), analysis is facilitated. In some emerging markets, local accounting standards may be utilized. Although IAS and GAAP may not be intrinsically superior to local accounting standards international investors or counterparties are unlikely to be familiar with their idiosyncrasies. Moreover, local accounting standards are sometimes characterized by reporting methods that are either unduly rigid and formalistic or allow banks excessive discretion in characterizing line items. More often than not, in comparison with IAS or GAAP, they tend to obscure rather than reveal banks' true financial condition. Problems with accounting standards include the use of peculiar definitions regarding the impairment and loss of financial assets such as loans. Non-performing loans may be defined in a lax manner which makes it difficult for the analyst to fathom the true asset quality of the bank, while masking the bank's probable real level of loan losses.

Inextricably linked to the problem of quirky accounting standards is the issue of consistent presentation of financial data. Consistent presentation of financial data across uniform fiscal years facilitate comparisons among banks. When it is not present, comparisons across markets become problematic. Where some banks define non-performing loans as those one day overdue and others define them as those 90 days overdue, comparison is made more difficult. Similarly, it is troublesome to compare banks that end their fiscal year in June and issue full financial reports then, with those that end their fiscal years in December. Of course, even

---

[5] Since the banks in question are often state-owned and in some cases probably technically insolvent, the fact that window dressing has not yet appeared to attempt to disguise their poor condition is of no great moment. The astute analyst would not be fooled in any case by the figures that finally do appear. Their delay only serves to confirm deficiencies in the bank's management and governance.

with a single accounting regime, inconsistency can occur as when a bank changes the way it reports particular data.

Consolidated Reporting

Another accounting standard issue concerns consolidation. Normally, it is best to analyze banks on a consolidated basis. The exception may be when the bank itself is but a minority subsidiary or affiliate in a much larger group. In such a case it would be appropriate to analyze the bank on an unconsolidated basis, although the creditworthiness of the larger group would be relevant in terms of possible shareholder support. Banks that report on a consolidated basis, including where appropriate unconsolidated financial statements, are less able to hide problem accounts in subsidiaries. Some Japanese banks have done this in the past, reporting financial and non-financial affiliates on an unconsolidated basis, thereby obscuring the magnitude of their financial difficulties.

Undisclosed Relevant Financial Items

As suggested in the preceding text box, banks frequently omit disclosure of items critical to effective credit analysis. These include most notably items relating to asset quality and non-performing loans, risk-weighted capital, and a comprehensive breakdown of income, expense, asset and liability items. Off-balance sheet activity is another element of financial condition that is frequently not fully disclosed.

Off-Balance Sheet Commitments: Major Categories

❑ Guarantees

❑ Documentary/trade credits

❑ Foreign exchange contracts (derivatives)

❑ Interest rate contracts (derivatives)

Corollary to the problem of failing to disclose is failing to disclose in sufficient detail. Disclosure of material information concerning a bank's financial condition can vary considerably in breadth and detail. While most banks will issue an income statement, balance sheet and cash flow

Basic Income Statement Data	Basic Balance Sheet Data
Audited, Consolidated & Unconsolidated	Audited, Consolidated & Unconsolidated Accounts
Interest Income	Liquid assets, by type: cash, central bank reserves, government and marketable securities, interbank assets (loans extended or deposits made)
Interest Expense	Other interest-earning securities, by type
Loan Loss Provisions	Total loans and advances, and composition of loan portfolio by sector, borrower type, and tenor
Non-interest income, categorized by components such as fees and commissions (showing fees and commission expense), trading gains (showing trading losses), dividend or investment income and exceptional gains	Other assets, by type, including trade bills, goodwill
Non-interest expense, categorized by components such as salary, occupancy, depreciation, and administrative costs	Fixed assets
Taxation	Total assets
Exceptional items (e.g. asset sales) and writedowns of assets	Deposits, whether retail or bank, whether current, savings or term and by tenor
Net profit	Borrowings, by type, seniority and tenor
Minority interest and profit attributable to shareholders	Other liabilities
Extraordinary items	Total liabilities
Dividends, common and preferred	Shareholders' equity (paid up capital, retained earnings, reserves); Minority interest
Retained earnings	Total liabilities and shareholders' equity

Other Important Data	
Asset quality	**Capital**
Accumulated loan loss reserves, categorized by general provisions and specific provisions	Shareholders' equity account
Non-performing loans, by classification, by type and/or geographic region; definition of non-performing loans	Tier 1 Capital
Accrued interest; interest in suspense	Tier 2 Capital
Composition of loan portfolio (concentration data)	BIS capital adequacy ratio
Restructured loans; relapse rate Foreclosed assets	Composition of regulatory capital Off-balance sheet exposure by category and instrument
Loan write-offs and write backs	**Key ratios**
Policies governing provisioning, write offs, write-backs; interest recognition	Return on assets or average assets
Related party lending	Return on equity or average equity
Expos. to affiliated companies	Net interest margin; Net interest spread
Expos. to directors/employees	Average yield on earning assets
Mkt value and book cost of trading securities; policy on valuation of investments; policies governing revaluation, depreciation	Average funding cost of interest bearing liabilities
Subsidiaries and holdings in investments	Efficiency ratio
Liquidity and Funding	Non-performing loan ratio; Collateral coverage of total and non-performing loans
Liabilities categorized by maturity and type	Loans to deposits
Assets categorized by maturity and type Foreign exchange exposure (assets and liabilities)	Liquid or quasi-liquid assets ratio

statement no less than annually, the quantity of information provided can run the gamut from a single line devoted to non-interest income, to paragraphs in appended footnotes describing the nature and sources of that revenue. Similarly, while disclosure of total non-performing loans is important, disclosure of the volume and non-performing loan ratio by product type (e.g. real estate mortgage loans, credit card lending) as well as the volume and proportion of foreclosed assets and restructured loans further assists the process of analysis.

Regulators vary in the amount of disclosure they require of banks. What disclosure facilitates bank analysis? At a minimum, the bank should disclose sufficient financial items so that an analyst can perform a basic ratio analysis. It is the rare bank that would not provide the basic data listed below, although in some so-called sub-emerging markets highly unusual financial statements based on local accounting mores or extremely limited itemization are occasionally seen.

Key Ratios

Although some ratios can be calculated with just the items above, others like the capital adequacy ratio cannot. Also, definitions of formulae and methods of calculation vary, so it is always helpful to obtain the bank's own ratio calculations. For example, the bank may calculate "average assets" or its "liquid assets ratio" on a monthly basis, while the analyst might only have access to end-of-year data. Bank calculations of the following ratios may be helpful.

❏ Return on assets or average assets
❏ Return on equity or average equity
❏ Net interest margin
❏ Average yield on earning assets, preferably by asset category (e.g. commercial loans, mortgage, interbank)
❏ Average funding cost of interest bearing liabilities, preferably by category (e.g. savings deposits, time deposits)
❏ Net interest spread
❏ Efficiency ratio
❏ Non-performing loan ratio
❏ Non-performing asset ratio

❑ Collateral coverage of total and non-performing loans
❑ Loan loss provisions to non performing loans and/or non-performing assets
❑ Capital Adequacy Ratio
❑ Tier 1, Capital Adequacy Ratio
❑ Loans to deposits
❑ Liquid or quasi-liquid assets ratio

Management's Projections and Attribution of Causes

The foregoing items comprise those that ideally will be disclosed in the bank's financial statements. In addition to these aforementioned line items and ratios, it is helpful if the analyst can obtain in discussion with management management's *projections* as to the following items and ratios:

❑ Net profits
❑ Loan growth
❑ Non-performing loans
❑ Non-performing assets (i.e. including restructured loans and foreclosed property)
❑ NPL ratio
❑ Capital Adequacy Ratio

As part of a bank review, the analyst may also look either to the annual report or from management directly for reasons or both concerning:

❑ Changes in net profit
❑ Changes in net interest income
❑ Changes in non I-interest income
❑ Changes in the volume of non-performing loans
❑ Changes in key ratios such as ROA, net interest margin, the CAR

Finally, in preparing a report, the analyst should look in the annual report or to management for management's view as to:

❑ The bank's franchise, brand equity, reputation and comparative advantage over its competition
❑ Risk management practices
❑ IT investment and innovation

❏ Branch expansion or rationalization

❏ Market share, customer penetration/retention, and market growth

❏ Quality of personnel, staff training, staff turnover and employee satisfaction

With the foregoing information, the analyst will have all the data reasonably necessary to prepare a workmanlike bank credit report.

Disclosure to the Central Bank

Since the nature of banking is that capital, liquidity and other financial ratios fluctuate in the course of doing business, most regulators impose a reporting requirement that banks calculate and disclose relevant ratios and other aspects of a bank's financial condition *to the regulatory authority* on a periodic basis. This does not mean that the results of such disclosure are made available to the public; indeed the information is often treated as expressly confidential and cannot be obtained from the authorities. This approach towards disclosure illustrates of the continuing dominance of paternalistic attitudes towards bank regulation — and data of this kind is reported considerably more frequently to regulators than to the public. The frequency of mandatory reporting varies globally, ranging from weekly in the US and other countries, to biweekly or every 15 days (e.g. Malaysia) to monthly (e.g. Taiwan).

Independence of Auditors and Freedom of Speech

When auditors are not independent, and analysts or commentators are castigated, or worse, if they speak out about a company or a country's problems, the true picture is obscured and risk-averse investors are prone to flee for the exits at the first sign of trouble. As Moody's has opined: "In some countries, it is illegal or imprudent to speak out publicly about the financial problems of an issuer of debt or equity. Without this public discussion, the other disclosure rules have much less value."[6]

PRUDENTIAL REGULATION

High quality bank supervision bolsters the strength of a banking system as a whole. The role of bank supervision, usually in the hands of the

---

[6] Special Comment, p. 5.

central bank, requires both insight into how banks are apt to go off the rails, and the authority and will to see that rules set down by bank regulators are enforced. Having discussed disclosure issues, we now turn to issues of substantive bank regulation, followed by related issues of enforcement. Broadly speaking, the body of substantive rules governing banks can be referred to as prudential regulation.

The second key element of bank regulation consists of the substantive requirements set down by the state entity responsible for the supervision of financial institutions. These are regulations designed to discourage banks from taking undue risks, and to encourage them to manage their operations prudently and maintain adequate financial strength. They include, for example, rules governing reserve requirements, capital requirements and prohibitions against or restrictions on activities such as related-party lending, engaging in non-banking business against lending, in the case of residential mortgage lending, more than a certain percentage of the appraised value of the real property securing the loan.

In an ING Barings report which examined bank regulation throughout Asia based on the extent to which regulators in countries throughout the region addressed specific facets of bank operations and minimum financial condition. Analysts proposed, based on their best judgment, a percentage weighting that each of the items would provide in assessing the regulators.[7] They included: capital requirements (40%), liquidity requirements (30%), credit risk (25%) and market risk (20%). In addition, maturity risk controls, exchange rate risk controls, and off-balance sheet controls each counted 5%, while deductions were made for policy loans (−5%), excessive reserve requirement (−5%) and a history of bankruptcies (−20%). While necessarily an arbitrary means of rating regulators — one could argue, for example, that excessive weight was placed on capital while a legal framework that facilitates bankruptcy is a sign of banking system health rather than weakness — it is nonetheless a useful framework for examining the ways that regulators attempt to shape bank behavior. It is also one worth bearing in mind as we survey the various forms of prudential regulation.

---

[7] ING Barings, Regulatory and Disclosure policies — Improved but still some weak spots, Banking Bullets, Feb. 1997.

Capital and Statutory Reserve Requirements

> Legal Reserve Requirements
> Capital Adequacy Requirements and Minimum Capital Requirements
> Off-balance Sheet Commitments (Contingent Assets and Liabilities)

Legal Reserve Requirements

Traditionally banks have been required to maintain a minimum level of reserves, normally expressed as a percentage of bank deposits, with the central bank. Originally, the rationale for the statutory reserve was to ensure that banks have a cushion with which to pay current liabilities. Other measures are now employed to mandate adequate bank liquidity, and the statutory reserve now functions more as an instrument of monetary policy rather than to back-up bank liquidity. When the statutory reserve is increased, liquidity is absorbed by the central bank since the funds placed on deposit are not available to lend. In addition, a bank's funding costs are effectively increased because the moneys placed in statutory reserve earn little or no interest. Since the deposits placed in reserve are unavailable to lend, the average cost of funds to the bank is raised. Statutory reserve requirements depend upon the monetary policy of the relevant country. The US, for example, has a minimum 3% reserve requirement on the first US$47 m of bank deposits, any excess being subject to a 10% requirement. Reserve requirements usually range between 0% and 15%.

Capital Adequacy Requirements and Minimum Capital Requirements

Banks are ordinarily required to meet absolute minimum capital thresholds and may also be required to meet regulatory capital ratios.[8] Minimum thresholds vary from country to country, and by type of bank. Their rationale is that a minimum critical mass of capital is required for a bank to be viable. To illustrate, in the Philippines, separate minimum capital requirements are applicable to each of several categories of banks including universal banks, commercial banks, savings banks and rural banks. Minimum capital requirements can also be used as incentives to encourage bank mergers. By raising capital requirements on a staggered basis

---

[8] India, for instance, requires banks to have a minimum total capital of one billion rupees.

industry consolidation is thereby encouraged. Ratio requirements attempt to related capital to the demands that may be placed upon it. The underlying regulatory intent is to ensure the maintenance of an adequate cushion of capital and liquidity to cover a bank's mistakes and the outflow of funds that may accompany them.

Ratio requirements have evolved from traditional ratios in the past to the increasingly widespread acceptance of the risk-weighted capital adequacy definition promulgated under the 1988 Basel Accord and its succeeding amendments. The so-called BIS Capital Adequacy Ratio, which we discussed in detail in Chapter 15, is frequently used as a benchmark. The BIS requires banks in OECD countries to meet a minimum 8% ratio. Technically, these have not been applicable to developing countries, although a large number have nevertheless adopted the BIS 8% threshold. The near universal adoption of what may be termed BIS-style capital adequacy requirements can be attributed to their being perceived to some extent as a panacea for all that ails banks.

Requirements may be phrased in terms of Tier 1 capital requirements (expressed as a ratio) or in terms of the CAR, which combines Tier 1 and Tier 2 capital. Some regulators even require higher minimums, no doubt out of the belief that more capital is better. Singapore, for example, until recently required its banks to have a minimum Tier 1 Capital Ratio of 12%. Certainly in emerging markets, an added cushion of capital may be desirable to compensate for the higher volatility, and regrettably the difficulties in supervising banks and enforcing prudential roles, in some countries.

Off-Balance Sheet Commitments

Simply put, off-balance sheet commitments refer to a bank's contingent liabilities. As they are incorporated within the BIS capital adequacy framework and assigned risk weightings in a similar manner to the bank's assets, they are regulated under BIS-style capital adequacy requirements.[9] In addition, regulators may place restrictions on particular types of off-balance sheet activity. Most often this occurs in connection with

---

[9] The rationale for treating off-balance sheet commitments as risk-weighted assets under the Basel Accord is that if the contingency occurs which triggers a financial obligation occurs, these must be funded in the same manner as a loan or other financial asset. Indeed, a commitment to provide a loan under certain circumstances in an off-balance sheet commitment even though the loan once extended becomes an on-balance sheet asset. Examples of off-balance sheet commitments include guarantees, letters of credit and various derivatives.

derivatives activity, such as the trading or dealing in interest rate or foreign currency swaps. Banks may need special licenses to deal in derivatives, and limits on such dealing may be imposed, frequently on a case by case basis. Licenses may also impose special and more frequent reporting to the regulatory authority.

Asset Quality: Lending Restrictions, Collateral Requirements and Limits on Foreign Currency Exposure

Restrictions on Intergroup/Insider Borrowing
Single Borrower Limits
Limitations on Real Estate Lending
Limitations on Margin or Share Lending
Limits on Foreign Currency Exposure
Collateral Requirements and Restrictions

Asset quality is probably the area of bank operations concerning which regulation is more critical. By limiting the tendency of banks to take on excessive risk in their loan portfolios and by ensuring that a bank takes account of the costs of its mistakes in extending credit through adequate loan loss provisioning, most of the difficulties banks might otherwise be likely to experience can be avoided. Once asset quality has started to erode, prompt measures must be undertaken to prevent further damage and the collapse of the bank as a whole. Regulation, broadly speaking, can be categorized into those measures that are designed to prevent asset quality from weakening (i.e. to prevent the bank from making such "mistakes" in extending loans), and those that are designed to repair any impairment that has already occurred.

In the first category then, are those which attempt to, for instance, reduce over-concentration of lending and impose collateralization requirements. In the second category, for example, are those that require specific provisions for certain classes of loans.

Restrictions on Intergroup, Related Party and Insider Borrowing

The existence of rules preventing significant lending to individuals or entities closely connected to a bank's shareholders, managers or staff is an important safeguard against the subversion of prudent credit standards. When banks use a substantial portion of depositors' funds to finance enterprises related to the bank's owners or employees, the risks to depositors are likely to far exceed any potential reward. Hence, regulations limiting the degree to which related parties can borrow from the bank and imposing arm's length dealing standards are highly desirable. Applicable directives may be phrased as a percentage of equity limitation (e.g. 5–25%), outright prohibitions or collateral requirements may be imposed. In reviewing such regulations, attention must be paid to the definition of related parties and the level of enforcement. The existence of such rules does not necessarily mean that they are strictly enforced.

Single Borrower Limits

In many jurisdictions, regulators limit the amount a bank may lend to any non-related entity or group. The purpose of such restrictions is to prevent an over-concentration of lending to a single individual, entity or group. Usually, these restrictions are expressed as a percentage of total capital, e.g. 25% of paid up capital (Hong Kong). Somewhat related to single borrower limits are restrictions on lending to the largest conglomerates and to certain sectors in South Korea in an attempt to create a more diversified economy and to cause bank loan portfolios to become more diversified.

Limitations on Real Estate Lending

Because financial history teaches that banks often run aground on the shoals of excessive real estate lending, and are left high and dry when the tide turns and asset prices sink, bank regulators may impose limits or guidelines on property-related lending. What is defined as property-related lending varies, but often excludes mortgage lending for owner-occupied housing, which is as a rule much less risky than lending for property development or investment. Note that such regulations are not infrequently circumvented in practice, sometimes inadvertently. Funds lent ostensibly for industrial purposes have been known to find their way into speculative property investment schemes.

Restrictions on real estate lending may be defined as a percentage of deposits or of total loans (e.g. 20% of total loans, Philippines). During times of approaching or burgeoning crisis, regulators may attempt to tighten restrictions on real-estate related loans, as this type of lending is closely associated with financial crashes.

Limitations on Margin or Share Lending

In some countries, an attractive business for banks is the practice of share or margin lending. This is the practice of lending to brokers or investors to finance investment or speculation in stocks. In share lending, loans are secured by equity securities, in a similar manner to the way that property investment is secured by a mortgage on property. Margin lending can refer to unsecured lending for the purchase of shares. Quite a number of jurisdictions forbid margin or share lending, Thailand, for example. Others constrain it to certain types of financial institutions, limit the percentage lent to a proportion of total loans (e.g. 15%, Malaysian commercial banks) or place an absolute cap on this type of lending (e.g. India).

Restrictions on Foreign Currency Exposure

It is not uncommon for regulators to restrict foreign currency risk, i.e. net exposure, to a percentage of capital (See Off-balance Sheet Commitments). Globally, a range of 10–15% as a proportion of Tier 1 capital (shareholders' equity) is usual. Regulators may also limit foreign currency lending and borrowing, or impose reserve requirements on foreign currency borrowing to constrain short-term foreign currency inflows.

Collateral Requirements and Restrictions

Regulators may require loans of particular types to be collateralized to a minimum degree. Real estate mortgage loans are often subject to such restrictions or guidelines. The requirement may be expressed as a loan to value ratio or as a collateral to loan ratio. For instance, in Hong Kong, banks are limited to a loan to value ratio on real estate mortgage loans of 70%. In other words, the loan may not exceed 70% of the appraised value of the property.

Restrictions may also be mandated on the type of collateral deemed acceptable. For instance, a bank may be prohibited from accepting its own shares or shares of a subsidiary as collateral. Or, collateral may be limited to certain types of real and personal property.

Asset Quality: Non-Performing Loans, Provisioning and Write-Offs

Definition of Non-Performing Loans
Interest Clawbacks and Interest Accruals
Mandatory Provisioning
Tax Deductibility of Provisions or Write Offs
Write Off Policies

Definition of Non-Performing Loans

Most regulatory schemes require banks to classify loans according to the degree of probability that they will default and become uncollectible. While some discretion may be allowed to the bank, regulators typically identify minimum thresholds based upon the amount of time that principal or interest remain unpaid or have been delayed. Broadly speaking, these definitions are referred to as definitions of non-performing loans, although the term *non-performing loan* may itself be a defined term. Regulators normally classify loans into four categories, excluding loans which are performing. Common terms for these categories are special mention, substandard, doubtful and loss. Note that a loan does not have to be overdue to be "classified." Special mention loans may apply to loans where the borrower is experiencing financial difficulties, but is nonetheless fully current in its payments, but not all regulators utilize the special mention classification. Note also that a loan may also be past due, without being deemed non-performing.

The customary international standard to define a non-performing loan is any credit which is past due more than 90 days. In many countries, especially emerging markets, looser definitions prevail, which of course tend to make the asset quality of the banks of that country appear better.[10] The fact that a loan is non-performing does not mean that a loan is a "bad loan," although in everyday parlance the terms may be used synonymously. A "bad loan" really means a loan that is in the impaired category ("doubtful" or "loss").

---

[10] A six month threshold instead of a three month threshold has been common in many emerging markets, although the trend is towards a general acceptance of the three month definition.

Cessation of Interest Accrual and Interest in Suspense

Cessation of interest accrual refers to the time from the loan becoming overdue after which banks are required to stop accruing interest when a loan is overdue. The international standard is three months (90 days), the same as the definition of a non-performing loan, but in some countries loans can be overdue six months or more before the bank is requires to cease interest accrual. In the case of a bullet or balloon payment (or a quarterly, semi-annual or annual payment), a payment overdue as little as one day can compel interest to cease accruing.

Interest Clawbacks and Interest Accruals

Interest clawbacks refers to the obligation to reverse the recognition of accrued interest in the income statement once a loan has been classified as non-performing. Regulations governing interest accruals determine under what circumstances a bank may no longer accrue interest. International best practice requires interest clawbacks of interest income accrued but not received when a loan is deemed non-performing. In some countries, however, banks have been permitted to omit interest clawbacks. This has the effect of inflating bank income. See Chapter 13 for more explanation on how interest accrual, interest in suspense and interest clawbacks work.

Mandatory Provisioning

Regulations sometimes provide for minimum general provisioning, applicable to performing loans, and specific provisioning applicable to "classified loans." The requirements concerning performing loans differ, but a general provisioning requirement of from 0.5–2% is not unusual. Specific provisioning is also subject to a great deal of variance, but the following are typical:

Loan Classification	Provisioning Requirement
Special Mention	No global standard, but countries generally range from 0–5%
Substandard	Global standard from 15–20%, but may range from 0–25%
Doubtful	Global standard is 50%, but may range from 20–100%, with 50–75% most common
Loss	Global standard is 100% to which nearly all jurisdictions conform

Write-Off Policies

Writing off loans is easy in some countries, difficult in others. The amount of time after which a write-off is mandatory also varies. In quite a number of emerging markets, regulations have often seemed to discourage write-offs. Prior to the Asian crisis, for example, the official policy in one country was that write-offs were not required for 21 months until after the loan became overdue, or following the end of litigation.[11] Tax treatment, as mentioned, will affect the inclination of banks to take write-offs. Also, in some countries as a matter of policy, write-offs may be discouraged, requiring approval of bank regulators for instance, or the requisite legal mechanisms for effecting write-offs cumbersome. As a general rule, easy write-offs are preferable, as otherwise, banks are dissuaded from declaring loans as losses and removing them from their books. When it is difficult for a bank to write-off impaired assets the negative impact on reserves and equity is thus obscured.

Tax Deductibility of Provisions or Write-Offs

The extent to which provisions or write-offs are tax deductible will affect banks' willingness to take them. In the United States and the UK, provisions are not tax deductible but write-offs are. In other markets, provisions may be deductible up to a percentage limit, but not write-offs.

Prudential Regulation: Liquidity Requirements

Minimum liquid asset ratios or other liquidity ratios
Restrictions on maturity mismatching of assets and liabilities
Restrictions on mismatching of foreign currency assets and liabilities

Liquidity as we have discussed is the proximate cause of most bank failures. Therefore, requiring banks to maintain a minimum degree of liquidity is of prime concern to bank regulators. Liquidity management, however, is among the more difficult areas of bank regulation, partly because liquidity needs can change so rapidly. Regulating liquidity is correspondingly difficult.

---

[11] Regulatory and Disclosure policies — Improved but still some weak spots, Banking Bullets, Feb. 1997, p. 18, citing Banking in the Far East, 1995 and regulatory authorities.

Control of liquidity, whether at the management level or as the regulator requires, as we have seen in an earlier chapter, involves assuring that the bank has an ample pool of liquid funds and that these are commensurate to the bank's probable liquidity needs. This is typically accomplished in two ways. First, bank regulators in many countries require banks to maintain a certain proportion of funds in liquid form in order to meet any current obligations, such as those resulting from the withdrawal of a substantial proportion of a bank's deposits. Liquid assets are those that are in the form of cash, or readily convertible to cash, such as government bonds or treasury bills. While loan to deposits is one measure of liquidity that is employed for this purpose,[12] as it measures non-liquid assets relative to the bulk of a bank's potentially loanable funds,[13] liquidity ratios that specifically measure liquid or current assets in proportion to total assets are more frequently utilized. Typical ratios range from 7–25%.

The second way in which management and regulators attempt to maintain adequate liquidity is by monitoring mismatches between assets and liabilities. Mismatches may be either in respect of a) maturity; or b) currency. As we have emphasized, fractional-reserve banking has an inherent liquidity risk in that virtually all banks have more comparatively illiquid assets such as loans than illiquid ones, while a large proportion of the bank's liabilities will almost certainly be demand deposits or other current or short-term liabilities. The challenge is to reduce this mismatch.

In addition, mismatching can occur in respect to the currencies of the bank's assets and liabilities. A bank may borrow in US dollars for example and then make loans in the local currency of the country in which the bank is situated. If the local currency devalues, the bank's need for foreign currency funds when the foreign currency liability comes due will suddenly have increased. In this respect, liquidity is closely to tied to foreign exchange risk, and banks must carefully manage this risk in order to avoid having a shortfall of foreign currency funds when those obligations become due.

Regulatory requirements in respect of asset-liability management correspond to each of the types of mismatch we have noted. First,

---

[12] E.g. Korea limits banks' loan to deposit ratio to be less than 100%.
[13] Funds borrowed from other banks or through the securities markets comprise most of the remainder.

supervisory authorities may limit the extent to which certain assets and liabilities classified by maturity may be mismatched. A rudimentary way to do this is by limiting the bank's loan to deposit ratio (loans are illiquid, deposits mainly demand or short-term obligations). Restrictions on loan to deposit ratios, when utilized, vary, but 100–120% is a common threshold. Second, open foreign exchange may be limited in an attempt to reduce foreign exchange mismatch. For example, the amount of any overnight foreign exchange position may be limited to a percentage of the bank's equity capital (e.g. 15–25%). Note, however, that banks may maintain matched foreign currency positions, but still be vulnerable to foreign exchange risk where they on-lend funds to local customers in foreign currency. Although technically that is the risk of the borrowers, if a major currency devaluation occurs and they have limited sources of foreign currency and are unable to find sufficient local currency to convert to foreign currency, their problem becomes the bank's problem. Finally, using the techniques described in Chapter 17, regulators may mandate ceilings on the level of mismatch permitted.

Another type of regulation which can facilitate bank liquidity is the existence of a deposit insurance program also discussed in Chapter 17. Whether implicit or explicit, such a program will reduce the likelihood of a bank run or smaller blips in demand for liquid funds, but as we have discussed it raises moral hazard issues as well. A related issue, although largely a matter of discretion rather than explicit regulation is the willingness of the central bank or monetary authority to function as a lender of last resort.

Restrictions on Bank Ownership Structure and Bank Equity Investment

> Limits on Individual Shareholdings in the Bank
> Restrictions on Bank Equity Investment
> Restrictions Bank Investment in Property

Limits on Individual or Single Group Shareholdings

To remove incentives for banks to channel depositors funds to loans to insiders, regulators may restrict the percentage of shares that may be held by any individual, corporation or corporate group. Alternatively, regulators may limit the percentage of voting shares that may be held by such individuals or entities.[14] In Asia, for instance, some jurisdictions have no limits on such shareholding (e.g. Hong Kong, Philippines), while have imposed restrictions on individual shareholdings (e.g. 20%, Singapore) and on corporate shareholdings (e.g. 10%, Thailand). In addition, percentages above a certain threshold may be subject to regulator approval.

Other Limits on Shareholding of Banks

To prevent domination of a local banking system by large foreign banks, regulators may impose foreign ownership restrictions, which can vary depending upon whether the shareholder is an individual or corporation. Generally these limit foreign shareholders to a minority position. Nationalism plays a role in the continuing existence of such restrictions. At the same time, the fear that large and efficient foreign financial institutions may drive local players out of existence is not without some justification. The Asian crisis has provided some impetus to deregulation, encouraging regulators in that region to allow foreign banks to hold majority positions as a way to bring in new capital and technology. An accompanying trend is to remove some or all restrictions on foreign ownership once a sufficient level of consolidation has occurred within local banking industries. In addition to outright restrictions on foreign ownership, the central bank may require its approval for investment in bank shares by an individual or group, foreign or domestic, above a certain percentage.

Restrictions on Bank Equity Investment

With the view that banks should confine their business to lending and avoid the risks of the equity markets, some regulators either prohibit banks from investing in stocks, or limit such investment to a proportion of bank capital. Typical limits range from 10% (Korea) to 40% (Singapore). Other regulations may prohibit or limit investment in other banks, and in non-bank businesses either financial or non-financial.

---

[14] India has no limit on individual or corporate shareholdings, but restricts voting rights exercisable to 1% of total shares.

Restrictions Bank Investment in Property

For the same reasons, some regulators forbid banks from investing in real estate, limit such investments to a proportion of bank capital (e.g. 25% of capital) or restrict the time period of applicable investments. Others, such as Hong Kong, mandate that foreclosed property be disposed of within a certain period time.

Adverse Aspects of Bank Regulation: Profitability Depletive Policies and Profitability Enhancement Policies[15]

Policy lending requirements	Government sanctioned
Excessive reserve requirements	bank cartels
High tax rates	

We have observed that profitability is the lifeblood of a bank, and that it is the foundation of a bank's financial strength. Internally generated capital is nothing more than retained profit (excluding dividend payout), and strong earnings enhance a bank's profitability. Thus government policies that tend to drain profits are inimical to a strong banking system. Property depletive policies include policy lending requirements (i.e. requirements or guidelines that a bank lend to certain companies or sectors determined by the government), excessive reserve require-ments (e.g. over 7%), and obviously, high tax rates. Note that policy lending requirements are not limited to so-called policy banks, but may be imposed on private commercial banks to one degree or another. These rules may be phrased affirmatively, for example that 20% of all lending must be directed to small businesses. Excessive reserve requirements are usually more a way for the government to obtain low cost or financing at bank expense (typically statutory reserves pay little or no interest) than a way to protect depositors and creditors.

Governments may also implement profitability enhancement poli-cies. Usually this is in the form of approving a cartel in which banks collude to maintain artificially high lending rates and artificially low deposit rates. While such policies may temporarily enhance bank

---

[15] See ING Barings, Regulatory and Disclosure policies — Improved but still some weak spots, Banking Bullets, Feb. 1997.

financial strength and creditworthiness, in the long run they are negative both for the economy and the banks involved. For the economy, high credit costs act as drag on growth — the cartel is in effect imposing a private tax on the economy — and for the banks they discourage the development of a credit culture, competitive skills, and innovation. Once implemented, such support is difficult to withdraw, and if withdrawn, the banks will find themselves ill-equipped to compete with their foreign counterparts domestically or regionally.

Regulatory Appraisal of Management

Although not easily subject to quantitative review, as with bank credit analysis itself, an effective bank regulatory agency is one that is not hesitant to appraise the quality of management in a fair and impartial manner. Bank regulatory authorities should also be willing adopt a consultative approach towards bank management, having the capacity to advise management on improving its practices where appropriate. At the same time, the authority should take an aggressive stance towards fraudulent or criminal activity such as money laundering.

SUPERVISION AND ENFORCEMENT

Supervision and enforcement are accomplished through regular bank examinations, review of disclosed information and the capacity to impose administrative sanctions, including shutting a bank down. In some jurisdictions, bank supervisory agencies are inadequately staffed and enforcement is consequently lax. In others, conditions may prevent bank examiners may be prevented from doing their job effectively. Poorly paid examiners may be prone to corruption or the examiners may be subject to lawsuits or other retribution from bankers who believe they are being unfairly targeted. In other jurisdictions, the bank supervisory agency may not, in practice, have the power to impose sanctions on errant banks, because the enforcement machinery is creaky or because the owners of the errant banks have the political clout to deflect sanctions that the agency attempts to impose. Ascertaining the quality of bank supervision is a largely subjective process, as the defects in bank supervision, by their nature, will tend not to be willingly revealed.

REGULATION OF BANKING: CREDITORS' RIGHTS

Effectiveness and Fairness of the Legal System

Whether a country has an effective legal system generally — one that is comparatively fair, consistent in application and which allows relatively speedy and cost-effective legal redress — a fundamental precondition to the efficient operation of banks. If those that borrow from a bank can renege on their debts with impunity, notwithstanding ability to pay, a financial institution can be brought to its knees, with grave consequences to the financial services industry as a whole. Of course, when economic conditions are rosy, it is in the interest of all parties to play by the rules. When conditions turn sour, however, the very economic survival of a debtor may be at stake, and the debtor may be inclined to skirt its legal obligations to repay a loan. Without an effective legal system, the debtor's problems become that of its bank, and if enough of the bank's customers take a similar position, the bank may collapse, with knock-on effects throughout the financial system as a whole. Specifically, the existence of insolvency and bankruptcy laws and related mechanisms for protecting creditors' rights are important components of long-term financial system health.

Foreclosure, Insolvency and Bankruptcy Law

The existence of an insolvency law that can be utilized to protect creditors' rights is critical to the ability of a bank to enforce its claims under a relevant loan or security agreement. In a number of emerging markets, insolvency laws though they may exist, are not infrequently archaic, little used or practically difficult to enforce. A dearth of judges with expertise in insolvency procedure, as well as a lack of specialized bankruptcy courts, may limit the ability of a bank to enjoy the benefit of legal process. A related barrier may be the policies and procedures embodied in extant law. Procedures may be cumbersome or biased in favor of debtors.

During the Asian crisis — in September 1998 — investment bank Warburg Dillon Read,[16] observing that international best practice afforded creditors the ability to foreclose on loan security within 3–6 months on average, estimated the following average times for such proceedings in

---

[16] The firm was absorbed by Swiss Bank and subsequently merged into UBS.

several Asian countries. The amount of time required varied anywhere from approximately 3 months in Singapore to as long as 5–10 years in Thailand.[17] It also observed at the time that "the main issue is not whether an insolvency law exists, but whether it is practiced and enforceable. Bankruptcy reforms in Thailand, previously noted, appear to have since reduced the time required considerably.

Like efficient and modern bankruptcy laws, simple and time-sensitive foreclosure procedures buttress the financial strength of banks. Procedures that permit foreclosure within three to six months are the international norm. In some markets, however, a borrower may have the right to redeem foreclosed assets for up to a year or more, or foreclosure procedures may be unduly cumbersome.[18] While a judgment may be forthcoming, it may be difficult for a creditor to seize and dispose of the subject collateral.

CHAPTER SUMMARY

In this chapter we have examined how the three key elements of an effective bank regulatory regime: 1) disclosure requirements that allow market forces to influence bank behavior and to act as a check on the tendency of bank management to overleverage bank capital and take excessive risks; 2) prudential regulations governing bank operations, together with an effective legal infrastructure; and 3) the enforcement capability of the bank regulatory authorities.

Effective disclosure means disclosure that is 1) timely and frequent; 2) comprehensible within an accounting standards that are generally accepted on a global basis; 3) comprehensive; and 4) is audited and reasonably accurate.

Effective prudential regulation means regulation that addresses in a meaningful manner operational issues in respect of a bank's: 1) maintaining adequate capital; 2) preventing asset quality problems and remedying them promptly if they do occur; and 3) maintaining ample liquidity.

Finally, an effective bank regulatory framework implies a legal system capable of affording creditors adequate legal protection and of protecting and enforcing creditors' rights.

---

[17] Warburg Dillon Read, Asian Banks Analyzer Supplement, Regulating the Asian Crisis, Sept. 1998, p. 22. Note that Thailand subsequently reformed its bankruptcy regime.
[18] See p. 507.

CHAPTER NINETEEN

THE DISTRESSED BANK, PART I: INTRODUCTION TO RESTRUCTURING[1]

The financial sector is the economy's plumbing system. A company's failure, even a big one like IBM's is like a broken sink, but a failure in the financial sector threatens the entire water supply.
— Charles Morris, *Money, Greed & Risk*

If you owe a bank £100, you have a problem. If you owe it £1 m, it has a problem.
— attributed to J.M. Keynes, Pennant-Rea and Emmott,
The Pocket Economist.

Distress in individual banks and banking crises are not uncommon. The failure of many small non-internationally active banks occurs without much notice being taken, but when the bank is a major institution or when a spate of bank failures takes place, it grabs the attention of the financial markets. The Asian crisis of 1997–98 was the most recent example of banking crisis in which numerous major and minor financial institutions had to be closed or taken over by the regulatory authorities. As the table below indicates, however, in the two decades prior to the Asian financial turmoil, there were a number of significant crises (and this is by

---

[1] The initial draft of the section of this book dealing with the distressed bank (Chapters 19–24) was kindly provided by Mr. Darren Stubing, Chief Bank Analyst at Capital Intelligence in Cyprus, a major specialist bank rating agency. Originally, the section was intended to be comparatively brief, but in view of the substantial amount of work done by Mr. Stubing and the timeliness and relevance of the topic, the author, using Mr. Stubing's original draft, expanded the manuscript he prepared into five chapters, adding a modicum of new material in the process. Mr. Stubing's draft, however, was invaluable in making this section of the book possible, and the author gratefully acknowledges his work and contribution.

Selected Banking Crises: 1982 to 1995

Country	Date	Cost as % of GDP	Industry NPLs %
Argentina	1982	13	43
Chile	1985	20	23
Norway	1988–92	4	6
Finland	1991–93	8	10
Sweden	1991–93	4	4
USA	1991	5	8
Japan	1990s	22	20
Venezuela	1994	13	57
Mexico	1994–95	12	44

Note that the NPL ratio and cost as a percentage of GDP is generally high in emerging market bank crises.

Source: SBC Warburg Dillon Read

Selected Major Bank Failures and Rescue: 1973 to 1992

Did Large Non-bank Depositors Lose Money?	Date	Bank	Country
No	1973	U.S. National	USA (Calif.)
Yes	1974	I.G. Herstatt	Germany
No	1974	Franklin National	USA (NY)
No	1980	First Pennsylvania	USA (Penna.)
No	1981	Banco Urquijo	Spain
No	1982	Banco Ambrosiano	Italy
Yes	1982	Penn Square	USA (Okla.)
Yes	1983	SMH	Germany
No	1983	FNB of Midland	USA (Tex.)
No	1984	Continental Illinois	USA (Ill.)
No	1985	Kronenbanken	Denmark
No	1985	Can. Commercial Bank; Northland Bank	Canada
No	1986–87	Continental Bank	Canada
No	1986	First Oklahoma; Bank Oklahoma	USA (Okla.)
No	1988	First City; First Republic	USA (Tex.)
No	1989	Cassa PratoCassa Prato	Italy
No	1989	M-Corp; Texas American	USA (Tex.)
No	1990	National Bancshares	USA (Tex.)
No	1991	Christiana; Den Norske; Fokus Bank	Norway
No	1991	Skopbank	Finland
No	1991	Forsta Sparbanken	Sweden
Yes	1991	BCCI	Luxembourg
No	1991	Bank of New England; Southeast Bancorp	USA (Mass., Fla.)
No	1992	Gota Bank	Sweden
Yes	1992	First City	USA (Tex.)

Source: Moody's Investors Service

no means a comprehensive list). Similarly, individual bank failures and bail-outs likewise occurred at frequent intervals, as the following, selected enumeration indicates.

THE CONSEQUENCES OF BANK FAILURE: THEORY AND PRACTICE

Applying everyday free market theory to banks, we might conclude that financial systems will benefit if weak banks are permitted to fail. By allowing bank shareholders, like other shareholders, to lose their investment when a bank collapses, the overall governance and performance of the banks that remain will tend to be strengthened. Supporting, i.e. subsidizing, weak banks distorts the market through creating unfair competition for the better managed financial institutions. Yet few governments actually allow their banks, at least their important banks, to collapse without a second thought.

While the theory of letting weaker firms fail so that capital can be most efficiently allocated to strong ones is generally sound, the "special" character of banks makes them an exception for nearly all governments. Their unique role — i.e. their important function in supplying credit, functioning as a transmission belt for government monetary policy, and as a payments mechanism — frequently persuades governments to view the troubled bank more sympathetically than they do the ordinary non-financial company that is experiencing difficulties.[2] Therefore, in practice, despite the lip service paid to the benefits of market outcomes, it is often the case that some banks are considered too big to fail without doing great damage to the healthy functioning of a country's financial system. As a result, governments frequently take extraordinary measures to prevent their country's most important banking institutions from collapsing.

Deposit Flight

In addition to the adverse effects already mentioned, a conspicuous early effect of a bank failure within a banking system and resulting loss of

---

[2] E. Gerald Corrigan, "Are Banks Special?" 1982 *Annual Report* Essay, Federal Reserve Bank of Minneapolis. In 2000, Mr. Corrigan, now a managing director at Goldman Sachs, reviewed his 1982 essay and restated his support for its general conclusion: that banking should be treated separately from other forms of commerce. See E. Gerald Corrigan: "Are Banks Special? A Revisitation," *Special Issue* 2000, Federal Reserve Bank of Minneapolis.

confidence is deposit flight. Deposit flight, whether to an offshore institution, or under the proverbial mattress, is what authorities want to prevent, since whatever direction deposits take when they leave a country's
banking system, the effect is not positive. The removal of liquidity from
the formal financial system makes it more likely that it will seize up. This
may ultimately force the central bank to put in place a blanket guarantee
on all deposits to restore confidence in the system.

Deposit flight is a common phenomenon in emerging markets. There
are many instances where authorities have had to resort to putting across-
the-board guarantees of deposits in place, most notably in Latin America
and, more recently, in Asia. The phenomenon can be quite severe. For
instance, the Argentine banking sector saw 18% of its deposits leave the
market within three months in 1995. In more volatile markets, systemic
deposit runs may occur, paralyzing the financial system.

The Example of Japan

Some countries go so far as to follow a policy of not allowing any bank
to fail in order to instill complete confidence in the market. For many
years, Japan, for example, did not let any of its banks go bankrupt. In
addition to temporary support provided by the government, banks in more
severe straits were kept alive through the so-called "convoy system" in
which strong banks were persuaded through "administrative guidance"
from the government to save weaker banks through timely mergers or
other forms of assistance. The nation's banks were seen as a convoy of
ships, each responsible for helping out their weaker cohorts so that all
could traverse rough seas together. Over-protection for banks in a particular system (i.e. where the authorities are very reluctant to liquidate banks)
often leads as it did in Japan to over-banked and inefficient markets. If
this policy is followed for too long, then weaknesses in the system may
increase, making it more difficult to restructure the sector later.

Reasons for Restructuring

The main reason then why central banks or financial authorities prevent
particular banks from failing is that they want to avoid the problems at
one or more banks leading to the impaired functioning of the financial
system as a whole. There is a justifiable fear that one troubled bank can
have a negative knock-on effect for the rest of the sector. The possibility

is what is termed systemic risk. A collapse of one institution may lead to problems at other banks in the sector through a deterioration in confidence that in extreme cases can give rise to a panic. Once sparked, a panic can lead to a paralysis of a country's financial system with catastrophic effects on the real economy. Keeping this ever-present possibility in mind, the government — often through the agency of the central bank — has to decide whether it is in the best interest of the system to: a) allow a particular financial institution to fail; or whether b) all things considered, it is more appropriate to support it and hence protect the rest of the sector, which may be seriously affected by bank failure.

Most countries fall somewhere in between what pure free market theory would call for and a policy of propping up all banks. To prevent the failure of important banks and rehabilitate them to normal functioning, the regulatory authorities may take a number of measures, including: recapitalization of the troubled banks, assist them in removing the burden of the bad loans on their books; assisting them in a search for a new owner; facilitating the merger with another bank; or even the nationalization of the bank as a prelude to privatizing it once its balance sheet has been cleaned up. The process whereby governments attempt to transform failing banks into healthy ones is broadly called "bank restructuring."

The process of bank restructuring is often expensive, as the table *Selected Banking Crises: 1982–1995* on page 426 indicates. The cost may be tens of billions of dollars and a significant chunk of a country is GDP. A government may very well not be able to bear the expense of fully restoring all banks to health, even if it were willing. Consequently, when a number of banks are adversely affected by financial turmoil, difficult decisions concerning which banks to rescue are faced. It may in the end be a matter of triage. Speaking of the Korean banking crisis, Paul Grela, now a banking analyst with Fitch Ratings, wrote:

> In any banking crisis, authorities will inevitably face difficult decisions on how to deal with distressed banks. ... In the Korean context the decision taken was ... (1) to close banks deemed beyond redemption; and (2) to support those banks under acute distress but considered 'vital to the sector.'[3]

---

[3] Gregory Root, Paul Grela, Mark Jones & Anand Adiga, "Financial Sector Restructuring in East Asia."

Weaknesses of Banks Can Exacerbate Financial Turmoil within a Market

Of the numerous banking sector crises over the last two decades many have led to both individual bank and banking sector restructuring. The recent banking sector problems during the Asian crisis (1997–98), particularly in Thailand, South Korea, Indonesia and Malaysia, provide clear and recent examples of how the governments concerned confronted the need to restructure and recapitalize their banks. Although exogenous factors such as economic downturns, international capital market turmoil, and currency devaluations may be immediate the cause of bank sector problems serious enough to warrant restructuring and recapitalization, often it is the inherent weaknesses of banks and banking sectors that exacerbates financial turmoil within a market leading to a crisis. Once the crisis takes hold, the shortcomings of the country's financial systems, which had hitherto been masked by rising prosperity and exuberance among investors, are fully exposed.

Bank restructuring tends to occur especially frequently in developing markets or economies in transition. The fragility of the banking infra-structure in these markets is apt to be reflected in phenomena such as weak regulation and supervision, poor corporate governance, capital requirements, elevated foreign currency exposure, and little or non-existent credit management and monitoring. By being aware of some of the factors and issues surrounding acute banking crises and the restruc-turing that inevitably follows, the analyst can, in fact, identify other banks and banking sectors that may face significant challenges in times of market turmoil. An awareness of the dangers banks face and what happens when things go awry is a great aid in analyzing banks that remain comparatively healthy.

THE CONTOURS OF BANK RESTRUCTURING: INDIVIDUAL OR SECTOR-WIDE

Individual banks may be restructured through state intervention, but this scenario is likely to be restricted to either cases where a bank is consid-ered too large to fail, is government-owned or is of national importance, or, where larger issues are at stake, such as the prevention of a systemic crisis. Probably most cases of bank restructuring involve the entire banking sector affected by a financial crisis. Such crises are typically characterized by a sharp rise in sector-wide non-performing loans (NPLs) or by deposit runs at bank, that can place the entire financial system of a country in a vulnerable position. The banking sector is at the heart of a country's economy and plays a crucial role in the smooth running of the economic system through the collection of savings and as facilitator of funds. If this vulnerability is not addressed, it may lead to depressed business activity and a paralysis of economic growth. When a country's banking sector is not functioning properly, its economic problems may be aggravated and recovery delayed. Japan is probably the best example of a country whose poor economic performance in the 1990s is in large part attributable to a weak financial sector and to the government's inability, at least as of the date of this working, to muster the political will to address its banking problems. In the first quarter of 2001, Standard and Poor's credit rating agency downgraded Japan's long-term yen-denominated and foreign currency debt, attributable in large part to the government's inability to muster such political will.[4]

Factors Leading to a Banking Crisis

There are many ingredients that when combined can ignite a banking crisis, triggering the need for a government response. These factors can be either internal or external.

Internal Causes of Bank Distress

Internal factors are specific to the bank in question, although they may be widely seen among banks in the country. They include:

❑ Poor management and corporate governance;

❑ Weak internal controls and supervision, accompanied by lack of disclosure and transparency;

❑ Aggressive lending practices, including politically driven and policy lending;

❑ Dearth of credit analytical skills and the absence of a credit culture;

❑ Spiraling bad debt and deteriorating profitability (which may have led to technical insolvency).

---

[4] *New York Times*, February 24, 2001.

Other factors may include:

❏ Excessive foreign currency borrowing;
❏ Large maturity mismatches;
❏ Fraud; and
❏ Related party exposure which may have turned non-performing because of problems at the group level.

The last may be hidden through opaque subsidiary companies.

External Factors Leading to Bank Distress

External factors are both macroeconomic and regulatory in nature. These once again are more often seen in emerging economies because of the volatility of the operating environment and the fragility of public institutions:

❏ Lax prudential regulations;
❏ Fragmented supervision and ineffective enforcement of existing regulations;
❏ Heavy-handed state intervention into the bank credit decisions (i.e. directed lending);
❏ Weak fiscal and monetary policies;
❏ High and/or volatile interest rate environments;
❏ High inflation;
❏ Excessive government borrowing and possibly;
❏ Over-reliance on short term funding.

Apart from internal and external factors, banking problems can be sector-specific in that characteristics pertaining to the market may be the cause of the weakness. A prime example of this would be a banking sector dominated by state banks. A sector where state banks have a heavy influence, say controlling over 25% of sector assets, is likely to lead to market distortions. Often this situation will increase funding costs for private banks as the government-owned banks can offer high rates of interest to depositors. The profitability of private banks will be squeezed on the other side as state banks are highly likely to provide soft loans to customers.

Symptoms of Sectoral Distress

Non-Performing Loans

Invariably, where bank restructuring is needed, problems have first occurred in the loan portfolio. Typically, NPLs will have risen considerably, and loan loss provisions will have not kept pace with the rise in bad debt. The result will be a triple burden: weaker earnings, a lower level of earning assets, and a rising carry-cost of bad debt. The gap between reserves and NPLs may in fact be greater than shareholders' equity. At this point, in technical terms, the bank will be insolvent. So long as liquidity is assured through external support, however, such technical insolvency will not prevent the bank functioning as a going concern.

Again, the magnitude of NPLs will vary from country to country, but generally, the level of bad debt will be much higher in emerging markets that are faced with the need for bank restructuring. For example, during the Asian crisis, bad loans rose to an estimated 70–80% for Indonesia, 50–60% for Thailand, and 30% for Malaysia (based on the gross three-month non-performing loan definition). In the case of developed countries, which have thorough restructuring processes, bad loans have tended to be up to no more than approximately 10% of gross loans, a level that is regarded as quite high in such countries.

Credit Squeeze

If a sharp economic recession, coupled with rising bad loans, has been one of the causes of banking sector problems, then banks will inevitably refrain from further lending activities, and may even call back some loans before maturity if the loan documentation permits. During a recession that has resulted in banking sector distress banks tend to focus on remaining as liquid as possible. This fact, combined with the fact that some weaker banks may have collapsed is prone to lead to a significant credit squeeze in the economy. The credit squeeze is likely to aggravate the poor state of the economy and even delay an eventual recovery. This was the main reason why the regulatory authorities required Malaysian banks to expand their loan portfolios by 8% per annum during 1999. As it happened, banks did not meet this quota, as they rightly focused on maintaining asset quality and balance sheet strength.

During a severe crisis, so many borrowers may default on their loans that misallocated credit remains frozen in real assets that have diminished in value and cannot circulate throughout the economy. When an asset bubble bursts, the difference between the value of the assets at their peak price and the value of the assets post-bubble represents wealth destroyed. The financial cost of bad loans in a banking sector can be substantial for a country. Indeed, it is this destroyed wealth that must be replaced through bank restructuring, and ultimately recapitalization. To liquefy these real assets and get the funds circulating again within the economy, banks must be willing to exercise their rights as creditors and compel the liquidation (i.e. sale) of these assets or the collateral taken as the underlying financial assets (the loans) diminish in value through legal process or negotiation.

The existence of an active market in the collateral, which is most often real estate, will allow the establishment of market clearing prices and permit the rapid recovery of a portion of the bad loans in the bank's portfolio. Evidence suggests that only about 40% of the value of bad loans is recovered from collateral attached to the loans.[5] Total recapitalization cost of bank restructuring in the recent Asian crisis was estimated by the IMF to be 30% of GDP for Indonesia and Thailand, and around 20% for Malaysia and South Korea. Authorities must endeavor to reduce the ultimate financial cost of sector restructuring on the economy, whilst as quickly as possible restoring confidence in the system. At the same time, the restructuring body must put in place a much stronger banking infrastructure to enable the sector to more adequately cope with financial turmoil in the future. We will discuss the method of calculating the cost of a recapitalization in the following chapter.

The Decision to Restructure and the Goals of Restructuring

As alluded to earlier the first decision bank regulators confront in the face of a failing financial institution is whether to attempt to save it at all. Concern about increasing moral hazard is frequently one that weighs heavily on the minds of the authorities (and if it does not, it should). If a bank is bailed out, it only encourages the expectation that the government will ensure bank owners and managers against their mistakes. This is likely to influence their future decision making and may plant the seeds for future banking system problems. The authorities should therefore see that the bank's existing owners and managers do not benefit from their lack of prudence. As ING Barings banking analyst James Fiorillo put it

---

[5] James Fiorillo, *Resolving Japan's Banking System Problems*, ING Barings, December 1997, p. 7.

in a 1997 report:

> The fact is, unless a regulator severely punishes a bank that comes to it for help by wiping out its shareholders' equity if it is privately owned, forcing it to shrink dramatically and ensuring that the managers responsible for the problems are sacked, it may aggravate the risks in a banking system.[6]

Moral hazard risks, of course, must be weighed against the damage to a country's economy that can ensue from a paralyzed banking system. The authorities must balance on one hand the issue of restoring confidence to the system, which may be plagued by deposit runs at banks, to the issue of moral hazard which may actually promote riskier banking activities in the future.

Often, however, there is not the luxury of a great deal of time for regulators to make a decision as to whether or not to provide assistance to a bank. As the need for such action most often arises during market turmoil, the decision to restructure must be made quickly in order to prevent exacerbating the situation or triggering adverse systemic effects that may worsen the situation. The case of the collapse of Barings Bank, discussed below, illustrates the time pressure the authorities must work under, although in that situation there was no systemic crisis at hand. The Bank of England had to take a decision concerning that fate of Barings over a mere weekend. Conversely Mr. Fiorillo, has suggested that a banking crisis may manifest in two waves, with the first signs of distress often not being dealt with comprehensively.

The objectives of bank restructuring are manifold, but the goal is simple. Fundamentally, it is to restore confidence to the financial system and to rehabilitate it to a healthy functioning. To accomplish this, improving a bank's or banking sector's solvency is a key objective. This entails evaluating the volume of loan losses, ascertaining the degree of new capital required. Restoration of solvency may be achieved either through direct recapitalization or through indirect recapitalization. Direct recapitalization involves: 1) funds injections from the government, present bank owners or new owners, domestic or foreign; 2) enabling the bank to raise funds in the capital markets; or 3) removing non-performing loans from the balance sheet (which has the effect of reducing capital requirements. Indirect recapitalization is accomplished by a) increasing the ability of

---

[6] See p. 434.

the bank to internally generate capital through operating or management restructuring; b) engaging in regulatory forbearance which reduces the burden on the bank's earning stream; or c) by implementing monetary policies that generally increase bank profitability. To prevent recurrence of the problem, another objective is to put in place systems both internally within banking institutions and externally through regulatory apparatuses to ensure that the country's banks stay on an even keel to perform their necessary economic functions.

Temporary Liquidity Support vs. Comprehensive Restructuring: Which and Under What Circumstances?

Let us here distinguish the provision of temporary liquidity support from comprehensive restructuring. The former is a familiar and common function of the central bank whereby it acts to provide a temporary infusion of cash to provide an otherwise healthy bank with the wherewithal as the official *lender of last resort* to deal with a temporary liquidity crunch where the banks solvency is not at issue.[7] The latter refers to a much longer and multifaceted set of policies and prescriptions to address the problem of one or more insolvent banks, whose sickness threatens to debilitate not only the financial system, but real economic growth. The regulators will distinguish between an illiquid bank (i.e. a bank facing temporary funding pressure) and an insolvent bank (technically negative net worth). We will now explore each of these remedies in more detail.

Temporary Liquidity Support

If the bank or banking sector has been affected by external forces, such as economic collapse, or market contagion, then the regulators and officials are likely to take a more lenient approach, when one or more banks are hit by difficulties. (Such difficulties usually manifest initially in the form of a liquidity shortfall, i.e. the inability to meet current obligations, for example, resulting from a withdrawal of an interbank credit line.) Complete restructuring will likely be forthcoming when the bank involved is one whose financial condition is otherwise relatively sound; i.e. it displays good capital, profitability and asset quality ratios. In less critical

---

[7] To be sure, some state-owned commercial banks may become addicted to this form of treatment, requiring ongoing infusions of funds.

situations, the bank may only need temporary liquidity assistance provided the central bank. Central banks are normally prepared to help illiquid banks by providing funds at heavy rates of interest, usually secured by collateral. Depending upon the severity of the bank's problems, the central bank may provide such liquidity while imposing specific requirements on the bank, tailored to the particular situation.

The authorities must also decide if the restructuring or support is to be conducted behind-the-scenes or in a public manner. The approach may be conducted confidentially if is thought to be in the best interest of the bank or banks in question. While disclosure is generally positive, there may be a legitimate fear of a panic that could lead to an epidemic of deposit runs in the sector that could even affect sound banks in the sector. Further justifying such an approach may be the belief that the problems the banks are facing will be short-term in nature. The provision of temporary liquidity is common throughout most markets and, indeed, it is one of the main roles of central banks. In the past, even the Bank of England has been known to provide temporary liquidity for institutions which are facing funding difficulties but are still, nevertheless, solvent. It had extended such assistance during the property collapse of 1973–74 and again in the recession of 1991–92, when it had "secretly supported about forty small banks" allowing them to recover their position.

Major and Comprehensive Restructuring

If the problems of one or more banks are very severe, liquidity support may be insufficient, and may in fact, just prolong the problem. Where non-performing loans have grown past a critical mass, e.g. 20–25% in emerging markets, 10–15% in developed markets, it may simply be impossible for a bank to earn itself out of its difficulties. A fresh infusion of capital may be required and major surgery on the ownership and organizational structure of the institution may also be necessary. Moreover, behavioral modifications may need to be made, lest the patient return to his bad habits and allow the problem to recur. Comprehensive restructuring is discussed in the chapters that follow.

The Errant Bank: When is Support Appropriate?

If there is only one bank in trouble and the causes of distress are bank-specific — for example, poor lending practices or risky banking activities that have not generally affected the sector as whole — the authorities are likely to take a much tougher approach. A harsher view may be especially appropriate when economic conditions are relatively sanguine and there is little risk of a panic. Indeed, the authorities may wish to make an example of the institution in such case, as a deterrent to others. While temporary liquidity support may be offered if the bank is otherwise in good shape, a bank in more serious difficulties may be allowed to collapse if there is the reasonable expectation that there will be little or no disruption to the financial system as a result.

This was the situation the Bank of England found itself in 1995 when Barings Bank, a more than two hundred-year old pillar of the banking establishment, was led into insolvency by the actions of rogue trader, Nick Leeson. Although there was precedent for a rescue — the Bank of England had rescued Barings in 1890 from an Argentinean securities issue gone bad — the circumstances in 1995 were quite different. In *All That Glitters*, a page-turning account of the Barings collapse, the two *Financial Times* journalists who authored the book capture the thinking of Rupert Pennant-Rea, the deputy governor of the Bank of England as to what course of action to take when he was first faced with the news of Barings' plight:

> … a single trader in Singapore had blown Barings apart. If that was so, there was no reason for depositors to think that because Barings collapsed, other banks might, too. What had happened was so extraordinary that it was by definition unrepeatable. That meant that the Bank should allow Barings to collapse, no matter how shocking that might be.[8]

Where, however, the sick bank is one that is simply manifesting in a more severe way problems that are endemic throughout the sector, either temporary liquidity support or more comprehensive restructuring may be appropriate. The relevant question is: given the costs, is a rescue required in the best interest of maintaining sector stability? If the restructuring course is taken, the shareholders should be properly penalized through either losing partial or total control of the institution. Depositors may also suffer, depending on the deposit guarantee policy in place at the time, and may even become shareholders in the bank on a pro-rata basis.

---

[8] John Gapper & Nicholas Denton, *All That Glitters: The Fall of Barings*, Penguin Books, 1997.

Exhibit 6-1

Restructuring Effects Gained Over Twenty Years at US Banks

		1980	1990	1995	1996	1997	1998
1	ROA	0.60	0.52	1.14	1.25	1.25	1.35
2	ROE	14.60	9.53	16.34	17.37	17.48	19.03
3	Net Interest Margin	2.81	3.67	3.90	3.93	3.85	3.79
4	Non-interest Rev./Net Revenue	23.0	39.0	39.2	41.1	42.9	44.9
5	Efficiency Ratio	61.0	67.0	60.9	58.7	58.9	56.5
6	Expenses/Average Assets	2.21	3.50	3.35	3.40	3.42	3.32
7	Net Charge Off	0.36	1.62	0.55	0.67	0.68	0.68
8	Reserve/Total Loans	0.96	3.03	2.44	2.29	2.09	1.99
9	Reserves/NPLs	73.0	72.0	181.3	216.3	235.5	216.0
10	Equity/Assets	4.00	5.63	6.31	6.20	5.89	6.10

Exhibit 6-2

Graphic Overview of Restructuring Effects Gained Over Twenty Years at US Banks

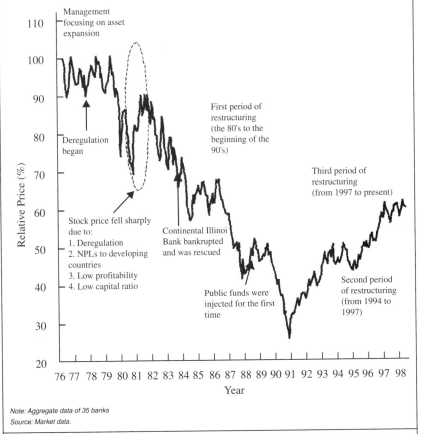

Note: Aggregate data of 35 banks
Source: Market data.

Source: Yukiko Ohara, "Simple US-Japan Restructuring Comparison Meaningless,"
Morgan Stanley Dean Witter, November 5, 1999

Longer Term Restructuring

Although we have been discussing restructuring in the context of dealing with the impact of a banking crisis, it is worth noting that some analysts use the term as well to refer to the response of the banking industry to long-term secular changes, which may also include periods of acute stress. This perspective can be helpful in seeing crisis-driven restructuring as part of a broader continuum of responses to changing conditions. In comparing the banking systems of the United States and Japan, Morgan Stanley Dean Witter analyst Yukiko Ohara took the long view, examining changes in the US banking industry over 25 years and discerning three phases of restructuring. (See diagram on the preceding page.) The first phase occurred during the 1980s when American banks sought improved efficiency over scale, cutting costs and unprofitable business lines. The second phase, from 1994 to 1997, marked a period of even more emphasis on shareholder value and profit maximization through market segmentation, database marketing and data mining enabled by increased information technology investment, and share buybacks. A third phase, which began in 1997, has emphasized industry consolidation, triggered in part by deregulation.

CHAPTER SUMMARY

This chapter introduces the subject of the distressed bank and bank restructuring. Bank restructuring is the process of rehabilitating banks into viable financial institutions able to fulfill their crucial economic roles. Absent the special character of banks embodied in their unique role in extending credit and financing economic growth, providing a place of safekeeping for individual savings, functioning as a payment system and acting as a transmission belt for monetary policy, they would be allowed to go bankrupt and be liquidated like any common corporation without a second thought. At least, they would be in quite a number of countries.

Banks do have this special nature, however, and because of it governments support banks. They do so through temporary infusions of capital whereby the central bank acts as a lender of last resort and also through major capital injections and restructuring exercises. The latter process is exceptionally costly, as the wealth that was destroyed through losses, whether the result of the actions of many credit officers making poor lending decisions or one rogue trader, must be effectively replaced.

In addition, structures must be put in effect to avoid recurrence, while preventing other banks from getting the idea that they will be bailed out should they, too, collapse.

Consequently, not all banks can or should be saved. The authorities must decide under what circumstances a bank will be nursed back to health and whether the game is worth the candle. Sometimes governments cannot muster the political will to take effective action at all, and sick banks linger in chronic illness, with deleterious effects to a nation's economy. The process of major and comprehensive bank restructuring is discussed in succeeding chapters.

CHAPTER TWENTY

THE DISTRESSED BANK, PART II: AIMS AND METHODS OF RESTRUCTURING

One type of financial institution is hugely more dangerous than all the rest, even though it claims to be the safest: the bank.

The Economist[1]

A banking crisis is an event. Bank restructuring is a process.
— Andrew Sheng, author of World Bank Publication titled Bank Restructuring: Lessons from the 1980s, cited in Roy I. Ramos, *A Tale of Four Bank Restructurings*, Goldman Sachs, January 7, 1999

Once the decision has been taken to rehabilitate one or more banks, the approach to restructuring should be coordinated and systematic. In parallel the authorities must also address the issue of corporate debt restructuring as the root of a bank's problems usually lies with corporate loans that have turned non-performing. The specific cause of a bank's, or the banking sector's, problems will, in turn, have a bearing on the approach adopted by the regulatory authorities in restructuring and recapitalizing the institutions in distress. In this context, the experience of regulators in the past is highly relevant. Andrew Sheng in his book, *Bank Restructuring: Lessons From the 1980s*, set forth a number of summary conclusions. Six of them listed below are particularly relevant to the discussion that follows.

---

[1] Freedom from fear? *The Economist*, September 11, 1999, p. 13.

Six Bank Restructuring Lessons from the 1980s[2]

1. Banks fail because of losses in the real sector, compounded by poor risk management and fraud

2. Bank losses often become quasi-fiscal deficits

3. Stopping the flow of future losses is critical

4. The method of loss allocation determines the success of the restructuring program

5. Success depends upon sufficient real sector resources to pay off losses, adequate financial sector reforms to intermediate resources efficiently and safely, and the budget's ability to tax "winners" and wind down "losers" without disturbing monetary stability

6. Rebuilding a safe and profitable banking system requires good policies, reliable management and a strong institutional framework.

Source: Bank Restructuring: Lessons from the 1980s, by Andrew Sheng, World Bank Publication; Goldman Sachs.

In other words, if I may take the liberty of paraphrasing Mr. Sheng:

❑ Banks fail because their customers suffer business setbacks as the real economy falters, in turn preventing them from paying back their loans to the banks;

❑ The resulting losses to banks prevent banks from playing their role in economic growth and therefore become the burden of the state;

❑ Unless bank losses are stopped, the burden and ultimate cost to the state simply becomes worse;

❑ Losses must be allocated in a way that is both fair and facilitates the process — bank shareholders, the individuals and corporations who borrowed, the depositors, and the government, i.e. the taxpayers, all must share the burden in some fashion;

❑ The degree to which a banking system can be successfully restructured depends in large part on the resources available, the underlying economic vitality of the country concerned, and the willingness to shut down unviable banks while undertaking effective reforms at those which show hope;

❑ The government must provide the framework to enable a stronger banking system to grow out of the one that has failed.

---

[2] Quoted in Roy I. Ramos, *A Tale of Four Bank Restructurings,* p. 7.

SUCCESSFUL BANK RESTRUCTURING: AIMS AND STRATEGY

Bank restructuring aims simply to restore the financial health of the banks which comprise the sector (by increasing equity, removing bad debt), improve confidence in the system thereby preventing deposit flight, and restore the banking sector to normal functioning. But how can this be accomplished? It is a chicken-and-egg problem. The economy has gone into recession, aggravated by poor risk management on the part of banks and inadequate government supervision, but the root problem is economic. Once banks have reached the level at which restructuring is required, they are beyond the ability to restore themselves to financial health. It is up to the government to take the necessary action.

Underlying any effective government policy is the will and leadership to take steps that are bound to cause pain to some. This requires a marshalling of the requisite political will. Restructuring must be made a priority. The government must maintain a fine balance between convincing the public of the seriousness of the problem without depressing public confidence further. How to maintain this balance is a matter of political leadership beyond the scope of this book. Suffice it to say, that some measure of support must be gathered; if the problem remains unaddressed, economic conditions are bound to deteriorate which will only make the task more difficult down the road. The government is going to have to pay the cost sooner or later.

This leads to the third of Sheng's lessons: stop the bleeding. Delaying bank restructuring and letting banks continue in their old ways only perpetuates the problem. Authorities should therefore prevent problem institutions from continuing to extend credit to delinquent borrowers. Unless this occurs, banks will not be able to return to financial health.

This leads to the next step: coming up with a fair and coherent plan that equitably balances loss allocation. This is easier said than done, and likely to be politically difficult as the affected groups have much to lose, and it would be so much more pleasant to have another group bear the loss. Shareholders of insolvent banks may be politically well-connected, and in countries where a comparatively small number of business groups and clans dominate both political and economic life, such individuals may be able to organize considerable resistance to giving up ownership of institutions with which they have been closely identified. Similarly, where major banks are insolvent, almost invariably the banks will have been lending to companies that are both major players in the economy and in default on their loans. These delinquent companies and their shareholders, not to mention their workers, may very well resist restructuring initiatives for two reasons. First, particularly if they are state-owned enterprises, they may have become dependent upon borrowing from banks to carry on their daily operations. Second, where bank restructuring is deemed necessary, it can be expected that corporate restructuring will not be far behind. Of course, one likely reason that these companies have not been able to perform their obligations to the bank — thereby leading to the bank's insolvency — is that they themselves are highly inefficient, if not loss-making enterprises, in need of new management and reorganization.

Bank depositors and other creditors of insolvent banks will, of course, be concerned that moneys owed to them are repaid, and may be anxious about any governmental actions that disturb the current order. Finally, in nearly all bank restructurings, taxpayers at large will ultimately have to bear a significant portion of recapitalizing problem institutions. Although it is ultimately in the public interest that banks be recapitalized, the public may be justifiably wary of public moneys being "given to" these institutions. While the public probably has no great love for the banks in trouble, they may not fully apprehend the consequences of letting the banking system collapse. Hence, convincing them that apparent subsidies to the banking system are necessary to the cause of long-term economic growth and prosperity may be a tough sell. Those who benefit economically from the status quo may attempt to characterize bank restructuring initiatives as antithetical to the national interest or in other ways that sway public passions (e.g. "Our banks are going to be sold to foreigners and we will lose control of our destiny."[3]).

Assuming an effective plan can be agreed upon, the next step is to begin the actual restructuring. This includes reform of the banks themselves through the installation of new management and the imposition of stronger banking regulations. To instill a new credit culture and to reduce moral hazard (so as to prevent the problem from recurring in five or ten years) existing shareholders should not be rewarded, but instead should be replaced in whole or at least in part. Notwithstanding that they find themselves in a difficult financial position, as the owners of the bank have benefited from risk-taking in the past, they should bear a large proportion of the cost of restructuring. Specifically, the actual losses of the banks should be tallied by applying international accounting

---

[3] This is not to say that there may not be a legitimate national interest in keeping the ownership of a portion of the banking system in local hands.

standards, if necessary. Next, operational restructuring of banks should be effected through management and staffing, and in the banks' organizational framework and operating procedures, particularly in respect of risk control. Third, the bad assets on the banks' books should be resolved through workouts of the banks' bad loans through negotiation with their corporate customers. Finally, with new management and procedures in place and a cleaned up balance sheet, it is time to recapitalize the banks through the injection of new funds (capital).

In addition, restructuring often goes hand-in-hand with macroeconomic and structural reforms. These encompass a wide range of policies including: 1) Regulatory and supervisory reforms, including tougher and enforced accounting and prudential standards (accompanied possibly by initial regulatory forbearance and the implementation of economic and regulatory policies that enable banks to improve their profitability); and 2) Increased transparency (i.e. disclosure) requirements, and in some cases reform of insolvency laws and regulations.

With that overview of the restructuring process, let us turn our attention to its specific steps.

Step 1: The government should establish appropriate agencies and institutions, if they do not already exist, to assess the damage in a rapid and preliminary manner, and create a plan for what needs to be done. In the next chapter we will discuss some of the ways in which institutional arrangements are structured to accomplish this task, so for the moment we will assume that agencies exist with that capacity. Both the system as a whole and particular institutions must be examined. Indeed, it will be difficult to obtain an accurate picture of the system as a whole without taking a close look at specific banks.

Bank restructuring as applied to particular institutions will ordinarily focus on key areas, including the asset base of the bank, its capital, and its earnings. Problems within the bank's assets need to be analyzed. To restore the bank's ability to lend profitably, it will invariably be necessary to remove non-performing loans from the balance sheet during the restructuring process and to infuse new capital. Earnings will need to be looked at closely as the bank or, if more than one is involved, the restructuring agency will want to improve profitability in the subject institution or across the sector as quickly as possible (again to improve reserves and lift provisions). Enhancing profitability will usually involve organizational and operational restructuring, such as the rationalization of activities, staff, distribution channels, and improving credit management policies and systems.

Step 2: Changes in Ownership and Management

Since existing shareholders are legally responsible for the losses of a troubled bank, there is a strong probability that these share-holders will be relieved of all or part of their ownership rights to the bank, although not necessarily without a struggle. The bank will be transfered to state ownership during a restructuring period, unless shareholders have significant resources or receive certain inducements to inject capital. The reasons for taking this action, as mentioned, are to reduce moral hazard by holding existing shareholders accountable for the policies they approved, and to reform the credit culture of the bank.

Some restructuring agencies will not give existing shareholders an option, taking over the bank immediately. In Latin America, restructuring initiatives dictated that the receipt of official aid required a complete change in bank ownership. In some other countries, however, it may not be politically feasible to remove the existing shareholders entirely, despite the fact that as shareholders, legally, the burden of loss is theirs. The extent of ownership retained in some cases may be substantial, while in others a face-saving arrangement is reached whereby the existing shareholders keep only a nominal stake in the restructured entity. Other restructuring strategies include adopting a transitional period in which bank shareholders are given additional time to raise capital. This is one of the policies the Thai restructuring agency has used.

A change of ownership, even if it occurs, may not be enough, however, to transform the bank's credit culture. The agency in charge of the restructuring process may need to effect more pervasive changes in the banking organization, either directly or indirectly. Again, in Thailand, for example, stricter loan loss provisioning requirements were to be phased in over a three-year period in order to give banks time to adjust to the new order. At each target point within the period additional capital is required. In addition, the Thai government offered to inject capital, but on the condition that banks would have to meet certain conditions, including tighter loan loss provisioning at the outset. Consequently, through this requirement, existing shareholders would see their capital dwindle before receiving any government funding.

Step 3: Changes in Operations

Changes in ownership and management may need to be accompanied by changes in operating procedures. At a minimum, as mentioned above, the bank must stop lending to delinquent borrowers, or at least begin to wean them from an incessant supply of credit. Other operational changes will naturally vary with the particular circumstances. If none is in place, for instance, a system of controls and internal audits should be implemented at the earliest stage and an accurate assessment made of the extent of the bank's financial problems. Applying accounting standards that conform to international best practice, the status of the bank's loan book should be clearly determined, as well as the amount of capital necessary to bring the more bank up to a benchmark capital adequacy level.

At the more routine operational level, the bank may be obliged by the authorities to create a credit committee and promulgate a written credit policy. Similarly, training of bank staff in modern bank operations may be undertaken or subsidized by the government. Mergers and acquisitions may be encouraged in the view that a fewer number of well-capitalized banks makes for a more robust and healthy banking industry than one comprising numerous smaller institutions. As a result of merger, or as a consequence of improved efficiency and the use of technology, the bank may also be encouraged to shed staff. Not surprisingly, in countries with a strong tradition of labor rights, trade unions may vehemently oppose such measures.[4]

Step 4: Regulatory Reform, Regulatory Forbearance

The lack of an effective prudential regulatory framework can contribute to a banking crisis. International best practice embraces an assortment of regulations including, to name a few, minimum capital adequacy requirements, the prohibition of related party loans (with limited exceptions), and requirement of full loan loss provisioning against anticipated non-performing loans, defined according to international standards. More often than not, the problem is not the absence of regulations, but a deficiency in enforcement. Fragmentation of supervision, where for example, two or more agencies share responsibility for bank regulation, can contribute to compliance problems. This, too, can be strengthened as part of a bank restructuring program.

---

[4] At the time of the writing of this book, Korean bank workers opposed to the merger of Kookmin and Housing and Commercial Banks were engaged in violent protest with the authorities over the planned consolidation.

Imposing such a regime on banks that have slid into chronic disability may not be possible, however, in the short-term. Minimal capital thresholds required of banks that have no capital, or full provisioning of banks that have no profits, would be pointless. Consequently, the authorities may decide to adopt a more conciliatory approach, working with the present management and owners to reach new prudential standards over time. Meant to be a transitional step, such regulatory forbearance broadly includes providing special dispensation for certain regulatory requirements (biding time while efforts are undertaken to improve the position of the bank), extending central bank credit and funding to banks, relaxing monetary policy, and aiding capital raising and diverting official or government deposits to a bank. Examples of relaxed regulatory requirements include lowering reserve requirements and minimum balance sheet liquidity, reducing capital requirements temporarily, and lowering provisioning requirements.[5] During the Asian crisis, an example of regulatory forbearance included the decision by the Bank of Thailand to reduce banks' Tier 1 capital requirement from 6% to 4.25%.

All of these relaxation steps can provide breathing space for a troubled bank through allowing more flexibility into its balance sheet. Many countries have employed these tactics, from those in Latin America in the 1980s and 1990s, to those in eastern and central Europe in the 1990s, to those in South East Asia in the more recent crisis. Adjusting monetary policy is a more radical move by the authorities. It is usually performed by adopting an aggressive monetary policy — lowering domestic interest rates in order to help widen margins for banks and fuel demand. A similar strategy was adopted by Malaysia as a response to its economic downturn in 1997–98. Banks' efforts to raise capital may be supported by the government and central bank, either through underwriting new equity issues by problematic banks or by supplying cheap loans for equity investments.

Step 5: The Management of Non-Performing Loans and Assets

Definition of NPLs

Bank restructuring is a long drawn-out process, one that is likely to take two to three years at a minimum. The extent of bad loans in the system

---

[5] Defined by Morgan Stanley Dean Witter analysts Wan Ismail and Rafael Bello, the term regulatory forbearance can be defined as the application of "greater tolerance when helping banks meet compliance standards during the recovery process. Wan Ismail & Rafael Bello, "The Bank Rehabilitation Process: Asia and Mexico Compared", Morgan Stanley Dean Witter, September 4, 1998, p. 5.

ought to be determined, insofar as possible, at the outset. Variables coming into play include the actual definition of a NPL (i.e. the length of time a facility can go unpaid before it is recorded as non-performing), whether the definition is on a gross basis or net of collateral, and is it taking into account issues such as accrued interest income. To aid the banking system in times of difficulties, the regulatory body may actually relax the definition of NPLs, which has the effect of reducing provisioning requirements while making the country's banks look relatively good compared with other countries that make use of a stricter definition. This was the case in Malaysia, which moved from a three-month definition to six-month. This gave banks breathing space, allowing them to record lower levels of bad loans and hence reduce the need for higher provision charges. This in turn boosted capital and reported bottom line profitability.

Valuation of Collateral

In looking at NPLs, both the bank and the restructuring agency will examine closely the collateral attached to the facility. The collateral will, or should, boost the amount recoverable thereby reducing net overall losses. However, in examining collateral it is important to take into account the legal system within the country. This may indeed be weak, as in the case of many emerging markets, with the bank or agency having difficulty pursuing both the defaulter and any collateral. The Asian crisis highlighted the weak legal systems in countries such as Indonesia and Thailand. Where the ability of the creditor bank to enforce its rights is weak, the non-payment mentality (i.e. can't pay, won't pay) is aggravated. Moreover, in many cases, the value of the collateral will be below the value booked.

Additionally, if the crisis is sector-wide, with many banks affected by NPLs, the value of collateral may fall due to a selling oversupply. Also, a large part of collateral may be connected to property and real estate. The value of such real estate is likely to fall sharply during a prolonged economic downturn thereby magnifying the net NPLs situation. Often spiraling property prices and rapidly increasing loan facilities to the property sector has been a major feature of economic boom times which, often, ultimately leads to a nasty correction for banks. This was the case in Thailand, which saw spiraling property prices throughout the 1990s, causing many assets to be valued excessively.

Removing Bad Assets from the Balance Sheet

One of the main decisions in bank restructuring programs is how to manage the bad loans of banks. A number of approaches are available. Leaving NPLs in banks may mean a less forceful approach in managing the bad assets, possibly through rescheduling or "ever-greening" loans and lower provisioning. In most cases, NPLs are taken out of the restructured bank's balance sheet and managed by a separate agency, often known as an *asset management corporation* (AMC). If the authorities intend to sell the troubled bank, removing bad assets from the balance sheet allows for an easier sale. An alternative option is one where a state-promoted agency — again often termed an AMC — purchases the NPLs from the bank but the bank still manages the bad loans with the two sharing in any recoveries. Yet another method sees the bank split into two institutions, a healthy bank with no NPLs and a bank that carries the bad debt. The bad bank in this case is an AMC by another name. This is the so-called good bank/bad bank approach. All of these approaches can in fact be seen as variation on the AMC theme.

The Asset Management Corporation Approach

The most common approach used during recent Asian banking crisis has been to set up a separate agency, i.e. an asset management company (AMC) to purchase all the NPLs from troubled banks. There are two basic types of AMC schemes: the centralized AMC and the decentralized AMC. The first refers to a national AMC that is responsible for the workout of bad assets on a nationwide basis. This type of AMC is normally owned, funded and guaranteed by the government.

The second type refers to an AMC that is linked to one or more specific financial institutions. The latter approach is akin to the good bank/bad bank approach and is more likely to be owned by the subject bank or perhaps a group of banks. Funding may be through the capital markets, possibly with government assistance. Each approach has its advantages and disadvantages. The centralized approach discussed below is suited to situations where there are a large number of banks facing loan problems or a substantial amount of bad debt across the sector.

Centralized vs. Decentralized AMCs

Selected Pros and Cons of Centralized and Decentralized Asset Management Corporations			
Centralized AMC Advantages	Disadvantages	Decentralized AMC Advantages	Disadvantages
More efficient use of limited workout talent and consultants	Inclination towards becoming a rigid and inefficient bureaucracy	More operational flexibility	Skill levels and ability to leverage consultants may be limited
Likely to have more authority to force workout; Concentration of creditor clout	If slower moving than decentralized AMC, potential for more deterioration of assets	Probably faster response time and less interruption in loan servicing	Lack of coordination with other AMCs
Potential economies of scale	Compensation of staff likely to be more like civil service than commercial bank limiting ability to draw and keep talent	Better local knowledge	Costly for individual bank to operate
Ability to pioneer new transactions	Risk of workouts/ asset sales being subject to political influence	Closer knowledge of debtors; relationship can aid in negotiation; ability to create new business opportunities	Risk of bank interference with workouts/asset sales
Standardization of due diligence and sale documentation; more attractive to investors			Fairness and disclosure issues; less attractive to investors
Source: Barents; Merrill Lynch			

However structured the AMC typically purchases the bad debt from distressed banks and places it on its own balance sheet. A national asset management corporation frequently will be granted special powers to accomplish its mission. As a result, the AMC has greater market resources to manage and recover bad loans, reschedule facilities where appropriate and negotiate on the settlement of bad debt from large corporations than an individual bank would have.

The AMC has to decide on its method and pricing of assets it is going to purchase. Some countries' AMCs buy bad loans based on a stable format, such as at a certain percentage of book value. Other AMCs will buy at a certain price that can be adjusted later on, dependent on the overall amount recovered. In Malaysia, the state AMC, Danamodal, has a specific price adjustment mechanism. Based on this method, if Danamodal is able to sell the acquired asset at a price higher than it paid the bank for the asset, then the bank receives 80% of the profit. As would be expected, a collateralized loan purchased would tend to bring a higher price than an uncollateralized loan.

To fund its purchases the AMC usually uses government-guaranteed bonds intending to sell the acquired assets before the government bonds mature. To aid sales and attract potential buyers of the assets, an AMC may guarantee buyers of impaired assets against losses (but at less than 100% and only for a certain period of time) as had happened in Thailand.

Roy I. Ramos, one of Asia's top bank analysts, lists six guiding principles and 23 specific measures that comprise an ideal bank restructuring program.

Step 6: Corporate Restructuring

Inextricably Intertwined with Bank Restructuring

An important element of the overall bank restructuring program involves the corporate sector. Corporate and bank restructuring are inextricably intertwined because in most cases delinquent corporate borrowers, and their inability (or unwillingness) to repay the money they borrowed underlie a bank's immediate liquidity problems. Most importantly, the banking system's non-performing assets are the corporate sector's defaulted liabilities. By selling these to an AMC, which in turn can sell the underlying collateral, or by using its power to force the delinquent corporations into bankruptcy and compel recovery of a portion of the value of those assets, liquidity can be restored to the financial system.

Bank and Corporate Restructuring Schematic

The diagram depicts some of the key interlinkages between bank and corporate restructuring and selected mechanisms for the restructuring of each.

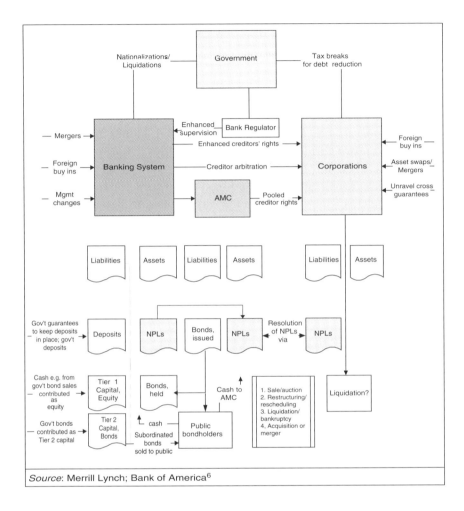

Source: Merrill Lynch; Bank of America[6]

Cyclical vs. Structural Distress

As with bank distress, the need for corporate restructuring may be acute or chronic. The acute need for corporate restructuring typically arises as a result of a financial crisis or panic. Corporate distress typically accompanies and is tied to bank distress, and together they necessitate the

---

[6] This schematic is a modified composite of two diagrams: one that appeared in Bank of America, Asia Financial Outlook, January 1999 at p. 14 (Dr. Andrew Freris, Daisy Shum and Ivy Lee) and one that appeared in Merrill Lynch, Asia Pacific Banknotes: Debt Restructuring in Asia, 1 April 1999.

restructuring of specific enterprises that require wholesale debt relief. The chronic situation arises in countries such as South Korea, Japan where over years or decades, the economic system has led to systemic or so-called structural problems. In economies where a large part of the corporate sector is still state-dominated, companies are likely to be run on non-commercial terms or are loss-making. In these countries, the whole corporate sector may need to be restructured, rather than just the debt-related restructuring of specific problem firms. China is an example of a country where the authorities have recognized the need to restructure both the state-owned enterprises and the state-owned commercial banks. But the problems which arise from the way China's economic system has evolved are so entrenched that the process may take a decade or more to accomplish. The Asian crisis also pointed to problems in corporate governance that gave rise to so-called "crony capitalism." This term encompasses a multitude of sins, ranging from: business transactions consummated for non-economic (e.g. political reasons); to unduly close cooperation between the government and private sectors engendering moral hazard; to the expropriation of wealth from minority shareholders by controlling shareholders; to corruption being seen as the price of doing business.

Victims of Circumstance Deserving of Aid

As with banks that find themselves in difficulty, the causes of corporate distress similarly vary. Like good banks caught up in a crisis, in some cases, otherwise good corporates may find themselves in difficulties due to weakened demand on the back of the weak economy and higher loan interest repayments as domestic interest rates rise. Or the company's problems may be more severe and it may be unable to service its debt and could be technically bankrupt. In the same way however, as the government might bailout a bank because it is "too big to fail," it may take the view that it may be more beneficial to allow the company to continue operating.

This not only may have less of an impact on the economy, but may also mean that banks with loans to the company will recover more of their exposure than would otherwise have been the case. For example, a bank with exposure to a struggling manufacturer is unlikely to force the closure of a factory as this would mean a sharp decrease in the manufacturer's value or net worth. Instead, the bank may well provide further funding for the corporate to enable it to survive, waiting for a possibly imminent recovery in the economy or for a possible sale. During Malaysia's economic crisis of 1997–98, for instance, the government took the approach that it needed to support some of the large industrial conglomerates in the country. It believed that allowing them to fail would have exacerbated the economic crisis, prolonged the recession, and added to the stock of bad loans in the banking sector.

Responsible for Their Own Misdeeds

In other cases, the corporates come to be in trouble because they over-leveraged themselves and channeled capital into unprofitable investments, even if the immediate cause of their troubles is an economic downturn. In such situations, drastic reorganization, in which existing management is replaced and portions of the company divested, or even liquided, may be viewed as the more appropriate course of action in order to free up the remaining capital that has become frozen in these unproductive investments by permitting some recovery to creditors.

Restructuring them embodies a variety of approaches that may range from mild, where existing management remains in place and terms of outstanding loans are renegotiated, to more severe forms in which new management is put in place, and subsidiaries and divisions are sold off or liquidated. Developed countries often have an effective legal and regulatory framework in place to facilitate restructuring. Emerging markets, however, often do not have the legal and regulatory mechanisms, such as effective foreclosure and bankruptcy laws, to facilitate more drastic forms of restructuring with the consequence that this course of action cannot be pursued and capital that could be redirected towards productive purposes stagnates. The Asian crisis demonstrated the fact that the legal infrastructure in a number of countries was ineffective to deal with restructuring needs.

Again, in such circumstances, recognizing the circumstances, a government may opt to bail out corporations that arguably should be restructured. To address some of the obstacles, several countries during the Asian crisis adopted approaches to corporate debt restructuring, sometimes setting up special agencies with sweeping authority to resolve restructuring issues that were formalized by law or regulation. The Thai authorities adopted formal principles for restructuring corporate debt in 1998. Other countries following similar guidelines included South Korea and Indonesia.

Illustration: Thai Corporate Restructuring

The principles of Thailand's corporate restructuring principles are highlighted below:

Thailand Corporate Debt Restructuring Principles

❑ To further the long-term viability of the debtor, the plan should achieve a business, rather than just a financial, restructuring.

❑ If the debtor's management is providing full and accurate information and participating in all creditor committee meetings, creditors "should stand still" for a defined (60 days) and extendable period. Restructuring should not be used to hide NPLs.

❑ Debt forgiveness should only be used as a last resort and only in exchange for stocks and warrants.

❑ A lead creditor institution (and within it, a specified individual) must be appointed early in the restructuring process to coordinate according to defined objectives and fixed deadlines. In major multi-creditor cases, a steering committee which is of a manageable size while representative of all creditors, should be appointed.

❑ Decisions should be made on information that has been independently verified.

❑ Creditors' existing collateral rights must continue.

❑ New credit extended on reasonable terms to help the debtor continue operations must receive priority status.

❑ Lenders should seek to lower their risk (e.g. through improved loan collateral), rather than to increase returns (e.g. by raising interest rates).

❑ Any creditor that sells his debt claim should ensure the buyer does not impede the restructuring process.

❑ Creditors should take account of the impact of any action on other creditors and on potentially viable debtors.

Source: Drawn from "A framework for corporate debt restructuring in Thailand." Published by the Board of Trade of Thailand, the Federation of Thai Industries, the Thai Bankers' Association, the association of Finance Companies and the Foreign Banks' Association. Extracted from BIS Policy Papers No. 6 — August 1999.

Indonesia's corporate restructuring effort was, however, far deeper, with the need for official assistance much greater. Authorities in

Indonesia established the Indonesian Debt Restructuring Agency (INDRA) in mid-1998 in order to aid Indonesian debtors to meet their foreign currency obligations. Indonesian corporate foreign currency obligations were substantial, reflecting both the extent of foreign borrowing and the increased repayment burden following the large-scale devaluation of the rupiah. Moreover, many Indonesian corporates did not generate any income in hard currency, thereby worsening their debt problems. INDRA acted as the intermediary between the Indonesian debtor and the foreign creditor in servicing debt that had been restructured or renegotiated. For INDRA to participate, the debtor and the creditor had to have agreed to restructure the loan facility to enable repayments, made in rupiah at a set exchange rate, to be spread over eight years or more with only interest paid in the first three years.

The approach taken by Indonesia was similar to that taken by some other countries, especially in Latin America, which implemented similar schemes whereby foreign debt was restructured over longer periods with significant grace periods granted. Foreign debt was also swapped for pre-denominated debt under a fixed government guaranteed exchange. Much of the mechanism adopted by corporate restructuring agencies utilizes the UK's informal framework for corporate restructuring where there is voluntary agreement among creditors to avoid placing companies into receivership. Banks devise a workout strategy in order to minimize losses.

CHAPTER SUMMARY

In this chapter we examine the bank restructuring process, why it is difficult and what is necessary for its success. In essence, financial sector restructuring is necessary because otherwise a country's economy cannot effectively function and grow, and recovery will be delayed. When the situation has progressed to the stage where comprehensive restructuring is required it is a corollary that the banks will be too far gone to restore themselves to financial health. Outside assistance, almost inevitably by the government, is required. It is not done for altruistic purposes.

Indeed, bank restructuring is a costly endeavor and one that becomes more costly the longer it is delayed. Consequently, the authorities must act quickly to stop the bleeding of banks through continued misallocated lending or banks tolerating the existence of unrecoverable loans.

This done, the damage must be assessed and the costs estimated. Inevitably, the burdens of restructuring will be painful and it is natural that each group affected will seek to avoid the bearing them. Shareholders will not want to lose their ownership stake, corporate borrowers will not want to pay or be forced into liquidation, depositors will not want to lose their savings, and taxpayers will not want to pay to recapitalize the banks. But only the depositors to some extent are likely to escape without too much pain, as their confidence in the banking system is essential to future economic health. It is therefore essential to bank restructuring that the government maintain the political will to effect the necessary changes and implement a fair and reasonable allocation of the economic burden. To see what happens when the problems are brushed under the carpet one need only look at Japan during the 1990s.

Once sufficient political support has been established, the actual process of restructuring can be completed. This ordinarily involves 1) changes in bank management and operations, regulatory reform (and possibly temporary regulatory forbearance), the removal of NPLs from the banks' balance sheets and the creation of appropriate mechanisms, such as asset management corporations or AMCs, to dispose of them, and finally corporate workouts and restructuring. The stage will then be set for sale of the troubled banks, their recapitalization or both which we discuss in the following chapter.

CHAPTER TWENTY ONE

THE DISTRESSED BANK, PART III: RECAPITALIZATION

Two types of advice books dominate the lists of non-fiction best sellers: how to get slim (i.e. Lose 50 lbs. and eat all you want) and how to get rich (i.e. Earn $10,000 a day in your spare time). Sadly absent is a much needed category for Asian bankers: how to rebuild a banking industry (i.e. Write-off your bad loans in 7 days without touching capital).
> — Robert Zielinski, "Asian Banking Crisis: Robert's Rules for Rebuilding" Lehman Brothers, July 16, 1998

The scale of Asia's banking crisis likely puts successful resolution beyond the scope of private capital inflows.
> — Keith Irving, "Asia-Pacific Banks: Progress & Issues in Bank Restructuring," Merrill Lynch, February 23, 1999

[I]t is increasingly obvious that thrifts will find raising capital about as easy as raising the dead.
> — Charles McCoy, The Wall Street Journal (1989)[1]

Recapitalization, as we have seen in the previous chapter, is but a small part of the whole bank restructuring process. While it is a critical part, capital alone is not enough to ensure the restoration of healthy banking. Merely injecting new funds into the bank will not address the underlying causes of the banking crisis or distress that engendered the need for recapitalization. The systemic roots of the problem are likely to be found

---

[1] Cited in Mills & Gardner.

in inadequate prudential regulation and bank supervision, a weak legal infrastructure, poor corporate governance, policy lending and deficient credit controls, deficient corporate governance and even in cronyism and corruption. These must be tackled in a coordinated way if recapitalization is not going to have be undertaken again in five or ten years. Having taken a bird's eye view of the restructuring process, we will now examine in more detail two of its critical aspects.

❑ First, how are the bad loans on the bank's books to be dealt with?

❑ Second, what methods are available to recapitalize the bank?

THE IMPORTANCE OF CAPITAL, REDUX

As we have discussed in detail in previous chapters, capital plays a critical role in the functioning of a bank. It has a number of functions of which, in the context of bank restructuring, the most important is the cushion it provides against economic shocks that diminish the value of a bank's assets. As highly leveraged entities, banks require sufficient capital to absorb the unavoidable fluctuation in the value of their loan and other financial assets that occurs when some borrowers inevitably default upon their loans. A bank without sufficient capital cannot function. It is like an overloaded car or a truck with a broken spring that is riding on its axles. With no cushion to absorb the shock, a single pothole can snap the axle and render the vehicle undrivable.

Needless to say, setting appropriate minimum capital requirements for banks, and then closely monitoring that banks maintain their *risk-weighted capital* above the minimum level, remain an important tool for bank supervisors to ensure that banks remain solvent and able to perform their intermediation role. If banks fall below the minimum requirement, supervisors must act quickly to ascertain how and when the banks will move their ratios above requirement. This, however, is easier said than done. In a number of emerging markets, countervailing pressures have long existed to expand lending at the expense of capital. Government policy in these countries may have kept profitability low — in effect, subsidizing the finance of industrial enterprises — so that banks were unable to grow capital internally. Or profits may have been heavily taxed with the same result. With the emphasis on growth, and depositors being given implicit or explicit guarantees that the bank would be kept afloat no matter what, capital at many banks in emerging markets has frequently been allowed to slip to dangerously thin levels.

The implementation of the 1988 Basel Capital Accord, although it only formally applied to a small number of OECD countries, has since come to be viewed as a benchmark for more than a hundred nations worldwide. The consequence has been some convergence in capital standards. Yet it is certainly arguable that real capital requirements are the greatest in the more volatile emerging markets, where a significantly greater cushion against economic shocks is needed. But the forms of supplementary (non-equity) capital permitted as Tier 2 capital, and the discretion allowed to regulators even in those countries that were obliged to meet the standards of the accord, mean that an 8% CAR in one country does not necessarily translate into the same level of safety as it does in another. Instead, the 8% benchmark has come to be seen as a kind of a seal of approval, one in which form has triumphed over substance. Yet in several countries, even this level has been unreachable for some banks.

When to Recapitalize

The 8% benchmark nevertheless at least serves as a common — if somewhat arbitrary — point of reference and banks that fall significantly below that level need to bolster their capital. The question of when to recapitalize is both simple and complex. It is simple in that banks that cannot meet the 8% requirement should be compelled to take steps to do so. It is complex in that within the setting of a troubled bank or banking sector, achieving that level is no real accomplishment unless more fundamental problems are addressed. For this reason, as part of an overall bank restructuring, no government capital should be infused into a bank unless it has made a commitment to address the problems that got it into trouble in the first place. In other words, among the items discussed in the previous chapter and in the first part of this (one such as the need to change management, reform operating procedures and address the bank's non-performing asset situation), recapitalization should be among the last to take place. It should be the carrot that causes the bank to do the hard work of reform before benefiting from government largesse.

Determining the Need: Calculating the Amount of Capital Required

---

How to Measure Recapitalization Needs

The Recipe:

- ❑ Calculate total loans net of provisions.
- ❑ Estimate the peak rate of NPLs.
- ❑ Estimate the recovery rate of NPLs taking account the degree of collateralization, the quality of the collateral and the efficacy of the legal system.
- ❑ Calculate the "black hole" i.e. Total NPLs (Peak Rate of NPLs × Total Loans) less recovery from NPLs (Total Loans × Estimated Recovery Rate). The "Black Hole" is the amount of capital that must be written off to compensate for outstanding bad loans.
- ❑ Calculate Net Worth (i.e. equity) of banks.
- ❑ Calculate Net Loans, i.e. Total Loans less Black Hole Cost.
- ❑ Calculate "Growth Capital" i.e. Tier One capital required to support Net Loans.
- ❑ Add Black Hole Cost + Growth Capital Need to get Total Capital Need. Then subtract existing Net Worth to obtain Recapitalization Requirement.

Example:

1. Total loans net of provisions = $2,021 m.
2. NPL Estimated peak ratio: 5%.
3. NPLs = 5% of total loans, or $101 m.
4. Est'd recovery rate = 50%.
5. Black hole cost = $101/2 = $50.5 m.
6. Net worth of banks = $375 m.
7. Net loans = Total loans less Black Hole Cost = $2,201 m less $50.5 = $1,971 m.
8. Calculate "Requisite Growth Capital" = Amount of Tier One capital necessary to support Net Loans at specified capital adequacy level e.g. 12%. Net loans $1,971 m × .12 = $236 m.
9. Add Black Hole Cost + Requisite Growth Capital, subtract Net Worth of Banks = $51 m + 236 m = $287 m less $375 = ($88 m).

In this case, there is no capital shortfall. The Net Worth of Banks exceeds the Black Hole Cost + Requisite Growth Capital. i.e. there is a capital surplus and hence no urgent need to recapitalize.

Note. This example represents Hong Kong in mid-1998.

N.B. Since NPL definitions vary regionally — though less so than before — NPLs should be adjusted to international standards i.e. a loan which has been overdue more than 3 months.

Source: Indosuez W.I. Carr Securities, Bank Recapitalization — Options & Policies, 15 July 1998. Analyst: Simon Maugham.

METHODS OF RECAPITALIZATION

There are a variety of ways to recapitalize banks. Assuming the bank's shareholders are not immediately willing or able to come up with new funds, various policy approaches are available to bank regulators. Each has both advantages and disadvantages and its suitability will vary depending upon the severity of the bank's capital shortfall and prevailing market conditions.

We will summarize them first and then explore them in greater detail. The main methods are as follows listed in order from greater to lesser intrusiveness.

❑ **Nationalization**. Fully or partially nationalize problem banks.

❑ **Consolidation**. Encourage or compel mergers and acquisitions within the banking sector.

❑ **AMCs**. Use the asset management corporation as a recapitalization vehicle.

❑ **Corporate Restructuring Workouts**. Use Debt equity swaps as a method of bank recapitalization.

❑ **Capital markets**. Facilitate capital-raising of banks through the issue of securities.

❑ **Monetary Policy**. Facilitate internal capital growth through monetary policy.

On the whole, the first three approaches contemplate much greater state involvement in the recapitalization process, while in the second three the hand of the government is less visible, and market mechanisms play a greater role. In the latter, the government functions more as a facilitator rather than as a direct participant in the recapitalization process. This set of tactics tends to be best suited to less severe banking crises or to supplement the former, which it follows is appropriate to more severe banking turmoil.

Government Recapitalization

A common method for recapitalizing troubled banks is for government agencies, or the government directly, to inject fresh capital into banks. This strategy has been a common feature of bank restructuring in the Asian banking markets over the last couple of years.

Nationalization

The most drastic of these approaches occurs where the government takes over or nationalizes the bank, displacing the existing shareholders. As the sole owner of the bank, the government injects new capital, cleans up the bank's bad assets either through direct write-offs or more commonly by transferring them to an asset management corporation (see below), and then ultimately privatizes the bank, selling it to an investor group. This is a workable and frequently-used approach, especially in emerging markets. There is a danger with this strategy, however, that privatization may be delayed too long, allowing problems to fester anew. When the banks are ultimately reprivatized, they may no longer be competitive.[2]

Partial nationalization may also occur whereby the government infuses capital into the bank in return for an ownership stake, or provides a "loan capital" to get the bank back on its feet without taking an equity interest in return. In such case, the original shareholders may or may not be replaced, but if not replaced their shareholdings will commonly be diluted either through the government taking a stake in the bank or through a strategic stake being sold to new investors. The new capital may take the form of cash or liquid assets or secondary capital, such as subordinated bonds. The subordinated bond approach is taken if the government decides it does not want a controlling stake in the bank. Other hybrid capital instruments can also be used, such as preference shares.

Use of the AMC as a Recapitalization Vehicle

The government may also recapitalize the bank through an asset management corporation discussed in the previous chapter. Recapitalization in such case is characterized as a value exchange whereby the bank "sells" its non-performing assets to the AMC at par value. Of course, the NPLs are in actuality worth a fraction of par, so this gambit kills two birds with one stone. First, mere disposal of the problem assets has the effect of automatically improving the bank's capital ratios — since assets have decreased while equity has remained the same. In addition, a back-door capitalization can be effected when the bank "sells" its bad loans to the

---

[2] Keith Irving, first vice prresident of Merrill Lynch suggested in "Asia-Pacific Banks: Progress and Issues in Bank Restructuring" (Merrill Lynch, February 23, 1999) that this is what happened to banks in Argentina and Mexico that were nationalized in the 1980s and reprivatized in the early 1990s, p. 30.

AMC at par, and contributes the increment between the purchase price and the real value of the NPLs to capital. Second — the government bonds have a lower risk weighting than the bad loans they replace.[3] A disadvantage, however, of the exchanging government bonds for bad assets approach is they do little to help the bank's liquidity position.

Pricing of NPL Purchases by AMCs			
Country	Pricing	Mode of Payment	Peak NPLs
Malaysia	30–50% discount to face value	Zero-coupon bonds	
Mexico	Face value; back door recapitalization	Zero-coupon bonds (non-tradable) to be replaced with coupon bearing tradable bonds	
South Korea	45% of face value (implicit subsidy)	Bonds	
China*	Face value; back door recapitalization		
Merrill Lynch and Central Banks (Feb. 1999) * China Construction Bank			

A Note on Government Bonds

In the majority of cases, recapitalization by the government is effected through the contribution of government bonds to the bank as capital. (Note that this approach is entirely different to the situation discussed below in which the bank itself issues subordinated debt itself as Tier 2 capital.) If zero-coupon bonds are supplied, the government does not have to provide any cash in the short term (as the entire interest and principal payment will be due in a balloon payment on the expiration of the bond), but the bank receiving this type of bond does not receive any immediate cash flow. This form of recapitalization is more cosmetic than real, especially where there are trading restrictions on the bond, although it does indicate government support for the bank.

---

[3] There is also the possibility that the bank may opt to characterize a portion of the funds realized from the asset sale as a capital gain than can be shifted into the capital account.

Illustration: Common Method of Government Recapitalization:
Non-Performing Assets for Government Securities

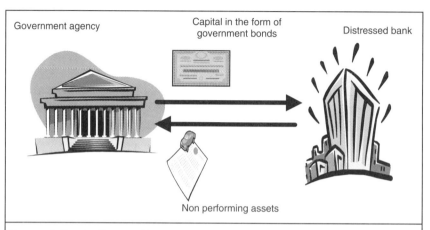

To recapitalize the distressed bank, the government issues debt—either with a continuing stream of coupon payments or with a zero-coupon at the end of the term of the instrument — an exchange for impaired assets, which are ordinarily nominally valued at or near face value. Thus, for example, a government issues to Distressed Bank a 10-year zero-coupon bond with par value of $10 m and an interest rate of 5%. As a result, $10 m in bad assets are removed from Distressed Bank's balance sheet, while $10 m is added as equity. Although the bank has received no liquid funds it has received the right to obtain a $10 m interest payment from the government in ten years. Since this right to receive $10 m 10 years hence, it has a present value that can be registered in the bank's capital account immediately. From an economic perspective, the net present value (and the purchase price) of the 10-year $10 m zero-coupon bond would be considerably less than $10 m. Precisely what amount would be recorded would depend on the accounting standards employed.

Receiving tradable bonds provides more flexibility for the bank in that it is able to sell them and receive the proceeds. The disadvantage is that the unreformed bank will be able to divert the funds immediately into lending. As a safety precaution, it may be desirable to restrict the selling of the bonds until after a certain length of time has elapsed. In some countries, so-called "tradable" bonds issued by the government may, in fact, not be liquid, due to the absence of a secondary market, and thus the banks may be forced to hold onto the bonds until maturity. While the bank will be able to receive any benefit of continuing interest payments, the capitalization is again largely cosmetic.

By way of illustration, two countries that have recently taken this approach are Malaysia and Thailand. Malaysia established Danamodal

Credit Lyonnais Restructuring: The Use of an AMC For Recapitalization

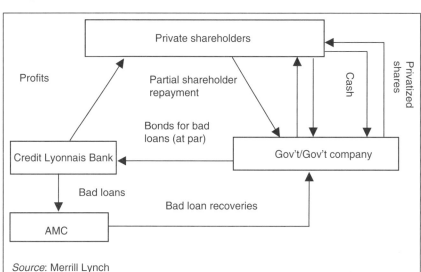

Source: Merrill Lynch

(see later section on Malaysian Bank restructuring), mainly funded from the issue of government guaranteed five- to ten-year zero-coupon bonds, to inject capital into weaker banks. Some of the stronger banks in Malaysia were required to subscribe to these bonds using funds released from a relaxation in their required reserve ratio.

As was the case in Malaysia, banks in Thailand receiving a capital injection were subject to certain conditions. Thai banks receiving capital support were required to meet tough loan loss provisioning rules. In addition, the new capital injected reduced the stake in the bank of existing shareholders. After the capital injections have raised the capital adequacy ratio to above 2.5%, any further capital injection would have to be met by equivalent amounts from the private sector. The new capital supplied by the government ranks above existing capital.

Mergers, Takeovers, and Bank Consolidation

Most restructuring programs aim ultimately for a consolidation of the banking sector in the belief that a smaller number of better capitalized and larger more efficient institutions will strengthen and stabilize the overall system. In a system-wide banking crisis, smaller banks tend to be more affected and vulnerable owing to their lower capacity to absorb shocks. Stronger banks in the sector are encouraged to buy weaker, smaller banks, either through gentle persuasion, or by offering financial incentives such as removing bad loans, injecting capital, tax breaks or funding.

Authorities managing a major restructuring program may also actively promote takeovers by foreign banks. This too has advantages, as it tends to lead to a stronger banking sector, with new expertise, skills and services, and foreign capital. Indeed, some argue that the side benefits brought by foreign banks in the form of improved banking technology and skills transfer is considerable. As analysts Wan Ismail and Rafael Bello of Morgan Stanley Dean Witter observe:

> Improved foreign participation is ... the most important element of banking reform.... Besides being the most effective means of recapitalization without overextending the public purse, greater foreign equity participation leads to greater board independence from majority (read, family) shareholders and increases the professionalism of bank management.[4]

However, most domestic authorities, particularly in transitional economies, do not want their banking sector to be dominated by foreign players. This is perfectly understandable given the colonial legacy quite a few of these countries still wish to put behind them. Some countries continue to actively limit the presence of foreign banks — for example, in Thailand, although foreign takeovers are permitted, the foreign bank can only own the shares for ten years. In Malaysia, the foreign ownership of banks is still limited at 30%.

But like their domestic counterparts, foreign banks may very well be unwilling to take on the role of bailing out the weak local institutions they are contemplating buying. They may require "loss protection" under which, for instance, the government may be required to compensate them if the volume of bad loans in the acquired local bank exceeds a certain threshold or proves to be worse than anticipated. Of course, in countries that have sharply restricted foreign ownership of domestic banks, the ability to obtain a banking license and gain entry into the country's

---

[4] Wan Ismail & Rafael Bello, "The Bank Rehabilitation Process: Asia and Mexico Compared," Morgan Stanley Dean Witter, September 4, 1998, p. 5.

banking market may prove a powerful incentive, and the cost of cleaning up the local bank's bad debts may be plausibly viewed as a premium to be paid to gain that access. Still a number of acquisitions of banks by foreign institutions have had to be abandoned because the government and the foreign bank could not come to terms on these issues.

Strong Bank—Weak Bank Merger

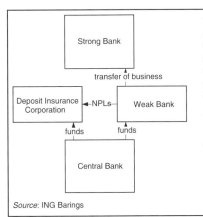

The strong bank-weak bank merger is one approach to recapitalizing a problem bank. Two weak banks, however, do not add up to one strong bank. It can work if the strong bank is sufficiently healthy, and particularly if the government provides some relief in the form of new capital and assistance in resolving NPLs.

This diagram, which depicts the insolvency of Hokkaido Takushoku of Japan in November 1997 as an illustration of this prototypical approach to recapitalization, was derived from an ING Barings report by banking analyst James Fiorillo, entitled "Resolving Japan's Banking System Problems: A Tough Mission for the Authorities — If They Choose to Accept It ...", 1 December 1997.

To be sure, mergers and takeovers, either by domestic or foreign banks, can be a far cheaper and more effective means for the regulatory authorities than supporting banks for lengthy periods, injecting capital and buying bad loans. Something cannot be created out of nothing, however. Unless the government injects some funds and relieves the weak bank of all or a portion of its NPLs, the merged banks still have the problem of the bad loans on their books, and while the capital of the larger, better capitalized bank may be able to absorb the loan losses, it will be diluted in the process. Also, the stronger banks may be reluctant, notwithstanding the incentives proffered, to absorb the weaker banks. Mergers under the best of circumstances have their share of difficulties and require a great deal of management energy to work. When the merger does not strengthen the franchise of the acquiring bank and is merely a way to shunt off a weak bank's problems onto a healthy institution, there is always the possibility that the scheme will backfire and that instead of one strong and one weak bank, what will be left is one large weak bank.

Debt for Equity: Corporate Restructuring

Banks will sometimes swap debt for equity stakes in companies that owe them money but are unable to pay. This obviates the need to classify exposures as NPLs as the debt is forgiven in exchange for the transfer of equity shares to the bank. Hence there is no need for a provisioning requirement. Debt for equity will also may provide a lifeline for the corporate, enabling it to remain in business, and, with the partnership of the bank, to improve operating performance. However, the frequent use of this approach will saddle the bank with significant non-bank equity participations and may, in the long-run, severely weaken the bank's performance. The analyst should also watch out for equity participations that are over-valued. As a general rule, they should be worth no more than the debt they replaced.[5] Some French banks in the past have been affected negatively by this approach. The analyst should be wary of situations where the bank is taking equity participations in group-related companies. This may only be to provide support for an insolvent group company.

Facilitate Bank Capital Raising Schemes in the Capital Markets

One reason that banks may have experienced problems is the difficulties they faced in raising outside capital. The capital markets, particularly the debt markets, are not well developed in many emerging markets, and the result in some cases may be an over-reliance on the controlling shareholders or the equity markets for finance. During a banking crisis, however, the market for bank stocks will almost certainly be near its nadir and that is hardly the best time to float new shares. This leaves the debt markets as an alternative, but as noted, these may be highly immature.

Often the government policymakers have not given the debt markets much concern and relied heavily on credit from banks to provide finance to growing industrial firms. The excessive demands placed upon banks in a rapidly growing economy, of course, may have contributed to the banking crisis in the first place. For a number of reasons, not the least of which may be to allow local banks to raise capital, the authorities may undertake to revive their debt markets during a banking crisis. The government itself may issue local debt, which will have the beneficial

---

[5] Irving at p. 35

effect of establishing a benchmark risk free yield curve, and the funds raised may also be channeled into bank recapitalization initiatives. By removing regulatory barriers and tax disincentives, and offering special inducements, local debt markets may become a viable vehicle for banks to raise new capital. Among the largest institutions, the international debt markets may also be utilized, although government guarantees may be a prerequisite for a successful underwriting.

The potential disadvantage of the use of local (and international) debt markets may be the high cost of capital, the lack of sufficient institutional investor demand, especially for local paper, and the fact that the Tier 2 capital, which subordinated debt provides, is a form of capital that is in major part cosmetic in nature.

Use of Macroeconomic Approaches to Foster Internal Capital Generation

Finally, by manipulating monetary and interest rate policy, regulators may be able to create conditions more conducive to bank profitability. By keeping the cost of funds low to banks but maintaining higher lending rates, the central bank may be able to fatten bank spreads, enabling them to more easily earn their way back to financial health. On the one hand, this type of recapitalization is largely invisible to taxpayers since there is no apparent government bailout. Politically, therefore, it is relatively painless. On the other hand, this type of policy does have real costs. The higher lending rates necessary to make it work mean a higher cost of credit to industry that is likely to dampen economic growth, and may even shift the problems of the banking sector to other sectors.

By definition, a banking crisis is one where banks are no longer able to earn their way back to full capital strength within a reasonable time period. Although manipulation of macroeconomic policy may speed the process, it will be inadequate to restore a severely impaired banking system to health and is best viewed as a supplementary method to be used in conjunction with the methods described above. As Keith Irving, head of bank analysis at Merrill Lynch in Hong Kong put it:

> The strategy of allowing ... banks to "earn their way out" of ... problems by charging super spreads will work only if the problems are small enough (e.g. Citibank and Barclays, with less than 10% NPLs).[6]

---

[6] Keith Irving at p. 57.

Summary of Recapitalization Policy Options

	Policy Option	Advantages	Disadvantages	
More intrusive	1. Nationalization of banks, assumption of bad debts and liabilities by the government i.e. the taxpayer.	Most clear cut way to *recap* banks.	Hard to hide that government is bailing out banks with taxpayers' money; political resistance may arise, justifiably, so when shareholders/managers get to keep their positions; cost may be onerous.	*Less market oriented*
	2. Encourage/force mergers of insolvent/weak banks with solvent/strong banks.	Accelerated consolidation of banking can build stronger, more efficient and more profitable banks better able to internally generate and externally attract capital. Works well when banks complement each other and synergies can be obtained; avoids need to use large amounts of taxpayer funds.	Two weak banks rarely make one strong bank: same problems may be perpetuated and entire banking system weakened; integration of operations can take large amounts of time and energy distracting from banking business; redundancies can cause fallout with trade unions and political resistance; heavy handed forced mergers can aggravate the above difficulties.	
	3. Create asset management corp. capitalized by the government to buy and dispose of bad loans and collateral.	If the AMC is effective, a relatively rapid method for disposing of bad loans.	Lack of funding, expertise and political will can hamper disposition of assets; where legal system is weak, well-placed individuals and firms can manipulate the system to buy back assets at a discount and escape debt. Artificial transfer pricing (rather than market clearing) mechanisms can sabotage positive benefits. Where purchase of bad debt is in exchange for government bonds, the bank's liquidity position is little improved.	

Table continued

Policy Option	Advantages	Disadvantages
Less intrusive 4. Facilitate restructuring via private asset sales and debt-equity swaps.	Another market-oriented solution that encourages banks to work out the optimal *recap* method.	If sale is with recourse to the bank, the problem remains; banks may be unwilling to give sufficient discounts to consummate transactions; restructuring of loans can merely mask underlying problems and postpone inevitable reckoning; political considerations can hinder deals. *More market oriented*
5. Facilitate capital raising in equity or subordinated debt markets, e.g. through removal of regulatory barriers, tax incentives, special inducements.	A market-oriented solution that encourages banks to work out the optimal recap method.	There may not be an adequate appetite for new paper, especially if many issues are required; costs may be high; if Tier 2 capital is raised, effect may be merely to make bank look better without providing the protection that Tier 1 capital does.
6. Fatten spreads through monetary and banking policy. Create fat spreads by 1) regulating interest rates; 2) inducing a steep yield curve. Effect is to enhance bank profits allowing them to "earn" their way out of the crisis.	Largely invisible to consumers and trade unions. Seems more "laissez faire" and therefore more appealing to int'l investment community.	High rates on borrowing and low interest rates on deposits discourage savings and function as a tax on economic growth. Will worsen difficulties of highly geared firms and individuals.

Source: Indosuez W.I. Carr Securities.

OTHER METHODS

Two other methods of dealing with problem banks are sometimes used, albeit less frequently than the foregoing methods. The first, open bank assistance, simply involves the infusion of new funds into the bank with no particular immediate effort to resolve its bad loans. It is sometimes been accompanied by full or partial nationalization, referred to above, or government guarantees. This method was used by the Japanese government initially in connection with Nippon Credit Bank in early 1997.

(The bank was later nationalized.) Under a government scheme, the Bank of Japan provided some funds and asked for contributions from commercial banks and insurance companies.

Another approach is outright liquidation. This method calls for putting the insolvent bank into receivership, taking over its assets and transferring them to another bank or to an AMC. This method is frequently used in the United States where 20% of insolvent institutions come to this end, and is also occasionally employed elsewhere. It was used by the Japanese government in 1996 when it shut down Hanwa Bank, a failed regional institution. A temporary new bank was created to handle deposit withdrawals and wind down Hanwa's business. Its assets were transferred to a special "bad bank" i.e. an AMC.[7]

A NOTE ON DEPOSIT INSURANCE SCHEMES AND THEIR MORAL HAZARD RISKS

Most authorities will put in place a full deposit guarantee policy in the face of a banking crisis, assuming one was not already there. However,

Problems with Wholesale Deposit Insurance Schemes: The Turkish Example

---

Deposit Insurance Schemes in Turkey

Turkey had an economic and banking crisis in the early part of 1994, with one of the main factors being a sharp and significant fall in the value of the Turkish lira. This placed pressure on banks that had borrowed heavily in hard currency. This pressure, exacerbated by rumors saw the collapse of three small banks, and this event triggered deposit runs at other banks, placing some on the point of collapse. To put stability in the system, the central bank announced a full 100% guarantee on all deposits. However, in the intervening period, many weak banks survived in Turkey on the back of this guarantee. They were able to attract deposits by offering rates a few percentage points above market average. This distorted the market and penalized the better, and lower-risk, banks. The Turkish central bank has only just capped the deposit guarantee in mid-2000, unfortunately probably two years or so later than it should have. During this period, eight banks have been taken over by the deposit insurance scheme, all weak banks that managed to survive for so long as a result of the scheme.

---

[7] ING Barings, cited above.

this policy does have risks if it is not quickly withdrawn, or reduced, when stability returns. If not, the promise of deposit insurance may weaken the whole sector. It also tends to attract more new banks to the sector, thereby overcrowding the market leading to further sector vulnerability. This scenario was common in Latin America, before sector restructuring occurred. Although full deposit insurance can quickly bring stability to a market, it is best if the authorities as soon as possible cap the amount guaranteed, at a reasonable level, so as to reduce moral hazard. Foreign bank creditors also may need to be guaranteed in certain market conditions in order to maintain banks' access to international markets. Without such access, funding may be squeezed. The support of foreign creditors has been seen in Korea where the government assumed responsibility for banks' foreign debt.

CHAPTER SUMMARY

In this chapter we reiterated the reasons for recapitalization and restated the reasons that recapitalization alone is an inadequate solution to a failed banking system. We then described how to calculate the recapitalization needs of a bank or bank. The core of the chapter was given over to a discussion of the six key methods of bank recapitalization and the advantages and disadvantages of each. Three of these methods require heavy governmental intervention. They are: nationalization, forced or incentivized consolidation; and the use of asset management corporations (AMCs) to recapitalize banks as well as to remove bad debts from the balance sheets of those institutions meant to be restored to viability.

The remaining three methods of recapitalization are more market-oriented. They are: facilitating debt equity swaps with corporate borrowers; facilitating the use of capital markets for bank recapitalization; and using monetary policy to enable banks to earn their way back to financial health more rapidly than otherwise. Two other methods which represent two extremes of tolerance for problem banks, open bank assistance and forced liquidation, were also mentioned. Finally, the impact of deposit guarantees on the recapitalization process was briefly discussed.

CHAPTER TWENTY TWO

THE DISTRESSED BANK, PART IV: ILLUSTRATIVE APPROACHES TO RESTRUCTURING — MALAYSIA AND SOUTH KOREA

Much analysis has been done on the root causes of the financial crisis that has swept Asia. Our view is simple: too much money was lent to the wrong people. A combination of financial liberalization, inflows of cheap money from overseas, and ill-conceived infrastructure projects caused bankers to be swept up with the times and go on a lending spree with little regard for risk.
— Robert Zielinski, banking analyst, "Restructuring Asia's Banks: The Process and Institutions Lehman Brothers," September 29, 1998

The definition of a 'non-performing loan' is a central question in efforts to recapitalize banks since it determines the amount of capital necessary to fulfill BIS requirements and maintain solvency.
— Dr. Andrew Freris & Daisy Shum, "A Survey of Banking Reform in Asia," Bank of America, July 1999

In this chapter, we shall explore in more detail the actual strategies, institutions and operations that were employed to deal with the Asian crisis of 1997–98. The purpose is to gain a more practical understanding as to how governments react to banking crises. The Asian crisis officially began in Thailand on July 2, 1997 with the devaluation of the Thai baht and rapidly spread throughout the region. Most badly effected were

Thailand itself, Indonesia, which saw and economic crisis trigger a political one with the ultimate deposing of President Suharto, and South Korea, which also saw political repercussions from the turmoil. Malaysia was arguably less severely affected.

Other countries experienced fallout from the crisis, but were not in the direct path of the storm — Singapore, Hong Kong (returned to Chinese sovereignty on June 30, 1997), Taiwan and the Philippines among them. Still others were only affected peripherally due to the relatively closed nature of their economies. China, Vietnam, and India fall into this category. Japan, of course, had been dealing with its own extended period of economic malaise since the crash of the Tokyo stock market at the end of the 1980s.

In hindsight, there is a fair degree of consensus that the Asian crisis was in large part a banking crisis. The East Asian economic miracle was essentially financed by bank lending. To be sure, capital markets have evolved to varying degrees of maturity in each of the countries that make up the region, but there has been a much greater reliance on bank lending in Asia than in other regions and the alternative forms of finance remain relatively nascent. Those countries with both weak or overstressed banking systems and freely trading currencies suffered the worst. One reason that Hong Kong, Singapore and the Philippines (the problems of the Philippines at the date of this writing are as much political as economic) survived comparatively unscathed is due in large part to the strength of their banking systems of the time the crisis hit. As at July 1997, banks in all three countries displayed robust financial indicators and regulation was reasonably good in all three, although the Philippines lagged behind particularly in terms of ongoing bank supervision and examination.

Each of the four countries we examine here utilized some form of the "asset management corporation" approach, in which a special entity was set up to assist in the resolution of bad loans.

MALAYSIAN BANK RESTRUCTURING PROGRAM

The Malaysian banking sector entered the 1997–98 Asian financial crisis in a relatively solid position. The 1980s banking crisis in Malaysia had led to a complete overhaul of banking legislation and supervision such that, prior to the crisis, Malaysia had adopted fully 22 out of the 25 BIS Core Principles of Banking Supervision. As of June 1997, the risk-weighted capital ratio of the banking system was 12% and net non-performing loans were 2.2%. With the onset of the Asian crisis in mid-1997, the Malaysian authorities adopted a thorough and preemptive approach to strengthen the resilience of the banking sector. Given the importance of the banking sector, and its role in the economy, stability in the domestic financial markets was perceived to be a crucial element in the economic recovery process. The approach involved the establishment of institutional arrangements to address the deterioration in banks' loan portfolios. This move was taken when the NPL ratio was still below 10% and the banking system was still adequately capitalized. The quick response to restructuring undoubtedly reduced costs at a later date.

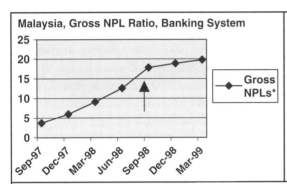

Malaysia, Gross NPL Ratio, Banking System

After Malaysia began its restructuring program in 4Q98, NPLs began flattening out. By July 2000, the banking system NPL ratio had fallen to 10.8% according to Bank of America's July 27, 2000 Asian Economic Brief. By that time, as a percentage of total NPLs, state agencies had absorbed 69.6%.

*NPLs on this chart are calculated according to the 3-month international standard.
Source: Bank of America

A National Approach to Restructuring and Recapitalization: The Institutions

Three specially formed agencies led the restructuring process. These included the national asset management company, Danaharta; a special purpose recapitalization agency, Danamodal; and the Corporate Debt Restructuring Committee (CDRC) to facilitate corporate debt restructuring. The three agencies operate on market-based principles.

Danaharta

Danaharta was formed in September 1998 and was intended to have a life of from five to ten years. Danaharta's task was to resolve the banks' NPLs by removing them from the banking system and disposing of them, together with acquired assets (i.e. collateral), in order to recover the maximum possible value. Danaharta focused on larger loans (over US$1.3 m) and gave priority to secured loans. In pursuit of its mission, Danaharta issued zero-coupon bonds or paid cash to selling banks in exchange for their bad loans, effectively replacing the bad assets on the bank's books with bonds or cash. The zero-coupon bonds were government guaranteed with yields approximating those of Malaysian government securities with similar tenures. For secured NPLs, the underlying collateral was valued by Danaharta's panel of independent valuers, while unsecured NPLs were acquired at a flat 10% of the principal outstanding of the NPLs.

A variety of methods were available to Danaharta for use in resolving NPLs. Dealing directly with the borrowers, Danaharta could restructure the loan, assist the borrower with additional funding, convert the debt to equity or even take over management of the borrower. Danaharta's normal profit-sharing arrangement stipulates that any excess in recovery values over and above Danaharta's acquisition costs plus directly attributable costs were shared with the selling financial institution on an 80:20 basis (80% financial institution and 20% Danaharta). Loan management efforts include loan rescheduling and debt/equity conversions. Banks were not obliged to transfer their bad assets to Danaharta, although strong incentives existed for them to do so. If they did not transfer them, they were obliged to write down the loans and then restructure them or pass them on to the Corporate Debt Restructuring Committee, discussed below.

By the end of December 1999, Danaharta had acquired and was managing NPLs with loan rights amounting to 45.5 billion Malaysian ringgit (RM) from the financial system, of which RM35.7 billion comprised the loan rights acquired from the banking system. The book value of the loans removed from the banking system amounted to RM34 billion, representing approximately 42% of NPLs in the banking system. The removal of these bad loans from the system reduced the NPL level to 6.6% of gross loans (based on the six-month non-international standard classification adopted by Malaysia during the crisis as a matter of regulatory forbearance) as at end December 1999 from 9% at end 1998. The overall weighted average discount rate for the acquired NPLs was about 56%. RM10.3 billion of nominal value zero-coupon bonds had been issued up to end December 1999 as consideration for the acquired loans. This was lower than the budgeted amount of RM15 billion.

Danaharta embarked on the secondary wave of NPL acquisition in late 1999. However, as the majority of bad loans had already been removed from the system, the amount of NPLs to be acquired was minimal. The secondary phase focused on facilities including unsecured loans granted to public companies and loans from banking institutions with net NPL ratios in excess of 10%. Danaharta has also entered the loan and asset management stage of the restructuring process. As at year-end 1999, RM17.6 billion of the loans and assets under its management had been restructured or disposed, with an average recovery rate of 80%. Danaharta also conducted two restricted open tenders to dispose of foreign currency loans and papers in August 1999 and December 1999 involving 43 accounts worth US$394 m. The first tender offering saw a recovery rate of 55% with the second at 71%. In regard to asset management, in December 1999, Danaharta conducted its first open tender exercise involving foreclosed properties. A total of 44 properties were included in the tender with indicative value of RM123m; 24 bids were successful for a total consideration of RM17.8m. The unsold properties were transferred to an asset subsidiary of Danaharta at the minimum bid price. Danaharta, in the view of most analysts, has been an effective agent in resolving the NPLs in Malaysia's banking system.

Malaysia: Restructuring Schematic

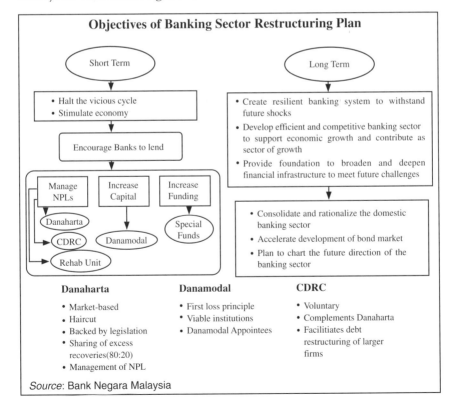

Objectives of Banking Sector Restructuring Plan

Short Term
- Halt the vicious cycle
- Stimulate economy

Encourage Banks to lend

Manage NPLs | Increase Capital | Increase Funding

Danaharta
CDRC | Danamodal | Special Funds
Rehab Unit

Long Term
- Create resilient banking system to withstand future shocks
- Develop efficient and competitive banking sector to support economic growth and contribute as sector of growth
- Provide foundation to broaden and deepen financial infrastructure to meet future challenges

- Consolidate and rationalize the domestic banking sector
- Accelerate development of bond market
- Plan to chart the future direction of the banking sector

Danaharta
- Market-based
- Haircut
- Backed by legislation
- Sharing of excess recoveries(80:20)
- Management of NPL

Danamodal
- First loss principle
- Viable institutions
- Danamodal Appointees

CDRC
- Voluntary
- Complements Danaharta
- Facilitiates debt restructuring of larger firms

Source: Bank Negara Malaysia

Danamodal

Created at the same time as Danaharta, Danamodal was set up to address the constraints faced by existing bank shareholders to recapitalize viable banking institutions to sound levels. Its mission was to both recapitalize the banking sector and assist in its consolidation, creating sustainably profitable institutions in the process. It was contemplated to have a limited life, recapitalizing the banking system within two years, and then over time disposing of its interests in the country's banks recovering all or part of the funds expended in recapitalization. To enable Danamodal to begin operations, Bank Negara Malaysia, the country's central bank, contributed seed capital. The intention at the outset was that the agency would ultimately widen its shareholder base by making equity available to a variety of investors. In October 1998, Danamodal obtained further funding by beginning a debt issuance program. (Additional financing was also effected through a US\$1.35 billion five-year loan to Malaysia at LIBOR + 290 bp.)

The funds raised were then provided to banks in need of recapitalization in exchange for irredeemable non-cumulative, exchangeable, convertible preference shares, non-redeemable cumulative preferred shares, subordinated bonds or other comparable securities. In the event that the net tangible assets of the recapitalization institution deteriorates further, Danamodal protects its investments through the use of a call option that enables it to acquire the remaining shares at nominal value. As at end July 1999, Danamodal had injected RM6.2 billion into ten banking institutions, increasing their risk-weighted capital ratio to 13%. By year-end 1999, the total capital injection into the ten institutions had fallen to RM5.3 billion following repayments by five institutions.

Corporate Debt Restructuring Committee: Mediator for Corporate Debt Restructuring

Contemporaneous with the creation of Danaharta and Danamodal, the Corporate Debt Restructuring Committee (CDRC) was established. Its purpose was to restructure corporate debt and work together with Danaharta in cases of defaulted or problem obligations to domestic banks, targeting borrowers that have viable business, have large debt obligations to more than one lender, and which are not under receivership. The CDRC does not have the power to compel workouts. Its role, instead, is to facilitate the restructuring of debt in the capacity of a mediator, and it therefore depends upon the cooperation of creditors and debtors. As at the end of

February 2000, the CDRC had completed the restructuring of 19 cases with debts amounting to RM14.1 billion.

Corporate restructuring in Malaysia does not seem to have been as sweeping as in South Korea, discussed in the next part of this chapter. In South Korea, the over-leveraging of the large conglomerates that dominated the economy became a political issue, particularly with the change in government at an early stage in the Asian crisis. In Malaysia, on the contrary, there was political continuity and government pursued an independent, if somewhat idiosyncratic, approach to economic reform. Measures aimed at stabilizing the currency at a fixed rate and controlling the country's capital account which were much criticized at the time. In hindsight, these measures appear to have had a beneficial impact and perhaps brought short- and medium-term relief to the corporate sector, mitigating the need for more far-reaching reform. The government also showed less reluctance to help companies deemed to be of strategic economic importance. Analysts criticized some of the so-called bailouts to companies seen as more politically well-connected than critical to Malaysia's economic survival.

Illustration: How the CDRC Works

Malaysia—CDRC and the debt restructuring workout process

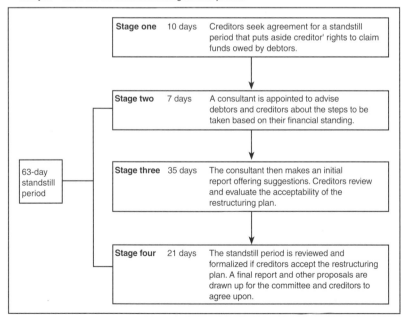

Source: CDRC Bank of America

How Danaharta, Danamodal and the CDRC Work Together

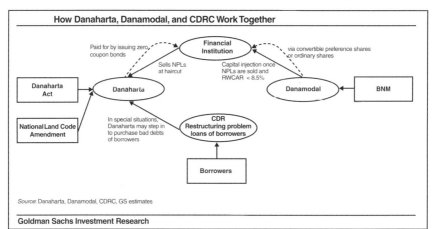

How Danaharta, Danamodal, and CDRC Work Together

Source: Danaharta, Danamodal, CDRC, GS estimates

Goldman Sachs Investment Research

Other Measures Employed in Malaysia's Financial Sector Restructuring

Consolidation: Bank Takeovers and Strong Bank–Weak Bank Mergers

Some banking institutions did suffer significant losses arising from high levels of NPLs and provisioning. In order to prevent further deterioration, Bank Negara Malaysia assumed control over the operations of four banking institutions: Kewangan Bersatu, MBf Finance, Sabah Finance and Sime Merchant Bank. This move was also aimed to preemptively contain any possibility of a systemic failure in the system. In addition, Bank Bumiputra Malaysia and Sime Bank, two of the larger domestic commercial banks, suffered severe losses, due again to significant NPLs and provisions. Because of their size and the potential impact of the two banks on overall system stability and market confidence, the two institutions were merged with stronger commercial banks. Bank Bumiputra was absorbed by Bank of Commerce and Sime Bank was acquired by RHB Bank. To ensure that the mergers would not weaken the strength of either Bank of Commerce or RHB Bank, the distressed assets of Bank Bumiputra and Sime Bank were removed to subsidiaries of Danaharta that were specifically set up to manage the bad assets of the two banks prior to the merger.

Comprehensive Program to Consolidate the Malaysian Banking System

Bank Negara Malaysia recognized the importance and need for consolidation in the banking sector. During strong economic growth periods in the late 1980s and early 1990s, the central bank's call for mergers was largely ignored, with only two market-oriented mergers completed subsequent to the mid-1980s banking crisis. In early September 1999, therefore, the Malaysian Finance Minister, Daim Zainuddin, together with Bank Negara, ordered the country's 22 banks, together with associated financial companies, to merge into six institutions under the leadership of six nominated anchor banks: Maybank, Multi-Purpose Bank, Bumiputra Commerce Bank, Perwira Affin Bank, Public Bank, and Southern Bank. It was felt that Malaysia's 58 financial institutions (21 commercial banks, 12 merchant banks, and 25 financial companies) with a total of 2,712 branches was too many for a population of 22 million. The aim was to make Malaysian banks big enough and efficient enough to withstand the further entry of foreign competitors in 2003, the year financial markets are due to be liberalized under a World Trade Organization pact. The plan, however, was met with significant protest as a couple of the larger and well-managed banks were not nominated as an anchor bank. On the back of perceived market difficulties and heavy lobbying, the government relented and gave all banks further time to arrange their own mergers. Following applications and negotiations, in February 2000, the central bank announced the finalization of the consolidation process, which saw the emergence of ten lead banks going forward. In addition to the original six, RHB, Arab Malaysian, EON and Hong Leong were selected.

Regulatory Initiatives

The central bank introduced a policy of indefinite regulatory forbearance to enable banks to more easily return to profitability. Policy changes included:

❑ Loosening the definition of NPLs from the international standard of three months to six months

❑ Reducing specific provisioning requirements on substandard loans

❑ Allowing restructured NPLs to be classified as performing if not in default for a continuous six months rather than the 12 months previously

❑ Relaxing limits on lending for purchasing shares and unit trusts

❑ Ordering banks to set up in-house "loan administration units"

SOUTH KOREA RESTRUCTURING PROGRAM

South Korea had long followed a policy of using its banking system to finance industrial development. Like Japan, to which its banking system bears some resemblance, directed lending was long a pervasive practice and for practical purposes part of public policy. Bank lending in South Korea was highly concentrated to the conglomerates known as *chaebol*, which had been the engines that drove the miraculous transformation of the country into an industrial powerhouse. By the mid-1990s, fed on a steady diet of cheap and seemingly never-ending bank financing, the *chaebol* had grown into gargantuan companies that had become obsessed with market share at the expense of profitability. Weighed down by their obligation to lend to the *chaebol* at razor thin spreads South Korean bank profitability was miniscule. Unable to generate capital internally, their capital adequacy was correspondingly marginal. These circumstances made the South Korean financial system highly vulnerable to outside shock, and when it came with the Asian crisis in the autumn of 1997, the impact was both sudden and dramatic.

Following an October 1997 announcement that it would establish a fund to assist local banks in writing off NPLs, in response to the financial crisis which hit the country hard toward the end of the year, South Korea embarked on an IMF-induced reform blueprint in December 1997. The Financial Supervisory Commission (FSC), the restructuring agency that was set up in April 1998, initially set out to identify and classify all financial institutions as either viable, non-viable or viable yet weak. The FSC orchestrated the closure and consolidation of many of these institutions, with an initial emphasis on the banks. The FSC initially moved to take into receivership the two most distressed banks — Korea First Bank and Seoul Bank. In January 1998, the government had already effectively nationalized Korea First Bank by taking a majority stake. The intention was to rehabilitate these institutions to the extent they could be auctioned off to new — preferably foreign — owners and negotiations began to dispose of them. The restructuring agency pursued reform and consolidation of the banking institutions via: 1) mergers; 2) fiscal support

(NPL sales and recapitalization); 3) fresh equity injections; 4) staff and branch redundancies; and, 5) management reform. Like Malaysia, South Korea implemented a variant of the AMC model of bank recapitalization. Fiscal support was engineered primarily through two agencies — Korea Asset Management Corporation (KAMCO) and Korea Deposit Insurance Corporation (KDIC).

The Institutions

Korea Asset Management Corporation (KAMCO)

In the classic AMC mode, KAMCO is a state-run enterprise charged with the responsibility to aggressively purchase bad loans at financial institutions with the ultimate aim of selling them back — ideally as performing loans — to the market. It had actually been established well prior to the Asian crisis, in 1992, for the purpose of resolving bad loans within the South Korean financial system. With the onset of the severe financial crisis in late 1997, it achieved a new prominence following its reorganization and the grant to it of new powers in November of that year. Modeled after the Resolution Trust Corp., the entity that was established in the United States to deal with the savings and loan crisis, KAMCO was essentially to take on the role of a "bad bank," acquiring the non-performing loans of financial institutions in exchange for government bonds, and disposing of the NPLs to maximize recovery on them. In this connection, it was responsible for managing collateralized assets and developing real estate in an effort to raise their value. An additional role for KAMCO was to include entering the foreign capital markets by packaging the assets of troubled banks into asset-backed securities. KAMCO acted quickly to acquire NPLs from ailing banks, purchasing 20 trillion won (W) bank assets with a face value of W44 trillion by end-1998. By September 2000, the total amount had risen to W76.7 trillion, with the expectation at that time being that perhaps another W20 trillion remained to be absorbed by the agency.

Korea Deposit Insurance Corporation (KDIC)

The principle function of KDIC is to provide protection to depositors of funds (both principal and interest) in the ROK's financial institutions. The maximum allowable deposit claim after year 2000 is limited to W20mn (US$15k). An additional role is to deal with extended, distressed financial

NPLs Bought by KAMCO, through End 1998

NPLs bought by KAMCO

(W bn)	Financial institutions	Face amount	Purchase price	Average purhase price (%)
26/11/97	KFB and Seoul Bank	4,394.3	2,910.3	66.2
28/11/97	30 merchant banks	2,698.8	1,755.5	65.0
12/12/97	30 commercial banks	3,951.0	2,474.3	62.6
19/02/98	2 fidelity & surety companies	2,816.6	412.1	14.6
23/07/98	Seoul Bank	1,040.0	498.9	48.0
31/07/98	KFB and Seoul Bank	1,133.5	606.6	53.5
30/09/98	5 closed banks	4,608.9	956.7	20.8
30/09/98	5 acquired banks	2,617.0	1,220.6	46.6
30/09/98	4 merged banks	4,873.9	2,355.4	48.3
30/09/98	9 banks	7,830.7	3,579.6	45.7
30/09/98	2 fidelity & surety companies	3,046.2	954.3	31.3
06/11/98	2 regional banks & NBFIs	496.9	261.6	52.6
29/12/98	Government-owned banks	4,530.0	1,903.0	42.0
Total		**44,037.8**	**19,888.9**	**45.2**

Source: KAMCO, CSFB

institutions by providing them with financial assistance or liquidating them. It is the South Korean counterpart of Danamodal in Malaysia, which, as discussed in the previous section, has as its purpose the rehabilitation and recapitalization of banks in that country.

KDIC is not capitalized; however it receives funding through a variety of channels that include:

❑ Insurance premiums and contributions from participating financial institutions.

❑ Deposit Insurance Fund bond issues.

❑ Government and central bank borrowings.

❑ Write-backs and recovery of funds extended to failed institutions.

The South Korean government committed US$50 billion through these agencies to support those institutions that deliver viable rehabilitation plans. Such plans must initially incorporate voluntary capital write-downs, new foreign capital inducements, installations of new boards and management, and wholesale reductions in costs stemming from both staff and branch redundancies.

The Financial Supervisory Commission (FSC)

Prior to the Asian crisis, South Korea's regulation of its banking system was fragmented. The Bank of Korea and the Ministry of Finance and

Economy, and several offices and departments within each, shared responsibility and coordination and accountability were lacking. The consequence was a deficient system of prudential regulation and bank supervision. In December 1997, as part of a regulatory initiative designed to give more autonomy to the Bank of Korea, a separate Financial Supervisory Commission was set up. It is fully responsible for licensing financial institutions, promulgating prudential regulations and through the FSS, described below, examining and supervising their operations. The FSC is under the office of the Prime Minister, but it in effect operates as an independent body. The FSC also oversees the Financial Supervisory Service (FSS), formerly the Financial Supervisory Board, which is charged with the examination and inspection of financial institutions under the guidance of the FSC, together with input from the Securities and Futures Commission. The FSS was designed to tie together the functions previously ineffectively handled by several bodies into a unified entity.

The Process of Restructuring in South Korea

Mergers

With the framework for bank restructuring in place by April, the government was able to begin the process in earnest. It closed five insolvent banks in June, which held on their books 7.3% of the country's bank loans. Rather than liquidating them, it allocated public funds to purchase the failed banks' NPLs and infuse new capital into the banks. It was then in a position to oversee a merger of the five resuscitated institutions with five healthy banks. Under the terms of merger deals involving weak or failed banks, the acquiring banks were obliged to assume only "good" loans, which are defined as those in the "normal" and "precautionary" categories. Additionally, the acquiring banks were offered an option to put-back to KAMCO any precautionary loans should such loans had turned bad prior to September 1999. The banks were also offered guarantees of subsidy from the KDIC up to end-March 1999 on unrealized losses on the assumption of securities portfolios, as well as the discretion on the assumption of fixed assets (branches and personnel). The acquiring banks were also promised the option to decline assumption of the performance-based trust accounts. On the liabilities side of the balance sheets, the acquiring banks were obliged to assume all obligations, excluding severance and pension provisions, with KDIC support for all net liability transfers.

Assets Assumed through P&A of Five Banks					
(W billion)			Government Capital Injection		
Acquiror	Exit Banks	Assets Taken Over	Make Up Hole	Preferred Shares	Subordinated Debt
Shinhan	Dongwha	6,945	1,574	293	146
Koram	Kyunggi	5,530	1,721	270	140
HCB	Dongnam	5,407	681	297	148
Kookmin	Daedong	4,073	1,065	200	100
Hana	Chungchung	2,766	774	460	70
Total		**24,721**	**5,815**	**1,519**	**604**
Source: Korea Deposit Insurance Corp.					

Goldman Sachs Investments Research

Following the initial forced mergers, a number of other banks also entered into voluntary mergers. In August, Hanil Bank and Commercial Bank of Korea, two of the country's largest banks, merged to form a new institution: Hanvit Bank. In September 1998, two other major banks, Hana Bank and Boram Bank, combined (surviving entity: Hana) while a short time later Kookmin Bank, and Korean Long Term Credit Bank also united (surviving entity: Kookmin).

Foreign Capital

Unlike Malaysia, which sought to solve its banking problems internally, South Korea at an early stage in the crisis recognized a need for greater foreign participation in the banking sector. In contrast to Malaysia, the country had a significant amount of foreign debt — a major reason that it opted for IMF assistance while Malaysia did not — and its banking problem was more grave. A majority foreign interest in Korea First Bank, which was the first bank to be taken over by the government in January 1998, was acquired by Newbridge Capital after protracted negotiations that finally led to a deal and to an initial investment in January 2000. Negotiations with HSBC for the purchase of an interest in the other bank made available to foreign holding, Seoul Bank, ultimately broke down after extended talks. In other cases, foreign banks took stakes ranging from a largely passive investment to more active, albeit minority owner-ship. (See table on the page 493.)

Some South Korean banks were also able to tap the foreign capital markets both for short-term and longer-term Tier 2 subordinated debt issues.

Chronology of Financial Sector Restructuring in South Korea

Date	Events
12/4/97	Korea adopts the IMF program
12/2/97	Business suspension of nine merchant banks
12/10/97	Business suspension of five more merchant banks (Daehan, Nara, Shinhan, Central, Hanwha)
12/12/97	FSC issues business improvement order to KFB and Seoul Bank
12/19/97	Business suspension of Shinsegi Investment Trust Company
12/29/97	Financial Reform Act passes the National Assembly
1/15/98	Capital reduction order on KFB and Seoul Bank
1/30/98	Government injects W1.5 trillion capital to each of KFB and Seoul Bank
1/31/98	Assets and liabilities of suspended merchant banks decided to be transferred to bridge merchant bank
2/17/98	License of ten merchant banks revoked
2/26/98	FSC issues business improvement recommendation to 12 banks with BIS ratios of less than 8%
3/23/98	Business suspension of Korea First Merchant Bank
3/16/98	License of Hansol Merchant Bank revoked
4/1/98	Financiat Supervisory Service launched
4/1/98	License of Daegu Merchant Bank revoked
4/15/98	License of Samyang Merchant Ban revoked
4/30/98	12 banks with less than 8% BIS ratio submit rehabilitation plan
5/15/98	Business suspension of Saehan Merchant Bank
5/18/98	License of Korea First Merchant Bank revoked
6/1/98	License of Coryo Securities and Dongsuh Securities revoked
6/12/98	Business suspension of Hangil Merchant Bank
6/29/98	Exit of 5 fragile banks through P&A, conditional approval on the rehabilitation plan of seven banks
7/4/98	Business suspension of KLB Securities
7/25/98	Business suspension of Korea Development Securities
7/31/98	Commercial Bank of Korea and Hanil Bank announce merger
8/11/98	Business suspension of four life insurance companies (Kukje, BYC, Taeyang, Coryo)
8/12/98	License of Saehan, Hangil Merchant Bank revoked
8/14/98	Business suspension of Hannam Investment Securities and Hannam Investment Trust Management
8/21/98	Transfer of four life insurance companies under suspension to four good companies through P&A
8/25/98	Kookmin Investment Trust Co. takes over Hannam Investment Trust
9/8/98	Hana Bank announces merger with Boram Bank
9/11/98	Kookmin Bank announces merger with Korea Long-Term Credit Bank
9/14/98	Capital reduction of Commercial Bank of Korea and Hanil Bank
9/25/98	Conditional approval of rehabilitation plan of two securities companies (SK and Ssangyong)
9/25/98	Rejection of rehabilitation plan of KLB securities and Dongbang Peregrine Securities
12/17/98	Chohung Bank announces merger with Kangwon Bank
12/30/98	Sale of Korea First Bank to New Bridge Capital of the United States
1/15/99	Injection of public money to five good banks to support their BIS ratios
2/22/99	Sale of Seoul Bank to HSBC

Source: Goldman Sachs.

Foreign Bank Alliances with Korean Commercial Banks

Main Foreign Alliances with Korean Commercial Baks				
Bank	Foreign partner	Stake (percent)	Date of initial investment	Scope of partnership
Korea First Bank	Nebridge Capital	51	January 2000	Full management control rests in Newbridge's hands.
Housing and Commercial Bank (H&CB)	ING Group	10	August 1999	Cooperation extends to mutual investments in ING's Korean life insurance subsidiary, and H&CB's investment trust subsidiary.
Kookmin Bank	Goldman Sachs Capital Partners	11.3	May 1999	Goldman Sachs is essentially a passive investor, although the strategic alliance offers Koomin access to Goldman Sachs's investment banking expertise.
Korea Exchange Bank	Commerzbank	27.7	July 1998	Two Commerzbank directors on the board, responsible for developing Korean Exchange Bank's corporate lending, credit analysis and capital market business; plans to help develop risk management, among other key areas.
KorAm Bank	Bank of America	16.8	March 1983	Bank of America has direct representation on the bank's credit committee and provides various advanced banking techniques; KorAm Bank adopted Bank of America's credit procedures and systems from its early days.

Source: Thomson Financial Bank Watch.

Corporate Restructuring

Corporate restructuring was also a major part of the government's reform program. Recognizing that the corporate sector had been too long dominated by the *chaebol*, revitalizing the small- and medium-sized enterprise sector became a priority. Funds were designated to help viable small- and medium-sized enterprises restructure their loans, while banks were offered both a carrot and stick to lend to such SMEs. While this did present dangers as being a form of directed lending, it was arguably a justifiable attempt to redress the imbalance that had long existed between the over-leveraged *chaebol* and other smaller firms that represented hope for future growth.

Meanwhile, various restrictions were placed on the *chaebol*. The 30 largest were prohibited from new cross-guarantees and existing cross-guarantees were to be terminated by 2000. Such cross-guarantees had enabled the *chaebol* to borrow on the basis that they were too big to fail. More significantly, interest on loans that were in excess of five times equity capital were made no longer tax-deductible. Government pressure under a new administration led the five largest — Hyundai, Samsung, Daewoo, LG and SK — to begin serious restructuring. Specific commitments were made to reduce the number of subsidiaries, reduce leverage, sell off assets, and raise new capital.

South Korean banks have been encouraged to restructure corporate loans through maturity extensions and interest holidays. However, this may only be postponing the classification of NPLs. A loophole also exists in some restructured assets. Officially banks must carry converted equity and convertible bonds at market values. However, with the lack of liquidity, market values are difficult to ascertain and banks can hold equity at any value. Convertible bonds are usually carried at very high values, leading to an overstatement of a bank's actual capital position. This will also encourage banks to hold onto converted equity stakes.

Prudential Regulation

Probably the most important step in improving prudential regulation of banks was the reorganization of the bank supervision function under a new and independent agency, the Financial Supervisory Commission. Together, the FSC and its affiliated agency, the Financial Supervisory Service (FSS), have tightened the regulation and supervision of South Korean banks. New capital adequacy requirements were imposed, more rigorous liquidity management rules were put into place, and extensive changes governing asset quality, including the definition of NPLs, provisioning requirements, and lending restrictions were set forth. Efforts were also made to improve disclosure, which had been less than adequate. The table below indicates some of the measures implemented to provide better transparency.

Recent Developments

More recently, in July 2000, the South Korean government's restructuring program has come under pressure from banking unions fearful of large-scale job losses as a result of planned mergers between banks. Plans to allow the creation of bank holding companies should speed up reform and promote bank mergers, thus leading to sector consolidation.

Kamco acquisitions to September 2000

	Amount purchased (A)	Purchased price (B)	Ratio B/A	Implied loss ratio
Ordinary loans (subtotal)	26.3	9.3	35%	65%
Secured	11.7	7.2	62%	38%
Unsecured	14.6	2	14%	86%
Daewoo/ITC	18.5	6.4	35%	65%
Restructured loans (subtotal)	31	13.8	45%	55%
Secured	18.7	10	53%	47%
Unsecured	12.3	3.8	31%	69%
Total	75.7	29.5	39%	61%
Source: Kamco				

Kamco acquisition by institutions to September 2000

Financial institutions	Face value (A)	Purchase price (B)	Ratio (B/A)	Implied loss ratio
Commercial banks	47.2	19.5	41%	59%
Merchant banks	2.7	1.8	67%	33%
Guarantee Insurance Corp	7	1.7	24%	76%
Insurance Companies	0.02	0.005	25%	75%
Securities Companies	0.1	0.06	60%	40%
ITC's & Savings	18.7	6.5	35%	65%
Total	75.7	29.5	39%	61%
Source: Kamco				

Disposition to date

Sales method	Face amount (Wtn)	Purchase price (Wtn)	Amount retrieved (Wtn)
International bidding	5.4	1.4	1.6
ABS Issuance	6.2	3.3	3.3
Foreclosure Auction	2.9	1.7	2.4
Kamco Auction	0.5	0.3	0.3
Individual loan sale	0.5	0.2	0.2
Sale to AMC, CRC	3.1	0.9	1.5
Others	5.7	2	3.1
Sub-total	24.3	9.9	12.4
Recourse & Cancellation	14.3	7.7	7.7
Source: Kamco			

Source: HSBC; KAMCO

Korea: Main Steps Taken to Improve Transparency

Publish data on usable foreign reseves twice a month
Publish data on external debt once a month
Provide monthly data on the consolidated central government's revenue, expenditure, and financing (effective July 1999)
Strengthen accounting standards to ensure full compliance by financial institutions with the minimum requirements of International Accounting Standard 30
Upgrade standards for disclosure, auditing, and accounting to the level of international best prcatice (effective January 1999)
Require listed companies to publish quarterly financial statments (as of Janauary 2000)
Require large business conglomerates to submit consolidated financial statements (effective year-end 1999)
Require the appointment of outside directors at listed companies (efffective February 1998)
Strengthen the rights of minority shareholders by allowing collective action and the right of appeal (effective May 1998)
Publish on an ongoing basis details of all public support for financial sector restructuring.

Source: Korea's Ministry of Financial and Economy.

Source: East Asia Bank Restructuring

In December 2000, a merger between Kookmin Bank and Housing and Commercial Bank was announced that precipitated protests by bank workers. In addition, plans were put forward to create a "corporate restructuring vehicle" to provide additional impetus to the process of corporate restructuring.

CHAPTER SUMMARY

This chapter discusses in somewhat greater detail the process of bank restructuring and recapitalization as implemented in two countries which were affected by the Asian crisis of 1997-98: Malaysia and South Korea. Both countries adopted an approach using an asset management corporation structure, but differed in how they implemented bank rehabilitation.

In Malaysia the problem was arguably less severe and the government was able to mobilize quickly to take action. It had the benefit of experience during the 1980s in dealing with a severe banking crisis and also had minimal foreign debt so did not need to involve the IMF or foreign banks. It was therefore able to pursue a policy of limiting capital flows that was much criticized at the time, but which in retrospect may have facilitated a more rapid economic recovery. Three agencies were created: Danaharta to purchase bad loans from the banks and dispose of them, Danamodal to recapitalize troubled banks and the CDRC to facilitate corporate restructuring. In addition, firm action was taken to force consolidation within the banking sector.

South Korea's problem was more severe as a consequence of higher foreign debt, a larger economy, and the fact that the banking system and the major conglomerates were more tightly linked. The South Korean government set up KAMCO, an AMC, while the KDIC functioned to support and recapitalize weak financial institutions. The FSC meanwhile focused on improving prudential regulation. More reliance was placed on foreign involvement and foreign entities were invited to bid for two nationalized banks: Seoul Bank and Korea First Bank. At the same time, the authorities encouraged consolidation within the sector.

CHAPTER TWENTY THREE

THE DISTRESSED BANK, PART V: ILLUSTRATIVE APPROACHES TO RESTRUCTURING — INDONESIA AND THAILAND

The definition of a 'non-performing loan' is a central question in efforts to recapitalize banks since it determines the amount of capital necessary to fulfill BIS requirements and maintain solvency.
> — Dr. Andrew Freris & Daisy Shum, "A Survey of Banking Reform in Asia," Bank of America, July 1999

Banks are actually no more accident-prone than other businesses. It's just that their gearing makes it more likely that mistakes will be fatal...
> — Martin Taylor, CEO of Barclays Bank[1]

Dumb lending is usually at the heart of any financial crisis.
> — Charles R. Morris

INDONESIAN BANK RESTRUCTURING

Indonesia was the hardest hit of all the Asian countries affected by the post-July 1997 financial havoc. It not only had to cope with one of the most severe of the banking system collapses, but the nation went through

---

[1]Cited *The Bankers*, p. 392.

a wrenching political crisis as well, which resulted in one of the longest serving rulers in the region, General Suharto, leaving office. In June 1997, just prior to the crisis, system-wide NPLs stood at about 13%, according to Indonesia's central bank. Total bank system NPLs rose quickly to 80% as the turbulence ensued, one of the highest figures reached in any banking crisis in modern times. If for no other reason, a brief description of the Indonesian experience is instructive.

Before things went awry, Indonesia's banking system was one of the weakest in the region, although the published financial indicators did not always tell the full story. Relaxation of controls over banking licenses in the 1990s resulted in a wave of new banks such that by 1997 Indonesia was perhaps the most over-banked country in the region with 162 private commercial banks. Although the appropriate bank regulations were largely in place, supervision was another matter. According to former Thomson BankWatch analyst Mark Jones,the Indonesian banking system was characterized by "rampant related-party lending by private commercial banks" and "politically driven lending by the state-owned banks." Coupled with weak bank supervision, the inability of creditors to exercise their rights, "poor and unreliable disclosure" and a sharp expansion of lending, the Indonesian banking system was an accident waiting to happen.

The Asian crisis had a profound effect on the viability of almost all Indonesia's banks. While the factors just mentioned were an explosive combination, the spark that triggered the collapse of the banking system in Indonesia was the economic dislocation resulting from a 70% devaluation of the rupiah within a space of just six months. This caused all but the most comprehensively hedged of Indonesia's many foreign currency borrowers to be unable to meet their loan obligations. Aggravating the situation was a rise in domestic interest rates from 12% pre-crisis to an average of 61% over the eight months ending November 1998, in what in retrospect was a misguided effort to support the rupiah. The consequence was that all but the most profitable of rupiah borrowers were unable to meet their loan obligations. Ultimately, these factors led to the quick collapse and closure of many banks which, along with mergers between state banks, led to wide-ranging structural changes as detailed in the table below. Notably, the state-owned banks' share of the system's assets has increased since the onset of the crisis — from 36% to 46% as at end-September 1999. The state banks have largely been the recipients of a flight to quality during the crisis. Incoming funds were mainly used by these banks to acquire central bank paper.

Structural Development of the Indonesian Banking Industry				
	Number of Banks		Assets/Sector Assets (%)	
Bank Type	30/6/97	30/9/99	30/6/97	30/9/99
State Owned Banks	7	4	36	46
Private National Banks	160	92	52	38
Foreign Banks	16	16	4	9
Joint-Venture Banks	28	25	5	5
Development Banks	27	27	3	2
Total	238	164	100	100
Source: Bank Indonesia				

IBRA and the Approach to Restructuring

Although the IMF began working with the government from an early stage and as early as November 1997 seventeen distressed banks were closed, financial system reform was slowed as political developments soon took center stage. The process of restructuring has thus been a protracted one. As was the case in Korea and Malaysia, the authorities employed a modified AMC approach. Because of Indonesia's high foreign debt, resolving foreign currency obligations was especially important. Also, as a consequence of the large number of insolvent banks, it was recognized early on that closure and consolidation would overshadow recapitalization initiatives (although recapitalization was undertaken selectively), and liquidation of insolvent banks was used in many cases.

Indonesian Bank Restructuring Agency (IBRA)

The institution with the lead role in driving banking restructuring, the Indonesian Bank Restructuring Agency (IBRA), was set up in January 1998. Its role was to rehabilitate the banking sector through various means, including recapitalization, restructuring and nationalization or liquidation and the transfer of assets either to it as an asset management corporation, or to a third party. A sub-agency, the Indonesian Asset Management Unit (AMU) was also established at the same time to actually handle the day-to-day asset management function with respect to bad loans and collateral.

Initially, the government was criticized for not giving IBRA enough power while at the same time it was alleged that political pressure was influencing its decisionmaking. To reduce political jockeying, the agency was put under the direct control of the president, and was also given more authority to effect bank restructuring. In the process of reaching settlements with some bank owners, IBRA became the steward of substantial corporate assets, the sale of which would help defray the costs of the agency's liquidity support for failed financial institutions.

In February 1998, IBRA provided liquidity support to 54 banks, although ultimately seven of them were deemed beyond help and were put into the hands of the AMU in August 1998. By end-1998, a total of 29 banks had been closed, and as of the date of this writing, that number had risen to 68, which represented about 14% of the banking system's total assets. Of these non-viable banks, most were closed in three blocks with the initial closures (previously mentioned) in November 1997, ten in April 1998, and 38 in March 1999. Included, however, were Bank Dagang Negara Indonesia (which was, prior to the crisis, the country's ninth largest bank and fourth largest private national bank representing 4% of the system's total assets) and Bank Umum Nasional (which was the eighth largest private national bank representing 2% of the system's assets).

State Banks

The existing state banks fell from seven prior to the crisis as a result of the merger of four state banks. Out of this merger, the state-owned Bank Mandiri was formed which, with 30% of the banking system's total assets, is now by far the largest bank in the country. At present, the government plans to sell off almost all of its bank holdings so as to generate funds in order to alleviate its domestic debt situation.

Surviving Private Banks and the Problem of Recapitalization

Of the 92 surviving private national banks, almost all have had to be recapitalized, in most cases, by a substantial amount. As a number of these banks' owners were unable or unwilling to recapitalize their banks, the government has been forced to provide the necessary recapitalization funds therefore gaining ownership of such banks in the process. More specifically, of the 92 remaining private national banks, 20 are now majority-owned by the Indonesian government by way of stakes ranging from 75% to 100%. Included in these 20 banks are the country's six largest private national banks (Bank Central Asia, Bank Internasional Indonesia, Bank Danamon, Bank Lippo, Bank Bali, and Bank Niaga) which together accounted for about 25% of the Indonesian banking system as at September 30,1999. Meanwhile, the other 14 private national banks now majority-owned by the Indonesian government are considerably smaller, together accounting for around 5% of the banking system. Hence, including the state banks, the government now wholly- or majority-owns 24 banks which together represent around 75% of the system's total assets. Over the coming year or two, it is the government's intention to aggressively sell off substantial stakes in these banks, including the state-owned banks, to both local and foreign investors. These sales began in 2000, with a public offering of 30% of Bank Central Asia, the largest private national bank which represents around 12% of the system's total assets. At the time of writing, the government is in the process of merging nine of these smaller banks into Bank Danamon.

The upshot was that, the government gained majority ownership of all 20 of these banks which, given that they included the country's six largest private national banks, accounted for around 30% of the banking system's total assets. Badly in need of fresh funds, they were recapitalized by the government via long-term rupiah-denominated bonds. Including the existing state-owned banks, the government obtained a majority stake in some 24 banks which represented some 75% of the banking system's total assets as at end March 2000.

The government holds no stakes in the 72 remaining private national banks, which represent around 9% of the system's total assets. These banks are generally quite small. They were able to survive largely on account of their high liquidity (usually due to exceptionally loyal customer bases) which enabled them to take advantage of the high interest rates available on central bank paper during the crisis. These banks also tended to have a low level of exposure to foreign currency borrowers.[2] Nevertheless, many of these banks did suffer considerably during the crisis and had to be substantially recapitalized by their owners during 1999. Many of these recapitalizations however were apparently insufficient and expectations are that a number of these 72 remaining smaller private national banks will be closed by the government over the coming year.

---

[2] In fact, prior to the crisis, many of the smaller private national banks did not have a foreign exchange license and were therefore effectively excluded from being able to enter the market of foreign currency lending to Indonesian corporations.

Recapitalization through Government Bonds

In common with the tack taken in Korea and Malaysia, Indonesia's national AMC, IBRA, recapitalized surviving banks largely with government bonds. Following the government's bailout of the banking system, which was due to be completed during 2000, most of the banks' NPLs will have been written off, and about 40% of the system's total assets will be in the form of government bonds. These bonds are largely risk free especially the bulk of the bonds carry floating rates of interest, and foreign exchange risk is excluded (the bonds are denominated in rupiah).

During 1999, the government issued IDR500 trillion in bonds in order to recapitalize the country's banking system. A further IDR145 trillion is expected to be issued over 2000 to complete the recapitalization program. Rather than issue these bonds to the public, the government is injecting these bonds directly into the banks. Around 43% of the bonds have been issued to the four state banks, 34% to the central bank, and 23% to the 20 private banks.

In terms of maturity and yield, the bonds issued to date are broken down as follows.

Maturity	Yield	Indonesian Rupiah—trillions
3 month to	floating rate of SIBOR + 2%	27
five year	floating rate of 91 day central	204
3–10 year	bank paper + 0%	
5–10 year/	fixed rate of 12% to 14%	51
20 year	floating rate of inflation + 3%	218
Total		500

The Indonesian government is planning to partly offset the interest and principal payments on the bonds through the privatization of state-owned corporations and asset sales by Indonesian Bank Restructuring Agency (IBRA). Many of the state-owned corporations, however, are in a poor financial state and the generation of substantial revenues from their privatization is unlikely. IBRA expects asset sales to generate a total of around IDR210 trillion over the next five years. This may prove optimistic with IBRA's track record of asset sales to date having been disappointing, largely due to a lack of foreign investor interest. IBRA's assets include: (i) stakes in some of Indonesia's largest corporates;

(ii) entire ownership of many smaller corporates; and, (iii) majority ownership of Indonesia's six largest private banks. These assets were acquired by IBRA as a result of:

❑ Assuming stakes in the companies previously owned by some of Indonesia's leading tycoons.[3]

❑ The transferal of loans and related security to IBRA from numerous banks in the country.

❑ Assuming ownership of some of Indonesia's major private banks following the government's recapitalization of these banks.

During 1999, several policy actions also helped banks rebuild capital. First, with the assistance of IBRA, they were able to write-off a very high level of NPLs, and second, the government injected into the banks as capital IDR207 trillion worth of rupiah-denominated government bonds specially issued by the government for this purpose (recorded under "Claims on the Central government"). Meanwhile, with regard to liabilities, the government effectively forgave the banks a large portion of their borrowings from the central bank. Overall, the loan losses incurred by the banks together with a further substantial negative level of net interest income over the year were largely offset by the government's injection of bonds and its debt forgiveness. Hence, the banks' equity position as at September 30,1999 was relatively unchanged from that nine months earlier.

Since September 1999, the government has injected another IDR75 trillion into the banks and it was expected to inject a further IDR145 trillion in 2000 — all in the form of specially-issued government recapitalization bonds. Also during 2000, the banks were expected to largely provide for and write off their remaining NPLs. Following this, the recapitalization of Indonesia's banks will be largely complete although the potential for the closure of a number of smaller private national banks may require the issuance of additional bonds. With regard to the quality of the banks' overall asset base, post-recapitalization, the system's total assets will be around 40% made up of recapitalization bonds. Of these bonds, around 80% will carry a floating rate of interest. All the bonds will be denominated in rupiah and issued by the government.

---

[3] Following the inability of these tycoons' banks to repay liquidity credits extended to them by the central bank during deposit runs early in 1998 and following the subsequent discovery that much of these banks' credits had been extended to related parties.

In view of these recapitalization efforts, it appeared that the overall quality of the banking system's asset base and capital base will, upon completion, have been sufficiently restored. Also, interest earned by the system on the bonds and the reasonable quality of the loan base, should ensure the system as a whole returns to a positive, albeit very low, level of profitability over 2000/2001. The banks, however, may find it difficult to sell their bond holdings on the open market due to a lack of domestic investor capacity and, particularly given the risk of rupiah devaluation, a lack of foreign investor interest. As such, over time, the bonds may constrain the banks' rupiah liquidity, which could limit their ability to engage in lending activities.

At present, the banks are only allowed to sell 10% of the recapitalization bonds they are holding. Over the next year or so, however, the banks are expected to be allowed to trade the remainder of their recapitalization bond holdings. It is questionable, however, whether the banks will ultimately be able to sell any sizeable amount of the bonds they are holding. The problem basically lies with the fact that: (i) the quantum of the bonds is far too high for the local market to absorb; and, (ii) foreign investors may not be prepared to purchase the bonds, given the foreign exchange risk incurred from holding the bonds. This, in turn, will limit the banks' profitability. At present, however, this is a longer-term risk given that demand for credit in Indonesia is currently low and is expected to remain so for some time to come.

Corporate Restructuring

By the end of 1997, corporate foreign debt had reached nearly US$80 billion. In August 1998, the Indonesian Debt Restructuring Agency (INDRA) was set up to help companies restructure their foreign debt. The concept was that INDRA would arrange voluntary workouts between Indonesian corporates and foreign creditors and in turn INDRA would help by providing foreign exchange at a comparatively low rate.

The "Jakarta Initiative" was launched in September 1998 and was an effort to reinforce INDRA by attempting to promote out-of-court workouts between debtors and creditors. On the one hand, debtors are required to disclose their accounts fully, while on the other they are offered assistance in restructuring their debts.

Prudential Regulation and Other Regulatory Changes

One of the most heralded pieces of regulatory reform during the restructuring process was the enactment of a new bankruptcy law in August 1998. The old law, based on Dutch colonial antecedents, was unwieldy and the accompanying legal proceedings inevitably long and drawn out. The liquidation of Bank Summa during the early 1990s, for example, took seven years to complete. Creditors were well advised by their lawyers to steer clear of bankruptcy proceeding. Given the precarious position many debtors found themselves in, it is not surprising that any

Illustration: Jakarta Initiative (Corporate Restructuring)

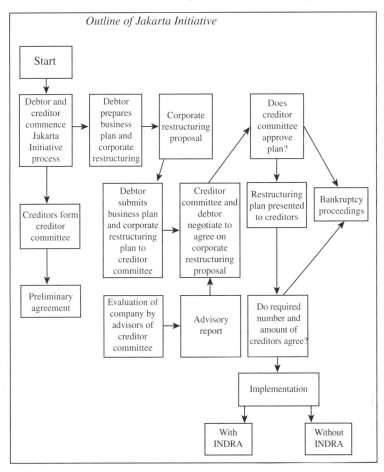

inclination to engage in stalling tactics was aggravated by the advantage the old law seemed to give borrowers. The new law considerably speeded up the process of restructuring and established a separate commercial court to handle bankruptcy matters. Under the best of circumstances, it will be some time before judges become familiar with new concepts and principles and a body of law and precedent protecting creditors' rights is built up. Nonetheless, the new law was widely regarded as being a positive step forward.

THAILAND'S RESTRUCTURING PROGRAM

We return to where the Asian crisis began: Thailand. Although also under IMF supervision from an early date, Thailand followed a somewhat different course than the other members of the "IMF 3" and Malaysia in its restructuring efforts. When the crisis began, the Thai banking sector, and the economy as a whole, were in highly leveraged positions. The ratio of total loans to GDP was very high and the banks had heavy exposure to foreign currency liabilities. In addition, Thailand had a large non-bank financial sector that was closely linked to the country's commercial banks, but which had outpaced them in profligate lending. Indeed, Thailand's financial system crisis can be said to have begun in its finance company sector, and it was the resulting erosion of confidence that contributed to a run on the baht and its ultimate "devaluation." In June 1997, prior to devaluation, the government closed 16 of the country's 91 finance companies and an additional 42 were shuttered in August (although in December, two were eventually allowed to resume operations). More finance companies, however, were closed since 1998, leaving just 23 at end 1999. Assets of the failed companies were taken over by the Financial Sector Restructuring Agency (FRA), discussed below.

The authorities' initial response was to restore stability to the banking sector and then focus on a market-led strategy to restructuring both the banking and corporate sectors. Established in 1985, the Financial Institutions Development Fund (FIDF), which is under the authority of the Bank of Thailand (BoT), resumed its role of providing liquidity assistance to local banks and financial institutions. As such, the FIDF also was set to become the primary government vehicle to facilitate bank recapitalization. The enabling legislation creating the FIDF was amended in August 1997 to provide a blanket, albeit temporary guarantee for depositors and creditors of financial institutions. Both measures were designed to stanch panic in the sector and allow the government to deal with reform of the financial system in an orderly manner.

Under the temporary program, the government, operating via the FIDF, guaranteed repayments to depositors and creditors in Thai baht. For depositors, the guarantee covered the full repayment of principal and interest, provided that the rate of interest did not exceed the average three-month deposit rate plus 3% per annum. For creditors the interest rate was minimum lending rate minus 4%. Excluded were directors, related parties or senior management. In the meantime, the government began work on setting up the Deposit Insurance Agency (DIA) to replace the blanket guarantee and develop a plan for a limited self-financed deposit insurance system. At the time of this writing, the Deposit Insurance Bill was undergoing final stages of review by legal experts. Under the plan, the government was to finance the start-up fund and DIA members would have to make an annual contribution accordingly to guarantee deposits.

In October 1997, the government established the Financial System Restructuring Authority (FRA) and the Asset Management Corporation. The latter was set up to buy NPLs from the finance companies, including those which had been closed, and the former was to auction the assets associated with the NPLs. A variant of the familiar AMC structure we have seen before, it should be emphasized that this structure was designed to deal only with the finance companies, and not with the NPLs held by Thailand's commercial banks.[4]

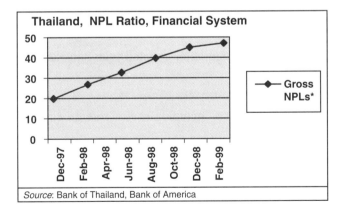

Source: Bank of Thailand, Bank of America

---

[4] Note that subsequent to the final preparation of this chapter a national AMC designed to target bank NPLs was proposed.

The banks were in serious difficulty when the Asian crisis hit, and arguably their condition helped precipitate it. While nominally profitable, they were among the least liquid in Asia and their capital strength was marginal. Excessively funding themselves with short-term foreign currency facilities, and then lending the proceeds to customers in either in local or foreign currency placed them in a precarious position in the event the baht, which had remained stable for many years, collapsed. When the baht did collapse on July 2, 1997, the consequences were traumatic.

Banks saw the quality of their assets deteriorate and their non-performing loans (NPLs) soared to around 50% of total loans, as the country slipped into a recession. Six of the weakest banks that were incapable of recapitalizing had to be taken over by the government. All the banks have recapitalized at least twice in the last two years. They all remain weakly capitalized as provisions for loan losses have consumed most of the new capital.

Restructuring the Banks

The Bank of Thailand remained a key player throughout the restructuring process, directly and working through the FIDF. The FRA and AMC, mentioned above, were concerned solely with the finance companies. (By July 1999, the FRA had auctioned most of the assets of the closed institutions and recovered about THB180 billion. The proceeds of the sale were repaid to creditors, the largest of whom was the FIDF.) The approach of Thai regulators shared many features of the other restructuring programs we have examined. Theirs was characterized by the following features.

❑ Tightening prudential regulation coupled with substantial regulatory forbearance

❑ Nationalizing the weakest banks

❑ Recapitalization of banks, including use of foreign capital

❑ Enactment of new bankruptcy and foreclosure laws

❑ Consolidation of the commercial banking sector

Bank AMCs

An additional variant of the AMC scheme we have seen elsewhere was brought into play. Instead of a national AMC program, the government enabled individual banks to set up their own AMCs to manage their bad assets. This is more like an internal debt recovery unit than the national AMCs with special powers that have been used in Malaysia and Korea, for instance. Unlike these AMCs, the subsidiary AMCs do not improve the bank's true capital position since the bad assets remain on its consolidated books.

The advantage to the banks is that they can segregate their bad assets and dedicate a particular operating company to manage them and maximize their value. This frees bank management to focus on managing the parent's banking business. In addition, AMCs are permitted under the Thai approach to hold and manage foreclosed assets for ten years, while banks are obliged to dispose of foreclosed assets as soon as possible. AMCs in theory can maximize the value of the assets better than banks because they are not under time pressure to get rid of assets at fire sale prices, and because they have a dedicated staff focused on managing those assets.

A number of Thai banks perceived some advantage in the AMC scheme and set up such units as indicated in the table below.

Bank	AMC	Date
Bangkok Bank of Commerce	Bangkok Commercial AMC	Jan 1999
UOB Radanasin	Radanasin AMC	Aug 1999
Thai Farmers Bank	Thonburi AMC; Chantaburi AMC	October 1999
Bangkok Bank Bangkok Metropolitan Bank	Tavee AMC BMB AMC	December 1999
Siam City Bank	SCIB AMC	
Siam Commercial Bank	Chatuchak AMC	
National Finance PCL	National Capital AMC	
Thai Military Bank	Thai Military AMC	
Source: Bank of America; Bank of Thailand		

Under the program, banks that transfer assets to the AMC have a choice of writing down the portfolio of NPLs to "fair market value" and the AMC purchasing the loan at that value or selling the loans at par value; or, selling the loan to the AMC at par value, but transferring reserves to the AMC to compensate for the estimated diminution in the value of the assets due to their non- performing status.

Tightening Prudential Regulation and Recapitalizing Viable Financial Institutions

The government introduced new loan classification and provisioning requirements; restructured the Bank of Thailand, also known as the BoT; and introduced new legislation — a new Financial Institutions Act and a new Bank of Thailand Act — to create a stronger supervisory regime. Tightening both regulation and supervision has been on ongoing process and new rules have been promulgated on an ongoing basis. The legal and regulatory infrastructure for bank supervision was being revised in 2000, with a new Banking Law under preparation. This law was expected to codify much of what the BoT has already begun to put in place to bring Thailand's regulatory standards up to international best practice.[5] Overall, the restructuring and recapitalization process is based on set time limits for the boosting of capital adequacy ratios and provisioning requirements.

Banks were also required to submit a recapitalization plan to the BoT. Most importantly, the government introduced a series of measures in August 1998 to restructure the financial system and provide public assistance to the banks. Two key provisions allowed viable financial institutions to recapitalize using public funds, in part, and enabled banks to establish private asset management corporations. Although utilization of the August 1998 capital support scheme has been limited, the government's commitment succeeded in building confidence in the Thai financial system among depositors and investors.

Meanwhile, the low domestic interest rate environment induced by the authorities has assisted the recovery of Thailand's economy. Within a year of introducing the scheme, private financial institutions had recapitalized by over THB250 billion.

---

[5] At the time of this writing, there were indications that some of the proposed revisions, and particularly those that enhance the independence of the BoT, are meeting resistance by the Ministry of Finance,

---

Thailand's Bank Recapitalization Program

BoT offers capital support for institutions in danger of falling below the minimum capital requirements. These are currently 4.25% for Tier 1 and 8.5% for Tier 1 and Tier 2 combined. There are two capital support schemes:

The Tier 1 Support Program requires that the applying institution present a comprehensive operational restructuring plan to the BoT. Such a program must contain measures to strengthen internal controls and risk management, measures to improve the resolution of NPLs, measures to improve revenues and strategies to cut costs. Most importantly, the institution must first set aside sufficient loan loss reserves to meet the end-2000 criteria laid down by the Bank of Thailand, i.e. reserves should meet the BoT guideline in full.

Following such provisioning, should the Tier 1 capital fall below 2.5%, the Ministry of Finance will provide funds sufficient to restore Tier 1 to 2.5%. The Ministry will then match-fund the further Tier 1 capital needed to bring the institution up to the regulatory minimum or above. Thus the institution must also raise additional Tier 1 capital from private sector equity investors. The additional governmental equity is provided in the form of preferred shares.

The Tier 2 Support Program is designed to help financial institutions to restructure problem debt more rapidly and to also help them to reactivate their lending. The amount of Tier 2 capital available equates to the total write-down on restructured loans in excess of previous provisioning plus 20% of any net increase in lending to the private sector. The capital is provided in the form of subordinated debt. In exchange, the institution must buy a corresponding amount of non-tradable ten-year government debt. There is a cap of 2% of risk-weighted assets.

The take-up under these programs has been lower than expected. Of the THB300 billion set aside, only THB48.8 billion has been utilized up to November 1999. Of this, THB41.38 billion has been Tier 1. It would appear that some banks are reluctant to undergo the extra governmental oversight that participation requires.

New Legislation to Strengthen Creditors' Rights

In addition, the government strengthened the framework for debt restructuring by introducing amendments to the Bankruptcy Law and Foreclosure Law. An act establishing a Bankruptcy Court has been passed. Time-bound enforceable processes for debt restructuring have been introduced to accelerate the pace of corporate debt restructuring.

Nationalization, Reprivatization and Liquidation

Instead of allowing the FIDF to extend unlimited credit, the government intervened and ordered the weakest banks to write down their share capital, change management and then recapitalized them by converting FIDF debt into equity.[6] Six of the pre-crisis commercial banks — Siam City Bank, Bangkok Metropolitan Bank, First Bangkok City Bank, Laem Thong Bank, Union Bank and Nakornthon Bank — were so treated. The banks, once nationalized, would be prepared for sale either to foreign investors or via a domestic privatization. This amounted to a significant relaxation of rules prohibiting foreign involvement in the Thai banking sector, necessitated by the crisis. Even prior to the government nationalizing the six distressed banks, the government had agreed to Development Bank of Singapore already acquiring a 51% interest in Thai Danu Bank and ABN AMRO acquiring 77% of Bank of Asia. These transactions were consummated in 1998.

Of the six nationalized banks, First Bangkok City Bank was acquired by the government-controlled Krung Thai Bank. Laem Thong Bank was merged with the new state-owned Radanasin Bank and Union Bank forms the nucleus of the new state-owned BankThai (although most of both assets and management come from Krung Thai Thanakit, a finance company). Radanasin Bank was set up in March 1998, as a 100% Ministry of Finance-owned entity, and was charged with bidding for the good assets of the closed finance companies to be disposed of by the FRA. (Note: The AMC was charged with acquiring their bad assets). The intention was to sell 75% of Radanasin, Nakornthon, Siam City and Bangkok Metropolitan to foreign investors. Two of these transactions have been completed, namely the sale of 75% of Nakornthon Bank to Standard Chartered Bank in September 1999 and the sale of 75% of Radanasin Bank to Singapore-based United Overseas Bank two months later.

In addition, one of the weakest banks, Bangkok Bank of Commerce was formally liquidated. Like a number of the finance companies, it had begun experiencing severe problems before devaluation.

---

[6] The FIDF also issued THB500 billion (US$13.5 billion) long-term bonds to replace the money borrowed in the short term money market. These and other monetary measures have assisted short-term money market rates to decline from its peak of around 25% in January 1998 to 1.3% in June 1999.

Corporate Restructuring

Individual banks endeavored to reach restructuring agreements with their own borrowers on a bilateral basis. In addition, the government established an umbrella framework to cover situations, mainly for large borrowers, where there are multiple lenders. The Corporate Debt Restructuring Advisory Committee (CDRAC) is a voluntary body. Both banks and borrowers can choose not to participate. However, after some initial reluctance by the foreign banks, all resident lenders have joined the scheme. Similarly, there is considerable moral suasion for borrowers to sign up; refusal to do so might well be viewed as an indication that the borrower was seeking to evade his responsibilities.

Initially CDRAC has been dealing with NPLs totaling THB1.5 trillion (US$40.5 billion). Of this total, THB178.5 billion has been restructured with a further THB137.5 billion agreed in principle. Another 850 large borrowers have recently signed up and together with 577 SME cases, bring the total under CDRAC overview to THB2.15 trillion. Total system NPLs have been given as THB2.70 trillion (US$73.0 billion) at May 1999 and THB1.98 trillion (US$53.5 billion) at end-1999, equivalent to around 40% of the financial system's credit.

NPLs in Thailand, December 1998 and December 1999

(THB billion)	Outstanding loans at		Non-performing loans at (as % of gross loans)	
	Dec 1998	Dec 1999	Dec 1998	Dec 1999
Private	3,063	2,894	1,240 (40.5%)	887 (30.6%)
State	1,660	1,682	1,037 (62.5%)	1,036 (61.6%)
Foreign bank branches	757	622	74 (9.8%)	61 (9.8%)
Total commercial banks	5,480	5,198	2,351 (42.9%)	1,984 (38.2%)
Finance companies	461	183	324 (70.2%)	90 (49.2%)
Source: Bank of Thailand				

Table: Creditors Rights Amendments

	Function	Purpose	Status
The Establishment of Bankruptcy Court Act	— Set up the Bankruptcy Court as a specialized court with specialized legal procedures. — Introduce specialized judges for Bankruptcy Court.	— Bring about more timely legal proceedings and verdict for bankruptcy cases. — Reduce the accumulated loss incurred between the two parties by reducing the time taken for hearing.	Enacted since April 8, 1999
The Amendment to the Bankruptcy Act	— Permit an individual person to be filed for indebtedness from debt valued at THB1 m. — Allow a business entity to be filed for indebtedness from debt of THB2 m. — Permit creditors to claim for debt repayment if such debts are for rehabilitating an insolvent debtor's business. — Allow debtors to retain fixed assets valued up to THB100,000. — Introduce new creditor classifications and groupings for the purpose of approving rehabilitation plans. — Reduce bankruptcy status to three years from ten years.	— Adjust upwards the value of indebtedness in line with developments in the economy. — Encourage debt restructuring process of insolvent businesses. — Eliminate the absolute power of certain creditors and debtors over the majority and facilitate the approval and adoption of rehabilitation plans.	Enacted since April 21, 1999

CHAPTER SUMMARY

In this chapter, we completed our discussion of bank restructuring and recapitalization with an examination of the process as it unfolded in Indonesia and Thailand. It can be seen that issues in bank restructuring and recapitalization are complex and there is no one formula that is necessarily best for any given individual bank or sector. Most restructuring programs are initiated following an economic or financial crisis which places certain banks or the banking sector under considerable strain. Perhaps the most widely accepted approach is the use of an asset management corporation, an independent agency, which buys bad debt from banks in exchange for government securities, sharing in any recoveries. By purchasing the NPLs, the AMC will enhance bank recapitalization, but capital may need to be further strengthened. Often another agency provides the additional capital by for example contributing government bonds, the proceeds of government bonds, or by facilitating the bank's own ability to raise funds in domestic and foreign capital markets.

In the majority of cases, banking sector restructuring also includes bank consolidation through both mergers and acquisitions, hopefully leading to a more efficient and competitive sector. Foreign institutions may be involved in some of the bank acquisitions due to their access to capital and financial resources. This also has the added benefit of enhancing the strength of the banking sector though the development of new products and services, and the transfer of expertise, technology and transparency.

In order to maintain confidence in the banking system, which in itself forms an integral part of the economy and payment system, the authorities must act quickly and decisively. The implementation of a blanket deposit guarantee policy has the immediate benefit of restoring depositor confidence, thereby helping to prevent any systemic crisis. However, what is important is that the blanket guarantee must be reduced as quickly as possible in order to prevent moral hazard. In association, the support and rescue of banks poses many issues and problems for bank regulators. It is prudent to provide temporary support to illiquid but solvent and otherwise viable banks. All things being equal, however, insolvent banks should not be supported. In times of a crisis, practical considerations are likely to be paramount. If the bank is deemed too big to fail — i.e., its perceived importance to the banking system and economy is so great that its failure would have grave and long lasting repercussions — then government support is probably necessary. Once the decision has been made to resuscitate a failing bank, what is important is that a solution be found expeditiously. If the institution is allowed to linger too long on intravenous liquidity support, it may never be able to return to full health.

Three major issues faced in the process of bank restructuring and which are inextricably linked are: the removal and management of non-performing loans, bank recapitalization, and corporate restructuring.

Finally, and possibly most importantly, banking sector restructuring must encompass the improvement and strengthening of banking regulation and supervision, corporate regulation, legal frameworks and systems, bankruptcy laws, accounting procedures, and bank management — although even with such moves there is no guarantee that a bank crisis will not occur again. Such measures, however, are likely to help to prevent a crisis and limit the magnitude of any banking system collapse.

CHAPTER TWENTY FOUR

RATING THE BANK, PART I: THE RATINGS INDUSTRY AND ITS RATIONALE

Credit ratings are used by investors as indications of the likelihood of getting their money back in accordance with the terms on which they invested.
— Fitch Ratings Brochure, October 2000

People say, in Mexico, the currency crashed, there was a financial crisis involving the government, so why can't that happen in Thailand? The answer is very simple. Because the fiscal position and financial position of Thailand is fundamentally different from that of Mexico.
— S&P report affirming Thailand's sovereign rating in April 1997, three months before the Thai baht was devalued sparking the Asian crisis.[1]

Sed quis custodiet ipsos custodies?
— Latin aphorism meaning "Who will guard the guards?"

BACKGROUND: ORIGINS AND DEVELOPMENT OF THE RATING INDUSTRY

The ratings industry had its origins in the mid-19th century when companies arose in the United States to provide merchants with credit information on customers. Towards the end of the century, the concept of merchant credit information agencies was adapted to the securities

---

[1] Quoted in "Risks beyond Measure," *The Economist*, December 17, 1997.

markets. Instead of serving merchants seeking information on the credit-worthiness of purchasers or sellers of goods, rating agencies provided a service for investors in bonds, offering views on the creditworthiness of debt issuers. *Poor's Manual*, which contained opinions on both equity and debt securities, was published in 1890. In 1909, John Moody published a book that evaluated the creditworthiness of railroad companies and the bonds that they issued, while distilling those evaluations into ratings symbols.[2] The rating symbols provided investors summary risk assessments designed to assist them in making decisions concerning which bonds to buy or sell and at what price,[3] a function that ratings continue to provide.[4] Moody's Investor Services (Moody's), incorporated in 1914, and Poor's Publishing Company, soon found a market in analyzing and evaluating investments in fixed-income securities, although Poor's (later Standard & Poor's) also covered equity securities. Both expanded as the capital markets evolved in the United States in the early 20th century, and were joined by competitors, including Standard Statistics Company in 1922, and Fitch Publishing Company in 1924.[5] Rating agencies originally charged subscribers a fee for obtaining rating information in contrast to the general present practice of charging for the rating itself, and thereby provided "unsolicited" rather than "solicited" (i.e. paid) ratings.

By the mid-20th century, corporate debt ratings were so well-established that institutional investors came to expect a rating from one of these two major agencies as a prerequisite to purchasing a fixed

---

[2] "In the Spring of 1909 I brought out the first edition of a new type of Railroad Manual which attempted to analyze railroad reports and rate their bond issues. While it raised a storm of opposition, not to mention ridicule from some quarters, it took hold with dealers and investment houses ..." Fifty Year Review of Moody's Investors Service, John Moody, 1950 quoted in "Moody's Credit Ratings and Research," (hereinafter "Credit Rating") Moody's Investors Service, (1995). Moody's original ratings were assigned to over 250 railroad issues, and by 1924 nearly the entire US bond market was rated. Moody's also rated foreign issuers of US dollar securities, including governments and corporations in Japan, China, Britain, Australia, Germany, France, Canada and Argentina.

[3] Moody's defines "a rating ... [as] an opinion on the future ability and legal obligation of an issuer to make timely payments of principal and interest on a specific fixed income security. ... The rating measures the probability that the issuer will default on a security over its life...." Credit Rating, p. 4. Note this definition refers to an issue rating in contrast to an issuer rating which refers to the generic ability of a company to fulfill its financial obligations.

[4] Counterparty risk ratings, which companies use to help establish risk exposure limits and for risk management purpose, are discussed below.

[5] Fitch and IBCA Ltd. merged in 1997. Duff & Phelps Credit Rating Co., which originally concentrated on researching public utilities, traces its origins to 1932, but did not begin to rate bonds until 1982.

income security from organizations other than the federal government.[6] In a sense, a rating assigned by a recognized agency came to be viewed as a passport into the bond and commercial paper markets. Ratings also became a means to distinguish between so-called investment-grade and non-investment grade securities for many institutional investors. The significance of this distinction between investment-grade and speculative-grade bonds (popularly known as "junk bonds," or more recently as "high-yield bonds") became more important as securities laws in the United States, which were strengthened during the 1930s, gradually came to give investment ratings a regulatory imprimatur in certain instances. For example, the US Banking Act of 1935 prohibited nationally-regulated banks from purchasing securities other than investment grade.[7] The imprimatur was strengthened in the US in the 1970s through the creation of the designation, Nationally Recognized Statistical Ratings Organization (NRSRO). The distinction came to be an important one in many instances. For example, when an NRSRO assigns an investment-grade rating to an offering of non-convertible debt or preferred stock, the issuer benefits from streamlined registration requirements.[8] Ironically, rating agencies themselves have not universally welcomed the incorporation of ratings into regulation, fearing a loss of independence and the erosion of credibility political pressures could bring to bear.[9] A belief that regulation would foster "rating shopping as also helped to foster this reaction, as we note below. Some of the controversy over the revisions proposed in 1999 to the 1988 Basel Capital Accord, discussed in Chapter 12 were the result of these concerns.

Beginning in the mid-1970s, the business model of the debt rating industry, which by then consisted of two major agencies previously mentioned, Moody's and Standard & Poor's[10] (S&P), as well as their competitors Duff & Phelps and Fitch, had begun to shift from one that was subscription fee-based to one to that charged issuers for the privilege of obtaining a rating. The change took some time to implement, and unsolicited ratings continued to be provided to a greater or lesser degree.

---

[6] In 1999, 95% of bonds issued in the US were rated.
[7] Partnoy, p. 688.
[8] Partnoy, n. 346.
[9] See e.g. See "Ratings Agencies as a Catalyst for Growth in Capital Markets," Moody's Special Comment, June 1997, ("Moody's June 1997 Comment").
[10] Poor's started rating securities in 1916. It merged with Standard in 1941 and was acquired by McGraw-Hill in 1961.

But by transferring the cost of a rating to the issuer and reframing the cost of a rating as part of the cost of borrowing in the capital markets — and a comparatively low one at that compared with underwriting, legal and accounting fees — rating agencies were able to hold down subscription costs and distribute ratings more freely to investors. Rating agencies, moreover by this time had become so ensconced (at least in the US) in shaping investor perception that they were usually able to justify their charge by asserting that a rating in most cases tended to reduce the cost of borrowing for the issuer, as compared to an unrated issue. The argument was made that even a modestly rated issue would fare more favorably than an unrated one, as the latter would be perceived by investors as intrinsically more risky. Although there is an apparent conflict of interest raised in a circumstance where the issuer pays for the rating fee, rating agencies have argued plausibly that they are constrained from showing bias toward those who pay the piper both by professional standards and because their business rests upon their credibility and reputation with investors. As Chester Murray, Moody's managing director for Europe said, "If we started inflating ratings to get business, it would become readily apparent to investors and our overall credibility as a rating agency serving the global credit markets would be at stake."[11]

Contemporaneous with this evolution in the industry, a number of specialist rating agencies that concentrated on particular industries, most notably the banking and insurance industries, were established. These included BankWatch in 1975, which was initially established as a division of boutique investment banking firm, Keefe, Bruyette and Woods, and IBCA, Ltd. in 1978.[12] Notable banking failures in the United States, such as that of Continental Illinois and others, provided the impetus for the creation of these specialist agencies. They were given further nurturance from the increasing concern about bank risk that came about in the 1980s

---

[11] Quoted in Katherine Morton, "Time to Face the Image Problem," Risk Publications, April 2000, http://www.riskpublications.com/credit/apr00/features/credcoverstory.htm. The Financial Times in a special report dated May 8, 1998 [citation below] cited in defense of the rating agencies a 1994 Federal Reserve Bank study which found that the discipline provided by concerns about their reputation kept agencies from inflating the ratings of their paying customers, and that a subsequent study "found little evidence that issuers shopped around for more favorable ratings." Other criticism of ratings agencies are discussed in a succeeding section of this chapter.

[12] I.B.C.A. was an abbreviation for "International Bank Credit Analysis." BankWatch was subsequently acquired in the mid-1980s by the Thomson Corporation. As referred to in the discussion of consolidation in the rating industry, IBCA ultimately merged in 1997 with Fitch under the ownership of Fimilac, a diversified French company. The new entity, Fitch-IBCA merged with Duff & Phelps to become Fitch in early 2000 and acquired BankWatch from Thomson in November 2000.

as a result of a number of causes: the Latin American debt crisis, anxiety about the use of off-balance sheet finance, deregulation and the latent savings and loan crisis, and finally the increasing prominence of Japanese financial institutions in world markets. The major agencies did not cover banks extensively during this period, unless they were major issuers of debt securities and coverage remained scant into the 1990s as most banks relied primarily on their depositors and the interbank market, rather than the capital markets, for funding.[13] Thus, at a time when credit information on international banks was limited, the specialist agencies provided a needed service to counterparties on a subscription basis.

These specialist agencies differed from the major agencies both in coverage, in the type of rating they provided and in the needs they fulfilled. Unlike the major agencies that became integral players in the capital markets, the specialist agencies were oriented towards counterparty and correspondent banking transactions, including trade finance. The major agencies were highly focused on the capital markets. In contrast, the specialist ratings tended to be used by credit officers at banks and corporations in one of their key tasks: establishing credit lines and limits for financial institution exposure, a function that took on increasing importance with the spread of derivatives for hedging and trading purposes. Their coverage was generally broader than the universe of financial institutions seeking to tap the capital markets for funding.

Moreover, there was relatively little incentive — at least, at first — for banks to pay to be rated as the business models of the major agencies generally required, so the specialist agencies initially relied on a subscription model of revenue to subsidize a wider range of coverage than that provided by the major rating agencies. This, of course, was the same approach the major agencies had taken in their early days. Ultimately, the specialist agencies also attempted to move to a paid rating revenue model, particularly in developed markets, but continued to rely heavily upon subscription revenue. In the case of paid ratings, they functioned in a similar manner to the major agencies, although usually instead of rating particular securities, they often focused on appraising the overall creditworthiness of financial institutions in respect to its outstanding obligations. Later, individual securities were rated, but often as generic classes of securities rather than as individual issues.

---

[13] Throughout the remainder of this chapter, I use the term major agencies to refer to Moody's, S&P, Duff & Phelps and Fitch.

The late 1980s and 1990s were characterized by global expansion within the ratings industry as equity and fixed income investment in emerging markets flourished. Sovereign ratings, which assessed the creditworthiness of governments, came into more widespread use. All agencies broadened coverage to meet customer demand with major players setting up overseas offices, while the secondary and specialist agencies grew primarily through acquisition and joint ventures. Thomson BankWatch, for example, acquired regional rating agencies located in Asia and Eastern Europe and formed joint ventures with local agencies in specific emerging markets. A related phenomenon was consolidation within the industry. Although the ratings industry based in the US was essentially an oligopoly, in the latter part of the 1990s consolidation occurred as both the general and specialist agencies recognized the virtues of size. Also motivating consolidation in the specialist rating industry was the consolidation of the banking industry itself, which went through an unprecedented wave of mergers and acquisitions during the decade.

This phenomenon of consolidation in the rating industry was epitomized with the merger of IBCA, a specialist rating agency, with Fitch in 1997. The amalgamation of Fitch-IBCA was followed by the acquisition of a secondary rating agency Duff & Phelps in early 2000 creating a third major rating agency renamed Fitch.[14] Both Duff & Phelps had a broad ratings business with some specialist niches including municipal bonds and later structured finance, securitization. This left Thomson Financial BankWatch as the surviving global specialist bank rating agency. Marginalized by the emergence of a "big three" each with increasingly strong bank coverage, and with little chance of being able to expand its franchise, in October 2000, the parent company of BankWatch sold the business to Fitch.

THE ROLE OF RATING AGENCIES: CRITICISM AND RESPONSE

Despite or perhaps because of their increasing importance in the capital markets, ratings agencies came under sharp criticism in the wake of the Asian crisis of 1997–98, particularly in terms of their sovereign risk ratings.[15] They were disparaged for failing to anticipate the Asian crisis,

---

[14] At the time, Duff & Phelps was the only publicly listed rating agency.

[15] See e.g. "On Watch: Much criticism has been leveled at credit-rating agencies for failing to spot impending crises. Yet the agencies are thriving." *Economist*, May 15, 1999; *Financial Times* Special Report: Asia in Crisis: Rating Agencies: Different Kind of Risk, May 8, 1998. http://www.ft.com/specials98/q2872.htm. For a trenchant academic criticism of the rating agencies,

its scope and magnitude. A conspicuous example was the case of South Korea, where major agencies maintained the country at the level of AA/AA+ even as the fixed income markets had largely factored in negative economic fundamentals.[16] They also caught flak for being too slow to downgrade their ratings and then over-reacting and being too sluggish in adjusting ratings upward when recovery began to take hold. Paradoxically, the agencies have also sometimes been criticized for being too strongly influenced by the market. Apart from the Asian crisis, concerns about the accountability of rating agencies have also been raised from time to time, prompting some governments, especially in certain developing countries, to call for their regulation.

Some Criticism is Warranted

While a degree of criticism of the rating agencies indeed has been warranted, and following the Asian turmoil, some agencies acknowledged to an extent the need to modify their methodologies in certain cases. At the time of the Korean downgrades, the *Financial Times* quoted the head of sovereign ratings at Fitch IBCA as declaring that all the agencies had been wrong on Korea.

> *"We've all been behind the curve on Korea," said Mr. Huhne. "We were all too focused on how low Korea's external debt was as a proportion of export receipts, so we underestimated the danger of a Korean default on its short-term debt."[17]*

---

see Frank Portnoy, "The Siskel & Ebert of Financial Markets?: Two Thumbs Down for the Credit Rating Agencies," *Washington Univ. Law Quarterly*, Vol. 77, No. 3, 1999. Portnoy is a professor at Univ. of San Diego Law School and a former derivatives trader for Morgan Stanley. An academic paper, "Rating Agencies: Are They Credible?" by Christoph Kuhner, mentions additional albeit less-often voiced criticisms. A particularly interesting one is the charge that rating agencies behave procyclically, i.e. express a herd mentality, in times of enhanced systemic risk. Prof. Nouriel Roubum has cited a number of articles critical of the agencies at his website under the heading. Rating Agencies. *Why Did They Fail to Predict Asian Crisis?* at http://www.stern.nyu.edu/globalmacro/asian_crisis/rating_agency.html.

[16] Moody's did not downgrade South Korea's bonds to below investment grade until December 10, 1997 "long after the press had reported that Korea's central bank was nearly out of foreign currency reserves." See S. Davies & L. Luce, "South Korea: Credit Rating Agencies Under Fire," *Financial Times*, December 12, 1997. S&P only downgraded Japan's Yamaichi Securities days before it went bankrupt on November 21, 1997. "Risks beyond Measure," *The Economist*, Dec. 13, 1997. Interestingly, when Moody's was earlier criticized for placing Thailand's short-term rating on review for a downgrade in May 1996, its critics contended that whatever problems there were had been solved and that the rating agency was behind the curve. Email from Kenny Hargrove, Asiabondportal.com

[17] S. Davies & L. Luce, "South Korea: Credit Rating Agencies Under Fire," *Financial Times*, December 12, 1997.

Another agency conceded that more emphasis was warranted concerning factors that had previously been given less attention such as short-term foreign borrowing by private firms (in contrast to public borrowing) in evaluating sovereign risk.[18] In addition, the agencies beefed up their international operations enabling them to monitor conditions in emerging markets more closely. Most have also provided more transparency about their rating process, posting detailed information about their methodologies on their websites and generally being more open to scrutiny than in the past. This said, while some criticisms were valid in part, it must also be observed that some of the carping was based on a misunderstanding of the function and purpose of ratings.

In this section we shall examine the some of the allegations which have been directed at rating agencies and provide a reasoned response based on the author's own experience working at a rating agency and functioning as a member of the rating committee evaluating Asian banks. It is hoped that two purposes are served by this discussion: first, that the reader may gain a better understanding of how rating agencies operate; and second, that the discussion will serve to elucidate what role they play in the financial industry.

What Is the Purpose of Ratings?

Broadly speaking, the purpose of default ratings[19] also termed debt ratings is, to quote Moody's, "to increase capital markets efficiency by assigning ratings to fixed income obligations."[20] Ratings do this by simplifying the credit risk evaluation process for investors through the application of an independent standard that results in the assignment of a rating symbol as a summary grade for the credit quality of the issuer's securities. Credit quality may refer solely to default risk (i.e. the risk that the issuer will not

---

[18] Other factors observed as having been given short shrift prior to the crisis include 1) the importance of a strong financial system and the negative economic impact of a fragile one, 2) the importance of the quality of investment as well as savings and investment ratios, 3) the speed with which contagion can spread in a global economy and a global financial market, 4) the importance of transparency and best practices in corporate governance in assuaging concerns over malinvestment 5) the inability of the IMF to respond appropriately and effectively to a crisis engendered by misallocation of private, in contrast to public, investment, and 6) the limitations of the "too big to fail" security blanket.

[19] "Default ratings" or the rating of the likelihood that an issuer will not default on its obligations with respect to a security or class of securities can be contrasted with a "counterparty risk ratings," which estimate the risk that an issuer will default on its obligations in general. The difference is discussed in more detail later in the chapter.

[20] *A Counterparty's Guide to Moody's Bank Ratings*, p. 3.

fulfill its financial obligations to the investor/creditor in accordance with the terms of the obligation), or it may encompass both "the probability of default and the magnitude of a possible loss associated with that default."[21] This enables investors and traders to quickly size up the perils associated with a particular fixed income security and price that risk more easily and accurately.[22] By exploiting economies of scale, rating agencies, like banks, are able to provide a service that single investors would ordinarily find prohibitive.

Regulators and the financial community at large appear to agree that the agencies perform a valuable service and generally enhance market efficiency. Indeed, the existence of local ratings is often seen as a pre-requisite to the development of debt capital markets in developing countries. For this reason, some regulators have mandated ratings in connection with local bond issuances. Rating agencies themselves, however, have argued against such policies (seemingly against their self-interest), contending that government mandated ratings promotes "rating shopping" and are a poor substitute for full disclosure by issuers and underwriters.[23] Better disclosure, they have argued, would tend to encourage additional sources of information and opinion about issuers.

Other Criticisms of the Rating Agencies and Corresponding Assumptions

As mentioned, certainly some criticisms of the rating agencies are not without merit and indeed were acknowledged by the agencies themselves. These — most notably the short shrift given to private indebtedness and the comparative importance of strong financial systems in stanching

---

[21] See Moody's June 1997 Comment, p. 3. This latter aspect is termed "severity" of loss.

[22] Moody's identifies four benefits of ratings to investors and three to issuers. To investors, ratings help investors 1) access markets by enabling them to gain comfort concerning the credit risk profile of unfamiliar markets and to focus on fixed income analysis rather than basic credit risk; 2) set credit risk limits and assist in portfolio weighting and diversification; 3) price risk premiums; and 4) provide general research support through the ratings reports issued in conjunction with ratings. Issuers arguably benefit by 1) obtaining broader access to capital over unrated institutions; 2) reduced funding costs over unrated institutions; and 3) assist in maintaining investor confidence. *Credit Rating*, p. 7–9.

[23] Rating shopping refers to the phenomenon whereby issuers canvass rating agencies and select the agency likely to award the highest rating. Moody's, for one, has argued against government policies that focus upon the rating agencies as a means to jumpstart their capital markets, asserting that such policies encourage rating shopping and that it would be better for governments to apply their efforts to promote full disclosure on the part of issuers and underwriters through appropriate regulations and penalties for non-compliance. See *Moody's June 1997 Comment*.

a crisis — generally had to do with refinements in the methodologies employed in assessing sovereign risk. Other criticisms were broader, and as we have suggested, often misconceived. They can be summarized roughly as follows and each corresponds to one or more myths about the rating business, some of which are mutually exclusive.

Criticism #1: The Fallibility Criticism

The first criticism is: the agencies *should* get it right, but they do not. This complaint is fortified each time an agency makes a supposedly bad call and is supported by a corollary that assumes that *rating agencies are (or should be) infallible.* When a company or country with a nominally good rating defaults, it is taken as evidence that the rating is wrong rather than as a probability event taken into account by the rating. A related assumption, that *rating agencies are (or should be) auditors*, may also come into play. If, to use a hypothetical illustration, Rating Agency X has affirmed the rating of Fobitron Inc. at single-A minus, and Fobitron defaults six months later after it is later revealed that the company has engaged in fraud, that its financial statements are deceptive and that most of its earnings are non-existent, Rating Agency X will be singled out for criticism notwithstanding that Fobitron Inc's financial statements were audited and certified by a major accounting firm. Finally, a third unsupported assumption may be made. This is that *rating agencies perform "rocket science,"* and are the experts whose opinion should be taken as gospel without question. In taking this view, however, the user of the rating gives great weight to what is after all a mere consensus opinion from the agency and little weight to other views. In the process, the rating is mystified and assumed to have been arrived at by methods and expertise far beyond the ken of sophisticated investors or creditors. By taking this view, the user of the rating is relieved of any responsibility in exercising independent judgment concerning the company in question. When nearly all the highly-paid analysts and strategists at investment banks failed to foresee the Asian crisis, those adopting this perspective would nonetheless find the rating agencies wanting for not predicting it as well.

Criticism #2: The Bad Faith Criticism

A second criticism is that unsolicited ratings are an evil as rating agencies exploit their market power to blackmail rated companies into taking ratings by assigning them highly adverse ratings if they do not pay for ratings mandates. This is the obverse of the criticism already discussed — that agencies favor those who pay the piper, i.e. those issuers which pay for ratings mandates. Implicit in this criticism is that *rating agencies are willing to risk their credibility by singling out issuers and extorting ratings fees (or currying favor)* from them.

Criticism #3: The Timeliness Criticism

This criticism holds that ratings are lagging indicators and provide little useful information to investors since they often react to rather than anticipate market events. An accompanying assumption is that *ratings are (or should be) leading indicators.* These criticisms assume an ideal that the traditional economics of the rating industry do not permit, but at the same time they point to ways in which the industry may evolve in the future.

Criticism #4: The Bias Towards/Obliviousness to the Market Criticism

This criticism posits that rating agencies are influenced too much or too little by market on other considerations. This charge either sees the rating agencies as being unduly influenced by market sentiment or too little influenced by them. Corresponding assumptions are: *market conditions are irrelevant to the financial health of a company* or, conversely that, *ratings should closely correlate to bond spreads.* Those who believe the former would fault the agencies for paying undue attention to market-moving events (notwithstanding that may ultimately reveal problems with or affect a firm's creditworthiness), while those who believe the latter would assert that the agencies are so detached from the market as to be meaningless. Those persuaded that ratings should closely correlate to bond spreads censured the agencies for not immediately downgrading sovereigns and corporate issuers during the early days of the Asian crisis when bond spreads skyrocketed, while those in the former camp would have agencies ignore market sentiment and be based entirely on fundamentals.

Let us now examine the enunciated criticisms above in more detail.

Validity of the Fallibility Criticism

Although "rating agencies hold an almost god-like status in global debt markets," misconceptions exist concerning the level and depth of information available to them.[24] In this context, a distinction must be made between solicited ratings, which sometimes (but not always) involve the disclosure of confidential (i.e. non-public) information, and unsolicited ratings which ordinarily are based on publicly available information and in some circumstances may not even include a visit with the issuer.[25] While the assignment of a solicited rating generally entails a more through review process than an unsolicited rating, the rating process even in the case of a solicited rating is *not* an audit. A solicited rating involves what is sometimes referred to as *due diligence*, but does not ferret into the level of detail which an auditor could be expected to pursue. Likewise, the testing and sampling of financial data is left to the bank's auditors. Neither does due diligence mean spending days poring through the books of a company the agency is rating. Nor does it involve a review of loan files, work which comes within the ambit of the bank examiner, not the rating agency analyst.

Rating agency analysts conduct an independent analysis, but do not independently extract raw financial data, reconstruct the elements of financial statements or test for error or malfeasance, although they may and often do reorganize data provided to them while "spreading" such statements into consistent standardized formats. At the same time, they also look for discrepancies or omissions in information. They may question, for instance, why a bank's net interest income rose despite a fall in lending, or whether an increase in provisioning charges was in anticipation of increased credit costs or an attempt to remedy loan losses that had already occurred. In the case of a solicited rating, agency due diligence ordinarily involves the completion of a questionnaire by the rated company, attested to by company officers. This may be followed by meetings between agency analysts, senior management and senior operational personnel. At these meetings, which normally would last for no more than one to two days (and may only amount to a few hours), agency analysts listen to the presentations by management concerning their business, and pose questions to management in turn. In addition, the solicited rating entails greater participation of the rated institution in the rating process, with concomitant contractual rights of review and appeal, which as noted can delay rating actions. Consequently, although agency

---

[24] IFR Asia, No. 174, "Time for a pan-Asian rating board?, p. 1, Sept. 2, 2000.
[25] Rating agencies do not always disclose which of their ratings are unsolicited, although S&P has begun the practice of designating unsolicited ratings as "pi" for "public information."

analysts cast a critical eye on the financial data with which they are provided, a rating is no guarantee against fraud, nor against inaccurate or misleading financial statements. Ratings are only as good as the information proffered, and consequently fraud by rated companies may escape undetected. As Robin Monro-Davies, CEO of Fitch IBCA has said in this context, "All rating agencies depend on people by-and-large telling the truth."[26]

This criticism of rating agencies is based upon a misconception of their role, their approach to credit analysis, and the service they offer to investors and institutional users. Rating agencies do not claim omniscience. From the rating agency perspective, a rating — whether a debt rating or a counterparty rating — is merely an independent and ultimately a subjective opinion concerning the creditworthiness of an issue or an issuer that is made for the benefit of an investor or counterparty.[27] According to this view, the designation of a rating is but one more piece of data that serves to increase the flow of information and liquidity in the financial markets. It should not be the sole source of an investor's decision. While a rating is forward looking, it is at heart an estimation of risk based on information available to the agency at the time the rating is issued.

The major rating agencies, nonetheless, have developed a good reputation on the whole for accuracy in their assessments. There is empirical evidence that suggests that their ratings correlate with statistical probabilities of default, and indeed their reputations to a large degree have been built upon this correlation. According to the data collected by the agencies over the past several decades, it is apparent that higher rated issues do default less often than lower rated issues. For example, Moody's observed in a 1995 publication that a mere 0.1% of Aaa rated issues had defaulted within five years from issue in contrast with 28% of B rated issues.

Spreads over US Treasuries, a common benchmark in the capital markets for an essentially risk-free rate, likewise corresponded to the higher risk premium that investors would be expected to demand

---

[26] Katherine Morton, "Time to Face the Image Problem," Risk Publications, April 2000, http://www.riskpublications.com/credit/apr00/features/credcoverstory.htm

[27] Note that the term "issuer" may either refer to the issuer of securities in the capital markets, or, in the rating industry context, simply to the rated entity (including counterparties) whether that entity has or has any plans to issue securities in the capital markets or not. In this sense, the meaning refers to the obligor with respect to any sort of financial obligation, including trade finance transactions, derivatives, bank deposits, or borrowers of bank loans.

from lower rated issues. In early 1994, for example, spreads of Aaa rated issues were 61 basis points over US Treasuries, while A3 issues were near 100 basis points, and B issues in the 400–550 basis point range.[28] Such spreads are not fixed, but move as the underlying benchmark moves. Spreads also tighten and widen with changing economic and market conditions, resulting in changing risk premiums paid for high risk (non-investment grade) securities relative to low risk (investment grade) securities.[29]

Correlation between Rating and Default Probability

Despite the awareness of the correlation between ratings and the probability of default or loss, historically there has been little attempt by rating agencies to calibrate ratings to any predetermined specific default probabilities. Indeed, the rating agencies generally eschew any representation that their ratings correlate with specific ranges of default risk. For instance, Fitch flatly states in its ratings definitions, "ratings imply no specific prediction of default probability," while observing in the next sentence, "However … it is relevant to note that over the long term, defaults on 'AAA' rate U.S. corporate bonds have averaged less than 0.10% per annum, while the equivalent rate for 'BBB' rated bonds was 0.35%, and for 'B' rated bonds, 3.0%."[30] In other words, the agencies do not attempt to define their ratings in terms of probabilities, as declaring, to use a hypothetical example, that a BBB rating for an issue means that bondholders can expect between a 3 to 7% probability of default within five years. Instead, the starting point for rating agencies is their qualitative ratings definitions, which as applied through the fundamental analysis of issuers and issues, subsequently have been empirically correlated with rates of default. In the parlance of the agencies, ratings are measures of relative risk, not absolute risk.

At the same time, for this reason primarily, it is correct to observe, as Moody's has, that ratings are not necessarily interchangeable among rating agencies, notwithstanding the use of the same or similar

---

[28] Spreads do not always correspond to ratings, especially over the short term. In early 1999, when non-investment grade Mexican bonds had lower spreads — 165 basis points over US treasuries — than those of Columbia, rated investment grade. On Watch, *The Economist*, May 15, 1999.

[29] *Credit Rating*, p. 5, 7. In February 1998, Moody's issued a "Special Comment," "Historical Default Rates of Corporate Bond Issuers, 1920–1997," which discussed Moody's experience with default rates in considerable detail.

[30] Fitch Ratings, October 2000, p. 1.

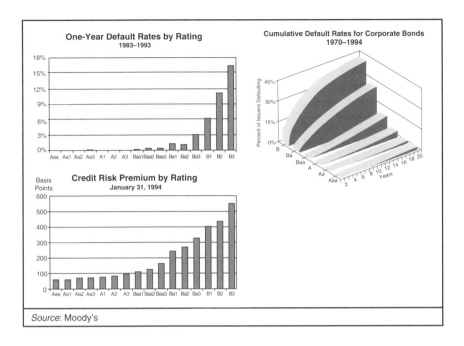

One-Year Default Rates by Rating
1983–1993

Cumulative Default Rates for Corporate Bonds
1970–1994

Credit Risk Premium by Rating
January 31, 1994

Source: Moody's

methodologies and symbologies. To be sure, the ratings of S&P and Moody's, the two leading players, are in fact regarded in such a way by the major market participants. But this assumption would only be correct if, for example, a single A rating (A2 in Moody's scheme) accurately correlated to the same or a similar loss expectation, e.g. an aggregate ten-year loss rate of 0.95%.[31] Ideally, all rating agencies would disclose the default rates associated with each of their symbologies. Such disclosure would enable market participants to use ratings more effectively by understanding the probabilities of default embodied in each rating symbol.

The Validity of the Bad Faith Criticism: Do Rating Agencies Exploit Their Position in the Market?

Because the judgments of rating agencies affect the cost of financing both of governments and corporations, it should not be surprising that the decisions of these private organizations has from time to time

---

[31] *Moody's June 1997 Comment,* p. 3.

come under public scrutiny. The accountability of the agencies has been questioned and occasionally calls are made to regulate their operations, without considering that by inevitably constraining the free flow of information, the cure is likely to be worse than any perceived disease. In this vein, criticisms are sometimes directed at unsolicited ratings. Of all the critiques of rating agencies, the assault on unsolicited ratings are probably the least warranted. Although the use of unsolicited ratings has been condemned by some, all the major general and specialist rating agencies began by offering unsolicited ratings[32] and without unsolicited ratings, agencies as we know them today would not exist. Moreover, unsolicited ratings add information in those markets where issuers or banks are unwilling to undergo the rating process or pay the fee, but where such information nevertheless in high demand by counterparties or investors.

The gist of the criticism of unsolicited ratings is that rating agencies issue a negative unsolicited ratings in order to persuade the rated entity to pay for a "solicited" rating. In simple terms, critics of unsolicited ratings seem to be suggesting that major agencies utilize their market power to extort ratings fees from unwilling institutions. At least in respect of reputable agencies (and this includes the major general and specialist rating agencies), this charge is almost certainly false. Although not obligated to do so, in the case of rendering unsolicited ratings, most of the rating agencies do attempt to make an informal visit to the institution being rated both as a matter of courtesy and to glean additional information. Since they have no contractual relationship with the issuer in such cases, they cannot compel the issuer to meet with them or to provide information. Nor can they reasonably be expected to spend a substantial amount of time on a *gratis* basis in an attempt to extract information from the issuer or accommodate all the issuer's suggestions. Their goal, however, is virtually always accuracy in the ultimate rating.

---

[32] One criticism appears to be rating agencies take a harsher view of rated companies in unsolicited ratings. It is true that unsolicited ratings are often more conservative than solicited ratings. The reason is not that agencies are attempting to punish companies that decline to pay for a rating, but that where there is doubt, the agencies will tend to err on the side of caution. Correspondingly, the more information provided to the agencies, the more transparent the disclosure process, the more comfort agency analysts will feel in giving the company the benefit of the doubt. In this context, however, it should be emphasized that in most cases the rating agencies do invite the participation of the rated companies, either through submission of questionnaires, informal visits, or informal reviews of the draft report. Those companies that refuse to cooperate in the process are not in a strong position to complain when the rating assigned does not meet their expectations.

While mostly unfounded, criticisms of agencies in particular circumstances have nonetheless given them some credence. In certain cases allegations have been made against particular agencies for attempting to punish issuers who refused to pay for ratings by publishing negative unsolicited ratings. Such abuses, if and when they have occurred, would be rightfully condemned. But it should also be borne in mind that issuers are apt to have a more glorified view of the rating that they deserve than a detached independent observer. It is also worth remarking that there may be a tendency for the agency analyst to give the issuer the benefit of the doubt — all other things being equal — in those instances where the issuer has provided a high level of disclosure and thoroughly answered all questions put to it. In the same manner, where in the case of an unsolicited rating, the issuer has not been very forthcoming with information, or places the burden of extracting that information on the agency analyst, it is not surprising that the agency analyst will tend to err on the side of conservatism, and properly so. As a matter of practice, less disclosure tends to be associated with higher risk. In the context of risk assessment, disclosure is not only the means by which the assessment is performed, it is also arguably a positive credit consideration in itself.[33]

The Validity of the Timeliness Criticism: Are Rating Agencies too Slow to Adjust Ratings?

The criticism that ratings are a "lagging indicator" has some merit, but it rests on a misconception as to the role of rating agencies and what they are attempting to accomplish in assigning a rating.[34] Certain — possibly unjustified — mystique has arisen concerning the process by which the agencies assign their ratings. For the moment it bears observing that at its core, however, the ratings process is a simple one. Agency analysts are merely credit analysts who apply traditional, albeit gradually evolving, models to assess the creditworthiness of the companies that they rate.

---

[33] Admittedly, the line between the benefit of the doubt offered to an issuer in connection with a solicited rating, where the issuer is effectively obligated to supply such information, and bias towards an unsolicited issuer for lack of disclosure can be a fine one.

[34] This criticism is not such a new one. Some commentators have observed that market players do not regard rating actions as early harbingers of change, and the agencies are seen more as confirming what is already known by market participants rather than providing new information to the markets on a timely basis.

What distinguishes the ratings agency analyst from other credit analysts is the consensual committee approach towards ratings assignments.[35]

Unlike securities analysts, rating agencies' opinions are invariably the product of a committee rather than being the calls of individual analysts. Although the lead analyst covering a particular institution will recommend a rating, that recommendation must be supported and the analyst's recommendation does not always prevail. The committee approach ensures a higher degree of consistency and helps to prevent bias in the rating process, but it also means that rating agency analysts may not be able to respond as quickly to changes in the credit environment as individual investment or credit analysts. The need to obtain consensus can slow the process and lead to more conservative adjustments than that of the individual analyst whose mission is to spot trading opportunities. In addition, when a rating is solicited, the company rated typically has the right to review and appeal the rating, although it has no right to change the rating. The review and appeal process can also slow down the assignment of a rating or a rating action (i.e. a rating change or affirmation).

To believe that rating agencies should be as on top of market movements as active participants is therefore based upon a misunderstanding of their role. Rating agencies do not perform fixed income analysis, attempting to prognosticate movements in yield curves in the short term. Investors and analysts who are close to the market — those for example who spend their working days in a dealing room — will likely be ahead of the agencies in spotting potential problems that may be reflected in short-term movements in credit spreads. Ratings, moreover, are not intended to measure market risk (e.g. changes in the market value of a security as a consequence of a change in prevailing interest rates), prepayment risk or the security's "potential for price appreciation."[36]

The Validity of the Bias Criticism: Are Agencies Too Little or Too Much Influenced by Market Considerations

This criticism is related to the previous criticism, for a lack of timeliness in ratings actions implies a lack of attention being paid to market-moving events. The rating agencies, as observed, were criticized for being too

---

[35] As noted below, this systematic process-oriented method of assigning ratings is designed to improve consistency and make ratings generally comparable on a global basis.
[36] *Credit Rating*, p. 6.

Changing Outlooks on the Philippines

In early 2000, the discrepancy between the Philippines' rating and the risk imputed by high bond spreads then prevailing came to the attention of analysts. While the Philippines was rated at BB+ by S&P and the equivalent Ba1 by Moody's, its sovereign bond traded at spreads more akin to a lower rated (putatively more risky) issues. "Why do bonds that we think are of high BB credit quality trade in the high four hundred basis point range, a level more suitable to bonds rated low BB or high single-B?" queried Salomon Smith Barney's head of sovereign credit research Stephen Taran in an article in FinanceAsia.com.[37] The overall view concerning the ratings of the various sovereign analysts and economists quoted in the article was that on fundamentals, the ratings were justifiable. Instead, it was market behavior that failed to recognize these comparatively positive fundamentals that appeared puzzling. The discrepancy was attributed largely to poor investor sentiment. The ratings assigned by Moody's and S&P to the country, though out of line with market perceptions, were not seen to be unfair.

Later, however, other commentators took the agencies to task for being too sensitive to market developments and for following the herd as market sentiment changes. Instead, the market was seen to be out of line with the fundamentals so astutely recognized by the agencies By the third quarter of the year, political sentiment had deteriorated considerably. In October 2000, S&P issued a negative outlook on the Philippines two weeks before affirming its rating at BB+. In an article in the same publication, the agency was indirectly criticized in a commentary by Desmond Supple of Barclays Asia. While Mr. Supple acknowledged the deterioration in the political climate which might result in the possible impeachment of President Estrada as a valid concern and a plausible reason for the change in outlook, he also implied that a possible downgrade would be driven by "the tendency of the rating agencies to follow the market."

As it turned out, the political situation in the Philippines did get worse before it got better. In the end the three major agencies held the rating at BB+ but with a negative outlook. With a new president in the country, the wind seems to be changing but as of the date of this writing none of the agencies have reversed their views.

slow in downgrading issuers as the Asian crisis gained momentum in late 1997 and bond spreads widened dramatically. Yet at times the agencies have caught flak from some for being insufficiently sensitive to market

---

[37] JTR Bentulan, *Buzzes like a BB+, trades like a B*, FinanceAsia.com, 16 August 2000.

sentiment, while others have praised them for steering a stable course. The Philippines provides an illustration as shown on the previous page.

Again, to believe that rating agencies should follow or ignore the market misconstrue's their role. If rating agencies are like large ships, slow to change course, fixed-income analysts can be analogized to speedboats able to zigzag several times as the debt markets move for each time a rating agency changes its view on a particular issuer. Their agility, however, is a function of their role. But neither can agencies ignore the market. Markets do affect creditworthiness, even when market perceptions are out of line with fundamentals. Rating agencies then cannot ignore the market, nor can they afford to be too sensitive to it without compromising their role. To a degree, the agencies are victims of the Heisenberg effect. Through the simple act of observing, and offering an opinion, they may change market dynamics.

Despite the criticism of the agencies, an understanding of their role actually provides opportunities for the fixed income analyst and his or her clients. As we will discuss in Chapter 26, an important part of the fixed income analyst's job is understanding rating agency dynamics as well as how market sentiment and appetite affects the pricing of securities.

Errors and Distortions in the Rating Process, Room for Improvement and the Evolution of the Ratings Industry

Although most of the criticisms slung at rating agencies are misdirected, there is, to be sure, room for improvement. As the rating agencies themselves say, investors and creditors should not place sole reliance on their opinions. This said, by virtue of the agencies' long tenure in modern capital markets (and often the regulatory imprimatur), their assessments — if not viewed as "holy writ" — still carry considerable weight, even when patently off the mark. While rating agency analysts are almost universally responsible professionals, they are not perfect. In short, rating agencies, being composed of human beings, make mistakes, but just as humanly are loath to admit them.[38] Moreover, even without making any single egregious error, over time organizational dynamics may allow ratings of a particular region, market or institution to become distorted.

---

[38] Admission of error could result in potential legal liability, although to date it has been asserted that no lawsuits against rating agencies for negligently assigned ratings have been successful. Rating agencies rarely issue corrections, and at least one agency had an unwritten policy not to do so.

Consistency among ratings is easier to achieve in theory than in practice, and once inconsistencies have occurred, the agency may be hesitate to make adjustments until an appropriate time for fear of sending the "wrong signal" to the market. In the interim, of course, the rating is not as accurate as it might be.

At the same time, while outside analysts may criticize a particular rating action, it is singularly difficult to prove when an error has been made, since rating assignments are in the end judgment calls that are rendered accurate or inaccurate only with the passage of time. Moreover, since in every rating category there is some possibility of default, a given rating assignment can hardly ever be shown to be definitively incorrect. Ratings can only be deemed incorrect in hindsight when an entire ratings category misperforms.[39] But there is almost always some window of opportunity before financial stress turns into default, and during that period the agency can re-rate the issuer.[40] As the agency will normally have a chance to correct a rating as the financial distress of the issuer is revealed, it would be extraordinary if such an obvious chink in the armor of agency credibility would be long left unrepaired.[41]

Why do errors arise? Resource limitations may be a factor. As companies run for profit, agencies pay keen attention to their expenses. Ideally, an analyst covering a given firm will regularly:

❑ Read the financial news for items potentially affecting or reflecting the firm's creditworthiness, including news about the company, its industry, regulation, and the economic and political environment;

❑ Examine interim financial reports including prospectuses and publicly available reports; and

❑ Keep in communication with the company's management concerning key developments.

To cover 10 or 15 banks is no problem. A rating agency analyst, however, may be responsible for covering as many as 30 to 40 institutions

---

[39] If an agency's higher rated issuers were defaulting at a higher rate of frequency than lower rated ones, something would clearly be amiss. Rarely are situations so clear cut, however, especially given the infrequency with which banks default.

[40] But not always. Reportedly, a Canadian life insurer, Confederation Life, was rated A+ one week and defaulted the next. On Watch, *Economist*, May 15, 1999.

[41] Strangely enough, some local rating agencies have undercut their credibility by failing to remedy obviously inaccurate ratings. In one Asian market, two issues that been defaulted upon the issuer remained listed as investment grade securities for months after the default.

in three or more countries.[42] Taking into account time required for spreading and analyzing financials, travel and bank visits, answering client inquiries, report preparation, ratings committee meetings and communications, report revisions, editing and proofreading, participating in ratings committee meetings, and related administrative responsibilities, marginal changes in administrative and research support levels can have significant impacts on the timeliness and quality of the risk monitoring process.[43] In other words, resource limitations may mean that day-by-day monitoring of institutions in certain markets is difficult (although the advent of the Internet has made it easier in some respects), and updating of reports on markets and banks can lag far behind the information available to the financial markets. A more extreme lack of resources can also make an agency vulnerable to seat-of-the-pants rating assessments in an attempt to rush rating assignments and reports to publication. These same resource limitations may allow the agency's ratings to become out of sync on a global basis, leading to inconsistencies — across regions for example — as mentioned above.

In addition, distortions can also occur when a highly persuasive individual or group of individuals may cause ratings in respect of particular markets or institutions under their purview to gravitate towards being overly pessimistic or optimistic. Also, a factor previously underweighted by agency analysts, such the ability of bank regulators to enforce their directives or the expectation that certain institutions would receive support from the authorities, may be revealed through circumstances to have been in error, compelling previous assumptions to be rethought. Finally, too much weight may be given to news reports by a rating committee sitting 10,000 miles away, without making independent investigation. This can lead to hasty actions that later prove to have been based on false premises.

Whatever their causes, once errors and distortions have occurred, remedying them can be problematic. For example, an agency may have leapt too quickly to downgrade or upgrade an institution or market, but may fear for the impact on its credibility if it corrects the action too quickly, notwithstanding that subsequent developments clearly show its inaccuracy. As we mentioned earlier, the agency may also worry about the

---

[42] Anecdotal evidence suggests that the larger rating agencies are able to provide more resources for staff and that consequently analysts at these agencies tend to spread less thin than at the smaller firms.
[43] At the same time, while compensation varies, it is a fact that levels of analyst compensation in the ratings industry are a fraction of that paid to analysts with investment banks of comparable stature.

signal a particular upgrade or downgrade may send to rating users about the market as a whole, irrespective of its applicability to the institution under review. If changes follow too rapidly on one another, the agency's credibility may be called into question. As a result, rating changes may become unduly cautious. Similarly, if distortions have occurred gradually on a systematic basis, it may be practically impossible for an agency to publicly recalibrate its ratings in one or more markets through across-the-board rating changes. The problem is exacerbated when paid ratings are involved, which require ordinarily require review by the rated entity.

The tendency towards caution is reinforced by the criticism agencies attract when their ratings are too optimistic. Overly pessimistic or excessively conservative ratings at worst will normally be regarded as erring on the side of prudence, and will rarely attract the same degree of censure. When a rating change is overdue, an event such as the disclosure of midterm financial results will often be viewed by the agency as a suitable time to make the change, the most recent figures supporting the decision to upgrade or downgrade the firm. In other words, needed recalibration or adjustment of inconsistent ratings can take place under cover of such events. Understanding these dynamics can assist the user of issuer and issue ratings to better anticipate rating changes and divine their meanings.

RATING THE BANK: BASIC DEFAULT PARAMETERS VS. COUNTERPARTY RATINGS

Methodology for Rating Banks: CAMEL Rules

The major and specialist rating agencies employ broadly similar methodologies to rating banks. Although rating symbologies and definitions vary, these agencies more or less follow the CAMEL model delineated in this book in assessing the financial condition of banks. In other words, all the major and specialist agency analysts apply a comparable approach to examining bank creditworthiness. To summarize briefly, this involves a review of the following items and, where applicable, associated ratios.

❑ Capital adequacy

❑ Asset Quality & Risk Control

❑ Management & Strategy and Banking Environment

❑ Earnings & Profitability

❑ Liquidity

Within this framework, which underlies a large portion of this handbook, there are of course variations as to how these elements of credit assessment are approached. The agency may assign percentage weightings to elements of financial performance and condition. For example, asset quality may be weighted as more important than capital, but such weightings generally reflect rather than guide actual practice. While some agencies utilize financial models to benchmark and calibrate their ratings, all avoid a purely mechanical approach to the rating decision.[44] Qualitative inputs based on the bank visit, the quality and coherence of managers' presentations, carry more weight than the layman might suspect. Indeed, it is often this qualitative input which adds value to the agency analyst's evaluation. Contrary to myth, none of the major general or specialist rating agencies have a "black box" into which data inputs are reconstituted as a rating assessment output.

In addition to these bank-specific factors, the sovereign risk rating of the country has an impact both through the sovereign ceiling, where applicable, and by providing a filter through which the bank's performance data is interpreted. Similarly, depending upon the type of rating — we discuss these in more detail in the following chapter — the banking environment, the capacity and willingness of the state to act as a lender of last resort and other systemic influences will affect the appraisal of bank creditworthiness.

The Common Factor: Emphasis on Process

What all the major agencies share is an emphasis on process: particularly the use of a committee approach, which we have alluded to earlier, in deciding what rating is appropriate. Based on relevant fundamentals (discerned through the comparison of a bank with its peers and historical performance and condition), the examination of the bank's financials for the likely causes of changes in that performance, the reasons for such changes proffered during meetings with management, as well as the prospects for the future gleaned from such meetings (or from third party opinions), the agency analyst can make an educated recommendation.

---

[44] "…Moody's ratings are not based on a defined set of financial ratios or rigid computer models. Rather, they are the product of a comprehensive analysis of each individual issue and issuer by experienced, well-informed, impartial credit analysts." Credit Rating, p. 14. The author's experience at BankWatch and discussions with a former Moody's analyst confirms this statement to be correct.

The opinions of other more detached analysts with experience in rating other banks functions as a check on an erratic ratings decision. To reiterate and as the agencies emphasize, a rating is merely an opinion, specifically an informed and consensual opinion based on fundamental analysis. By and large, this approach has served the agencies and their customers well.

CATEGORIES OF RATINGS: DEFAULT OR ISSUE-SPECIFIC AND COUNTERPARTY OR ISSUER

Fundamentally, there are two types of ratings. The first is the traditional default or issue (-specific) rating which rates the risk of default on fixed income securities issued by any corporate entity. Default ratings, which may also be termed public debt ratings (public because they are most often used in the public securities markets) or more simply debt ratings, attempt to assess the risk that the issuer of such obligations will not perform the financial obligations of the issue in accordance with their terms. In addition to funding their lending and other business activities from deposits, banks frequently borrow in the capital markets, issuing short-term or medium-term paper to investors. Although unrated corporate debt issues are sometimes successfully offered, particularly in the high-yield market and in certain local currency markets, as was observed previously, a rating usually is a pre-requisite for a corporate issuer to successfully obtain funding. At least this is the case in order to obtain an interest rate approaching the benchmark rate obtained by prime issuers. Since for banks, the cost of funding is extremely critical to its profitability, a rating is normally a *de facto* prerequisite for a bank that wishes to obtain funding in the capital markets, particularly in the international debt markets.

Debt ratings, which are the bread-and-butter of the major agencies, are in principle issue-specific, and take into account the terms and covenants of the legal instrument that constitutes the debt obligation, as well as the financial strength of the issuer and other relevant factors. As defined by S&P, an issue credit rating is:

" ... a current opinion of the creditworthiness of an obligor with respect to a specific financial obligation, a specific class of financial obligations, or a specific financial program (including ratings on medium term note programs and commercial paper programs). ... It takes into consideration the creditworthiness of guarantors, insurers, or other forms of credit enhancement on the obligation and takes into account the currency in which the obligation is denominated."

According to S&P, an issue rating measures both the "capacity and willingness" of the borrower to fulfill its financial obligation in accordance with its terms. In evaluating the likelihood of repayment, the agency looks at the terms of the obligation, creditors' rights afforded under relevant bankruptcy and insolvency law. Senior debt will normally be rated higher than junior or subordinated debt, which ranks lower in priority in the case of insolvency. The primary customers for default rating information are institutional investors such as pension funds and insurance companies that purchase debt obligations of corporations, as well as the investment banks that underwrite issues and traders who speculate in fixed-income securities. As noted, Moody's and S&P are the main providers of default ratings, although with the agglomeration of Fitch, and Duff & Phelps with BankWatch[45] to become the new Fitch, the last is becoming a rival to these two. At the same time, specialist agencies such as BankWatch have attempted to make inroads into this territory, with a limited degree of success.

Counterparty risk ratings, which were once the province of the specialist agencies focus on the ability of the issuer to satisfy its obligations generally, irrespective of the terms of any particular debt obligation. BankWatch, for instance, defined its issuer rating as an indicator of the probability of "future problems arising and the ability of the company to address such adversity." Commercial banks are obliged to deal with financial institutions worldwide, especially in trade finance transactions, such as letters of credit, and are the primary customers for counterparty rating.

The Sovereign Ceiling: Impenetrable or Not?

The concept of the sovereign ceiling, adopted to a greater or lesser degree by all rating agencies, refers to the notion that a corporate entity, whether public or private, cannot be rated higher than the sovereign rating, i.e. the rating assigned to the country in which the corporation is based. The rationale for the sovereign ceiling is that the sovereign has the power to compel other issuers to default by, for example, imposing a moratorium

---

[45] Prior to its acquisition by Fitch, BankWatch attempted to make inroads into this territory, with an extremely limited degree of success.

on foreign currency transfers, mandating exchange controls, limiting access to foreign currency, or imposing other restrictions.[46] To illustrate, if Bank X located in Country Y, which is rated BB, the highest rating that could be assigned to X is BB. In practice, it would likely be assigned a rated below that unless it was a 100% state owned bank with the full expectation of government support or possessed of an extremely high financial condition.

The sovereign ceiling is most applicable to foreign currency obligations, since it is foreign currency transfers that are most likely to be restricted should a particular country experience macro economic problems. Some agencies assign a separate local currency sovereign rating that may serve as a ceiling for local currency debt issues. Not all rating agencies believe that the sovereign ceiling should be a rigid constraint, and allow that in some cases an individual bank could have a rating higher than that of the sovereign. This exception to the rule applies most often in respect to local currency ratings, and is considerably rarer in the case of foreign currency ratings. In addition, special purpose vehicles used in structured finance transactions, when located offshore and pumped with special credit enhancements, will not be subject to the sovereign ceiling.

In theory, the sovereign ceiling would apply to both debt ratings and to counterparty ratings. In practice, it is usually not directly applicable to counterparty ratings, irrespective of whether they are based solely on financial strength or incorporate some element of state support. The reason is that counterparty ratings characteristically employ a different ratings scale than that characteristic of sovereign and issue (debt) ratings and are therefore not directly comparable. (Counterparty ratings often use the A–E scale rather than the AAA to C scale generally used for sovereign and debt ratings.) For example, Bank X conceivably could have a counterparty rating on the latter scale of A, even though its foreign currency debt rating would be restricted to BB. The sovereign rating, however, may have an indirect impact upon a counterparty (issuer) rating and agencies have addressed the relationship between the sovereign ratings and counterparty ratings in different ways as will be seen during the discussion of the methodologies of major generalist and specialist rating agencies.

---

[46] See Peter Jordan, Gabriel Torres & Christopher Huhne, "Rating Above the Sovereign Ceiling, Fitch IBCA Special Report, June 18, 1998.

THE BANK RATING PROCESS

The Rating Process

The process of rating banks and other corporations and institutions some-times appears to be a formidable one, shrouded in more mystery than is justified. In fact, it is comparatively simple. Assuming that the agency has already rated some institutions in the subject market, the process ensues as follows:

Data Collection

The bank's latest financial statements and annual report are collected, and "re-spread" into a standard form used by the agency.

Request for Supplementary Data

A questionnaire requesting supplementary information is sent to the bank.

Bank Visit

A meeting is arranged between one or more agency analysts and one or more senior bank staff. Such bank visits ordinarily will last from about one hour to a full day, depending upon whether the rating is solicited or unsolicited, and whether the bank has been rated in the past or is a first time rating. Meetings for ratings with banks on an unsolicited basis are ordinarily the briefest, as the analytical team or a single analyst may have a meeting with an individual that will usually last up to one to two hours. In the case of solicited ratings, ratings of banks previously visited will normally range from one to four hours in duration, and analysts may meet with bank management sequentially. First time ratings will normally range from two hours at a minimum to one to two full days.

Bank visits may involve a prepared presentation by management or take the form of a question and answer session with the agency analysts. Topics typically discussed include:

❑ the bank's history, franchise, management philosophy and strategy
❑ review of latest operating results
❑ explanation of causes of significant aspects in the financial statements, such as a steep rise or decline in line items or operating ratios

❑ discussion of any extraordinary and other specific line items in the financial statements

❑ investment in information technology, branch expansion or other major fixed investments

❑ discussion of risk management procedures and policies

❑ regulatory developments, the competitive landscape, new products and services, subsidiaries, potential acquisitions or divestments

❑ capital raising activities

Analysis and Report Preparation

The analysts prepare a draft report, normally within one to two weeks of the visit, which may be sent to the rated institution for initial review. At this stage, depending on the agencies policy the report may or may not include a ratings recommendation.

Rating Committee Review

The analyst(s) who have prepared the report decide on a ratings recommendation, taking into account quantitative and qualitative inputs. This ratings recommendation, together with supporting documentation and the draft report, is submitted to a ratings committee, either in person, by conference call, or via email, and a consensus is reached. The ratings committee, typically composed of analysts with relevant experience, will ordinarily include from three to seven or more members. The major and specialist rating agencies eschew the use of outside committee members both for reasons of efficiency and consistency.

Additional Review and Rating Dissemination

Once a consensus has been reached, the rating will be disseminated, in the case of solicited ratings with the right of review by the rated institution.

Time Required

Unless a first time rating, the entire rating process to this point will in most cases be accomplished within one month. Where the rated institution has the right of review, this may include the right to appeal the rating or the right to prevent the distribution of the rating. Such reviews may, of course, extend the duration of the process several weeks or more.

First-time ratings, i.e. those which have not been previously covered by the rating agency in solicited or unsolicited form, tend to be the most time-consuming, as the agency analysts must familiarize themselves with the company from the ground-up. Follow up requests for information may be necessary as well. The entire process is likely to take anywhere between one to two months.

Rating Actions and Changes

Ratings reviews of issuers and long term issues will as a rule be performed on an annual basis. Significant changes in the issuer's performance or financial condition, as well as changes in market conditions, regulatory enactments, and macroeconomic indicators, may trigger an ad hoc review. Some agencies will announce a review publicly and couple the announcement that the outlook for the issuer is positive, negative or stable (or applying comparable language). When the outlook is indicated to be positive or negative, the implication is that the rating if changed at all, will be respectively upgrade or downgraded within the near term. When the review is completed, the changed rating will be announced, or the current rating will be affirmed.

Agencies will also generally announce the assignment of new rating or a discontinuation of an old one. A ratings discontinuation does not necessarily imply anything negative. The rating may be an unsolicited rating that the agency deems no longer cost-effective to cover, or it may be a solicited one where the issuer has determined that the cost of maintaining the rating is no longer worth the benefits. In some instances, a bank's declining financial condition may lead it to the conclusion that it would be better to no rating than a highly negative one.

The Cost of a Rating

Rating costs vary considerably. The major rating agencies charge upwards of US$40,000 for an initial rating, and depending upon the size of the institution and issue being rated, the cost can exceed US$100,000. Of course, the major agencies will rate some institutions on an unsolicited basis, particularly where only an issuer rating — in contrast to an issue rating is involved. Maintenance fees for ratings may be lower than the initial cost, where the duration of the issue exceeds one year. Unsolicited ratings are most frequently offered to major state-owned commercial banks, where the cost of a rating may be prohibitive. The ratings fees of local and specialist agencies varies considerably. The cost can range from a few thousand dollars to fees comparable to those of the major agencies.

Trends in the Rating Industry

The rating agencies have sought to improve their timeliness and accuracy through changes in methodology and beefing up of overseas operations. Arguably, consolidation in the industry will lead to increased economies of scale and better ratings. Despite the major agencies having formed local ventures to supply local debt ratings, some local markets and as well as niche areas remain not well served by credible rating agencies. Recent developments in technology including the Internet as well as changes in bank regulation can be expected to affect the rating industry. Distribution of ratings via the World Wide Web has become increasingly important as a link between the agencies and their users. While the big 3 can be expected to dominate the international capital markets, local, regional and specialist agencies may be able to find viable niches and address customers not well served by the majors. While qualitative judgments will continue to be important in the rating process, it can also be expected that technology will enable the use of more sophisticated quantitative and statistical methods to assist in making rating assignments.

CHAPTER SUMMARY

Ratings measure the risk of default and the risk of loss from that default. Traditionally, what is measured is the relative risk of default rather than an absolute level of risk tied to a specific mathematical default probability. Retrospective studies, however, demonstrate that the relative risks embodied in a ratings symbol do tend to correlate over time with particular mathematical probability indicators. Ratings assist investment and risk managers to select securities and establish exposure limits consonants with the needs of their particular institutions. Benchmarked against a sovereign risk rating, i.e., the risk of default by a government, ratings help to establish a yield curve and assist investors in pricing securities. Similarly, by providing an independent view of the credit risk entailed in exposure to various institutions and securities, ratings assist risk managers in avoiding losses and in allocating capital effectively.

The ratings industry developed in the early 20th century, and has evolved to encompass two primary types of ratings: debt ratings and counterparty ratings. The former rate the default risk of specific fixed-income security issues, such as bonds or commercial paper and were traditionally the province of the major agencies. The latter rate the default risk attributable generally to an institution, often financial institutions, and were traditionally the province of the specialist agencies. Since the 1970s, major rating agencies have shifted the cost of performing ratings from investors to issuers. Most international debt ratings are now solicited or paid ratings. Unsolicited ratings are still performed by the agencies in certain circumstances. The industry expanded rapidly in the 1980s and the 1990s saw both its globalization and consolidations. Three agencies presently dominate the ratings of international debt issues: Moody's, S&P and Fitch. Other regional specialist and local agencies fill various niches, including regional bank counterparty ratings and local currency debt markets.

Various criticisms have been lodged against rating agencies, and the failure of the major agencies to anticipate the Asian crisis of 1997–99 heightened such criticisms. The primary charges made against rating agencies are that they are often wrong, that they exploit their market power, that ratings are lagging indicators, and that they are biased. While some criticisms are justified, in respect of the major international agencies, most are not and are based upon a misconception of the rating agencies' role. Rating agencies are not auditors, nor are they infallible. Neither do they perform rocket science. Rating agencies typically utilize mainstream analytical methods to assess fundamental credit risk. In the case of financial institutions, the familiar CAMEL model, utilized together with peer group and trend analysis, is the primary tool used in assigning a rating.

Although the agencies do not draw attention to their mistaken judgments, they are not perfect, nor should they be viewed as such. Unsolicited ratings generally add information to the market, and although occasionally abuses have been alleged, they are most certainly extremely infrequent. Rating agencies do not attempt to monitor daily changes in bond spreads, and it is unreasonable to expect that they should be better able than other sophisticated market participants to predict market moves or market developments, including panics or contagions. Finally, while rating agencies may be biased towards prudence and caution, they have every reason not to demonstrate any consistent and detectable bias towards identifiable parties as it would undermine their credibility and hence the market for the services they provide.

The assignment of ratings is a labor-intensive and somewhat time consuming procedure, which is characterized by an emphasis on process. For this reason, ratings cannot be expected to be as timely as some market participants would wish. Nonetheless, demand by the users of ratings may to lead towards a greater emphasis on faster and more frequent ratings actions, as well as an increased use of quantitative methods and risk measures in the future.

CHAPTER TWENTY FIVE

BANK RATING TYPES AND SYMBOLOGIES: A USER'S GUIDE

By distilling analysis into a single symbol, a rating system inherently suppresses information.
— Moody's Special Comment: Moody's Approach to the Credit Analysis of Banks and Bank Holding Companies, April 1993.

INTRODUCTION

Within the two broad categories of ratings mentioned in the previous chapter, each rating agency has come up with its own rating types, definitions and symbologies. There are many parallels among them, yet the rating types and symbols are not completely equivalent, and are not necessarily equivalent to each other. This section will discuss the rating types and symbologies of the major rating agencies and key specialist agencies before comparing their rating methodologies.

To reiterate, rating agencies categorize ratings into issue and issuer ratings, short-term and long-term ratings, and foreign currency and local currency ratings. *Issue*[1] ratings refer to specific securities issues and the accompanying legal instruments, while *issuer*[2] ratings refer to the overall willingness and capacity of the issuer of financial obligations to fulfill those obligations. *Issue* ratings are distinguished by priority, i.e. senior debt versus subordinated debt versus preferred shares, while *issuer* ratings are single ratings. (In the case of insolvency, senior debtholders

---

[1] Also known as default, public debt or debt ratings.
[2] Also known as counterparty ratings.

are paid out of the assets of the issuer that remain before subordinated bondholders and preferred shareholders). *Issuer* ratings will generally take account of external support, whether in the form of explicit guarantees or implicit shareholder or state backing. *Issue* ratings may or may not do so, depending upon how the rating category is defined. Sovereign risk ratings, although they may refer to specific instruments, are usually classified as *issuer* ratings.[3]

Normally, sovereign risk ratings and long-term issue ratings and employ a rating scale with the greatest number of gradations, or "notches." Short-term issue ratings typically utilize an abbreviated four-notch scale, while financial institutions issuer ratings fall somewhere in between. Whether an issue or issuer is evaluated in respect of foreign or local currency does not ordinarily make any difference in the form of the rating scales utilized. Below we will examine the rating symbologies of the three major rating firms — Moody's, S&P and Fitch and two specialist agencies, BankWatch (recently absorbed by Fitch), as well as that of Capital Intelligence, a regional specialist agency.

Typical Utilization of Rating Scales

	Issue (and Sovereign Risk Ratings)	Issuer
Long-Term	Broad scale, many (18+) gradations	Mid-sized scale, medium number of gradations
Short-Term	Narrow scale, few (often 4) gradations	

MOODY'S INVESTOR SERVICES

Moody's offers four types of ratings that address the risks of bank obligations. They are:

❑ Default Ratings

❑ Bank Deposit Ratings

---

[3] Sovereign risk ratings as applied to sovereign bonds and comparable obligations are effectively equivalent to issuer ratings since sovereigns are immune from bankruptcy courts and consequently the concept of priority and subordination is meaningless in the sovereign context. Likewise, covenants are effectively unenforceable, so the focus is nearly always on sovereign capacity and willingness indicators rather than on issue-specific considerations.

❑ Counterparty Ratings

❑ Bank Financial Strength Ratings

Default Ratings

Like all default ratings, Moody's default ratings are issue-specific. They encompass both long term (one year or more) and short-term ratings (less than one year). The long-term ratings employ Moody's well known Aa-C scale, which has nineteen gradations or "notches" in ratings parlance. The short-term default ratings are divisible into only four notches, as the table below indicates.[4] Long-term ratings are *issue-specific*, while in Moody's case, short-term ratings are *generic issue* ratings that apply to short-term obligations "in any market anywhere in the world." The rationale is that short-term obligations are typically unsecured and are without covenant protection.

Bank Deposit Ratings

In addition to the standard default rating which Moody's has offered since it began operations in the early part of the 20th century, the agency in 1985 introduced a bank deposit rating, which it regards as a subcategory of default rating. Although a default rating, bank deposit ratings are assigned to issuers and assess risk of default of the issuer with respect to bank deposits generally. In this context, bank deposits can be thought of as a form of senior debt. Moody's Bank Deposit Ratings do not only take account of the financial strength of the bank, but also consider the prospect of external support from a government or parent. But Moody's does not "impute a head office guarantee in the absence of an explicit undertaking."[5] These ratings utilize the same symbology as Moody's Default Ratings. As is the case with Default Ratings, Bank Deposit Ratings are subject to a sovereign ceiling with respect to foreign currency deposits. In the case of foreign branches of rated banks, the branches are subject to the sovereign ceiling of the host country rather than that of the country in which the parent bank is domiciled.

---

[4] Moody's Prime/Not Prime rating scale was introduced in 1972 and was designed for use with commercial paper issues.

[5] Ibid. p. 5.

Counterparty Ratings (Subsumed into Default Ratings)

Moody's also introduced a category of ratings called Counterparty Ratings in 1994, that were designed to assess counterparty risk in the derivatives market. Subsequently, this category of ratings was dropped.[6]

Bank Financial Strength Ratings

Also in 1994 Moody's introduced the Bank Financial Strength Rating. This rating was very similar to the issue and counterparty ratings that had been the mainstay of the bank specialist rating firms, i.e. BankWatch, I.B.C.A. and Capital Intelligence.[7] (See table on the next page.) Employing identical A to E scales, the type of rating was specifically addressed to the needs of "interbank market and counterparty credit departments." It addressed the risk management concerns of banks generally and specifically assisted banks in setting line of credit with institutions and in establishing country risk limits. Unlike the bank deposit rating, it does not take account of external support and is solely addressed to the stand-alone financial condition of the bank.

STANDARD & POOR'S

S&P's bank ratings include, in addition to standard default (i.e. issue) rating, a "Counterparty Credit Rating" which it defines as a type of *issuer* credit rating. Another type of issuer rating is a sovereign risk rating. An issuer rating, according to the agency, is "a current opinion of an obligor's overall financial capacity (its creditworthiness) to pay its financial obligations." As such, it is non-issue specific and is very much akin to Moody's Bank Financial Strength Rating. Like Moody's Bank Financial Strength Ratings, S&P's counterparty credit ratings do *not* take account of external

---

[6] They were launched, according to the agency, because customers were using issue-specific default ratings to assess the risk of a counterparty's failure to perform financial agreements such as swaps, options, forwards and letters of credit. The ratings were devised because it was believed that such agreements might not be treated in the same manner as senior unsecured debt in all jurisdictions due to varying laws and regulations. The agency therefore felt it needed a new category of rating to take account of differences in regulatory regimes and the corresponding likelihood of enforceability in the event of liquidation. Although Counterparty Ratings considered the regulatory framework affecting financial contracts, they were not intended to examine particular contracts employed by particular issuers. Emphasis was placed on applicable law and regulation, and on risk management controls and systems employed by the rated institution. The agency acknowledged that in the case of banks, Counterparty Ratings were typically the same as default and bank deposit ratings.

[7] As noted elsewhere, BankWatch and IBCA (Inter Fitch IBCA) are now part of Fitch.

Table: Moody's Default, Bank Deposit and Counterparty Ratings Scales

	Long-Term	Short-Term (n.b. no short-term Counterparty Ratings)	
Investment Grade	Aaa		Prime
	Aa1		
	Aa2	P1	
	Aa3		
	A1		
	A2		
	A3	P2	
	Baa1		
	Baa2	P3	
	Baa3		
Speculative Grade	Ba1		Not Prime
	Ba2		
	Ba3		
	B1		
	B2	Not Prime	
	B3		
	Caa*		
	Ca		
	C		

support or credit enhancement. The agency's long-term counterparty credit rating make use of the agency's standard AAA to CC ratings symbology. The agency has also added special symbols R, SD and D, indicating "under regulatory supervision," "selective default" and "default" to indicate problem banks in various stages of present or prospective default. The agency's short-term counterparty credit rating employ an A-1 to C scale, together with the R, SD, and D designations. S&P also utilizes subscripts "pi" to indicate ratings based on "public information," i.e. unsolicited ratings.

S&P Counterparty Credit Rating with Moody's Approximate Equivalent in Italics

	Long-Term, Counterparty, S&P (19 + 3 notch)	Long-Term, Moody's equivalent (19 notch)	Short-Term, Counterparty, S&P (7 notch)
Investment Grade (3 or 10 notch)	AAA	Aaa	A1+
	AA+	Aa1	A1
	AA	Aa2	
	AA−	Aa3	A2
	A+	A1	
	A	A2	A3
	A−	A3	
	BBB+	Baa1	B
	BBB	Baa2	
	BBB−	Baa3	
Speculative Grade (1 or 9 notch)	BB+	Ba1	C
	BB	Ba2	
	BB−	Ba3	
	B+	B1	
	B	B2	
	B−	B3	
	CCC+	Caa	
	CCC	Ca	
	CC	C	
Default	R	= C	R
	SD		SD
	D		D

Source: Moody's & S&P

THE SPECIALIST AGENCIES: FITCH IBCA (NOW FITCH), AND CAPITAL INTELLIGENCE

Previous to 1997, IBCA and Thomson BankWatch dominated the specialist bank rating industry, with Cyprus-based Capital Intelligence maintaining a strong franchise in covering financial institutions in the Middle East. IBCA, which had previously been acquired by a diversified French company, Fimilac, merged with Fitch that year and subsequently acquired Duff & Phelps in early 2000. In October 2000, BankWatch was acquired by the group. At the time of writing, the succeeding entity, Fitch, was in the process of harmonizing the rating methodologies and symbologies among the constituent rating firms. It can be expected, however, that Fitch IBCA's bank rating methodology, described below, will remain largely intact leaving no global specialist bank rating agencies, although arguably the larger Fitch groups still encompasses such a group. Only Capital Intelligence remains as a regional specialist rating agency with a niche in coverage of Middle East financial institutions.[8]

The Ratings of the Former Thomson Financial BankWatch: A Post-Mortem

Thomson BankWatch (Thomson Financial BankWatch) absorbed by Fitch in November 2000, was like the other agencies in that it made a distinction between issuer and debt ratings. Debt ratings, however, are almost without exception not assigned to specific securities, but to classes of securities only. As such, no account was taken of non-customary covenants or provisions in specific securities. BankWatch's basic issuer rating used an A to E scale (as comparable to Moody's *Bank Financial Strength Rating* and Fitch-IBCA's *Individual Rating*), and had a 12–18 month time horizon.

Unlike Moody's bank financial strength ratings, BankWatch's issuer rating considered both financial strength and external support. Although the rating scale resembled Moody's Financial Strength Rating, the rating was more akin to Moody's Bank Deposit Rating, insofar as the Moody's rating took account of explicit external support.

---

[8]Although BankWatch was purchased from Thomson by Fitch in October 2000, and at the time of this writing it appears that the BankWatch franchise and methodology will be subsumed under that of Fitch, a description of the BankWatch rating approach is retained for heuristic purposes. For this reason, the BankWatch approach is described in the past tense.

In the case of BankWatch's ratings, shareholder and government support was frequently imputed even when not explicit. In this, BankWatch ratings differed from the other agencies.[9] In addition, BankWatch also assigned a short-term issuer rating, in which even more weight was given to external support, both implicit and explicit. This "TBW" (or in the case of emerging markets loosely defined, the agency's short term local currency — i.e. LC) rating ranged from 1 to 4, with 1 being best. BankWatch also assigned a variety of debt, i.e., default ratings for senior debt and subordinated debt ratings using a scale similar to S&P's.

Also unlike the other agencies, BankWatch utilized both a global rating scale and a so-called emerging market rating scales. The latter was designed to avoid the problem of rating compression. Rating compression occurs when a global scale, such as that which Moody's employed, was applied to emerging market countries. In countries with low sovereign risk ratings or weak banking systems, even the best bank may be no more worthy than a "D/E" on a global scale. This will tend to mask real differences in creditworthiness among institutions within a single market. BankWatch therefore came up with the idea of using two types of emerging markets scales. The first was called the intra-country issuer (IC) rating. This term, which implied that the rating puts the best banks in a country at the top of the scale and the worst at the bottom, was actually a misnomer.[10] What it actually meant was that banks with the same intra-country issuer, or IC rating were thought to be roughly comparable across borders within emerging markets very loosely defined (e.g., all of Asia except Japan fell into "emerging markets").

For example, a bank rated IC-C in the Philippines was regard as having a similar level of creditworthiness as one rated IC-C in Peru. The rating compression problem is was not entirely avoided by the use of this approach. In some countries the degree of latitude in ratings assignment was still highly constrained. But it did appear to allow for more gradations in credit quality than a purely global scale. BankWatch also used a numerical scale called a Credit Evaluation Rating, that paralleled the intra-country issuer rating. The CE rating, which applied mainly to unsolicited ratings of smaller institutions or banks in sub-investment grade

---

[9] Both BankWatch's issuer (intra country issuer and short term ratings take account of external support. The agency, however, notes that "Short-Term Debt Ratings put a greater emphasis on the likelihood of government support."

[10] Cf. At the time of this writing all the domestic banks in Thailand covered by BankWatch are rated IC-D.

countries in Asia, was in the process of being phased out at the time of BankWatch's sale. Although there was a plausible logic behind the rating system, in practice a dual-rating scale proved to be confusing, if not problematic.

How the issuer ratings converted to intra-country issuer ratings within the BankWatch scheme was not precisely articulated in the agency's literature. The issuer and intra-country issuer ratings effectively operated on two different tracks, with North American, Japanese and Western European banks occupying the "global scale" and banks in the remainder of the world on the so-called IC scale. By comparing the distribution of ratings, as well as how the 260 global senior debt ratings were assigned, it was possible to see how the two issuer scales worked together and how they corresponded with debt ratings.[11] An empirical observation suggests that the two issuer scales did not unify in a coherent and systematic way into a true global rating scale, but appeared to be essentially the same scale with minor differences in rating assignment due to sovereign and systemic risk considerations.[12]

Fitch—IBCA (Fitch) Ratings

Fitch employs two counterparty-style ratings: the Fitch (IBCA) individual rating and the Fitch (IBCA) support rating. The former, which is based on A to E scale, is similar to the issuer rating that was employed by Thomson BankWatch's issuer rating, and to Moody's bank financial strength rating. In contrast to the practice used by Thomson BankWatch, Fitch's individual bank rating does not take account of government or shareholder support within its issuer rating, but instead utilizes a separate support rating which rates the strength and likelihood of external support on a 1

---

[11] To illustrate, AAA debt ratings most often corresponded to issuer ratings of A, but were linked to issuer ratings as low as B. A long term debt rating of "A" corresponded to an issuer (i.e. global issuer) rating ranging from C/D to B, but also to IC ratings ranging from IC-B to IC-A. The lowest investment grade rating of BBB- corresponds to issuer ratings from C/D to B, but also to IC ratings from IC-C/D to IC-A/B.

[12] In practice, the adjustments made due to these considerations varied according to the sovereign risk rating. As a general rule, issuer and intra-country issuer ratings were identical or nearly so for sovereign ratings of AA- and above. For countries where the sovereign risk rating is between A+ and BBB, a downward adjustment of one ratings notch would ordinarily be made in the intra-country issuer rating versus the issuer rating. For non investment grade countries, the adjustment could be as much as two notches or more. These were not hard and fast rules, but did seem to account for most of the differences between the two scales.

Rating Scale of the Former Thomson Financial BankWatch

BankWatch, Issuer, 9 notch scale	BankWatch Debt approximate equivalent, 20 notch scale	Short-Term (Local Currency) Issue. & approximate equivalent, 4 notch scale
A	AAA	
A/B	AA+	
	AA	1
B	AA−	
	A+	
B/C	A	2
	A−	
C	BBB+	
	BBB	3
C/D	BBB−	
	BB+	
	BB	
D	BB−	
	B+	4
	B	
D/E	B−	
	CCC+	
	CCC	
E	CC	
	D (Default)	

Distribution of BankWatch Issuer and "Intra Country" Issuer Ratings, mid-2000 (prior to acquisition of BankWatch by Fitch)

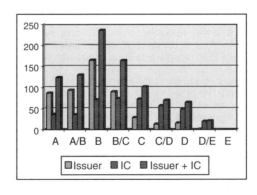

to 5 scale. These ratings may be qualified by a "T" designation in respect of ratings from 2–5 that indicate potential transfer risk or political risk "which might prevent support for foreign currency creditors." Also, unlike the Thomson BankWatch scheme, it is purely global in nature.[13]

Fitch-IBCA Rating Scale

Fitch IBCA, Issuer, 9 notch scale	Fitch IBCA International Long Term Debt, approximate equivalent, 22 notch scale	Fitch IBCA International Long Term Debt, approximate equivalent, 7 notch scale
A	AAA	F1+
A/B	AA+	
	AA	F1
B	AA−	
	A+	
B/C	A	F2
	A−	
C	BBB+	
	BBB	F3
	BBB−	
C/D	BB+	
	BB	B
	BB−	
D	B+	
	B	
	B−	C
D/E	CCC+	
	CCC	
	CC	
E	DDD (Default)	D
	DD	
	D	

---

[13] There is surely some merit in separating the probability of external support from that of transfer risk. For example, it may be highly probable that external support will be provided by a strong parent bank to its subsidiary, but if government regulations prohibit payments in foreign currency to a bank's creditors, they will be the victims of transfer risk.

In addition to its Bank Individual and Support Ratings, Fitch IBCA assigned international long term credit ratings on a scale from AAA–D, and international short-term credit ratings on a scale from F1+ to D.[14]

Capital Intelligence

CI employs three types of ratings: and a foreign currency rating, a domestic strength rating, and a support rating. The foreign currency ratings are

Capital Intelligence, Domestic Strength, 20 notch scale	Capital Intelligence, Foreign Currency, Long-Term, 20 notch scale	Capital Intelligence, Foreign Currency, Short-Term, approximate equivalent, 7 notch scale
AAA	AAA	A+
AA+	AA+	
AA	AA	A1
AA−	AA−	
A+	A+	
A	A	A2
A−	A−	
BBB+	BBB+	
BBB	BBB	A3
BBB−	BBB−	
BB+	BB+	
BB	BB	B
BB−	BB−	
B+	B+	
B	B	
B−	B−	C
C+	C+	
C	C	
C−	C−	
D	D	D

---

[14] The Fitch system makes explicit some distinctions that were blurred in the BankWatch regime and has the virtue of clarity, while the BankWatch approach, for all its ambiguity, had the advantage of being able to distill all ratings inputs into single ratings symbol.

capped at the sovereign rating ceiling for the country and includes all sovereign risk factors. The foreign currency rating also factors in the support element related to the bank with that exception. Its scheme is very similar to Fitch IBCA's, with some minor variations.

COMPARISON OF THE DEFINITIONS AND SYMBOLOGIES

Although the rating agencies will claim that their rating scales are not directly comparable with each other, as can be seen, all rating agencies employ quite similar rating definitions and symbologies. Whatever difference exist would therefore seem to lie in the nuances of the methodologies used by each agency and how they are applied in practice. Among the common elements are separate ratings for issuers and issues, and separate long- and short-term issue ratings. Scales for issues are usually AAA to C or D for long-term issue ratings, with + or − designations for most of the ratings range, and a more compact scale (4 or 7 notch) for short-term issue ratings.

Issuer (i.e., counterparty) ratings either follow the nine notch A to E scale (Moody's, BankWatch, and Fitch IBCA) or the 19–22 notch AAA

Comparison of Rating Scales and Symbologies

	S&P	Moody's	Fitch IBCA	BankWatch	CI
Issue, Long-Term	Long-Term Issue: 20 notch, AAA to D scale	19 notch, Aaa to C scale	20 notch, AAA to D scale	20 notch, AAA to D scale	20 notch, AAA to D scale
Issue, Short-Term	Short-Term Issue: 7 notch A1+ to D	4 notch, Prime to Not Prime scale	7 notch F1+ to D	4 notch, 1 to 4 scale	7 notch A1+ to D
Issuer/Counter-Party	Counterparty: Long-Term, 22 notch, AAA to D, Short-term, 7 notch A1+ to D	Bank Financial Strength Rating: 9 notch A to E scale	9 notch A to E scale	9 notch A to E scale (corresponding scales, including 1, 1.5 to 5 scale for "emerging markets")	20 notch, AAA to D scale
Support	None	None. N.B. Bank Financial Strength Rating does not incorporate external support	Yes. "T" designation refers to transfer risk.	No. BankWatch ratings incorporate external support. Support has greater weighting in short term ratings.	Yes.
Remarks					

Fitch IBCA's and CI's external support ratings

Fitch-IBCA Definition*	CI Definition	Common aspects
1 A bank for which there is a clear legal guarantee on the part of the state OR a bank of such importance both internationally and domestically that, in our opinion, support from the state would be forthcoming, if necessary. The state in question must clearly be prepared and able to support its principal banks.	Government-owned or clear legal guarantee on part of the state, or of such importance to the country, that the state would provide support in case of need. The state must clearly be able, and willing, to provide support.	Government-owned with high likelihood of support explicitly undertaken (or strongly implied), or Private bank that is "too big to fail", i.e. almost assured of support combined with the ability of state to provide support.
2 A bank for which, in our opinion, state support would be forthcoming, even in the absence of a legal guarantee. This could be, for example, because of the bank's importance to the economy or its historic relationship with the authorities.	Government support extremely likely despite absence of written guarantee. There may be some uncertainty regarding the state's willingness or ability to provide support. A private bank which has extremely strong ownership.	Government support likely, although not as certain as in category 1. Bank may be: government owned in part or whole, but support less likely than in category 1. private but highly likely to receive government support or private but with extremely strong shareholders or parent company.
3 A bank or bank holding company which has institutional owners of sufficient reputation and possessing such resources that, in our opinion, support would be forthcoming, if necessary.	Owners of very good reputation and resources, and which can provide clear support.	Generally a private bank with strong shareholder(s) or a strong parent likely able and willing to provide adequate support.
4 A bank for respect of which support is likely but not certain.	Support is likely but not certain.	Generally a private bank for which shareholder or parent support is more probable than not, but in respect of which capacity for support may or may not be wholly sufficient.
5 A bank, or bank holding company, for which support, although possible, cannot be relied upon.	No clear support and/or support cannot be relied upon.	Support is not probable or if forthcoming likely to be inadequate.

Source: respective websites

*A 2, 3, 4, or 5 Support rating may be qualified by the suffix "T". This indicates significant existing or potential transfer risk of economic and/or political origin which might prevent support for foreign currency creditors.

Rating Definitions: Condensed				
S&P Issuer & Issue Scales	S&P's Issuer & Issue Definition. Ability to meet financial commitments is:	Moody's Issue Scale	Moody's Default Rating Definition	BankWatch Debt (Issue) Scale
AAA	Extremely strong capacity	Aaa	Best quality. Carry the smallest degree of investment risk and are generally referred to as "gilt edged." Interest payments are protected by a large or by an exceptionally stable margin and principal is secure. While the various protective elements are likely to change, such changes as can be visualized are most unlikely to impair the fundamentally strong position of such issues.	Ability to repay principal and interest on a timely basis is extremely high.
AA+ AA AA–	Very strong capacity	Aa1 Aa2 Aa3	Judged to be of high quality by all standards. Together with the Aaa group they comprise what are generally known as high-grade bonds. They are rated lower than the best bonds because margins of protection may not be as large as in Aaa securities or fluctuation of protective elements may be of greater amplitude or there may be other elements present which make the long-term risk appear somewhat larger than the Aaa securities.	Very strong ability to repay principal and interest on a timely basis, with limited incremental risk compared to issues rated in the highest category.
A+ A A–	Strong but is somewhat more susceptible to the adverse effects of changes in circumstances and economic conditions than obligors in higher-rated categories.	A1 A2 A3	Possess many favorable investment attributes and are to be considered as upper-medium-grade obligations. Factors giving security to principal and interest are considered adequate, but elements may be present which suggest a susceptibility to impairment some time in the future.	Ability to repay principal and interest is strong. Issues rated a could be more vulnerable to adverse developments (both internal and external) than obligations with higher ratings.

Table continued

Rating Definitions: Condensed				
BBB+ BBB BBB−	Adequate but adverse economic conditions or changing circumstances are more likely to lead to a weakened capacity of the obligor to meet its financial commitments.	Baa1 Baa2 Baa3	Medium-grade obligations (i.e. they are neither highly protected nor poorly secured). Interest payments and principal security appear adequate for the present but certain protective elements may be lacking or may be characteristically unreliable over any great length of time. Such bonds lack outstanding investment characteristics and in fact have speculative characteristics as well.	The lowest investment-grade category; indicates an acceptable capacity to repay principal and interest. BBB issues are more vulnerable to adverse developments (both internal and external) than obligations with higher ratings.
BB+ BB BB−	Less vulnerable in the near term than other lower-rated obligors	Ba1 Ba2 Ba3	Judged to have speculative elements; their future cannot be considered as well-assured. Often the protection of interest and principal payments may be very moderate, and thereby not well safeguarded during both good and bad times over the future. Uncertainty of position characterizes bonds in this class.	While not investment grade, the BB rating suggests that the likelihood of default is considerably less than for lower-rated issues. However, there are significant uncertainties that could affect the ability to adequately service debt obligations.
B+ B B−	More vulnerable than the obligors rated 'bb', but the obligor currently has the capacity to meet its financial than higher-rated commitments. Adverse business, financial, or economic conditions will likely impair the obligor's capacity or willingness to meet its financial commitments.	B1 B2 B3	Generally lack characteristics of the desirable investment. Assurance of interest and principal payments or of maintenance of other terms of the contract over any long period of time may be small.	Issues rated B show a higher degree of uncertainty and therefore greater likelihood of default issues. Adverse developments could negatively affect the payment of interest and principal on a timely basis.
CCC+ CCC	Currently vulnerable, and is dependent upon favorable business, financial, and economic conditions to meet its financial commitments.	Caa	Of poor standing. Such issues may be in default or there may be present elements of danger with address respect to principal or interest.	Issues rated CCC clearly have a high likelihood of default, with little capacity to further adverse changes in financial circumstances.

Table continued

Rating Definitions: Condensed				
CC		Ca	Are speculative in a high degree. Such issues are often in default or have other marked shortcomings.	CC is applied to issues that are subordinate to other obligations rated CCC and are afforded less protection in the event of bankruptcy or reorganization.
DDD (Default)		C	Lowest rated class of bonds, and issues so rated can be regarded as having extremely poor prospects of ever attaining any real investment standing.	Default
DD D				

to C or D scale (S&P and CI). Issuer/counterparty, with the exception of S&P's scheme which utilizes essentially the same rating scales ratings for issuer and issue ratings, are not divided into long and short term. Three of the agencies, Fitch IBCA and CI, separate external support from intrinsic financial strength into a five-notch scale, although Moody's does not explicitly rank external support. BankWatch incorporates external support into its issuer ratings. It also states that support is given more weight in respect of short-term ratings.

Bank Issuer/Counterparty Ratings in Layman's Terms

Consensus characteristics of A to E rated banks can be inferred as follows:

A Banks

The strongest banks, nearly always major institutions, characterized by excellent financials, healthy and sustainable franchises, and a first-rate operating environment. Nothing to worry about.

B Banks

Solid banks, usually important institutions, operating in good economic and banking environment. May be some minor weaknesses, but no serious ones. Not perfect, but still basically nothing to worry about.

Comparison of BankWatch Issuer, Fitch IBCA Individual & Moody's Bank Financial Strength Ratings

	BankWatch	Fitch (IBCA)	Moody's
A	1. Exceptionally strong balance sheet and earnings record, 2. excellent reputation, 3. very good access to its natural money markets. 4. Any weakness or vulnerability mitigated by the strengths of the organization.	A very strong bank; outstanding: profitability and balance sheet integrity, 1. franchise, 2. management, 3. operating environment, or 4. prospects.	**possess exceptional intrinsic financial strength.** Typically, they will be 1) major institutions with 2) highly valuable and defensible business franchises, 3) strong financial fundamentals, and 4) a very attractive and stable operating environment.
B	**Company is strong with a solid financial record** and is well-received by its natural money markets. Some minor weaknesses may exist, but any deviation from the company's historical performance levels should be limited and short-lived. The likelihood of significant problems is small, yet slightly greater than for a higher-rated company.	**A strong bank. There are no major concerns** regarding the bank. Characteristics may include strong profitability and balance sheet integrity, franchise, management, operating environment or prospects.	**strong intrinsic financial strength.** Typically, they will be important institutions with valuable and defensible business franchises, good financial fundamentals, and an attractive and stable operating environment.
C	Company is inherently a sound credit with no serious deficiencies, but financials reveal at least one fundamental **area of concern that prevents a higher rating.** Company may recently have experienced a period of difficulty, but those pressures should not be long-term in nature. The company's ability to absorb a surprise, however, is less than that for organizations with better operating records.	**An adequate bank which, however, possesses one or more troublesome aspects.** There may be some concerns regarding its profitability and balance sheet integrity, franchise, management, operating environment or prospects.	**good intrinsic financial strength.** Typically, they will be institutions with valuable and defensible business franchises. These banks will demonstrate either acceptable financial fundamentals within a stable operating environment, or better than average financial fundamentals within an unstable operating environment.
D	**Company financials suggest obvious weaknesses,** most likely created by asset quality considerations and/or a poorly structured balance sheet. A meaningful level of uncertainty and vulnerability exists going forward. The ability to address further unexpected problems must be questioned.	**A bank which has weaknesses of internal and/or external origin.** There are concerns regarding its profitability and balance sheet integrity, franchise, management, operating environment or prospects.	**adequate financial strength, but may be limited by one or more of the following factors**: a vulnerable or developing business franchise; weak financial fundamentals; or an unstable operating environment
E	Very serious problems exist for the company, creating doubt about its continued viability without some form of **outside assistance**, regulatory or otherwise.	A bank with very serious problems which either requires or is likely to require external support.	Possesses very weak intrinsic financial strength, requiring periodic outside support or suggesting an eventual need for outside assistance. Such institutions may be limited by one or more of the following factors: a business franchise of questionable value; financial fundamentals that are seriously deficient in one or more respects; or a highly unstable operating environment.

C Banks

Inherently sound banks but with one or more significant problems such as below-average asset quality, liquidity, profitability or capital strength. Can be roughly average banks in an average environment, above average banks in a weak operating environment, or somewhat below average banks in a first-rate operating environment. Banks with at least one conspicuous weakness that bear watching.

D Banks

Banks with one or more obvious but potentially solvable problems. D banks may be major banks operating in fragile environments, or significantly weaker institutions in fairly strong operating environments. Banks with relatively degrees of vulnerability. Nonetheless in some countries, there may be no better.

E Banks

Banks with very serious problems that will require government or other help to survive. Problem banks. Outside support if not already available will likely soon be needed.

Comparing Ratings on the Basis of the Probability of Default

In the previous chapter, we saw that ratings could be historically correlated to default rates. The two largest rating agencies, Moody's and S&P have maintained the most detailed records of default rates within the their ratings universe over decades.

Although the two tables are not strictly comparable as the Moody's data breaks down rating categories into "+" and "−" categories, i.e. suffixes "1" and "3", the probabilities derived from both agencies relative risk assessments are remarkably close. The Aaa category for Moody's, equivalent to S&P's AAA rating, shows nil defaults in years 1 and 2 following the rating assignment, and the probability for year 5 varies only by 0.01%. Years 3 and 4 show more significant variations, but the differences are nonetheless minimal. Examining Moody's Baa2 rating, which corresponds to S&P's BBB rating, again the probabilities are still quite close. At the B2, i.e. B level, the deviation between the two becomes more substantial, with Moody's B2 rating appearing to reflect a higher risk security than that of S&P's B rating. It should be emphasized that the parameters of the data are not clearly specified and that it may

Moody's Cumulative Bond Default Rates, 1996						S&P Average Cumulative Default Rates					
Years	1	2	3	4	5	Term	1	2	3	4	5
Aaa	0.00	0.00	0.00	0.07	0.23	AAA	0.00	0.00	0.07	0.15	0.24
Aa1	0.00	0.00	0.00	0.31	0.31						
Aa2	0.00	0.00	0.09	0.29	0.65	AA	0.00	0.02	0.12	0.25	0.43
Aa3	0.09	0.15	0.27	0.42	0.60						
A1	0.00	0.04	0.49	0.79	1.01						
A2	0.00	0.04	0.21	0.57	0.88	A	0.06	0.16	0.27	0.44	0.67
A3	0.00	0.20	0.37	0.52	0.61						
Baa1	0.06	0.39	0.79	1.17	1.53						
Baa2	0.06	0.26	0.35	1.07	1.70	BBB	0.18	0.44	0.72	1.27	1.78
Baa3	0.45	1.06	1.80	2.87	3.69						
Ba1	0.85	2.68	4.46	7.03	9.52						
Ba2	0.73	8.37	6.47	9.43	12.28	BB	1.06	3.48	6.12	8.68	10.97
Ba3	3.12	8.09	13.49	18.55	23.15						
B1	4.50	10.90	17.33	23.44	29.05						
B2	8.75	15.18	22.10	27.95	31.86	B	5.20	11.00	15.95	19.40	21.88
B3	13.49	21.86	27.84	32.08	36.10						
						CCC	19.79	26.92	31.63	35.97	40.15
Source: Moody's						Source: S&P CreditWeek, Apr. 15, 1996					

be that other factors, such as time factors, e.g. what proportion of the ratings in each pool referred to issues made just prior to the great depression of the 1930s. Nonetheless, the data is interesting not only in that is enables the user to obtain some indication about the probability of default associated with each rating category, but it shows evidence of ratings anomalies where better rated issues occasionally exhibited higher rates of default than their lower rated counterparts.[15]

	Yr 1	Yr 2	Yr 3	Yr 4	Yr 5
Moody's Aaa	0.00	0.00	0.00	0.07	0.23
S&P, AAA	0.00	0.00	0.07	0.15	0.24
Variance	0.00	0.00	−0.07	−0.08	−0.01
Moody's, Baa2	0.06	0.26	0.35	1.07	1.70
S&P, BBB	0.18	0.44	0.72	1.27	1.78
Variance	−0.12	−0.18	−0.37	−0.20	−0.08
Moody's B2	8.75	15.18	22.10	27.95	31.86
S&P, B	5.20	11.00	15.95	19.40	21.88
Variance	3.55	4.18	6.15	8.55	9.98

---

[15] This is visible in the table drawn from Moody's table which shows a greater number of rating categories.

How Rating Reports Compare

Rating agencies ordinarily support the ratings they assign to banks with analytical reports. These reports, which may vary from 2 to 12 or more pages in length, also share broadly similar features. The specialist agencies, including BankWatch, Fitch-IBCA and CI, with their orientation towards the needs of institutional credit risk managers tend to provide more background information and to elaborate on the reasons supporting their assessments. This is because, for such users, the decision concerning credit limits requires inputs additional to the mere rating symbol. Most such credit professionals apply their own institutional rating model to this process, but may have limited access to additional investment research typically available to institutional investors. In contrast, for the major agencies, with their orientation towards such traders and investors in fixed income securities, the emphasis has traditionally been upon the rating symbol as embodying the major portion of the credit evaluation. Such investors turn to fixed income analysts for additional issuer information to assist in the buy/sell decision rather than to the rating agency, as well as for information concerning the extent to which the issue is over or under rated by major agencies.

The elements of bank reports of both the major and specialist agencies are nonetheless quite similar in many respects. The first page tends to be in the nature of an executive summary, including summary factual data and often contact information. While the "executive summary" of the first page may be followed by additional background information, most of the succeeding text will be given over to a financial analysis: describing, examining the relationships among the key credit criteria, and rendering assessments of relative performance and creditworthiness.

Illustrative Reports

Examining some reports on Asian banks at random will illustrate some of the distinctions among the major and specialist agencies.

S&P on Hua Nan Commercial Bank (Taiwan), 1997

S&P's report on Hua Nan Commercial Bank Ltd. of Taiwan, issued in February 1997 just prior to the Asian crisis, begins with current ratings information on the bank, summary financial data encompassing three years of data on assets, loans, deposits, equity, operating income and net income. The bulk of the first page of the report is taken up by the rating rationale, which justifies S&P's "public information" rating on the bank on the basis of its "solid market position and franchise," "reasonable shareholder profile," and shareholder support. Negative factors identified, including intensifying competition and hefty property exposure, implicitly detract from the overall rating. Profitability measured by return on assets, net interest margin are just "fair" on a global scale. Asset quality is still satisfactory, but could be on the rise from low levels, according to the report, while merely average capital ratios and a lackluster property market contribute to the agency's concern. The provincial government is indicated as being the majority shareholder and affords the bank some "capital support," and possible privatization within the next several years presents some uncertainties. The agency's primary anxiety, however, is "competitive pressures" that may adversely affect profitability and asset quality. This is mitigated, though, by the bank's "solid franchise" and the expectation of continued strong economic performance. Following a discussion of the bank's history and ownership, the nature of its business and franchise, as well as its scale and scope, the remaining three pages of text address ownership and legal status, strategy (branch expansion and movement towards greater customer orientation), asset quality (loan growth, loan composition, non-performing loans ratio), profitability (trends in net income growth, profitability and expense ratios, description of income composition), asset-liability management (i.e. funding and liquidity) and capital (capital ratios and quality of capital). Quantitative data include key financial items (more detailed than page one) for a five-year period, key ratios for five years, a five-year balance sheet and a five-year income statement.

Moody's on Metrobank (1999)

Moody's report on Metrobank, a major Philippine bank, is briefer than the S&P report. Summary ratings data, as well as ratios and financial items for a five-year period are included on the front page. The bottom third of the page includes a brief rating rationale which notes the bank's rapid growth and dominance in middle market lending that have rendered it vulnerable to asset quality problems following the Asian crisis. Profitability is expected to decline in the wake of rising loan loss provisions. A one-sentence ratings outlook (affirmed as negative) and a one-sentence description of recent results are also included on the first page. The remainder of the report, sans financials, follows an unstructured narrative format. The negative outlook on the bank is related to the general economic slowdown in the Philippines and the bank's rapid expansion into the vulnerable middle market. This is followed by a one paragraph description of the bank, and by a longer discussion of the bank's asset quality problems, its historically above average profitability, strong capital position, professional management and concentrated ownership.

Fitch IBCA on Hong Kong and Shanghai Banking Corp. (2000)

The first page of the Fitch IBCA report on the largest bank in Hong Kong includes ratings data, summary financial data (assets, equity, net income, ROA, ROE, leverage), and analyst contact information. The narrative begins with a background paragraph describing the bank's dominant role in Hong Kong, and its subsidiaries. The second paragraph discusses the legal structure of the bank (Hong Kong subsidiary of UK-based holding company) and the probability of support for the bank from the authorities. Finally, an assessment of the bank is made indicating that the rating is being upgraded based on "improving asset quality, strong capital ratios, and sound core operations." The rest of the paragraph supports these statements with reference to the bank's enhanced financial performance (growth in net profits, reduced provisioning requirements, etc.) and rising asset quality. The remainder of the report, interspersed with financial tables illustrating specific points, fleshes out the various elements of the CAMEL model. Topics addressed follow the outline below:

> Profile (history, ownership, strategy, disclosure)
> Performance (profitability and earnings)
> > Revenues
> > Non-Interest Income
> > Operating Expenses
> > Exceptional Items
> > Loan Loss Provisions
> > Prospects
> Risk Management (credit policies and procedures, loan growth and composition, NPLs)
> > Credit Risk
> > Market Risk & Asset/Liability Management
> Funding & Capital

The text of the report is followed with three pages of balance sheet, income statement and ratio analysis.

Thomson Financial BankWatch on Wells Fargo & Co. (December 1999)

BankWatch's report on Wells Fargo & Co., the holding company of Wells Fargo Bank, one of the largest banks in the US, was illustrative of its the agency's bank profiles. The profiles followed a standard template, normally varying in length from three to six pages in length, although longer reports are were sometimes provided for complex or problematic institutions. Unsolicited ratings of banks in emerging markets may might be limited to reports of one page of text. Financial data was limited confined to one page of "spreads" including income statement data, balance sheet data, and ratio analysis. However, the text of the report may be interspersed with financial tables and graphs at the discretion of the analyst.

As is the case with the reports of the preceding agencies, the first page constitutes an executive summary including the bank's ratings, analyst contact data, the bank's rating history, summary financial data (ROA, Capital Adequacy ratio, Assets, Deposits, Equity, Net Income), a rating rationale, and a SWOT analysis. The heart of the executive summary is the "rating rationale," which supplies the salient reasons for the rating assignment, affirmation or change. In the case of Wells Fargo, the rating rationale focuses on the credit impact of the bank's recent merger with Norwest Corporation and the bank's overall strong capital and liquidity. Strengths (broad franchise, alternative delivery channels, excellent capital, liquidity and asset quality), weaknesses (some businesses are interest sensitive, goodwill a drag on profitability), opportunities (cross selling, reinforcement of strong brand) and threats (impact of potential recession, especially on consumer and small business franchises) are enumerated below the rating rationale.

Page two and the first part of page three include a discussion of key developments (e.g. merger and appointment of new CEO), business description, management and information technology. The remaining two pages of text elaborate on the remaining CAMEL elements: i.e. Profitability [Earnings], Asset Quality, Capital, Funding & Liquidity.

Capital Intelligence on Standard Bank of South Africa (July 2000)

Capital Intelligence's report on Standard Bank of South Africa, one of the big four South African banks, issued in July 2000 is typical of the agency's report format. The first two pages form the executive summary. The first page consists of the bank's ratings, key balance sheet and profit and loss numbers, key financial ratios, and positive and negative factors. The half-page text on the first page describes the bank profile and rating rationale. The second page consists of a summary of the financial analysis focusing on asset quality, capital, liquidity and profitability. The middle part of the report incorporates non-financial factors of the analysis including bank ownership and support, background, market environment, strategies, operations, management, and systems and controls. The final part of the report includes a detailed financial analysis consisting of five pages, looking at asset quality, capital, liquidity and profitability. In addition, for the previous four-year period, a breakdown of the balance sheet and profit and loss statement, and indicating percentage movements is included together with 45 performance ratios. The overall report, including the two-page executive summary, runs to 14 pages, with two pages of financial spreads. Standard Bank of South Africa is the largest subsidiary of Standard Bank Investment Corporation Limited (Stanbic). Stanbic is the holding company for the interests of the Standard Bank Group. Accordingly, the report looks at both Standard Bank of South Africa and Stanbic. The report comments that Standard Bank, and its parent, Stanbic, possess a very strong domestic banking franchise, with noted market positions in retail, commercial and corporate banking. International operations are an important contributor to group profitability. Asset quality is sound although the bank has experienced a rise in non-performing loans during 1998/99 as domestic interest rates rose to 26% and disposable incomes were squeezed. However, domestic interest rates have fallen sharply and NPLs have now peaked. The capital position is solid and liquidity is comfortable, although the bank does rely on wholesale funding.

Profitability is good despite operating expenses to gross income remaining high, largely on account of the wide branch network. Profitability was also affected by a high provision charge, but is expected to be reduced further this year. Nedcor's (Nedcor is a domestic competitor) hostile bid approach for Stanbic in late 1999 rejuvenated the bank and much operational and strategic headway has been made over the last six months, focusing on profit improvement, cost control and alternative distribution channels. Following the banning of the bid, Capital Intelligence expects Standard Bank to emerge as an even stronger competitor and performer, capitalizing on the work which has been done recently in exploiting its key strengths. Foreign currency ratings of BBB- long-term and A3 short-term were capped at the sovereign level for South Africa.

The domestic strength rating of A+ reflected Standard Bank's strong market position and financial profile.

Ten Frequently-Asked Questions about Ratings

1. What does it mean when a rating agency drops a rating?

In short, nothing. Rating agencies drop and add coverage for many reasons. Most rating agencies are in business for profit, and they seek to fulfill customer needs. If a rating is solicited, i.e. paid, the issuer itself may decide to terminate the rating, or may wish that it continues, but no longer feels a business need to pay for a rating. It may be that the bank no longer needs access to the capital markets, or it may have decided to change or limit the rating agencies which it pays for a rating. If the bank is mainly interested in establishing correspondent banking relationships, its management may believe that the bank's reputation is strong enough so that it can do without a paid rating. This leaves the question of whether the rating agency will want to continue to offer the rating on an unsolicited, i.e. unpaid, basis. It may offer some unsolicited ratings in the hope that the institutions covered will eventually seek a paid rating, or because the institution is so important that investors and subscribers will make requests for coverage. Conversely, the agency may have covered a bank for some time on an unsolicited basis, and come to the realization that investors and customers have little interest in the bank. For instance, the bank may once have been internationally active, but has changed its strategy to focus on a domestic retail business. Finally, the rating agency may have dropped coverage for internal reasons or policies. It may wish to allocate more resources to paid ratings, or it may have a policy not to provide separate coverage of majority owned subsidiaries the parent of which it already rates.

2. What does it mean when a bank is not rated?

Again, very little, except that the bank is probably not a very important financial institution. The key rating agencies want to cover the banks in which investors or subscribers have an interest, either on a solicited or an unsolicited basis. Small banks, banks which do not need to access the capital markets for funding, or banks that are publicly-owned but second-tier institutions may feel no need for a rating, and rating agencies may feel that the end-users of their rating services are not much interested in the institution. In such a case, it will not be rated.

3. How long does the rating process take?

Time varies considerably depending upon whether the rating is solicited or unsolicited, and whether if unsolicited, a bank visit will be scheduled. If unsolicited, and no visit is deemed necessary (or if the rated institution does not make time available), a rating recommendation and a report supporting the recommendation can be completed in a day or less. Upon approval by the ratings committee, a rating may be assigned in less than a week. This, however, is the exception. Most unsolicited ratings and all solicited ratings entail a bank visit, and in the case of solicited ratings the bank has the right of appeal if it disagrees with the rating. The entire process can take from several weeks to one to two months. Most time consuming of all is likely to be a first time rating, since the rating request may not coincide with the routine visit of analysts to the region in which the bank is located. In addition, the due diligence required is likely to be more intensive in the case of a first time rating, and the ratings committee is also likely to require more time to deliberate.

4. What are rating agency analysts most concerned with when they visit a bank?

First and foremost, analysts are keen to discern whether the bank has any hidden problems, such as latent not performing loans or other potential problems in its security or loan portfolio that could impair capital. Asset quality is in most cases the preeminent concern. The analysts will attempt to form an opinion concerning the sustainability of the bank's franchise, the coherence of manage-ments strategy and a general impression of the quality of bank's management. The agency analysts are likely to have reviewed financial statements before meeting with the bank, and will be looking for explanations of any apparent anomalies, such as sharply increasing expenses amid a contracting loan book, or declining profitability despite rapid loan growth. In addition to explaining historical performance, the analysts will seek to supplement the past year's financial statements with more up to date interim financial data as well as management's projections for the current year. The analysts may seek to gauge management's overall view of the industry and business conditions, and seek clarification concerning future plans, which are likely to have been glossed over in the annual report.

5. What's the difference between the quality of a solicited and unsolicited rating?

In theory, there is no difference, other than that one is paid for by the issuer and the other is not. Rating agencies as a rule try to be fair and do not skew the rating against an issuer just because the rated institution is not a paying customer. Neither do they favor paying customers. The rating industry is the exception to the aphorism that "he who pays the piper calls the tune." By the same token, it is certainly the case that the more comfortable the agency analysts get with the managers of the rated institution, and the more disclosure that has been provided, the more likely that rated company will receive the benefit of any doubt. This is not really a function of payment — the analysts in any case are salaried professionals who certainly receive no benefit from the fact that an issuer is paying for the rating — but rather a function of the degree of interaction between the analysts and the issuers' managers that may give rise to a certain degree of confidence in management. Of course, it can always go the other way. More contact can lead to strengthening or confirmation of negative intuitions or perceptions.

6. How do I know whether a rating is solicited or unsolicited?

Some agencies disclose this information, while others do not. For example, it was not BankWatch's policy to disclose whether a rating was paid or not, although through certain signals it was possible to determine with some degree of accuracy which ratings were unsolicited. On the one hand, paid ratings were always "full reports" rather than abbreviated ones, and assigned issuer ratings rather than CE ratings. Thus, short reports or CE ratings could always be read as unsolicited. Some full reports and issuer ratings were unsolicited as well, so one could not be certain which were solicited and which were not. In the case of Moody's, the first press release accompanying the rating assignment will indicate whether a rating is solicited or not, but after that there will be no additional designation. S&P employs a so-called "pi" designation to indicate unsolicited ratings based on "public information."

7. How many analysts will visit the bank?

Normally two. Indeed, it is policy at the major agencies to send at least two analysts on a bank visit. The specialist agencies, however, have sometimes suffered from a shortage of resources and have been known to send only one analyst on a bank visit, particularly for unsolicited ratings.

8. What's the best way to make a good impression on agency analysts?

A whole sub-profession, known as ratings advisory, developed within the investment banking industry to enable issuers to obtain the best rating possible. Fair and full disclosure is better than one-sided disclosure that denies problems and is likely to be perceived as a "whitewash." If problems exist, but there are mitigating circumstances, these should be highlighted. For example, if capital levels at the end of the most recent financial year were low, and the bank has since raised new capital or has plans to do so, these developments should certainly be mentioned. Formal presentations, using Powerpoint slides, can be helpful in establishing a context for the discussion and answering some questions that are likely to come up in any case. Whether slides or used or not, some sort of opening remarks and presentation is usually the better strategy, as to leave all the initiative on the side of the analysts can be taken to imply that the bank is seeking to disclose as little as possible. Having information at the ready makes a good impression and saves the analysts the hassle of having to follow up to obtain it later. If information is promised to be delivered, follow up promptly. It is often helpful to have one bank officer designated as the "point man" who will be responsible for responding to agency requests.

9. How are rating decisions decided?

By committee. The analytical team will offer a rating recommendation that will either be agreed to not agreed to by the committee. The lead rating analysts may be grilled by the committee in an attempt to air all concerns, or in other cases a consensus may be reached fairly quickly. Where there is disagreement, different agencies may resolve them differently. Decision may be by majority vote or a consensus may be required to change the rating. More senior committee member are likely to have the final say, or at the very least their positions will carry more weight informally, if not formally.

10. Why does Moody's use a different symbology than S&P and how do you convert the scale from one to the other?

The two scales are essentially the same scale. The lower-case "a" used in the Moody's scale is simply a cipher for the capital letter which denotes the rating category. Hence "Baa" in Moody's parlance corresponds with S&P's "BBB," "Aa" corresponds with "AA" and so on. Instead of "+" and "–" symbols used by S&P, Moody's uses "1" for plus and "3" for minus, while "2" is neutral. Thus, "Ba3" is "BB–," "Baa2" is "BBB" and so forth. Why did Moody's choose such a peculiar symbology? The apocryphal story is that the scale currently used by S&P was actually first used in the US by Moody's. When Moody's ran into financial difficulties in the early 20th century, it is said that the company sold the rights to the symbology to S&P, and was compelled to come up with a new symbology. The present symbology was the result.

SOME OBSERVATIONS ON THE RATING INDUSTRY

Rating agencies, as we have seen, have become ensconced as independent evaluators of the creditworthiness of issues and issuers. Some have attempted to make a case that rating agencies do not adequately fulfill this role and should either be eliminated or more strictly regulated, while others have attempted to improve on the rating agencies in providing timely and independent credit data. One field of endeavor has been the quest for better ways to quantitatively model and predict default. Much of this effort has gone into predicting corporate insolvencies in developed markets, most notably the United States, which certainly can be said as being one of the most, if not the most, transparent market in the world. Altman's Z-score model is one attempt to create a quantitative model of risk by identifying key ratio variables that were correlated to default risk. Another model is the EDF, for expected default frequency, developed by KMV Corporation. The EDF model incorporates securities pricing data. In brief, KMV's model, which like Altman's Z Score is not specifically addressed at financial institutions, rests on the proposition that "when the market value of a firm drops below a certain level, the firm will default on its obligation."[16] Equity prices are utilized to assist in determining the market value of the firm. This limits the applicability of the KMV model to publicly listed companies, although the firm offers an analogous model that can be applied to non-listed companies by valuing the company on the basis of operating income times a multiplier.

The limited disclosure characteristic of banks in emerging markets, variances in accounting regimes and the greater weight that qualitative factors take on in emerging markets has limited their application in the global banking universe. Still, the long-term trend is towards greater disclosure worldwide.

Although sophisticated quantitative approaches such as those of KMV are not widely established among credit professionals, most of whom still apply a "human expert" approach to credit assessment as embodied in the methods of the rating agencies, they suggest that with improved collection and disclosure of data, ever growing computing power, and amid more volatile markets, credit assessment is likely to take on an increasingly quantitative cast. While fundamental and qualitative analysis as employed by most of today's credit analysts is unlikely to be discarded, it will probably be supplemented by greater use of equity and bond pricing data and other quantitative performance measures in an attempt to improve the accuracy and timeliness of risk assessment.

---

[16] Caouette, John B., Edward I. Altman, Paul Narayanan, *Managing Credit Risk, The Next Great Financial Challenge*, John Wiley & Sons, Incorporated, October 1998.

CHAPTER SUMMARY

In this chapter, we examined the various ratings symbologies employed by the major agencies and the specialist agencies. Although there are sometimes puzzling variations among the symbologies of the various agencies, the similarities are stronger than their differences. Nevertheless, it is important to be aware of what those differences are — whether external support is incorporated into the rating, for instance — and how they may affect the rating designation. Key variables in determining the rating scale employed are whether the rating is short-term or long-term, and issue-specific or issuer. Local currency scales typically replicate foreign currency scales. Additionally, the agencies may employ idiosyncratic symbols for specific purposes, e.g. S&P's use of the "pi" designation to indicate unsolicited ratings based on public information.

Not only are the symbologies quite similar among the various agencies, so are rating definitions. Remarkably, the probabilities of default corresponding to each of Moody's and S&P ratings categories are also fairly comparable. No doubt this corresponds to modest differences in methodology and its application among the entities rated. A greater degree of difference can be found in the reports that support the ratings. Styles, the scope of information provides, and financial details vary considerably.

CHAPTER TWENTY SIX

FIXED INCOME ANALYSIS APPLIED TO FINANCIAL INSTITUTIONS[1]

One of the problems with sovereign bond strategy is that it partly relies on second guessing the rating agencies.
— Desmond Supple, FinanceAsia.com, Oct 23, 2000

Fixed income analysis of bank securities parallels fixed income analysis of other corporate securities. As such it has four key elements:

❑ Determining *fundamental fair* value;

❑ Taking account of the *market and technical factors* that can influence bond pricing, including credit rating dynamics;

❑ Understanding the *capital structure* of a bank, i.e., the priority of the investors' claims relative to other bondholders and other creditors, together with the concomitant implications for pricing;

❑ Identifying *relative value* or the discrepancy (market inefficiency) between fundamental fair value and current market price as affected by market and technical factors and rating dynamics.

One of the objectives of this chapter is to demonstrate how important it is to understand that credit fundamentals, which determine the *true or underlying creditworthiness* and hence *fundamental fair value* of fixed income issues, are only one component of bond pricing, and hence are only one component of fixed-income analysis. Changes in bond prices can result from changes in credit fundamentals, but are just as likely to

---

[1] This chapter was kindly provided by Andrew Seiz, a fixed-income analyst covering financial institutions with Goldman Sachs. The author wishes to express his gratitude to Mr. Seiz and to Goldman Sachs for this contribution.

result from changes in the market environment. It is critical to differentiate between the two. By so doing and by making sound judgments concerning both, fixed income analysis can lead to successful investment recommendations.

CREDIT ANALYSIS VS. FIXED INCOME ANALYSIS

We have already discussed analysis of credit quality in the preceding chapters as we delineated the application of the CAMEL model to the credit evaluation of banks from a risk management perspective. The analysis of banks from a fixed income perspective is essentially the same as that from pure credit (or risk management) perspective. As mentioned, however, fixed income analysis of bank securities must take into consideration additional market-related and technical factors. Such factors, described in more detail below, can drive pricing of an issue quite independently of changes in fundamental credit quality. Indeed, a challenge for a fixed income analyst is to identify what may be driving pricing on a particular bond — fundamentals or technicals — and to recommend investment action accordingly.

Table: Criteria for Credit Analysis and Fixed Income Analysis of Banks

Applicable to	Specific Factor	Underlying criterion
Credit analysis and fixed income analysis	Credit fundamentals	True creditworthiness
	Sensitivity to credit rating dynamics	Rating dynamics
	the liquidity of specific bank issues	
	the external liquidity environment	Liquidity
	the nature of the investor base	
Fixed income analysis only	Relative value	Anomalies between true credit worthiness and market perception
	The level of subordination of the bond	Legal priority of the investors' claim

Market and technical factors chiefly include:

❑ *Ratings*; the impact of nominal credit ratings and rating actions;

❑ *Liquidity-related influences*; including the liquidity of specific bank issues and issues which fall into particular ratings categories, the overall liquidity environment, as well as the nature of the investor base which translates into the strength of the appetite for purchasing and trading particular categories of fixed income securities;

❑ *The level of subordination of the bond*; or how far down the totem pole the investors' claim is should the issuer default; and

❑ *Relative value*; or the difference between fundamental fair value as based on true creditworthiness, and current market value as affected by liquidity concerns, extant credit ratings and investor sentiment.

DIFFERENTIATING BETWEEN AND WEIGHTING CREDIT FUNDAMENTALS AND MARKET/TECHNICAL FACTORS

Although we have distinguished between credit fundamentals and market/technical factors as way to understand how fixed-income analysis of financial institutions differs from credit analysis in the risk management context, in practice the division between these influence is not always so clear cut. In fact, the market is affected by changes in creditworthiness, and of course the appetite of the market for the securities issues of a bank influences that bank's creditworthiness. Nor should the importance of fundamental credit analysis as a highly critical component of fixed income analysis be underemphasized. Often very marginal improvements in fundamental credit quality can result in dramatic improvements in investor sentiment and contribute to substantial spread rallies. Indeed, the immediate developments that can fuel a spread rally may result in significant real credit quality improvements only much later and only if banks concurrently adopt other initiatives. So, among the difficulties involved in fixed-income bank analysis is determining which real changes in credit quality will have an impact on the market, and in turn, which market developments will have implications for spreads and short- and long-term credit quality. Spreads can move in the opposite direction to real or perceived changes in credit quality.

Essentially, there is little difference between the risk management approach to credit fundamentals and that employed in a fixed income analytical setting, although there is some difference in focus. The differences mainly have to do with the fact that the fixed income analyst must consider the impact of debt subordination (an item that we categorize here as a technical factor) on the risk of default and probability of recovery.

Rating Dynamics: The Use and Impact of Credit Ratings and Rating Actions

The real and perceived creditworthiness of an issue affects its price in two ways. First, irrespective of the issuer's true creditworthiness, which a credit rating (and indeed any form of credit analysis) can only approximate, a rating to the extent it is trusted by the market carries weight and informs investors' perceptions of the credit risks associated with the issuer and the issue. Credit ratings can clearly have a discernible impact on spreads for bank issues as they affect investors' perception of the risk of the security and their corresponding appetite for it. Such ratings, as we have seen, are determined on the basis of credit fundamentals, i.e. the CAMEL methodology discussed previously.

Here the analyst's understanding of what is likely to trigger a rating change and what the impact will be are equal to or of greater importance to taking an independent view as to the true creditworthiness of the issue. Rating changes may be anticipated by a change from a neutral to favorable or negative outlook, or may occur suddenly, often due to an external shock or a secular event. While each rating agency utilizes roughly the same approach when assessing bank creditworthiness, differences may arise both as to nominal ratings and the timing of rating changes. Sensitivity to these differences, gained over time through experience, is therefore a skill to be cultivated on the part of the fixed income analyst.

Even if a rating action is largely anticipated, the final move is likely to result in some price movement. Spreads on bank issues also typically anticipate and react to sovereign rating movements. Ratings can also have a large impact on trading/market technicals — particularly when a rating action enables or prohibits a new class of investors from buying a credit. This is most apparent when the rating moves into or falls below investment grade. Since credit rating changes can be important drivers of pricing, anticipating such changes is an important part of fixed income analysis.

Market and Technical Factors

Liquidity

As enumerated in the table on the page 586, in addition to credit fundamentals and rating dynamics, there are five salient aspects of fixed
income analysis that must be considered when evaluating bank paper.
The first three — the liquidity of specific bank issues, the external
liquidity environment, and the nature of the investor base — pertain to
the liquidity of the security under review. Liquidity in this context refers
to the ease with which the security can be sold and is both a function of
the structure of the particular debt market, as well as investor appetite for
similar securities and the supply of such paper on the market. In other
words, overall supply and demand will strongly influence liquidity. All
other things being equal, higher levels of liquidity will tend to reduce
spreads, while lower levels of liquidity will increase them.

Ascertaining the liquidity of specific bank issues is an art that
requires paying close attention to the market: who is buying, who is
selling, and why? To understand the market, the fixed-income analyst
must be in close proximity to it, and for that reason fixed-income analysts
are often situated on a bank's trading floor, within earshot of the
institution's traders.

Relative Value: Cheap, Rich or Fairly Valued

The primary objective of traditional credit analysis of financial institutions
is to assess the risk of a counterparty defaulting. While this is also the
key task for a fixed income analyst, the focus is more opportunistic.
Anticipating changes in underlying credit quality can result in spread
changes and thus investment opportunities. The nexus between
underlying credit quality and rating actions also comes into play here.

Pricing of bank issues on a primary or secondary basis is done via
relative value. This is usually a combination of comparing the bank's
credit profile, ratings, and trading levels with those of other bank issues
or relative to a sovereign benchmark. For instance, an analyst would
typically identify value in Korea's sovereign banks — Korea Development Bank, Export-Import Bank of Korea, Industrial Bank of Korea —
by comparing trading levels and the credit profiles against one another
and also against a similar-maturity sovereign benchmark. The incremental spread of a non-sovereign issue over its sovereign benchmark is a

measure of the "compensation" an investor requires (at a particular point of time) for assuming the additional risk. Relative value can also be measured among banks in different jurisdictions and among different parts of a bank's capital structure.

Fixed income analysis attempts to assign a value to a bond issue and identify whether it is cheap, rich or fairly valued. This will be a function of where the bond is trading relative to issues from banks that have similar characteristics in terms of ratings, size, and country of domicile. For instance, Bank Alpha and Bank Beta are both located in Country X, and are of similar asset size. Both are rated BBB. Spreads will likely be the same or very similar. If Bank A, however, is reasonably ascertained by a fixed income analyst as being relatively more creditworthy on a fundamental basis than Bank B, the analyst may believe that the general market may soon take a similar view and perhaps that Bank B may soon be upgraded. In such a case, a recommendation to buy the security may follow since the spreads offered may be higher than the underlying creditworthiness would warrant. When this perception becomes general, then the price of the paper is apt to rise as spreads narrow. An investor will gain both appreciation in the value of the bond while benefiting from a higher coupon spread than the security's true credit risk warrants.

Beyond determining fundamental and relative credit worth, among the main challenges for a fixed income analyst is to identify trends in credit quality. To illustrate, the analyst may believe that Bank Alpha does not at present have superior credit quality to Bank Beta, but that steps it is planning to recapitalize and improve its business franchise will have that effect. In such an instance, the analyst may also recommend that investors purchase the paper of Bank Alpha.

DETERMINING FUNDAMENTAL FAIR VALUE IN THE CONTEXT OF DEBT SUBORDINATION AND GOVERNMENT POLICY

Bank Capital Structure and the Uneasy Position of Subordinated Debt Holders

Banks issue both senior and subordinated debt, both of which rank lower in priority than the claims of depositors. Typically, senior debt issues are short- to medium-term (under 5 years) and provide funding for the bank, while longer-term issues are subordinated, ranking below the claims of senior debtholders and are issued for capital raising purposes. The reason for this structure is in part because the Basel Accord, which we discussed in Chapter 12, permits subordinated debt to count as Tier 2 capital, subject to the limitations we discussed in that chapter, including most significantly the proviso that the issues must be five years or longer in maturity.[2]

Evaluating the fundamental fair value of a subordinated bank issue is inherently difficult. The trade-off for such an investment is typically binary, particularly in emerging markets or distressed situations. As banks are regulated entities, some form of government intervention is warranted in the event of a bank failure — either through nationalization or a government-administered wind-down — to ensure systemic stability and avoid deposit runs. In such a bankruptcy/break-up scenario, it would generally be expected that the true recovery rate on subordinated debt would be zero. As entities that are, on average, leveraged up to 12 times, the Tier 1 and Tier 2 capital providers that are at the lowest end of the capital structure would stand to get zero even if the recovery rate for the bank's assets is a highly unlikely 90%. As a result of systemic considerations, retail depositors are usually protected — through either deposit insurance or government guarantees. Shareholders of the bank in theory will almost certainly wiped out entirely. Senior and subordinated creditors lie between these two extremes and can, in theory, be subject to losses. The position of subordinated creditors is usually more uncertain, as a result of where the instruments stand in a bank's capital structure and their status as Tier 2 capital. At the end of the day, whether such creditors are protected is at the discretion of the regulators.

Break-Up Valuation of Developed Market Corporates Can Be Quite Accurately Determined: The Impact of Government Intervention

For distressed corporate bond issues in developed markets, fundamental fair value can be reasonably accurately determined from, for instance, a break-up analysis of the asset base. Transparent financial statements and legal processes render it more likely that a price assigned to a bond issue is based on credit/financial fundamentals (although the often limited liquidity of the issues can see technical factors being at play). The

---

[2] This is not to say that banks will not on occasion issue longer-term debt for funding rather than for capital building purposes.

break-up value is ultimately what a bondholder of a distressed developed market corporate issuer must rely upon. Because of the solicitous attitude governments often take towards banks, financial institution bond issues are not so easily analyzed.

Nationalization Scenarios Can Be Positive or Negative

In the case of distressed bank sitations, investors in *distressed* subordinated debt must essentially determine if there is a risk of the bank being closed and if so what will be the treatment of creditors in such a scenario. While the risk of a particular bank being shut down is a direct function of its credit quality, creditors in a liquidation scenario are subject to policy risk. Regulatory interventions can be characterized by government nationalizations, which can, in the near term, be positive for creditors. However, nationalizations raise uncertainties about the future status of the bank for which a number of scenarios are possible: liquidation, sale to a foreign bank/investor, acquisition by a local bank.

Treatment of Subordinated Obligations May Be Uncertain

Some scenarios can clearly be positive developments for creditors — purchase of a controlling stake in the nationalized bank by a foreign bank with no transfer or change in the status of the debt obligations of the former. Others can be negative — separation of the bad assets and subordinated obligations of the bank into an asset management corporation (AMC or "bad" bank), with the good assets, deposits, and senior liabilities transferred to a "good" bank or an existing healthier financial institution. In the case where subordinated obligations are transferred to a bad bank, the likelihood of such creditors experiencing losses is quite high.

Government Policy Risk Can Be a Key Element in Subordinated Debt Analysis

Policy risk should not be underestimated as a driving factor in the valuation and analysis of subordinated debt, especially in banking systems under stress. As a result of the financial crises in Thailand, Malaysia, Indonesia, and South Korea, the respective monetary authorities extended blanket guarantees for the deposits and, in most cases, the senior liabilities of banks and finance companies in their systems. The nature of the guarantees has varied in terms of tenor and which currency a foreign obligation would be repaid. Also, in some countries, most notably Thailand, subordinated obligations have been excluded from the guarantee.

Bank Closures Pose Greatest Risks to Subordinated Creditors

Closure of a financial institution poses the biggest risk to subordinated creditors. In the context of the Asian crisis, we have seen two very different approaches being taken by the Thai and Korean monetary authorities with respect to the obligations of banks being closed/ liquidated. As part of its overall consolidation drive, Korea's Financial Supervisory Commission (FSC) orchestrated the take over of five troubled banks by five stronger counterparts. This saw the country's largest deposit-taker, Kookmin Bank, acquire selective assets and the bulk of the liabilities of Daedong Bank — a small nationwide bank that specialized in lending to small- and medium-sized enterprises. This included a $50 million subordinated 2006 FRN that now is an obligation of Kookmin Bank.

Foreign Currency Subordinated Bondholders of Thailand's Bangkok Bank of Commerce Were Less Fortunate

Foreign currency subordinated creditors of troubled Bangkok Bank of Commerce in Thailand were treated quite differently. The government nationalized the bank in April 1998 together with three other banks as a result of deposit runs each was experiencing. One of the banks, First Bangkok City Bank, was acquired in its entirety by state-owned Krung Thai Bank. Two other banks, Siam City Bank and Bangkok Metropolitan Bank, are being auctioned for sale to foreign banks. Bangkok Bank of Commerce has effectively been liquidated, with its "good" assets being transferred to Krung Thai Bank and its bad assets remaining at Bangkok Bank of Commerce, which is now an asset management corporation (AMC). Deposits and senior liabilities were also transferred to Krung Thai Bank, but subordinated liabilities were kept at the AMC. Thisincluded a DM100 million 1999 subordinated floating rate note (FRN) (puttable in October 1998), on which the bank has since defaulted. Bondholders have recourse only to assets in the AMC, and we would expect the recovery value on such notes to be zero.

Senior and Subordinated Debt Ratings

Breakdown of Bank Capital Structure in Descending Order of Seniority

Instrument	Example
Senior secured credits	Loan secured by specific assets
Deposits[3]/senior unsecured credits	USD senior FRNs, USD FRCDs
Lower Tier II subordinated dated[4]	Local currency sub debentures, USD sub FRNs/bonds
Upper Tier II subordinated perpetual[5]	Perpetual subordinated debt
Preference shares Common stock	SLIPS/CAPS
Source: Goldman Sachs Fixed Income Research	

Impact of the Level of Subordination

Subordinated Debt—An Avenue for Capitalization

The credit markets have enabled banks to tap a relatively cheap source of capital-subordinated debt. Such debt counts as Tier 2 capital in a bank's risk-adjusted capital adequacy ratio, and in most jurisdictions, interest

---

[3] Moody's typically rates its foreign currency deposit ceiling lower than the senior debt ceiling for emerging market sovereigns. The rationale given is that deposits are in registered form, so they are easier to reschedule vis-à-vis senior debt, which is in bearer form and held by investors in a variety of different jurisdictions. Prior to October 1997, Moody's rated foreign currency FRCDs issued by banks in Asia against the senior debt ceiling rather than the deposit ceiling, with the reason being that as bearer instruments FRCDs resemble debt instruments more closely than deposits. This policy changed in October 1997 following the agency's review of the legal standing of FRCDs, which prompted Moody's to rate these issues against the deposit ceiling rather than the senior debt ceiling. One of the reasons for the change could have been the lack of cross-default language in the prospectuses of these FRCDs.

[4] Lower Tier 2 subordinated dated securities would incorporate the bulk of the dollar subordinated debt that has been issued by the Thai banks. According to the Basel Accord, treatment as Tier II capital is permitted until five years before the maturity of the note, at which point Tier II capital amortizes by 20% per year. For instance, for a 10-year lower Tier 2 dated subordinated note, a bank would lose 20% of the face value of the note that could be counted as Tier 2 capital, beginning in Year 6 for each year until maturity. This was one of the reasons why Bangkok Bank administered a Yankee bond exchange in January — to lengthen the maturities of its dollar subordinated notes, particularly the 7.25% 05s, and thus delay the effective depletion of its Tier 2 capital.

[5] Often Upper Tier 2 instruments contain a loss absorption provision — i.e., in the event that losses by the bank wipe out common and preferred equity, perpetual subordinated bonds can be used to absorb losses. Also they often contain an interest deferral clause.

costs or coupon payments for these obligations are tax deductible. A variety of forms of these instruments have developed to provide bank issuers with the cost savings inherent in debt products but also to provide certain flexibility available in equity products. To the extent that the different features have implications for the level of subordination, they will affect ratings and pricing.

Various Features of Subordinated Debt Instruments

Interest deferral or "skip" provisions permit an issuer to miss coupon payments without a bondholder being able to call an event of default. Loss absorption provisions, while less common, enable a bank to write down a portion of the debt obligation in much the same way that net losses in any given year are borne by shareholders (holders of such securities would typically bear losses only after common shareholders have been completely wiped out). Bondholders are forced to take a haircut on the face value of their notes at maturity.

Upper Tier 2 vs. Lower Tier 2

The different forms of subordinated debt result in an Upper or Lower Tier 2 designation. The latter are dated instruments — for banks in Asia, the most common maturity has been ten years — with fixed or floating coupon payments and often with call features in Year 5, after which the coupon "steps up" by a designated amount. The Tier 2 capital treatment of subordinated debt begins to amortize by 20% each year, five years before the maturity date of the instrument. The call features provide the banks with the option to refinance and extend the period for which the notional amount of the subordinated note can be counted as Tier 2. Upper Tier 2 instruments can be perpetual and/or obtain various skip provisions.

Tier 1 Qualifying Instruments

Perpetual preferred securities are essentially synthetic Tier I debt instruments. They enable Tier I-qualifying capital to be raised in a tax-efficient manner — at the same time from a capital structure risk perspective, the bondholder is just one step above common stockholders. In Asia, Japanese banks have been significant issuers of these instruments via US dollar-denominated "OpCo preferred" securities. In 1999, Thai banks were active issuers of SLIPS/CAPS products, which are baht-denominated Tier I-qualifying instruments that were primarily sold to the banks' depositors.

Pricing Implications of Subordination

The level of subordination will affect the level of credit protection for the bondholder and the nature of the investor base. Also, as we discuss below, in distressed situations it could have implications for potential government support. Disparities on these fronts become more apparent the further down the credit curve one moves — i.e., the lower the credit quality of the issuer, the greater will be the spread and ratings differential between different parts of the capital structure.

BANK CREDIT ANALYSIS AND TECHNICAL CONSIDERATIONS

Fixed income analysis of banks is typically complicated by technical factors. Particularly in emerging markets, bonds issued by banks are usually quite illiquid — issue sizes and trading volumes are relatively small, bid-asked spreads are wide, and large portions of the issue can sit with buy-and-hold investors and simply not trade. As such, prices or spreads can be quite volatile and it may be difficult to determine "fair value" for a specific issue. Determining relative value can be even more difficult — relative spreads for a group of bank issues can be inconsistent with the relative credit quality of the banks and be more a reflection of the nature of the buyers and size of the issues.

External Factors Affecting Pricing

Pricing movements for bank issues can therefore be at odds with credit quality developments for a bank. As with credit markets in general, external factors can have a huge impact on pricing. As predominantly an over-the-counter market, corporate bond issues can be held hostage to the willingness of dealers to provide liquidity, which is a function, among other things, of their own risk appetite. The events culminating in the crisis conditions of global financial markets in October 1998 clearly demonstrated the immense impact that emerging markets contagion can have on the financial community and thus on the pricing and liquidity of fixed income issues.

Buyers of FRNs vs. Buyers of Sub Debt

The nature of the investor base will often be a large determinant of the spread for a particular bank issue. Traditional investors in Asian bank floating rate notes (FRNs) have largely been commercial banks in the region, whether local or the Hong Kong or Singapore subsidiaries of European or, to a lesser extent, U.S. banks. Maturities have typically been three or five years, with the notes representing senior obligations of the issuing banks. Issue sizes in most cases have been relatively small: $50–150 million, with the "float" — i.e., the proportion that is actually traded — being a fraction of this. Bank buyers have usually bought such instruments as a proxy for a bilateral or syndicated obligation to the issuer and thus have largely had a buy-and-hold approach.

Senior vs. Subordinated Spread Differential

The senior-subordinated spread differential has become more apparent quite recently with bonds issued by Thai banks and has been driven primarily by technical developments. Flush with liquidity in a low interest rate environment and with a limited capacity and appetite to lend domestically in size, many Thai banks have been buying back their own senior FRN issues — i.e., retiring them before maturity. This has resulted in a strong bid for and spread tightening on such issues. The Tier 2 capital treatment permissible for subordinated obligations and the need for Thai banks to continue to bolster their capital bases has resulted in the Bank of Thailand prohibiting local banks from directly buying back "sub debt."

Relationship between Share Price and Subordinated Debt

Emerging markets subordinated debt can lie in somewhat of a gray area in a bank's capital structure. Although it fundamentally represents a borrowing obligation, local laws may often not recognize it as such. Moreover, defaults on subordinated obligations do not always trigger a cross-default on other senior obligations of the issuer. Upper Tier 2 or Tier 1-qualifying instruments often contain coupon skip provisions and thus can be likened to equity.

Deeper Subordination Usually Results in Stronger Share Price—Sub Debt Relationship

Usually, the more deeply subordinated or lower rated a bank, the greater the correlation between share and subordinated debt prices. Deeper subordination and lower ratings imply more equity-like characteristics and associated risks. For a lower rated bank — especially one rated below investment grade — the differential between senior and lower Tier 2 subordinated ratings is typically at least two notches, reflecting the higher risk profile of the bank and/or the country of domicile and the higher uncertainties for subordinated creditors. For banks at very low ratings levels (single-B range), subordinated creditors can face unique uncertainties vis-à-vis senior creditors — for instance, as mentioned above, the Bank of Thailand excluded subordinated obligations from its blanket guarantee of deposits and credits in the Thai banking system. Moreover, since very low credit ratings reflect financial distress, the risks of nationalization involving a write-down of existing shareholders and/or liquidation are high. This raises uncertainties for subordinated creditors.

Should There be a Correlation?

Subordinated creditors, like senior creditors, should be most concerned about a bank being liquid so that outstanding obligations can continue to be serviced. This will be a function of domestic depositor and local and foreign creditor confidence in the institution, which in turn will be a function of its credit quality. Liquidity arises as a more important consideration vis-à-vis solvency: As we have observed before, a bank can be "technically" insolvent and still continue to operate if depositors and creditors believe that it will remain a going concern. This is a common characteristic of selected development/government banks in Asia, which have high levels of problem loans and poor operating performance yet benefit from their typically large size and government support.

Subordinated Bondholders Should be More Concerned about Solvency vis-à-vis Senior Creditors

Because of their relative position in a bank's capital structure, subordinated creditors should be more concerned about solvency than senior creditors. The greater the level of shareholders' equity or the higher a bank's Tier 1 risk-weighted capital adequacy ratio, all else being equal, the more cushion for subordinated bondholders. Any Tier 1

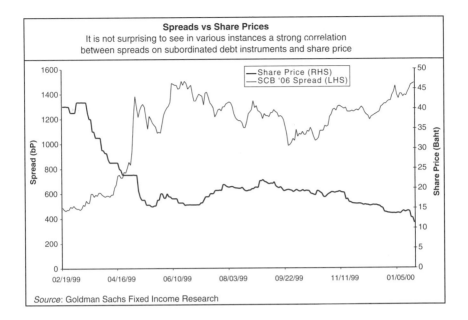

Spreads vs Share Prices
It is not surprising to see in various instances a strong correlation between spreads on subordinated debt instruments and share price

Legend:
— Share Price (RHS)
— SCB '06 Spread (LHS)

Source: Goldman Sachs Fixed Income Research

capital raising or rights issue that may dilute existing shareholders and therefore negatively affect a bank's share price should be viewed quite positively by subordinated bondholders. In this case, share prices and spreads on subordinated issues should not necessarily move in the same direction.

CHAPTER SUMMARY

This chapter explores credit analysis of financial institutions in the context of the fixed income markets, with an emphasis on emerging economies. The chapter explores how traditional credit analysis can be applied to evaluating bonds issued by banks and subsequently, making investment recommendations of those bonds. Fixed income analysis of financial institutions attempts to apply traditional bank credit analysis techniques to evaluate the fair value of the debt obligations issued by such entities. A number of factors can influence this analysis beyond fundamental credit evaluation — where in a bank's capital structure the instrument lies, the nature of the investor base, and the external spread/market environment. Differentiating spread movements resulting from changes in fundamentals vs. changes in market conditions is a critical challenge in fixed income analysis and usually forms a significant rationale behind an investment recommendation.

CHAPTER TWENTY SEVEN

E-BANKING: THE INTERNET AND THE FUTURE OF THE BANK

Credit ratings will continue to come under pressure by those banks which fail to respond to the strategic challenges raised by the Internet ... [which] has significantly reduced barriers to entry in the industry and undermined traditional banking models, which have historically relied upon costly branch networks to distribute their products.

— Ian Linnell, Glen Grabelsky, Bridget Gandy,
Internet Banking: Separating the Myths from Reality, Fitch IBCA,
Financial Institutions Special Report, May 2000

We believe that the Internet will re-write the rules for financial services.

— Grant Chan, Lehman Brothers banking analyst,
Online Banking in Hong, March 27, 2000

The IT revolution will likely make banks marginal institutions in economic development. ... [A] bank is a product of an inefficient market.

— Andy Xie, *Bankless Economies: Banks and the IT revolution,*
Morgan Stanley Dean Witter, Asia Pacific

The advent of the Internet in the 1990s will profoundly change the financial services industry. These changes may not occur in the catalysmic and revolutionary fashion as some participants in the financial markets may once have imagined. Yet even as the Internet bubble has burst, established players as well as new entrants have been making investments in technology that will dramatically reshape the industry. As much as money, the stock in trade of financial intermediaries is information. They use economies of scale gained from performing many transactions and spreading fixed expenses over them to reduce the cost of information. By reducing information costs, financial institutions can overcome to a great degree asymmetry of information ("differences in knowledge ... that affect ... bargaining power") that act as obstacles to transactions. It is this ability which gives banks their comparative advantage and enables them to perform their intermediation role while making a profit. Although the fee or spread charged for performing these functions is comparatively low, banks use high leverage to generate rates of return attractive to investors.

THE CONSULTANTS' VIEW: BLOWN TO BITS

Perhaps most significantly, the Internet reduces the cost of information dramatically and in so doing substantially alters the dynamics of the banking industry. Precisely how this development will manifest is by no means certain, but various commentators and analysts who have examined banks' prospects and business models suggest that significant changes are in the offing. In *Blown to Bits*, authors Philip Evans and Thomas Wurster posit that the Internet has broken the fixed linkage between "richness" (the quality, depth and customization) of services and their reach (the number of end-user to whom they can be cost-effectively provided).[1] Banking, they observe, is particularly vulnerable to disintermediation, a phenomenon that indeed first became part of everyday business jargon in the context of banking.

> Twenty years ago, corporate banking was a "spread" business ... [Banks'] business model required them to form deep relationships with their corporate customers. ... [T]hen, thanks to technology, corporate customers got access to the same financial markets banks used: reach and information symmetry transformed the relationship. Banks were disintermediated. ... Capital now flows directly from the ultimate lender to the ultimate borrower through the capital markets [leaving bankers merely] to rate the risk, give advice, make markets and serve as custodians.[2]

Evans and Wurster now see banking as again vulnerable to disintermediation, this time affecting the retail customer. The trade-off between richness and reach, they argue, has been broken since customers no longer need the physical proximity of a retail branch to obtain the

---

[1] Wurster, Thomas S. and Philip Evans. Blown to Bits: *How Economics and Information Transforms Strategy*. Havard Business School Publications, October 1999.
[2] Evans & Wurster, Blown to Bits, p. 49–50.

information about products and services, comparative pricing data of loan and deposit rates, financial planning information, and advice concerning investments that are now available at free or at low cost from numerous sources. Indeed, in some respects, the Internet has made possible a greater richness than a depositor was ever able to obtain from the local bank branch, including 24-hour bank statements and transacting ability and realtime stock quotes. They believe that something like what has happened in corporate banking will replicate itself in retail banking, with open standards financial software enabling consumers to pick and choose among a broad range of financial service providers and easily change accounts among them.

> Customers will be able to contact any financial institution for any kind of service or information. They will be able to maintain balance sheets on their desktop, drawing on data from multiple institutions. They will be able to compare alternative product offerings and sweep funds automatically between accounts at different institutions. They will be able to announce their product requirements and accept bids.[3]

Further, the authors of *Blown to Bits* see electronic bill presentment, allowing consumers to pay emailed bills at the press of a button, as the "killer app" that will provide the impetus for a mass migration to online banking. In this brave new world of retail banking, the role of banks will be transformed. Evans and Wurster envision the banks of the future, no longer as "an integrated business where multiple products are originated, packaged, sold and cross-sold through proprietary distribution channels," but as "navigators" or product specialists.

INTERNET BANKING MODELS: THE EQUITY ANALYSTS' VIEW

Four major Internet banking models have been distinguished.[4] Lehman Brothers analyst Grant Chan in *Online Banking in Hong Kong: Rewriting the Rules*, identifies the following Internet banking strategies:

1) another channel

2) strategic integration

3) head to head competition

4) pure play

---

[3] cite p. 46
[4] Grant Chan, *Online Banking in Hong Kong: Rewriting the Rules*, March 27, 2000, p. 9.

The Internet Merely as an Alternative Channel

One approach to coping with the challenges wrought by the Internet is for bank managers to look upon it as an additional channel to source customers and distribute product.

Integration of the Internet into the Existing Business Model

This approach takes the alternative channel one step further, using technology to data mine and aggressively market and cross-sell products as part of an integrated strategy. It requires additional investment and planning than the alternative channel model.

Creation of a Standalone Internet Bank in Conjunction with an Incumbent Bank

Some banks have sought to embrace the Internet by creating an entirely new institution that is affiliated with an existing bank, but also competes against it.

Standalone Internet Bank

This model applies to non-bank investors that wish to compete with banks by creating a so-called "pure play" or standalone Internet bank. It implies the reduction of a physical presence to a minimum to

---

The Egg

Perhaps the most well-known example of an Internet pure play in the banking arena is "The Egg," a standalone Internet bank. Established by UK-based insurance group Prudential in 1998, The Egg has no branches and operates solely as a Web-based and phone banking depository institution. Instead, it operates out of a call center headquarters in Derby, England, where it is has a staff of 1,500. By offering higher deposit rates than the competition, The Egg was able to attract US$11 billion in deposits in 12 months from 700,000 customers, notwithstanding that it does not operate an ATM network nor offer checking accounts. (It does offer credit cards and personal loans.) Interestingly, the high deposit rates are effectively a loss leader. Instead, the business strategy of the parent is to use The Egg to acquire customers and cross-sell insurance, investment and personal credit products.

cut occupancy and staff expense, and is the most aggressive of the four in shedding the traditional banking model.

The Lehman Brothers analyst believes that, at least in the Hong Kong market, Internet will have a positive impact on the returns and valuation in the longer term through improved productivity and the ability to cross-sell services.

A RATING AGENCY PERSPECTIVE: THE FITCH IBCA VIEW

Although by no means as visionary in their approach as Evans and Wurster, the bank rating agency Fitch IBCA, in a report entitled "Internet Banking: Separating the Myths from Reality,"[5] also concludes that the Internet will have far-reaching effects on the banking industry and over the longer term significant impact on creditworthiness and credit ratings.

In what at the date of publication is one of the few efforts to examine the impact of the Internet on banks from a credit perspective, Fitch IBCA analysts Ian Linnell, Glen Grabelsky and Bridget Gandy discern a number of positive and negative implications that the Internet, and more broadly "e-commerce," will bring about.

Specific Implications

Lower Operational and Entry Costs vs. High Investment Costs

Although it requires high investment costs, it seems certain that the Internet will reduce operating costs to existing banks. The Fitch IBCA report suggests that a mature standalone Internet bank could have a cost-income ratio of 15%, much less than the 60–65% for traditional commercial banks.[6] But the same factors that allow banks to cut expenses will also lessen entry costs for new competitors. Institutions that traditionally have relied upon a branch network to source deposits and distribute products may find their legacy of a large branch network a burden rather than a boon. The establishment of such networks is a costly and labor intensive process, and a physical branch network is costly to maintain as well as being somewhat inefficient, since each branch involves some degree of replication in administrative functions. Occupancy and compensation expense are a bank's primary non-interest expense and both tend to be

---

[5] Internet Banking: Separating the Myths from Reality, May 2000.
[6] p. 606.

Structural Implications of E-Commerce on the Banking Industry According to Fitch IBCA

Positive Implications	Negative Implications	Ratings Implications
1. Low costs	1. Erosion of distribution as a barrier to entry	1. Reduced profitability
2. Improved data mining and customer segmentation	2. Improved data mining and customer segmentation	
3. Individual customer pricing and financial packaging	3. Margin and profitability pressure	2. Further consolidation
4. Cross border potential	4. Increasing competition	
5. New revenue lines border expansion	5. New entrants border expansion	3. Greater cross
6. Online brokerage	6. Impact on traditional products	
7. Business-to-business	7. E-payments under pressure	4. Mono-line players
8. Exploiting brand value	8. Consumer empowerment	
9. Internet service providers	9. The value of brands in financial services	5. Existing leading players in a strong position
10. Improved capital flexibility	10. Increasing transparency and the role of aggregators	
11. Improved culture	11. High investment costs	6. Need for a credible e-commerce strategy
		7. Increased polarization of ratings

Source: Fitch IBCA, May 2000

swelled by a large branch network, although the ability to source deposits cheaply and to increase sales and distribution has usually made the large branch network a cost-effective proposition.

Nevertheless, distribution and operational costs on a relative basis should fall over time providing cost advantages to both incumbents and new entrants. Lower entry costs do not benefit only non-incumbents. Few banks offer a full range of services in all markets, and the Internet holds the promise of existing players being able to relatively rapidly leverage their existing infrastructure into new revenue lines or existing revenue lines into new markets. In many emerging markets, however, Internet penetration is still comparatively low and migrating customers to the Internet will lag until Internet access is ubiquitous.

The Internet then is a benefit to banks generally, and from a cost perspective may be of greatest initial benefit to new entrants who will not risk cannibalizing their own customers by setting up banks that depend on Internet rather than physical access. Standalone banks, however, do have one critical deficiency: getting cash to customers. Although cash in card form shows a great deal of promise, paper and metal currency are likely to be with us for some time to come, and may never be replaced entirely. Without a physical ATM network, standalone banks have been hindered in their ability to capture customers from incumbent banks.

Yet by lowering the costs of entry into the banking sector, new entrants will be encouraged. In many countries, however, regulatory restrictions on banking licenses and regulators' interest in maintaining the integrity of the banking system can be expected to prevent a flood of new banks being established. Ultimately, the Internet will probably not make a large branch network entirely obsolete, but will almost certainly reduce the advantages of such a network— banks may simply not need as many branches as previously. It can be anticipated that banks will be able to get by with a smaller number of full branches and the trend to mini-branches and kiosk banking can be expected to grow. These costs advantages over the longer term, however, are lessened in the short-term as banks are forced to make major and costly investments in equipment and train staff to prevent their rivals from gaining a huge competitive advantage through technology.

Online brokerage is one area where banks can exploit new business opportunities and where the cost efficiencies of the Internet are not [author to fill in]. Until the repeal of the Glass Steagall Act in the US in 1999, banks in that market were limited in their ability to act as brokers for securities and mutual funds, but with that barrier removed, some banks have entered the field. The Fitch report notes that it is estimated that by 2002 some 30% of all US investors will have an online account. While in that market online brokerages have tapped much of the trade, Europe has also been fertile ground for the development of online brokerage services by incumbent banks.

The Commoditization of Bank Products vs. Individual Pricing and Bundling

Despite the efficiency gains and new business opportunities, the Fitch IBCA analysts observe that the Internet is likely to increase profitabilty pressure on banks and reduce margins. The ability of customers to obtain pricing data on the Internet, compare prices, and with the aid of Web-based software agents locate the best prices at any given moment does not bode well for bank profits. Financial products are largely fungible commodities, and although there is the potential for banks to provide added-value non-fungible ancillary products, their core business is highly vulnerable to "commoditization." This is because the Web enables the creation of much more expansive virtual "financial supermarkets" than any one institution could conceivably. Indeed, their report sees "increasing transparency and the role of 'aggregators'" as having negative implications for banks supply and adding "impetus to the forces of commoditization." The "customer empowerment" that the Internet affords is placed in the report in the same category. The knowledge and flexibility that the Web reduces "endowment effect" that has benefited particularly those institutions in countries "where a customer is more likely to change their spouse than their bank."

To some extent, techniques such as individual pricing and financial packaging will be able to neutralize the trend towards commoditization. Individual customer pricing refers to a technique facilitated by technology whereby the price charged to a customer for a specific product or service varies according to the customer's overall relationship with the bank. Sometimes referred to as "dynamic pricing" this technique could mean that customers who do a lot of business with the bank and who are viewed as highly profitable could be charged less than "ordinary" customers. As the Fitch IBCA analysts put it, new technologies permit "much greater individual pricing based on a customer's overall economic value to the bank, i.e. length of relationship, amount of products held, and risk profile." It could also mean that customers who were adjudged to be less-price sensitive than others could be charged a higher price for the same service. Dynamic pricing also enables price changes to be effected rapidly, altering over much shorter time frames than that to which customers are presently accustomed, except when buying or selling securities. However applied, individual or dynamic pricing could make pricing more opaque by rendering it more difficult for customers to compare prices among banks and other institutions. Conceivably, this could counteract the scenario suggested at the beginning of this chapter that bank products and services could be transformed into commodities for which bank customers let out bids.

Related to individual customer pricing is the ability of banks, in their capacity as financial supermarkets, to bundle attractive combinations of products. Like the integrated travel services agency that is able to bundle a package of air fare, accommodation, meals and transfers more cheaply than the sum of its component parts, such "financial packaging" as Fitch IBCA refers to it will certainly be attractive to some customers and again may be an antidote against the commoditization of bank products and services. Although some bank customers may, like some travelers, prefer to search and bargain individually for each travel service they purchase, banks may have an advantage over "mono line providers" in attracting customers who prefer the convenience and "bargain" that comprehensive packages provide.

While the Fitch IBCA analysts regard the concept of financial packaging as advantageous to banks, permitting them to "reduce the influence of pricing," it is not certain that banks will be able to retain this advantage. Financial products by their nature tend to be much more fungible than products in which customer satisfaction is predicated on many factors, any number of which may be intangible. Banks may have to compete with brokers or assemblers who are able to piece together bundles that are highly competitive with bank offerings. Bundling may offer short term advantages, but if assemblers appear, more sophisticated customers may be drawn towards putting together their own combinations of products and services from financial service providers rather than simply taking what is on offer from a particular institution.

Data Mining and Customer Segmentation—A Two-Edged Sword

As the Fitch report mentions, "new technology significantly enhances the ability of institutions to segment and mine their customer databases."

In other words, banks will be able to use customer data to market their products more effectively, and presumably increase sales. Data mining has already been used to reduce unprofitable customer relationships, sometimes with perverse effects. Some US banks have introduced additional fees and charges on their supposedly "unprofitable" customers with the end-result that they have lost more business than they anticipated and have seen their stock prices suffer as a result. Over time, it can be expected that banks will be able to refine their use of data mining both to optimize sales and to encourage less-profitable customers to migrate to institutions to whom they constitute a niche market, e.g. community banks.

The Fitch report sees data mining and data segmentation, however, as "a double edged sword" which can be used by new players, including those from outside the banking industry, to capture bank customers. Insurance companies, mortgage brokers and lenders, and fund management companies are among those who may, by utilizing the same data mining and customer segmentation technology available to banks, be able to target specific bank customers and provide them with alternative offering. In this way, they will be able to compete aggressively in specific profitable product niches, leaving less profitable product lines to the banks themselves. Data mining and segmentation technology thus cuts both ways, opening up new opportunities for sales on the one hand, and increasing competition on the other. As the cost of the relevant software and hardware falls, these tools will become ubiquitous and will become less of a competitive factor than they appear to be today.

The Value of Brands: Another Two-Edged Sword

According to *Blown to Bits* authors Evans & Wurster, "a brand is nothing but rich, product-specific information acquired, retained and believed by the customer independent of any specific act of consumption."[7] Although a brand encompasses many intangible "feelings, associations [and] memories," it is analogous to a rating symbol in that it represents a distillation of multitude of variables and judgments. While a rating symbol is abstract and re-usable, a brand, however, is unique. There is only one Sony, although some may see Sharp or Toshiba as adequate or even as superior substitutes.

---

[7] p. 162.

In the view of the Fitch IBCA analysts, financial services brands, traditionally associated with values like security, have functioned as barriers to entry to lesser-known financial institutions. The rapid spread of new brands through the Internet, such as E-Trade in the online stock brokerage arena, suggests that as a barrier to entry brands may be less formidable than previously thought. The commoditization of financial services products and the accompanying emphasis on pricing may lead to a de-emphasis in the importance of brands. At the same time, the Fitch IBCA analysts acknowledge that brand value may have special importance for potential customers in the financial services context, especially for those particularly concerned about the potential for fraud. Well-established banking brands are associated with "stability, longevity and trust," and it is certainly plausible that until some of the issues relating to security and criminal activity on the Web are more fully resolved that blue-chip names in banking will hold an advantage over newcomers.

There is certainly a great variety of opinion, however, as to how the Internet will affect brands and considerable uncertainties remain. Some argue that existing brand names, whether of financial institutions or other companies, are not readily transferable to the Web. In the provocatively titled, *The Eleven Immutable Rules of Internet Branding*, marketing consultants Al and Laura Ries argue the victors of the "Internet bank war" will not be those that are identical to those who dominate the offline banking world — "Citibank.com, Chase.com or BankofAmerica.com," — but instead will be won by "Internet-only bank start-ups, like Wingspanbank.com."[8] A number of analysts, however, have been critical of the standalone Internet banking model for reasons including its lack of a cash delivery mechanism and Wingspanbank has, judging by some of their reports, not been a raging success.

B2B (Business to Business), E-commerce and Other Implications of the Internet

One of bank's most important traditional roles is providing a payments mechanism. This mechanism functions both domestically, through checking accounts for example, and internationally, where letters of credit are

---

[8] p. 15.

a common way to pay for goods from overseas. The facilitation of e-commerce i.e. online commerce via the Internet provides new opportunities for banks to extend their role as payments facilitators. Online B2B exchanges, whether open or community based, will ultimately require online payments mechanisms. While credit cards function well at the consumer level, for businesses where the payments range from less than $10,000 to millions of dollars more sophisticated methods will be required. Online letter of credit processing, which is already in a formative stage, is one element of the type of services that will ultimately be on offer. Banks, partly because of their existing customer relationships, are well-positioned to take a major role in providing online procurement systems, and various online software solutions to small and large businesses alike and this is an area where banks have considerable opportunities.

Other impacts of the Internet on banking are varied. The Fitch IBCA report mentions two notable areas where the Web may have an additional positive influence on banks.

Corporate Culture

First the innovative thinking required to adapt to the information age potentially has positive side benefits. The Internet can shake up banks' traditional and sometimes stodgy culture. As the Fitch IBCA analysts put it, "the positive experiences of establishing an Internet banking capability can be … applied to their traditional businesses."[9]

Capital Flexibility

Second, creation of an Internet banking unit creates new capital raising options as the possibility exists that these units can be spun off as separate companies. In view of the mid-2000 dot com bust, however, this viability option is in doubt.

Rating Implications

What does all this mean to banks from a rating perspective? Although there are some bright spots in terms of the Internet's impact on the banking industry, on the whole it is a disruptive technology that is

---

[9] p. 8.

likely to shake up rather than strengthen the sector. The Fitch IBCA analysts observe several salient rating implications flowing from the Internet.

1. Negative Earnings Impact

The general impact is to have an overall negative affect on earnings by squeezing margins through increased competition and sophistication among customers. Financial products are intrinsically vulnerable to commoditization, a process the Internet will hasten.

2. More Consolidation Nationally and Globally Favoring Major Full Service Incumbents

Margin pressure, the costs of investing in Internet technology, and the increased ease of cross border transactions will give further impetus towards existing trends towards consolidation and globalization. Major existing players able to leverage their existing infrastructure and capital to this end will be well positioned to succeed in the new financial economy. The Fitch IBCA analysts believe that "mono-line" specialists will have a much tougher time competing in the new environment.

3. Need for a Credible E-Strategy

Whatever the eventual consequences of the Internet, banks that ignore it do so at their peril. Banks will no longer be able to rely on the status quo way of doing things and will have to move more rapidly to compete in a more quickly changing economy. Banks that actually attempt to delineate a coherent strategy to deal with the challenges the Internet presents will be more likely to succeed in the evolving business environment.

4. Polarization of Ratings

The Fitch IBCA analysts believe that greater differentiation will be seen between those banks that are responding to changes in the banking industry and those that are sitting still or clinging to obsolete business models. Over time, this will be reflected in their credit ratings with a trend towards polarization in ratings between the "winners" and those left behind.

Looking at Internet Banking from the Credit Analyst's Perspective

Although the Internet brings new opportunities and challenges to the banking industry, it does not mean that the traditional principles of credit analysis no longer apply. It should be obvious that to be viewed as creditworthy, a bank which employs the Internet as part of its strategy whether as a pure play standalone Internet bank or as merely another channel, needs to achieve profitability, preserve asset quality, keep a capital cushion, display good management, attract deposits and maintain liquidity.

To be sure, a pure play Internet bank may have certain operational cost advantages, but these may be outweighed by start-up and marketing costs. At the same time, an incumbent bank which begins to invest heavily in Internet technology will see its efficiency ratios suffer in the short-term, but the long-term benefits of such investment should be kept in mind by the analyst. As with other aspects of bank credit analysis, Internet

Internet Banking Scorecard	
1. Available Channels PC Internet banking SIM mobile banking WAP mobile banking PDA banking	**5. Cross Selling of Financial Services** online stock broking online life insurance online non-life insurance online mutual funds
2. Transacting Capability balance inquiry funds transfer wire transfer to 3d parties account activity/history bill presentment bill payment credit card account activity	**6. Financial Portal** loan calculators personal financial planning modules news stock quotes Microsoft Money/Quicken compatibility
3. Customer Service email to banks email alerts internet phone online status of loan applications	**7. Community** online shopping online lifestyle flight information travel hotels & restaurant information
4. Online Lending online loan applications online loan approvals	**8. Ease of Use** personalized web pages demos online help
Source: Goldman Sachs	

strategy ought not be viewed in isolation, but must be seen in the context of the banking environment. In a market where Internet penetration is less than 1% and connection costs are high, a huge investment in Web banking would make less sense than in a market where penetration is 70% and broadband connections are commonplace. What a bank's peers are doing will of course have an impact on the consequences of investing or not investing in technology.

A bank's approach to the Internet therefore is one additional facet of bank operations that should be on the agenda of the bank analyst as he or she visits a bank or reviews its annual report. In a report entitled "E-Finance in Asia, Part 4," Roy Ramos and his bank analysis team at Goldman Sachs surveyed 19 banks in Asia and compared their Internet capability in eight major categories. This scorecard provides some useful parameters to consider when examining a bank's Internet strategy.

In addition to the bank's retail oriented strategy, its offerings in e-commerce and business-to-business services such as payment gateways and trade finance form an important component of assessment of bank operations.

CHAPTER SUMMARY

This last chapter of the *Bank Credit Analysis Handbook* is intended merely to provide a brief introduction to the impact of the Internet on the banking industry. This is clearly an aspect of banking that is in a state of rapid flux, and it is difficult to predict how the Internet will ultimately change the landscape of financial services. Most commentators and analysts agree that the Internet poses a threat to banking in its traditional form. But standalone Internet banks have had limited success to date, and it seems more likely that the more successful incumbent banks will simply integrate and adapt the Internet into their existing business models as a means to both reduce costs and offer new services. The jury is still out on whether the overall impact on the industry will be positive or negative. Whatever the outcome, the role of the Internet in a financial institution's business strategy deserves attention and close monitoring by the bank credit analyst.

Appendix A: Sources and Further Reading

GENERAL SOURCE MATERIAL AND
CHAPTER 1. THE ROLE OF THE BANK CREDIT ANALYST:
ASSESSING THE CREDITWORTHINESS OF BANKS

Hale, Roger H., *Credit Analysis: A Complete Guide*, John Wiley & Sons
    (1983, 1989)

A very useful introduction to credit analysis is *Credit Analysis: A
Complete Guide* by Roger H. Hale. Written by a New York banker who
was inspired to write it following his participation as an instructor credit
training program in Asia, this book, first published in 1989 remains a
useful and practical guide to credit analysis. Although the book is
targeted to analysts and credit officers working for banks, one chapter is
devoted to the analysis of banks and a case study concerning the collapse
of Franklin National Bank reprinted from *Fortune* magazine is also
included.

R. Taggart Murphy, *The Real Price of Japanese Money*, Westfield and
    Nicholson, 1996.

Although its title is a bit misleading, banker R. Taggart Murphy in
The Real Price of Japanese Money explains the tectonic movements in
the world's financial system that resulted in monetary policy and financial flows during the 1980s, catalyzed in part by the disruptive role of
Japanese banks. In Chapter 2, "The Credit Decision," Murphy discusses
how Western banks view credit and how this perspective contrasted with
Japanese banks. The book also provides an excellent background to the
Plaza Accord of 1985 and the Basel Accord of 1988, as well as Japan's
bubble economy and it aftermath.

Mayer, Martin, *The Bankers: The Next Generation: The New Worlds of Money, Credit and Banking in an Electronic Age*, Truman Talley Books/Dutton, New York, 1997.

A financial journalist who published a best-selling account of the commercial banking industry over two decades ago, Martin Mayer updated his earlier 1997 work. Though it concentrates on banking in the United States, this is not a major disadvantage since Mayer is thereby able to show in cross-section the evolution of a financial system that has undergone tremendous changes during the intervening period, sharing many of the developments that other systems have seen including deregulation, disintermediation, a banking crisis, and diversification. Rich with quotes, Mayer's *The Bankers: The Next Generation* is good for gaining a flavor of the sector.

For a discussion of the changing role of the equity analyst and critiques, the following may be helpful:

Lashinsky, Adam, "What a Research Analyst Is (And What an Analyst Is Not)," *TheStreet.com*, 6/19/00 (1st of a 3 part series).

Morgenson, Gretchen, "Rating the Analysts Who Rate the Market," *International Herald Tribune*, July 19, 1999.

"Worth the Paper Its Printed On?" *Euromoney*, December 1997.

For readers wishing to gain a better understanding of the role of financial institutions, a university level textbook is the best choice. Among those consulted during the preparation of this book include:

Hubbard, R. Glenn, *Money, The Financial System and the Economy*, 2nd Ed., Addison-Wesley, 1996.

Mishkin, Frederic S., *Financial Markets, Institution and Money*, HarperCollins, New York, 1995.

Thomas, Lloyd B., *Money, Banking and Financial Markets*, Int'l. Ed., Irwin McGraw Hill, Boston, 1997.

The rationale for treating banks differently from non-financial corporations.

Corrigan, E. Gerald, "Are Banks Special?" 1982 *Annual Report* Essay, Federal Reserve Bank of Minneapolis.

Corrigan, E. Gerald, "Are Banks Special? A Revisitation," *Special Issue* 2000, Federal Reserve Bank of Minneapolis.

An explanation of why banks deserve special treatment can be found in numerous textbooks. An insightful essay on the topic was one written by E. Gerald Corrigan in 1982 just as financial deregulation was sweeping the United States. In 2000, Mr. Corrigan, now a managing director at Goldman Sachs, reviewed his 1982 essay and restated his support for its general conclusion: that banking should be treated separately from other forms of commerce.

The Money Multiplier Concept and the Role of Banks in Monetary Policy

The money multiplier concept can be found in numerous textbooks concerned with economics and money and banking. Prof. Mishkin discusses the topic in Chapter 20, *Determinants of Money Supply of Financial Markets*, as does Prof. Thomas in Chapter 13, *The Deposit Expansion Process: A Simple Analysis, in Money, Banking and Financial Markets*. Both texts were cited in the previous chapter.

Banking Risk and Moral Hazard

Addressed in all most any textbook on banking or bank management. Mishkin devotes Chapter 16 of his text to the topic, for example to bank risk. Bank management textbooks are also extremely helpful resources not only for this specific topic, but also for the entire subject of bank operations. One of the best textbooks on bank management is entitled exactly that *Bank Management: Text and Cases* by George H. Hempel, Donald G. Simonson and Alan B. Coleman. This text addresses nearly every facet of bank of running a bank with one of five parts of the book devoted entirely to managing the loan portfolio. (A somewhat lighter international version of this text is also available in paperback.) Of course, this book like others on bank management, is not written from the analyst's point of view but from the banker's. Nonetheless, they are extremely valuable in gaining an understanding of the trade-offs the bank manager faces and what considerations guide his or her decisions. Two other textbooks I found helpful were *Commercial Bank Management* by Peter S. Rose and *Managing Financial Institutions: An Asset Liability Approach* by Mona Gardner and Dixie Mills.

Hempel, G., Simonson, D. and Coleman, A., *Bank Management: Text and Cases*, 4th Ed., John Wiley & Sons, Inc., New York, 1994.

Rose, Peter S., *Commercial Bank Management*, McGraw-Hill, 1996.

Shanmugam, B., C. Turton, and G. Hempel, *Bank Management*, John Wiley & Sons, 1992. (international edition for Hempel, Simonson and Coleman)

Gardner, M. & Mills, D. *Managing Financial Institutions: An Asset/ Liability Approach*, 2nd Ed., Dryden Press 1991, Harcourt Brace 1998.

For readers wishing to delve further into bank risk, additional references are given under Chapter 19 on the page 629, where other sources on bank risks and risk management are also included.

Banking Crises

One way to understand risk in banking is to read some accounts of banks and banking systems that have gone wrong, as well as those books dealing with financial crises. Among my favorites are:

Delhaise, Philippe F., *Asia in Crisis: The Implosion of the Banking and Finance Systems*, John Wiley & Sons, 1998.

For a highly insightful and accessible account of the Asian crisis and the role weak and risk-prone banking systems played in its unfolding, I would highly recommend *Asia in Crisis: The Implosion of the Banking and Finance Systems* by Philippe Delhaise. Mr Delhaise, my former boss, was a banker in emerging markets for many years and a founder of the predecessor to Thomson BankWatch Asia, the regional division of what was the world's leading specialist bank rating agency until its acquisition in late 2000.

Gapper, J. & Denton N., *All That Glitters: The Fall of Barings*, Penguin Books, 1996.

In *All That Glitters: The Fall of Barings*, *Financial Times* journalists John Gapper and Nicholas Denton explain just what went wrong at Barings and how poor risk management allowed rogue trader Nick Leeson to bring this venerable institution to ruin.

Kindleberger, Charles, *Manias, Panics and Crashes: A History of Financial Crises*, 3rd Ed., John Wiley & Sons, 1996.

A classic on the topic of financial crises is *Manias, Panics and Crashes: A History of Financial Crises* by Charles Kindleberger. Although not specifically focused on banking, banks are implicated in nearly all periods of extreme financial distress. One of the virtues in reading Kindleberger's book is that we can see how the same patterns repeat themselves, if somewhat differently each time. From this vantage point the analyst or investor can at least contemplate the possibility that the euphoria of the moment might give way to less sanguine conditions.

Morris, Charles R., *Money, Greed and Risk: Why Financial Crises and Crashes Happen*, Random House, 1999.

Money, Greed and Risk: Why Financial Crises Happen by Charles R. Morris takes a more contemporary view of the boom-bust cycle with greater emphasis on the US financial history.

Wood, Christopher, *The Bubble Economy: Japan's Extraordinary Speculative Boom of the '80s and the Dramatic Bust of the '90s*, The Atlantic Monthly Press, New York, 1992.

The Bubble Economy by Christopher Wood told the story of how Japan's "second rate financial system" aggravated both in the late 80s boom in the country and the early 90s bust. Published in 1992, this account by a former financial journalist and later investment bank strategist presaged Japan's lost decade and the financial weaknesses which are still being played out.

General Sources

The Economist newspaper — an American would call it a magazine — is an excellent source of news from an economic perspective, with excellent coverage on issues affecting banking and financial institutions. I developed the *Economist* habit while working for the Economist Intelligence Unit, a sister organization — the weekly issues were free to contributors — and regard it as a must-read for analysts. One fund manager told me that he found a valuable idea in nearly every issue. Coverage of developments in the banking industry insofar as they affect the larger markets is first-rate. In this chapter, two articles were cited.

"Freedom from fear? *The Economist*, September 11, 1999, p. 13.
"Handle with Care," *The Economist*, October 3, 1998.
"The Business of Banking," *The Economist*, October 30, 1999.

Other sources cited in this chapter which the author found stimulating and generally helpful in preparing this book include:

Grier, Waymond A., *The Asiamoney Guide to Credit Analysis in Emerging Markets*, Asia Law & Practice, Hong Kong 1995 (focus on corporate credit analysis).

Palmer, Howard, *Bank Risk Analysis in Emerging Markets*, Euromoney Publications (emphasis on trade credit risk), March 1998.

Standard & Poor's Rating Service, "Sovereign Credit Ratings: A Primer," December 1998.

Zielinski, Robert, Lehman Brothers, "New Research Techniques for the New Asia," December 14, 1998.

The following may prove helpful to those like myself who focused on the humanities and social sciences rather than on business matters in their undergraduate educations.

Brealey, Richard A. and Myers, Stewart C., *Principle of Corporate Finance*, 5th Ed., McGraw Hill, 1996.

Brett, Michael, *How to Read the Financial Pages: A Simple Guide to the Way Money Works and the Jargon*, 3rd Ed., Century Business, 1992.

Not actually consulted in the course of writing this book, but looks useful nevertheless. See Chapter 13, "Banks, borrowers and bad debts."

Coggan, Philip, *The Money Machine: How the City Works*, 3rd Ed., Penguin, 1995.

To gain a better understanding of financial statements, the following are recommended:

Rice, Anthony, *Accounts Demystified: How to Understand and Use Company Accounts*, FT Pitman, 1997.

Tracy, John A. *How to Read a Financial Report: For Managers, Entrepreneurs, Lenders, Lawyers and Investors*, John Wiley & Sons, 5th Ed., 1999.

White, Gerald I., Sondhi, A.C., Fried, Dov, *The Analysis and Use of Financial Statements*, John Wiley & Sons, 1994.

Useful sources for financial terminology and concepts, which aided as well in the preparation of the Glossary (Appendix D) included the following:

Fitch, Thomas, Barron's *Dictionary of Banking Terms*, 3rd Ed., Barron's Educational Series, March 1993.

Nobes, Christopher, *Pocket Accounting*, The Economist Books, 1995.

Hindle, Tim, *Pocket Finance*, The Economist Books, 1997.

Ryland, Philip, *Pocket Investor*, The Economist Books, 1997.

For some popular treatments of the games accountants play, the following may be of interest. Although most of the examples are of non-financial corporations, some of the same concepts apply to banks.

Griffiths, Ian. *Creative Accounting: How to Make Your Profits What You Want Them to Be*, Unwin, 1986.

Schilit, Howard M., *Financial Shenanigans: How to Detect Accounting Gimmicks & Fraud in Financial Reports*, McGraw Hill, 1992.

Although detecting fraud from financial statements alone may be a stretch, at least those reported in most emerging markets, the underlying principles are sound and some of Schilit's seven key financial shenanigans apply to banks. Shenanigan No. 2, for example, boosting income with one-time gains is not an unknown phenomenon among banks in certain markets.

Smith, Terry, *Accounting for Growth: Stripping the Camouflage from Company Accounts*, Century Business, 1992.

Focus is on UK companies.

A primer to bank credit analysis and useful for understanding some disclosure issues is Robert Morris Associates, *A Guide to Analyzing Foreign Banks*. Robert Morris Associates is now the Risk Management Association.

CHAPTERS SIX AND SEVEN: EARNINGS & PROFITABILITY

The major rating agencies are excellent sources of information on the methodology of bank credit analysis as well as credit analysis generally.

Profitability is a major concern of all the agencies when evaluating bank creditworthiness. Moody's, S&P and Fitch all provide excellent material, which at present, is freely available at their website. Especially noteworthy are the following:

Rating Methodology Bank Credit Risk (An Analytical Framework For Banks In Developed Markets), Moody's Investor Service, April 1999 (48 pp.)

Rating Methodology Bank Credit Risk In Emerging Markets (An Analytical Framework), Moody's Investor Service, July 1999 (36 pp.)

Financial Institutions Criteria, Standard & Poor's, January 1999, (195 pp.)

In addition, materials produced by regulatory agencies, although often prepared for bank examiners, are of benefit to the analyst. Again, these materials are of benefit not just in analyzing profitabilty but in all aspects of bank credit analysis. A good example is:

Federal Reserve System, Division of Banking Supervision and Regulation, *Commercial Bank Examination Manual*, 1994 (over 1000 pp.)

Analysis of profitability is also the preeminent concern of equity analysts, although as we have mentioned equity analysts place more emphasis on valuation. Unfortunately, much of their work is not easily accessible as the distribution of the material is restricted.

For a discussion of profitability from an equity perspective, the following may be of assistance.

Hooke, Jeffrey C., *Security Analysis on Wall Street: A Comprehensive Guide to Today's Valuation*, Methods, John Wiley & Sons, 1998.

CHAPTERS EIGHT–TEN: ASSET QUALITY

Many of the sources already mentioned were helpful in the preparation of these chapters on asset quality. For a description of the business cycle, Kindleberger and Gwartney and Stroup, cited above, are good sources. In addition, the following were among the sources consulted:

Calverley, John, *Pocket Guide to Economics for the Global Investor*, Irwin, 1995.

Kettell, Brian. *What Drives Financial Markets*, FT Prentice Hall, 1999.

In addition, economists working for investment banks occasionally produce interesting material on this topic. The following report, cited in the chapter, is an excellent example.

Dr. Jim Walker, "Asianomics: The Unbearable Knowledge of Impotence: From Austria to Asia," Credit Lyonnais Securities Asia, 11 May 1998.

Finally, Paul Krugman has written insightfully about the Asian crisis and the perils of attaching moralistic value to recessions. See, for example:

Paul Krugman, *Return of Depression Economics, xxx.*

Concerning bank provisioning and accounting for loan losses, the following were especially useful.

Paitoon, C. & Ti, B. Salomon Smith Barney, *Bank Accounts Made Easy, Vol I: Recognition of Interest* Income, Feb. 9, 2001.
BankWatch, *Fundamentals of Bank Credit Analysis* (CD-ROM)
Development Bank of the Philippines, "Bank Reserve Accounting, "Supplement of FY99 Annual Report.

Other sources cited in these chapters include:

G. Root, P. Grela, M. Jones and A. Adiga, "Financial Sector Restructuring in East Asia," don't have the cite for this one.
David Stimpson, Editor, *Moody's Investor Service – Global Credit Analysis*, IFR Books (1995).

CHAPTER ELEVEN: CAPITAL: CUSHION AGAINST LOSS

CHAPTER TWELVE: CAPITAL ADEQUACY: THE BASEL ACCORD AND PROPOSED CHANGES

Many of the sources already mentioned were relevant to the discussion of capital. Additional sources that were particularly valuable included:

"Bank Capital: A Vale of Tiers," Fitch IBCA, October 1997. (A very well-written discussion of bank capital and its evolution under the Basel Accord.)

Special Report: "Tier 3 Capital – Well-named and unloved," Fitch, July 2000.

Special Report: The Rise And Rise Of Preference Share Capital In Europe "Horses For Courses," Fitch IBCA, May 2000.

The various rating agencies have produced a number of reports relevant to bank capital, as well as commentary on the proposed revisions to the Basel Accord. Selected material includes:

"A New Capital Adequacy Framework Consultative Paper Issued by the Basel Committee on Banking Supervision," Duff & Phelps Credit Rating Co., June 1999.

"Implications for Banks of the Basel Committee's New Capital Adequacy Proposals (June 1999)," Moody's Special Comment, June 1999.

"Everything you wanted to know about Fitch IBCA and the BIS/Basel rules but were too afraid/too baffled to ask" (a dialogue between a searcher after truth and Fitch IBCA), Fitch IBCA, undated.

Special Report: "Bank Regulatory Capital: A Critical Review of the New Capital Adequacy Paper Issued by the Basle Committee on Banking Supervision and its Implication for the Rating Agency Industry," Fitch IBCA, March 2000.

The Bank of International Settlements website is the source for information concerning the Basel Accord an excellent source of material of material on bank regulation and analysis generally. Selected papers available at the site include:

"Capital Requirements and Bank Behavior: The Impact of the Basle Accord," April 1999.

"International Convergence of Capital Measurement and Capital Standards," July 1988 (original Basel Accord).

"International Convergence of Capital Measurement and Capital Standards" (July 1988, updated to April 1998), April 1998 (updated original accord).

"A New Capital Adequacy Framework Consultative Paper Issued by the Basel Committee on Banking Supervision," issued for comment by March 31, 2000, Basel. June 1999 (first proposal for new accord).

The following were particularly helpful in understanding the variant types of Tier 2 capital:

"Special Corporate Study — Financial Institutions, Asian Bank Subordinated Debt — A Primer," JPMorgan, Tokyo, January 24, 2000.

Additional sources cited in this chapter include:

Tim Noonan, "Running on the Spot," *South China Morning Post Magazine*, October 1, 2000.

CHAPTER THIRTEEN: FUNDING AND LIQUIDITY, PART I: LIQUIDITY AND ASSET LIABILITY MANAGEMENT

CHAPTER FOURTEEN: LIQUIDITY & FUNDING, PART II: FUNDING THE BANK AND RATIO ANALYSIS

Note: These chapters were prepared by Darren Stubing, Chief Bank Analyst at Capital Intelligence.

Dresdner Kleiwort Benson Global Fixed Income Credit Research Note, April 2000.

CHAPTER FIFTEEN: MANAGEMENT AND THE BANK VISIT

Although Palmer, supra, includes a chapter on bank management entitled: "Banks in emerging markets — A management grid matrix," there is relatively little information available on evaluating bank management from the analyst's perspective. In addition to the bank management textbooks, the Federal Reserve System's Commercial Bank Examination Manual, and the RMA guide to analyzing foreign banks, another helpful source in preparing this chapter was:

Comptroller of the Currency, Administrator of National Banks, *Comptroller's Handbook: Large Bank Supervision*, July 1998.

For further reading on corporate governance issues, see:

Mathur, A. and Jimmy Burhan, *The Corporate Governance of Banks: C-A-M-E-L-I-N-A-C-A-G-E*, Asian Development Bank.

CHAPTERS SEVENTEEN AND EIGHTEEN: THE BANKING ENVIRONMENT

Basel Committee on Banking Supervision, "Core Principles for Effective Banking Supervision," April 1997.

Beers, David T. And Cavanaugh, Marie, Standard & Poor's Rating Service, "Sovereign Credit Ratings: A Primer," December 1998.

Bessis, Joel, *Risk Management in Banking*, John Wiley & Sons, 1998.

Cade, Eddie, *Managing Banking Risks: Reducing Uncertainty to Improve Bank Performance*, Amacom, 1999.

Cook, Timothy Q. and Rowe, Timothy D., *Instruments of the Money Market*, Federal Reserve Bank of Richmond, 6th Ed., 1986.

Holliwell, John, *The Financial Risk Manual: A Systematic Guide to Identifying and Managing Financial Risk*, FT Pitman, 1997.

ING Barings, "Regulatory And Disclosure Policies — Improved But Still Some Weak Spots, Banking Bullets," Feb. 1997.

Interagency Country Exposure Risk Committee, Country Risk Management Subgroup [USA], Common Practices for Country Risk Management in US Banks, November 1998.

JP Morgan Emerging Markets Bank Research Team, "Special Corporate Study — Financial Institutions: Bank Sector Risks to Emerging Economies," November 7, 1997.

Martin, Todd et al., Asian Banks Analyser Supplement: Regulating the Asian Banking Crisis, Warburg Dillon Read, September 1998.

Moody's Investors Service, "Moody's Approach to Analyzing and Rating Emerging Market Banking Systems: Argentina as a Case Study," July 1997.

Morgan, Donald P., "Judging the Risk of Banks: What Makes Banks Opaque," Federal Reserve Bank of New York, September 14, 1997.

Selzer, Donald E., Special Comment, "Disclosure And Transparency: Failures In Both Emerging And Established Markets," Moody's Investors Services, May 1998, based on material delivered in a speech to the US Securities and Exchange Commission, International Institute for Securities Market Development, April 29, 1998, Washington, D.C.

V, Raja, "Strengths and Weaknesses of the Regional Banking System," Bank of America, July 1999.

CHAPTERS NINETEEN–TWENTY FOUR: THE DISTRESSED BANK

Barents, The Role of Asset Management Companies in East Asia, Conference on "Systemic Resolution of Corporate and Bank Distress in Crisis-Affected East Asian Countries," (undated).

Clarion Securities, "Why Asian Banks Should Write Off NPLs and Recapitalize Fast," September 25, 1998.

Fiorillo, James, "Resolving Japan's Banking System Problems," ING Barings, December 1997

Fitch IBCA, "Asian Bank Restructuring: A Comparative Analysis, Part II," 1999.

Freris, Dr. Andrew & Daisy Shum, "A Survey of Banking Reform in Asia," Bank of America, July 1999.

Freris, Dr. Andrew with Daisy Shum and Ivy Lee, Bank of America, *Asia Financial Outlook*, January 1999.

Gapper, John & Nicholas Denton, *All That Glitters: The Fall of Barings*, Penguin Books, 1997.

Goodhart, C, P Hartmann, D Llewellyn, L Rojas-Suarez and S Weisbord (1988): *Financial Regulation: Why, How and Where Now?* Routledge/Bank of England — London. IFR Asia Pacific Report, Restructuring Asia, March 1999.

Irving, Keith, "Asia-Pacific Banks: Progress & Issues in Bank Restructuring," Merrill Lynch, 23 February 1999.

Matanachai, Wanna, Ramos Roy I., and Wanglee, Paul, "Bank and Debt Restructuring, Part II, Thai Debt Restructuring II," Goldman Sachs, December 1, 1998.

Maugham, Simon, "Bank Recapitalization — Options and Policies," Indosuez W.I. Carr Securities, July 15, 1998.

Merrill Lynch. "Asian-Pacific BankNotes, Focus: Debt Restructuring in Asia," April 1, 1999.

Moody's Investors Service, "Recovery, Restructuring and Reform: Moody's Outlook for Asian Banks," May 2000.

Ramos, Roy I. et al., "A Tale of Four Bank Restructurings," Goldman Sachs, January 7, 1999.

Ramos, Roy et al., "Asia's Twin Banking Crises," Goldman Sachs, February 9, 1998.

Ramos, Roy et al., "Fixing Asia's Banks, Part 1: Asian Bank NPLs," Goldman Sachs, September 16, 1998.

Root, Gregory, Grela, Paul Jones Mark & Adiga Anand, "Financial Sector Restructuring in East Asia."

Wan Ismail & Rafael Bello, "The Bank Rehabilitation Process: Asia and Mexico Compared, " Morgan Stanley Dean Witter, September 4, 1998.

Zielinski, Robert "Restructuring Asia's Banks: The Processes and Institutions": Lehman Brothers, September 29, 1998.

Zielinski, Robert and Kunishige, Nozomu "Japan's Banking Crisis: Don't Solve the Problem": Lehman Brothers, September 10, 1998.

Zielinski, Robert, "Asian Banking Crisis: Robert's Rules for Rebuilding": Lehman Brothers, July 16, 1998.

CHAPTERS TWENTY FOUR AND TWENTY FIVE: RATING THE BANK

"Ratings Agencies as a Catalyst for Growth in Capital Markets," Moody's Special Comment, June 1997.

"Risks beyond Measure," *The Economist*, December 17, 1997.

Bentulan JTR, "Buzzes like a BB+, trades like a B," *FinanceAsia.com*, 16 August 2000.

BIS Policy papers No. 6 — August 1999: "Bank Restructuring in Practice."

Caouette, John B., Edward I.Altman, Paul Narayanan, *Managing Credit Risk, The Next Great Financial Challenge*, John Wiley & Sons, October 1998.

Financial Times Special Report: "Asia in Crisis: Rating Agencies: Different Kind of Risk," May 8, 1998.
http://www.ft.com/specials98/q2872.htm.

Fitch IBCA, "Bank Rating Methodology," April 1998.

Golin, Jonathan, "Rating Financial Institutions: The Thomson BankWatch Approach," paper submitted to the APEC Consultative Group Workshop, The Credit Rating Industry in APEC Economies: Critical Issues for Capital Markets Development, ADB, February 8–9, 1999, Manila, Philippines.

IBCA, "Sovereign Comment: Sovereign Ceilings and Sovereign Ratings," May 1997.

IBCA, "Sub-National Rating Methodology," (undated).

IFR Asia, No. 174, "Time for a pan-Asian rating board?" p.1, Sept. 2, 2000.

Jordan, Peter Gabriel Torres & Chirstopher Huhne, "Rating Above the Sovereign Ceiling," Fitch IBCA Special Report, June 18, 1998.

Kealhofer, Steven et al., "The Use and Abuse of Bond Default Rates," KMV Corporation, March 3, 1998.

Mariano, Roberto, "An Assessment of Credit Rating Services in APEC Economies: A Background Paper for the APEC Consultative Group Workshop," The Credit Rating Industry in APEC Economies: Critical Issues for Capital Markets Development, ADB, February 8–9, 1999, Manila, Philippines.

Moody's Investors Service, "A Counterparty's Guide to Moody's Bank Ratings."

Moody's Investors Service, "Moody's Approach to the Credit Analysis of Banks and Bank Holding Companies," April 1993.

Moody's Investors Service, "Promoting Global Consistency for Moody's Ratings," May 2000.

Morton, Katherine, "Time to Face the Image Problem," Risk Publications, April 2000.

On Watch, *Economist*, May 15, 1999.

Partnoy, Frank, "The Siskel & Ebert of Financial Markets?: Two Thumbs Down for the Credit Rating Agencies," *Washington Univ. Law Quarterly*, Vol. 77, No. 3, 1999.

"Rating Agencies: Are They Credible" by Christoph Kuhner, Pretto, Christina, "Rating Services in a Global Economy," Standard and Poor's Credit Week, December 16, 1998.

Sheehan, Paul, "ABCs of AMCs," Lehman Brothers, March 7, 2000.

Supple, Desmond "S&P's About Face," Financeasia.com, October 23, 2000.

CHAPTER TWENTY SIX: FIXED INCOME ANALYSIS

Note: This chapter was prepared by Andrew Seiz, Fixed Income analyst at Goldman Sachs.

Additional reading

Fabozzi, Frank J., ed., *The Handbook of Fixed Income Securities*, McGraw Hill, 1997.

CHAPTER TWENTY SEVEN: E-BANKING: THE INTERNET AND THE FUTURE OF THE BANK

Chan, Grant, "Online Banking in Hong Kong: Rewriting the Rules," Lehman Brothers, March 27, 2000.

Evans, Philip and Wurster, Thomas S., *Blown to Bits: How the New Economics of Information Transform Strategy*, Harvard Business School Press, 2000.

IFR Special Report, Internet, March 2000.

Ismail, Wan and Tham, John, "Identifying Realities in Asian Banking, E-Commerce and Technology Investment," Morgan Stanley Dean Witter, March 2, 2000.

Linnell, Ian et al., "Internet Banking: Separating the Myths from Reality," Fitch IBCA, May 2000.

Rajpal, A. and Wong, W., "Hong Kong: Banking — The Internet — Market Ready, Players Missing," March 8, 2000.

Ramos, Roy et al., "E-Finance in Asia, Part 3," Goldman Sachs, March 29, 2000.

Ramos, Roy et al., "E-Finance in Asia, Part 4," Goldman Sachs, March 29, 2000.

Ramos, Roy et al., "E-Finance in Asia, Part 5," Goldman Sachs, July 7, 2000.

Ramos, Roy et al., "E-Finance in Asia, Part 6–B2B and Banks in Asia," Goldman Sachs, July 7, 2000.

APPENDIX B: BANK ANALYSIS TOOLBOX — RATIO COMPENDIUM

A note on the more than 90 ratios that follow.

❏ With the exception of *leverage*, *debt to equity* and other indicators specified to be multiples rather than fractions, ratios are generally expressed as a percentage to two decimal places.

❏ *Unless otherwise specified*, terms like shareholders' equity and liquid assets refer to *total* shareholders' equity and *total* liquid assets. Because the terms *total loans*, *gross loans*, and *net loans* have specific meanings, these terms are specified more particularly.

❏ Note that throughout *The Bank Credit Analysis Handbook*, we define *total loans* as the face value of all loans and advances, including financial leases; *gross loans* as total loans plus unearned interest income; and *net loans* as total loans minus loan loss reserves. Loans in this context means *total loans* and *advances*, including *leases*.

❏ *Net income* normally refers to net income *excluding* extraordinary items, but at the analyst's option or where *extraordinary items* are not disclosed, the *reported* net income figure may be used. As used in this book, *Non-interest expense* excludes loan loss provisioning.

❏ *Deposits* refer to customer and bank deposits; *customer deposits* to non-financial institution deposits only.

❏ Where *average assets* is the denominator of the ratio, it can be used as a component of a Dupont analysis as a way to compare earnings drivers and earnings' destroyers. Although on some ratios there is consensus concerning whether a numerator or denominator are averaged, in respect to others it is up to each analyst or analytical team to make a determination. Variations where common have been indicated. Where not specified, period-end figures should be assumed.

❏ Note that *ratios are mere tools* and are only as good as the data supplied. Variations in methods of defining or calculating ratios are responsible for most discrepancies. Although there may be legitimate reasons for using one definition or formula over another, there is no good reason for being inconsistent.

CAPITAL INDICATORS

Capital indicators measure capital strength, the extent of a bank's ability to absorb and rebound from economic shocks.

Key Ratios

Indicator	Formula	Remarks
BIS Capital Adequacy Ratio	Tier 1 Capital + Tier 2 Capital / Risk Weighted Assets	The so-called BIS Capital Adequacy Ratio (also known as the Total Capital BIS ratio, the BIS CAR, etc.) is the method of calculating capital established in the Basel Accord of 1988, as amended during the 1990s, and which has since been adopted in some fashion by over 100 countries. Note that there are many local variations on how the ratio is calculated, so that the indicator may not be strictly comparable in all respects on a cross-border basis, although it represents a major advance in global uniformity of capital adequacy measurement over the heterogeneity that existed before. The benchmark minimum CAR is 8% although some countries impose higher minimums. Note also that although the benchmark minimum will remain at 8%, a new accord (commonly referred to as Basel 2) will provide alternative means of calculating the ratio. The new accord, assuming final approval by end 2001 is expected to be in force by 2004.
Equity to Assets	Shareholders' Equity/ Total Assets	A rough-and-ready measure of capital strength, which makes no allowance for risk weightings. Note that some analysts use average assets as the denominator and in some cases average shareholders' equity as the numerator.
Equity to Loans	Shareholders Equity / Total Loans (and Advances)	Since using loans separates out a major class of risk assets from total assets, this measure represents an improvement over the straight equity to assets ratio.
Internal Growth Rate of Capital (IGRC)	Net profits (attributable to shareholders) less dividends /Shareholders Equity	Also known as Internal Capital Generation Ratio (so also abbreviated ICGR), Equity Generation Rate, and Capital Formation Rate. Note the following: 1) average Shareholders' Equity may also be used in the denominator; 2) dividends refer to cash dividends; 3) some analysts prefer to calculate the

Table continued

Indicator	Formula	Remarks
		ratio using the dividend payout at the beginning of the year, rather than the dividend proposed in the annual report; and 4) the IGRC should be viewed in perspective, taking account of asset growth and relative capital strength.
Leverage	Assets/Shareholders' Equity	Note that: 1) some analysts use average assets as the numerator and /or average shareholders' equity as the denominator; 2) leverage is the inverse of equity to assets and is a multiple rather than a fraction, and is also equivalent to the equity multiplier used in Dupont analysis. See also *debt to equity ratio* in supplementary ratios below.
Tier 1 Capital Adequacy Ratio	Tier 1 Capital / Risk Weighted Assets	Calculated based on Tier 1 capital only,which is generally equivalent to shareholders' equity. The Basel Accord imposes a 4% minimum. Minimums vary by jurisdictions. Also known as Tier 1 Capital to Risk Adjusted Assets.

Supplementary Ratios (Capital)

Indicator	Formula	Remarks
Adjusted Equity + Reserves to Loans	(Shareholders' Equity + Loan Loss Reserves − 50% of NPLs)/ (Loans − 50% of NPLs).	Used by Moody's. Measures core capital plus loan loss reserves to loans, assuming a 50% recovery rate on existing NPLs.
Debt to Equity	Total Liabilities / Shareholders' Equity	An alternative leverage measurement, the debt to equity ratio is used more often in corporate credit and equity analysis than in analysis of financial institutions, although some bank analysts do employ it.
Dividend Payout Ratio	Declared Cash Dividends/Net Income	This ratio corresponds to the IGRC, but shows if any unused equity generation capacity exists. Note that in the case of a bank holding company, a dividend paid to the parent may disguise a debt service component. It can be instructive to compare the payout between a bank subsidiary and a bank holding company with the payout of the holding company to its shareholders and with that of other subsidiary banks to the parent company.
Equity Growth	(Shareholders' Equity in Yr 2 − Shareholders' Equity in Yr 1)/ (Shareholders' Equity in Yr 1)	Significant equity growth rate should accompany significant asset growth. When asset growth outpaces equity growth, capitalization becomes weaker. When material growth in equity capital is observed, the analyst should ascertain its course: internal generation, infusion from existing shareholders, a new offering of shares, or a merger or strategic investment.
Equity to Deposits	Shareholders' Equity/ Deposits	Once a popular measure of capital strength, this traditional ratio is little used today as it ignores subordinated debt funding and the risk weighting of assets. It is included for reference only.

Table continued

Indicator	Formula	Remarks
Equity to Risk Assets	Shareholders' Equity/ Risk Assets	Note this ratio is a traditional ratio and is unrelated to risk-*weighted* assets as defined under the Basel Accord. Liquid Assets are defined as cash or cash equivalent, or easily liquefiable, including cash, marketable securities, and interbank deposits Risk assets are defined as total assets minus liquid assets. A variant is equity to risk assets plus off-balance sheet items.
Off-balance sheet items to average assets	Off-balance sheet commitments Average Assets	Takes account of the proportion of off-balance sheet items to the size of the bank. Variant ratio use Basel risk weightings when calculating off balance sheet items or measure off-balance sheet items against shareholders' equity.
Primary Capital Ratio	(Common equity + perpetual preferred stock + loan loss reserves + minority interest + convertible or redeemable debt)/ (total assets + loan loss reserves)	Used by Moody's.
Surplus Capital	(Total CAR minimum × risk-weighted assets)/ (risk-weighted assets)	Used by Nomura analysts to measure a bank's extra capital beyond the required minimum. If no minimum Tier 1 ratio is stated, the total minimum is used or ` another figure can be designated.
Sustainable Growth Rate	(Retained earnings/ Minimum CAR) Risk weighted assets	Nomura's ratio divides retained earnings by the minimum applicable capital adequacy ratio by risk weighted assets to see how fast the bank can grow without deterioration in its minimum CAR.
Term Debt to Equity	(Subordinated Debt + Non Perpetual Preferred Stock + Other Indebtedness) / (Equity Capital)	This ratio indicates to what extent a bank has tapped its capacity to issue debt.

ASSET QUALITY INDICATORS

Capital indicators measure capital strength, the extent of a bank's ability to absorb and rebound from economic shocks.

Indicator	Formula	Remarks
Dead bank ratio	Loan loss reserves + Shareholders equity NPLs + Foreclosed Assets + Restructured Loans	Rough and ready conservative measure of overal cushioning for problem loans. Note that this ratio assumes the worst case for problem loans, i.e. that all problem loans will be 100% losses, foreclosed assets will have zero value and all restructured loans will also immediately relapse. If < 1.0 suggests solvency problems.
Loan Growth	(Total Loans in Yr 2 − Total Loans in Yr 1) Total Loans in Yr 1	Rapid loan growth can be a sign of burgeoning asset quality problems raised by a bank expanding its loan book more rapidly than it can prudently evaluate prospective borrowers, especially as the swelling of the loan book will tend to dampen the bank's NPL ratio. Watch out for sustained loan growth over 20% per annum in emerging markets, unless a new bank growing from a small base.
NPL coverage	Loan Loss Reserves/NPLs	This key ratio indicates the degree to which problem loans are covered by loan loss reserves. A variant of this ratio includes shareholders' equity in the numerator. Rule of Thumb: > 100% ample; 75–100% good; 50–75% fair; < 50% problematic; <25% weak.
NPL ratio	NPLs/ Total Loans	NPL stands for non-performing loans. But how are they defined? This can be the source of much confusion. Nomura's banking analysts have come up with an interesting solution. They refer to an international standard NPL ratio, which they call the IAR for *impaired assets ratio*. This ratio defines an NPL by the international standard of overdue 3 months or more. They also allow for a "local standard" ratio which they refer to as the *headline NPL ratio*. Another point of confusion can be the denominator. Some analysts (including Nomura's) use the term "gross advances" as the denominator of the ratio. Our approach, however, has been to use *total loans*, which we adhere to here. Note that throughout the *Bank Credit Analyst Handbook* we have used *total loans* to refer to the face value of loans and gross loans to refer to their face value *plus* unearned interest income. Whatever approach is used, it is important to be clear both about how the numerator and denominator of this ratio are defined. Note that in developed markets NPLs >10% indicate severe problems, possibly irreparable without outside assistance; in emerging markets >20% is the rough equivalent.

Supplementary Ratios (Asset Quality)

Indicator	Formula	Remarks
Asset Quality Ratio	Operating profit after provisions/ Operating profit before provisions	Used by Nomura. An indicator of credit costs calculated by comparing loan loss provisioning to earnings before taxes and provisions.
Blended recovery ratio	Estimated Collateral Value + Recovery from NPLs + (Rescheduled loans less haircut due to relapse)/ NPLs	Defined by Nomura as based on international standard NPLs. Note recoveries from NPLs exclude recoveries on sale of collateral to avoid double counting. Note also that NPLs minus the elements of the numerator is equal to net economic loss, i.e. NPLs less (estimated collateral value + recoveries on NPLs + rescheduled loans net of relapse)= net economic loss on problem loans.
Change in NPAs	NPLs + Foreclosed Assets (+ Restructured Loans) Year 2/ NPLs + Foreclosed Assets (+ Restructured Loans) Year 1	Measures growth in problem assets in absolute terms. May be useful counter-point to NPA ratio when assets are growing rapidly.
Change in NPLs	(NPLs Year 2)/(NPLs Year 1) minus 1	Measures growth in problem loans in absolute terms. May be useful counter-point to NPL ratio when assets are growing rapidly.
Collateral Cover	Estimated collateral value/NPLs	Defined by Nomura as based on international standard NPLs.
Consumer loan exposure	Consumer loans/total loans	Like real estate loans, high yielding consumer loans are apt to turn sour at a more rapid rate than many other credits when economic conditions deteriorate.
Direct Cover	Specific Provisions + General provisions over minimum + Estimated Collateral Value/NPLs	Defined by Nomura as based on international standard NPLs. See also Collateral Cover, Total Cover.
General Provisioning Ratio	General loan loss reserves/Total Loans	Ignores specific provisioning. Little use alone, but helpful for comparative purposes in showing how aggressively a bank is provisioning. Determining why requires more digging.
Gross Write Offs to Average Loans	Gross write offs/ Average Total Loans	Bank write-offs are not always in line with actual loan losses.
Loan Loss Coverage	(Earnings Before Provisions and Taxes (net operating income))/ (Net write offs)	Also referred to as Earnings Coverage of Loan Losses. Indicates how much write-offs could be increased before the bank would incur a loss. Some definitions would include loan loss provisioning in the numerator.
Loan Loss Provisioning to Average Assets	Loan loss provisioning/Average Assets	Comparative ratio used in Dupont analysis.

Table continued

Indicator	Formula	Remarks
Net write-offs to loans	Net write offs/ Average Total Loans	Links write-offs to recoveries. May mean that clean up of loan book is finished or has not yet begun. Net write-offs are equal to write offs less recoveries.
NPA Coverage	Loan Loss Reserves/ NPLs + Foreclosed Assets + Restructured Loans	Note that this ratio assumes a worst case for problem loans and treats all problem loans as 100% losses, foreclosed assets and all restructured loans as having zero value.
NPA ratio	(NPLs + Foreclosed Assets + Restructured Loans)/ (Total Loans)	Alternative calculation includes foreclosed assets in denominator.
NPLs plus foreclosed assets to total loans plus foreclosed assets.	(NPLs + Foreclosed Assets)/ (Total Loans + Foreclosed Assets)	Takes account of NPLs which have recently been written off, but which remain on the bank's books as foreclosed assets.
NPLs to Equity plus Loan Loss Reserves	(NPLs)/ (Loan Loss Reserves + Equity)	Similar to NPL coverage but includes equity and is inverted.
Real estate exposure	Non residential real estate loans/ total loans	Real estate exposure has often been lethal to banks, so keeping tabs on the extent to which a bank is exposed to this cyclical industry can be useful in assessing asset quality.
Recoveries to Loans	Recoveries/Average total loans	Also known as write backs to loans.
Recoveries to write offs	Recoveries/Gross write offs	If a bank is highly aggressive in write offs this ratio may look unduly positive.
Specific Provision Cover	Specific Provisions/NPLs	Defined by Nomura as based on international standard NPLs.
Total Cover	(Specific Provisions + General provisions over minimum + Estimated Collateral Value + Recovery from NPLs + (Rescheduled loans less haircut due to relapse))/(NPLs)	Defined by Nomura as based o n international standard NPLs. Note recoveries from NPLs exclude recoveries on sale of collateral to avoid double counting.
Total Provisioning Ratio	Loan loss reserves/Total loans	Little use alone, but helpful for comparative purposes in showing how aggressively a bank is provisioning. Determining why requires further inquiry. Variant ratios are *Loan loss reserves to gross loans* and *loan loss reserves to net loans*.

EARNINGS, PROFITABILITY & EFFICIENCY INDICATORS

Key Ratios

Indicator	Formula	Remarks
Average Cost of Funding	(Gross Interest Expense)/ (Average Interest Bearing Liabilities)	Also known as *Cost of Interest-Bearing Liabilities, Funding Cost*. Note that Interest Bearing Liabilities = Borrowings + Interest-Bearing Deposits. Moody's attempts to adjust income on a tax-equivalent basis.
Average Gross Yield	(Gross Interest Income)/ (Average Interest Earning Assets)	Also known as *Yield on Average Earning Assets, Earning Asset Yield*.
Change in Net Income	[(Net Income Year 2)/ (Net Income Year 1)] minus 1	Watch out for changes off a low Income base which look better than they are.
Cost to Assets	Non Interest Expense/ Average Assets	Also known as *Cost Margin*. A less variable indicator of operating efficiency than the *Efficiency Ratio*, which fluctuates with changes in income.
Efficiency Ratio	Non Interest Expense Net Interest Income + Non Interest Income	Also known as *Cost to income ratio*. Usually varies between 40–70%. Over 80% is unduly uncommonly low. Moody's refers to an *overhead ratio*, which adjusts interest income on a tax-equivalent basis.
Net Interest Margin	(Net Interest Income)/ (Average Earning Assets)	Actually, return on average earning assets. Shows the profitability of the bank's interest-earning business. Key profitability ratio. If it is declining look for a compensating decline in non-interest expense or provisioning charges.
Net Interest Spread	Average Gross Yield minus Average Cost of Funding	Also known as a bank's *spread*, or *Interest Spread*. Key interest of profitability of interest income business.
Return on Assets	(Net Income)/ (Average Assets)	Also known as Return on average assets. As a general rule, when referring to ROA one is referring to return on average assets. Rule of thumb: 1–2% good; 0.5–1.0% mediocre; < 0.5% poor; >2.0% very high: watch out for excessive risk taking.
Return on Equity	Net Income/ Average Shareholders' Equity	Also known as Return on average equity. As a general rule, when referring to ROE one is referring to return on *average* equity. Easily manipulated by increasing or reducing leverage. Note: some analysts exclude the preferred shareholders' dividend when calculating this ratio.

Supplementary Ratios

Indicator	Formula	Remarks
Breakeven Yield	(Non interest income − Non interest expense)/ (Average Assets)	Excludes non-recurring items. Shows profitability of non-interest income business.
Earning Assets to Assets	Average Earning Assets/ Average Assets	Indicator of the weighting of the bank's business towards interest-earning activity as opposed to non-interest income.
Effective Tax Rate	Income Tax/ Pre-Tax Income including Extraordinary Items	Indicates relative tax bite.
Exceptional Items Ratio	Net operating income less provisions/Pre-tax earnings	Shows what proportion of pre-tax income from exceptional items.
Loan Yield	Loan Interest/Average Loans	Supplemental to *Earning Asset Yield.*
Loans to Earning Assets	Average Loans/Average Earning Assets	Indicates how heavily weighted the bank's interest earning business is towards lending, but note that securitization of loans in markets where this is an option offers opportunities to profit from origination and servicing without keeping loans on the bank's books.
Net income to employees	Net income/number of employees	Net customer loans, customer deposits, and branches can also be measured on a per employee basis.
Non-Interest Contribution to Revenues	Non interest Income/ Operating Income	Also known as *Other Income to Total Income.* A measure of income diversification. A happy medium between too little and too much, and a steady contribution is best. Nomura uses an inverse ratio known as *the Business Mix Ratio* which divides operating income by net interest income.
Non-interest income to average assets	Non interest income/ Average assets	A comparative indicator of contribution of non-interest income to operating income.
Operating Margin	Net operating income/ Net income	A variant efficiency ratio utilizes net operating income *after* deduction for non-interest expense other than provisions.
Payout Ratio	*See Dividend Payout Ratio under Asset Quality Indicators*	
Pre-provision return on assets	Operating Income/ Average Assets	Measure of core profitability.
Pre-tax Profit Margin	Pre-tax Net Income/ Operating Income	An overall profitability indicator, but provisioning policy needs to be considered.

Table continued

Indicator	Formula	Remarks
Pre-tax return on assets	Pre-tax Income/ Average Assets	
Pre-tax return on equity	Pre-tax Income/ Average Shareholders' Equity	
Provisioning to Average Assets	Loan Loss Provisioning/ Average Assets	Another way to gauge credit costs.
Provisioning to Net Write Offs	Loan Loss Provisioning/ Net Write Offs	Shows to what extent a bank is building up its reserves. Puts provisioning charges in context.
Provisioning to Operating Income	Loan Loss Provisioning/ Operating Income	Provides an indicator of how deeply provisioning costs are cutting into profits.
Staff expense to Operating Income	Staff expense (including pension costs)/Operating Income	Alternatively, net operating income or net income may be used as the denominator.
Tax Management Ratio	Pre-tax earnings/Net income (after tax)	Indicates comparative tax bite.

LIQUIDITY AND FUNDING INDICATORS

Key Ratios

Indicator	Formula	Remarks
Liquid assets ratio	Liquid assets/Assets	Broadly, liquefiable assets divided by total assets. How liquefiable assets are defined depends to some degree on the jurisdiction. Liquid assets generally include: Cash, Marketable Securities, Government Securities, Interbank Deposits, and Short Term Marketable Securities. Also known as quasi-liquid assets ratio. The term quasi-liquid assets is often loosely defined and the difference between liquid assets and quasi liquid assets may be nonexistent. When it is defined with precision, the difference still usually is one of judgment, the term quasi-liquid an attempt to include categories of assets which are generally liquid but which may not be in certain cases.
Liquidity Ratio	(Interbank assets, funds lent pursuant to securities repurchase agreements, trading account assets, short-term securities)/ (Deposits + funds borrowed pursuant to securities repurchase agreements + commercial paper and short term debt issued)	In other words, liquid assets divided by short term liabilities. N.B. Banks may not offer adequate disclosure to calculate properly.
Loans to Deposits	Net Loans/ Deposits	Rule of Thumb: 70–90% is acceptable; 90–100% marginal; over 100% risky; 60–70% conservative; below 60% perhaps excessively conservative. Alternative ways to calculate this ratio are 1) to substitute customer deposits for total deposits; or 2) to substitute customer loans for total loans.

Supplementary Ratios

Indicator	Formula	Remarks
Asset Structure Ratio	Average Assets/Average Total Loans	Inverse of the loans to asset ratio; useful also for discerning the business mix of the bank.
Change in Purchased funds	[(Purchased Funds Year 2)/ (Purchased Funds Year 1)] minus 1	Look out for a sharp increase in the use of purchased funds.
Current Ratio	(Cash & cash equivalent + interbank assets + short term investments)/Deposits	Also known as the liquid assets to deposit ratio: Liquid Assets / Deposits. Note that this ratio is another way of looking at the loan to deposit ratio. This is the other liquid assets to deposit ratio. 25–50% is acceptable. Under 25% is risky, over 50% highly conservative.
Foreign Currency Assets to Foreign Currency Liabilities	FX Assets/FX Liabilities	Measures extent of foreign currency assets and liability mismatch.
Foreign Currency Loans to Foreign Currency Deposits	FX Total Loans/FX Deposits	Measures mismatch between FX deposit funding and FX loans. Net loans may also be used in the numerator.
Funding Structure Ratio	Average Customer Deposits/ Average Liabilities	Shows the diversification of funding. Compare with the various purchased funds ratios which also look on reliance on funding other than deposits.
Interbank Assets to Interbank Liabilities	Interbank Assets (deposits or placements with other banks)/ Interbank Liabilities (borrowings from other banks)	Measures degree to which bank is a net lender in the interbank market (preferable) or a net borrower.
Liquid Assets to purchased funds	Liquid Assets/Purchased Funds	An indicator of liquidity if lenders of purchased funds refused to roll them over.
Loans to funding	Total loans/Deposits + Borrowings	Also known as Loans to Deposits and Borrowings.
Loans to Stable Funds	Net Loans total customer deposits + official deposits + medium / long-term liabilities (borrowings) + free capital funds	Similar to loans to funding, but does not include short-term borrowing. Free capital funds is defined as shareholders' equity less minority interest less fixed assets. The ratio illiquid assets to core funding sources is a variant of this ratio.
Pledged Government Securities to total Government Securities	Government Securities pledged as collateral/ Government Securities	One measure of the extent to which government securities are truly liquid assets.
Purchased Funds Ratio	Purchased funds/Total loans plus investement securities	Alternatively the ratio of purchased funds (i.e. large time deposits — over US$100,000), funds borrowed under

Table continued

Indicator	Formula	Remarks
		securities repurchase agreements, interbank borrowings, commercial paper and short-term borrowings) to liabilities may be used. Purchased funds are more costly and more apt to flee than customer deposits. Any loss of confidence can spark an outflow and a liquidity crunch.
Purchased Funds to Earning Assets	Purchased Funds/Average Earning Assets	A comparative measure of purchased funds utilization.
Quasi-liquid assets ratio	See *Liquid assets ratio*	
Securities and Other Holdings to Funding	Securities and Other Holdings Deposits + Borrowings	BankStat ratio. Securities and other holdings are defined as Government Securities, Treasury Bills, Other Securities and Investments, as well as Long-Term Equity Investments and Equity Investments in Subsidiaries and Affiliates.

SOURCES

BankStat Ratio Definitions.

ING Barings, Asian Banking Sector Strategy, May 1997, Appendix 1, Banking Ratio Definitions.

Moody's Investors Service, Global Credit Analysis, IFR Books, 1995.

Moody's Investors Service, Rating Methodology: Bank Credit Risk, Appendix, Financial Ratios, April 1999.

Moody's Investors Service, Sample Ratios: Banks and Bank Holding Companies, undated.

Nomura Asia, Banking Guidebook: Nomura's Standardised Financial Statements and Ratios, November 1, 1999.

Nomura Asia, Nomura Equity Return Decomposition, November 8, 1999.

Thomson BankWatch Ratio Definitions, undated.

Thomson BankWatch, Survey of Asia's Commercial Banks, 1997.

Appendix C: The New Basel Capital Accord: The January 2001 Proposal Due For Implementation By 2004

In July 1999, the Basel Committee on Banking Supervision issued a preliminary consultative proposal to revise the 1988 Capital Accord to remedy the numerous deficiencies that had become apparent in the decade it had been in effect.[1] After receiving over 200 comments concerning the June 1999 proposal, which had recommended placing substantial emphasis on the use of external ratings to gauge risk-weighting of bank assets, the Committee issued a new final consultative proposal in January 2001. While there are significant changes from the June 1999 proposal, there is also much as well that remains unchanged. Similarly, many of the concepts from the original 1988 Capital Accord remain intact.

As the Committee has observed, the original accord used a one-size-fits-all approach to establishing minimum levels of capital adequacy, reflected in a single indicator — the capital adequacy ratio — that was intended to capture all relevant variables into a single number. The new methodology, in contrast, takes a three pronged approach to risk management that provides a more flexible approach to risk assessment that permits greater emphasis on internal rating systems. The three prongs, or in the Committee's language, "three pillars," are: a minimum capital requirement, strong supervisory review, and the use of market discipline. Not only is the first component, which under the old accord was in danger of becoming purely formalistic in nature, more refined, but it also is to be supplemented and reinforced by a new emphasis on effective

---

[1] See Chapter 12, Capital Adequacy: The Basel Accord and Proposed Changes for background to the original accord and its revisions.

bank supervision and the use of market mechanisms to enhance bank soundness.

1. MINIMUM CAPITAL REQUIREMENT: THE CAPITAL ADEQUACY RATIO

While the capital adequacy ratio concept remains — 8% is still the international benchmark minimum — the formula now measures not just credit risk and market risk (the focus of the previous risk-weighting calculus), but operational risk as well. Market risk is also more fully integrated into the capital adequacy formula than in the past. Looking at the previous method for calculating the capital adequacy ratio and the revised one, it can be seen that the *numerator*, or how *capital* is calculated, is the same as before. What is different is the *denominator*. Here a variety of methods are now permitted to calculate not only the credit risk of bank assets where one prevailed before, but a similar menu is allowed for the components of market risk and operational risk. (See illustration below.)

The first Pillar: minimum capital requirement

How capital adequacy is measured

$$\frac{\text{Total capital (unchanged)}}{\text{Credit risk} + \text{Market risk} + \text{Operational Risk}} = \text{the bank's capital ratio (minimum 8\%)}$$

Menu of approaches to measure credit risk

Standardised Approach (a modified version of the existing approach)
Foundation Internal Rating Based Approach
Advanced Internal Rating Based Approach

Menu of approaches to measure market risk (unchanged)

Standardised Approach
Internal Models Approach

Menu of approaches to measure operational risk

Basic Indicator Approach
Standardised Approach
Internal Measurement Approach

Source: Basel Committee on Banking Supervision

Notably, in terms of credit risk, the existing approach to weighting assets is retained as one option, but in a modified form. A greater refinement in the current risk weighting approach is achieved, largely through the use of external ratings. It is expected, however, that most larger banks will opt for the more complex and more sophisticated internal ratings approaches. The use of the internal ratings approach is subject to a number of hurdles that the banks must surmount in order to establish the credibility of their internal rating systems. Banks that opt of the internal ratings based (IRB) approach will be required to comply with "strict methodological and disclosure standards."[2] In addition, greater consideration will be given than before to credit risk mitigation, including the use of collateral, guarantees, credit derivatives and other similar credit enhancement techniques than in the past. While the method of calculating market risk is largely unchanged, operational risk under the new accord will be given a weighting equal to approximately 20% of the denominator, which will need to be taken into account in meeting the overall capital requirement.

2. BANK SUPERVISION AND MARKET DISCIPLINE

The two other pillars of bank soundness place more of a burden on bank supervisors than in the past. The stress in the original accord was placed mainly on banks meeting mandated standards of capital strength. Now a burden is being placed upon regulators as well, calling upon them to have "sound internal processes in place" as well as to impose strict disclosure requirements so that market discipline can work more effectively.

The impact of the new accord

It is likely that the new accord will go into effect at end-2001 with relatively little further modification. Most of the earlier criticisms targeted at the use of external ratings appear to have been addressed, and the industry response to the new proposal to date has been mainly favorable, although one commentator has noted its "byzantine complexity."[3] By its

---

[2] Secretariat of the Basel Committee on Banking Supervision, The New Basel Capital Accord: an explanatory note, January 2001.
[3] Peter Toerman et al., European Banks — Basel 2: Changing the Banking Landscape, Morgan Stanley Dean Witter, February 6, 2001, p. 1. [Banking Landscape]

terms, the new accord will be implemented by 2004. Although the accord is only binding upon the same member countries as previously, in light of the history of the first accord, there is clearly an expectation that the new accord will also be widely adopted on a global basis. As before, countries have some degree of discretion in the extent to which they implement the new scheme, and this is obviously the case with respect to the countries upon which the accord is not binding. The Committee observes however that the World Bank and IMF "use the Basel Committee's standards as a benchmark in conducting their missions" implying that non-member countries have some incentive to accept the new scheme.[4] It is possible, however, that some such countries may opt to stay with the present system.

As for the impact on banks themselves, various analysts have observed that the new accord redresses a bias under the previous accord in which, given the extremely broad risk buckets, high-risk, high-yield retail and consumer banking was favored. More finely-tuned risk weightings will allow banks with strong corporate banking portfolios to allocate less capital then before. In other words, returns on equity will rise on a relative basis for corporate banking and fall for retail banking, including credit cards, but likely excluding mortgage lending which has a comparatively low default rate.[5]

Looking at the European banking landscape, Morgan Stanley Dean Witter bank equity analysts see the winners in the new Basel accord as banks with strong positions in corporate banking and capital markets, as well as those banks which have strong franchises in mortgage banking. Banks that are heavily retail-oriented or which have weak corporate portfolios will be the losers.[6] In Asia, Lehman Brothers banking analysts view the new accord as favoring large players that are capable of meeting new requirements for internal ratings based risk assessment, while banks that are mediocre credits will be priced out of the interbank markets. In addition, some entire countries with weak sovereign credit ratings will "be shut out of the international market."[7]

---

[4] Secretariat of the Basel Committee on Banking Supervision, The New Basel Capital Accord: an explanatory note, January 2001.
[5] Banking Landscape, p. 1–3, 16.
[6] Ibid.
[7] Paul Sheehan & Grant Chan et al., The End of Capital as We Know It, Lehman Brothers, January 18, 2001, p. 1.

Appendix D: Glossary

BANK CREDIT ANALYSIS HANDBOOK
ANNOTATED GLOSSARY: AAA TO Z-SCORE

*Money is not complicated. The principles behind financial transactions are simple
enough. It is usually the detail that confuses by obscuring the principles*[1]

*For most people, trying to determine whether a financial institution is sound is
as frustrating as trying to decipher a foreign language.*[2]

Half the battle of understanding how bank credit analysis works is understanding the jargon which bankers, analysts, and investors use, sometimes without understanding each other. In addition, because banking is a global business there are also variations from country to country in the meanings of terms and a large variety of terms which stand for essentially the same thing. Too often, the users of these terms believe that their usage of the terms is the only right way and the usage of the same term with a slightly different meaning is wrong, even when that usage is prevalent in another country. I myself have taken that attitude in the past. When I first came to Hong Kong, I thought that an editor who used the term "corporate" as a noun was making a profound grammatical error, and having been trained as a lawyer thought I was on firm ground to say so. Little did I know that in British usage, a corporate is what Americans would more often call a corporation.

Common everyday business terms may have peculiar meaning in the banking context. Deceptively simple terms like "capital," or "reserves" can have numerous meanings depending upon what is being referenced

---

[1] Michael Brett, How to Read the Financial Pages: A Simple Guide to the Way Money Works and the Jargon, 3rd Ed., 1987, 1991.
[2] Leonard M. Apcar, Staff Writer, *The Wall Street Journal* (1987), quoted in Mills & Gardner at p. 647.

and how the word is used. Other terms have one or more synonyms that may allow for more stylistic variety in writing analytical reports, but can cause confusion to the reader, for example: *net profit* and *net income*; *net worth* and *shareholders' equity*; *income statement* and *P&L*; *off-balance sheet accounts* and *contingent accounts*. Likewise, there are some commonly used terms which have several apparent synonyms that are broadly similar in meaning but which may have particular nuanced denotations depending upon the jurisdiction in which they are used. Have you ever been perplexed as to just what is the difference between a *non-performing loan*, a *classified loan*, an *overdue loan* (or a *past-due loan*), a *non-accrual loan*, an *impaired loan*, a *problem loan* and a *bad loan*? How about the difference between *gross loans*, *total loans* and *net loans*? If so, the succeeding glossary which is designed to be an integral part of this handbook may help.

Bank analysis is difficult enough without suffering confusion about the meaning of terms being used. For better or worse, English has become the common language of international business. While it may be impossible to agree on standard terms for all banking concepts, it is my hope that this glossary will help to provide a frame of reference to understanding the many variations in terminology, as well as when applicable their underlying concepts. In this way, perhaps it will assist the reader when discussing topics in this book to clarify the meaning intended by those communicating. Although English is the *lingua franca* of the banking world, its participants come from many different backgrounds and, as a result, may be more familiar with terminology used in one market than with terminology which is more often used in another.

While I accept that different terms are in common use and have no desire to impose my own preferences, where usage may lead to confusion, I have not hesitated to say so. Two examples may suffice. *Operating income* in reference to banks usually refers to *net interest income* plus *non-interest income*. Sometimes, however, the term is used to refer to *net* operating income, which is something quite different. Likewise, *non-interest expense* most often refers to *operating expenses* but excludes *loan loss provisioning*. Sometimes, however, it is used to mean operating expenses *plus* loan loss provisioning costs. To my mind, this latter definition only provides fertile ground for confusion.

This glossary is by no means intended to be comprehensive, but to include the most common terms as applied in a financial context, abbreviations that may prove puzzling to the novice, and terms which, as discussed, have numerous synonyms or which are easily confused. I have attempted to offer practical definitions and where feasible have provided illustrations. The focus is on vocabulary encountered in bank analysis rather than in bank operations, but naturally there is some overlap. A variety of terminology from the spheres of corporate, bank equity and sovereign risk analysis are also included, and are marked with the words (corporate) (equity) or (sovereign) where they are mainly applicable to those areas of analysis. I have not shied away from including some very basic terms such as *bank*, *money* and *income* both as a reminder of first principles and as an aid to students.

A note on the sources of these definitions: they are primarily based on my experience performing credit analysis in Asia and on the knowledge I gleaned during that period and in the process of researching this book. In some cases, the definitions are based on my understanding of the concepts embodied in the terms. In other cases, I have consulted the outside sources, synthesized the definitions proffered and reworded them in my own language. Occasionally, I came across an explanation of a term or quotation I could not resist using and these are properly attributed by footnote. In the process of compiling this glossary, it is entirely possible that errors and omissions occurred. I welcome any thoughts from readers that may enable its further refinement.

AAA. The highest credit rating in a number of commonly used default rating symbologies (rating scales which attempt to measure the relative risk of default on a long-term financial assets such as bonds). According to Standard & Poor's, a AAA rating indicates that the "the obligor's capacity to meet its financial commitment on the obligation is extremely strong." The equivalent rating under the Moody's Investor Services scheme is Aaa. Note that the major rating agencies do not have an *AAA*+rating or its equivalent. Note also that other rating scales are applied by the dominant rating agencies in other contexts such as to measure counterparty risk, or the risk of default on short-term securities.

Above-the-line. (Corporate). Above the bottom line. Top line revenue refers to revenue prior to deduction for expenses.

Absolute credit risk. The risk of default expressed as a numerical probability. See *relative credit risk.*

Acceptance. See *Banker's Acceptance.*

Accrual basis. Accounting for income or expenses when earned or incurred irrespective of whether they have been received or paid. The rationale is to match expenses incurred with the revenues that result. Customarily, an income or expense item is earned or incurred at the time the underlying obligation to pay has been created. The income or expense item may be said to "pass through" the income statement at the time it was accrued, unless reversed prior to the date of the income statement.

Accrued interest payable. Interest owing on loans or other financial assets and thereby "passed through" the income statement, but which has not yet been remitted by the bank.

Accrued interest receivable. Interest accrued on loans or other financial assets and thereby "passed through" the income statement, but which has not been received by the bank.

Acid test ratio. (Corporate). Quick ratio.

ADB. Asian Development Bank, headquartered in Manila, Philippines.

Adjusted core return on assets. Refers to a ratio used by Moody's to measure a bank's ability to earn itself out of difficulties. The ratio is: core profits (i.e. EBPT) less consumer net charge-offs less preferred share dividends divided by risk-weighted assets plus securitized loans. Moody's views consumer net charge offs as essentially an expense associated with consumer lending and preferred share dividends essentially as a funding expense akin to interest paid on fixed income obligations. Securitized loans are seen as a funding mechanism and are thus added to assets notwithstanding their off-balance sheet accounting treatment. Another adjusted ratio used by Moody's is return on risk-weighted assets plus "managed receivables" i.e. securitized credit cards.

Advance. A loan, but often connoting either short-term lending, e.g. a bridge loan, or lending against a pre-existing line of credit.

Adverse selection. The tendency for those at greatest risk for the risk insured to seek insurance or the tendency of those most at risk for default to seek a loan.

Affiliate. A company can be said to an *affiliate* or *associate* of the another if the latter holds a substantial proportion e.g. 20% or over of the company's shares. See *Subsidiary.*

AFTA. ASEAN Free Trade Area.

ALCO. Asset liability management committee.

Allowance for loan and lease losses. Loan loss reserves; a reserve against bad debts.

AMC. An asset management corporation.

Analyst. One who evaluates companies for investment or risk management purposes.

Appetite. Demand. (Frequently used in the bond markets.)

ARM. Adjustable rate mortgage.

ASEAN. Association of Southeast Asian Nations.

Asset bubble. A boom period marked by speculative excess and investor euphoria that tends to occur during an economic upswing just prior to its peak, during which the prices of real or financial assets rise to unprecedented level. An asset bubble may be triggered by low real interest rates and easy credit, a material in technology (e.g. the introduction of automobiles, radio) that suggest that society has entered a new economic era. Frequently heard words during an asset bubble are: "this time it's different" and "there are no more business cycles."

Asset inflation. A rapid rise in the prices of real or financial assets fueled by a manic investor psychology, cheap and easy credit, and the prevalence of the "greater fool theory." See *malinvestment; greater fool theory*.

Asset liability management. The process of managing assets and cash flow to maintain the ability to meet current liabilities as they come due. The term liquidity management is another term for *asset liability management*.

Asset management corporation. Abbreviated as AMC, the asset management corporation is a mechanism for off-loading the bad assets (i.e. impaired loans) of banks into a separate entity to facilitate the management and disposal of those assets, restructuring and workouts with the borrowers, and foreclosure and management of any accompanying security, as well as to free banks' balance sheets in order that they may achieve minimum capital adequacy standards. A variety of approaches to asset management corporations have been tried, including the national AMC approach, localized AMCs and AMCs which are little more than debt management *affiliate*s of banks. In general AMCs are funded by the government through the issue of debt instruments. The AMC then buys the bad assets of the bank at their face value or at some discount to it. The removal of the bad assets in itself will improve the capital ratios of the banks, but further "back door" recapitalization can be effected where the value paid for the banks' assets exceeds their mark-to-market value. The rationale for an AMC is thus fourfold. First, it provides a way to get bad assets off banks' books and improve banks' capital ratios. Second, it can be used to help recapitalize banks through backdoor recapitalizations or through direct cash injections. Third, since it is a specialized agency devoted to bad asset management, it can achieve economies of scale and leverage expertise gained to improve the recovery potential. Fourth, as government agencies, sometimes endowed with special powers, the AMC may have more clout with debtors than banks would have acting in their individual capacity.

Asset quality. *Asset quality* refers to the ability of a bank's assets, especially its loans, to continue to perform according to their terms and generate net interest income for the bank. The ratio of *non-performing loans* to total loans is a common quantitative measure of *asset quality.* The ratio of *non-performing loans* to total or gross loans is a typical measure of *asset quality.* More broadly, an evaluation of a bank's *asset quality* encompasses not only quantitative measures of the proportion of problem assets, but also the more qualitative elements, including its approach to provisioning against those assets, lending strategies, credit review policies and procedures, loan portfolio composition, and underlying *credit culture.*

Asset trading. In banking, usually refers to the sale and purchase of loans. Although loans are generally viewed as illiquid assets, banks may be able to trade quality loans, usually those with blue-chip or top-tier companies, with one another, assuming there is no prohibition to doing so in the loan agreement. The reason for doing so may be that a bank desires to reshape its loan portfolio to achieve better diversification. See also *syndicated lending.*

Asset. An item owned or held having value. Categories of assets include (tangible) fixed assets, such as real property or equipment, intangible assets, such as patents, trademarks, or goodwill, and financial assets, such as loans or securities, that represent claims against other parties.

Assets. See *Asset.* Assets, usually as reported by the bank in its financial statements, although analysts in some cases may refer to assets subject to adjustment for bank revaluations and other accounting techniques that may have been undertaken by management. N.B. In some countries, reported assets may include off-balance sheet commitments such as letters of credit, guarantees and acceptances.

Associate. An associated company; an *affiliate*. As a general rule, a company of which 20–50% of the shares are owned or controlled by another is an associated company (*associate* or *affiliate*) of that company. One in which 50% or more of the shares are owned or controlled by another is a *subsidiary*; one in which less than 20% of the shares are owned or controlled by another is a mere trade investment. A company 100%-owned by another is a wholly-owned *subsidiary*. See *subsidiary*.

Asymmetry of information. That a borrower or issuer of debt or equity ordinarily knows more about the potential risks and intentions of participants in his business than does a lender or investor is referred to as an *asymmetry of information*.

Audited financial statements. Financial statements that have been audited by a certified auditor, usually a major accounting firm or in some cases a state agency, stating that the financial statements present a true and fair picture of the company's financial condition, or words to that effect.

Authorized but unissued shares. Shares that are authorized by a bank's or corporation's charter, but are unissued. Treasury shares are shares which have been issued by the bank, but have been reacquired, for example, out of the bank's surplus funds. (The purpose of reacquiring stock may be to have stock available for acquiring other entities, for distribution to employees as bonuses, to acquire the shares of troublesome shareholders, or to generally increase earnings per share and hence the stock's market value.) Both categories are shares that belong to the corporation and are not held by any particular shareholder. Because there is no immediate effect on capital or assets, authorization alone of the issue of common stock is not construed as a formal accounting event. Likewise, *authorized but unissued shares* do not appear as a line item, although their disclosure is generally required on the balance sheet. In contrast, treasury shares do appear as a line item. They are, however, neither an asset nor a part of shareholders' equity. Instead, to prevent distortion of dividends paid to shareholders, the corporation not being deemed a shareholder in its own shares, treasury shares are deducted from shareholders' equity. This does not, however, affect the amount of shareholders equity available for distribution to shareholders upon liquidation. A number of jurisdictions do not permit treasury shares and require that repurchased shares be cancelled.

Authorized capital. Sometimes referred to as *share capital, authorized share capital,* or *nominal capital, authorized capital* refers to the amount of capital authorized to be issued by a corporation. *Authorized capital* will always be equal to or greater than *issued capital. Authorized but unissued shares* are shares already authorized to be issued, usually without further shareholder approval.

Average assets. Usually total assets in the current year plus total assets in the previous year divided by two. However, *average assets* may refer to any time-weighted asset calculation, e.g. average of quarter or monthly assets. Average assets is often used in asset-based ratios to avoid distortions in ratios caused by comparing, for example the income earned over the course of a year with year-end assets or to smooth out sharp changes from year to year due to rapid expansion or contraction of lending. For the same reasons, the same principles of calculation apply to *Average Earning Assets, Average Interest-Bearing Funds,* etc.

Average equity. The shareholders' equity of a bank averaged over a period of time. In the absence of more precise data is available, the average can be obtained by summing the current year's shareholders' equity and the past year's shareholders' equity and dividing by two. See also *Average assets.*

Average interest-bearing liabilities. The earnings-bearing liabilities of a bank averaged over a period of time. In the absence of more precise data, the average can be obtained by summing the current year's interest-bearing liabilities and the past year's and dividing by two. See *Average assets.*

Average interest-bearing deposits. See *Average interest-bearing liabilities.*

Average interest-earning assets. The earning assets of a bank averaged over a period of time. In the absence of more precise data is available, the average can be obtained by summing the current year's earning assets and the past year's and dividing by two. See also *Average assets.*

Average investment securities. See *Average interest-earning assets.*

Average. *adj.* When referring to *average assets, average loans, average interest-bearing liabilities,* etc. the term *average* refers to time-weighted averaging. This can be done using any time period, but in bank credit analysis it is most frequently done on a yearly, semi-annual or quarterly basis. For example, to find the *average assets* on an annual basis, add the total assets at the end of the most recent fiscal year and the prior year, and divide by two.

Average Loans. Usually total loans in the current year plus total loans in the previous year divided by two. See also *Average assets*.

B & DD expense. *Bad and doubtful debt expense*; The amount charged to the income statement for bad and doubtful debts, i.e. *loan loss provisioning*.

Backtesting. The process of verifying that the results predicted by a model conform with the actual results, and if not, observing how they differ.

Bad bank. See *Good bank/bad bank*.

Bad debt. A debt that is or is expected to become uncollectible.

Bad loan. A bad debt in reference to a loan made by a bank; i.e. a loan which is expected not to be collectible in full; as commonly used the term bad loan encompasses a broad ranging of meanings, sometimes referring to a *non-performing loan*, and at other times used as a narrower synonym for an *impaired loan* or just for a *loss loan*.

Balance of payments. A country's overall *balance of payments*, or its official reserve transactions balance, is equal to its *current account* plus its *capital account*. The sum represents the change in a country's *foreign reserves*. Normally, the sum of a country's *current account* and its *capital account* is near zero. If it is positive, that means that foreign reserves increased; if negative, they decreased.

Balance sheet management. The process of maintaining sufficient *capital adequacy* and *liquidity* to meet any foreseeable shocks which a bank must absorb to continue functioning as a *going concern*.

Balance sheet. A comprehensive statement of a company's assets and liabilities — what it owns and what it owes (or, to be more precise, the claims on what it owns) — at a given moment, usually the end of the fiscal period, e.g. December 31. Also known as a *statement of condition*, a *statement of resources* etc.

Bank deposit rating. A type of rating provided by Moody's Investor Service among other agencies which evaluates the relative risk of default of a bank in respect to its deposits. Moody's bank deposit rating takes into account both bank financial strength and explicit external support.

Bank holding company. A company hat has one or more bank subsidiaries.

Bank of International Settlements. Founded in 1930, the BIS as it is popularly known, is the bank for central banks. It accepts deposits from an making loans to its member banks, acts as a source of information for issues related to international capital movements, and provides a voice for the views of central bankers generally. Its headquarters in Basel, Switzerland has also provided a forum for the Basel Committee on Banking Supervision, a group composed of the regulators from the Group of Ten (G10) countries which has been active since the mid-1980s in promoting uniform rules on bank capital adequacy, risk management and bank supervision. See *Basel Committee*. The fruits of their efforts produced the 1988 Basel Accord on Capital Adequacy and an accompanying formula for calculating bank capital adequacy, popularly known as the *BIS ratio* or the *BIS capital adequacy ratio*, which has been adopted by bank regulators and banks worldwide. Although the two organizations are separate, the Bank's website is a source for material on the *Basel Accord*. See www.bis.org.

Bank run. A bank run is a panic in which depositors, fearing that a bank is experiencing financial difficulty, flood a bank's offices demanding the return of their deposits. A line outside a bank's offices is often associated with a bank run. Because of the nature of *fractional reserve banking* whereby depositors' funds are used to make illiquid loans, even the most solvent and liquid bank is vulnerable to a bank run, unless it has access to immediate sources of liquid funds from a lender of last resort such as the central bank. This vulnerability also explains why public confidence is so critical to an effectively functioning banking system.

Bank. A financial intermediary, usually deposit-taking and typically highly-leveraged, which usually earns its income primarily from the spread between the cost it pays for funds and the price at which it lends or invests those funds. As an intermediary, the bank takes advantage of its perceived creditworthiness to attract funds and through expertise and informational advantages gained as a result of experience and deal flow, substitutes its credit judgment for those of the ultimate suppliers of funds (e.g. depositors). The bank adds value by exploiting economies of scale, knowledge and technology access to information, and by offering convenience and peripheral services to the suppliers and users of funds. Intensified competition and the reduced cost of information, however, have caused banks to rely increasingly on fee income and other forms of non-interest revenue to achieve their profit targets.

Bankers' acceptance. A negotiable instrument, usually arising from a letter of credit transaction, in which is a draft drawn on a bank and marked "accepted."

Banking crisis. A situation characterized by a loss of confidence which threatens or causes the breakdown of a banking system's ability to function in its usual role as a source of credit, a payments mechanism and as a vehicle for monetary policy. A banking crisis is typically accompanied by *capital flight* (i.e. the withdrawal of deposits from banking institutions in the country affected) and a *liquidity crunch* (i.e. a contraction of bank lending resulting from a loss of deposits and other funding, erosion of capital, a perceived high risk lending environment, and in some cases high interest rates. In severe cases, a banking crisis may be preceded or followed by major currency devaluations, failures of large companies, a dramatic drop in economic growth (or even economic contraction) and political turmoil. The Asian crisis of 1997–98, especially as it affected Thailand, Indonesia and South Korea, was in large part a banking crisis.

Banking environment. The business and regulatory environment in which a bank operates. Key variables include: sovereign risk, including macroeconomic and political factors; phase of the economic cycle; level of competition and degree of consolidation; extent to which lending and other banking business opportunities are diversified; the existence of banking cartels; ease of entry into in the market; quality of bank regulation, supervision and enforcement; legal framework and status of creditors' rights; prevailing bank net interest margins; prevailing bank capital adequacy, NPL level and loan growth, prevailing liquidity levels and sources of funding.

Bankruptcy. The legal status of being insolvent or unable to pay debts; legal proceedings pursuant to which a *bankruptcy* court takes over the assets of the debtor and appoints a receiver or trustee to administers them.

Basel 2. Refers to the second major revision of the Basel Accord, for which a first consultative document was issued in June 1999 and a final consultative document in January 2001, with approval scheduled by end-2001 and final implementation by 2004.

Basel Accord. The Basel Capital Accord of 1988, formally entitled "International Convergence of Capital Measurement and Capital Standards," as amended. Sometimes referred to as the 1988 Accord, the 1988 Basel Capital Accord and so on.

Basel Committee. The Basel Committee refers to the Basel Committee on Banking Supervision, a panel of regulators from the Group of Ten (G10) countries that usually convenes at the Bank of International Settlements (BIS) in Basel, Switzerland. The Committee established the first international standards on the capital adequacy of banks in 1988, in the form of a risk-weighted capital adequacy ratio (CAR). Although the standards and the CAR have nothing to do with the BIS per se, for convenience' sake the ratio is often referred to as the BIS ratio, the BIS capital adequacy ratio, or as the BIS CAR.

Basis point. One hundredth of a percent (0.01%). Abbreviated *bp*.

Basis risk. See interest rate risk.

Bear market. A period of declining stock prices; when the relevant stock market index has fallen 20% or more from its peak.

Behavioral risk. Operational risks related to human error or frailty. See Crime Risk, Legal Risk; Compliance Risk.

Behest lending. (Philippines) Refers to lending (usually from state-owned or controlled banks) motivated by political influence.

Benchmark yield curve. The yield curve; the yield curve established for a particular country using the most risk-free securities, typically government treasury bills and bonds, as a benchmark. When the government is not a major issuer of securities, a quasi-governmental entity or the most highly creditworthy corporate issuer may be used as a substitute.

Beta, short for *beta coefficient*, measures an investment's vulnerability to systematic risk, i.e. the degree to which the risk of an (equity) investment correlates to that of the relevant market generally. A beta of 1.0 means that the price of the stock will move in line with the market, a beta of less than 1.0 means that it when the market goes up or down, it will move less than the market as a whole, while a beta greater than one means that it will move more than the market as a whole.

BHC. A bank holding company.

Bid-offer spread. A way in which financial intermediaries make profits in the capital, foreign exchange and money markets. The difference between the price at which a bank is willing to sell an asset or security and the price at which the same bank is willing to buy the same asset or security represents its bid-offer spread.

Bill of exchange. A payment order in which the drawer requests a drawee (e.g. a bank) to pay a certain amount to a certain person or bearer (the payee) on a particular date or under specified conditions, for example upon the receipt of certain documentation.

Bill. 1. A bill of exchange or similar instrument; a payment order; a draft. Bills receivable are assets to a bank; bills payables are liabilities. 2. A bill of lading 3. A type of US government fixed income security having a tenor of one year or less.

BIS capital adequacy ratio. Total capital divided by risk-weighted assets as both are defined under what is commonly referred to as the 1988 Basle Capital Accord (see *Basel Accord*), as subsequently amended and as modified by the relevant local banking authorities. The Accord and the ratio actually have nothing to do with the BIS other than the fact that the Basel Committee usually holds its meetings at the bank and that materials concerning the Accord and the rules issued thereunder are available from the bank or at its website, www.bis.org.

BIS ratio. The BIS capital adequacy ratio.

BIS. Bank for International Settlements.

Black hole cost. The cost of bank recapitalization represented by banks' collective problem loans losses, so-called because the non-recoverable amount of loan losses have disappeared into the proverbial black hole. Total estimated peak NPLs "minus recovery is the black hole cost," where recovery is equal to an estimated recovery rate times total estimated peak NPLs.[3] Example: Analyst X expects peak NPLs in Tropicola's commercial banking sector to reach 32%. Outstanding commercial loans net of provisions equal $100 billion, and X estimates a recovery rate on NPLs of about 40%. Total NPLs = $32 billion, recovery = $32 bn. × 0.4 or $12.8 bn. The black hole cost is $32 billion − $12.8 billion or $19.2 billion.

Bond. A long-term fixed income security, long-term meaning having a maturity date of at least one to five years, depending upon the definition employed. Banks frequently issue subordinated bonds with a term of five years or greater for capital raising and sometimes for funding purposes. These bonds are subordinated or junior to the obligations of the bank to its depositors.

Bond rating. A rating associated with a particular bond. See *rating*.

Book capital. Shareholders' equity.

---

[3] Simon Maughan, "Bank Recapitalization: Options & Policies," Indosuez W.I. Carr Securities, July 15, 1998, p. 3.

Book value. The value of an item as reported in a company's balance sheet, i.e. as recorded on the firm's "books."

Boom. n. A period of economic expansion in which the economy is growing at an above average rate.

bp. Basis point.

Breakeven yield. The difference between non-interest income (excluding exceptional items) and non-interest expense divided by *average assets*.

Budget deficit. (Sovereign). The shortfall in government tax revenues compared to the amount a government spends in a given time period. Large budget deficits are viewed negatively by sovereign risk analysts, as they are thought to provide an impetus for inflation.

Building society. A type of deposit-taking financial institution that engages in long-term mortgage lending primarily to finance owner-occupied residential property (UK). The US equivalent is a *savings and loan society* or *savings and loan association*, frequently abbreviated to an "S & L." See *Mortgage Bank, Savings Bank, Savings-and-Loan, Thrift Bank.*

Bull market. A sustained period of generally rising stock prices. (e.g. 2 years according to Charles Henry Dow).

Business cycle. The sequence of recovery, upswing, downturn, recession during which business activity as reflected in various economic indicators predictably rises and falls. The timing of business cycles and the change from one phase into another, however, is largely unpredictable. Procyclical indicators tend to rise during recovery and fall during a recession, while countercyclical indicators tend to fall during recovery and rise during a recession. Leading indicators are usually at the forefront of changes in the business cycle, while lagging indicators follow those changes.

Business risk. See *operational risk.*

Buy-side. Used mainly to refer to an analyst who is employed by an investment fund — a mutual fund, pension fund or hedge fund, for example — whose role is to select securities or other assets to buy, sell or hold. The counterpart to buy-side analysts are sell-side analysts, who are employed by investment banks. Many buy-side analysts have previously worked as sell-side analysts.

Call. 1. To demand early repayment of a loan; 2. To exercise a call provision in a bond indenture and redeem the security early by repaying the investors pursuant to that provision.

CAMEL. The acronym for the mainstream approach to credit analysis of financial institutions, referring to the five key elements of credit assessment: Capital (Adequacy), *Asset quality*, Management (Competency), Earnings (and Profitability) and Liquidity (and Funding). Sometimes used as a noun as in "Orange Bank has good CAMELs."

CAMELOT. An acronym devised by banking analyst Roy Ramos of Goldman Sachs in Hong Kong to represent a model used for equity analysis purposes. "O" stands for operating environment and "T" for transparency. See *CAMEL.*

Capital account. 1. Net foreign investment plus net foreign credits (short-term and long-term) 2. "A country's international transactions arising from changes in holdings of real and financial capital assets (but not income on them, which is in the current account). Includes foreign direct investment (FDI), plus changes in private and official holdings of stocks, bonds, loans, bank accounts, and currencies."[4]

Capital Adequacy Ratio. Abbreviated CAR. See *BIS capital adequacy ratio.*

Capital and reserves. Shareholders' equity.

Capital Asset Pricing Model. A theory which states that the return on any investment will be the risk-free return rate plus a premium for systematic risk (risk associated with the market in which the asset trades) plus an additional premium for specific risk (risk specific to the asset). See *systematic risk; specific risk.*

Capital consumption allowance. (Sovereign). See depreciation.

Capital formation rate. Internal growth rate of capital.

Capital goods. (Sovereign). Investment goods as opposed to consumption goods.

Capital markets. The market for long-term securities which encompasses equity securities and fixed income securities with a term of one year or greater.

Capital. 1. Shareholders' equity; equity capital. 2. A buffer against financial institution *insolvency* as defined by regulatory authorities; regulatory capital. 3. Shareholders' equity plus loan capital (debt); long term capital. 4. That which can be used to produce goods and services. 4. After labor and land, the third factor of production. 5. Wealth or money.

Capital reserves. Restricted surplus. The portion of shareholders' equity which is not distributable until liquidation.

Capitalize. To treat as an investment rather than as a cost or expense.

---

[4] Deardorff's Glossary of International Economics, http://www-personal.umich.edu/~alandear/glossary/.

CAR. 1. Capital Adequacy Ratio as defined under the Basel Accord. 2. Capital-at-risk, a synonym for Value-at-Risk or VaR (also VAR).

Cash flow statement. See *Statement of Cash Flows*.

Cash flow. Earnings before interest payments, taxes and depreciation. Because of the nature of the banking business, cash flow is little used in bank credit analysis relative to corporate credit analysis; however, it assumes greater importance in the analysis of bank holding companies.

Cash. 1. Funds that can be readily spent or used to meet current obligations; legal tender, coins; 2. Cash and cash equivalent.

CD. Certificate of deposit.

CEEs. Credit equivalent exposures.

Certificate of deposit. Abbreviated CD. Receipt for a deposit of funds for a specific period of time at a stated interest rate. Certificates of deposits may be either negotiable (transferable to a new holder before maturity) or non-negotiable. In the US, negotiable CDs usually have denominations of at least US$100,000.

CFROI. (Equity) Cash flow return on investment.

Chaebol. A Korean conglomerate. *Chaebol* have dominated the South Korean economy since the 1960s. Major *chaebol* include Hyundai, Samsung and LG.

Charge-off. Write-off.

Chart of accounts. A uniform system for coding accounts for use in management or financial reporting.

Chinese wall. Institutional barriers blocking communication concerning sensitive information between, for example, a bank's corporate finance department and its proprietary securities trading unit.

CHIPS. Clearing House Interbank Payments System. An electronic funds transfer system which permits the international transfer of funds among eligible financial institutions.

Church and state. The credit assessment function and the business development function.[5]

City bank. (Japan). Large Japanese private banks located in the country's major cities.

Classified loans. A term which ordinarily refers to loans that are problematic, i.e. that fall into one of several categories other than

---

[5] Cades, p. 81.

"pass" or "normal," i.e. fully performing and expected to continue to do so. Examples of classifications from least to most problematic include: specially mentioned, substandard, doubtful, and loss.

Claw-back provisions. See *interest income clawback provisions.*

Clean opinion. An unqualified opinion; that is, an opinion without any additional qualifications or limitation.

Clean up the balance sheet. In reference to balance sheet management, a bank during times of financial stress or unfavorable economic conditions may be said to be "cleaning up its balance sheet" "rebuilding it balance sheet" or in a "consolidation phase." These three phrases ordinarily mean that a bank is engaged in one or more of the following: calling in loans or refusing to grant new loans in order to improve its nominal capital adequacy and liquidity; recognizing loan losses and writing off bad loans against existing loan loss reserves and if need be capital; or attempting to increase loan loss reserves and capital through any combination of measures, including reduced dividends to shareholders, the issue of subordinated debt as Tier 2 capital or rights issues or public offerings. In more extreme cases, cleaning up the balance sheet may involve major restructuring initiatives such as setting up an asset management corporation to facilitate the disposal or workout of bad assets and foreclosed assets or a government infusion of funds. See *restructuring.*

Clean. Unsecured; as in a "clean loan."

Clearinghouse. An institution in which claims among members are settled through offsetting payments.

Closed capital account. Countries (e.g. China) which severely restrict the movement of inbound and outbound capital through administrative rules and the imposition of taxes are said to have a closed capital account. A closed capital account is typically coupled with restrictions on the convertibility of the country's currency. In practice, the openness of a country's capital account is a matter of degree, and governmental restrictions are sometimes evaded. In the past, most emerging countries maintained closed capital account, but many have liberalized them, although some, such as Malaysia, have resumed certain restrictions. See *open capital account.*

Collateral cover. An *asset quality* indicator which measures the value of collateral securing a bank's problem loans against the bank's problem loans, i.e. The estimated value of collateral securing NPLs divided by NPLs.

Collateral. Assets, e.g. real property securing a loan. If the borrower defaults on a loan obligation, the creditor can through judicial means, as for example through foreclosure, take full title to the property.

Commercial paper. Short-term unsecured debt, usually with a maturity of 270 days or less, issued by a corporation or a bank holding company. (Rare) Corporate debentures; in some countries, commercial paper may refer to longer dated debt issues of one year or more.

Common equity. Shareholders' equity excluding that of preferred shareholders.

Common shares. Ordinary shares that have no preferential right to receive defined dividends.

Competition risk. The risks affecting a bank's business brought about by the action of existing competitors, the entry of new ones, or the inability of the bank to keep pace with its rivals. Examples include: the risk of change in strategic alliances, the new product initiatives from the competition, the risk of more sophisticated foreign banks entering the market, and the risk of key staff being poached by competitors. Competition risk is a category of operational risk.

Compliance risk. The risk to capital or earnings arising from non-compliance with prudential and other relevant laws and regulations leading to civil or criminal liability. Violation of such laws and regulations can lead to fines, civil damages, the voiding of contracts and may diminish the reputation of the bank. Compliance risk is a category of legal risk and a sub-category of operational risk.

Compound interest.

Consolidated financial statements. Financial statements which incorporate the results of a company's subsidiaries. Note: In bank credit analysis, unless the bank is a small part of a larger industrial group, it is preferable to analyze its consolidated financial statements.

Consolidation. 1. Mergers and acquisitions among banks in a particular market, reducing the number of banks in the sector. Consolidation is sometimes encouraged by regulatory authorities in the belief that a small number of comparatively large and financial strong banks create a more robust and stable banking system than one made up of numerous smaller institutions. See also *Clean up the balance sheet.*

Consumer lending. Includes auto finance, personal loans, home equity finance, credit card finance and may include home mortgage finance.

Consumer Price Index. Often abbreviated CPI, this is a measure of the rate of inflation, which itself is a fundamental parameter of sovereign risk. The consumer price index measures the price of a "shopping basket" of goods and services against the cost at a base date. The change in the price of the goods expressed as a percentage corresponds to the rate of inflation. In the US, the composition of the shopping basket is as follows: Housing 42%; Food 18%;Transportation 17%; Medical Care 6%; Apparel 6%; Entertainment 4%; Other 7%.

Consumption goods. Goods for consumption purposes as opposed to for investment.

Contagion. The transmission of a financial crisis from one country to another largely through a loss of confidence manifested in changes in the sentiment and behavior of investors, consumers and investors and a belief that the country affected may be vulnerable to the same malady as that already affected.

Contingent account. Off-balance sheet account.

Contingent liabilities. Also referred to as off-balance sheet obligations, these are liabilities that are contingent upon certain events taking place. For example, a guarantee of a customer's performance only becomes a firm obligation upon the contingency of the customer defaulting on the primary obligation.

Contributed capital. Paid in capital.

Convertible bonds. Bonds that can be converted to ordinary or common shares upon certain conditions. Companies typically issue convertible bonds when their share price is expected to rise as investors will accept a lower coupon rate in the expectation that they may be able to convert the bonds into shares and realize a gain. Convertible preferred shares may be issued for similar reasons.

Convoy system. Refers to the policy which prevailed in Japan for many years whereby the government through "administrative guidance" would direct stronger banks to assist weaker banks through transactions which benefited the weaker banks including merger. Convoy refers to the image of a naval convoy in which each ship protected the other.

Cooking the books. Creative accounting, but with a somewhat stronger connotation of deceptiveness or possible illegality. See *creative accounting*.

Core capital. Tier 1 Capital.

Core customer deposits. Customer deposits (as opposed to (inter)bank deposits).

Core deposits. Customer deposits (as opposed to (inter)bank deposits); the sum of demand deposits, interest-bearing checking accounts, savings deposits, money market accounts and time deposits (in the US excluding brokered deposits and time deposits having a denomination of US$100,000 or more).

Core earnings. Net income excluding deductions for provisioning and taxes. Also known as: *core profits, underlying profits, earnings before taxes and provisions and EBPT*, for *earnings before taxes and provisions.*

Core profitability. Underlying profitability; Core earnings divided by *average assets.*

Corporate governance. While the term "corporate governance" refers literally to the manner in which a corporation is governed and decisions are undertaken, in practice it has a normative connotation, with (good) corporate governance referring to corporations (and banks) that: 1) make decisions for the benefit of shareholders (not management); 2) make decisions on the basis of commercial (i.e. for profit) criteria; and 3) protect the rights of minority shareholders (rather than approving corporate actions that unfairly benefit the majority or controlling shareholders at the minority's expense). In contrast, "bad" corporate governance refers corporations that: 1) make decisions for the benefit of management or another interest other than shareholders as a whole; 2) allow non-commercial criteria (e.g. related- party and insider transactions, political favoritism, cronyism, corruption to infiltrate the corporate decision-making process; or 3) allow majority shareholders to trample the rights of minority shareholders. Corporate governance is affected by applicable legal and regulatory regime in which the corporation operates, the articles and bylaws governing the corporation, and the actions undertaken by the board of directors, management and the shareholders in attempting to influence corporate policies.

Corporate lending. Refers to lending to large corporations in contrast to small and medium sized firms, which are known as the "middle market."

Corporate. n. A corporation.

Cosmetic restructuring. Restructuring of problem loans by a bank which in fact is the mere rescheduling or deferral of the loan obligation for appearance' sake (e.g. to make the banks problem loan ratio appear better), without reference to the viability of the debtor's business.

Cost of funds. The rate the bank pays to borrow funds that it re-lends to customers (i.e. borrowers). The cost of funds is usually calculated by dividing average interest payable over a particular time period, e.g. one year, by the average interest bearing liabilities. Cost of funds can also be calculated for specific classes of funds such as the *Cost Of Deposits*, the *Cost Of Interbank And Money Market Items* and the *Cost Of Long Term Borrowings*.

Cost of interest-bearing liabilities. Cost of funds.

Cost to income ratio. Non interest expense as percentage of operating income. See *Efficiency ratio*.

Cost-margin. Non-interest expenses (excludes loan loss provisions) to *average assets*.

Counterparty risk rating. A credit rating of a counterparty that attempts to measure its ability to satisfy its obligations generally, irrespective of the terms of any particular debt obligation; an issuer rating.

Counterparty. The other party in a financial contract that involves credit risk. The term often refers to a party that upon the occurrence of some contingency is likely to come under a financial obligation to pay money to the party extending credit. Two banks will often be counterparties to each other. Examples of counterparty risk include derivatives transactions, such as foreign exchange swaps, and trade finance transactions, such as letters of credit. A counterparty is similar to an obligor or borrower except that the term counterparty connotes *contingent* credit exposure, while an obligor typically has a *fixed* credit exposure.

Counter-trade. A form of barter trade used in trading with countries that lack ample hard currency; the acceptance by the seller of goods as full or partial payment instead of currency.

Country grading. An internal rating of country risk, i.e. of the country in which, or with which, a bank has exposure.

Country risk. The range of risks emerging from the political, legal, economic, and social conditions of a country that have adverse consequences affecting investors and creditors with exposure to that country, and may also include negative effects on financial institutions and borrowers in that country. Country risk analysis is similar to sovereign risk analysis, but where sovereign risk analysis focuses on the risk of the government defaulting on its obligations (e.g. bond issues), country risk embraces the risks affecting creditors, investors and borrowers within and without the country, including those affecting direct and portfolio investors. Among such risks are: destruction of property through war or civil disorder, nationalization or expropriation, "creeping [i.e. gradual] expropriation," the imposition of moratoria on foreign currency remittances and similar actions. See *sovereign risk, transfer risk.*

Coupon rate. The *yield* on a bond based on the face value (value at maturity). Sometimes shortened to *coupon.* In the past, bond interest was received by clipping coupons in exchange for which the bondholder was entitled to specific payments of interest.

CPI. Consumer price index.

Crawling peg. An exchange rate regime in which a fixed rate is automatically adjusted gradually and periodically according to a generally predetermined scheme. Also known as *sliding parity.*

Creative accounting. Using the use of discretionary standards in accounting to enhance profits (preferably showing steadily increasing revenue rather than erratic earnings), improve capital ratios and generally obscure financial problems that the company may be facing. Banks have many opportunities to use creative accounting techniques including among them: over- or under-provisioning for loan losses, under-disclosing problem loans, and characterizing non-recurrent transactions as recurrent and vice-versa. A more euphemistic term for creative accounting and one with a less pejorative connotation is "window dressing."

Credit costs. With respect to a class or portfolio of interest-earning assets, the costs ultimately equal to the losses incurred. In the short-term, credit costs represent the sum of provisioning and write-offs in connection with that pool of assets.

Credit crunch. A shortage of credit resulting from an unwillingness on the part of banks to lend due to heightened uncertainty, a riskier business climate, deteriorating *asset quality* or monetary and economic policy changes. A credit crunch will not necessarily be self-rectifying since the level of interest rates at which lending would again become economically attractive may be so high as to attract only the most undesirable borrowers. Also termed a *credit squeeze.*

Credit culture. The attitudes, values, and internal rules and the enforcement of those rules that govern a financial institution's credit policies and the behavior of its staff concerning the extension of credit and the recovery of funds owed to the institution. "A strong *credit culture* will achieve a prudent equilibrium between business development and quality control, and not merely a sales bias that pays lip service to such checks and balances."[6]

Credit cycle. The business cycle from the bank's perspective, focusing on credit standards and the accumulation and reduction of *non-performing loans*. See *business cycle*. During recovery and an economic upswing, credit standards tend to become looser as bankers are confident about the economy's prospects and borrowers enjoy strong income and plausible growth prospects. During a recession, bankers tighten lending standards not only because pessimism prevails, but also because they need to "clean up their balance sheets" by provisioning against and writing off NPLs. This may lead to a credit crunch and exacerbate the liquidity problems of borrowers, causing some marginal ones to fail. The expansion and contraction of lending together with rise and fall in *non-performing loans* characterizes the credit cycle.

Credit enhancement. Provisions included in debt agreements to enhance the creditworthiness of the borrower and provide additional comfort to the creditor against the risk of default. They are often incorporated into derivatives' contracts, structured finance or asset-backed securitization transactions. Examples include over-collateralization, guarantees, credit downgrade triggers, and netting agreements, which provide for the set-off of liabilities between two counterparties.

Credit equivalent exposures. Under the Basel Accord capital adequacy framework, the product of a bank's off-balance sheet items times the applicable credit conversion factors.

Credit grading. Also known as *internal credit risk rating*. The internal rating of bank loans. Credit grading models vary from the simple to the complex and take account of varying mixes of quantitative and qualitative data, and are used as tools in assisting a bank in managing its loan portfolio, in pricing loans and in provisioning for them, as well as in assessing capital and liquidity needs.

Credit risk modeling. The process of modeling credit risk across an institution's business lines by product, counterparty or borrower type and geographic region to assist it in pricing credit products and making credit decisions, assessing capital and liquidity needs, and allocating resources for collection efforts. In contrast to market risk modeling,

---

[6] Cades, p. 79.

credit risk modeling is complicated by limitations on data including: 1) the fact that most assets which are subject to credit risk, e.g. loans, are not marked-to-market; 2) the comparative infrequency of default events; 3) the absence of a comprehensive historical record of default events owing to the private character of many credit transactions; and, 4) the relatively long time horizons associated with credit transactions. Model validation is correspondingly more difficult and is typified by the "use of simplifying assumptions and proxy data."[7] The end result of a credit risk model is the generation of a bell curve (probability density function of losses) representing the probabilities of (unexpected) credit loss as measured by the distance from the mean (expected losses). A given point X will be ascertained that is sufficiently improbable that a corresponding level of allocated economic capital will be sufficient to cover the risk of such a loss within a given confidence interval. Credit risk models can be either conditional, i.e. incorporating data about the state of the economy, or unconditional.

Credit risk. The risk of loss through default on financial obligations. Credit loss may embody both the probability of default as well as expected loss in the event of default (the default-mode paradigm) (mark-to-market paradigm).

Credit scoring. Credit grading as applied to consumer or retail lending. Relative to credit grading, credit scoring tends to be more quantitative. See *credit grading*.

Credit unions. Member-owned institutions whose purpose is to take deposits and provide financing within the membership.

Credit. 1. From the Latin, credere, meaning "to trust, believe:" a) trust in one's integrity on money matters and one's ability to meet payments when due," b) one's financial reputation or status."[8] 2. "lender's agreement to advance funds"[9] 3. the borrower 4. a loan or advance 5. in accounting, a decrease in assets or an increase in liabilities or equity; example: When a bank credits a customer's account, it increases the amount, which to the bank is an increased liability. 6. (Sovereign) Recorded as positive (+) in the balance of payments,

---

[7] See Credit Risk Modelling: Current Practices and Applications, Basle Committee on Banking Supervision, Basle, April 1999.

[8] *Webster's New World College Dictionary*, 3rd Ed., Macmillan, 1997, p. 325.

[9] Thomas Fitch, *Dictionary of Banking Terms*.

any transaction that gives rise to a payment into the country, such as an export, the sale of an asset (including official reserves), or borrowing from abroad.

Creditmetrics™. A type of proprietary credit risk modeling system developed by J.P. Morgan which employs a discounted contractual cash flow approach (i.e. present value is calculated as the discounted value of future contractual cash flows) to model current and future marked-to-market values of assets, where the discount rate is determined by the default probability linked to a correspondingly rated corporate bond (applying debt ratings from the major rating agencies).

Criminal risk. Also *Crime Risk*. 1. The risk of being a victim of crime including, among others, fraud, embezzlement, computer crime, and robbery. 2. The risk that an officer or employee engages in activity subjecting the bank to criminal liability. N.B. If the activity is non-criminal and the bank is merely subject to the risk of civil liability, the risk would be more appropriately classified as compliance risk or legal risk. Criminal risk is a category of operational risk. The collapse of Barings Bank in 1995 can be attributed to activity that can be classified as criminal, aggravated by poor risk controls.

Crony capitalism. An economic system in which government and business interests collude to facilitate business transactions which benefit each other. The term embodies a variety of activities ranging from rent-seeking behavior, to the exploitation of minority shareholders to graft and corruption.

Cross-border risk. Country risk.

Cross-rate. Exchange rate of two currencies that will be calculated by reference to a third currency. For example, the cross rate between the Australian dollar and the Mexican peso will probably be calculated using the US dollar exchange rate as a reference currency, since the market for direct foreign exchange transactions between holders of Aussie dollars and Mexican pesos will likely be thin.

Cumulative preference shares. Preferred (preference) shares in which shareholders are entitled to receive dividends unpaid in previous years as a result of insufficient net profit in those years.

Currency basket. A portfolio of currency holdings, usually reserve currencies, that are typically used as the benchmark for pegging a currency. For example, prior to July 1997, the Thai baht was pegged to an unspecficied basket of currencies which included the US dollar and Japanese yen.

Currency board. A form of exchange rate regime in which a special agency is given the role of pegging the local currency to a specified foreign currency at a specified rate with the mandate to back each unit of the local currency at that rate. Hong Kong is an example of a locality with a currency board, the Hong Kong Monetary Authority, which among its other responsibilities backs the Hong Kong dollar at the rate of 7.8 to each US dollar.

Currency peg. An exchange rate regime in which the government attempts to peg or fix the exchange rate through a variety of means ranging from the use of a currency board to various forms of intervention. Prior to the Asian Crisis of 1997–98, Thailand attempted to peg the Thai baht at approximately 25 baht per US dollar. The peg was abandoned on July 2, 1997, a date often used to mark the start of the crisis.

Currency risk. Refers to exposure to fluctuation in currency exchange rates that may have an adverse effect on a bank's market position. Synonymous with foreign exchange risk.

Current account balance. Exports plus net transfer income minus imports.

Current account balance. Gross savings less gross investment.

Current account. A demand account; a checking account. An account from which funds may ordinarily be withdrawn on demand and which pays little or no interest.

Current account. (Sovereign) Merchandise trade balance (exports plus imports) + services balance (non factor services e.g. freight, tourism, insurance) + capital services (e.g. interest receipts, profit remittances) + labor services (workers' remittances + unilateral transfers.

Current yield. The interest payable on a fixed income security divided by its price. The current yield will diverge from the coupon rate of a security, depending upon the price paid for the security; i.e. whether it is a discount from the security's face value or a premium to its face value.

Customer deposits. Deposits other than interbank deposits. Customer deposits typically include short-, medium- and long-term deposits, foreign currency deposits, cash margins placed with the bank as collateral, and certificates of deposits. N.B. In the US, customer deposits has a specific definition which generally includes domestic deposits in denominations of under US$100,000.

Customer. User of a bank's services generally, but sometimes meaning those who use a bank's financing services in contrast to mere depositors.

Customer loans. Bank loans and advances other than interbank loans.

Daylight exposure. Intra-day exposure.

Dead bank ratio. Colloquial analyst term used to refer to the ratio of the sum of bank equity capital and loan loss reserves to problem assets. If equity capital and loan loss reserves exceed problem assets, the bank is generally solvent; if not, it is insolvent or very close to it.

Deal flow. The flow of transactions which gain significance not only from the revenue they produce, but in the market and related information they provide that can be arbitraged to provide a financial institution with a competitive advantage.

Debenture. An unsecured corporate debt issue. (N.B. in British usage, debentures are secured loans having a fixed term and a fixed interest rate.)

Debt rating. A default rating.

Debt ratio. (Sovereign). Public sector debt to GDP; national government debt to GDP. See also Total Debt to GDP. (Corporate) Long term debt divided by long-term debt plus equity.

Debt. Borrowing; long-term liabilities, usually in the form of loans from banks or other entities, fixed income securities issued (e.g. bonds, floating rate notes). Such long-term liabilities are sometimes referred to as loan capital.

Default rating. A rating which rates the default risk of a particular securities issue, and may also take into account the severity of the default, i.e. the degree of loss in the event of default.

Default risk. The risk that the issuer will not fulfill its financial obligations to the investor/creditor in accordance with the terms of the obligation. Depending upon how it is defined, it may encompass not only the probability of loss but also the magnitude of the loss.

Default. The material breach of an agreement to perform a contractual obligation, most frequently, in the financial context, the obligation to pay or repay interest or principal.

Deflation. General decrease in prices; a period of declining prices.

Delta. The correlation between the change in the price of a derivative and the change in the price of the underlying asset.

Depositor. An individual or company which deposits funds with (i.e. lends funds to) a bank, a large of portion of which the bank uses to lend to its customers.

Deposit flight. The outflow of bank deposits within a country's financial institutions into governmental, foreign or offshore institutions perceived as more secure, or into cash, hard currency or tangible assets such as gold, usually as a result of a decline in confidence in the country's banks. Deposit flight is a common phenomenon in countries with shaky banking systems and which lack effective deposit insurance systems, and may be a precursor to systemic bank runs that may paralyze a country's financial systems. See *Flight to Quality*; *Bank Run*.

Depository institution. A financial institution which take deposits; a bank.

Depreciation. 1. The cost of replacing a capital good or investment, often estimated by formula which may or may not reflect the actual cost of replacement or the useful life of the investment; amortization. (Sovereign)When applied in a sovereign risk context, the term *capital consumption allowance* is sometimes used to refer to depreciation. 2. Decline in value, e.g. of a currency. A currency that depreciates relative to a benchmark currency falls in value, while one which appreciates rises in value.

Deregulation. The reduction or elimination of regulations designed to protect financial institutions from competitive market forces that are viewed as detrimental to bank health and economic efficiency. Examples of deregulation include removal of constraints ceilings or floors on interest rates, prohibitions against the entry of foreign banks into a market. Note that deregulation can leave a previously regulated sector prone to excessive risk taking and that excessive deregulation without reasonable quality of bank supervision is likely to be a recipe for disaster.

Derivatives. Synthetic financial instruments which derive from an underlying asset or pool of assets. There are two types: standardized exchange-traded instruments, and over-the-counter (OTC) instruments. Common examples of OTC derivatives include interest-rate swaps (of the interest payments of two bonds) and currency futures, while stock market index options are a type of exchange-traded derivatives. Derivatives are probably best used for hedging purposes, i.e. laying off (reducing) risk, but can also be traded. Depending upon how they are structured derivatives can also be highly complex, and comparatively unsophisticated institutions have allegedly been victimized in particular transactions. The high leverage that derivatives afford, the high notional amounts (that do not take account of netting, i.e. offsetting positions) and the potential for systemic risk being created have given rise to anxiety about their use. This has been aggravated by headline cases in which companies or other entities have suffered great losses (e.g. the Orange Country, California *bankruptcy*) have given derivatives a perhaps not quite deserved notoriety. Standardization of derivative contract terms under uniform contracts promoted by trade organizations such as ISDA have reduced the need to customize transactions and has also diminished legal uncertainty about enforceability, while facilitating their purchase and sale. A bank which engages in significant derivatives activity should have suitable risk control mechanisms in place and be able to explain them coherently to the analyst.

Devaluation. (Sovereign). Often used to refer to a rapid or sudden depreciation of a currency, especially as a result of government intervention or change in policy.

Direct investment. In contrast to portfolio investment, which is normally a short- to medium-term investment in marketable financial assets usually through an exchange, direct investment refers to long-term, often comparatively illiquid, equity investments in local companies or projects.

Directed Lending. Similar to policy lending, the term direct lending implies the situation where a commercial bank (i.e. a non-policy bank) is directed by the authorities to lend to specified sectors or entities. See *Policy lending*.

Dirty float. A managed float; a floating exchange rate managed through intervention by the central bank, whereby the bank buys or sells foreign exchange or uses other means to maintain the country's currency within a stable range. A clean float is a floating exchange rate in which governmental intervention is absent.

Disclosure. Disclosure refers to the degree to which a bank reveals details concerning its financial condition, performance and operations. A high level of disclosure allows market mechanisms to operate, providing incentives for the bank to achieve an optimal balance of performance (maximizing sustainable returns) and creditworthiness (minimizing risk). The high leverage under which banks operate, the importance of maintaining confidence in the banking system, and other factors incline many banks to provide the minimum disclosure.

Disinflation. Not to be confused with deflation, disinflation refers to the squeezing out of excess inflation from an economy, usually through a policy of tight money and austerity for a period sufficiently long to change investor, worker and consumer expectations.

Disintermediation. The phenomenon whereby as an economy evolves into a mature state, savers have an increasing variety of choices other than bank accounts (e.g. mutual funds) into which to place their savings, each with varying risk/reward tradeoffs but which often provide higher yields than banks, while borrowers similarly have more opportunities to source capital (e.g. through the capital markets, venture capitalists), in many cases more cheaply than bank loans, resulting in a decline in bank deposits and bank loans as a proportion of total savings and total investment respectively. Even in mature economies, the integral role of banks in the payment system has ensured them a continuing place as financial intermediaries. Moreover, in some cases, banks have welcomed disintermediation at it has allowed them to focus on more profitable non-interest income (for example, through asset securitization) rather than on less profitable interest income generating activities, such as traditional lending.

Diversification. Not putting all your eggs in one basket. The principle that a portfolio in which assets are variegated into different industry sectors, geographic regions and firms will embody less overall risk than one in which assets are concentrated into a few sectors, regions and firms.

Dividend payout ratio. Total dividends paid out to shareholders as a percentage of net profit (attributable to shareholders). Dividends paid out to preferred shareholders are included in the calculation of this ratio.

Documentary credits. See *documentary letter of credit.*

Documentary letter of credit. A legal instrument whereby an (issuing) bank agrees to pay, on behalf of the bank's customer, a beneficiary upon the submission to the issuing bank of documents specified by the terms of the letter of credit (L/C). By means of the L/C, the customer (the account party) in effect is able to substitute the bank's creditworthiness for its own, thereby facilitating international trade. L/Cs are issued in favor of a definite beneficiary; state a fixed or determinate amount; specify the means of and conditions governing payment to the beneficiary and have a definite expiration date. Also referred to as a *commercial documentary letter of credit.*

DOSRI loans. Insider loans (Philippines), referring to loans to directors and associated persons

Doubtful loan. 1. A loan which is overdue and in respect to which some measure of loss is probable. 2. A loan for which principal or interest payments have been overdue for some fixed period of time, e.g. more than 6 months or 180 days, but less than one year.

Duration. 1. The expected or average life of an instrument such as a subordinated bond or a mortgage loan, in contrast to its nominal maturity. 2. (Fixed Income). A measure of the sensitivity of the price of a fixed income security to a change in prevailing yields, expressed as a percentage.

Earned capital. Retained earnings; undivided profits. See *Earned surplus.*

Earned surplus. Retained earnings; undivided profits. N.B. Not to be confused with surplus.

Earning assets. Interest earning assets, i.e. the sum of a bank's assets that earn interest, such as loans and investments in fixed-income securities, i.e. interest earning assets. Can also be defined as total assets less fixed assets and non-interest earning assets such as cash in the vault and non-interest earning reserves on deposit with the central bank. For most banks, the vast majority of its assets will be in the form of earning assets.

Earning rate. See *Yield on average earning assets.*

Earnings before taxes and provisions. Net income before taxes and provisions. May be abbreviated as EBPT. Also referred to as "core profits" or "underlying profits."

Earnings per share. Net profit attributable to common shareholders, i.e. net profit after tax, minority interests, extraordinary items and dividends payable on preferred shares have been deducted divided by total outstanding shares. Abbreviated as EPS.

Earnings. Net income; profits.

EBIT. (Corporations). Earnings before deduction of interest, tax and minority interest; EBIT includes exceptional items and income from associates.

EBITDA. (Corporations). Cash flow; cash earnings; literally, earnings before interest (payments), taxes, depreciation and amortization. EBITDA is a key measure of a corporation's ability to service its debt and is therefore a principal indicator of corporate creditworthiness. Because of the nature of the banking business, it is not generally applicable to the credit analysis of financial institutions.

EBPT. Earnings before provisions and taxes.

Economic capital. A term which with reference to banking refers to the difference between assets and liabilities on a marked-to-market basis sufficient to cover expected losses within a given confidence interval, which risk-weighting calculations attempt to approximate.

EDF. Expected default frequency.

EDR. Expected default rate.

Efficiency ratio. 1. Cost to income ratio (i.e. Non-Interest Expense to Operating Income) 2. Non-interest expense to net income

EGR. Equity generation rate. See *internal growth rate of capital.*

Elasticity. The responsiveness or sensitivity of one variable to another.

Emerging market. A term coined in 1981 by Antoine W. van Agtmael, an employee of the International Finance Corporation, an "emerging market" is broadly synonymous with the terms less developed country (LDC) or developing country, but has the connotation that the country is taking steps to reform its economy and increase growth with aspirations of joining the world's developed nations that are characterized by high levels of per capita income among various relevant indicia. Leading emerging markets at present include, among others, the following countries: China, India, Malaysia, Indonesia, Turkey, Mexico, Brazil, Philippines, Chile, Thailand, Russia Poland, Argentina, Hungary, Peru, Vietnam, Nigeria, Czech Republic, Egypt, and South Africa. Somewhat more developed countries, such as South Korea, are sometimes referred to as NICs, or newly-industrialized countries.

EPS. Earnings per share.

Equity and reserves to loans. Shareholders' equity plus loan loss reserves to total loans. The combination of shareholders equity and loan loss reserves in a ratio is more commonly seen in the "dead bank ratio" which compares this deep measure of cushioning ability with NPLs. See *dead bank ratio.*

Equity generation rate. Internal growth rate of capital.

Equity risk. The risk to a bank from holding equity securities. As a result of both tradition and law, US and British banks have avoided investing in equity securities. In contrast, banks in continental Europe and Japan adopted an approach to banking in which it was customary for banks to maintain long-term holdings in the shares of their customers, and, in the case of Japan particularly, in the shares of members of the corporate group of which the bank was a part.

Equity securities. Equity shares. Equity shareholders are the owners of a company, entitled to a share of dividends and, on liquidation, of shareholders' equity (the net worth of the company).

Equity shares. Common stock; ordinary shares.

Equity. Shareholders' equity.

EU capital adequacy directive. Capital requirements imposed by the European Union in January 1996, which applied capital risk-weighting principles to foreign currency risk, repos, reverse repos and interest rate position risk, equity position risk and to underwriting.

EU. European Union.

Eurodollars. US dollar deposits and other dollar denominated assets held or issued offshore.

EVA™. (Equity) Stands for economic value-added analysis; a method of measuring profits by taking into account the cost of all capital, including debt and equity. The end result is similar to other methods that establish "hurdle rates" for firm investments. Example: A company's *subsidiary*'s total capital is $10 m and its average cost of capital is 9% per annum. If the *subsidiary* earns $1 m, its EVA will be $100,000 ($1 m less $900,000); i.e. it created $100,000 in value. If it earned $800,000, its EVA would be negative $100,000; i.e. it destroyed $100,000 in value.

Event risk. Usually an event such as a rating action which subjects a bank or its counterparty to interest rate or market (pricing) risk.

Exceptional item. An item on the income statement which should properly be itemized separately in order to present a fair and accurate view of the company's recurrent income, which is mostly applied to an unusually large one-off expense or income item resulting from ordinary business activities that are not expected to recur. The 1989 (UK) Statement of Standard Accounting Practice defined an exceptional item as "material events which derive from events or transactions which fall within the ordinary activities of the company and which need to be disclosed separately by virtue of their size or incidence if the financial statement are to give a fair and true view."[10] In practice, the terms "exceptional items" and "extraordinary items" are often used loosely as synonyms. See *Extraordinary item.*

Expected default rate. The expected rate of default for a certain class of financial asset over a specified time period, expressed as a probability. An expected default rate is a measure of absolute credit risk, while a credit grading or a credit rating is ordinarily a measure of relative credit risk.

Expert systems. Systems which attempt to model and replicate the knowledge of credit experts by codifying them into sophisticated

---

[10] Quoted in Terry Smith, *Accounting for Growth: Stripping the Camouflage from Company Accounts*, p. 64.

flow charts or neural network/artificial intelligence software programs in order to allow less-expert staff to achieve similar results in credit evaluation and judgment. Also known as knowledge-based systems and rule based systems.

Exports. Domestically produced goods and services sold to foreigners.

Exposure. The total amount loaned or committed to a particular borrower, or the total risk of loss arising from a transaction with a particular counterparty.

External debt. Cumulative local or foreign currency borrowings by the domestic public and private sectors from foreign (non-resident) individuals and entities.

External position. Refers to the relative size of a government's external account. It may be measured by such indicators as the amount of external debt or the current account deficit.

External support. The implicit or explicit willingness of either a government or government agency, or in the private context, a parent company or shareholder to come to the aid of a troubled bank by injecting capital or liquidity, or in the case of government, exercising regulatory forbearance.

Extraordinary item. A significant expense or income not expected in the ordinary course of business, i.e. a non-recurrent income or expense item. An example of an extraordinary item for a bank might be the gain from the sale of a *subsidiary*. Similar to an extraordinary item is an exceptional item, one which is of unusual magnitude but nonetheless occurring within the ordinary course of business. The 1989 (UK) Statement of Standard Accounting Practice defined an extraordinary item as "material events which derive from events or transactions that *fall outside the ordinary activities of the company* and which are therefore expected not to recur frequently or regularly."[11] See *Exceptional item.*

Factors of production. The primary factors of production are: land, labor and capital.

FASB. Financial Accounting Standards Board.

FDI. Foreign direct investment.

Fed. The Federal Reserve System, which functions as the central bank of the United States.

---

[11] Quoted in Terry Smith, *Accounting for Growth: Stripping the Camouflage from Company Accounts*, p. 64.

Federal Open Market Committee. Comprised of the Board of Governors of the Fed and the presidents of five of the 12 regional Federal Reserve banks, the FOMC meets eight times a year to determine whether to raise, lower or maintain current interest rates. The Fed determines interest rates by changing the rate at which banks may lend their excess mandatory reserves to other banks. It also uses *open market operations* to supplement its decision to supplement its decision on interest rates. To lower rates, the Fed will purchase government securities, such as Treasury bills, on the open market which injects money into the banking system. To increase rates, it sells government securities, which pulls money out of the banking system.

FIDF. Financial Institutions Development Fund (Thailand). The FIDF's role is to provide liquidity to Thai financial institutions.

Finance company. A lending institution that does not take retail deposits. Instead, finance companies fund themselves through large wholesale deposits or through the capital markets. In the US, finance companies traditionally targeted the working class and lower middle class, who otherwise did not have access to credit. The expansion of credit cards and the diversification of banks have impelled finance companies to compete directly with banks, and also to specialize.

Financial accounting. The branch of accounting that deals with accounting for external reporting purposes in contrast to accounting for internal managerial purposes. The latter is called management accounting.

Financial crisis. A substantial disruption in financial markets typified by one or more of the following: a plunge in asset prices, capital flight, a credit crunch and the collapse of numerous financial and non-financial companies. A financial crisis is often catalyzed by an economic or a political shock and accompanying change in perception which results in a loss of confidence in financial institutions, major moves in interest rates or foreign exchange rates and business, investor and lender uncertainty.

Financial intermediary. An institution which plays a middleman role between the savers of capital and users of capital, channeling funds from the savers to users and earning some recompense for its trouble. A commercial bank is the classic financial intermediary. Other financial intermediaries include finance companies, life insurance firms, and mutual funds.

Financial leverage. See *leverage*.

Financial risk. Refers to the possible non-compliance by a borrower or counterparty with contractual credit terms as a result of incapacity or unwillingness.

Financial strength. Refers to the overall financial condition of a bank or corporation as reflected, in the case of a bank, in its core profitability, *asset quality*, liquidity, capital and management capability. Financial strength is essentially equivalent to an entity's core creditworthiness, leaving aside only external support and possibly willingness to pay (a factor customarily implicitly assessed in evaluating management).

Financial supermarket. Universal banking American-style; a colloquial term for a company which offers a diverse range of financial services such as banking, insurance, mortgage finance, brokerage and trust banking services. As US banking law has been liberalized during the 1980s and 1980s, the evolution of financial supermarkets has been widely predicted.

Financials. Financial statements.

Fiscal policy. A government's policy towards revenue (taxation) and spending is its fiscal policy. See *monetary policy*.

Fixed assets. Premises, equipment, fixtures, furnishings, vehicles, computers and other similar items constitute a bank's fixed assets, which are often subject to depreciation. Fixed assets are non-earning assets, but, somewhat controversially, were deemed 100% risk-weighted assets under the 1988 Basel Accord. Note that fixed assets may be also be categorized as intangible, examples of which are the value of patents, copyrights and trademarks.

Fixed capital formation. (Sovereign). Fixed investment. The amount of fixed investment is a key component of a country's GDP. See *Net fixed investment*.

Flight to quality. During times of financial turmoil, fear of bank and corporate failure will cause depositors and investors to shift their deposits and investments to banks and companies that appear safe from collapse, although which may offer lower yields and, in the case of equity investments, potential for upside gain.

Floating charge. A general lien on all of a company's assets.

Floating exchange rate. An exchange rate regime in which the exchange rate between a country's currency and other currencies varies with market supply and demand.

Floating rate note. In contrast to a fixed-rate note, the interest rate of a floating rate note varies according to a widely-accepted index or benchmark rate such as LIBOR (London Interbank Offered Rate, a short-term interbank rate); often abbreviated as FRN.

FOMC. Federal Open Market Committee.

Footings. An amount equal to a bank's total assets.

Foreclosed assets. Assets including collateral acquired through foreclosure or other legal proceedings on a borrower's default; essentially synonymous with OREO (other real estate owned).

Foreclosure. A legal procedure to enforce pledged security (collateral).

Foreign exchange line. A foreign exchange trading facility; A line of credit in foreign currency.

Foreign exchange risk. The risk arising from holding foreign currency assets or liabilities which may as a consequence of a change in foreign exchange rates cause the value of the assets to decline and that of the obligations constituted in the liabilities to rise.

Foreign exchange. 1. the exchange, trading or dealing of the currency or funds of one nation for that of another 2. foreign currency or foreign money.

Forex. Foreign exchange, as in foreign exchange trading gains, i.e. net gains from dealing in foreign currencies, also referred to as *forex income*.

FRA. Financial Sector Restructuring Authority. Established in October 1997 to rehabilitate Thailand's finance companies.

Fractional reserve banking system. The customary form of banking system prevalent worldwide in which banks need only keep of fraction of their deposits in reserve and may lend out the remainder.

Franchise. Business or banking franchise; a bank's business, e.g.: "Citibank has a strong franchise in retail banking."

Free capital funds. Total capital less financial and non-financial subsidiaries less fixed assets.

Free funds benefit. The difference between the net interest margin and the net interest spread, which is accounted for by shareholders' funds, non-interest bearing deposits and other non-interest bearing liabilities. These non-interest bearing funds tend to be relatively stable, but as interest rates rise, they generate a free funds benefit that tends to increase the difference between the net interest margin (which represents return on average earning assets) and the net interest spread (which represents the actual spread between interest-bearing assets and interest-bearing liabilities), typically causing the former to rise more rapidly than the latter. Also known as the "non- interest bearing deposit and capital margin."

FRN. Floating rate note.

Funding book. A bank's "portfolio" of funding, i.e. the composition of its deposits and other funding. The funding book is the balance sheet counterpart of a bank's loan book, as the bank's deposits and other financial liabilities fund the bank's loans and its other financial assets, such as securities.

Funding Cost. See *Cost of funds.*

FX. Foreign exchange; forex.

FY. Fiscal year.

GDP Price Deflator. (Sovereign). The adjustment ratio that accounts for the difference between real (price-adjusted) GDP and nominal GDP.

GDP. Gross domestic product.

Gearing. Leverage.

General provisions. Provisions (i.e. loan loss reserves) based on a fixed percentage (e.g. 1%) of gross or total loans and set aside as a matter of policy. General provisions, sometimes called *statistical provisions*, do not correspond to identified loans deemed problematic, and thus contrast with *specific provisions* made for such identified problem loans.

Generic issue rating. A credit rating applicable to a class of securities issues (e.g. subordinated debt issues) as opposed to a specific issue, e.g. Dao Heng '07.

Gold standard. A type of exchange rate regime in which each unit of currency is backed by a specified amount of gold.

Good bank/bad bank. Another name for the asset management corporation (AMC) structure. The asset management corporation in which a bank's "bad" assets are placed is the "bad bank." Usually the original bank takes the role of the "good bank" retaining those assets which continue to perform. See *Asset management corporation.*

Goodwill to deposits. A ratio obtained by dividing a bank's retail (i.e. customer or core deposits) by the difference obtained through subtracting the book value of the bank's equity from its market capitalization.

Goodwill to loans. A ratio obtained by dividing a bank's gross loans by the difference obtained through subtracting the book value of the bank's equity from its market capitalization.

Goodwill. The difference between the net asset value of a company and the price paid to acquire the company. Goodwill is attributable to the value of the company's organization and franchise, its relationships with customers, suppliers and employees and the value of the company's brands and reputation in the marketplace.

GPAs. (Sovereign) gross problematic assets (as used by Standard & Poor's); non-performing assets.

Gross domestic product. Often abbreviated as GDP, this is a key measure of a country's overall economic activity encompassing the total market value of goods and services produced within a country during a specific time period. Note that GDP is based on the purchase price of the goods and services by end-users and as it measures current production excludes the sale of second-hand goods, transfers of income, and pure financial transactions (e.g. sale of stock). Per capita GDP is an indicator of the country's relative state of development, while the GDP growth rate reflects the health of its economy. GDP is formally defined as $C + I + G + NX$ $(+ Residual)^*$, where C = personal consumption expenditure (comprised of durable and non-durable goods + services), I = gross private domestic investment (comprised of residential and non-residential fixed investment + change in business inventories + depreciation), G = government expenditures and gross investment (including defense and non-defense), and NX = net export of goods and services (exports less imports).[12] Note that GDP includes all production within a country, while GNP, i.e. gross national product, refers to the production of a country's nationals including those employed overseas. Usually the two indicators are nearly identical, but significant variation exists in those countries that export a significant portion of their labor such as the Philippines.

Gross fixed investment. Capital goods expenditure.

Gross impaired and *non-performing loans*. NPLs including restructured NPLs that are now performing. Also referred to as "impaired assets and non-accrual loans." Net impaired and NPLs equals Gross Impaired and NPLs less specific provisioning.

Gross investment. Capital goods expenditure + changes in business inventories.

---

[12] These and other formulas marked with an asterisk were sourced from http://www.stern.nyu.edu/~nroubini/bci.

Gross loans. The face value of all loans in the bank's portfolio plus unearned income. Unearned income is the "unamortised portion of interest income on the loan books."[13] To illustrate, Berry Bank makes an interest-only loan to Smith having a face value of $1,000 and payable annually at the simple interest rate of 8%, which is the only loan on its books. At the time of making the loan, the bank would make the following entries on the bank's books. Debit loans (an asset) $1,000, credit cash (an asset) $1000 and credit unearned income (an asset) $400, which is the amount of interest that will accrue over the loan's five-year term. If Berry Bank sets aside general loan loss provisions of which $10 is attributable to the Smith loan, then Berry Bank has gross loans of $1400, total loans of $1000 (face value of its loans) and net loans of $990.

Gross National Product. The total encompassing the total production of goods and services by a country's nationals, abbreviated as GNP. In the past, GNP was a more popular indicator of economic activity, but it has gradually been subsumed by GDP, with refers to the total production of goods and services within a country. See *Gross Domestic Product*.

Gross savings. (Sovereign). GNP less consumption.

Headline NPL ratio. The NPL ratio reported in the media. (According to the banking analysts at Nomura, this refers to NPLs as defined by local standards.) It is prone to vary depending upon who is being quoted and how the term is being defined. Official NPLs as reported by the central bank have been known to vary from those estimated by bank analysts.

Herstatt risk. The manifestation of settlement risk leading to a systemic breakdown in a settlement or financial payments system. In 1974, a small German bank, Bankhaus Herstatt, active in foreign exchange trading was required to shut down having not completed its end of a number of forex transactions with several counterparty banks in New York, leaving the banks which had irrevocably paid out funds on their end of their respective transactions in a precarious position. The CHIPS settlement system was subsequently interrupted and financial institutions were unable to settle transactions for a period of time.

---

[13] "For example, a US$10,000 loan that is priced on an interest only basis of 10% for five years would accrue $5000 over its life. The initial accounting entry on the bank's books when the loaned was booked would be to debit loans of US$15,000 and credit cash of US$10,000 and unearned income of US$5,000. ING Barings, Banknotes, 8 March 1999, p. 60.

High grade. As in *high grade* securities; *investment grade.*

HKMA. Hong Kong Monetary Authority.

Hot funds. Interbank deposits. See *Purchased funds.*

IAR. Impaired Asset Ratio.

IBST. Income before securities transactions (and excluding extraordinary gains and minority interest).

IGRC. Internal growth rate of capital.

Illiquid assets to core funding sources. Loans to deposits.

Illiquid assets. 1. broadly refers to loans or to other often comparatively illiquid assets such as foreclosed assets and fixed assets. 2. BHCs: loans plus advances to and investments in subsidiaries.

Illiquid. Not liquid; refers to assets which are not easily converted to cash.

Impaired Asset Ratio. 1. Loosely, a synonym for the more commonly used term, NPL ratio, or *non-performing loan* ratio. 2. (US) doubtful and loss loans to total loans.

Impaired assets and non-accrual loans. See *Gross impaired* and *NPLs.*

Impaired loan. 1. (US) A loan classified as doubtful or loss. 2. Loosely, a problem loan; a *non-performing loan.*

Imports. Foreign-produced goods and services purchased domestically.

Income statement. The income statement indicates and itemizes total revenues and expenses for a particular time period, e.g. one year, to calculate net income (i.e. net profit) for the period. Net income is the "bottom line." The income statement is also known as the "profit and loss account" or the "P&L." It can be viewed as an extension of the balance sheet explaining the factors contributing to net income for the relevant period, in the same way that a footnote covering loan loss reserves explains why that item changed. Note that the income statement and the balance sheet are linked as retained earnings appear on the balance sheet as an increase in shareholders' equity.

Income. Incoming funds; revenue (received).

Industrial production. (Sovereign). The part of GDP attributable to industrial activity, in contrast to, for example, agricultural activity.

Industry risk. The risk of industry decline or collapse affecting a bank's customers, and thereby indirectly the bank, due to secular factors (e.g. textile industry, shipbuilding in the US) or to a calamity affecting bank customers (e.g. epidemic affecting farmers' livestock).

Inflation. 1. The rate of increase in prices, usually measured by indicators such as the CPI (consumer price index) and the PPI (producer price index). 2. Sustained and substantial increase in prices. A persistent rate of inflation over 5% might be said to constitute an inflationary environment. In general, inflation is the result the money supply increasing at faster rate than production of goods and services.

Insolvency. The state of being insolvent, i.e. where liabilities exceed the value of a firm's assets. Often used synonymously with the term *bankruptcy*, *insolvency* connotes a financial condition that typically precedes the formal condition of *bankruptcy*, while *bankruptcy* connotes the connotation of a legal status of being unable to repay debts.

Insolvency risk. See *Solvency risk*.

Institutional investors. Major players in most equity markets and particularly debt and money markets, institutional investors include banks, major corporations, pension funds, mutual funds, hedge funds and governmental agencies.

Intangible property. A form of property whose value inheres in what it represents rather than in its physical nature.

Interbank assets. Interbank assets include time deposits with banks, placements, deposits due from banks, certificate of deposits and asset backed securities.

Interbank deposits. Interbank assets, i.e. deposits placed with other banks.

Interbank borrowings. Deposits from financial institutions. Also known as, "hot money." Generally equivalent to *interbank liabilities*.

Interbank liabilities. Interbank liabilities should include deposits from banks, call loans from other banks, *vostro* accounts, overdrafts, funds borrowed from banks, repurchase agreements, drafts and remittances outstanding.

Interbank market. The market for interbank funding. Banks with more deposits than lending opportunities may place the funds in the interbank market. Other banks with more lending opportunities than deposits will borrow such interbank funds to lend to their customers. In other words, they will obtain funding for loans in the interbank market. From a credit perspective, it is better for a bank to be a net lender in the interbank market than a net borrower, since borrowers pay more for funding and that funding is highly volatile and subject to rapid withdrawal in case of sudden change in market sentiment.

Interest earning assets. See *Earning assets*.

Interest expense. Interest paid on all interest bearing liabilities such as deposits and bonds. Does not include preferred share dividends.

Interest in suspense. A type of reserve account similar to loan loss provisioning in which accrued but unpaid interest income is accumulated in an interest in suspense account, which is not deemed to be interest income. The impact on the bottom line is the same as provisioning.

Interest income clawback provisions. Reversals of interest income already accrued but not received. Prudential regulatory provisions that require a bank to make an adjustment for interest previously accrued where a loan have become non-performing and interest income recorded has not in fact been received.

Interest income. Revenue generated from loans to customers, interest-bearing deposits with other institutions, or from fixed income securities. Interest income can refer more particularly to *gross interest income*, i.e. before the deduction of *interest expense*, or to *net interest income*, i.e. after the deduction of *interest expense*.

Interest rate risk. The risk that a change in prevailing interest rates will adversely affect a bank's portfolio. Example: By funding long-term residential mortgages on short-term deposits, US' savings and loans were vulnerable to interest rate risk in the early 1980s when prevailing interest rates shot up and depositors were able to obtain significantly higher yields in money market funds. To compete for deposits, S&Ls ultimately had to offer similarly high interest rates, sometimes resulting in negative interest spreads, or invest in very high risk junk bonds. Note that there are various types of interest rate risk. One type is open-position risk which is the risk that rates for issues of varying tenors may all shift in parallel simultaneously (i.e. the yield curve will move up or down but its shape will not change). Another type is yield curve risk. This is where the shape of the yield curve changes, with or without an overall shift in rates. A third type is basis risk, which occurs where the yield curves for different types or grades of assets may change their relationship to one another, causing differential spreads to tighten or widen.[14]

Interest rate sensitivity analysis. Also called *mismatch/gap management*. A form of liquidity analysis, mismatch/gap management goes beyond simple maturity matching (comparing the maturities of assets and liabilities) to look at when interest rates will reprice. The gaps

---

[14] See Cades at p. 150.

between the interest-sensitivity of the assets and liabilities, based on defined time periods, or "buckets," is then calculated and compared with peers. In other words, the tenor of the asset is not determinative; example: if a five-year term loan is floating rate, but reprices quarterly, it would be classified as a 3–6 month interest sensitive asset. If the amount of assets repricing exceeds liabilities (i.e. funding) repricing, there is a *positive gap*; if it is less, there is a *negative gap*. Equilibrium is called a *zero gap*. Note that interest rate sensitivity analysis is complicated by the possibility of extreme variations within each "bucket" potential causing the gaps to widen sharply at particular intervals, and the fact that the actual interest sensitivity of some liabilities, such as savings accounts may be discretionary and therefore difficult to determine.

Interest rate sensitivity. Refers to both the nominal frequency (e.g. every three months) with which financial assets and liabilities, such as loans and deposits, reprice as well as to the intensity of the preference of the obligors and obligees in respect of those assets and liabilities. For example, some passbook account holders may maintain relatively small deposits accounts even if the interest rate is significantly lower than other comparable accounts. Those depositors can be said to be not very "interest sensitive." In contrast, for a creditworthy business borrowing $200,000 a difference of one-quarter of a percentage point in interest could be a deal breaker.

Interest sensitivity. Interest rate sensitivity.

Interest spread. See *Net interest spread*.

Interest. The rent paid for borrowing principal; the cost of borrowing money. Interest rates vary with supply, demand, the present and anticipated rate of inflation, and the creditworthiness of the borrower. The yield curve, compiled from the benchmark yield on notes and bonds of varying terms (usually issued by the relevant government which it is presumed will not default on securities issued in its own currency), represents the risk-free interest rate, on top of which a premium is charged the borrower depending upon its creditworthiness. See *Japan premium*. The *real interest rate* is the nominal (face) interest rate less the rate of inflation. Example: If the nominal risk-free rate of interest is 8% and the rate of inflation is 5%, the real interest rate is 3%. While the nominal interest can never in practice be negative, under certain somewhat unusual circumstances, negative real interest rates may prevail on occasion. See also *negative spread*.

Intergroup lending (borrowing). Where a bank is part of a larger corporate group, lending from the bank to its *affiliate*s or parent company constitutes intergroup lending.

Internal credit risk rating. See *credit grading*.

Internal growth rate of capital. Net profit less dividends (i.e. retained earnings) divided by shareholders' equity (or average shareholders' equity). This ratio links profitability with the ability of the bank to bolster its capital strength. The higher the dividend payout, the lower the internal growth rate of capital will be. Abbreviated as *IGRC*. Also referred to as the *Internal Capital Generation Ratio (ICGR), the Equity Generation Rate (EGR)* and the *Capital Formation Rate.*

Inventory investment. (Sovereign). Goods which were produced but which were unsold during a specific time period.

Inverted yield curve. A negative or downward sloping yield curve. See *yield curve*.

IRB. Internal rating based (approach).

Islamic banking. A type of banking practised in some Islamic countries or countries with large Muslim populations. As Islam prohibits interest, various mechanisms for banking and finance have been devised which are deemed to conform with Islamic law. These mechanisms take the form of direct investment or a partnership in which bank and borrower share in the profit or loss. Islamic banks can be found in countries such as Indonesia, Malaysia, Bangladesh, Pakistan and Iran. In some countries, such as Bangladesh, Islamic banking and non-Islamic banking co-exist, sometimes within the same banking organization.

Issue rating. A credit rating of a debt issue; also known as a public debt rating or a default rating.

Issue. Securities which have been offered for sale are collectively referred to as an issue.

Issuer rating. A credit rating of an issuer or a counterparty.

Issuer. An entity, such as a bank or corporation, which issues securities.

Issue-specific rating. A credit rating of a specific debt issue in contrast to a class (e.g. short-term notes) of issues. The latter can be termed a *generic issue rating*.

Japan premium. The premium paid by Japanese banks in the interbank and fixed income markets attributable to their marginal financial condition.

Joint-stock bank. 1. In Europe, a joint stock bank refers to a privately-owned bank as opposed to a public law bank deemed to have implicit or explicit state support 2. Vietnam. A semi-private bank; that is, a bank that is part privately-owned and part owned by state or quasi-state organizations or state-owned enterprises.

KMV Credit Monitor. A system and service for predicting default of listed companies developed by KMV of San Francisco, California. Applying a structural model of firm value, KMV's model is based on the assumption that a company will default when its liabilities exceed the market value of its assets.

Law of Large Numbers. "If a random variable is observed many times, the average of these will tend toward the expected value (mean) of that random variable."[15] Example: As a bank makes more and more loans having certain characteristics, e.g. owner-occupied home mortgage loans, loan to value under 70%, borrower employed more than x years with an income of y times the amount borrowed, etc., the default rate on that pool of loans will tend towards an average default rate. Knowing the average default rate of a loan with the given characteristics, the bank will be better able to predict future default rates and more accurately price the loan to cover its credit costs and earn a profit.

LBO. Leveraged buyout.

LDC. Less developed country.

Legal capital. The par value, or stated value in the case of no-par stock, of common stock multiplied times the number of shares issued. Legal capital is not available for distribution to shareholders, except upon the liquidation of the corporation.

Legal reserves. See *primary reserves*.

Legal risk. Also *Legal and regulatory risk*. A category of operational risk as a result of a variety of causes, including: an adverse change in law or regulation; the risk of being a defendant in time-consuming or costly litigation; the risk of an arbitrary, discriminatory or unexpected adverse legal or regulatory decision; the risk that the bank's rights as creditor will not be effectively enforced (see sovereign risk); the risk of ineffective bank supervision (see systemic risk); or, the risk of penalties or adverse consequences incurred as a result of inadvertent errors in documentation (see compliance risk). Example: court decisions finding certain swaps transactions in the UK were

---

[15] D. Downing, *Dictionary of Mathematics Terms*, Barron's, 2nd ed., 1995.

found to have entered into transactions without proper authority un-enforceable could be viewed as a form of legal risk.

Leverage. 1. A multiple rather than a fraction obtained by dividing total *average assets* by average equity, often excluding revaluation reserves. 2. Gearing. N.B. In the case of non-financial enterprises, leverage is often calculated by dividing the company's debt by its equity, i.e. the debt-equity ratio. In the case of a bank, total liabilities (including deposits and borrowings) would be used in the calculation. 3. v. To apply financial leverage. 4. v. to take advantage of (a competitive edge).

Liability. A claim on an entity's assets.

LIBOR. London Interbank Offering Rate.

Liquid assets. 1. Assets, generally of a short term, that can easily be converted into cash, including cash itself, deposits with the central bank (but generally not mandatory reserves), treasury bills, other (marketable) government securities, interbank funds sold (i.e. inter-bank deposits or placements) and negotiable certificates of deposit issued by first-rate banks, securities purchased under resale agree-ments (reverse repos), and if marketable, commercial paper and other short-term fixed income investments; 2. BHCs: cash and cash equiva-lent, securities, interbank assets and deposits in bank subsidiaries.

Liquid. adj. Easily and predictably convertible into cash, normally with-out incurring a burdensome cost or loss in the conversion process.

Liquidate. 1. pay off or settle, for example through the conversion of assets to cash in order to make payment as "to liquidate a loan" or "the loan is self-liquidating since on the sale of goods financed by the loan, the borrower is able to pay it off." 2. to terminate or wind up a company by selling off all its assets and distributing the proceeds to creditors, and if any is remaining, to shareholders.

Liquidity management. The process of managing assets and cash flow to maintain the ability to meet current liabilities as they come due. The term *asset liability management* is another term for liquidity management.

Liquidity problems. A lack of liquid funds; cash flow problems.

Liquidity risk. The risk that a bank will not have sufficient liquid funds to meet its current obligations, such as deposit withdrawals. The risk of "running short of cash," liquidity risk is closely linked to and in a sense the other side of the coin of credit risk, since a borrower's liquidity risk is a lender's credit risk, which in turn is the lender's liquidity risk, which in turn is a credit risk for the lender's creditors. Liquidity risk is also closely linked to *solvency* risk as both are characterized by an inability to fulfill financial obligations. "But illiquidity is temporary, and *insolvency* permanent."[16]

Liquidity standby line. A type of credit enhancement used in asset securitization transactions.

Liquidity. 1.The capacity to fulfill obligations as they fall due. In bank analysis, liquidity is measured by in various ways, primarily by: a) the proportion of liquid or quasi-liquid assets to total assets; b) the relationship between comparatively illiquid assets i.e. loans to comparatively stable funding sources i.e. deposits; and c) the degree to which assets and liabilities are mismatched in terms of maturity and interest sensitivity. Other liquidity ratios which are sometimes used include variations of item b): e.g.. the relationship between liquid assets and volatile funding, i.e. liquid assets to purchased funds. Note that liquidity is inversely correlated with profitability, since liquid assets, having a low risk, are characterized by low yields. 2. (Equity) Marketability; ease with which an asset, such as shares, can be disposed of on the market. Example: "Bank X's shares do not have much liquidity. Their free float is comparatively low at 10% and daily trading is thin."

LLPs. Loan loss provision(ing) set aside for the year or relevant period.

LLRs. Loan loss reserves, cumulative stock.

Loan and lease allowance. Loan loss reserves.

Loan capital. Debt as opposed to equity (mainly British usage); also called *loan stock*. *Loan capital* ordinarily consists of long-term borrowings or debt issues, and represents the debt component of a company's capital structure, in contrast to equity or share capital. Subject to certain limitations, loan capital (e.g. subordinated debentures) can form part of regulatory capital.

Loan grading. Credit grading; the internal rating of loans by a bank in terms of their creditworthiness. See also *credit grading*.

Loan loss allowance cover. NPL coverage.

Loan loss coverage. Differs from loan loss allowance cover (NPL coverage). Refers to net operating income (EBPT) divided by net write-offs for the year. The resulting multiple reflects the extent to

---

[16] Cades, p. 56.

which write-offs could be expanded without creating an operating loss on a pre-tax pre provision basis.

Loan loss provisioning. The amount charged to the income statement for specific and general provisioning for the relevant period. Loan loss provisions, in contrast, refer to the cumulative stock of loan loss reserves.

Loan loss provisions. Loan loss reserves.

Loan loss reserves. The cumulative stock of loan loss reserves after new provisioning has been added and write-offs have been subtracted.

Loans. Total loans, i.e. loans and leases minus loan loss reserves and unearned (interest) income. In some countries (e.g. US) "loans" may refer to gross loans, i.e. loans prior to deduction for loan loss reserves, while in others (e.g. Japan) loans may encompass such off-balance sheet items as guarantees.

Loans. When used in ratios, ordinarily refers to *total loans* unless otherwise specified.

Long-term capital employed. Long-term debt plus equity.

Long-term. More than five years.

Loss loan. Loans deemed uncollectible; notwithstanding that some recovery may ultimately be obtained, loss loans can no longer be considered viable assets on the bank's balance sheet.

Loss rate given default. Degree of loss in the event of default. Sometimes abbreviated LGD. See *severity*.

Lower Tier 2 Capital. Ordinary subordinated debt that qualifies as Tier 2 Capital under the Basel Accord. While in general Tier 2 capital may not exceed Tier 1 capital, in the case of qualifying subordinated debt (so-called lower tier 2 capital), the ceiling is 50% of Tier 1 capital. Thus, so-called "upper tier 2 capital" has evolved as a favored means of banks wishing to issue subordinated debt that qualifies as Tier 2 capital when they have reached their ceiling on ordinary subordinated debt. See *Upper Tier 2 Capital.*

M1. The narrowest monetary aggregate, consisting of cash, coin, travelers' checks and checking accounts (demand deposits).

M2. A broader measure of money than M1, including M1 as well as overnight funds, dollars outside the US, money market accounts, and small denomination time and saving accounts.

M3. The broadest measure of the money supply, includes large denomination time deposits as well as some other items.

Macroeconomic imbalance. A situation where two or more macroeconomic indicators appear to show a disparity or divergence which is likely to be unsustainable without disrupting some other economic variable, for example a high level of domestic credit (i.e. loan) growth coupled with modest economic growth as reflected in the GDP growth rate.

Malinvestment. Misallocated investment; usually refers to the excessive investment in real estate, golf courses, and other "white elephants" using a speculative boom at the expense of more productive uses of capital. Malinvestment is typically caused by cheap and plentiful credit that temporarily distorts cost-benefit projections. It is often exacerbated by tax incentives and a regulatory framework that further distort the anticipated benefits, and aggravated by name and related party lending on the part of banks, poor bank supervision, and a euphoric boom mentality.

Mark-to-market. To revalue to the market price; to adjust the value of an asset (or liability) on the balance sheet that is readily liquefiable (i.e. marketable) to the prevailing market value rather than indicating its historical, or book, cost, which is the customary accounting convention. A mark-to-market paradigm as used in credit risk modeling means taking into account credit deterioration short of a complete default, i.e. a higher probability of default or slow payment, which would be reflected in the market price, actual or hypothetical.

Market depth. Liquidity.

Market expectations. Market expectations, for example as to the creditworthiness of an issuer, may be reflected in indicators such as the issuer's spread relative to issuers having a comparable credit rating, or in terms of a country specifically, in the forward exchange rate.

Market risk. As affecting banks, the risk that a change in interest rates, foreign exchange rates and in the case of derivatives, equity prices, will adversely affect a bank's financial position, normally through diminution of the value of assets it holds relative to matching liabilities. See also *Market/position risk*.

Market sentiment. The view of the market or of market participants generally; market psychology.

Market socialism. A type of economic reform sometimes adopted by countries of a Marxist-Leninist persuasion in which market mechanisms are used to supplement and to a large extent replace a command economy. Market socialist reforms are nonetheless often accompanied by rhetoric concerning the ultimate triumph of socialism and usually without forsaking a commitment to one-party rule under a communist party that eschews political dissent or political pluralism.

Market/position risk. Market and interest-rate risk. A term sometimes used as a "counterpoint to credit risk." Interest rate position risk can be defined as the risk that changes in interest rates will lead to price movements in fixed income securities with an adverse effect upon the party bearing the risk.[17] See *Market risk*.

Market-maker. A market participant who is willing to quote two way prices for financial securities and who either has such securities in his inventory or is willing to bear the risk that he can obtain them and sell them at a profit to a customer.

MAS. Monetary Authority of Singapore.

Maturity matching. A form of liquidity analysis, maturity matching compares the maturities of assets and liabilities, based on defined time periods, or "buckets." The gaps or differences between the volume of assets and liabilities for each bucket is then calculated and compared with peers.

Medium/long term liabilities. Medium/long-term liabilities includes loans and notes with more than one year to maturity.

Medium-term. One to five years.

Middle market. The market for middle-sized corporate lending. In a given country, companies that are not among the largest 100–1000 companies.

Minority interests. Adjustments made in consolidated financial statements to account for the portion of shares held by shareholders other than the company in subsidiaries that are not wholly-owned by the company.

MIS. Management information systems.

Monetary aggregates. The constituents of the money supply; M1, M2 etc.

Monetary policy. A government's policy towards the supply of credit (and therefore interest rates, and the money supply (and therefore prices) and the money supply comprises key aspects of its monetary policy. See *fiscal policy*.

Monetize. To transform assets into money.

Money laundering. The process of converting the monetary proceeds of illegal or criminal activity (dirty money) into apparently legitimate

---

[17] Cades, p. 17.

funds (clean money). In general, the process involves making cash deposits into a variety of bank accounts, which may be opened using bogus identification, then mixing the funds through a web of complex transactions, often with legitimate funds under cover of an otherwise lawful business, so that its origins can no longer be traced except with extreme difficulty.

Money market. The market for short-term debt instruments, including federal funds, repos and reverse repos, treasury bills, interbank placements, negotiable certificates of deposit, bankers' acceptances, and commercial paper.

Money multiplier effect. The expansion of the money supply through the extension of private credit, which is a natural consequence of a fractional reserve banking system. If banks are required to maintain x% of their deposits on reserve with the central bank, the money supply will in theory multiply by the initial excess reserves times the reciprocal of the reserve requirement or 1/x%. In this way, the banking system acts as a transmission belt for government monetary policy. Example: If the reserve requirement is 10%, then the remaining 90% of that may be lent out, which becomes a deposit at another bank and then 90% of that deposit can be lent out and so on down the line until, again in theory, the money supply will expand by ten-fold. That is, if $100,000 is deposited, it will add as much as $1 m to the money supply. In practice, friction in the system and money escaping from the formal financial system will keep this ratio considerably lower.

Money. 1. A medium of exchange, usually legally established, used to pay for goods and services. See *money supply*. Money functions as a means of payment, standard or value and as a store of value.[18]

Moral hazard. The risk that those who are insured against the risk of loss, such as banks that expect to be bailed out if they fail (or that because of a deposit insurance program have no need to worry about the loss of funding), will as a result take greater risks than they would otherwise.

Mortgage backed securities. Bonds backed by a stream of revenue from a pool of mortgage loans. Mortgage backed securities, begun in the US in the 1970s, were one of the first widespread forms of asset securitization. See *securitization*.

---

[18] Lloyd B. Thomas, *Money, Banking and Financial Markets*, Int'l ed., Irwin-McGraw Hill, 1997, p. 19–20.

Mortgage bank. 1. A bank which specializes in originating mortgage loans for resale to other banks or investors and which earns the bulk of its income from origination fees, profits on the sale of the mortgages and fees for servicing the mortgage. Also known as a mortgage company. 2. A thrift institution.

Mortgage. A debt instrument used normally to finance the purchase of real estate and which is secured by that real estate. In some markets, mortgages are traded in a secondary market. A second mortgage refers to a similar debt instrument but one in which the lien securing the debt is junior or subordinated to the first mortgage. For example, a homebuyer may obtain a mortgage loan equal to 70% of the value of the house she is buying secured by the value of the entire property. Later to finance the construction of a garage, she may take out a second mortgage on the property equal to 10% which is also secured by the value of the entire property. If she default on the loan, either mortgagee may foreclosed, sell the house and obtain repayment out of the proceeds. The first mortgage holder gets paid first, and assuming sufficient funds remain, the second mortgage holder obtains repayment out of the remainder.

MFN. Most favored nation status.

Municipal bonds. Bond issued by sub-national or local government units.

NALs. Non-accrual loans. For practical purposes, NPLs. In the US, NPLs encompass restructured loans and foreclosed assets. Hence, the term non-accrual loan there refers to the subset of loans referred to as NPLs in international practice.

Name lending. The practice of lending to customers based on their perceived status within the business community rather than on the basis of credit analysis assessing their ability to service additional debt.

NCOs. Net charge-offs; net write-offs.

Negative equity. Used most often in the context of mortgage lending to describe the situation where, due to falling property prices, the principal owed on a mortgage loan is less than the value of the real estate securing it. In such circumstances, from an economic perspective, the borrower's liability exceeds that the market value of the asset. Without considering the potentially adverse effects on the borrower's credit record, the borrower has an economic incentive to default in this situation, particularly where the loan is on a non-recourse basis. In practice, the consequences of default, including the stigma that may attach, coupled with the fact that shelter is a human necessity and the likely hope that prices will ultimately rise may impel the borrower to continue to make payments.

Negative gap. See *Interest rate sensitivity analysis.*

Negative interest spread. Where a bank's cost of funding exceeds its cost of lending. This can occur under unusual circumstances where a temporary rise in short-term funding rates may exceed longer term lending rates.

Negative yield curve. An inverted or downward sloping yield curve. See *yield curve.*

Negotiable. Transferable to another party; tradable. A negotiable instrument is a financial obligation that meets certain requirements that render it negotiable, i.e. transferable to another party who assumes the same rights as the original holder and becomes a holder in due course.

Net assets. Assets less liabilities, i.e. net worth, shareholders' equity.

Net book value. The value of an asset on the balance sheet after any adjustments, e.g. depreciation, loan loss provisions

Net borrower in the interbank market. A bank which has more interbank liabilities than interbank assets.

Net charge-offs. Net write-offs.

Net exports (Sovereign). Exports minus imports.

Net external debt. External debt minus less external assets, but not including equity investments.

Net external liabilities. The sum of external debt, cumulative inward direct and equity investment less cumulative outward direct and equity investment, public sector foreign real and financial assets and official reserves.

Net fixed investment. Net fixed investment is equal to the sum of *net residential investment, investment in structures, and investment in producers' durable equipment. Net private domestic investment* is equal to net fixed investment plus the net change in inventories. *Gross private domestic investment* is equal to *net private investment* plus *capital depreciation.*

Net foreign liability. The extent to which foreign currency liabilities are not matched by foreign currency assets; i.e. foreign currency assets less foreign currency liabilities.

Net government debt. The difference between a government's debt and the sum of government deposits, official reserves, funds lent, and pension fund assets.

Net impaired and non-accrued loans. See *Non-performing loans.*

Net interest income. The difference between (gross) interest income and interest expense. (Net Interest Income = Total Interest Income − Total Interest Expense.)

Net interest margin. Return on average earning assets, calculated by dividing net interest income by average earning assets. The net interest margin measures the profitability of a bank's interest-earning business. Also referred to as NIM, the net interest margin roughly correlates to the net interest spread.

Net interest spread. The difference between the yield on average earning assets (gross interest income/average earning assets) and the cost of funds (gross interest expense/average interest-bearing liabilities).

Net investment. (Sovereign). Gross investment minus depreciation.

Net lender in the interbank market. A bank that has more interbank assets than interbank liabilities.

Net loans. Total loans less (total) provisions.

Net loans. Total loans less loan loss provisions applicable to the period.

Net occupancy expense. See *Occupancy Expense.*

Net operating income. Net interest income + non-interest income − non interest expense, and generally prior to deduction for loan loss provisioning. See *Operating Profit.*

Net purchased funds. See purchased funds.

Net realizable value. The value that can be realized on the sale of particular assets.

Net-Something. After deducting something from something else. Net x is x less y (something else). Confusion can arise from not specifying or understanding what is being deducted and what that item is being deducted from.

Net worth. Assets less liabilities; shareholders' equity.

Net write-offs. The total of loans and leases written off minus amounts recovered from loans and leases written off in the same year. The ratio, Net write-offs to *average assets,* may be used to compare the write-off policies among peer banks.

NIC. Newly industrializing country.

NIM. Net Interest Margin.

Non-interest expense. Administrative and general expenses; i.e. expenses other than the cost of interest the bank is paying on its interest-bearing liabilities. Two major categories of non-interest expense are staff compensation and occupancy. Non-interest expense includes depreciation, but depending upon whose definition is being used, may or may not include provisioning expense. The author's preference is to *not* include provisioning expense as a non-interest expense.

Non-accrual loans. Loans on which the recording of interest received has been suspended, which in many jurisdictions will normally occur after a loan is overdue more than 90 days. Roughly speaking, a non-accruing loan is synonymous with a *non-performing loan*, but there may be technical differences depending on the market. In the US, a non-accrual loan is formally defined as loans which are either: a) maintained on a cash accounting rather than on an accrual basis as a result of impairment in the borrower's financial condition; b) are not anticipated to return interest and principal in full; or c) principal or interest in 90 days or more overdue, with a limited exception for loans that are well-secured and in the process of collection.

Non-current loan. An overdue loan. Note that a non-current or overdue loan technically refers to a loan that is overdue a day or more. In contrast, a non-accrual loan refers to a loan on which the bank is no longer accruing interest (i.e. reporting putative interest as interest income), which is ordinarily a loan that is more than 90 days overdue. Generally speaking, the terms *non-accrual loans*, *impaired loans*, and *non-performing loans* can be used synonymously.

Non-interest income. Revenue generated by a bank that is other than *interest income*. For this reason, it is sometimes referred to as *other income*. Net interest income is typically composed of fees and commissions, e.g. from trust activities, letters of credit, and gains from foreign exchange or securities trading.

Non-interest revenue. Non-interest income.

Non-performing assets. The sum of NPLs, restructured loans, and foreclosed assets.

Non-performing loan. A *non-performing loan*, or NPL, is a loan with respect to which a bank will not be able to recover the amount due (i.e. principal + interest) under the terms of the relevant loan agreement. The international standard for a *non-performing loan* is one which is 90 days or more overdue in payment of interest or principal. The terms *non-performing loan*, *problem loan*, and *impaired loan* are often used synonymously, although technically an impaired loan includes only loans classified as loss (bad) and doubtful. Note that generally speaking, the term *non-performing loan* encompasses all non-performing customer advances, including leases.

Nostro account. A due-from-foreign bank account.

Notch. In the context of credit ratings, a notch refers to one rating upwards or downwards. For example, if an issuer rated BB receives a new rating BB +, and BB + is the next highest rating after BB, the issuer has obtained a one-notch ratings upgrade.

NPA. Non-performing asset.

NPL coverage. The ratio of loan loss reserves to *non-performing loans* expressed as a percentage; loan loss reserves divided by NPLs.

NPL ratio. The ratio of *non-performing loans* to total loans expressed as a percentage; total loans divided by NPLs. As a rule of thumb, a ratio over 10% in developed markets and over 20% in emerging markets denotes a bank with severe and possibly irremediable *asset quality* problems.

NPL. *Non-performing loan.*

NPV. Net present value.

Obligee. Lender; creditor.

Obligor. Borrower; debtor

Occupancy expense. A major component of non-interest expense, occupancy expense refers to a bank's costs arising from the use of its premises, furniture, fixtures and equipment. *Net occupancy expense* refers to *Occupancy Expense* minus rental income.

Off-balance sheet accounts. Contingency accounts.

Off-balance sheet finance.

Off balance sheet item. A contingent item.

Off-balance sheet risk. The risk incurred by a bank's contingent liabilities, often referred to as off-balance sheet commitments. These include guarantees, standby letters of credit and other obligations, which come to life upon the occurrence of some event, often a default event.

Official deposits. Deposits or borrowings from central governments/ banks.

Official reserves. The market value of the foreign currency and gold held by the central bank.

Offshore banks. Usually owned by non-resident financial institutions, these are banks established in certain "offshore" financial centers. Their function is to accept deposits from foreign banks and make loans in the essentially unregulated Eurocurrency market. They are generally prohibited from accepting local deposits and engaging in local banking business.

Offshore. With reference to a particular country, outside the borders of that country.

Opacity. Non-disclosure. (Opposite of Transparency.) See *transparency*.

Open capital account. An investment or economic regime which permits the conversion of "local financial assets into foreign financial assets and vice versa at market determined rates of exchange."[19] A country with an open capital account places little or no restrictions on inbound or outbound investment, nor does it place material restrictions on the free conversion of its currency into another currency.

Open market operations. See *Federal Open Market Committee*.

Open position risk. See *interest rate risk*.

Open position. An unhedged position.

Operating income. 1. Net interest income plus non-interest income. Note that *net operating income*, also sometimes referred to as operating profit, is operating income minus non-interest expense. 2. Net operating income. Sometimes the term operating income is used to refer to what is defined here as net operating income. To avoid confusion, this usage is not recommended.

Operating margin. (Corporations). EBIT divided by sales.

Operating profit. 1. Net operating income, i.e. (net interest income + non-interest income − non interest expense). 2. Net operating income minus loan loss provisioning. If this definition is used, the term *pre-provision operating profit* will be used to specify operating profit before the deduction of loan loss provisions.

Operating revenue. Operating income.

OREO. Other real estate owned. Essentially synonymous with foreclosed assets.

Other income. Non-interest income; income other than (net) interest income.

Other operating income. Other income; non-interest income.

Overbanked. A banking sector that has too many banks. Note: How many banks are too many is an unresolved question, but current thinking among many regulators is that a smaller number of well-capitalized institutions leads to a more stable banking system and one in which its members have the critical mass to compete effectively in local, regional and global markets. See *consolidation*.

---

[19] Reserve Bank of India, (1997) Report of the Committee on Capital Account Convertibility, Mumbai, p. 4, quoted in Benu Schneider, *Issues in Capital Account Convertibility in Developing Countries*, Overseas Development Institute, London, June 2000.

Overcapitalized. Higher capital ratios than warranted given prevailing returns and historical experience leading to reduced return to shareholders and less availability of credit. Under-leveraged.

Overcollateralize. A means of credit enhancement used in asset securitizations whereby the collateral of the special purpose vehicle (SPV) well exceeds the assets transferred to the SPV.

Overdue loan. Technically, an overdue loan is one that is overdue in respect of principal or interest payments by one day. In practice, overdue loans are sometimes loosely but inaccurately used to refer to as *non-performing loans*. Overdue loans are sometimes referred to as *non-current loans*.

Overhead ratio. *Cost to income ratio; efficiency ratio.*

Overheating. An economy which is growing at an unsustainably rapid pace is said to be overheating. An overheating economy provides fertile ground for *inflation* to take hold with often deleterious effects.

P & L. Profit and loss (account).

Paid-in capital. The amount of the assets paid in by shareholders in exchange for shares of ownership, i.e. contributed capital. Also referred to as paid-in surplus.

Paid-up capital. Paid in capital.

Par value. The nominal or face value of a corporation's shares, often set at a figure like $1.00, far below their actual worth.

Par. Par value; face value. Note that the par value of a stock is usually far below its actual value, but the par value of a bond refers to the amount that will be repaid to the investor at maturity.

Participating preference shares. Preferred (preference) shares in which the amount of the dividend may be increased when certain performance conditions are achieved.

Past due coverage. NPL coverage.

Pawnshop mentality. Usually used pejoratively to describe an approach to credit review that focuses solely on the purported value of collateral as justification for making a loan, in contrast to the borrower's ability to generate positive cashflow adequate to satisfy its financial obligations.

Paying rate. Cost of funds.

Peer group analysis. Examining how the financial indicators of a given bank or company compare with similarly-situated banks or companies, i.e. its peer group. Peer group analysis is sometimes referred to as benchmarking.

Peer group. Banks of a similar size and type to the subject bank, e.g. Japanese regional commercial banks. A peer group may range considerably in size and scope. Typically, a bank is compared with 3–15 other banks.

PER (or PE). Price Earning Ratio.

Percentage change in net income. Net profits in Year 2 divided by Net profits in Year 1) minus 1; i.e. Growth in Net Interest Income.

Performing Loan. 1. A loan which is not overdue more than 90 days; i.e. a loan which is not classified as non-performing. 2. A loan which is fully current and not overdue. 3. A loan which is deemed to have performing status, such as a restructured loan for which payments have resumed and have been maintained on a current basis for some fixed period of time.

Perpetual non-cumulative preferred shares. Preferred shares of the type that 1) do not require management to make up dividends missed during years where profits were insufficient, and 2) do not provide the shareholders with a right of redemption. This type of preferred shares therefore more closely resembles common equity than debt. Perpetual non-cumulative preferred shares for this reason were classified, with common (ordinary) equity under the 1988 Basel Accord as Tier 1 capital.

Policy bank. A bank established to further government policies and the loan portfolio of which reflects that purpose. Examples include banks whose mission is to promote agricultural development, community development or industrial development. See *policy lending*. Note that a bank does not need to be a policy bank to be obliged to engage in policy lending.

Policy lending. Lending in furtherance of governmental policies, in contrast to purely commercial purposes. As a consequence of government ownership, policy banks may not have as their purpose to achieve profits for stockholders, but instead to further a governmental policy, such as agricultural or industrial development, and be obliged by their charter or by law or regulation to lend all or a portion of their available funds to that end. Private commercial banks may also be obliged by the government to engage in some degree of policy lending.

Portfolio investment. Investment in financial assets, often through an exchange, in contrast to direct investment. Portfolio investment is generally liquid with a short- to medium-term time horizon, while direct investment is generally made other than through an exchange, is comparatively illiquid, is longer term, and connotes the taking of an active role in managing the investment.

Positive gap. See *Interest rate sensitivity analysis.*

PPI. Producer Price Index.

Precautionary loan. A special mention loan.

Preference shares. Preferred shares.

Preferred shares. Also called preference shares, these are shares that in contrast to common or ordinary shares give the holder a preferential right to a defined dividend ahead of common shareholders, provided sufficient net profits exist out of which to pay such dividends. Preferred shareholders also rank above common shareholders (but below creditors) in the event of the liquidation of the company and subsequent distribution of its assets. As they resemble both debt and equity in some respects, preferred shares can be said to be a hybrid between the two. Some forms of preferred shares so closely resemble debt that regulators classify them as such for regulatory purposes.

Premium on paid-up capital. See *share premium.*

Pre-provision earnings. Net operating income; net earnings before provisions and taxes.

Pre-provision operating profit. Net operating income also known as earnings before provisions (and taxes), or EBPT. An income statement item (or one that can be calculated therefrom) which reflects core earnings strength. Equivalent to: (Net income + Non-interest income) – Non-interest expense (not including loan loss provisions). EBPT as a percentage of *average assets* (pre-provision ROA) is a key measure of core profitability.

Pre-tax profit. Net profit before deduction (or credit) for income or profits tax. Other taxes will have been included in non-interest expense and previously deducted.

Price earning ratio. Abbreviated PER or PE.

Primary market. The market for new issues of fixed income securities or public offerings of equity securities.

Primary reserves. Also known as *legal reserves.* Reserves which the central bank or monetary authority requires to be placed with it in a reserve account as security for depositors. Although these may be listed on a bank's balance sheet under the category as "cash and due from banks," such reserves are not normally available to the bank during the ordinary course of business. Some banks show these reserves as a special line item. Primary reserves, it should be noted, typically pay little or no interest, and thereby provide a source of finance for governments. The term secondary reserves is sometimes used to refer to a minimum level of liquid assets a bank is required to maintain on its balance sheet. Such funds are not kept with the central bank, although some countries may mandate that banks hold a certain portion of non-negotiable government securities, which essentially amounts to the same thing.

Prime rate. The interest rate, usually announced publicly, at which a bank or banks are willing to lend to their best (prime) customers. The importance of the prime rate has declined in countries such as the United States where the best potential bank customers now have direct access to the debt markets.

Probability density function of losses. See *credit risk modeling.*

Problem loan. Generally, a *non-performing loan*, i.e. one that is more than 90 days overdue and which would be classified as substandard, doubtful or loss. A synonym for a problem loan is a *troubled loan.* However, the term problem loan sometimes may be also used more broadly to encompass loans that are just one or few days overdue as well as loans still current but where the borrower is perceived likely to experience problems making full repayment of principal and interest problematic. Both types of loans, i.e. those not yet deemed non-performing (or non-accrual) but which nonetheless are perceived as potentially problematic, may fall under the formal loan classification of *special mention.* Problem loans may also include restructured loans.

Producer Price Index. A measure of the rate of inflation, which itself is a fundamental parameter of sovereign risk. The producer price index (PPI) measures the price of a "shopping basket" of wholesale goods and commodities against the cost at a base date. The change in the price of the goods expressed as a percentage corresponds to the rate of inflation. Unlike its counterpart, the consumer price index (CPI), it does not account for the cost of services.

Productivity. (Sovereign). Together with investment, the main determinant of economic growth.

Profit and loss account. Income statement. Abbreviated as *P & L.*

Proprietary trading. Trading on the bank's own account, including the taking of open (unhedged) positions. While most banks may have temporary unhedged positions in the ordinary course of dealing on behalf of customers, proprietary trading differs from the former in the volume, frequency and duration of such positions. Sustainable success at proprietary trading is likely to be elusive, although a bank may benefit from sophisticated quantitative analytical capabilities and the intuitive qualities that the most astute traders have. At best, trading income is likely to be erratic. During the 1990s, most major banks became more risk-conscious and reduced their reliance on proprietary trading.

Provision (v.) To set aside or deduct an amount from operating income to cover expected or identified loan losses.

Provision for Losses to *Average assets.* Loan loss provisioning to *average assets*, a measure of credit costs.

Provision to pre-provision. Loan loss provisioning divided by earnings before provisions and taxes.

Provisioning. Amounts set aside or deducted from operating income in a given period to cover expected or identified loan losses.

Provisions. Loan loss reserves. The accumulated stock of specific and general provisions comprise total provisions.

Prudential ratios. Ratios, generally relating to capital strength or liquidity, mandate as minimum requirements by a country's central bank or monetary authority. The capital adequacy ratio, originally defined by the 1988 Basel Accord has been adopted in some form by more than 100 countries and is the classic example Other prudential ratios include ratios governing minimum paid-in capital, reserves, and liquidity.

Public debt rating. A default rating assigned to an issue, such as a subordinated bond, issued in the publicly-traded debt markets.

Public sector debt to GDP. (Sovereign). The debt ratio. Total public sector debt divided by GDP; also may be referred to (more narrowly) as national government debt to GDP.

Public sector debt. The sum of government debt, the debt of state-owned enterprises (other than state-owned banks and other financial enterprises), and private sector debt guaranteed by the government.

Purchased funds. Bank funding obtained through the interbank market, including large and uninsured certificates of deposit, foreign deposits and short-term borrowings. Purchased funds generally refer to funding other than customer deposits and long-term borrowing. They generally include the following: time deposits > US$100,000, interbank borrowings, overnight funds, repos, commercial paper issues and other short-term debt. *Net purchased funds* means purchased funds net of money market assets. Also known as hot funds, hot money, confidence funding.

Pure risk. One-directional risk (downside only); Also called static risk, in contrast to dynamic or two-way (upside and downside) risk.

QOQ. Quarter-on-quarter. See *YOY*.

Qualified opinion. A qualified auditors' opinion, meaning one in which the auditor has expressed reservations concerning the presentation of audited financial statements. N.B. From the analyst's viewpoint, a qualified auditors' opinion is a red flag.

Qualifying capital. Balance sheet items eligible to be included as capital when calculating the Basel Committee (BIS) capital adequacy ratio.

Quality of earnings. Sustainability of earnings.

Quasi-liquid assets. Assets which include liquid assets (i.e. assets that can be converted into cash with little difficulty), but quasi-liquid assets may encompass a broader range of assets than liquid assets, or categories of assets which are normally easily liquefiable, but which may not be in specific indeterminate instances. Quasi- liquid assets may include marketable securities issued by non-governmental entities (e.g. corporations) and other assets that are relatively easily liquefiable.

Quick ratio. (Corporate). Current assets to current liabilities; i.e. (cash + accounts receivable + marketable securities) divided by current liabilities. The rule of thumb is that this ratio should be 1.0 or higher.

RAROC. Risk adjusted return on capital, a measure of return developed by Bankers Trust, a major US bank, in the 1970s which attempts to take into account the riskiness of the assets and the credit costs used to generate net income. It is sometimes abbreviated in other ways, but the meaning is the same.

Rating. A measure of the relative risk of default (and the severity of default) associated with a particular securities issue, issuer or other financial asset.

Rating action. An announcement by a rating agency upgrading, down-grading or affirming a rating or changing the rating outlook in respect to an issuer from any category, i.e. positive outlook (positive watch) or negative outlook (negative watch), or neutral, to another category. See *rating outlook*.

Rating migration. With respect to an issuer (counterparty) or issue, the movement from one rating (symbol) to another during a given time horizon.

Rating shopping. The phenomenon whereby issuers in search of the best rating approach multiple rating agencies and award the ratings mandate to the agency which it believes will offer the best rating at the best price. It has been argued that rating shopping is a danger where ratings are required by law as a precondition for issuing securities. Rating shopping appears to occur mainly in local markets where the agencies lack credibility and the rating functions mainly as a formal requirement and is not closely scrutinized by investors.

Rating symbol. A rating symbol is commonly one or more letters or numbers or the combination of the two, employed by a rating agency or internally by a bank or corporation, which represent the distilled assessment of the creditworthiness of a bank (or other issuer or counterparty) by the organization conducting the evaluation. Examples of rating symbols are: AAA, Ba, E, P-3.

Rating symbology. A grading system or systems employed by a rating agency or internally by a bank or corporation to rank issuers or counterparties in terms of their relative creditworthiness. An examples of a rating symbology is A, A/B, B, B/C, C, C/D, D, D/E, and E, which is commonly used to rate financial institutions as counterparties.

Ratings compression. Refers to the limitations of global rating scales in making distinctions in the credit quality of banks in low-rated countries, a phenomenon that is often exacerbated by the sovereign ceiling. For example, if Country X is rated single-B, the highest debt rating available to a bank's debt issue would ordinarily be B or lower, notwithstanding the financial strength of the bank. This would allow for relatively few gradations among issues. Similarly, in such a country, it would not be unusual for many of the banks to be at a D level or below on a global basis, absent any consideration being given to external support. As such, gradations would be limited to three — i.e. D, D/E and E. The lack of gradations might make it impossible to distinguish among the banks within the country with any degree of refinement.

REACQ. Real estate acquired (in satisfaction of debts).

Real exchange rate. Exchange rate adjusted for inflation or deflation.

Real GDP. GDP adjusted for inflation or deflation. Non-adjusted GDP is known as nominal GDP.

Real interest rate. The nominal interest rate minus the rate of inflation. In a deflationary environment, real interest rates may be exceptionally high since the nominal interest can never fall below zero. Example: If the prevailing interest rate is 1%, but prices are deflating (declining) at the rate of 5%, the real interest rate is 6%. Between

1975 and 1994, real interest rates in major countries around the world averaged between 1–4%.[20]

Real net worth. The net worth (shareholders' equity) of a firm expressed in purchasing power terms, i.e. the market value (capitalization) of the firm.

Real. True; in finance, meaning in most cases, as adjusted for inflation or deflation.

Recapitalization. In the banking context, the injection of new capital into a bank. In the case of a problem bank or banks, restructuring is likely to include, but not be limited to, recapitalization. Recapitalization may involve the straightforward infusion of cash into the bank by shareholders or the government, or it may involve accounting legerdemain designed primarily to improve confidence by creating the appearance of improved capital strength.

Recession. An economic downturn or slowdown; in the US, a recession is more precisely defined as being at least two consecutive quarters in which GDP has declined. A depression is a prolonged and severe recession, characterized by many company bankruptcies, high rates of unemployment, lower income per capita, and price deflation.

Redeemable preferred shares. Preferred shares in which the holders have the right to demand the return by the company of the funds invested after some certain period of time.

Regulatory capital. Bank capital as defined by regulators (having authority over the subject bank), often pursuant to the international standards established by the Group of Ten's Basel Committee on Bank Supervision, which may include balance sheet items other than shareholders' equity (net worth), including subordinated debt, loan loss reserves, and hidden reserves.

Regulatory forbearance. The relaxation of prudential regulatory standards, such as minimum capital requirements or definitions of *non-performing loans*, that are designed either to improve performance at the expense of financial strength, or to make the bank's performance or financial condition appear better than it would be had prior regulations been applied.

Regulatory risk assets. Assets calculated on a risk-adjusted basis as defined by the regulatory agency having authority over the subject bank, or more generally as defined under the Basel Accord.

---

[20] L. Thomas, Money, Banking & Financial Markets, p. 126.

Related party lending. Lending by a bank to its officers or staff, or their families. Related party lending may also include lending to corporations within a larger conglomerate or group of which the bank is a member. The terms insider lending and related party lending are largely the same.

Relative risk. The risk of default of a financial asset or class of financial assets compared with another, often expressed as a symbol. For example, Bank X rates loan Y as "B," a lower quality than "A" loans but a higher quality than "C" rated loans. The term relative risk is often used in respect of credit agency ratings or internal bank credit gradings. See *absolute risk, expected default rate.*

Repayment culture. A country's *credit culture*; the propensity for borrowers within a particular country to repay their debts relative to those in another country. A country's repayment culture may be influenced by the legal and regulatory framework, social, political and cultural considerations.

Repos. Repurchase agreement; a form of short-term secured borrowing using securities as collateral. See *repurchase agreement.*

Report of condition. Balance sheet.

Report of income. Income statement.

Reputation risk. The risk to earnings or capital from a diminished ability to maintain existing business relationships or generate new ones coming as a result of negative public opinion. Certain business are particularly vulnerable to reputation risk, including fiduciaries such as asset managers, and independent credit rating agencies.

Rescheduled loan. A loan in which the terms of payment have been altered, usually made more lenient to the borrower. Various reasons may play a part in the decision of a lender to reschedule a loan — the desire to reduce its own overall ratio of *non-performing loans*, for example. Note: There may be no difference between a restructured and rescheduled loan, but in the case of a restructured loan the connotation is that the borrower's business remains viable and that its capacity to repay under the terms originally agreed has been adversely affected by circumstances beyond its control; with regard to the term rescheduled loan, this connotation is considerably weaker and in some circumstances the implication may be that the borrower has adjusted the terms of borrowers' obligations purely to improve the appearance of its own *asset quality.*

Reserve currency. One of a number of currencies in which governments maintain their foreign reserves, e.g. US dollars, Euros, British pounds (sterling) Japanese yen; hard currency.

Reserves. 1. Loan loss reserves, a contra-account to loans, which are a category of assets. Loan loss reserves are designed to cover a bank's credit costs arising from non-performing or bad loans. 2. Equity reserves, form a part of shareholders' equity, are separate and distinct from loan loss reserves; 3. Primary reserves; i.e. reserves required to be maintained with the central bank as security for depositors. 4. Secondary reserves refer to the base minimum of liquid assets a bank may be required by regulatory authorities to maintain. See also *foreign reserves, loan loss reserves, primary reserves and secondary reserves.*

Restructured loan. 1. A loan to a viable borrower which due to circumstances beyond its control it is unable to repay according to the original terms, and which has been readjusted by mutual agreement between the bank and borrower to permit the borrower to continue as a going concern. 2. A rescheduled loan. Note that in some countries, a loan that has been restructured will no longer appear on the books as a *non-performing loan.* Banks in such countries have a strong incentive to restructure a loan without regard to the borrowers ultimate ability to satisfy its debt in full.

Restructuring. (Loans). See *restructured loan.*

Restructuring. (Banks). Refers to the process whereby an insolvent bank (or bank approaching *insolvency* is restored to financial health. Restructuring may apply to an individual bank or to entire banking system. A number of methods may be employed including, for example, an injection of new capital, change of ownership or management, changes in the organizational framework, improvements in risk control procedures and the removal of bad loans from the bank's books, often by means of a special entity formed for that task, e.g. an asset management corporation. At the level of the banking system as a whole, a special restructuring agency may be created, prudential regulations enhanced and reforms in *insolvency* laws implemented. Successful bank restructuring is often accompanied by corporate restructuring. See *restructuring* (Corporations).

Retained earnings. Accumulated net after-tax profits that have not been distributed to shareholders by way of dividends.

Retained profit. Retained earnings.

Return on assets. Actually, return on *average assets*, often abbreviated as ROA. A profitability indicator that measures the bank's ability to efficiently employ its assets. It is calculated by dividing net profit by the bank's assets, or more commonly, by its *average assets*. See *average assets*. Note that ideally ROA and ROE (return on equity) should be calculated using a measure of net income that excludes: 1) extraordinary items; 2) exceptional securities gains; and 3) deduction for minority interest. Both methods of calculating ROA, i.e. on the basis of reported net profit and net profit after making adjustments for the three foregoing items, are acceptable. But it is important to be clear on what figure was used to calculate ROA when comparing banks.

Return on capital employed. Commonly used to evaluate the return of non-financial enterprises, return on capital employed is equal to the sum of shareholders' equity, net debt (debt minus cash) and tax payable. N.B. "Capital" in this context is defined broadly to mean all financing, whether debt or equity.

Revaluation. 1. An upward adjustment in the value of something; the counterpart of writing down assets that have diminished in value. For example, a company may decide to revalue certain assets, usually limited to land and buildings, when their market value has increased. Like assets that are marked to market, this is an exception to the historical cost accounting convention under which assets are reported at the price at which they were purchased. When assets are revalued, their value is increased and the corresponding entry on the liability side of the balance sheet is the create of a revaluation reserve. 2. A change in the value of something. See *devaluation.*

Riding the yield curve. The tactic of purchasing a bond when interest rates are comparatively high, enjoying the benefit of the high interest payments for a time, and then selling the security for a gain when interest rates fall.

Rights issue. An offering of shares to existing shareholders in order to raise additional capital. By offering existing shareholders the right to obtain additional shares by subscribing additional capital, a rights issue ordinarily enables shareholders to avoid the dilution in their holdings that could occur through an offering of shares to the public at large.

Risk appetite. Demand for assets of a particular risk profile; the demand for assets in light of a desired portfolio weighting.

Risk assets. Assets calculated on a risk-adjusted basis as defined by the regulatory agency having authority over the subject bank, or more generally as defined under the Basel Accord. For example, under the Accord, residential mortgage loans had a risk weighting of 50%. Therefore, in calculating total risk assets, total residential mortgage loans would be just half of their nominal amount.

Risk premium. The premium paid by an issuer to issue securities perceived as riskier than other securities, otherwise comparable. The risk may be specific to the issuer or systematic. See *Japan premium*.

Risk segmentation. The categorization of borrowers into discrete segments or "risk buckets" based on observable criteria.

Risk. 1. "Exposure to uncertainty of outcome."[21] 2. "The possibility of suffering harm or loss."[22]

Risk/reward trade off. The exchange of higher credit costs for higher yield and vice versa. An understanding of the risk/reward trade off implies being able to price credit costs accurately.

Risk-free rate. The rate of interest, which represents the time value of money, that in most cases corresponds to the benchmark yield on notes and bonds of varying terms issued by the relevant government, as it is presumed government debt in its own currency is risk-free. Interest is comprised of the risk-free interest rate plus a premium is charged the borrower depending upon its creditworthiness. For example, in the case of US dollar borrowing, if the risk-free rate interest rate is 5% per annum, a borrower rated BB, may perhaps pay 8–9% in interest. See *interest*.

ROCE. Return on capital employed.

ROPOA. (Philippines). Foreclosed assets. (stands for "real or other property owned or acquired").

RORAC. Return on risk-adjusted equity capital. The concept implicit in RORAC is to apply the risk-weighting concept used, for example, in the Basel Accord for capital adequacy purposes, to profitability analysis.

RTGS. Real-time gross settlement.

RWA. Risk-weighted assets.

S&L. Savings and Loan.

Savings. Surplus resources set aside.

---

[21] Cades, p. 2.
[22] The American Heritage Dictionary, 3rd Edition.

Secondary market. The market for fixed income and equity securities that have already been issued; "second-hand" securities.

Secondary reserves. See *primary reserves; reserves.*

Secular. Long-term trends or developments, e.g. industrialization, the rise of the Internet.

Securities house. An investment bank.

Securities purchased under resale agreements. Collateral taken for a repo transaction. See *repo.*

Securities sold under repo agreements. Collateral given for a repo transaction. See *repo.*

Securitization. The process of converting traditionally illiquid financial assets such as loans into marketable securities. Mortgage backed securities, which achieved popularity in the US in the 1970s, were one of the first forms of asset securitizations. Pools of mortgage loans were packaged and the revenue from the interest payments of the borrowers was used to provide interest income to the holders of the securities. Other types of assets, including auto loans and credit card receivables, can also be used to create asset pools to back such securities, which are unsurprisingly often termed asset-backed securities. Securitization creates a secondary market for mortgage loans and also enables a bank with a good customer franchise to originate many more loans than its capital could otherwise support. The bank can sell such loans to arrangers of asset securitizations, booking an origination fee, and potentially a profit on the sale as well as income from servicing the loan, in the process and thereby increasing its profitability.

Seignorage. The profit the government realizes from the printing of paper money or the minting of coin; the difference between the cost of printing or minting and the face value of the notes or coins. A fractional-reserve banking system reduces a government's seignorage since the banking system itself creates money through the money multiplier effect.

Self-liquidating. A type of credit that contains the means for its own payment at maturity. Examples would be: an agricultural loan for seed and fertilizer secured by the crop; a bankers' acceptance (secured by the goods purchased).

Sell-side. Used mainly to refer to analysts who work for an investment bank supporting the bank's brokerage business. Sell-side analysts include fixed income and equity analysts who often specialize by sector or country. They prepare primary proprietary research for the benefit of institutional, and sometimes, retail investors.

Sensitivity analysis. A determination of the sensitivity (response, degree of change) of results (output) to changes in parameters (inputs).

Settlement risk. Risk of loss arising from a counterparty's being unable or unwilling to complete its end of a transaction within the period required for settlement. Settlement risk arises from the gap between the time payment is made and delivery is received during which time a counterparty may, for instance, become insolvent or be blocked from making payment. The longer the time gap, the greater the risk. Real-time settlement, if and when implemented, offers a way to minimize if not eliminate settlement risk.

Severity. The expected loss in the event of default. Also referred to as *loss in the event of default.*

Share premium. The amount realized on the sale of authorized shares in excess of their par value (mainly British usage); premium on paid-in capital.

Shareholders' equity. Net worth, or assets minus liabilities.

Shareholders' funds. Shareholders' equity.

Sharpe ratio. A ratio originally developed by William F. Sharpe of Stanford University in 1966 to measure for the performance of mutual funds, for which he proposed the term *reward-to-variability ratio.* The ratio attempts to measure the degree to which excess returns on a portfolio were the result of judicious stock picking or merely the result of excessive risk-taking.[23]

Short-term. One year or less.

Sick bank. A vague term used to describe a bank with impaired capital that will have difficulty earning its way back to financial health, and may therefore need external support in the form of a substantial infusion of liquidity, capital or both.

Sinking fund. A mechanism sometimes required by bond indentures (agreements) in which the issuer is required to make regular payments into a custodial account, the "sinking fund," in order to ensure it has the wherewithal to redeem the bond at maturity, i.e. repay the bondholders their principal. In some cases, a sinking fund

---

[23] The Sharpe Ratio, William F. Sharpe, Stanford University, The Journal of Portfolio Management, Fall 1994. See http://www.stanford.edu/~wfsharpe/art/sr/sr.htm.

requirement may be satisfied through the issuer's purchase of the bonds on the open market.

Sliding parity. See *crawling peg*.

SME. Small- or medium-sized enterprise.

SOCB. State-owned commercial bank.

SOE. State-owned enterprise.

Soft loan. A subsidized loan, i.e. one at below-market interest rates, often granted by development agencies or multilateral institutions to developing countries.

Solvency. The extent to which a bank's capital (and current retained profits) provides an adequate cushion for any losses which may arise in its loan or securities portfolio; the state of being solvent. "[T]he capacity to meet external liabilities in full by realizing assets at current value."[24] A highly solvent bank is one that is well-capitalized, having comparatively high volume of capital relative to its assets. A insolvent bank is one in which losses from the bank's portfolio are greater than the bank's capital. There are several measures of relative *solvency*, of which the most common are the equity to assets ratio and the BIS capital adequacy ratio. See *technical insolvency*. While illiquidity is the proximate cause of most bank failures, depositors and creditors will tend to have less confidence in an undercapitalized bank, which will therefore have more difficulty maintaining adequate liquidity. *Solvency* and liquidity are thus linked.

Solvency risk. The risk that (a bank's) liabilities will exceed its viable assets (i.e. total assets less bad assets) plus equity capital. Another way to put it is the risk that the difference between a bank's total assets and its viable assets exceeds equity capital such that not all creditors are likely to be paid in full.

Sovereign ceiling. The principle that the debt rating of a rating of a company or bank based in a country cannot exceed the sovereign rating of the country itself, on the grounds that because of the power to impose restrictions on transfer payments and undertake other restrictive measures that may be imposed during times of economic distress, a company can be no more creditworthy than the government which has authority over it. Rating agencies, on occasion, do make exceptions to the sovereign ceiling, and in the case of asset

---

[24] Cades, p. 24.

securitizations and other forms of structured finance, special arrangements including credit enhancements can circumvent the sovereign ceiling. Note the sovereign ceiling primarily applies to default ratings and not to general counterparty or financial strength ratings.

Special deposits. Reserve account with the central bank or monetary authority (UK). See *primary reserves*.

Special mention loan. A loan not necessarily even overdue but one in which the borrower is perceived to be experiencing difficulties that may impair its ability to repay the loan in full or on a timely basis. Depending on the jurisdiction, a special mention loan may or may not be considered a problem loan or one which requires that specific provisions be set aside.

Specially mentioned loan. Special mention loan.

Specific provisions. Provisions (i.e. loan loss reserves) set aside to provide for (credit costs) associated with identified problem loans. The amount provided will vary with loan classification; e.g. 50% of face value for loans classified as "doubtful." Specific provisions contrast with general provisions.

Specific risk. The risks associated with a particular assets or equity investment as opposed to the system as a whole. In theory, diversification can eliminate all specific risks since the effects of specific risks of particular assets will tend to cancel each other out. See *systematic risk*.

Speculative risk. Two directional risk, i.e. there can be an upside or a downside. Also called dynamic risk. Antonym: pure risk, static risk.

Spot market. The market for items priced for immediate delivery.

Spread. (v.) To spread a bank's financial statements means to transpose the line items of the its components into a standardized and objective format to facilitate analysis.

SPV. Special purpose vehicle.

Stable funds. Total customer deposits plus official deposits plus medium-/long-term liabilities plus free capital funds.

Stand-alone financial condition. Financial strength, i.e. core financial capacity, excluding external support.

Standard deviation. A basic concept of statistics found frequently in literature on risk management, the standard deviation refers to "a rough estimate of the average distance of the values of the random variable form the expected value (mean)" calculated by taking the positive square root of the variance.[25] Assuming a normal bell curve, the one-sigma rule provides that approximately 68% of the values in a distribution will lie within one-standard deviation of the mean, the two sigma rule that 95% will lie within two standard deviations and the three sigma rule that 99% will lie within three standard deviations.

Standby letter of credit. In contrast to a documentary letter of credit, the standby letter of credit does not necessarily have anything to do with foreign or domestic trade. It is instead a type of guarantee whereby an issuing bank undertakes on behalf of its customer (account party) to pay specified sums on the default or non-performance of its customer. Unlike the documentary letter of credit, there is no presentation of proper trade documentation involved nor an exchange of goods; rather, the beneficiary must merely evidence the default or non-performance by the account party. A stand by letter of credit is not self-liquidating and is ordinarily riskier than a documentary letter of credit, particularly if uncollateralized.

State support. External support provided by a government.

Statement of Cash Flows. A financial statement which reports the source and uses of a company's funds. Highly useful in the analysis of non-financial companies, because of the nature of the banking business cash flow analysis is little used in analyzing financial institutions.

Statement of Changes in Capital Funds. Statement of Stockholders' Equity.

Statement of Condition. A balance sheet. See *balance sheet*.

Static risk. See *pure risk*.

Statistical provisions. General provisions.

Stocks. 1. Shares. 2. Inventory (UK).

Structural NPLs. *Non-performing loans* arising from deficiencies from the structure of an economy resulting from rules which shape the way in which firms, financial institutions, and others interact. In this context, structural is the antonym for cyclical. Impliedly, structural NPLs do not diminish of their own accord but require government intervention and reform to reshape the regulatory regime which channels economic activity.

Structural. adj. (Sovereign). As opposed to cyclical; resulting from basic problems in the structure of an economy, including the types of

---

[25] Lloyd Jaisingh, Statistics for the Utterly Confused, p. 153, McGraw Hill, 2000.

industries which dominate the economy and restrictions on the factors of production, including obstacles to capital flowing into more productive sectors (e.g. government policies that favor certain sectors, extensive cross shareholding agreements, undeveloped capital markets), on labor mobility (e.g. restrictive labor laws, immigration policies), and on the use of land (e.g. ineffective *bankruptcy* and foreclosure laws).

Structured finance. Asset backed or future flows-based securitizations, mainly; structured finance refers to finance secured by certain assets or cash flows rather than based on the intrinsic creditworthiness of the issuer or borrower.

Sub-emerging market. A term sometimes informally applied to a country that is on the borderline of being an emerging market with respect to its commitment to economic reform and market-based mechanisms, as well as with respect to investor sentiment.

Subsidiary. A company-owned 50% or more by another company, or in which the company holding the shares has a controlling interest, is the *subsidiary* of that company.

Substandard loan. An overdue loan, generally more than 90 days in arrears, in respect to which the borrower is experiencing difficulties that may threaten its ability to make payment in full.

Supplementary capital. Tier 2 capital; secondary capital; non-core capital; capital other than shareholders' equity.

Surplus. Paid-in capital for shares in excess of their par or stated value. Also referred to as *paid-in surplus*. See *share premium*.

Suspend (interest). See *interest-in-suspense*.

Sustainable growth rate. The rate at which a bank can grow while generating sufficient capital internally to maintain a prudent level of core capital adequacy. Most banks will be hard pressed to sustain growth rates of greater than 20% without an infusion of outside capital or unusually high spreads, perhaps due to a cartel like situation. Illustration: Assume a prudent level of Tier 1 capital is 5%, that total asset are equivalent to risk assets, ROA (on a non-averaged basis) of 1%, no NPLs and that 1/4 of all net profit is paid out to shareholders. The sustainable growth rate of would be (Total Assets × ROA × dividend payout at a % of net profit × leverage) divided by Total Assets, where leverage = 1/Tier 1 ratio. a) Assume year-end assets of $100 m, equity of $5 m, net profit of $1 m. If 1/4 is distributed to shareholders, then $750,000 is available to boost shareholders' equity which can support an increase in assets of $\$750,000 \times 20$ or $\$15$ m. The bank can grow its assets at 15% per year while maintaining its Tier 1 capital ratio at 5%. b) Assume the same except ROA is 0.8%, dividend payout is ½ and the Tier 1 capital ratio is 4%. The sustainable growth rate equals ($\$100$ m $\times 0.008 \times$ ½ $\times 25$) = $\$10$ m/ $\$100$ m or 10%.

Swap. A type of derivative transaction that is usually in the form of either an interest rate swap or a currency swap or both. Example: UVW, Inc., a large creditworthy US company, issues a 5-year $\$10$ m bond paying a fixed rate. XYZ Ltd., a second-tier British company issues a 5-year $\$10$ m bond paying a floating rate. UVW's CFO prefers floating rate funding fearing a fall in interest rates. XYZ Ltd. desires the stability of fixed rate funding. Through a bank, which acts as an intermediary and collects a fee for its services, they swap their obligations to pay interest, making adjustments for the rates in a mutually agreeable fashion through the bank.

Systematic risk. 1. Risk which affects assets on an across-the-board basis; general market risk; systematic risk is often used to refer to the penchant for all share prices to move in the same direction. In a bull market, for example, a rising tide lifts all boats, and even marginal stocks register price rises. However, in a bear market, the opposite occurs and even the soundest companies tend to lose market value. In other words, systematic risk is the general risk of holding shares, or a diversified portfolio of shares in a market, risk that can cannot be diversified away. It can also be applied to non-equity assets such as bank loans or bank subordinated debt. In these cases, systematic risk would be the risk that an economic recession or events affecting a particular country (country risk) will have a general impact, for example causing overall default rates to rise. *Specific risk*, in contrast, refers to the element of risk embodied in the shares of a particular company but which is not correlated with the market as a whole. Investment in shares inevitably involves taking on systematic and specific risk. 2. The risks affecting a system generally. To an insurer, an earthquake is systematic risk; a house with defective foundations that collapses is a specific risk

Systemic risk. The risk of the breakdown of banking system due to financial institution default creating a chain reaction of further defaults, as one domino falling can cause a whole row to fall. Contributing factors include: the structure of the banking system; the regulatory regime; the quality of bank supervision; the quality of bank management and risk control; as well as, secular factors and external shocks. Systemic risk is closely related to sovereign risk and to industry risk.

Tangible common equity. Common equity (shareholders' equity of the bank's common or ordinary shareholders) excluding intangible items such as goodwill.

Technically insolvent. Technical *insolvency* occurs when, usually as a result of loan losses, the value of a bank's earning assets declines to a level less than its liabilities, not including shareholders' equity. A technically insolvent bank may continue to operate for years or decades, so long as it is not legally obliged to close and it is provided continuing external liquidity support (e.g. through cash emergency infusions or loans from a central bank).

Tenor. Tenor refers to the term of a loan or security.

Term structure of interest rates. A matrix that describes the relationship between interest rates and the term, credit rating and priority of fixed income securities.

Terms of trade. (Sovereign). Average export prices to average import prices, which provides an indication of a country's relative capacity to purchase the imports that it needs.

Thrift Bank. See *thrift institution.*

Thrift institution. Sometimes referred to informally as a "thrift," a thrift institution is a deposit-taking institution that focuses on financing the purchase of owner-occupied residences through mortgage loans. This type of institution got its name from its mission of promoting personal thrift leading to home ownership. See also *savings and loan, building society, mortgage bank.*

Tier 1 Capital. Defined core capital under the 1988 Basel Accord as amended, roughly equivalent to shareholders' equity. Its constituents are generally as follows: paid-up common (ordinary) share capital, perpetual non-cumulative preferred shares, disclosed reserves, minority interest, and current profit/loss but excluding goodwill and intangible assets.

Tier 2 Capital. Defined supplementary capital under the 1988 Basel Accord as amended, typically composed in large part by long-term subordinated debt.

Tier 3 Capital. So-called trading book ancillary capital under the Basel Accord which consists of medium-term debt. Somewhat rarely used.

Too big to fail syndrome. The failure of a single bank can lead to a collapse of a financial system, with potentially dire consequences. The idea behind the notion of "too big to fail" is that a bank of certain size will be highly likely to cause such a collapse. Hence, governments in such circumstances believe that the cost of bailing out a large bank is less than the economic damage that could result from letting nature take its course.

Total bad and doubtful expense. Provisioning (expense) plus write-offs. See *B&DD expense.*

Total capital employed. Refers to average shareholders equity plus average debt.

Total deposits. Customer or core deposits plus deposits from financial institutions (interbank deposits).

Total loans. The face value of loans prior to the deduction of provisioning, sometimes referred to more specifically as *total loans net of provisions.* See also *gross loans* and *net loans.*

Total provision cover. Also known as NPL coverage.

Total published equity. Reported shareholders' equity, generally including preferred shares and minority interest.

Trade balance. Exports minus imports.

Trade deficit. Negative trade balance; the excess of imports over exports.

Trade finance. The finance of import and export transactions, often by means of a loan to a vendor secured by a letter of credit.

Trading book. The trading portfolio which is on the bank's own account, as opposed to being for customers' accounts. Under the EU capital adequacy rules, which came into effect in1996, trading book activity is subject to certain capital requirements.

Trading gains. A major component of non-interest income, trading gains refers to a bank's net gains from trading in foreign exchange and securities.

Trading revenue. See *trading gains.*

Tranche. From the French for slice, a tranche is one of two or more borrowings as part of a single loan facility or debt issue.

Transfer payments. (Sovereign). Taxes, premiums and other funds collected by governments and transferred to beneficiaries in the form of pension payments, unemployment benefits and other remittances.

Transfer risk. The risk that remittances in respect of cross-border financial obligations will be blocked, limited or delayed.

Transparency. Disclosure.

Treasury bills. Short-term fixed income securities (bonds) issued by the government; e.g. US Treasury bills.

Treasury notes. Long-term fixed income securities with, in the case of US government securities, a term of from one to ten years. The term note is applied to US Treasury notes as a convention. Fixed income securities with a one-year term or greater are also referred to as bonds.

Treasury stock. Issued shares that have been reacquired by the corporation. Many jurisdictions do not permit treasury shares on the grounds that a corporation cannot own its own shares.

Trend analysis. Examining how a given financial indicator, e.g. net interest margin, has changed over a period of time. A three- to five-year time period is typically used.

Trust bank. A bank that manages assets or investments held in trust accounts (often inheritances) as a fiduciary to the trust beneficiaries. Depending on the jurisdiction, trust bankers may also provide investment advisory services as well as some commercial banking services, while some commercial banks offer trust services.

Undercapitalized. Over leveraged.

Underground economy. The transactions that go unrecorded in official statistics due to illegality or to evade taxes.

Underlying profit. Earnings before provisions and taxes; i.e. net interest income plus non-interest income less non interest expense (excluding provisioning and taxes).

Underlying profitability. Underlying ROA. Pre-provision, pre tax profit, also known as earnings before provisions and taxes or EBPT, divided by *average assets*; underlying profit divided by *average assets*, expressed as a percentage. Underlying ROE, correspondingly, is pre-provision, pre tax profit return on average equity. Note that underlying profitability is sometimes referred to as *core profitability.*

Underlying ROE. See *underlying profitability.*

Underwriter. An entity such as an investment bank that arranges an offering of a security issue on behalf of the issuer and distributes it to the public through other banks and securities houses. Although it depends upon the jurisdiction, circumstances and applicable securities laws, the underwriter typically buys the issue from the issuer and accepts some or all of the risk that the issue may not fetch the specified purchase price in the market.

Undivided profits. Retained earnings. Also known as earned surplus.

Unit trust. British term for *mutual fund*.

Universal banks. Commercial banks which offer a comprehensive range of financial services including investment banking, cash management, asset management, brokerage, insurance and others. Universal banks may be subject to special licensing criteria in their home jurisdictions. Until the Glass-Steagall Act was repealed by the US Congress, American banks were highly restricted in the activities in which they could engage, and were unable to function as universal banks. The universal banking model is more prevalent in Europe where commercial banks generally have been permitted to engage in a wider range of financial services businesses; however, only the largest banks tend to operate as universal banks and may not offer all services in all markets.

Unrated issue. An issue that has not been rated by a credit rating agency.

Unsecured. Without collateral, as in an unsecured or clean loan.

Upgrade. A rating action in which the rating assigned to an issuer or issue is raised by one notch or more, e.g. from A- to A.

Upper Tier 2 capital. Long-term or perpetual subordinated debt with equity-like characteristics that enable it to escape the 50% ceiling on Tier 2 capital imposed by the 1988 Basel Capital Accord. These equity-like characteristics derive from the fact that bondholders of such debt are subject to interest payment deferral and losses under certain defined circumstances.

Volatility. Variability from an expected outcome; a key measure of risk.

Vostro account. Account used by a bank to describe a demand deposit account maintained with it by a bank in a foreign country. It is the vostro account of the other bank and used mainly to arrange foreign exchange transfers between the two banks.

Vulture fund. Funds that specialize in trading distressed assets at a deep discount.

Warrants. A security which entitles the holder to purchase a certain amount of shares at a certain price on (or before) a certain future date. Warrants are sometimes bundled with other securities, such as bonds, to make them either more marketable or to reduce the cost of issuing of issuing them. For example, during the early 1980s many Japanese companies whose share prices were rising rapidly issued bonds with attached warrants that allowed the bondholder to purchase a specified number of shares at a fixed price on a specified date. Given the rising stock prices, bondholders could benefit from the difference between the exercise price and the actual price of the shares prevailing on that date, and therefore were willing to accept a lower yield on the bonds.

Wealth effect. The notion that when stock ownership becomes widespread and stock prices rise, consumption increases based on the perception on the part of a large segment of consumers that they are wealthier as a consequence of rising but as yet unrealized gains that translate into higher net worth.

Wealth. 1. To an individual, net worth. 2. To a nation, the stock of assets, including money, real property, financial assets and so on.

Wholesale banking. In contrast to retail banking, wholesale banking is mainly concerned in dealing with large or highly creditworthy organizations, including major corporations, government agencies, and sound financial entities, including banks and institutional investors. Typical wholesale banking products include: lending (wholesale lending), asset financing, repos and reverse repos, structured finance, securitization, and derivatives. Wholesale mortgage banking is specifically concerned with the purchase of mortgage loans originated by other institutions.

Wholesale lending. Lending to large or highly creditworthy organizations, including major corporations, government agencies, and sound financial entities, including banks and institutional investors.

Working capital. (Corporations). Current assets less current liabilities.

WRAs. Risk-weighted ("weighted risk") assets.

Write back. v. Show as a recovery; n. a recovery.

Write down. To adjust the value of assets on the balance sheet to reflect their actual value more accurately. Loans are ordinarily written down by charging provisions against the expected loss.

Write off. v. Write down an asset e.g. a loan to zero on the expectation that it will no longer be repaid. Also can be used as a noun.

WTO. World Trade Organization.

Yield curve risk. See *interest rate risk.*

Yield curve. The risk-free interest rate for fixed-income securities with varying maturities. Usually government issues serve as a benchmark to ascertain a benchmark yield curve that assists in pricing securities of lesser credit quality. Yield curves can be established for varying grades of securities ranging from AAA to "junk" quality (below BBB). The yield curve, depending upon whether it is mildly upward sloping, steeply upward sloping, downward sloping ("negative," "inverted"), or humped may serve as an economic indicator. A mildly upward sloping yield curve implies normal growth; a steeply upward sloping yield curve, fast growth; a downward sloping yield curve, recession and a humped yield curve, slow growth or a flattening business cycle. The term structure of interest rates is reflected in the benchmark yield curve, while their risk structure is reflected in the yield curves of various grades of investments. See also *interest rate risk; term structure of interest rates.*

Yield on average earning assets. Total interest income divided by total average earning assets. Also known as the earning rate or the earning asset yield.

Yield on earning assets. Yield on average earning assets.

Yield. Return on a financial asset as percentage of price. In respect to an interest-earning asset, yield will ordinarily be defined as the return divided by the average balance (e.g. average earning assets), but in certain cases the purchase price or the market price of the asset (e.g. bonds) may be used. Yield may also be calculated for classes of financial assets, e.g. *yield on government securities, yield on inter-bank and money market items, yield on performing loans.*

YOY. Year-on-year. Used to compare change over a 12-month period. Also abbreviated as *Yoy* and *y-o-y.*

Zero gap. See *Interest rate sensitivity analysis.*

Zero-Coupon Bond. A bond which pay no coupon rate of interest, but which is sold at a deep discount from its face value, which the holder receives on maturity. Effectively, the holder receives the entire interest payment at that time in a balloon payment. For example, a zero-coupon bond with a ten-year term having a face value of $1,000

[26] Simon Maughan, Bank Recapitalization: Options & Policies, Indosuez W.I. Carr Securities, July 15, 1998, p.3.

[27] Deardorff's Glossary of International Economics, http://www-personal.umich.edu/~alandear/glossary/.

[28] Cades, p. 81.

[29] Cades, p. 79

[30] See Credit Risk Modelling: Current Practices and Applications, Basle Committee on Banking Supervision, Basle, April 199.

[31] Webster's New World College Dictionary, 3rd Ed., Macmillan, 1997 p. 325

[32] Thomas Fitch, Dictionary of Banking Terms,

[33] Quoted in Terry Smith, Accounting for Growth: Stripping the Camouflage from Company Accounts, p. 64.

[34] Quoted in Terry Smith, Accounting for Growth: Stripping the Camouflage from Company Accounts, p. 64

[35] These and other formulas marked with an asterisk were sourced from http://www.stern.nyu.edu/~nroubini/bci.

might be purchased for \$400, which would result in an effective interest rate of about 9.6%.

Z-Score. The Altman Z-Score refers to a model developed by Edward Altman which attempts to aggregate financial ratios to create a score capable of predicting corporate defaults. $Z = (1.2 \times (\text{working capital}/\text{total assets})) + ((1.4 \times (\text{retained earnings}/\text{total assets})) + ((3.3 \times (\text{EBIT}/\text{total assets})) + (0.6 \times (\text{market value of equity}/\text{book value of debt})) + (1.0 \times (\text{sales}/\text{total assets}))$. A Z-score over 2.99 denotes a firm in the "non-bankrupt" sector while one below 1.81 denotes one in the bankrupt sector. The Z-Score model set forth above is applicable generally to non-financial corporations.

---

[36] "For example, a US\$10,000 loan that is priced on an interest only basis of 10% for five years would accrue \$5000 over its life. The initial accounting entry on the bank's books when the loaned was booked would be to debit loans of US\$15,000 and credit cash of US\$10,000 and unearned income of US\$5,000. ING Barings, Banknotes, 8 March 1999, p. 60.

[37] See Cades at p. 150.

[38] D. Downing, Dictionary of Mathematics Terms, Barron's, 2nd ed. 1995.

[39] Cades, p. 56

[40] Cades, p. 17.

[41] Lloyd B. Thomas, *Money, Banking and Financial Markets*, Int'l ed. Irwin-McGraw Hill, 1997, p. 19–20.

[42] L. Thomas, Money, Banking & Financial Markets, p. 126.

[43] Cades, p. 2.

[44] The American Heritage Dictionary, 3rd Edition

[45] The Sharpe Ratio, William F. Sharpe, Stanford University, The Journal of Portfolio Management, Fall 1994. See http://www.stanford.edu/~wfsharpe/art/sr/sr.htm.

[46] Cades, p. 24.

[47] Lloyd Jaisingh, Statistics for the Utterly Confused, p. 153, McGraw Hill, 2000.

INDEX